LANDLORD & TENANT LAW

LANDLORD & TENANT LAW

General Editor

Dr Gabriel Brennan

OXFORD

UNIVERSITY PRESS

Great Clarendon Street, Oxford, OX2 6DP,
United Kingdom

Oxford University Press is a department of the University of Oxford.
It furthers the University's objective of excellence in research, scholarship,
and education by publishing worldwide. Oxford is a registered trade mark of
Oxford University Press in the UK and in certain other countries

© Law Society of Ireland 2018

The moral rights of the author have been asserted

Fourth edition 2007
Fifth edition 2010
Sixth edition 2014
Impression: 9

Public sector information reproduced under Open Government Licence v3.0
(http://www.nationalarchives.gov.uk/doc/open-government-licence/open-government-licence.htm)

Published in the United States of America by Oxford University Press
198 Madison Avenue, New York, NY 10016, United States of America

British Library Cataloguing in Publication Data

Data available

ISBN 978–0–19–878811–9

Printed in Great Britain by
CPI Group (UK) Ltd, Croydon, CR0 4YY

Links to third party websites are provided by Oxford in good faith and
for information only. Oxford disclaims any responsibility for the materials
contained in any third party website referenced in this work.

Disclaimer

PREFACE

Our aim in writing this book is to provide trainee solicitors with a comprehensive text dealing with all the fundamental aspects of landlord and tenant law. The primary focus of the text is to prepare trainee solicitors for practice. Where necessary academic law is referred to; however, it is assumed that readers have a basic knowledge of land law and contract law.

This text is designed for the guidance of trainee solicitors attending the Law Society's Law School. It is anticipated that the text will provide a foundation for their learning and also assist them once their training period is concluded and they have entered the solicitor's profession. Indeed it is hoped that the text will provide assistance to all practitioners in the area of landlord and tenant law. If utilised in practice, the sample forms and precedents included in the text should be adapted as appropriate to the transaction in question.

The text reflects Law Society recommended practice, which, like all aspects of law, is constantly evolving. The law and practice are stated as at 1 April 2018.

While every effort has been made to ensure that the text is accurate the authors would be grateful to learn of any errors or omissions. Any comments or queries on this manual should be sent to the editor at the Law Society.

Thanks to all my colleagues who gave their support and special thanks to my wonderful family.

Gabriel Brennan
The Law School
May 2018

AUTHORS

Dr. Gabriel Brennan is a solicitor with the Law Society. She is co-editor and co-author of the Law Society's *Conveyancing* manual and is editor and co-author of this *Landlord & Tenant Law* manual. She lectures and tutors in all areas of property on the Law Society's Continuing Professional Development, Diploma and Professional Practice Courses. She is a longstanding member of the Law Society Conveyancing Committee and eConveyancing Task Force and co-chairs the eSignatures Working Group. Gabriel was formerly in practice with Abercorn Solicitors.

Sean Brodie has lectured on the Law Society's VAT and landlord and tenant law modules on the Professional Practice Courses and on the Law Society's Diploma in Commercial Conveyancing. He has also lectured on VAT for the Irish Tax Institute and is co-author of *Value Added Tax* published by the Irish Tax Institute. He is currently a partner with Price-waterhouseCoopers where he advises on all aspects of VAT. Prior to joining Pricewater-houseCoopers he worked in the office of the Revenue Commissioners.

Having been a partner in one of the big five firms for 15 years **Michelle Linnane** moved to an international company to advise its pension fund on its property portfolio. She currently provides a specialist service as a consultant in all areas of property to colleagues and firms throughout the country. She is a lecturer and tutor on the landlord and tenant and conveyancing modules on the Professional Practice Courses in the Law School and has been a co-author of this manual on landlord and tenant law since its first edition in 2000 and is also co-author of the Law Society's manual on *Complex Conveyancing* (published by Bloomsbury Professional). She served as external examiner to the Law School from 2000 to 2015. She has lectured on Diploma and Certificate courses run by the Law Society as well as giving lectures to the DSBA. Michelle is also qualified as an attorney at the New York Bar (1990) and as a solicitor in the UK (1994).

David Soden is a lecturer and tutor on the Law Society's conveyancing, landlord and tenant law, professional practice and conduct, skills and civil litigation modules on the Professional Practice Courses. He has carried on practice as a sole practitioner in Dublin since 1997, following stints as an assistant solicitor in two mixed practices where he specialised mainly in civil litigation.

ACKNOWLEDGEMENTS

While the individual authors are, of course, solely responsible for the contents of the manual, we would like to express our gratitude to the many colleagues who so ably assisted us in this project.

In particular thanks are due to Arthur Cox, Solicitors for kindly allowing us to use their precedents.

OUTLINE CONTENTS

1   Introduction   *1*

2   Categorisation of Tenancies   *14*

3   Licences   *19*

4   Other Relationships Involving Land   *36*

5   Taking Instructions/Essential Contents of a Lease   *45*

6   Residential Tenancies Acts 2004 to 2016   *59*

7   Residential Tenancies Board   *91*

8   Repairs   *104*

9   Termination   *118*

10   Statutory Reliefs   *140*

11   Ground Rents   *179*

12   Commercial Leases   *225*

13   Value Added Tax   *253*

14   Housing (Private Rented Dwellings) Act, 1982   *273*

DETAILED CONTENTS

Table of Statutes   *xvii*

Table of Regulations and EU Law   *xxiv*

Table of Cases   *xxv*

1   Introduction...1

1.1   General...1

1.2   Definitions...2

1.3   Historical Background and Early Legislation.......................5
Historical Background   The 18th century
The 17th century   The 19th century

1.4   Recent Legislation 9
the 20th century   Landlord and Tenant (Amendment)
Landlord and Tenant (Amendment)   Act, 1994
   Act, 1980   The 21st century

1.5   Conclusion...12

1.6   Recommended Reading...13

2   Categorisation of Tenancies 14

2.1   Introduction 14

2.2   Fixed Term/Term Certain 15

2.3   Periodic Tenancies 15

2.4   Tenancy at Will..16

2.5   Tenancy at Sufferance 16

2.6   Statutory Tenancy 17

2.7   Tenancy by Estoppel..17

2.8   Temporary Convenience Lettings.......................................17

2.9   Conclusion..18

3   Licences **19**

3.1   Introduction 19
        Bare licence   Contractual licence
        Licence coupled with an interest   Estoppel licences

3.2   Characteristics of a Licence 22

3.3   Example Car Park Licence 26

3.4   Example of Licence of Concession Area 29

3.5   Conclusion 35

3.6   Recommended Reading 35

4   Other Relationships Involving Land **36**

4.1   Introduction 36

4.2   Servant/Employee 36

4.3   Lodger/Guest 36

4.4   Hirer 37

4.5   Conacre 37
        Generally   Characteristics of conacre

4.6   Agistment Holder 39
        Meaning   Characteristics of agistment
                                                     example of agistment agreement

4.7   Franchise 40

4.8   Rights of Residence 41

4.9   Caretaker 43
        Meaning   Example of a caretaker's agreement

5   Taking Instructions/Essential Contents of a Lease **45**

5.1   Taking Instructions 45

5.2   Instruction Sheet 46

5.3   Pre-lease Enquiries 48

5.4   Covenants and Conditions in a Lease 48

5.5   Essential Contents of a Lease 49
        Date of commencement of the term   Habendum
        Parcels   Reddendum

5.6   Practical Procedure when Drafting a New Lease 50
        Introduction   What happens in practice

5.7   Agreement for Lease 56
        Contents of the agreement   The limitations of an agreement
                                                     for lease

5.8   Residential Tenancy Agreements 57

DETAILED CONTENTS

6   **Residential Tenancies Acts 2004 to 2016** **59**

6.1   Introduction 59

6.2   Commencement 59

6.3   Application of the Act 59
Exceptions to the application
of the Act

Exceptions to the application
of Part 4 only

6.4   Interpretation of the Act 62
Definition of 'dwelling'
Definition of 'tenancy'
Definition of 'Part 4 tenancy'
Definition of 'public authority'

Other section 4 definitions
Definition of 'landlord',
'tenant' and 'lease'

6.5   Service of Notices 65

6.6   Tenancy Obligations of Landlords and Tenants—Part 2 65
Part 2, Chapter 1—Landlord's
obligations

Part 2, Chapter 2—Tenant's
obligations

6.7   Offences—Section 9 70

6.8   Redress under Part 6—Section 119 70

6.9   Rent and Rent Reviews—Part 3 71

6.10   Security of Tenure—Part 4 73
Termination of residential tenancies
Termination of Part 4 tenancies
Termination of fixed term tenancies

Further Part 4 tenancies
Part 4 and multiple occupants
Part 4—miscellaneous matters

6.11   Termination—Notice Periods and Other Procedural
Requirements—Part 5 83
Scope and interpretation
Contents of the termination notice
Period of notice to be given
Additional requirements and procedures
where the tenancy is sub-let

Miscellaneous matters
Time limit for disputing a notice of
termination
Prohibitions under section 184
Overview of termination periods

7   **Residential Tenancies Board** **91**

7.1   Introduction 91

7.2   Establishment and Composition of the RTB 91

7.3   Functions of the RTB 92
Resolution of disputes
Registration of particulars
Advice to the minister on policy

Development and publication of
guidelines for good practice

7.4   Overview of Changes to the 2004 Act 103
The 2015 Act

The 2016 Act

8   **Repairs** **104**

8.1   Introduction 104
2011 Bill

8.2   Common Law 105

8.3   Statute 106

Housing (Miscellaneous Provisions)
    Act, 1992
Deasy's Act, 1860, section 42
Landlord and Tenant (Amendment)
    Act, 1980, section 65

Landlord and Tenant (Amendment)
    Act, 1980, section 87
Miscellaneous statutes
Landlord must be notified
Conclusion

8.4   Sample Covenants to Repair 111

Residential
Commercial

Interpretation of covenants
    to repair

8.5   Remedies 116

The landlord's position

The tenant's position

9   Termination **118**

9.1   Introduction 118

Forthcoming reforms

9.2   Notice to Quit 119

Situations where a notice is not
    required
Who may serve the notice?
Form and contents of the notice
Length of notice

Upon whom and how should the
    notice be served?
Waiver of notice
Sample notices to quit

9.3   Forfeiture... 126

General
Basis for forfeiture
Sample proviso for re-entry
Section 14 and statutory restriction
    on right to forfeit

Forfeiture—the procedure
Relief against forfeiture

9.4   Other Forms of Termination... 132

Effluxion of time
Merger
Demand for possession *per* Deasy's
    Act, 1860, section 86
Decree or warrant for possession *per*
    Deasy's Act, 1860, section 78
Execution of a judgment or decree for
    possession *per* Deasy's Act, 1860,
    sections 52 and 66

Surrender
Occurrence of a stated event
Court order
Derelict sites and dangerous premises
Exercise of an option
Liquidator's disclaimer *per* the
    Companies Act, 2014, section 615

9.5   Legal Proceedings 136

Ejectment civil bill on title based on
    forfeiture
Ejectment for non-payment of rent

Ejectment civil bill for overholding
Ejectment for deserted premises

9.6   Summary of Practical Steps 139

10   Statutory Reliefs **140**

10.1   Introduction 140

Tenements: section 5

DETAILED CONTENTS

10.2   Right to a New Tenancy 144
    Business equity   Restrictions on right to a new
    Long possession equity   tenancy
    Improvements equity   Procedure for claiming a new
    Terms of a new tenancy   tenancy

10.3   Compensation for Improvements... 158
    General principles   Improvement notice

10.4   Compensation for Disturbance... 159

10.5   Practical Steps... 160

10.6   Provisions Relating to Covenants in Leases.............................. 161
    Covenants against alienation: section 66   Covenants against making
    Covenants restrictive of user: section 67   improvements: section 68
                                                       Forthcoming changes

10.7   Prescribed Forms 163
    Form No 1   Form No 8
    Form No 2   Form No 9
    Form No 3   Form No 10
    Form No 4   Form No 11
    Form No 5   Form No 12
    Form No 6   Form No 13
    Form No 7   Form No 14

11   Ground Rents **179**

11.1   Historical Background 179

11.2   Right to Buy Out Freehold... 180
    Introduction   Restrictions on the right
    Test under the 1978 Act

11.3   Right to a Reversionary Lease 188

11.4   Procedure for Purchasing Fee Simple....................................... 189
    1967 Act procedure—All property   Registration
    1978 Act procedure—Dwellinghouses   Merger

11.5   Practical Steps... 198
    1967 Act Procedure   1978 Act Procedure

11.6   Calculation of Purchase Price on Arbitration 199
    Expired lease   Lease with less than 15 years to run
    Yearly tenancy or lease with more than   or rent subject to review within
       15 years to run of residential premises   the 15 years of residential premises
       less than one acre   less than one acre
                                                      General

11.7   Abolition of Ground Rents: No 1 Act of 1978................................ 202

11.8   Prescribed Forms 203
    1967 Act procedure   1978 Act procedure

11.9   Sample Notice of Application for Arbitration to the County Registrar 219

11.10 Ground Rents—Guidelines for Ground Rents Purchase Scheme 221

12   Commercial Leases **225**

12.1   Introduction 225
'Fri' lease   Procedure
Shopping centres

12.2   Service Charge Clauses in Commercial Leases 226
General   Potential areas of dispute
Determining the amount of the service   Certification of the charge
  charge   Apportionment of charge among
Services to be included in the lease   tenants

12.3   Rent Review Clauses in Commercial Leases 234
General   Interpretation of rent review clause
Time is not of the essence   Sample clause re basis for review
Provision for independent review   Recording the revised rent
Basis for reviewing rent

12.4   Alienation (Assignment and Sub-letting) 240
General   Assignment
Restrictions   Sub-letting
Statutory/common law   Partial assignment or sub-letting

12.5   Change of user 246
General   Statute/common law

12.6   Insurance 248
Who effects the insurance—and why?   What are the insured risks?
What is the amount of the insurance   Subrogation
  and the rate?

12.7   Repair 250
Advising the client

12.8   Registers 251

13   Value Added Tax **253**

13.1   General 253
Background   Accounting for VAT
How VAT operates   Input credit—VCA part 8 chapter 1
What is subject to VAT?   Records

13.2   Lettings 258
Introduction   Surrenders and assignments of
General approach   ten-year+ leases granted pre-1 July
'New' lettings after 1 July 2008   2008 (Category 3—'Legacy Leases')
  (Categories 1 and 2)   Lease granted by a person who
                                                        has a waiver of exemption in
                                                        place on 1 July 2008 (Category 4)

13.3   Summary 269
Transfer of business

13.4   Miscellaneous 271
Rent to buy   Lettings by mortgagee in possession,
Completion of residential properties—   liquidator or receiver
  Revenue concession

14   Housing (Private Rented Dwellings) Act, 1982..........................**273**

14.1   'Controlled Dwellings'...273

14.2   Housing (Private Rented Dwellings) Act, 1982......................................273

14.3   Jurisdiction..273

14.4   Statutory Protection 274

14.5   Practical Concerns 274

14.6   Entitlement under the 1980 Act (as amended)......................................275

14.7   Entitlement under the Ground Rents Legislation 276

14.8   Implications...276

Appendices **278**

1   Tenancy Registration Form RTB1...278

2   Approved Housing Bodies Tenancy Registration Form RTB2 286

3   Notes on Service Charge Clauses in Commercial Leases.......................294

4   Standard Rent Review Clauses...300

5   Agreement for Lease 308

6   Lease..341

7   September 2011 Practice Note Revised VAT Special Condition 3 And
       Pre-contract VAT Enquiries 382

8   VAT on Property: Amendments to Pre-contract VAT Enquiries and
       Special Condition 3 (August 2011) 384

9   VAT Special Condition 3 February 2014 Edition.....................................385

10   Pre-contract VAT Enquiries February 2014 Edition 392

Index...*417*

TABLE OF STATUTES

Act of Union 1800 . . . 1.3.4
Adoption Acts 1952–1998 . . . 6.10.2.2
Arbitration Act 1954 . . . 12.3.3
Arbitration Act 1998 . . . 12.3.3
Building Societies Act 1989 . . . 8.3.1
Civil Law (Miscellaneous Provisions) Act
    2008 . . . 10.2.5.2, 12.1.1
  s 47 . . . 1.4.3, 4.9.1, 5.2, 10.1, 10.2.5.1,
    10.2.5.3
  s 48 . . . 10.1
Civil Partnership and Certain Rights and
    Obligations of Cohabitants Act 2010
  s 172 . . . 6.10.2.2
Companies Act 1963 . . . 10.1.1.2
Companies Act 1990
  s 31 . . . 5.2
  s 48 . . . 9.2.2
  s 51 . . . 9.2.5.3
  s 615 . . . 9.1, 9.4.11
  s 615(5) . . . 9.4.11
Companies Act 2014
  s 48 . . . 9.2.2
  s 51 . . . 9.2.5.3
  s 615 . . . 9.1, 9.4.11
  s 615(5) . . . 9.4.11
Conveyancing Act 1881 . . . 9.3.4, 9.3.6.2
  s 5 . . . 4.2
  s 6 . . . 5.5.2
  s 6(1) . . . 5.5.2
  s 14 . . . 9.3.4, 9.3.5.1, 9.3.5.2
  s 14(1) . . . 8.5.1.1, 9.3.4, 9.3.5.1
  s 14(2) . . . 9.3.6, 9.3.6.1
  s 14(6), (8) . . . 9.3.4
Conveyancing Act 1892 . . . 9.3.6.2
  s 2(2) . . . 9.3.4
  ss 4, 5 . . . 9.3.6.2
Deasy's Act *see* Landlord and Tenant Law
    Amendment Act (Ireland) 1860 (Deasy's
    Act)
Derelict Sites Act 1990 . . . 9.4.9
Family Home Protection Act 1976 . . . 9.4.6.2
  s 7 . . . 9.2.5.4
Finance Act 1999 . . . 6.10

Finance Act 2001 . . . 1.4.4
Finance Act 2002 . . . 1.4.4
Finance Act (No 2) 2008 . . . 13.2.5
Finance Act 2012 . . . 5.6.2.5
Fines (Payment and Recovery) Act 2014 . . . 2.1
Harbours Act 1946 . . . 10.2.1.1, 11.2.3
Health Act 1970 . . . 6.4.4, 10.2.1.1
Health (Eastern Regional Health Authority) Act
    1999 . . . 6.4.4
Housing Act 1988
  s 9(2) . . . 6.3.1, 6.3.1.1
Housing Acts 1966–1988 . . . 8.3.1
Housing Acts 1966–2004 . . . 8.1
Housing Finance Agency Acts
    1981–1988 . . . 8.3.1
Housing (Miscellaneous Provisions) Act
    1992 . . . 5.8, 8.1, 8.3.1, 8.3.1.1, 8.3.1.2
  s 6 . . . 6.3.1
  s 6(2) . . . 6.3.1.1
  s 16 . . . 9.2.1, 9.2.3, 9.2.4.1
  s 16(2) . . . 9.2.3
  s 17 . . . 8.3.1.3
  s 17(1) . . . 8.3.1.1
  s 18 . . . 6.6.1, 6.6.2, 8.3.1.2, 8.3.1.3
  s 18(1) . . . 8.3.1.2
  s 20 . . . 8.3.1.3
Housing (Miscellaneous Provisions) Act
    2002 . . . 8.1
Housing (Miscellaneous Provisions) Act
    2009 . . . 8.1, 8.3.1, 8.3.1.2
  s 20 . . . 6.3.1.1, 6.10.2.2
  s 100 . . . 6.3, 6.6.1, 7.3.2.3
  s 100(2) . . . 6.3.1.1
  s 100(3)(b), (c) . . . 7.3.2.3
  s 100(4) . . . 7.3.2.3
  s 100(5) . . . 7.3.2.3
Housing (Private Rented Dwellings) Act
    1982 . . . 8.3.1, 14.1–14.8
  Part II . . . 6.3.1, 7.3.2, 14.6
  s 2(1) . . . 14.4
  s 7(2) . . . 14.4
  s 8 . . . 14.6
  s 8(2)(b) . . . 2.8

TABLE OF STATUTES

s 13 . . . 14.2
s 13(1)(a) . . . 14.6
s 20 . . . 9.2.6.1
Housing (Private Rented Dwellings)
       (Amendment) Act 1983 . . . 14.3
Interpretation Act 2005 . . . 11.2.2.2
Land Act 1965
   s 12 . . . 1.4.4
   s 45 . . . 1.4.4
Land Act 2005 . . . 1.4.4
Land and Conveyancing Law Reform Act
       2009 . . . 1.2, 1.4.4, 1.5, 5.4, 5.6.2.2,
       9.3.4, 9.4.6, 12.3.1
   Part 4 . . . 4.8
       s 3 . . . 1.2, 1.3.4.1, 2.4, 2.5, 2.9, 5.4, 5.5.2,
           11.2.2.2
       s 9(2) . . . 1.3.1
       s 11 . . . 1.2
       s 11(1) . . . 1.2
       s 11(2) . . . 4.8
       s 11(2)(c)(ii) . . . 4.8, 6.3.1.1
       s 11(6) . . . 1.2
       s 11(7) . . . 1.4.4
       s 12 . . . 1.2, 2.1
       s 13(1), (2) . . . 1.2
       s 14 . . . 1.2, 2.1
       s 51 . . . 1.3.4.3, 9.4.6
       s 51(2), (3) . . . 1.3.4.3
       s 62(2) . . . 1.2
       s 67 . . . 1.2
       s 67(1) . . . 1.2
       s 71 . . . 5.4, 5.5.2
       s 127 . . . 5.4, 5.5.2
       s 132 . . . 1.4.4, 2.1, 12.3.1, 12.3.5
       s 132(3) . . . 12.3.1
       s 133 . . . 2.1
   Schedule 2 . . . 1.4.4
Land Law (Ireland) Act 1881
   s 5 . . . 4.5.1
Landlord and Tenant Act 1931 . . . 1.4.1, 1.4.2,
       4.9.1, 9.5.3, 10.1.1.2, 10.2.1.2, 10.2.2,
       10.2.6, 10.4, 10.7.1
   Part III (ss 19-23) . . . 6.3.1, 10.2.2
   Part V (ss 46–54) . . . 11.2.2.4
   Part VI (ss 55–59) . . . 8.3.3
       s 5 . . . 8.3.3.2s 55 . . . 8.3.3, 8.4.3.3
Landlord and Tenant Acts . . . 3.2, 10.2.5.3,
       10.2.5.4
Landlord and Tenant Acts
       1931–1994 . . . 12.3.6.1
Landlord and Tenant Acts
       1980–1984 . . . 1.4.4
Landlord and Tenant (Amendment) Act
       1980 . . . 1.1, 1.4.1, 1.4.2, 1.4.4, 2.6, 2.8,
       3.1, 3.2, 4.9.1, 6.10.6, 8.1, 8.3.1, 8.3.3.2,
       9.2, 9.5.3, 10.1, 11.2.1, 11.2.2.3,
       11.2.2.4, 12.1.1, 12.3.6.2, 14.5, 14.6
   Part I (ss 1–12) . . . 10.1
   Part II (ss 13–29) . . . 6.3.1, 10.1, 10.2, 10.2.2,
       10.2.4, 10.4, 10.7.1

Part III (ss 30–44) . . . 10.1, 11.2.3, 11.3
Part IV (ss 45–63) . . . 10.1, 10.2.3, 10.2.5.6
Part V (ss 64–69) . . . 8.3.3, 10.1, 12.5.2
Part VI (ss 70–88) . . . 10.1
s (1)(a)(iii) . . .10.1.1.2
s 3 . . . 10.1.1.1, 10.1.1.3, 10.1.1.4, 10.2.1.1,
       10.2.5.6
s 3(1) . . . 10.2.4
s 4 . . . 10.2.5.5
s 5 . . . 1.2, 2.6, 2.8, 3.2, 8.3.4, 10.1.1,
       10.1.1.2, 10.7.1, 10.7.5, 14.6
s 5(1) . . . 10.1.1.1
s 5(1)(a)(iii) . . . 10.1.1.2, 14.6
s 5(3) . . . 10.1.1.2
s 13 . . . 1.4.3, 6.10, 10.1, 10.2.1.1, 10.2.4.1,
       10.2.5.3, 10.5
s 13(1)(a) . . . 6.3.1, 10.2, 10.2.1.1, 10.2.4.1,
       10.2.5.2, 10.2.5.3, 10.4, 14.6
s 13(1)(b) . . . 10.2, 10.2.2, 10.2.5.4, 10.4
s 13(1)(c) . . . 10.2, 10.2.3
s 13(2) . . . 10.2.1.2
ss 14, 15 . . . 10.1.1.1
s 16 . . . 10.1, 10.2, 10.2.4
s 17 . . . 1.4.3, 10.1, 10.2.5,
s 17(1) . . . 10.2.5.6, 10.4, 10.5
s 17(1)(a) . . . 10.2.2, 12.1.1
s 17(1)(a)(iiia) . . . 10.2.5.2, 10.2.5.3
s 17(1)(a)(iiib) . . . 10.2.5.4
s 17(2) . . . 10.2.5.6, 10.4, 10.5, 10.7.1
s 17(2)(a) . . . 10.3.2, 10.4
s 17(2)(a)(i) . . .10.2.5.6
s 17(3) . . . 10.2.5.6, 10.4
s 17(4) . . . 10.2.5.6
s 18 . . . 10.2.4, 10.7.1
s 20 . . . 9.1, 9.5.3, 10.2.2, 10.2.6, 10.7.1,
       10.7.2
s 20(1) . . . 10.7.1
s 20(2) . . . 10.7.1, 10.7.2
s 20(2)(a)(ii) . . . 10.7.2
s 20(2)(c), (d) . . . 10.7.2
s 20(3) . . . 10.7.1
s 21 . . . 6.3.1, 9.5.3, 10.2.2, 10.2.6
s 21(2) . . . 3.2, 10.2.6
s 21(3) . . . 10.2.6
s 22 . . . 10.7.3, 10.7.4
s 22(1) . . . 10.7.3, 10.7.4
s 22(2)(a), (c) . . . 10.7.4
s 23 . . . 1.4.3, 10.1, 10.2.4.1
s 23(2) . . . 10.2.4.1
s 23(5) . . . 10.2.4.2
s 23(7) . . . 10.2.4.3
s 27 . . . 10.2.1.2, 10.2.4.1
s 28 . . .10.2.6
s 34 . . . 11.3
s 35 . . .11.3
s 36 . . .11.3
s 39 . . .11.3
s 45 . . . 10.2.3, 10.3.1, 10.7.1, 10.7.5,
       10.7.9
s 46 . . . 10.3.1, 10.7.1

s 46(1) . . . 10.7.5
s 46(1)(a), (b) . . . 10.7.1
s 47 . . . 10.3.1
s 48 . . . 10.3.2, 10.7.5
s 48(1) . . . 10.7.5
s 48(2) . . . 10.7.5–10.7.8
s 48(2)(a) . . . 10.7.6
s 48(2)(b) . . . 10.7.7
s 48(2)(c) . . . 10.7.8
s 48(3) . . . 10.7.5–10.7.8
s 48(4) . . . 10.3.2, 10.7.5, 10.7.6, 10.7.8
s 48(5) . . . 10.7.5, 10.7.6, 10.7.8
s 49(1), (2), (4), (5) . . . 10.7.9
s 50 . . . 10.3.2, 10.7.6, 10.7.10
s 51(1) . . . 10.3.2, 10.7.7
s 51(2) . . . 10.7.7
s 51(4) . . . 10.7.7
s 52 . . . 10.3.2, 10.7.8, 10.7.10
s 54 . . . 10.7.1
s 54(2) . . . 10.3.2, 10.7.5
s 55(1)–(3) . . . 10.7.10
s 55(4), (5) . . . 10.7.11
s 55(6) . . . 10.7.10, 10.7.11
s 56 . . . 10.7.2
s 56(1) . . . 10.7.1
s 58 . . . 10.1, 10.4, 10.7.1
s 58(1) . . . 10.4
s 58(1)(b) . . . 10.4
s 58(2) . . . 10.4
s 58(4), (5) . . . 10.4
s 60 . . . 9.4.8, 10.1, 10.2.5.6, 10.7.12
s 60(2) . . . 10.2.5.6, 10.7.12
s 60(3)–(6) . . . 10.7.12
s 61 . . . 6.8
s 65 . . . 8.3.3, 8.3.3.1, 8.5.1.2, 10.6
s 66 . . . 10.6.1, 12.4.3
s 67 . . . 10.6.2, 12.5.2
ss 68, 69 . . . 10.6.3
s 70 . . . 11.2.3
ss 71, 72 . . . 11.2.2.4
s 73 . . . 11.2.2.1
s 74 . . . 1.2
s 78 . . . 9.3.6.2
s 78(2) . . . 9.3.6.2
s 83 . . . 10.2.6, 10.7.1
s 84 . . . 10.7.1, 10.7.13
s 84(1) . . . 10.7.13
s 84(2), (3) . . . 10.7.14
s 85 . . . 1.4.3, 4.9.1, 10.1, 10.2.1.2,
    10.2.5.1
s 87 . . . 6.8, 8.3.4
Landlord and Tenant (Amendment) Act
    1984 . . . 1.4.4
s 3 . . . 11.3
s 7 . . . 11.4.1.4, 11.6, 11.6.4
s 7(3) . . . 11.6
s 7(4) . . . 11.6.1
s 9 . . . 11.2.2.5
s 14 . . . 10.2.5.5
s 15 . . . 10.2.4.2

Landlord and Tenant (Amendment) Act
    1989 . . . 10.2.4.1
Landlord and Tenant (Amendment) Act
    1994 . . . 1.4.3, 5.2, 9.2, 10.1, 10.2.1.1,
    10.2.1.2, 12.1.1
s 3 . . . 10.2.1.1, 10.2.4.1
s 3(2) . . . 10.2.1.2
s 4 . . . 1.4.3, 4.9.1, 10.2.5, 10.2.5.1, 10.2.5.2,
    10.2.5.4
s 5 . . . 10.2.4.1
Landlord and Tenant (Ground Rents) Act
    1967 . . . 11.2–11.9
s 3 . . . 11.2.2.1, 11.4, 11.8.1.1
s 3(1) . . . 11.2.1, 11.2.2.1, 11.4
s 3(2) . . . 11.2.2.1, 11.4
s 3(3) . . . 11.2.2.1, 11.4
s 4 . . . 11.2.2.4, 11.2.3, 11.4.1, 11.8.1.1, 11.9
s 5 . . . 11.4.1.2, 11.8.1.1
s 6 . . . 11.2.1
s 6(1) . . . 11.4.1.1
s 7 . . . 11.4.1, 11.8.1.2
s 7(1) . . . 11.8.1.2, 11.9
s 7(2) . . . 11.8.1.3
s 8 . . . 11.4.1.2, 11.9
s 8(4) . . . 11.4.1.2
ss 9, 10 . . . 11.4.1.3, 11.8.1.4
s 11 . . . 11.4.1.2, 11.4.1.5, 11.8.1.5
s 12 . . . 11.4.1.5, 11.8.1.5
ss 13, 14 . . . 11.4.1.5
ss 15, 16 . . . 11.4.1.5, 11.8.1.6
s 17 . . . 11.2.1, 11.4, 11.4.1.2
s 17(2), (3) . . . 11.4.1.2
s 19(1)–(3) . . . 11.4.1.3
s 21 . . . 11.4.1.6
s 21(1) . . . 11.8.2
s 21(3) . . . 11.4.1.6
s 22 . . . 11.4.1.2
s 23 . . . 11.4.1, 11.4.2.2
s 29 . . . 10.6.3
s 31 . . . 11.4.1.7
s 33 . . . 11.4.1.8
s 35 . . . 9.3.4
Landlord and Tenant (Ground Rents) Act 1978
    (No 1 Act of 1978) . . . 8.3.1, 11.7
s 2 . . . 11.7
s 2(4) . . . 11.7
Landlord and Tenant (Ground Rents) (No 2)
    Act 1978 . . . 3.1, 11.2–11.10
Part II . . . 6.3.1, 11.2.2.1, 11.2.2.4, 11.4.2.1,
    11.8.2.1–11.8.2.4, 11.9
Part III . . . 11.2.3, 11.4, 11.4.2, 11.4.2.4
s 3 . . . 11.2.2.1
s 4 . . . 11.2.3
s 7 . . . 11.2.2.1, 11.4
s 8 . . . 11.2.2.1, 11.2.3
ss 9–16 . . . 11.2.2.1, 11.4
s 9 . . . 11.2.2.1, 11.2.2.2, 11.2.2.4,
    11.2.2.5, 11.2.3, 11.3, 11.4, 11.4.1,
    11.4.2.1, 11.5, 11.9, 14.7
s 9 (4) . . . 11.2.2.2

TABLE OF STATUTES

s 10 . . . 11.2.2.1, 11.2.2.2, 11.2.2.4,
   11.2.2.5, 11.3, 11.4, 11.4.1, 11.4.2.1,
   11.5, 11.9
s 12 . . . 11.2.2.4
s 14 . . . 11.2.2.3, 11.8.2.4
s 15 . . . 11.2.2.5, 11.4, 11.5, 14.7
s 15(e) . . . 11.2.2.5
s 16 . . . 11.2.3, 11.7
s 16(2) . . . 11.2.3
s 16(2)(c) . . . 11.2.3
s 16(2)(f) . . . 11.2.3
s 16(3) . . . 11.2.3
s 17 . . . 11.6
s 18 . . . 11.4.2
s 19 . . . 11.4, 11.4.2, 11.4.2.1, 11.7
s 20 . . . 11.4.2, 11.4.2.1, 11.4.2.2, 11.8.2.1,
   11.8.2.5
s 21 . . . 11.4.2, 11.4.2.2, 11.8.2.2, 11.8.2.6
s 21(1) . . . 11.4.2.2, 11.8.2.2, 11.8.2.4
s 21(2) . . . 11.4.2.2
s 21(4), (5) . . . 11.4.2.2
s 22 . . . 11.4.2.1, 11.4.2.2, 11.4.2.7, 11.8.2,
   11.8.2.1, 11.8.2.2, 11.8.2.4–11.8.2.6
s 22(1) . . . 11.8.2.3
s 22(1)(a) . . . 11.4.2.1
s 22(1)(b) . . . 11.4.2.2
s 22(2) . . . 11.4.2.3
s 22(5), (6) . . . 11.4.2.3
s 23(4), (5) . . . 11.4.2.4
s 24 . . . 11.4.2.6
s 24(3) . . . 11.4.2.6
s 27 . . . 9.3.6.3
s 28 . . . 11.4.1.7, 11.6.1
s 28(1), (2) . . . 11.4.2.5
s 28(2)(a)–(c) . . . 11.4.2.5
Landlord and Tenant (Ground Rents)
   (Amendment) Act 1987 . . . 11.2.2.1
Landlord and Tenant (Ground Rents) Act
   2005 . . . 11.2.3
Landlord and Tenant (Ireland) Act
   1870 . . . 9.2.3
Landlord and Tenant Law Amendment Act
   (Ireland) 1860 (Deasy's Act) . . . 1.3.4.1,
   1.4.4, 5.5.4, 8.1, 8.1.1, 8.5.2.5, 9.1.1
s 1 . . . 1.3.4.1
s 3 . . . 1.3.4.1, 1.3.4.3, 1.5, 3.1, 3.2
s 4 . . . 1.3.4.1, 1.3.4.3, 1.5, 2.1
s 5 . . . 2.3
s 6 . . . 9.2.4.4
s 9 . . . 1.5
s 40 . . . 8.1.1, 8.5.2.5, 12.2.4.8
s 42 . . . 8.1.1, 8.2, 8.3.2
s 48 . . . 6.8
s 52 . . . 9.1, 9.2.1, 9.4.5, 9.5.2
s 60 . . .9.5.2
s 66 . . . 9.1, 9.4.5
s 71 . . .9.5.2
s 72 . . . 9.5.3
s 78 . . . 9.1, 9.2.1, 9.4.4, 9.5.4
s 86 . . . 4.9.1, 9.1, 9.4.3

Landlord and Tenant Law Reform Bill 2011
   (draft) . . . 1.2, 1.3.4.3, 1.4.3, 1.4.4, 1.5,
   2.1, 2.3, 2.4, 2.5, 2.6, 3.1, 3.2, 5.4, 5.5.4,
   8.1.1, 8.3.7, 9.1.1, 10.1, 10.1.1.1,
   10.2.4.2, 10.6.4, 11.1, 12.2.4.5, 12.3.1,
   12.3.5, 12.6.3
Part 2 . . . 3.2
Part 3 . . . 1.5
s 3 . . . 1.5
Landlord and Tenant (Reversionary Leases) Act
   1958 . . . 1.4.2, 11.7, 11.2.2.4, 11.2.3,
   11.7
Local Government Act 1941 . . . 10.2.5.6
Local Government Reform Act 2014
   s 32 . . . 5.6.2.7
Local Registration of Title (Ireland) Act,
   1891 . . . 1.3.4.3, 1.4.1
Notices to Quit (Ireland) Act 1876 . . . 9.2.3
Planning and Development (Housing) and
   Residential Tenancies Act 2016 . . . 1.1,
   1.4.4
Part 3 (ss 30–50) . . . 6.1
s 37 . . .1.4.4, 2.6
Prohibition of Forcible Entry and Occupation
   Act 1971
   s 2 . . . 9.3.5.4
Registration of Deeds Act (Ireland)
   1707 . . . 1.3.2
Registration of Deeds and Title Act
   2006 . . . 1.4.4
s 9 . . . 1.4.4
s 32 . . . 11.2.2.2
s 64 . . . 5.6.2.1
s 76 . . . 11.2.3
s 77 . . . 11.4.2.5
Registration of Title Act 1964 . . . 1.4.1
s 3 . . . 5.5.2
s 24 . . . 11.4.3
s 72 . . . 3.5, 5.6.2.6, 11.4.2.5
s 81 . . .4.8
s 104 . . . 5.6.2.1
Registration of Title Act 1972
   s 72 . . .3.5
Renewable Leasehold Conversion Act
   1849 . . . 1.2
Rent Restrictions Acts 1960–1981 . . . 8.4, 14.1
Rent Restrictions Act 1960 . . . 14.1
Residential Tenancies Act 2004 . . . 1.1, 1.2,
   1.4.4, 5.8, 6.1–6.11, 7.1–7.4, 8.1, 9.1,
   10.1, 10.2.5.4, 14.6
Part 1 (ss 1–11) . . . 6.1
Part 2 (ss 12–18) . . . 6.1, 6.6
   Chapter 1 (ss 12–15) . . . 6.6.1, 6.6.1.2
   Chapter 2 (ss 16–18) . . . 6.6.2
Part 3 (ss 19–24) . . . 6.1, 6.9, 7.3
Part 4 (ss 25–56) . . . 1.1, 1.4.4, 2.6, 6.1, 6.2,
   6.3.2, 6.4.3, 6.10, 6.10.1, 6.10.2,
   6.10.2.1, 6.10.2.2, 6.10.2.3, 6.10.3–
   6.10.6, 6.11, 6.11.1, 6.11.8, 9.1, 9.4.1,
   10.2.2, 10.2.5.4

Chapter 1 (ss 25–26) . . . 6.10
Chapter 2 (ss 27–32) . . . 6.10
Chapter 3 (ss 33–39) . . . 6.4.3, 6.10.2,
    6.10.2.2, 6.10.4
Chapter 4 (ss 40–42) . . . 6.10.2, 6.10.4
Chapter 5 (ss 43–47) . . . 6.10.4
Chapter 6 (ss 48–53) . . . 6.10.2.2, 6.10.5
Chapter 7 (ss 54–56) . . . 6.10.6
Part 5 (ss 57–74) . . . 5.8, 6.1, 6.10.2,
    6.10.2.2, 6.10.2.3, 6.10.3, 6.11, 6.11.1
Chapter 2 (ss 62–64) . . . 6.11.2
Chapter 3 (ss 65–69) . . . 6.11.3
Chapter 4 (ss 70–72) . . . 6.11.4
Chapter 5 (ss 73–74) . . . 6.11.5
Part 6 (ss 75–123) . . . 5.8, 6.1, 6.3.1.1, 6.6.1,
    6.6.1.1, 6.8, 6.9, 6.10.2.1, 6.10.5, 6.10.6,
    6.11.2, 6.11.4, 7.3, 7.3.1.4
Chapter 8 (ss 115–120) . . . 6.8
Part 7 (ss 124–148) . . . 6.1, 6.6.1, 7.3,
    7.3.1.1, 7.3.1.2, 7.3.2, 7.3.2.1
Chapter 2 (ss 134–148) . . . 7.3.2.2
Chapter 3 (ss 139–145) . . . 7.3.2.3
Part 8 (ss 149–181) . . . 6.1, 7.2
Part 9 (ss 182–202) . . . 6.1
s 1(d) . . . 6.5
s 3 . . . 6.3.1.1
s 3(1) . . . 6.3
s 3(2) . . . 6.3, 6.3.1, 6.3.1.1, 7.3.2, 8.1,
    8.3.1.1, 8.3.1.2, 10.2.2, 14.6
s 3(2)(c) . . . 6.3.1.1
s 3(2)(h) . . . 6.3.1
s 3(2A) . . . 6.3.1.1
s 3(4) . . . 6.3.1.1, 6.4.3, 6.6.2
s 3(5) . . . 6.3.1.1
s 3(6) . . . 6.3.1.1
s 3A . . . 6.3.1.1
s 3B . . . 6.3.1.1
s 4 . . . 6.4, 6.4.5, 10.2.5.4
s 4(1) . . . 6.4.1, 6.4.3
s 4(2) . . . 6.4.1
s 5 . . . 6.4, 10.2.2, 10.2.5.4
s 5(1) . . . 6.3.1.1, 6.4.2, 6.4.6, 14.6
s 5(2) . . . 6.4.6
s 6 . . . 6.5, 6.11.1
s 6(1)(d) . . . 6.5
s 6(2), (3) . . . 6.5
s 6 (5), (6) . . . 6.5
s 9 . . . 6.7, 7.3.1.7, 7.3.2.3
s 9(3) . . . 6.7
s 9(4), (5) . . . 6.7
ss 12–18 . . . 6.6
s 12 . . . 5.8, 6.6, 6.6.1, 8.1, 8.4.1
s 12(1)(a) . . . 6.6.1
s 12(1)(b) . . . 6.6.1, 8.3.1.2
s 12(1)(b)(i), (ii) . . . 6.6.1
s 12(1)(ba) . . . 6.6.1
s 12(1)(c)–(i) . . . 6.6.1
s 12(2) . . . 6.6.1, 8.3.1.2
s 12(3) . . . 6.6.1
s 12(4) . . . 6.6.1, 6.6.1.2

s 12 (4)(a)(i) . . . 7.3.2.3
s 12(4)(b) . . . 7.3.2.3
s 12(5) . . . 6.6.1
s 13 . . . 6.6.1
s 14 . . . 6.6.1
s 14(2)–(4) . . . 6.6.1
s 15 . . . 6.6.1.1
s 16 . . . 5.8, 6.6, 6.6.2, 8.1, 8.4.1
s 16(a)(i), (ii) . . . 6.6.2
s 16(b) . . . 6.6.2, 8.3.1.2
s 16(c)–(e) . . . 6.6.2
s 16(f) . . . 6.6.1, 6.6.2, 6.8
s 16(g)–(n) . . . 6.6.2
s 17 . . . 5.8, 6.6.2
s 17(1) . . . 6.6.2.1
s 17(1)(a), (b) . . . 6.11.3
s 17(3), (4) . . . 6.6.2
s 18 . . . 6.6
s 18(1)–(3) . . . 8.4.1
s 19 . . . 6.9
s 19(1) . . . 6.9
s 19(3)–(7) . . . 6.9
s 19(4) . . . 6.6.1, 6.9
s 20 . . . 6.9
s 20(3) . . . 6.9
s 21 . . . 6.9
s 22(1), (2) . . . 6.9
s 22(3) . . . 6.9, 7.3.1.1
s 23 . . . 6.9
s 24(1) . . . 6.9
s 25 . . . 6.3.2, 6.4.3, 6.10, 6.11.1
s 25(3) . . . 6.3.2
s 25(4) . . . 6.10
s 25(5)–(7) . . . 6.3.2
s 26 . . . 6.4.3, 6.10, 6.10.1, 6.10.3, 6.10.6,
    6.11.1
s 27 . . . 6.10
s 28 . . . 6.4.3, 6.10, 6.10.2.2
s 28(1), (2) . . . 6.4.3
s 28(2)(a) . . . 6.10.2.1
s 28(3) . . . 6.4.3, 6.10.5
s 29 . . . 6.4.3, 6.10, 10.2.5.4
ss 30–32 . . . 6.10
s 33 . . . 6.11.8
s 34 . . . 6.10.2, 6.10.2.1, 6.10.6, 7.3.1,
    9.4.1, 10.2.2
s 34(a) . . . 6.10.2.1, 6.10.4, 6.10.6, 6.11.8
s 34(b) . . . 6.10.2.1, 6.10.4, 6.11.8
Table . . . 6.10.2.1, 6.10.6, 10.2.2
s 35 . . . 6.10.2.1
s 35(9)(b) . . . 6.10.2.1
s 35A(2) . . . 6.10.2.1
s 35A(3)(a) . . . 6.10.2.1
s 36 . . . 6.10.2, 6.10.2.2, 6.11.8, 9.4.1
s 37 . . . 6.10.2.2, 6.11
s 37(1), (2) . . . 6.10.2.2
s 38 . . . 6.10.2.2
s 38(4) . . . 6.10.2.2
s 39 . . . 6.3.1, 6.10.2.2, 9.4.1
s 39(1) . . . 6.10.2.2

s 39(3) . . . 6.10.2.2
s 39(5) . . . 6.10.2.2
s 41 . . . 6.10.4, 9.4.1
s 41(1)–(3) . . . 9.4.1
s 42 . . . 6.10.2.3, 6.10.4, 6.10.6
s 43 . . . 6.10.4, 9.4.1
s 45 . . . 6.10.4
s 46 . . . 6.10.4
s 47 . . . 6.10.5
s 48 . . . 6.10.5
s 49 . . . 6.10.5
s 50 . . . 6.10.5
s 50(6) . . . 6.10.5
s 50(7) . . . 6.10.5
s 51 . . . 6.10.5
s 51(2) . . . 6.10.5
ss 52, 53 . . . 6.10.5
s 54 . . . 6.10.6
s 55 . . . 6.10.6
s 55(1), (2) . . . 10.2.2
s 56 . . . 6.10.6
s 56(2) . . . 7.3.1
s 56(6) . . . 6.10.6
s 57 . . . 6.11.1
s 57(b) . . . 6.11.1
s 58 . . . 6.11.1
s 59 . . . 6.11.1
s 60 . . . 6.11.1
s 61 . . . 6.11.1
s 62 . . . 6.11.2, 6.11.4
s 62(1)(b) . . . 6.11.5
s 62(1)(c) . . . 6.11.2
s 62(1)(f) . . . 6.11.2, 6.11.3
s 63 . . . 6.11.2
s 64 . . . 6.11.2
s 65 . . . 6.11.3
s 65(4) . . . 6.11.1, 6.11.2, 6.11.3
ss 66–69 . . . 6.10.2.2
s 66 . . . 6.10.2, 6.10.2.3, 6.11.2, 6.11.3,
   6.11.8
s 67 . . . 6.10.2.3, 6.11.3, 6.11.8
s 68 . . . 6.10.2.2, 6.10.2.3, 6.11.3, 6.11.8
s 68(4) . . . 6.11.3
s 69 . . . 6.10.1, 6.11.3
s 70 . . . 6.11.4
s 70(3) . . . 6.11.6
s 71 . . . 6.11.4
s 72 . . . 6.11.4
s 72(1), (2) . . . 6.11.4
s 73 ...6.11.5
s 74 ...6.11.5
s 75(3) . . . 7.3.1
s 75(4) . . . 6.9
s 75(4)(b) . . . 7.3.1
s 76 . . . 7.3.1
s 76(2) . . . 7.3.1.1
s 76(4) . . . 6.10.5, 7.3.1
s 77 . . . 7.3.1, 7.3.3
s 77(2) . . . 6.6.1.1, 7.3.1
s 77(4) . . . 6.6.1.1

s 78(1) . . . 6.9
s 78(1)(b), (c) . . . 6.9
s 78(2), (3) . . . 6.11.4
s 80 . . . 6.11.6, 7.3.1.1
s 81 . . . 6.11.4, 6.11.6, 7.3.1
s 81(2) . . . 6.11.6
s 81(3) . . . 6.11.2
s 82 . . . 7.3.1.1
s 82(5) . . . 7.3.1.7
s 83 . . . 7.3.1.1, 7.3.1.2
s 84 . . . 7.3.1.2
s 85 . . . 7.3.1.2
s 86(1), (2) . . . 6.9
s 88 . . . 6.9, 7.3.1.1
s 94 . . . 7.3.1
s 95(4) . . . 7.3.1.7
s 96 . . . 7.3.1.4
s 96(6) . . . 7.3.1
s 97(2)–(7) . . . 7.3.1.5
s 97(4)(b) . . . 7.3.1.4
s 99 . . . 7.3.1.7
s 100 . . . 7.3.1, 7.3.2.3
s 102 . . . 7.3, 7.3.1.6
s 102(1) . . . 7.3.1
s 103 . . . 7.3.1.6
s 104(5), (6) . . . 7.3.1.6
s 108 . . . 7.3.1.7
s 109 . . . 7.3.1.3
s 115(2)(b) . . . 6.9
s 116 . . . 6.11.4
s 117 . . . 7.3.1.7
s 118 . . . 6.10.6
s 118(2) . . . 6.10.6
s 119 . . . 6.8
s 119(1) . . . 6.8
s 121 . . . 7.3.1.4, 7.3.1.7
s 123(1)–(3) . . . 7.3.1.7
s 124 . . . 7.3.1.7
s 124(7) . . . 7.3.1.7
s 126 . . . 7.3.1.7
s 126(3) . . . 7.3.1.7
ss 127–148 . . . 7.3.2
ss 127, 128 . . . 7.3.2.1
s 135(2) . . . 7.3.2.3
s 136 . . . 7.3.2.2
s 137 . . . 7.3.2.2
s 139 . . . 6.9, 7.3.2.2
ss 143–145 . . . 7.3.2.3
s 144 . . . 7.3.2.3
ss 146–148 . . . 7.3.2.3
s 147(A) . . . 7.3.2.3
s 149 ...7.2
s 151 . . . 7.3
s 151(1)(g) . . . 6.9
s 151(3) . . . 7.3
s 152 . . . 7.3.4
ss 153–155 . . . 7.2
s 153(4) . . . 7.2
s 157 . . . 7.3
s 159(3) . . . 7.3

s 160 . . . 7.2
s 182 . . . 6.10.6
s 182(1) . . . 7.3.1
s 184 . . . 6.11.7
s 186 . . . 6.6.2, 6.10.3
s 187 . . . 6.6.1
s 187(2) . . . 6.6.1
s 191 . . . 10.2.5, 10.2.5.1, 10.2.5.4
s 192 . . . 10.2.2, 14.5
s 192(2) . . . 10.2.2, 10.2.3, 14.6
s 192(3) . . . 10.2.2
s 193(a) . . . 8.3.2
s 193(b) . . . 9.3.4
s 193(d) . . . 10.6.1, 10.6.2, 10.6.3
s 193(e) . . . 9.2.3
s 195(4) . . . 7.3.1
s 199(1) . . . 10.4
s 199(2) . . . 9.4.8, 10.2.5.6
s 201 . . . 8.3.1.3
Schedule, para 8(2) . . . 7.3.1
Residential Tenancies (Amendment) Act
    2009 . . . 7.3
Residential Tenancies (Amendment) Act
    2015 . . . 1.1, 1.2, 1.4.4, 6.1, 6.4
s 1 . . . 6.3.1.1
s 2(c) . . . 6.3.1.1
s 3 . . . 6.3.1.1
s 4(1) . . . 6.4.3
s 9 . . . 6.3.2
Residential Tenancies Act 2016 . . . 1.1, 1.4.4,
    2.6, 6.1, 6.9, 7.1, 7.3.3, 7.4, 7.4.2, 9.4.1
s 4 . . . 6.6.2
s 33 . . . 6.6.1, 6.9
s 34 . . . 6.6.9
s 35 . . . 6.9
s 36 . . . 6.6.1.1
s 37 . . . 1.4.4, 6.10
s 37(1) . . . 6.4.3
s 37(3) . . . 6.4.3
s 40 . . . 6.10.2.1
s 41 . . . 6.10.4, 6.10.6
s 49 . . . 7.3.1.7
Settled Land Acts 1882–1890 . . . 4.8
State Airports (Shannon Group) Act 2014
s 37 . . . 6.4.4

State Property Act 1954 . . . 1.3.1
Statute of Frauds (Ireland) 1695 . . . 1.3.2
s 2 . . . 1.3.4.3
Succession Act 1965
s 73 . . . 1.3.1
s 111 . . . 4.8
Taxes Consolidation Act 1997
s 380B(2) . . . 6.10
s 380C(4) . . . 6.10
s 380D(2) . . . 6.10
Town Tenants (Ireland) Act 1906 . . . 10.7.1
Urban Renewal Act 1998
s 7 . . . 9.4.8, 10.2.5.6
Value Added Tax Consolidation Act
    2010 . . . 13.1.1
Part 3
    Chapter 1 (ss 19–23) . . . 13.1.3.2,
        13.2.3.1
    Chapter 3 (ss 25–28)... 13.1.3.2
Part 4
    Chapter 1 (ss 29–31) . . . 13.1.3.3
    Chapter 3 (ss 33–35)... 13.1.3.3
Part 6, Chapter 1 (ss 46–51)... 13.1.3.4
Part 8
    Chapter 1 (ss 59–62) . . . 13.1.5
    Chapter 2 (ss 63–64) . . . 13.2.3.3
Part 9, Chapter 2 (ss 66–73) . . . 13.1.4.2
s 2 . . . 13.1.3.2
s 20 . . . 13.1.3.2
s 22(c) . . . 13.1.3.2
s 46(1)(a)—(d) . . . 13.1.3.4
s 64(12) . . . 13.2.3.3
s 85(1) . . . 13.2.3.3
s 95 . . . 13.2.4, 13.2.4.1
s 95(8) . . . 13.2.4.1
s 95(8)(a) . . . 13.2.4.1
s 96(8) . . . 13.2.5
s 97 . . . 13.2.3.1
s 97(4) . . . 13.4.1
Schedule 1 . . . 13.1.3.1, 13.1.3.4
Schedule 1, para 11 . . . 13.2.3.1, 13.4.1
Schedules 2, 3 . . . 13.1.3.4
VAT Act 1972 . . . 13.1.1
s 7A(4) . . . 13.4.1
Schedule 1 . . . 13.1.3.1, 13.4.1

TABLE OF REGULATIONS AND EU LAW

Regulations

European Communities (Energy Performance of Buildings) Regulations 2012 (S.I. 243/2012) . . . 6.6.1

European Communities (Protection of Employees on Transfer of Undertakings) Regulations 2003 (S.I. 131/2003) . . . 3.4

Housing (Private Rented Dwellings) (Standards) Regulations, 1984 (S.I. 337/1984) . . . 8.3.1.2

Housing (Registration of Rented Houses) Regulations 1996 (S.I. 30/996) . . . 1.4.4

Housing (Rent Books) Regulations 1993 (S.I. 146/1993) . . . 6.6.2, 8.1, 8.3.1.1, 8.3.1.3
Schedule . . . 8.3.1.1

Housing (Rent Books) Regulations 1993 (Amendment) Regulations 2004 (S.I. 751/2004) . . . 8.1, 8.3.1.1

Housing (Rent Books) (Amendment) Regulations 2010 (S.I. 357/2010) . . . 8.1, 8.3.1.1

Housing (Standards for Rented Houses) Regulations 1993 (S.I. 147/1993) . . . 8.3.1.2

Housing (Standards for Rented Houses) Regulations 2008 (S.I. 534/2008) . . . 8.3.1.1, 8.3.1.2

Housing (Standards for Rented Houses) (Amendment) Regulations 2009 (S.I. 462/2009) . . . 7.3.4, 8.3.1.2

Housing (Standards for Rented Houses) Regulations 2017 (S.I. 17/2017) . . . 6.6.1, 6.6.2, 8.1, 8.3.1, 8.3.1.1, 8.3.1.2

Land and Conveyancing Law Reform Act 2009 (Commencement) (Section 132) Order 2009 (S.I. 471/2009) . . . 12.3.1

Land Registration Rules 2012 (S.I. 483/2012) . . . 5.6.2.1, 9.4.6.1

Landlord and Tenant (Ground Rents) Act 1967 (Forms) Regulations 1967 (S.I. 43/1967) . . . 11.4.1, 11.8.1

Landlord and Tenant (Ground Rents) (No 2) Act 1978 (Fees) Order 1984 (S.I. 194/1984) . . . 11.4.2.4

Landlord and Tenant (Ground Rents) (No 2) Act 1978 Regulations 1978 (S.I. 219/1978) . . . 11.4.2, 11.8.2
Schedules 1, 2 . . . 11.8.2

Landlord and Tenant Regulations 1980 (S.I. 272/1980) . . . 10.2.6, 10.7

Local Government Reform Act 2014 (Commencement of Certain Provisions) (No. 2) Order 2014 (S.I. 146/2014) . . . 5.6.2.7

Planning and Development (Housing) and Residential Tenancies Act 2016 (Commencement of Section 49) Order 2017 (S.I. 590/2017) . . . 7.3.1.7

Residential Tenancies Act 2004 (Commencement) Order 2004 (S.I. 505/2004) . . . 6.2, 6.4.3, 10.2.2, 10.2.5.4

Residential Tenancies Act 2004 (Commencement) (No 2) Order 2004 (S.I. 750/2004) . . . 6.2, 10.6.1

Residential Tenancies Act 2004 (Prescribed Form) Regulations 2016 (S.I. 150/2016) . . . 7.3.2.2

Residential Tenancies Act 2004 (Prescribed Form) (No. 2) Regulations 2016 (S.I. 217/2016) . . . 6.9

Residential Tenancies (Amendment) Act 2015 Commencement Order (S.I. 151/2016) . . . 6.3.1.1

Residential Tenancies (Amendment) Act 2015 (Commencement of Certain Provisions) (No. 2) Order 2016 . . . 6.3.1.1

State Airports (Shannon Group) Act 2014 (Shannon Commercial Enterprises Transfer Day) Order 2014 (S.I. 396/2014) . . . 6.4.4

EU legislation

Council Directive 2006/112/EC (Recast Sixth VAT Directive) . . . 3.2, 13.1.1

TABLE OF CASES

A O'Gorman & Co Ltd v JES Holdings Ltd,
31 May 2005, High Court
(unreported) . . . 11.2.2.2, 11.2.2.4, 11.6.4
Addiscombe Garden Estates Ltd v Crabbe
[1958] 1 QB 513 . . . 3.2
Aherne v Southern Metropole Hotel Co Ltd
[1989] ILRM 693 . . . 10.4
Allied Dunbar Assurance plc v Homebase
Limited [2002] 27 EG144 . . . 12.4.2
Argy Trading Development Co Ltd v Lapid
Developments Ltd [1977] 3 All ER
785 . . . 12.6.2
Atkinson v King [1878] 2 LR (Ir) 320 . . . 3.1.2

Bank of Ireland v Fitzmaurice [1989] ILRM
452 . . . 10.2.5.1
Barry v Registrar of Titles and the Honourable
Hemphill (ex tempore) [1992] ILRM
62 . . . 11.2.2.5
Basham, Re [1986] 1 WLR 1498 . . . 3.1.4
Bashir v Commissioner of Lands [1959] 3 WLR
996 . . . 5.4
Baumann v Elgin Contractors Ltd [1973] IR
169 . . . 10.2.6
Bellew v Bellew [1982] IR 447 . . . 3.2
Bernard v Meara (1862) 12 Ir Ch R
389 . . . 1.3.4.3
Blake v Hogan (1933) 67 ILTR 237 . . . 9.3.6.4
Boylan v Dublin Corporation [1949] IR
60 . . . 4.4
Brendan Flynn v James McMahon, 3 May
2001, Circuit Court
(unreported) . . . 10.1.1.
British Railways Board v Mobil Oil Co Ltd
[1994] 1 EGLR. 146 CA . . . 12.3.1
Brown v Davies [1958] 1 QB 117 . . . 8.4.3.2
Burns v Morelli [1953– 54] Ir Jur Rep
50 . . . 12.4.3

Canty v Private Residential Tenancies Board
[2007] IEHC 243 . . . 6.11.1, 6.11.3

Carroll v Mayo County Council [1967] IR
364 . . . 44.3
Carton v McManus (1962) 96 ILT 92 . . . 2.8
Chaloner v Broughton (1865) 11 Ir Jur (NS)
84 . . . 8.4.3.2
Chandler v Kerley [1978] 2 All ER 942 . . . 3.1.3
Chartered Trust plc v Davies [1997] 2 EGLR
83 . . . 8.5.2.4
Cleve House Properties v Schildof [1980] CLY
1641 . . . 12.2.4.1
Concorde Graphics Limited v Andromeda
Investments SA (1983) 265 EG
386 . . . 12.2.2
Conquest v Ebbetts [1896] AC 490 . . . 8.5.1.2
Cowan v Factor [1948] IR 128 . . . 8.2
Cue Club Ltd v Navaro Ltd, 23 October 1996,
Supreme Court (unreported) . . . 9.3.6.1,
9.3.6.4
Cullen v Cullen [1962] IR 268 . . . 3.1.4
Cuprum Properties Limited (Acting by its Joint
Receivers and Managers Tom O'Brien
and Simon Coyle) v Murray [2017]
IEHC 699 . . . 10.2.4
Curoe v Gordon (1892) 26 ILTR 95 . . . 9.2.6

Davies v Hilliard (1967) 101 ILTR 50 . . . 4.9.1
Dease v O'Reilly (1845) 8 Ir LR 52 . . . 4.5.2
Dickeson v Lipschitz [1972] 106 ILTr
1 . . . 9.3.6.4
Digital Hub Development Agency v Keane &
Ors [2008] IEHC 22 . . . 11.2.3
Dolan v Corporation of the Corn Exchange
Buildings Company of Dublin [1973] IR
269 . . . 10.2.5.6
Dorothy Blake v Attorney-General [1982] IR
117 . . . 14.1
Driscoll v Riordan [1885] 16 LR IR 235 . . . 2.8
Dursley v Watters and Castleblaney Plant Hire
Ltd [1993] 1 IR 224 . . . 10.1.1.1

Earl of Meath v Megan [1897] 2 IR 477 . . . 2.3

TABLE OF CASES

Edward Lee & Co Ltd v N1 Property
    Developments Ltd . . . 10.2.5.6
Ennis v Rafferty (1938) 72 ILTR 56 . . . 9.3.6.4
Errington v Errington and Woods (1952) 1 KB
    290 . . . 3.2

Farrell v Wine (1973) 107 ILT & SJ
    222 . . . 10.2.1.2
Farrelly v Doughty (1881) 15 ILTR
    100 . . . 9.4.2
Fenlon v Keogh (Per Rep of Anna Keogh), 10
    February 1997, High Court
    (unreported) . . . 11.2.2.2
Fetherstonhaugh v Smith, 12 February 1979,
    High Court (unreported) . . . 8.3.6
FG Sweeney Ltd v Powerscourt Shopping
    Centre Ltd [1985] ILRM 442 . . . 9.3.5.1,
    9.3.6.1
Finchbourne Ltd v Rodrigues [1976] 3 All ER
    581 . . . 12.2.2, 12.2.5
Fitzgerald (Trustees of Castleknock Tennis Club)
    v John Corcoran [1991] ILRM
    545 . . . 11.2.2.3
Fleming v Brennan [1941] IR 499 . . . 8.3.2

Gallagher v Earl of Leitrim [1948] Ir Jur Rep
    23 . . . 10.2.5.6
Gatien Motor Co Ltd v Continental Oil Co of
    Ireland Ltd [1979] IR 406 . . . 3.2, 4.9.1,
    10.2.1.2
Gilligan v Silke [1963] IR 1 . . . 8.3.3.2
Gleniffer Finance Corporation Ltd v Bamar
    Wood & Products Ltd [1978] 2 Lloyd's
    Rep 49 . . . 12.6.2
Gooderham & Worts v Canadian Broadcasting
    Corp [1947] AC 66 . . . 805.1.2
Groome v Fodhla Printing Co [1943] IR
    380 . . . 8.3.3, 8.4.3.1– 8.4.3.3

Harrisrange Limited v Duncan [2002] IEHC
    117 . . . 9.3.5.4
Heatons Wholesale Ltd v Anthony McCormack
    [1994] 2 IR 400 . . . 11.4
Hill v Barclay (1810) 16 Ves 402 . . . 8.5.1.3
Horne v Struben [1902] AC 454 . . . 5.5.2
Hurst v Picture Theatres Ltd [1915] 1 KB
    1 . . . 3.1.3
Hussein v Mehlman [1992] 2 EGLR
    87 . . . 8.5.2.4
Hynes v Walsh, June 1994, Circuit Court
    (unreported) . . . 9.2.7.2

ICC Bank plc v Verling [1995] 1 ILRM
    123 . . . 5.3
Ickendel Ltd v Bewley's Cafe Grafton Street Ltd
    [2013] IEHC 293 . . . 12.3.1

International Drilling Fluids Ltd v Louisville
    Investments (Uxbridge) Ltd [1986] 1 Ch
    513 . . . 12.4.3
Irish Glass Bottle Company Ltd v Dublin Port
    Co [2005] IEHC 89 . . . 10.6.2
Irish Shell & BP Ltd v Costello Ltd [1981] ILRM
    66 . . . 3.2, 4.4
Irish Shell & BP Ltd v Costello Ltd (No 2)
    [1984] IR 511 . . . 1.3.4.2, 3.1, 4.4
Irish Telephone Rentals v ICS Building Society
    [1991] ILRM 880 . . .

Jacob Isbicki & Co Ltd v Goulding & Bird Ltd
    [1989] 1 EGLR 236 . . . 12.2.3,
    12.2.4.3
Johnston and Perrott Ltd v Cantrell, 3 May
    2001, Circuit Court
    (unreported) . . . 10.2.5.6
Jones v Luke Gardiner Ltd, 17 May 1999
    (unreported) . . . 10.2.5.6

Keating v Carolin [1968] IR 193 . . . 11.2.2.2
Kehoe and Kehoe v C J Louth & Son [1992]
    ILRM 282 . . . 11.2.2.5
Kelaghan v Daly [1913] 2 IR 328 . . . 4.8
Kelly v Woolworth & Co Ltd [1922]
    2 IR 5 . . . 4.4
Kenny Homes and Co Ltd v Leonard, High
    Court, 11 December 1997 (unreported)
    and Supreme Court, 18 June 1998
    (unreported) . . . 3.2, 10.1.1.1, 11.4.1.2
Killeen v Baron Talbot de Malahide [1951]
    Ir Jur Rep 19 . . . 11.2.2.2
King's Leasehold Estates, Re (1873) LR 16 EQ
    521 . . . 5.5.3

Lace v Chantler [1944] KB 368 . . . 2.1, 5.5.3
Linders Garage v Syme [1975] IR 161 . . . 9.5.3,
    10.2.6
Lister v Lane [1893] 2 QB 212 . . . 8.4.3.2,
    8.4.3.3
Londonderry and Lough Swilly Railway Co Ltd
    v Gillen, 7 May 1984, High Court
    (unreported) . . . 10.2.6
Lovelock v Margo [1963] 2 QB 786 . . . 9.3.6.4
Lurcott v Wakely [1911] 1 KB 905 . . . 8.4.3.2,
    8.4.3.3, 12.2.4.5
Lyle v Richards [1866] LR 1 HL 222 . . . 5.5.2
Lyons v Johnston (1944) 78 ILTR 19 . . . 9.2.6

M50 Motors Ltd v O'Byrne, 3 May
    2001 . . . 10.2.1.1
MacGinley v National Aid Committee [1952] Ir
    Jur Rep 43 . . . 4.4
Madigan v Attorney-General [1982] IR
    117 . . . 14.1

Mark Rowlands Ltd v Berni Inns Ltd [1985] 3 WLR 964 . . . 12.6.4

Mason v Leavy [1952] IR 40 . . . 10.1.1.1

Maurice E Taylor (Merchants) Ltd v Commissioner of Valuation [1981] NI 236 . . . 44.5.1, 4.5.2

McCarthy, Bolding and Cambridge v Larkin High Court 18 February 2009 (unreported) . . . 10.2.5.6

McCutcheon v Wilson (unreported) . . . 2.8

McEvoy v O'Donnell [1946] Ir Jur Rep 38 . . . 8.4.3.2

McGill v Snodgrass [1979] IR 283 . . . 3.1.3

Meagher & Anor v Luke J. Healy Pharmacy Ltd [2010] IESC 40 . . . 12.4.3

Mealiffe v GN Walsh Ltd [1986] IR 427 . . . 10.2.6

Meier and anor v Lynch . . . 9.5

Metropolitan Properties Ltd v John O'Brien and the Commissioners of Public Works in Ireland [1995] 2 ILRM 383 . . . 11.2.2.2, 11.2.3

Michael Terry v Edward J Stokes [1993] 1 IR 204 . . . 10.1.1.1

Minister for Communications, Marine and Natural Resources v Figary Watersports Development Company Limited [2015] IESC 74 . . . 9.5.2

Mint v Good [1951] 1 KB 517 . . . 8.2

National Bank v Keegan [1931] IR 344 . . . 4.8

National Maternity Hospital v McGouran [1994] 1 ILRM 521 . . . 3.2

Norwich Union Life Insurance Society v Gestetner Duplicators Ltd, 14 February 1984, High Court (unreported) . . . 12.2.3

Nynehead Developments Ltd v R H Fibreboard Containers Ltd [1997] 2 EG 139; [1999] 1 EGLR 7 . . . 8.5.2.4

O'Flaherty v Kelly [1909] 1 IR 223 . . . 4.6.1

OHS Ltd v Green Property Co Ltd [1986] IR 39 . . . 10.6.2, 12.2.4.7, 12.5.2

O'Reilly v East Coast Cinemas Ltd [1968] IR 56 . . . 8.3.3.2

Ò'Siodhachain v O'Mahony, 31 October 2002, High Court (unreported) . . . 3.2

Perfect Pies Ltd (In Receivership) v Chupn Ltd [2015] IEHC 692 . . . 10.6.1

Plant v Oakes [1991] 1 IR 185 . . . 10.2.1.1

Post Office v Aquarius Properties Ltd [1987] 1 All ER 1055 . . . 8.4.3.2

Powell v Dillon (1814) 2 Ba & B 416 . . . 1.3.4.3

Proudfoot v Hart (1890) 25 QB 42 . . . 8.3.2, 8.4.3.2

PRTB v Judge Linnane [2010] IEHC 476 . . . 6.3.1.1

Public Trustee v Westbrook [1965] 1 WLR 1160 . . . 9.3.6.4

Quirke v Folio Homes Ltd [1988] ILRM 496 . . . 14.2

Rainbow Estates Ltd v Tokenhold Ltd [1998] 2 All ER 860 . . . 8.5.1.3

Ravenseft Properties Ltd v Davstone (Holdings) Ltd [1980] QB 12 . . . 8.4.3.2

Regis Property Co Ltd v Dudley [1959] AC 370 . . . 8.4.3.2, 12.2.4.1

Reox Holdings PLC v Cullen and Davidson [2012] IEHC 299 . . . 12.3.1

Rice and Kenny v Dublin Corporation [1947] IR 425 . . . 10.6.1

Riverside Automotive v Blackhawk Automotive [2005] 1EGLR 114 . . . 8.4.3.2

Ryan v Bradley [1956] IR 31 . . . 10.2.5.6

Scales v Vandeleur [1914] 48 ILTR 36 . . . 8.2

Secretary of State for the Environment v Possfund (North West) Limited [1997] 2 EGLR 56 . . . 12.2.4.4

Shell-Mex and BP Ltd v Manchester Garages Ltd [1971] 1 WLR 612 . . . 3.2

Shirley & Ors v A O'Gorman & Co Ltd & Ors (2006) IEHC 27 . . . 11.6.4

Shirley & Ors v A O'Gorman & Co Ltd & Ors [2012] IESC 5 . . . 11.6.4

Siney v Dublin Corporation [1980] IR 400 . . . 8.2

Smith v Coras Iompair Eireann, 9 October 2002, High Court (unreported) . . . 3.2

Sotheby v Grundy [1947] 2 All ER 761 . . . 8.4.3.2

Spencer v Godwin (1815) 4 M & S 265 . . . 9.3.2.3

Square Management Limited & Others v Dunnes Stores Dublin Company [2017] IEHC 146 . . . 3.1.2

St Albans Investment Co v Sun Alliance & London Insurance Ltd [1983] 1 IR 362 . . . 12.2.4.6, 12.6.2

Staghold Ltd v Takeda [2005] 3 EGLR 45 . . . 12.2.3

Stapleyside Company v Carraig Donn Retail Limited [2015] IESC 60 . . . 10.2.5.6

Star Energy UK Onshore Limited v Bocardo SA [2009] EWCA Civ 579 . . . 5.5.2

Street v Mountford [1985] AC 809 . . . 3.1, 3.2

Tangney v Kerry County Council (1946) 80 ILTR 127 . . . 4.5.2

TABLE OF CASES

Twil Ltd v Kearney [2001] 4 IR
476 . . . 10.2.1.1

Ultraworth v General Accident Fire & Life
Assurance Corporation [2000] 2 EGLR
115 . . . 8.4.3.2

Walker v Hatton (1842) 10 M & W
249 . . . 8.4.3.2
Walsh v Lonsdale (1882) 21 Ch D 9 . . . 1.3.4.3
Wanze Properties (Ireland) Ltd v Mastertron
Ltd [1992] ILRM 746 . . . 10.6.2, 12.5.1,
12.5.2
Warren v Keen [1954] 1 QB 15 . . . 8.2

Waucob v Reynolds (1850) 1 ICLR 142 . . . 4.3
Whelan v Madigan [1978] ILRM
136 . . . 8.4.3.3
Whipp v Mackey [1927] IR 372 . . . 3.1.3,
9.3.6.4
White v Mitchell [1962] IR 348 . . . 9.2.7.2
Whyte v Sheehan [1943] Ir Jur Rep 38 . . . 3.2
Wigoder & Co Ltd v Moran [1977] IR
112 . . . 9.5.3, 10.2.6
William Bennett Construction Ltd v Greene
[2004] 2 ILRM 96 . . . 5.5.2
Winter Garden Theatre (London) Ltd v
Millennium Productions Ltd [1948] AC
173 . . . 3.1.3
Wood v Leadbitter [1845] 13 M and W
838 . . . 3.1.2

CHAPTER 1

INTRODUCTION

1.1 General

The law of landlord and tenant is one of the most important areas of land law and it continues to hold a central role in Irish social and political history. Today, land and, in an urban area, the property on it, is a valuable commercial asset. The purpose of this manual is to look at the essential characteristics of the relationship of landlord and tenant, the different situations where that relationship can exist, the rights and obligations arising in such a relationship and also how the relationship is created and can be determined.

Examples of the most common situations involving a landlord and tenant relationship are:

(a) A tenant or lessee who wishes to purchase the freehold interest in the land or property which he currently holds under a lease. If the lessee is able to establish a statutory right to acquire the freehold interest, this is a factor which would determine the purchase price. Such a price is considerably below the open market value that the lessee would have to pay if he did not have a statutory right. The acquisition of superior interests is the subject of **chapter 11**.

(b) A lessee wishes to sell or purchase land or premises which are held under a lease. If acting for a vendor it would be important to ensure that all the covenants of the lease have been complied with, in particular, those requiring payments to the landlord, not only of rent but other payments which might be reserved to the landlord under the lease, eg service charge, reimbursement of the insurance premium or, if the premises are not separately rated, payment to the landlord of a proportion of the total rates based on the floor area occupied by the tenant.

If a client wishes to purchase a property held under a lease it is important to examine the terms of that lease and, in particular, any onerous or restrictive covenants, the length of term unexpired, the user, any rent review provisions and to be able to advise on same. The essential terms of a lease are the subject of **chapter 5**.

(c) Taking instructions to draw up a commercial lease, including any special conditions peculiar to the particular letting; agreeing amendments with the tenant's solicitors and proceeding through the different stages to completion and registration (see **chapter 12** with particular reference to commercial leases).

(d) Disputes which may arise between the parties during the term, eg the extent of the tenant's liability under the repairing covenant (see **chapter 8**).

(e) The determination of non-residential tenancies and the effect of such determination on the landlord's title (see **chapter 9**).

(f) The determination of tenancies covered by the Residential Tenancies Act 2004 and amending legislation, in particular the Residential Tenancies (Amendment) Act 2015 (the '2015 Act') and the Planning and Development (Housing) and Residential Tenancies Act 2016 (the '2016 Act') (see **chapter 6**).

(g) Security of tenure and rights of renewal provisions provided by statute governing the landlord and tenant relationship under the Landlord and Tenant (Amendment) Act, 1980, as amended (see **chapter 10**).

(h) Security of tenure arising under Part 4 (ss 25–26) of the Residential Tenancies Act 2004 as amended by the 2015 Act and the 2016 Act (see **chapter 6**).

1.2 Definitions

The following definitions, listed in alphabetical order, are some of the terms in common use with reference to landlord and tenant law and are included only to assist in following the text. They are not intended as a comprehensive guide.

Many have now been redefined by the provisions of the Land and Conveyancing Law Reform Act 2009 ('the 2009 Act') which, bar one section, came into force on 1 December 2009. This was a major piece of legislation and forms part of a comprehensive reform and modernisation of land and conveyancing law. The 2009 Act updates and simplifies the law and the conveyancing process and also facilitates the introduction of an eConveyancing system. Because of the sweeping changes introduced by the 2009 Act it will be constantly referred to throughout the manual.

Agistment: a right to graze animals on another's land. It is a licence and creates no estate or interest in land.

Agreement for lease: a declaration of intent between two or more persons which sets out the rights or duties each has in relation to an agreement to take a lease of premises/land.

Alienation: the transfer of immovable property from one person to another. It is often interchangeable with the word assignment.

Appurtenant: attaching to land, eg an easement.

Assignment: deed passing a leasehold interest from a lessee to a party who takes on the mantle of the lessee. Such party ('the assignee') or new lessee takes subject to all the rights and liabilities of the original lessee.

Assurance: conveyance, assignment or transfer of property.

Bare licence: permission to do something which would otherwise be illegal. It does not need consideration. Such a licence is always revocable.

Conacre: right to plant or harvest crops on another's land. It is a licence and creates no estate or interest in land.

Demise: the grant of a tenancy or lease.

Demised premises: the property which is let or leased.

Ejectment: legal proceedings for the recovery of the possession of land.

Fee farm grant: fee simple estate (subject to a rent). It is defined in s 3 of the 2009 Act as any (a) grant of a fee simple, or (b) lease for ever or in perpetuity reserving or charging a perpetual rent, whether or not the relationship of landlord and tenant is created between the grantor and grantee, and includes a sub-fee farm grant. Existing fee farm grants are not affected by the 2009 Act but under s 12 the creation of a fee farm grant at law or in equity is now prohibited.

Fee simple: the largest estate in land that a person can have. Prior to s 67 of the 2009 Act it was essential to use the correct words of limitation in order to convey a fee simple estate. Section 67 abolishes the need for words of limitation in conveyances of unregistered land. Section 67(1) provides that a conveyance without such words will nevertheless convey whatever estate or interest the grantor has unless a contrary intention appears.

Fee tail: freehold estate of inheritance confined to descendants of the initial grantee. It was created by the words of limitation 'heir' followed by some words of procreation. Section 13(1) of the 2009 Act provides that the creation of a fee tail of any kind at law or in equity is prohibited and s 13(2) provides that from 1 December 2009 any instrument purporting to create a fee tail in favour of any person vests in that person a legal fee simple or, as the case may be, an equitable fee simple.

Fixtures and fittings: items annexed to the property by the lessee/occupier and removable by him. Trade fixtures are those chattels which are used by the lessee/occupier exclusively in the course of its business/profession. The draft Landlord and Tenant Law Reform Bill 2011 ('the draft 2011 Bill') (see **1.4.4** and **1.5**) proposes to replace both the common law and existing statutory provisions and simplify the law on this point.

Forfeiture: the termination of an interest in property as a result of breach of covenant or wrongdoing on the part of the lessee.

Freehold: the general term used to describe a fee simple, fee tail, fee farm grant, life estate and lease for lives renewable forever. Section 11(1) of the 2009 Act provides that the only legal estates in Ireland which may be created or disposed of are the freehold and leasehold estates specified by s 11.

Gale day: the day on which a periodic payment of rent is due. There are normally four gale days in each year for the payment of yearly rents and historically these were linked to religious feast days: 25 March, 29 June, 29 September and 25 December (feasts of the Annunciation, Saints Peter and Paul, Michael the Archangel and the Nativity respectively).

Ground rent: rent calculated without reference to the value of buildings on the land. It is a nominal amount and is found in leases granted for a long period of time, eg 300 years.

Habendum: (*habere*: to have): the clause in a deed which defines the estate to be taken by the purchaser. This has effectively disappeared by virtue of s 62(2) of the 2009 Act.

Improvement notice: the notice a business tenant serves on his landlord when he proposes to carry out improvements to the property.

Indenture: deed to which there are two or more parties. The origin of the word arose due to the freehand indentation of the paper in early times, which made the deed unique and avoided the risk of fraud.

Lease: this is defined by s 3 of the 2009 Act as a noun meaning an instrument creating a tenancy; and as a verb meaning the granting of a tenancy by an instrument. The expression 'lease' denotes an interest for a longer period of time whereas 'letting agreement' or 'tenancy agreement' is used in the context of a shorter period, eg one year. The term 'lease' also tends to be used in the context of commercial property versus a 'letting agreement' for residential property.

Lease for lives renewable forever: a lease granted for the term of certain lives, usually three, which contains a condition that when the last of the lives 'dropped out', ie died, the grantor would grant a renewal of the lease for a new life/lives on payment of a sum of money called a renewable fine. The Renewable Leasehold Conversion Act 1849 gave such lessees the right to obtain fee farm grants from their lessors in place of their leases. Surviving leases for lives renewable forever, not converted into fee farm grants under the 1849 Act, have automatically been converted into fee simple estates by s 74 of the Landlord and Tenant (Amendment) Act, 1980, such fee simple estates being deemed to be grafts on the previous interests. Section 14 of the 2009 Act prohibits the future creation of various categories of leases for lives or for a combination of lives and a period of years.

Lessee/Tenant: 'lessee' is defined by s 3 of the 2009 Act as meaning the person, including a sublessee, in whom a tenancy created by a lease is vested and the word 'tenant' means the person, including a subtenant, in whom a tenancy is vested.

Lessor/Landlord: section 3 of the 2009 Act defines 'lessor' as meaning the person, including a sublessor, entitled to the legal estate immediately superior to a tenancy created by a lease. The word 'landlord' means the person, including a sublandlord, entitled to the legal estate immediately superior to a tenancy.

Licence: an authority to do something which would otherwise be wrongful or illegal.

Licence coupled with an interest: a permission to do something which would otherwise be wrongful or illegal in order to exercise another right granted, ie right to fish. It may be revoked only in accordance with its terms.

Life estate: an interest in land for the period of the lifetime of a named party. The interest determines (ie ends) on the death of that life. Section 11(6) of the 2009 Act provides that life estates will no longer be legal estates and will vest as equitable interests only.

Notice of Termination: this is a specific form of notice under the Residential Tenancies Act 2004 (as amended by the 2015 Act).

Overholding: this arises where a tenant or occupier of land remains on or in possession of same after the expiration of the original term.

Parcels: the part of a deed setting out the description of the property/land, its location, physical extent and dimensions.

Parol: oral (not written).

Predecessors in title: the persons who previously held the same interest in the land.

Premium: capital sum or fine paid by the tenant to the landlord on the granting of a lease.

Quiet enjoyment/Possession: usual covenant in a lease that a lessee will have quiet enjoyment of the property without a claim from the lessor or a third party, ie the lessor covenants he has title to grant the lease.

Rack rent: rent which reflects not only the value of the land but also any building on it, ie full market rent. Section 3 of the 2009 Act defines 'rent' as including a rent payable under a tenancy or a rent charge, or other payment in money or money's worth or any other consideration, reserved or issuing out of or charged on land, but does not include interest.

Recital: clause in a deed which recounts the previous ownership of the land and explains the context of the present transaction.

Reddendum: ('that which is to be paid') the clause in the lease/tenancy agreement which specifies the rent which is payable and the time and manner of its payment.

Reverse premium: capital sum or fine paid by the landlord to the tenant on the granting of a lease to induce the tenant to enter the lease.

Reversion/Reversionary interest: the residue of all estate left in the grantor or lessor which does not commence in possession until the determination of some particular estate granted by him, eg when a freehold owner granted a lease, the fee simple interest which he retained was a reversion and on the expiration of the term of years demised by a lease it reverted to the lessor.

Sub-letting/Underletting: a lease created by a lessee out of his leasehold interest for a period less than the period held by him under his lease.

Tenement: defined by the Landlord and Tenant (Amendment) Act, 1980, s 5. For the purpose of statutory or business tenants a tenement means a premises consisting wholly or partially of buildings, or of an identified portion of a building, or of land covered partly by buildings where the land not covered by buildings is subsidiary and ancillary to the buildings. Such premises must be held by the occupier on a tenancy and the tenancy must not have been expressed to have been made either for the temporary convenience of either party or to be dependent on the continuance in any office or employment or appointment of the tenant. Under the draft 2011 Bill (see **1.4.4**) it is proposed that the concept of 'tenement' be dropped so that a tenant who runs a business on land without buildings (eg a car park or farming activities) would be entitled to statutory reliefs provided other conditions are met such as holding under a tenancy and continuous occupation for the relevant period.

Tenure: the manner whereby tenements are held. Today it is the relationship between one person and his reversioner, eg tenant and landlord.

Term: a fixed period of time for which an interest in land is granted.

Terms: the covenants and conditions of the agreement (whether oral or written).

Waiver: the renouncing, disclaiming, forbearance or abandonment of a claim to a right or benefit. It may be express or implied.

Wayleave: the right over another's land to facilitate the supply of utility services, eg gas, water, electricity.

1.3 Historical Background and Early Legislation

1.3.1 HISTORICAL BACKGROUND

Prior to the introduction of the feudal system of tenure into Ireland by the Normans in the 12th century, Brehon law ruled and continued to influence Irish society until the 17th century (save for the area around Dublin known as 'the Pale').

The feudal system believed that a private person or body could not own their land outright and that all land was held ultimately from the Crown. The system did not recognise the relationship of landlord and tenant and grants of land for a period of years were regarded as creating personal contracts only.

Section 9(2) of the 2009 Act states 'in so far as it survives, feudal tenure is abolished'. However the section makes it clear that the abolition of feudal tenure does not affect the position of the State under the State Property Act, 1954 and s 73 of the Succession Act, 1965.

Professor Wylie, in his book *Irish Land Law* (5th edn) states that landlord and tenant law is a mixture of four basic elements, which are paraphrased below:

(a) English common law, being principles based on the feudal system introduced into England by the Normans and developed over the centuries by conveyancers and judges;

(b) English statute law, which includes statutes passed at Westminster for both England and Ireland and statutes passed exclusively for Ireland;

(c) Irish statute law, ie statutes passed in Ireland for the whole of Ireland or for either the Republic of Ireland or Northern Ireland; and

(d) Irish common law, in the sense of principles developed by Irish conveyancers and judges.

1.3.2 THE 17TH CENTURY

The 17th century saw the completion of the conquest of Ireland begun by Henry II, the imposition of English common law and the displacement of the ancient Irish law. This century also saw the rapid decline of the feudal system of landholding.

During the 17th century, the creation of leasehold estates in Ireland arose as a direct result of the confiscation and resettlement of Irish land. The social, political and economic upheavals during this century marked the foundation of modern land law legislation, which began with the Statute of Frauds (Ireland), 1695. The Registration of Deeds Act (Ireland), 1707 was also passed, which introduced the system of registration of deeds.

1.3.3 THE 18TH CENTURY

As the larger estates became more and more subdivided, the lot of the small tenant-farmer worsened. Usually, he held under a very short lease or a periodic tenancy from year to year. In addition to paying his rent he had to pay a tithe owed to the established Church of Ireland. There was no incentive to improve a holding, as the landlord would claim it on the termination of the tenancy or use the improvement as a reason for demanding a higher rent. Any attempt to increase the size of farms was usually done by conacre and agistment letting. These social and economic conditions led to agrarian disturbances in the latter part of the 18th century and legislation was passed to suppress and outlaw the various groups that formed to agitate against the large landowners, eg the Whiteboys.

1.3.4 THE 19TH CENTURY

After the Act of Union, 1800, the principal concerns of the Irish Members of the Parliament of Westminster were: (a) a resolution of the land problem in Ireland where relations between absentee landlords and their tenants were worsening and (b) Home Rule. Economic disaster for Ireland, including the famine, spurred on the desire for reform.

1.3.4.1 Introduction to Deasy's Act, 1860

The Landlord and Tenant Law Amendment Act (Ireland), 1860, known as Deasy's Act, was a major piece of legislation, designed to consolidate much of the legislation passed in the previous century in Ireland. Deasy's Act is of fundamental importance and could, in fact, be described as the basic foundation of present landlord and tenant law. The Act, however, only went part of the way to protecting the position of the tenant. It regulated the laws of the contracts referred to in s 3 and amended the law relating to ejectments. It made no provision for renewals of leases, compensation for improvements or disturbance on termination of a tenancy.

One section in particular had a major impact and is the reason why the basis of our landlord and tenant legislation differs from that in the UK to this day. This was s 3.

Section 3 provides:

> the relation of landlord and tenant shall be deemed to be founded on the express or implied contract of the parties, and not upon tenure or service, and a reversion shall not be necessary to such relation, which shall be deemed to subsist in all cases in which there shall be an agreement by one party to hold land from or under another in consideration of any rent.

It is important to examine the constituent elements of s 3. This provides:

(a) the relationship of landlord and tenant is deemed to be founded on the express or implied contract of the parties; and

(b) the relationship is deemed to subsist where there is an agreement by one party to hold land from or under another in consideration of any rent.

Section 4 of Deasy's Act, 1860, provides that:

> *every lease or contract with respect to lands whereby the relation of landlord and tenant is intended to be created for any freehold estate or interest or for any definite period of time not being from year to year or any lesser period, shall be by deed executed, or note in writing signed by the landlord or his agent thereunto lawfully authorised in writing.*

Section 1 of Deasy's Act, 1860, defines 'lease' as: 'any instrument in writing, whether under seal or not containing a contract of tenancy in respect of any lands, in consideration of a rent or return'. Section 3 of the 2009 Act defines it as an instrument creating a tenancy.

Thus, to create the relationship of landlord and tenant, the parties must intend to create it and they must comply with the formalities laid down by law.

1.3.4.2 Intention

Whether the parties intended to create the relationship of landlord and tenant can be deduced by the written agreement entered into, or sufficient evidence acceptable to a court of any oral agreement or the actions of the parties in relation to the land.

No clear objective criteria have been established by the courts when determining the intention of the parties to create the relationship. The terms of a written agreement will be examined by the court, but it will not determine the matter exclusively based on the written agreement as it is aware that the agreement may not represent the true intention of the parties. In some cases the parties may not be in an equal bargaining position when reaching the agreement. The courts are careful to examine other factors to seek the true intention. In the case of an oral agreement, intention to create the relationship will be deduced from the words and behaviour of the parties as given in evidence to the court: *Irish Shell & BP Ltd v Costello Ltd (No 2)* [1984] IR 511.

1.3.4.3 Formalities

There are two relevant statutory provisions relating to the formalities necessary for the establishment of a lease.

As already stated at **1.3.4.1**, s 4 of Deasy's Act, 1860, provides that the relationship of landlord and tenant in respect of any freehold estate or interest, for any period of time more than a year, shall be executed in writing.

Previously s 2 of the Statute of Frauds (Ireland), 1695, provided that contracts for the future creation of the relationship of landlord and tenant and involving an interest in land be evidenced by a note or memorandum in writing signed by the party against whom it was sought to enforce the contract. This note or memorandum did not need to be a contract in the formal sense as long as it set out the essential terms of the lease/tenancy and there was sufficient evidence of an unconditional and complete agreement between the parties as to the terms. Correspondence has been deemed sufficient evidence: *Powell v Dillon* (1814) 2 Ba & B 416. Examples of such essential terms are:

(a) identity of landlord and identity of tenant;

(b) a clear description of the premises to be let;

(c) rent or any fine/capital sum/premium/reverse premium to be paid by the landlord or tenant in consideration of the grant;

(d) an indication of commencement of the term sufficient for a court to ascertain a date;

(e) duration of term.

If there is any ambiguity, parol evidence can be forthcoming. However, if the terms are, in the view of the court, still uncertain they will not be enforced: *Bernard v Meara* (1862) 12 Ir Ch R 389.

The 2009 Act has repealed s 2 of the Statute of Frauds (Ireland), 1695, and replaced it with s 51. This re-enacts the substance of s 2 and states that, subject to subsection (2), no action shall be brought to enforce any contract for the sale or other disposition of land unless the agreement on which such action is brought, or some memorandum or note of it, is in writing and signed by the person against whom the action is brought or that person's authorised agent. Section 51(2) makes it clear that equitable doctrines, such as part performance or estoppel will continue to be available. Section 51(3) provides that payment of a deposit, and reference to such in the written evidence of the contract, is not necessary in an enforceable contract, unless there is an express agreement otherwise.

There is a distinction to be drawn between a contract/agreement for lease and the actual grant of a lease. A contract/agreement governing an interest in land (including an agreement to grant a lease) was governed by s 2 of the Statute of Frauds (Ireland), 1695, and is now governed by s 51 of the 2009 Act. The actual grant of a lease or a tenancy is governed by s 4 of Deasy's Act, 1860. The distinction is not so important today as it is not standard practice to have an express contract or agreement for lease in advance of the actual grant, particularly where a short-term lease or a commercial lease in a standard form is proposed to be granted. However, where commercial premises are under construction (such as an office block or an industrial unit) or a major development is planned (such as a shopping centre or an industrial estate) a developer is likely to want future tenants to commit themselves to take a lease in the development and will have prepared the draft lease. In such cases the opportunity to renegotiate or vary the terms is limited. Such a contract or agreement for lease will have the draft lease attached, initialled by the parties to show their agreement to its terms.

The rules embodied in s 51 of the 2009 Act and ss 3 and 4 of Deasy's Act, 1860 might be summarised as follows:

(a) A tenancy for a certain period of, say, six months, or which by its term can run periodically from year to year or less need not be in writing. If there happens to be a written tenancy agreement, the signature of the tenant alone will act as an estoppel.

(b) If the lease is for a term of more than one year it must be in writing signed by the landlord, or his authorised agent or it will not be a valid agreement enforceable by either party. This only applies to commercial leases as residential tenancies are now governed by legislation introduced in 2004. See **chapter 6**.

(c) In the case of an agreement under which a tenant has entered into possession, which could be construed as a contract for a future lease for more than one year, it must be in writing signed by the party to be charged therewith, ie if it is signed only by the tenant it may then be proved as to its terms against the tenant but not against the landlord. Section 51 of the 2009 Act applies as it is an agreement not an actual grant.

Failure to comply with the formalities to create the relationship results in the agreement being unenforceable at statute or common law. In equity, the agreement could be enforceable if there has been a sufficient act of part performance by the application of the maxim 'equity regards as done what ought to have been done'. The rights of the parties are equitable only until a formal lease is executed, if necessary as a result of a decree of specific performance. Until that happens the parties' positions are still governed by the terms of the informal lease but their rights are equitable only unless and until a formal lease is executed: *Walsh v Lonsdale* (1882) 21 Ch D 9.

The draft 2011 Bill (see **1.4.4**) proposes to repeal and replace Deasy's Act and largely re-enacts the provisions of s 3 but recasts them with modifications as recommended by the Law Reform Commission. For further reference to proposed changes see **1.5**.

Other legislation passed during the 19th century included various Land Acts vesting title in tenant purchasers with the aid of monies advanced by the State. It was important that an effective title registration system be established providing security of title. This led to the Local Registration of Title (Ireland) Act, 1891, which established a system of registration of title that was compulsory for state-aided tenant purchasers and voluntary as regards other landowners. The Land Registry was established to provide a secure and reliable title registration system for recording transfers of ownership, mortgages, leases and other legal interests.

1.4 Recent Legislation

1.4.1 THE 20TH CENTURY

The Landlord and Tenant Act, 1931, gave certain rights of renewal to tenants and provided, inter alia, for the following:

(a) a tenant who proved an 'equity' got a new lease for 21 years at a rent agreed between the parties or in default of agreement fixed by the court;

(b) a right to compensation for loss of goodwill and removal expenses for disturbance, available for premises used wholly or substantially for business purposes;

(c) a right to compensation for improvements on leaving the premises based on the capitalised value of the addition to the letting value resulting from that improvement;

(d) renewal was to be at a fair rent;

(e) a tenant was not entitled to a new lease where the landlord required possession for development or it would not be consistent with good estate management. Compensation would be payable.

The Landlord and Tenant Act, 1931, was repealed by the Landlord and Tenant (Amendment) Act, 1980.

The Registration of Title Act, 1964 repealed and replaced the Local Registration of Title (Ireland) Act, 1891. The principle objective of this Act was 'the gradual extension of compulsory registration to all land in the country'. This has now happened so that as at 2017 93 per cent of the land mass and almost 90 per cent of legal titles are registered in the Land Registry.

1.4.2 LANDLORD AND TENANT (AMENDMENT) ACT, 1980

The 1980 Act re-enacts the provisions of the Landlord and Tenant Act, 1931, and the Landlord and Tenant (Reversionary Leases) Act, 1958, with some alterations that broaden the scope of tenants' relief. It sought to remove certain inequities that arose from the interpretation of provisions of the Landlord and Tenant Act, 1931. It is a major piece of legislation very relevant in practice today (see **chapter 10**).

1.4.3 LANDLORD AND TENANT (AMENDMENT) ACT, 1994

The 1994 Act amended ss 13, 17, 23 and 85 of the Landlord and Tenant (Amendment) Act, 1980. Section 13 deals with the right to a new tenancy. Section 17 contains certain restrictions on the right to a new tenancy. Section 23 provides for the rent and the duration of the term to be set by the court in the absence of agreement between the parties and s 85 provides that any provision contracting out of the 1980 Act would be void.

The strict position of s 85 of the 1980 Act was changed by s 4 of the 1994 Act, which allowed a tenant of office premises only to contract out of its right to a new tenancy. This was subject to certain conditions being met and it applied to business premises used only as an office. However, there was no definition of what constituted 'an office' in the 1994 Act and s 47 of the Civil Law (Miscellaneous Provisions) Act 2008 ('the 2008 Act') extended the renunciation to all business tenancies. One of the cases where a tenant is not entitled to a new tenancy is where the tenant has renounced in writing, whether for or without valuable consideration, an entitlement to a new tenancy in the premises and has received independent legal advice in relation to the renunciation. The draft 2011 Bill (see **1.4.4**) proposes to replace s 17 of the 1980 Act and s 47 of the 2008 Act.

1.4.4 THE 21ST CENTURY

Towards the end of the 20th century the economic boom which had begun some ten years earlier led to escalating house prices and dramatic increases in rent for private accommodation. The Residential Tenancies Act, 2004 ('the 2004 Act') implemented almost all of the reforms recommended by the Commission on the Private Rented Residential Sector established in 1999, and the Finance Acts of 2001 and 2002 implemented those recommendations relating to tax and supply incentives approved by the Government.

The 2004 Act, in conjunction with the 2015 Act and the 2016 Act, is a major piece of legislation. These Acts relate to private residential lettings only. The most significant changes for landlords and tenants brought about by the 2004 Act are:

(a) the establishment of the Private Residential Tenancies Board (PRTB), now renamed the Residential Tenancies Board (RTB) under the 2015 Act, as its jurisdiction was extended beyond the private rented sector to include certain tenancies in the voluntary and co-operative housing sector;

(b) a user-friendly dispute resolution service consisting of mediation, adjudication or a Tenancy Tribunal instead of using the courts;

(c) certain minimum obligations that apply to all tenants and to all landlords are set out;

(d) security of tenure on the basis of four-year cycles as contained in Part 4 of the 2004 Act. This security has been extended to six years under s 37 of the 2016 Act;

(e) procedures to be followed to terminate a tenancy to which the 2004 Act, as amended by the 2015 Act, apply;

(f) the establishment of a new tenancy registration system and repeal of The Housing (Registration of Rented Houses) Regulations 1996 (SI 30/1996), which previously required registration with local authorities.

These changes are examined in more detail in **chapters 6** and **7**.

The Land Act, 2005 ('the 2005 Act') repealed both s 12 (relating to sub-division of lands) and s 45 (vesting in qualified persons) of the Land Act, 1965. It also provided for the automatic discharge of land purchase annuities of €200 pa or less.

As part of the reforms to pave the way for the introduction of an electronic registration and conveyancing system the Registration of Deeds and Title Act 2006 ('the 2006 Act') was enacted. Its purpose was to restructure and modernise land registration systems in the State, update and modernise the law relating to registration of deeds and reform the law relating to registration of title to land. Section 9 established the Property Registration Authority, which now manages and controls the Registry of Deeds and the Land Registry. The Registry of Deeds is being phased out due to compulsory registration of titles in the Land Registry.

Just as the 2004 Act, as amended by the 2015 and 2016 Acts, is a major piece of legislation so is the 2009 Act, which is the culmination of work commenced in 1987. It has transformed Irish land law and the practice of conveyancing. To quote Professor John C W Wylie in his lecture on the CPD subject 'The Land and Conveyancing Law Reform Bill/Act 2006/2009' given on 21 September 2009: 'the fact is that the Act has many truly radical and far-reaching provisions which go beyond anything achieved in other common law jurisdictions'. The 2009 Act has put Ireland at the forefront in modernising its laws and greatly facilitates the introduction of eConveyancing. All sections save s 132 (the section relating to rent reviews) came into force on 1 December 2009. Section 132 came into force on 28 February 2010.

The 2009 Act is not a codification of the law; rather it is a consolidation. An example is s 11(7) which states that nothing in the 2009 Act affects judicial recognition of equitable interests.

The principle objectives of the 2009 Act may be briefly summarised as follows:

(a) Repeal of old statutes. The Act, in Schedule 2, provides for the repeal—in whole or in part—of about 150 pre-1922 statutes and they are replaced, where appropriate, with statutory provisions more suited to modern conditions. The Act also repeals certain provisions in Acts post 1922 which are no longer required.

(b) It consolidates in one Act most of the statutory provisions which underlie the Irish conveyancing and land law system.

(c) It introduced possibly the most up-to-date substantive law in the common law world as a result of this major 'root and branch review'.

(d) The use of plain language in the drafting of the Act so as to keep its provisions as clear and straightforward as possible.

In addition to all this new legislation a general reform of landlord and tenant law has been under consideration for some time by the Law Reform Commission. The result is the publication of two consultation papers, one on Business Tenancies (LRC CP 21–2003) and the other on the General Law of Landlord and Tenant (LRC CP 28–2003), and the Report on The Law of Landlord and Tenant (LRC 85–2007) published in November 2007. This contains the final recommendations together with a draft Bill. As already stated, this is part of a much larger programme of reform being undertaken which is designed to prepare the way for the eventual introduction of a system of electronic conveyancing. Its recommendations include consolidating Landlord and Tenant Acts including Deasy's Act and the Landlord and Tenant Acts, 1980 to 1984.

In a press release dated 19 April 2011 the Minister for Justice, Equality and Defence published an information paper and a draft general scheme in the Landlord and Tenant Law Reform Bill 2011 ('the draft 2011 Bill') (www.justice.ie) and invited submissions. The purpose of the Bill is to update and reform the general law relating to landlord and tenant and will involve (i) the repeal of at least 35 pre-1922 statutes, some dating from the 17th century, and the introduction of a streamlined statutory framework more suited to modern conditions; (ii) an updated statutory redress scheme to replace the former old 'eviction' remedies which will be abolished; and (iii) clarification of the rights and obligations of landlords and tenants.

Thus the draft 2011 Bill proposes overriding obligations to be imposed by statute, which the parties cannot contract out of, and default obligations which would operate in the absence of an express provision or agreement to the contrary or as a variation of the statutory provision. It covers termination of tenancies and rights to a new tenancy and compensation. Schedule 1 also sets out precedent rent review provisions. For example, the tenant has an obligation to pay rent while the landlord is obliged to give good title, possession and quiet enjoyment and also to repair and insure. Deasy's Act, 1860, is repealed in its entirety and considerable parts of the 1980 Act (see **chapter 10**) are replaced. Some of these changes are mentioned in subsequent chapters, where relevant, but it should be noted that an inspection of www.justice.ie in January 2018 showed that draft 2011 Bill had yet to be published and its status in the spring/summer 2017 legislative programme states 'Heads approved, work is continuing'. The draft 2011 Bill is expected to undergo pre-legislative scrutiny. Hence there may be significant changes to its provisions as it moves through the legislative process before enactment. As the Minister said when launching the consultation process, 'a modern landlord and tenant code applicable to business tenancies is essential for our economic recovery and while attention has, quite understandably, been focused in recent times on problems associated with "upward only" rent reviews, the entire landlord and tenant code needs to be updated to make it "fit for purpose" in the 21st century.'

1.5   Conclusion

In general terms, it can be said that the law of landlord and tenant is governed by common law and by statute law, the latter operating to impede the freedom of both landlord and tenant to contract as they might wish in certain areas.

It is important to distinguish between the relationship of landlord and tenant and other relationships concerned with the use of land which are similar to it, eg a licence. This is due to several considerations, one being that a landlord may have remedies available to him against a user only if that user is a tenant, eg remedies for recovery of rent, or a right of distress. A tenant has an interest in land which entitles him to exclusive possession for the period of his tenancy, a right he may assert against third parties as well as the landlord. A tenant may dispose of, or deal with this interest, eg by assignment or sub-letting subject to the terms of the agreement. Other users or occupiers of land frequently have only 'personal' rights in respect of the land, which they cannot pass on to third parties. These rights are considered in more detail in **chapters 2, 3** and **4**.

Section 3 of Deasy's Act, 1860, is the starting point for modern law and distinguishes the Irish concept from its English counterpart in that it is founded on contract rather than tenure and the draft 2011 Bill retains this principle. An obligation to pay rent is necessary in all cases for the creation of a tenancy and the grant of a tenancy without a reversion would be void both at law and in equity. Hence the provisions of s 3 of Deasy's Act are largely re-enacted in the draft 2011 Bill but incorporating modifications as recommended by the Law Reform Commission.

Part 3 of the draft 2011 Bill replaces ss 4 and 9 of Deasy's Act. It provides that tenancies shall be created at law only in a document signed by (a) the landlord or (b) an agent authorised in writing by the landlord. This requirement does not apply to (a) a tenancy for a recurring period not exceeding one year or (b) a tenancy for a fixed period not exceeding one year unless the grant includes provision for a renewal or extension which, if exercised, would result in the period as renewed or extended exceeding one year.

Hence the rule in s 4 of Deasy's Act that writing is required for the creation of a tenancy, subject to some exceptions, is retained. It is also clear that a tenancy for one year can be created orally, thereby resolving judicial uncertainty as to the effect of s 4 of Deasy's Act. It does not apply, however, where exercise of an option to renew or other provision results in the combined period exceeding one year. The intention in the draft 2011 Bill is to capture any provision which enables the initial term to be renewed or extended so that the combined terms exceed one year.

A new statutory framework for landlord and tenant law is a logical sequel to, and will complement, provisions in the 2009 Act which modernise the law relating to land ownership and the conveyancing of land.

1.6 Recommended Reading

Ross, M, *Commercial Leases* (Issue 15, June 2006, Butterworths).

Wheeler, D H, 'The Land and Conveyancing Law Reform Act 2009: Significant Changes or Mere Tweaking?' (2009) 14(3) CPLJ 62.

Wylie, J C W, *Landlord and Tenant Law* (3rd edn, 2014, Bloomsbury Professional).

Wylie, J C W, *The Land and Conveyancing Law Reform Act 2009: Annotations and Commentary* (2009, Bloomsbury Professional).

Wylie, J C W, *Irish Land Law* (5th edn, 2013, Bloomsbury Professional).

CHAPTER 2

CATEGORISATION OF TENANCIES

2.1   Introduction

Historically, a lease was regarded as a mere contractual right to use another's land. A leasehold interest was treated in the same way as furniture or livestock and was regarded as personal property. It could be seized by a sheriff on foot of a judgment obtained by a creditor in respect of a debt. Hence, on purchasing a leasehold interest, a solicitor would carry out a sheriff's office search to ensure that no judgment had been lodged for execution against the personal goods of the vendor. Section 133 of the Land and Conveyancing Law Reform Act 2009 ('the 2009 Act') abolished the power of the sheriff to seize a tenancy under a writ of *fieri facias* or other process of execution save in relation to a tenancy wholly or partly used for business purposes. Hence the necessity as a purchaser or mortgagee of commercial property to continue to carry out sheriff office searches against commercial or partly commercial leasehold property and a Practice Note dated March 2012 of the Law Society Conveyancing Committee advised it as standard practice to carry out these searches. The position changed with the passing of the Fines (Payment and Recovery) Act 2014 ('the 2014 Act'). This provides that a court which has imposed a fine of not less than €500 can appoint a receiver, ie a sheriff or an approved person, and that receiver can seize real property. As a result, a Law Society Practice Note of January/February 2017 states that it is now necessary to carry out a search in the receiver/sheriff's office prior to closing a sale or a mortgage against all property, both leasehold and freehold.

There are two types of sheriff, an Ordinary Sheriff and a Revenue Sheriff and searches with both should be done when a sheriff's search is required. The Ordinary Sheriff is the County Registrar, run by the Courts Service. The Revenue Sheriffs are government appointees. There are currently 16 Revenue Sheriffs in Ireland whose primary responsibility is to collect taxes on behalf of the Collector-General.

The main distinction between a leasehold and a freehold is that a leasehold has a definite and predetermined duration either in years, months or weeks. *Lace v Chantler* [1944] KB 368, decided that a lease granted for 'the duration of the war' was void for uncertainty as to its duration. A tenancy from year to year is saved from being uncertain because each party can give notice to the other to determine at the end of any year. The term continues until determined as if both parties had made a new agreement at the end of each year for a new term for the following year.

Section 4 of Deasy's Act, 1860, requires leases and tenancies to be in writing if they are to create the legal relationship of landlord and tenant 'for any freehold estate or interest or for any definite period of time not being from year to year or any lesser period'. This envisages two types of lease:

> (a)   one granted for a freehold estate eg lease for lives renewable forever; a fee farm grant. However, s 12 of the 2009 Act prohibits the creation of a fee farm grant at law or in equity or a lease for life or lives renewable forever or for any period which is perpetually

renewable. This does not affect any fee farm grants created prior to 1 December 2009 (the commencement date of the 2009 Act save for s 132). Section 14 of the 2009 Act provides that a grant of a lease for life or lives and any contract for such a grant made after the commencement of the 2009 Act is void both at law and in equity.

(b)   one granted for a definite period of time or successive definite periods, eg fixed-term tenancies or periodic tenancies for a period less than a year.

The previous chapter referred to the draft general scheme of Landlord and Tenant Law Reform Bill 2011 ('the draft 2011 Bill') (see **1.4.4**) and the changes proposed in it. One of these is that s 4 of Deasy's Act will be replaced, though it retains the requirement that writing is required for the confirmation of a tenancy at law signed by a landlord or an agent authorised by the landlord. It will not apply to a tenancy for a recurring period not exceeding one year or a tenancy for a fixed period not exceeding one year unless the grant includes a provision for a renewal or extension which, if exercised, would result in the period, as renewed or extended, exceeding one year.

Today most tenancies fall into two broad categories: a tenancy for a fixed term or a tenancy from year to year or other periodic tenancy.

The following categories of tenancies will be examined in this chapter:

(a)   fixed term or term certain;

(b)   periodic;

(c)   at will;

(d)   at sufferance;

(e)   statutory;

(f)   by estoppel.

2.2   Fixed Term/Term Certain

A tenancy may be created for any fixed term, no matter how long or short. Leases for very long terms, eg 999 years, are not uncommon. A fixed term is certain in the sense that from the outset it is known when it will determine.

On the expiration of the fixed term the lessee's interest ends automatically and the lessor is entitled to possession.

Another example of a lease for a fixed term is a reversionary lease. This is a lease for a term which is to take effect some time in the future. It was common to grant such a lease during the currency of an existing lease with the term to commence from the expiration of the subsisting term. Examples can be seen in many of the old Pembroke Estate titles. Such a reversionary lease does not affect the operation of the pre-existing lease.

The rent reserved in such long leases is generally a small amount, eg £30 pa. This is known as a ground rent (to distinguish it from a rack rent reserved in a lease for a shorter term of commercial (or residential) premises).

2.3   Periodic Tenancies

A periodic tenancy may be a tenancy from year to year (ie yearly tenancy) or a tenancy for successive periods of less than a year (eg weekly or monthly tenancies). In periodic tenancies, each period is automatically renewed and will continue indefinitely beyond the initial period until terminated by notice to quit. The periods of notice are set by statute and common law. A tenancy from year to year, although initially for a term of one year, will therefore continue from year to year indefinitely until ended by either party or their respective successors giving notice of the termination. Usually a tenancy from year to year arises by implication and there is a long line of authority to the effect that where a tenant for a fixed term at a yearly rent holds over after expiry of that term he or she is presumed to be a tenant from year to year. In the case of *Earl of Meath v Megan* [1897] 2 IR 477, Gibbon LJ said:

> '[W]here any tenant holds under a lease or agreement in writing, for a term which comes to an end, and he continues in possession without making any fresh agreement, there is a presumption that all the terms of the agreement continue to apply, except so far as they are rendered inapplicable by the changes of the tenancy.'

A tenancy from year to year can also arise by virtue of s 5 of Deasy's Act, 1860, which provides:

> *in case any tenant or his representative after the expiration or determination of the term agreed upon in any lease or instrument in writing, shall continue in possession for more than one month after the demand of possession by the landlord or his agent, such continuance shall, at the election of the landlord, be deemed to constitute a new holding of the said lands from year to year, subject to the former rent and to such of the agreements contained in the lease or instrument as made to be applicable to the new holding.*

Section 5 confers a 'right of election' on the landlord. This election can only be made following the lapse of more than one month after demand for possession by the landlord followed by events which would give rise to either the operation of s 5 or the raising of the presumption of a new tenancy. This would be applied by the court as a matter of law if the facts warrant it.

The draft 2011 Bill (see **1.4.4**) does not contain any equivalent section to s 5 of Deasy's Act.

[A periodic tenancy may also be created for any successive period other than a year. Tenancies from week to week or from month to month are commonplace and may be created expressly or by implication. The type of periodic tenancy is determined by the manner in which the rent is reserved and not the way in which the rent is actually paid] Therefore, a tenancy under which the rent is reserved weekly is deemed to be a weekly tenancy, if reserved monthly it would be a monthly tenancy.

2.4 Tenancy at Will

Such a tenancy is only of historic interest now. It concerned a person in possession of land for an indefinite period with the consent of the owner. Either party could determine the arrangement at any time and such tenancies were without rent.

The definition of 'tenancy' in s 3 of the 2009 Act specifically states that it does not include a tenancy at will. The draft 2011 Bill (see **1.4.4**) in its definition of 'tenancy' in s 3 also excludes a tenancy at will.

2.5 Tenancy at Sufferance

Again, this type of tenancy is of historic interest only. It could arise by operation of law only and occurred if the tenant continued in possession at the end of a lease or tenancy without paying rent and without the landlord's consent or dissent. Such a tenant differed from a trespasser in that the original entry was lawful and it differed from a tenancy at will in that the occupation was without the landlord's consent.

There was no relationship of landlord and tenant and the person in possession was called a 'tenant' only because his original occupation of the land was under a contract of tenancy. Section 3 of the 2009 Act states in its definition of 'tenancy' that it does not include a tenancy at sufferance. The draft 2011 Bill (see **1.4.4**) in its definition of 'tenancy' in s 3 also excludes a tenancy at sufferance

2.6 Statutory Tenancy

Various statutes confer on tenants the right to remain in possession of property subject to the terms decreed by that statute.

There is the right of a tenant who is applying for a new tenancy under the Landlord and Tenant (Amendment) Act, 1980, to remain in possession pending the outcome of his application. This applies to both residential and business lettings provided the subject matter of the existing tenancy was a tenement as defined in s 5 of that Act.

The draft 2011 Bill (see **1.4.4**) replaces parts of s 5 of the 1980 Act and drops the concept of 'tenement'. It will apply to tenancies generally subject to specific restrictions.

Part 4 of the Residential Tenancies Act 2004 provides relief to persons who have been in occupation of a dwelling under a tenancy for a continuous period of six months, subject to certain exceptions. The purpose of Part 4 is to provide security of tenure to residential tenancies based on four-year cycles, now extended to six-year cycles by virtue of s. 37 of the Planning and Development (Housing) and Residential Tenancies Act 2016 (see **chapter 6**).

2.7 Tenancy by Estoppel

A tenancy by estoppel is based on the legal principle of estoppel, under which a party who has induced another to rely on his representations is precluded from subsequently denying the truth of those representations. For the purpose of the relationship of landlord and tenant, it is confined to the parties to the purported tenancy agreement themselves and persons claiming under them. It does not apply where a party holding a title superior to the landlord asserts his rights against the tenant.

Where the doctrine of estoppel applies to a purported tenancy agreement the parties are treated as subject to the same rights and obligations that they would have had if the tenancy agreement had been fully valid. The covenants are enforceable between the parties and their successors, ie the landlord may claim the rent reserved and recover possession as a landlord. If the landlord subsequently acquires title, where his title at the time of the purported grant of the tenancy agreement was defective, this is said to 'feed the estoppel' and the tenant is then deemed to have the original purported tenancy validated.

2.8 Temporary Convenience Lettings

Lettings for temporary convenience arise where a dwelling (in the case of a residence) or premises (in the case of business or commercial use) is expressed to be let for temporary convenience or to meet a temporary necessity of the landlord or the tenant. Such lettings, if they are genuinely made for such purposes, fall outside the legislation affording statutory protection and rights to such occupiers.

Under the Housing (Private Rented Dwellings) Act, 1982, s 8(2)(b) excludes a dwelling 'let bona fide for the temporary convenience or to meet a temporary necessity of the landlord or the tenant'. This exclusion applies only to the restrictions on the landlord's right of recovery and retention of possession by the tenant.

In the case of premises with business or commercial user such lettings were excluded from the provisions of the Landlord and Tenant (Amendment) Act, 1980. The temporary convenience or temporary necessity of the landlord or the tenant must be bona fide and a court is entitled to seek evidence of the temporary nature of the arrangement. If it considers the arrangement too vague, it may refuse to accept that such an arrangement is excluded from the security of tenure provided by the legislation.

As the description implies, this type of letting is generally made for a short period of time or to meet a temporary necessity of the landlord and the tenant. There is no definition of temporary convenience though some guidance may be had from such case law as exists.

In *McCutcheon v Wilson*, unreported, but quoted in *Driscoll v Riordan* [1885] 16 LR Ir 235, Fitzgibbon LJ stated:

'Every letting is in a sense for the convenience or to meet a necessity of one or other or both of the parties; but the temporary convenience or necessity contemplated here must, I think, be something special, peculiar to the party or parties or to the holding, collateral to, or possibly even irrespective of the quantity or quality of the tenant's interest, not expected to continue to exist at another time or in other hands, and must be shown to have formed the motive of the letting at the time.'

In *Carton v McManus* (1962) 96 ILT 92, it was held that a mere statement of temporary convenience is not enough. The letting must actually be for temporary convenience.

This type of letting may be employed to avoid statutory controls and in particular the renewal rights which accrue under the Landlord and Tenant (Amendment) Act, 1980, as amended. A letting for temporary convenience is specifically excluded from the definition of a 'tenement' in s 5 of the 1980 Act. Each case will, however, be determined on its own particular facts.

There is no restriction on the length of such a letting. The courts will seek evidence to support a claim that the letting is for a genuine temporary convenience. It is the motive which is significant rather than its duration.

When drafting an agreement for the genuine temporary convenience of the parties it is important to set out the nature of the temporary convenience in the clearest terms in the agreement. A common reason for such a letting is where the landlord is occupying the premises but does not need all of it for his or her own use in the short term and the tenant is seeking to set up a business in the area and does not wish to commit himself or herself to a long-term lease. Another example would be where a tenant has sold his or her previous premises in the area and is seeking more suitable long-term accommodation but wishes to continue business in the area while seeking such accommodation. It should be noted that a temporary convenience letting does not grant statutory protection and rights to a tenant.

In the event of a dispute between the parties and the matter coming before the courts, the courts will look closely at the agreement to see whether the letting is a genuine or bona fide temporary convenience letting.

2.9 Conclusion

It can be seen that there are a wide range of agreements which can affect land. All of the above can apply to both business/commercial premises, eg manufacturing, retail, offices, as well as residential premises.

CHAPTER 3

LICENCES

3.1 Introduction

The essential point about a licence is that it does not transfer any estate or interest in the land to the licensee. As the word 'licence' suggests, it is in fact permission by an owner of land to allow another person to enter that land. Without the licence such entry and occupation of the land would amount to trespass.

As an article by Dr Albert Power in the Law Society *Gazette* August/September 2004 points out:

> 'a lease brings with it, potentially, statutory rights of renewal, compensation for disturbance, compensation for improvements, enforceability of covenants between successors to the original parties, covenants implied by statute and—in principle—the freedom by the occupier to assign his interest. A licence enjoys none of these things. It neither creates nor transfers an interest in lands. In its essence, it is a mere permission'.

As we have seen in **1.3.4.1**, s 3 of Deasy's Act, 1860 provides that the relationship of landlord and tenant is deemed to be founded on the express or implied contract between the parties and to arise where one party agrees to hold land from another party 'in consideration of any rent'. In the case of a lease and a licence both derive from contract, both involve occupation and both feature payment of money; in the case of a lease it is described as 'rent' and in the case of a licence it is generally described as 'licence fee'. It is important to be able to distinguish that the agreement under examination is either a lease or a licence because, as we have seen, a lease brings with it statutory rights and protection. A licence does not have the benefit of this and, most importantly, a licence does not create an interest in land. As Henchy J stated in *Irish Shell & BP Ltd v John Costello Ltd (No. 2)* [1984] IR 511:

> 'In all cases it is a question of what the parties intended, and it is not permissible to apply an objective test which would impute to the parties an intention which they never had.'

One must objectively look at the relationship between the parties to see which path they have chosen. Lord Templeman in *Street v Mountford* [1985] AC 809, states:

> 'If the agreement satisfied all the requirements of a tenancy, then the agreement produced a tenancy and the parties cannot alter the effect of the agreement by insisting that they only created a licence.'

In the case of a lease, a tenant may qualify for important statutory rights under the Landlord and Tenant (Ground Rents) (No. 2) Act, 1978 and the Landlord and Tenant (Amendment) Act, 1980. These include the right to a new tenancy, the right to a reversionary lease and the right to buy out the fee simple interest in the property. In contrast a licensee is excluded from these statutory rights. He has no entitlement to a new licence, no right to a reversionary lease and no right to buy out the freehold interest.

Statutory rights are also covered by the draft Landlord and Tenant Law Reform Bill 2011 ('the draft 2011 Bill') (see **1.4.4**) and will be covered in more detail in **chapter 10.**

Licences are one of the most difficult and confusing areas of property law. One of the reasons for this is that judges have resorted to the concept in a number of very different situations to solve the particular problem before them. In the commercial world an example would be a short-term occupation of business premises where it is not intended that the relationship of landlord and tenant be created, eg where a person requires short-term accommodation to carry on a business while looking for more long-term suitable premises in the immediate area. The term 'licence' has been used regularly in the past to avoid the effects of legislation restricting rent or to evade the renewal rights provided for in the Landlord and Tenant (Amendment) Act, 1980.

There are different categories of licence, with different incidents applying to them. The main categories are set out below.

3.1.1   BARE LICENCE

A bare licence is a mere personal permission to do something such as enter specific land or property. No payment is made and it is revocable at any time by the licensor. The licensee is entitled to reasonable notice to enable him or her to leave with his or her belongings. If the licensee does not do so he or she then becomes a trespasser. If reasonable notice is not given and the owner of the land forcibly removes the licensee, this action constitutes an assault, as the existence of the licence prevents the licensee from being a trespasser.

As the licence is personal to the particular licensee he or she cannot transfer his or her right to be on the land to a third party. A bare licence is not binding on successors in title who may subsequently acquire the land.

3.1.2   LICENCE COUPLED WITH AN INTEREST

A licence coupled with an interest arises where a person is granted an interest in another's land, eg the right to shoot game or cut down and remove trees. If the licence was not granted the licensee would not be able to enter onto the land to exercise his or her interest. This type of licence is irrevocable as long as the grantee's interest exists. Clearly, if the right to cut down and remove trees was granted and there were no further trees to cut down, then the licence to enter the land to exercise that interest will automatically terminate. The interest had to be granted by deed as otherwise such a licence could be readily revoked. If it was revoked the licensee became a trespasser and could not seek damages (*Wood v Leadbitter* [1845] 13M and W838). However, if it was clearly intended that the licence was to continue until the subject matter of its enjoyment no longer existed, then even if not granted by deed, equity looked on the licence as irrevocable and would permit an injunction to restrain its revocation (*Atkinson v King* [1878] 2 LR (Ir) 320). This type of licence can be transferred to another and it is binding on third parties.

In *Square Management Limited & Others v Dunnes Stores Dublin Company* [2017] IEHC 146, the High Court held the purported assignment of licences in a deed dated 22 January 1991 was null and void and of no legal effect. The 1991 deed had sought to effect a bare assignment of the licences which in each case was a licence coupled with an interest. The court quoted from *Megarry & Wade*: 'at common law such a licence is both irrevocable and assignable but only as an adjunct of the interest with which it is coupled. It therefore has no independent existence merely as a licence.'

3.1.3 CONTRACTUAL LICENCE

A contractual licence is created by contract. The power of revocation is governed by the terms of that contract. There is no proprietary interest in the land. It is not necessary that the contract be an express one: *Chandler v Kerley* [1978] 2 All ER 942. Such a contract may be implied but there must be a clear intention of a contractual relationship being created.

In *McGill v S* [1979] IR 283, an unmarried couple were living together in a house which had been bought and restored by one of them. The court held that when the owner went abroad and ceased his association with his partner he was entitled to recover possession from her.

The recognition of a contractual licence was established in the case of *Hurst v Picture Theatres Ltd* [1915] 1 KB 1. In this case, the plaintiff was removed from a cinema in the mistaken belief that he had not paid for admission. The English Court of Appeal held that this was an actionable assault as the plaintiff had not become a trespasser through the purported revocation of his licence. Buckley LJ observed that where a licence is created by contract it is revocable in accordance with the terms of that contract. In this case, the plaintiff had not been in breach and he was entitled to remain in the cinema for the duration of the film. He had not been a trespasser when he was ejected as the purported revocation of his licence was ineffective.

The distinct nature of a contractual licence was recognised in *Whipp v Mackey* [1927] IR 372, where it was stated that a licensor can be prevented by injunction from acting upon a purported revocation which is in breach of contract.

In *Winter Garden Theatre (London) Ltd v Millennium Productions Ltd* [1948] AC 173, the contract provided for a licence to hold plays and concerts in a theatre owned by the defendant. In the Court of Appeal, Lord Greene stated that a licence could not be considered separately from the contract which created it. He further stated:

> 'A licence created by a contract is not an interest. It creates a contractual right to do certain things which otherwise would be a trespass ... In considering the nature of such a licence and the mutual rights and obligations which arise under it, the first thing to do is to construe the contract according to ordinary principles.'

This principle was agreed in the House of Lords although they reversed the decision on another ground.

It makes sense that a contractual licence must be dependent on the most objectively identifiable conditions to be determined on the facts of each case. An oral representation could constitute a contractual licence, but if there was a lack of certainty which would result in holding an indeterminable and inconclusive relationship as a valid contract, then the relationship would be one of a licensee at will and not a contractual licensee. See the comments of Gannon J in *McGill v Snodgrass* [1979] IR 283.

3.1.4 ESTOPPEL LICENCES

In certain circumstances a licensor may be estopped from revoking a licence relating to land unless the successor is a bona fide purchaser of the legal estate without notice. The principle of estoppel is where, as a result of a person making a representation to another who acts on that representation, the representor can subsequently be prevented from denying the accuracy or effectiveness of the representation. Estoppel is recognised both at law and in equity and the court has a wide discretion as to how it will give effect to the 'equity'.

The case of *Cullen v Cullen* [1962] IR 268 involved a breakdown of family relations brought about by the father's mental illness. One of the sons had erected, at his mother's suggestion, a portable house on the father's land which was run as a family business. This had been done after his mother had asked his father's permission and the father had stated she could do what she liked as he planned to transfer the land to her. However, he made it a condition that the transfer was subject to the mother and the sons signing a statement that he was sane and they would not get an order for his committal. Kenny J considered the position of the son in relation to the house erected on the land and he held that the son could not invoke proprietary estoppel because he had not been mistaken as to the ownership of the land when he constructed the house. He could not require his father to convey the site to him, but the father was precluded from asserting any title to the site by the doctrine of promissory estoppel.

In *Re Basham* [1986] 1 WLR 1498, the court stated that to successfully invoke the doctrine of proprietary estoppel there needs to be proof that an assurance was given and has been relied on by the plaintiff to her detriment.

An estoppel licence is personal to the licensee.

3.2   Characteristics of a Licence

A form of agreement described as a licence was often used by parties who wished to avoid the effects of statutory restrictions, particularly in relation to renewal rights arising in a landlord and tenant relationship. The document offered by the owner of the land may be described as a licence and employ licence terminology. There is no problem where the intention of both parties is to create a licence for genuine purposes. However, the words used in the document, or the label used to describe the relationship between the parties, is not conclusive and a body of extensive case law has been built up by the courts when determining if an agreement is a tenancy or a licence. As this is often difficult to determine, a court will look closely at the terms of the agreement described as a 'licence' to see if it is, genuinely, a licence and not an attempt by one or both parties to avoid statutory rights. In other words, the court will attempt to determine the reality of the bargain made between the parties, ie the true nature of the agreement rather than the label given to it by the parties; see *Esso Ireland Ltd & Ireland Roc Ltd v Nine One One Retail Ltd* [2013] IEHC 514. Lord Templeman in *Street v Mountford* [1985] AC 809 observed:

> 'The consequences in law of the agreement, once concluded, can only be determined by consideration of the effect of the agreement. If the agreement satisfied all the requirements of a tenancy, then the agreement produced a tenancy and the parties can not alter the effect of the agreement by insisting that they only created a licence.'

In *Smith v Coras Iompair Eireann* [2002] IEHC 103, the applicant had appealed against a decision of the Circuit Court dismissing an application for a new lease under s 21(2) of the Landlord and Tenant (Amendment) Act, 1980. The applicant operated a shop under the railway arch at Tara Street Railway Station, Dublin, by an agreement dated 4 December 1991. The agreement was described as a licence for a period of ten years commencing on 1 July 1991. The periodic payments were described as 'an annual licence fee'. Furthermore, clause 10 stated *'Nothing in this licence shall be construed as giving the licensee any tenancy in or right to possession of or any right or easement over or with respect to any part of the property'*. Both parties understood what was offered was a licence agreement. The applicant had exclusive possession and the respondents neither entered the premises nor did they hold a key. The applicant had invested a significant sum of money in the business including a payment of IR£75,000 to the respondent as a premium and had further spent a sum of IR£25,000 on fitting out the premises. On the conclusion of the ten-year agreement the applicant sought a new tenancy under the terms of the 1980 Act. The application was dismissed by the Circuit Court. Peart J allowed the Appeal and declared that the applicant was entitled to a new tenancy. Peart J held that apart from the one clause that characterised the agreement as a licence, the entire document was a standard commercial lease. If that one clause was deleted and the 'licence labels' replaced with 'tenancy labels', then according to Peart J it would bear a significant resemblance to any normal tenancy agreement. Payments were in effect rent, the grantee had exclusive possession, the grantee had invested heavily in the business and, taken altogether, the grantee clearly had more than a 'mere personal privilege'. Peart J cited extensively in favour of his decision from the speech of Lord Templeman in *Street v Mountford* [1985] AC 809:

> 'If the agreement satisfied all of the requirements of a tenancy, then the agreement produced a tenancy and the parties cannot alter the effect of the agreement by insisting that they only created a licence.'

Hill and Redman's *Law of Landlord and Tenant* (Vol 1) Issue 28 October 1998, states that 'the cardinal rule is to seek an objective assessment of the intention of the parties ... The correct course is to consider all the relevant circumstances and then to ask whether a reasonable onlooker would regard the transaction as a lease or a licence.'

As stated above, the labelling of a document as a lease or as a licence will not, per se, suffice to place it into either category. The following are the main elements that may differentiate a licence from the other types of interest which can be created in land:

(a)   There is no interest in land. It confers personal rights only and cannot be assigned.

(b)   Exclusive possession. In certain circumstances a licensee may have exclusive possession of land: *Bellew v Bellew* [1982] IR 447, but in many cases the licensee does not have sufficient 'control' to amount to possession, eg lodgers, hotel guests. While exclusive possession is not conclusive proof as to the existence of a tenancy it has been held to be a prerequisite. Kenny J stated in *Gatien Motor Co Ltd v Continental Oil Co of Ireland Ltd* [1979] IR 406: 'when determining whether a person in possession of land is to be regarded as a tenant or as being in some other category, exclusive possession by the person in possession is undoubtedly a most important consideration but it is not decisive. A person may be in exclusive possession of land but not be a tenant.'

In his Article *Law Reform Commission Land Law Update* (2004) 9(1) CPLJ 8 Trevor Redmond discusses the Consultation Paper on General Law of Landlord and Tenant (LRC CP 28–2003) and notes that the Law Reform Commission agrees with the remarks of Kenny J in *Gatien Motor Co Ltd v Continental Oil Co of Ireland Ltd* to the effect that exclusive possession is not a conclusive criterion and he further goes on to state 'according to the case law the concept of exclusive possession is treated as a negative criterion only in that its absence in a particular case will rule out a tenancy, but its presence will not necessarily result in a ruling in favour of a tenancy. Its presence will simply be regarded as one factor, but not necessarily the determining one, pointing to a tenancy.' The Law Reform Commission recommends that any statutory guidelines should include the requirement of exclusive possession.

In the case of *National Maternity Hospital v McGouran* [1994] 1 ILRM 521, a hospital allowed an individual to occupy part of the building for use as a coffee shop. The agreement was stated to be a licence and it was expressly laid down that there was no exclusive possession and the plaintiff was entitled to substitute another suitable premises within the hospital. The hospital administrators were entitled to come into the coffee shop whenever they wished. In practice, Mrs McGouran was the sole keyholder. Morris J took the clause negating exclusive possession at face value so under the first principle laid down in *Irish Shell & BP Ltd v John Costello Ltd* [1981] ILRM 66, the agreement could not have been a lease. In *Whyte v Sheehan* [1943] Ir Jur Rep 38, Shannon J stated:

> 'If it is clear from the document that it was intended to part with an estate in the property and to confer an exclusive right of occupation, so that the grantor had no right to come upon the premises without the consent of the occupier, a tenancy or demise is created although no words of letting are used, and although the remuneration is not spoken of as rent.'

In *National Maternity Hospital v McGouran* [1994] 1 ILRM 521, Morris J held that the fact that the occupation was specified as non-exclusive and the premises where the grantee's trading activities took place were liable to be substituted by other premises at the behest of the hospital meant that there could not be a tenancy. Although the grantee could be said to have had 'exclusive possession' to the extent that she was the sole keyholder, '*the reality is that the hospital continued to operate and exercise dominion*'.

Kenny Homes and Co Ltd v Leonard High Court 11 December 1997 (unreported) and Supreme Court 18 June 1998 (unreported) involved a licence of a petrol filling station to facilitate the hire of equipment and sale of produce manufactured by the grantor. The licensee was the sole keyholder but, according to Costello P, the licensors 'had contractual rights over the site which they could enforce at any time'. Occupation of the site by the licensee was not exclusive possession, because, in successive written agreements they had specifically agreed otherwise.

(c) Although a bare licence is revocable, other types of licence, especially those coupled with an interest or a contractual licence or an estoppel licence, may not be revocable.

(d) Since the licensee occupies with the consent of the licensor he cannot be in adverse possession to the licensor so time does not run.

(e) The agreement must be examined to see whether it contains terms usually found in a lease.

(f) The expressions actually used by the parties to describe the transaction should be examined. However, these will not be conclusive.

(g) What monetary payments, if any, are reserved? Does it appear to be in fact rental payments payable on certain dates throughout a calendar year?

(h) Does a special relationship between the parties exist, eg a family relative?

(i) Did the licensee previously occupy the premises before the present arrangement? If so, on what basis?

(j) What is the degree of formality surrounding the transaction? The greater the formality, the stronger the inference that a tenancy is intended to be created.

(k) The capacity of the grantor to grant a tenancy.

(l) The degree of control kept by the licensor over, and in possession of, the premises.

(m) Is there a right for the licensor to enter the premises?

(n) Are there any repairing obligations? It is inappropriate for a licensee to be obliged to carry out repairs: *Addiscombe Garden Estates Ltd v Crabbe* [1958] 1 QB 513.

The foregoing are merely guidelines, which may be helpful in clarifying whether a licence or a tenancy exists. It may be difficult, however, to reach a definite conclusion.

At a Law Society Continuing Legal Education seminar on *Landlord and Tenant Law* on 29 August 2000, Buckley J stated:

'There is no doubt that the question of whether premises have been leased or licensed continues to give rise to difficulty. A significant number of the cases which have come to the courts have involved the attempt by landlords to avoid tenants claiming a new tenancy under the Landlord and Tenant Acts. This was particularly important in the years when a tenant was entitled on renewal to a 21-year lease at a fixed rent, which gave the tenant, particularly at times when rents were steadily increasing, a very substantial equity in the property. A major category of these cases involved filling stations.

Oil companies owned the sites, the tanks, the equipment and the buildings on the site, but did not wish to operate them through employees. Accordingly they would enter into agreements with the operators under which the operators were entitled to use the site, tanks, buildings and equipment for the sale of petroleum products, all of which were supplied by the oil company ... In two leading cases ... the issue of whether these types of agreement were licences or leases came before the Supreme Court.'

The two leading cases on the issue of whether these types of agreement were licences or leases are *Gatien Motor Co Ltd v Continental Oil Co of Ireland Ltd* and *Irish Shell & BP Ltd v Costello Ltd* [1981] ILRM 66. Both these cases went to the Supreme Court and the leading judgment was given by Griffin J each time. In the *Irish Shell & BP Ltd* case, Griffin J said one had to consider whether it was a personal privilege given to a person (and hence a licence) or the granting of an interest in land (and hence a tenancy). Whether an agreement is in fact a licence depends primarily on whether it is personal in its nature or not. In this case the oil company was trying to protect its interest by inserting a number of provisions in the agreement which were more appropriate to a lease than a licence and hence Griffin J concluded that the true nature of the agreement was that of a lease. Examples of clauses which he gave as influencing his decision were the restriction on assignment (not appropriate in a licence), a provision for hiring equipment with no reference to a workshop and a clause very similar to a re-entry clause.

In *Shell-Mex and BP Ltd v Manchester Garages Ltd* [1971] 1 WLR 612, Lord Denning stated that the transaction must be looked at as a whole in order to find out if it was intended to create the relationship of landlord and tenant or the relationship of licensor and licensee.

The case of *Ò'Siodhachain v O'Mahony* High Court 31 October 2002 (unreported) was concerned with whether a document constituted a lease where no rent was payable and there was a question of undue influence. The facts briefly were that the defendants owned a farm which included a dwelling-house. They resided in a nearby village. In August 1998 they unsuccessfully attempted to sell the land at public auction. Shortly after the abortive auction the plaintiffs met the defendants and became friendly. Subsequently, financial matters were discussed and two contracts were drawn up. The first one was prepared by the plaintiffs and signed after an all-night discussion. The defendants agreed to purchase a property in County Cork owned by one of the plaintiffs and the plaintiffs agreed to purchase part of the farmland together with the farmhouse. The agreement was set out as an exchange of properties and, inter alia, incorporated a 15-year lease of the farmhouse. The plaintiffs moved into the farmhouse and remained there without paying any rent or purchase monies to the defendants. It was subsequently agreed that the defendants would be relieved of their obligation to proceed with the purchase of the property in County Cork. The plaintiffs remained in the farmhouse. In 2000 a contract was drawn up by the defendant's solicitor for the sale of the farm to the plaintiffs for IR£220,000 with a deposit of IR£22,000. The contract was returned with a deposit of IR£100 and the solicitor advised the defendants not to sign the contract and to seek possession of the farm. They issued a notice to quit. The High Court held that at no time was the relationship between the parties an equal one. The plaintiffs had considerable legal experience, but Mr O'Mahony was educationally disadvantaged and his wife was isolated and vulnerable. From the facts there was a relationship of confidence and trust by the defendants in the plaintiffs such as might give rise to a presumption of undue influence. The court found that actual undue influence was proved and hence the contract signed following the all-night discussion was not enforceable. In relation to the defendants' claim for possession the court found that the plaintiffs occupied the farm as permissive occupants only. Their entitlement to remain terminated with the notice to quit.

It would seem that this is the first case in Ireland where an agreement was described as a lease but found to be a licence. Most of the cases which arise concern 'licences' that are found to establish leasehold rights. Here it is unlikely that the plaintiffs could have established leasehold rights in circumstances where they were not paying any rent or other consideration to the defendants.

Another example of the creation of the relationship of a licensor and licensee is in the case of a car parking licence. Such a licence cannot give rise to a claim for a new tenancy because there is no building which would constitute a 'tenement'. A clear example of how such an agreement could not be held as a lease but only as a licence is a provision whereby the landlord reserves the right to change the car parking space and for the landlord to implement such changes.

The draft 2011 Bill (**1.4.4**) replaces parts of s 5 of the Landlord and Tenant (Amendment) Act, 1980 and drops the concept of 'tenement'. It would no longer be necessary to have buildings on the land to acquire statutory rights of renewal provided other conditions are met.

Another use of a licence is within a department store, supermarket area or a shopping centre where the owner grants a licence to use a space as a concession. An obvious situation which comes to mind is in a department store in the cosmetics department where different cosmetic companies each occupy a space in the department to market their particular brand. The essential element to such an agreement is the reservation of the right by the owner of the store to move the location of the particular stand within the department store.

A good licence agreement will acknowledge that the rights are personal to the licensee and the licensee will undertake to co-operate with the licensor in the management and control of the property.

In its Consultation Paper on General Law of Landlord and Tenant (LRC CP 28–2003) the Law Reform Commission addressed the problematic area of the lease/licence distinction and noted that there was considerable uncertainty in law and in practice due to case law. The Commission referred to the cases of *Smith v Coras Iompair Eireann* [2002] IEHC 103 where it was held that the operator of the shop had in fact entered into a tenancy agreement from the outset and the difficulty in reconciling this decision both with s 3 of Deasy's Act and the decision in *Kenny Homes and Co Ltd v Leonard* High Court 11 December 1997 (unreported), Supreme Court 18 June 1998 (unreported). It should be noted that *Smith v Coras Iompair Eireann* related to a commercial arrangement whereas the cases of *Street v Mountford* [1985] AC 809 and *Errington v Errington and Woods* (1952) 1 KB 290) involved residential arrangements. The Commission recommended that it should only be open to a court to disregard the terms of the agreement where there is evidence that unfair advantage is being taken, or that a party is being deprived of rights which could be reasonably expected to arise.

The draft 2011 Bill at Part 2 deals with the fundamental issue of when the relationship of landlord and tenant as opposed to some other relationship such as licensor/licensee exists. It states a tenancy shall be created at law only in writing signed by the landlord or the landlord's agent authorised in writing. Two exceptions are a tenancy for a recurring period not exceeding one year and a tenancy for a fixed period not exceeding one year unless the grant includes a provision for renewal or extension which would result in the period exceeding one year.

Accountancy Ireland, April 2016 vol. 48 no. 2 has an article on the VAT treatment of the supply of a letting service which is exempt from VAT, but in contrast the supply of a licence is subject to VAT at 23 per cent. The difference between a lease and licence for VAT purposes must be determined in accordance with the EU VAT Directive 2006/112/EC and the European Court of Justice case law.

3.3   Example Car Park Licence

Note in particular clause (2) where the licensor can substitute spaces, clause (10) referring to a licence fee and clauses (11) and (13).

THIS LICENCE is made on

BETWEEN

(1)   having its registered office at   in the City of   (hereinafter called 'the **Licensor**') of the one part; and

(2)   (hereinafter called 'the **Licensee**') of the other part.

WHEREAS:

1. The Licensor is the owner of the car park site at [   ] (**'the Car Park'**) as more particularly delineated on the map or plan annexed hereto and thereon edged blue.

2. The Licensor has agreed to grant to the Licensee a Licence to use car parking space(s) numbered [   ] (the **'spaces'**) in the Car Park upon the terms and conditions hereinafter more particularly set out.

NOW IT IS HEREBY AGREED AND DECLARED by and between the parties hereto as follows:

(1) The Licensor hereby licenses and authorises the Licensee its servants and agents to use the space(s) edged red on the map or plan annexed hereto in the Car Park for the term of these presents which spaces are numbered [   ].

(2) The Licensor shall allocate to the Licensee the spaces to be used by the Licensee and may from time to time and at any time during the period of this Licence allocate to the Licensee another or other spaces in the Car Park for use in accordance with these presents in substitution for one or more of the spaces then allocated to the Licensee.

(3) The spaces shall be used for the parking of private motor cars only and shall not be used for any other purpose between the hours of 8 am and 6 pm on Mondays to Fridays inclusive and not more than one such motor car shall at any one time be parked in any one space allocated by the Licensor to the Licensee.

(4) The Licensee shall not obstruct or suffer any obstruction in the Car Park or do anything which will create or cause a nuisance in the Car Park and shall not drop any litter in same.

(5) The Licensee shall ensure that the entrance gate to the Car Park is locked by him on each occasion upon which he enters or leaves the Car Park in order to prevent any unauthorised persons entering the Car Park. In the event of the Licensee failing to lock the said entrance gate and having received notice of such failure from the Licensor, its servants and agents, the Licensor shall be at liberty to terminate this lcence upon the Licensee's continuing failure to lock the said entrance gate.

(6) The Licensee hereby covenants with the Licensor that he/she/it will repair and make good any damage caused to the Car Park by him/her/it or his/her/its employees, servants and agents of which notice in writing shall be given by the Licensor to the Licensee within 14 days of the giving of such notice or such other period as the notice may specify, and on the Licensee's failure to comply with such notice the Licensor may carry out the work referred to therein and recover the cost thereof on demand from the Licensee.

(7) This Licence shall continue for a term of [   ] year(s) from the   day of   , 20[   ] unless sooner determined in accordance with the provisions hereof.

(8) The Licensee covenants to pay the Licensor during the said term of the Licence the sum of €[   ] payable on the signing hereof.

(9) The Licensee covenants to pay to the Licensor on demand a proportional sum for rates payable in respect of the Car Park such proportion to be the same as that which the spaces the subject of the Licence bear to the total of the car parking

spaces which are let in the Car Park, and the certificate of the Licensor shall be conclusive as to the number of such spaces which are let.

(10) In the event of this Licence continuing for more than one year it shall in the absence of a new Licence be deemed to be a Licence determinable by one month's notice in writing by either party and the Licensee covenants with the Licensor to pay to it during the remainder of the period of the Licence such licence fee as may be payable in accordance with the provisions hereof.

(11) The Licence hereby granted shall be personal to the Licensee and shall not be assignable.

PROVIDED ALWAYS and these presents are upon this condition that if any covenant on the Licensee's part herein contained shall not be performed or observed then and in any such case it shall be lawful for the Licensor at any time thereafter to re-enter upon the spaces or any part thereof in the name of the whole and thereupon this Licence shall absolutely determine but without prejudice to any claim by the Licensor in respect of any antecedent breach of any covenant or provision herein contained and on the happening of any of the said events it shall also be lawful for the Licensor to determine this Licence by giving to the Licensee or sending by registered post to its place of business last known or to its registered office a Notice to determine same and to vacate the spaces within fourteen days of the said Notice the said Notice expiring on any day of the week and upon the expiration of such Notice the Licence hereby created shall be deemed to have been duly determined by such Notice and the Licensor shall thereupon be entitled to occupation of the spaces as of its former estate and as if the Licence hereby created had never existed.

(12) The Licensee will pay to the Licensor the stamp duty on this Licence and Counterpart and VAT if any payable on the granting thereof or the licence fee receivable hereunder.

(13) The Licensor shall be at liberty at any time to terminate this Licence on giving to the Licensee not less than three calendar months' notice in writing whereupon the Licensee shall cease to use the space(s) and this Licence shall be null and void and of no further force or effect but without prejudice to any claim by either party against the other in respect of any antecedent breach of any covenant or condition herein contained.

(14) If the Licensee shall fail to pay any sum reserved or made payable hereunder within seven days of the day and in the manner herein prescribed for the payment of same such unpaid sum shall bear interest from the day or days on which the same shall become due to the date of actual payment (after as well as before any judgment) at a rate which shall exceed the three month Dublin Inter Bank Rate by four per centum or if there should be no such rate the corresponding or nearest appropriate rate thereto at the date upon which the said sums fall due or become payable of/or if there shall be no such rate twenty-four per centum.

(15) The Licensor accepts no responsibility for any loss or damage to any vehicle or its contents or for any loss or injury to any persons or property caused by any person or persons or use of any vehicle or vehicles while in the Car Park or while entering or leaving same.

IN WITNESS whereof the parties hereto have hereunto executed these presents the day and year first herein **WRITTEN**

PRESENT when the Common Seal
of the **Licensor**
was affixed hereto:

SIGNED AND DELIVERED
by the **Licensee**
in the presence of:

28

3.4   Example of Licence of Concession Area

Note in particular recital (B) and clauses 4 and 6.

THIS AGREEMENT is made the   of   two thousand and

BETWEEN   whose registered office is at   (hereinafter called the 'Company') of the one part and   whose registered office is situate at   (hereinafter called '   ').

WHEREAS:

(A)   The Company owns a retail department store (hereinafter referred to as the 'Store') in   trading as   .

(B)   The Company has agreed to grant an exclusive licence to   to occupy part of the Store for use as a shop upon the terms and subject to the conditions contained herein.

NOW IT IS HEREBY AGREED AS FOLLOWS:

HEADINGS

1.   Clause headings are inserted for convenience only and shall not affect the construction of this Agreement.

DEFINITIONS

2.   'Termination Date', the date of termination of this Agreement.

'Transfer Regulations', the European Communities (Protection of Employees on Transfer of Undertakings) Regulations 2003.

POSITION AND AREA

3.   The Company hereby grants an exclusive licence to   to occupy part of the Store for use as a shop under the name   (the said part of the Store to be hereinafter called the 'Licensed Premises').

4.   The floor area of the Licensed Premises and its layout and position within the Store shall be mutually agreed between the parties.

It shall be lawful for the Company to change the location of the Licensed Premises at any time on giving sixty days prior written notice of that intention specifying the new location in the Store to be used, provided always such new location is comparable as to floor area and quality as the previous location in the Store.

The fixtures, fittings or other equipment necessary for the operation of the Licensed Premises, but with the exception of a till, will be provided by and shall remain the sole property of   .   shall bear all costs related to installation of its fixtures and fittings, signage and any other items necessary for the operation of the Licensed Premises. The Company shall provide a till for the use of and will maintain the fixtures and fittings provided by and all other fixtures and fittings and all lighting necessary for the use of the Licensed Premises in a good state of repair at its own expense. No right of title ownership or lien shall be claimed by the Company or its receivers upon such fixtures and fittings **NOTWITHSTANDING** that the said fixtures or other equipment may be fixed to the Company's premises for the purpose of safety, decorative appearance or to connect to the services of the Company's Store as required.

5.   The Company shall pay all rents, rates, insurance (including property insurance) and other outgoings in respect of the Licensed Premises and at its own expense shall provide all heating, lighting, cleaning and other services required in respect of the Licensed Premises.

LICENCES

6. Nothing contained in this Agreement shall create or be construed as creating the relationship of Landlord and Tenant between the Company and   .

7. Neither party shall describe itself or purport to act as agent or representative of the other.

8. Nothing contained herein shall or shall be deemed to create any joint venture or partnership between the parties or create any tenancy or any other proprietary interest in respect of the Licensed Premises.

9. The Company shall permit its customers, servants and agents during the continuance of this Agreement at all reasonable times during ordinary business hours to have full and free right of access to and egress from the Licensed Premises through the doors, entrances and passages of the Store as may be necessary and convenient for the purpose of its business permitted by this Agreement but not for any other purpose.

MERCHANDISE

10. All merchandise to be sold in the Licensed Premises shall be supplied by   which shall be responsible for maintaining and supervising reasonable supplies and quality control of such merchandise.

11. The Company shall provide such services and make such facilities available at the Store as are necessary to enable items of stock to be moved in, to and out of the Licensed Premises at all reasonable times.

12. All stock whether in the Licensed Premises in the possession or under the control of the Company shall at all times until sold remain the property of   .

STAFF

13.   shall, at its own cost, recruit and employ staff to work in the Licensed Premises (hereafter referred to as the 'Staff') who shall for all purposes be employees of   .

14. (a)   shall ensure that the Licensed Premises is staffed adequately at all times to fully and effectively conduct its trade within the Licensed Premises.

   (b)   shall take all measures necessary to comply with all provisions, requirements, rules, regulations, statutory or otherwise relating to such employment and use of all Licensed Premises and shall comply with all rules, regulations and provisions whether statutory or otherwise relating to the Store in so far as same may apply to.

STAFF DISCOUNT

15. The Store staff will receive 15 per cent discount off full retail price purchases on purchases made for personal use only within   .   Staff will receive 15 per cent discount off full retail price purchases on purchases made for personal use only within Store departments. The Company will enjoy full commission on the net value of a staff purchase sale within.

TRANSFER OF UNDERTAKINGS

16. The Company and acknowledge and agree that the termination of this Agreement for any reason may constitute the transfer of an undertaking for the purposes of the Transfer Regulations.

17.   hereby agrees to fully indemnify and hold harmless the Company against all claims, judgments, decrees, orders, awards, costs, liabilities, demands and expenses howsoever arising under, or by virtue of, the application of the Transfer Regulations and any resulting transfer to the Company pursuant to the Transfer

Regulations of members of the Staff or any other person engaged by or on behalf of   whether arising by reason of or in relation to:

(i) the termination by on or before the Termination Date of the contract of employment of any member of the   Staff;

(ii) anything done or omitted to be done in respect of the employment of any member of the   Staff in the period up to and including the Termination Date;

(iii) any breach by on or before the Termination Date of its obligations under the Transfer Regulations;

(iv) the termination by the Company after the Termination Date of any member of the   Staff or any person engaged by or on behalf of who is deemed to transfer to the employment of the Company pursuant to the Transfer Regulations; or

(v) in the event the Company elects to continues the employment of any member of the   Staff or any other person engaged by or on behalf of who is deemed to transfer to the employment of the Company pursuant to the Transfer Regulations after the Termination Date, any additional cost incurred by the Company in providing the   Staff or any other person, pursuant to the Transfer Regulations, with terms and conditions of employment which are inconsistent with the Company's standard terms and conditions of employment.

18. In the event the Transfer Regulations apply to the termination of this Agreement,   hereby undertakes to provide the Company with such information regarding the   Staff and any other person engaged by or on behalf of   as the Company may reasonably require in order to give effect to the foregoing provisions.

ACCOUNTING AND STORE ACCOMMODATION CHARGE

19. The Company shall be responsible for the safekeeping of all takings of the Licensed Premises from the time that the Company shall remove takings from any till installed in the Licensed Premises (which it shall do at least once daily) where such till is used by   in respect of the business conducted in the Licensed Premises; or

20.

(a) The Company shall pay through Banker's Automated Clearing System (or failing that by cheque) to a sum representing the retail sales value of merchandise sold in the Shop (including deposits taken) for the monthly accounting period less a commission of [   ] % based on the Retail Sales Value excluding Value Added Tax ('VAT') to be received by   on or before the tenth day of the following month (the 'License Fee'). Retail Sales Value shall mean the aggregate prices at which merchandise is sold to the customer including VAT less the retail price of goods or deposits returned and refunds given in. If the Company fails to remit the moneys due by the due date then it shall pay interest on the overdue balance at the rate of 4% above the base rate of [   ] Bank for the time being. Such interest shall be calculated from the due date until the actual date of payment.

(b) If any dispute shall arise between the parties as to the amount of the Licence Fee such dispute shall be determined by an independent chartered accountant agreed between the parties or in default of agreement on the application of either party as nominated by the President of the Institute of Chartered Accountants in Ireland. The independent chartered accountant will act as an expert and not as an arbitrator. His fees will be borne equally by both parties and his decision shall be final and binding on both parties in the absence of manifest error.

(c) VAT on sales in the Licensed Premises shall be the liability of   who shall account to the Revenue Commissioners for VAT in respect of all such sales.

21. The Company shall render monthly statements to   in respect of amounts remitted including:

(i) a deduction of the cost of telephone calls as provided in Paragraph 25 hereof.

(ii) a deduction of any expense properly incurred by the   Staff in the course of their employment and paid by the Company.

DELIVERY AND INSURANCE

22.   shall at its own expense deliver stock to the Store and shall be responsible for insuring the stock while in transit to the Store.

23. The Company shall be responsible for all stock when the Store is closed and the Company shall take out and maintain full insurance in respect of all such stock against loss or damage from any cause during this time.

EXPENSES

24.   shall at its own expense supply all carrier bags required for the Licensed Premises.

25. The cost of telephone calls made by staff from any telephone in the Store whether installed in the Licensed Premises or not shall if local be borne by the Company but otherwise shall be borne by   .   shall maintain a record of all calls made by its staff and the cost of which will be subject to reconciliation at any time.   shall install a direct 24-hour telephone line for the exclusive use of   .

INDEMNITY

26.   shall be liable and shall indemnify the Company against any expenses, liability, loss, claim or proceedings incurred by the Company arising in whatever manner from the activities and operations of   , its employees, servants, agents, invitees or licensees unless due to the negligence of the Company or its employees.

(a) The Company hereby indemnifies and shall continue to indemnify   and   hold harmless and hereby indemnifies and shall continue to indemnify and hold harmless the Company from and against all and any costs, claims, actions, demands and damages from and against all and any costs, claims, actions, demands and damages that arise from:

(i) all and any actions, claims and demands (and all costs and expenses related thereto) in connection with the use of the Licensed Premises by employees, invitees and customers of either the Company or   , as the case may be;

(ii) any and all actions, claims, demands (and all costs and expenses related thereto) based on any infringement or alleged infringement of any third party intellectual property rights in consequence of the unauthorised use or possession by   of any intellectual property of the Company or vice versa; and

except where such costs, damages and liabilities arise from the gross negligence or wilful default of   or the Company or of any employee of   or the Company.

(b) Any such liability shall be limited to a maximum of €[   ].

27. Covenants
    hereby further covenants and agrees as follows:

(a) To keep accurate books of accounts on all its sales from the Licensed Premises and to make the said books available for inspection by the Company at reasonable times and on reasonable notice.

(b) To keep its stand, stall, counters and furniture on the Licensed Premises properly stocked and regularly open and properly attended to during such hours as the Store is open and use its best endeavours to make the same attractive for the sale of the particular articles hereby authorised to be sold by   .

(c) To observe and conform to all rules and regulations (including those relating to receiving and store policy) made from time to time by the Company for the proper management and control of the Store in accordance with the principles of good estate management and to fully co-operate with the Company and its servants and agents in their management control of the Licensed Premises.

(d) Not to purport to assign, sub-license or deal with or dispose of any of its rights under this agreement which rights are personal to   .

(e) To give notice in such places as the Company may from time to time in writing require that the business is operated under Licence from the Company and is separate from the Company.

(f)   shall adequately insure against the risks of Employers and Products Liability and shall also effect insurance against defamation, false imprisonment and wrongful arrest to such level as shall be agreed from time to time between the Company and   .   shall adequately insure its stock counters, stands, fittings, stalls, cash and customers' property against all risks including (but without prejudice to the generality of the foregoing) fire, water and sprinkler leakage damage and shall produce such policies and premium receipts to the Company's authorised representatives on request.

ADVERTISING AND WINDOW DISPLAY

28. The Company shall from time to time during each year (where possible at times chosen by   ) allocate a reasonable amount of space in the window displays of the Store for the display of the merchandise sold in the Licensed Premises.

29. The Company shall during this Agreement use its reasonable endeavours to encourage and promote sales in the Licensed Premises by all appropriate means including interior display and advertising.

DURATION

30. The term of this Agreement shall be for a minimum period of twelve months from the date trading commences and thereafter shall continue until terminated by either party giving to the other not less than six months' notice in writing or on such terms as may be agreed between the parties during the continuance of this Agreement.

This Agreement shall immediately terminate (but without prejudice to any rights already accrued to the parties) by either party giving to the other written notice in the event of:

(i) Any material breach of any of the provisions herein contained which remains unrectified after a period of 14 days have elapsed from the first written notification of the breach and in this regard any breach of this Agreement by which in the reasonable opinion of the Company is injurious to the goodwill of the Company or in the reasonable opinion of the Company adversely affects the business of the Company in any way shall be deemed a material breach: or

(ii) Either party closing business or becoming insolvent or distress or execution being levied upon its property or a receiver thereof being appointed: or

(iii) Either party going into Compulsory or Voluntary Liquidation or an order being made for its dissolution other than for the purpose of reconstruction or amalgamation.

31. If the Licensed Premises or any part thereof shall be damaged by any force majeure event or by any of the insured risks so as to be unfit for occupation and use (provided the insurance has not been vitiated nor payment of any insurance monies refused by reason of any act or default of) then the Licence Fee (or a fair proportion thereof) shall be suspended until the Licensed Premises shall again be rendered fit for occupation and use. In the event that the Licensed Premises shall not have been rebuilt and/or reinstated within twelve months following damage and/or destruction, either party shall have the right to terminate this Agreement on the giving of two months' written notice to the other.

CURRENT LIST PRICE

32. Merchandise shall be offered for sale to the public in the Licensed Premises at the prices appearing in 's price list for the time being in force and which reserves the right to alter at any time without notice.

33. shall use its best endeavours to ensure that any sales, discounts, and/or promotional offers occur at the same time as the bi-annual sales of the Company. shall inform the Company of the level of any sales discounts and shall agree the form of any sales and/or promotional offer advertising.

ALIENATION

34. shall not purport to assign, license or deal with or dispose of any of its rights under this Agreement.

FORCE MAJEURE

35. The parties shall not be in breach of this Agreement if any total or partial failure to perform their respective obligations arises from any act of God, fire, act of Government or State, war, civil commotion, labour dispute or any other reason whatsoever beyond their control. If either party is unable to perform its duties and obligations as a direct result of the matters referred to above for a period in excess of 60 days the other party shall have to terminate the Agreement on one month's written notice.

GOVERNING LAW

36. This Agreement shall be deemed to be subject to the laws of the Republic of Ireland and the parties submit to the jurisdiction of the Irish Courts.

AS WITNESS the hand of the duly
authorised representative of the parties hereto:

SIGNED BY ....
as the authorised
representative of   Limited

SIGNED BY ....
as the duly authorised
representative of   Limited

3.5   Conclusion

Licences cause difficulties for conveyancers for several reasons:

(a)   Many licences are informal and, if they are in writing, are not with the title documents. If verbal, as there is no documentary evidence, their existence is not apparent in the investigation of title.

(b)   If title to the land is registered a licence would be a burden affecting property without registration (Registration of Title Act, 1972, s 72) and would need to be disclosed in a s 72 declaration by a vendor/mortgagor.

(c)   If the licensee is in possession a purchaser may be put on constructive notice of the possibility of the existence of a licence. If the licensee is not in exclusive possession it is often difficult for a purchaser to discover his or her existence.

As Dr Albert Power in his article in the Law Society *Gazette* August/September 2004 states:

'Lawyers who advise clients seeking to enter legal relations that involve occupancy and on-going payment need to be clear in advance as to what the relationship is—then advise and draft accordingly. To proceed otherwise is the wrong way, and done at peril.'

3.6   Recommended Reading

Harpum, C, Bridge, S and Dixon M, *Megarry & Wade: The Law of Real Property* (8th edn, 2012, Sweet & Maxwell).

Hill, H A, *Hill and Redman's Law of Landlord and Tenant*, Vol 1 (issue 28, 1998, LexisNexis/Butterworths).

CHAPTER 4

OTHER RELATIONSHIPS INVOLVING LAND

4.1   Introduction

A number of other relationships between parties involving land and possession of it have come before the courts from time to time to determine whether the relationship of landlord and tenant has been created. The following are some of these relationships.

4.2   Servant/Employee

A servant or employee may be permitted to occupy the employer's property. Often it is a term of the contract that the property is occupied as part of the job, eg watchman.

Sometimes occupation depends on the agreement entered into between the employee and employer. It is not uncommon for a multinational employer to own properties in Ireland which senior employees on secondment and their families are permitted to occupy. Such occupation by an employee is often on a licence agreement which is terminable on ceasing employment with the company or the secondment ending. In some cases the employee signs a tenancy agreement with the employer and pays a sum of money to occupy the premises. Frequently, this is a sum which does not represent the current market rent but is intended to cover the overheads of the employer in maintaining the house and grounds. The tenancy would be for the period of secondment and dependent on the employee remaining with the company.

4.3   Lodger/Guest

The case of *Waucob v Reynolds* (1850) 1 ICLR 142 stated that possession by a lodger does not mean that the householder loses occupation. Such occupation is under the control of the owner of the home and the terms of occupation are determined by contract.

Professor Wylie, in *Landlord and Tenant Law* (3rd edn, 1997, Butterworths) at p 60, states, 'It is the retention of control by the owner over the premises occupied by the lodger and the lodger's lack of possession independent of the owner which distinguishes a lodger from a tenant.' This also applies to hotel guests. In *Carroll v Mayo County Council* [1967] IR 364, Henchy J stated 'in the case of a lodger or hotel guest, the occupier of the room may have the exclusive use of it as far as third parties are concerned, but the landlord or hotelier concurrently occupies and uses the premises for the purposes of his business and is therefore the rateable occupier'.

4.4   Hirer

No tenancy is conferred on a hirer: at most, it is a licence to use premises for a specific purpose. Possession remains with the owner.

In *Kelly v Woolworth & Co Ltd* [1922] 2 IR 5, rooms were hired for four hours for a whist drive and a dance. Ronan LJ stated 'it is absurd to think that by a hiring for four hours for a dance the parties intended that an estate should pass ... The defendants never parted with their estate or with the possession and occupation of the rooms.' This decision was followed in *Boylan v Dublin Corporation* [1949] IR 60, where rooms had been hired for a whist drive. In *MacGinley v National Aid Committee* [1952] Ir Jur Rep 43, a right to use rooms was subject to the keys being kept by the owner's agents and Maguire J held that the owners had not parted with possession.

In *Irish Shell & BP Ltd v Costello Ltd* [1981] ILRM 66 and *Irish Shell & BP Ltd v Costello Ltd (No 2)* [1984] IR 511, a petrol station and adjoining car park had been occupied continuously for over 30 years under successive 'hiring and licence agreements' granted by the owners, Irish Shell Ltd. Costello J held that the agreements made it clear that no tenancy had ever been created and the Supreme Court confirmed this. The wording of the documentation was of paramount importance in achieving this result, which ran counter to a number of other decisions where the underlying facts were very similar.

4.5   Conacre

4.5.1   GENERALLY

Conacre is a right to sow and harvest crops on another's land. The agreement is either done on an informal basis between the parties, or drawn up by the local auctioneer, usually on one page. Use of such an arrangement is very common and usually agreed on a seasonal basis and never for a full 12 months. This was to allow the land to be rested or fertilised. The owner of the land was regarded as retaining general possession and, at most, the taker of the land was regarded as having a special possession for that particular period. The sum of money agreed for the use of the lands is paid in two parts, one when the taker of the land is allowed access to it and the final payment made at the end of the agreement when the landowner takes back full possession.

Conacre is peculiar to Ireland and arose because of the economic and social conditions of agricultural workers in the 19th century. A landowner would give access to a portion of his land that was sufficient for the tenant to plant, cultivate and harvest a crop which supported and fed their families. Traditionally, the occupation lasted for 11 months, which gave the tenant the necessary time to plant, cultivate and remove the crop. The tenant had access to, and use of, the land but did not own the crop until, at the end of the period, he or she paid the landowner either in money or in kind or by working for the landowner. After payment was made to the landowner, the tenant was free to remove the crop and had no further involvement with the land. Importantly, as the landowner remained in legal ownership and possession of the land he or she continued to enjoy the parliamentary franchise, the right to vote.

Under s 5 of the Land Law (Ireland) Act, 1881, the protective rights available to a statutory tenant did not apply to a conacre tenant.

As a conacre letting is created by contract it depends on the terms of the contract. Such an arrangement has some common features with a licence and with *profits à prendre*—though the latter must be created by deed. In the course of judgment in *Maurice E Taylor (Merchants) Ltd v Commissioner of Valuation* [1981] NI 236, it was stated 'the owner now merely has a claim in debt for the rent and no longer has any lien or charge on the crop or a right to prevent the removal'. Conacre enables a farmer to extend his or her farming activities without investing or borrowing capital to do so. Nowadays such a letting can comprise several fields and the landowner rarely exercises any control over the land save perhaps to stipulate what crop may be grown or that the land is to be fertilised. He or she does, however, retain the right to recover the land at the termination of the letting.

A conacre letting is often used where a farmer retires or dies leaving a widow who wishes to keep the farm to pass on to her children when they are adult. Often the land would be let on conacre year after year, frequently to the same person. This practice would continue until the deceased farmer's children were of an age to run the farm themselves.

4.5.2   CHARACTERISTICS OF CONACRE

(a)   The user of the land has no interest in it and no legal estate arises or is created.

(b)   It is a mere right of user for a limited purpose.

(c)   It arises by contract either oral or written.

(d)   The landowner no longer has any lien on the crop but merely a claim in debt for the 'rent'.

(e)   Payment is not to be deemed to be rent nor to be recoverable as such—*Dease v O'Reilly* (1845) 8 Ir LR 52.

(f)   A conacre holder is not considered to have sufficient possession of the land to be in rateable occupation: *Tangney v Kerry County Council* (1946) 80 ILTR 127. The test for rateable occupation is who is in 'paramount' occupation. In *Maurice E Taylor (Merchants) Ltd v Commissioner of Valuation* [1981] NI 236, a company grew potatoes on a large tract of land taken in conacre. The company carried on the business of shipping seed potatoes and its buildings were situated 10–20 miles away from the land. The question arose whether the company occupied the land for rating purposes. Gibson LJ stated:

> 'I am satisfied that the decisions of the Irish courts in the last century to the effect that a conacre tenant is not in occupation of the land for rating or other purposes have been overtaken both by the changes in the nature of conacre lettings and also by law. The facts found by the Lands Tribunal established that the company has exclusive occupation of the various plots for the purpose of growing and harvesting the potatoes. It also has the right to exclude all other persons, including the owners of the land, from the lands taken during the period of the take. Whereas, in earlier days, the land owner retained paramount occupation of the land it is now clear that if there is any question of paramount occupation which would only arise in the case of some rather exceptional contract, it now resides in the tenant.'

Most conacre holdings today still lack the element of exclusive possession and control and hence the conacre holder cannot be said to have 'paramount' occupation.

4.6 Agistment Holder

4.6.1 MEANING

Agistment is the right to graze livestock on another's land. In *O'Flaherty v Kelly* [1909] 1 IR 223, Holmes LJ stated:

'[I]t is a letting of a right in the nature of a profit à prendre subject to which the occupation of the soil remains in the person who makes the letting ... The legal status of the agistor is that of a person who is entitled to the grazing of land which is in the possession of another.'

It is the hiring of the ground that is involved. In the same case, FitzGibbon LJ stated:

'[S]uch a hiring, in law, is an agistment contract, and nothing more. The possession and occupation of every estate and interest in the land remain wholly and entirely in (the land owner).'

As with a conacre agreement there are similarities with a licence and with a *profit à prendre*, eg pasturage. However, the latter must be created by deed whereas an agistment agreement lies in contract. The land is not let for a full 12-month period so as to allow it to 'rest' before its use again. As with conacre, the general possession of the land remains with the landowner and the party taking the land under such an arrangement could be described as having a special possession of the land for the purpose of the agreement together with the right of entry/exit to same.

4.6.2 CHARACTERISTICS OF AGISTMENT

(a) The user of the land has no interest in it and no legal estate arises or is created. The accepted view is that agistment is a right only to graze livestock and there is no right to exclusive possession. It does not involve sub-letting and the landowner remains the rateable occupier.

(b) As agistment is deemed a grazing contract, any money payable under it cannot be regarded as rent. It is common for a lump sum to be paid either at the beginning or end of the contract or, as is more usual in practice, half of the total sum is paid midway through the contract and the balance paid at the end of the contract.

(c) It is usual for the owner to remain responsible for maintaining and repairing the fences.

4.6.3 EXAMPLE OF AGISTMENT AGREEMENT

An example of an agistment agreement is as follows:

SIR

I propose to take the grazing of your land at [insert address] containing [state area of land] from the   day of   20[ ] to the   day of   20[ ] for which I agree to pay the sum of €[   ] to be paid in two equal instalments of €[   ] each on the   day of   20[ ] and   day of   20[ ].

I further agree not to allow any horses, donkeys, goats or bulls on said lands, and I will preserve and keep all the fences and gates thereon in good order and repair, and preserve the trees thereon from injury, and I undertake to remove all my stock from said lands upon the said   day of   20[ ].

And I hereby declare that nothing in this Agreement shall in any way prevent you from removing my stock off said lands, and treating same as trespassers, at the determination of this Agreement, and nothing herein contained shall in any manner whatsoever be taken or deemed to have created me a tenant of said lands, but merely affording a right of agistment, as aforesaid.

I hereby undertake to remove all weeds that shall grow in or upon said premises during the time aforesaid, and to keep all the fences thereof in proper and good repair; and if at any time weeds shall be allowed to remain, or any of the fences allowed to remain out of repair after receiving one week's notice thereof from you, you may enter upon said premises and rectify the same accordingly, and recover any expenses incurred thereby from me, which I undertake to pay, and you may at any time enter upon said lands to inspect the same. And I undertake not to remove any manure off the premises, or the leaving of any hay that I may bring thereon for the purpose of feeding cattle.

Dated this   day of   20[ ]

Signed:

To [the party taking the land]

I accept the above proposal.

Signed:

The reference to horses and donkeys is that the manner in which these animals crop grass results in more damage/wear and tear to the land than cattle or sheep. A bull is a dangerous animal. Consequently third parties have a greater responsibility when entering the land to prevent it escaping.

4.7   Franchise

Franchising is a common form of business agreement now widely used and it involves a businessman/businesswoman or company/firm allowing another to exploit its trademark or product. Such agreements cover a wide range of consumer goods. Franchises can range from petrol filling stations, concessions within large stores, service facilities such as carpet cleaning, fast-food outlets, etc. These agreements are basically trade agreements whereby the franchisor receives payment based on the annual turnover figures of the franchisee's business.

It should be noted that a franchise agreement simpliciter is a straightforward business agreement which does not involve the use or occupation of premises owned by one or other of the parties. If a franchisor owns the premises from which the franchisee is to trade the matter of what arrangement is entered into between the parties regarding the premises must be considered. Is a lease to be granted by the franchisor to the franchisee? If so, for what period of time? It is unlikely that a franchisee would want to take a lease of premises for a period less than the statutory minimum required for him or her to obtain renewal rights on its expiration. He or she would not want to spend the capital sums generally required in fitting out the premises to the universal specifications required by the franchisor and spend time and effort in building up goodwill and business to find then that he or she has to seek alternative premises when the short-term lease expires.

Likewise, a franchisee would be reluctant to take a licence of a premises as it would not give security and any lending institution would not favour such an arrangement and would not advance money on the security of a licence. If the franchisee owns the premises from which he or she wishes to operate the franchisor's business he or she is in a stronger position in that, if the franchise agreement ends, he or she can still continue to trade in another business or realise his or her capital investment by selling the premises or creating an income by letting it to another party. If the franchisee does not own a premises, in practice, he or she may prefer to borrow the capital either with or without the aid of the franchisor in order to acquire a legal interest in separate premises from which he or she will operate the franchise. In the event of the franchise agreement terminating the franchisee still has premises from which to trade or to sell in order to recoup some of his or her capital.

4.8 Rights of Residence

It was common in Ireland for rights of residence to be created either by will or family settlement—such rights are registered as burdens on a folio relating to title registered in the Land Registry. Today such rights are becoming less frequent by way of testamentary disposition as the surviving spouse is often left sufficient money to purchase another property.

Often a farmer's will would leave the land and dwellinghouse on it to children or other relatives who would run the farm with a right of residence reserved in the farmhouse, or part of it, as a means to provide for the widow during her lifetime. Section 111 of the Succession Act, 1965, which gives the surviving spouse a legal right to a proportion of the estate, has reduced this practice.

An example of a provision in such a will is 'I give devise and bequeath my house [and its contents] to [name] subject to the right of residence of [name] for life.'

Rights of residence also arise in relation to farm holdings where the landowner, during his or her lifetime, transfers the property comprising the land and the farmhouse to his or her son or daughter and reserves a room or rooms in the property for himself or herself and his or her spouse or the survivor of them to reside in for their lifetime.

An example of such a right registered in the Land Registry as a burden on a folio would be 'the right of [insert name] to reside in the dwelling house during his or her life'. This is a pure right of residence. An example of such an entry on the folio where other rights are included would be 'the rights and privileges specified in instrument no [insert no] in favour of [name] and [name] and the survivor of them during his or her life.' This ensures that if her husband predeceases her, the widow has the right to remain for her lifetime.

There is often coupled with this right of residence a right of maintenance and support which is expressed in a monetary sum, usually an annual amount to be paid by the son or daughter to the parent, which is intended to cover clothing, food, fuel, entertainment and incidental expenses. This is known as an annuity and is registered as a separate burden.

If a specified room or rooms are indicated, this becomes a special right of residence. Some grants of residence specify that such a right is to be a charge on the property.

In *National Bank v Keegan* [1931] IR 344, Kennedy CJ stated that 'the general right of residence charged on a holding is a right capable of being valued in moneys numbered at an annual sum and of being represented by an annuity or money charge'. This is a 'case in which the exclusive use during her life of a specified part of the holding comprising two rooms is given to the beneficiary. If this benefit were given to her by a deed or a will, I think that it is clear that she would hold an estate for life in the property, legal or equitable, according to the terms of the instrument.'

Efforts to explain the nature of a general right of residence can give rise to the following issues:

(a) Previously if a life estate were created then, in effect, the person with the right of residence had all the powers of a tenant for life under the Settled Land Acts, 1882–1890, including the power of sale. Clearly, this was probably never intended by the deceased landowner. The 2009 Act repeals the Settled Land Acts, 1882–1890, and Part 4 of the Act provides that in future legal title to land will always reside in the holder of a fee simple in possession. Estates such as a life estate will operate in equity only.

In relation to land registered in the Land Registry, as a result of Part 4 of the 2009 Act, where a life interest is created a trust comes into operation and the legal estate is held by the trustees. Hence if a life estate is created in relation to registered land, whether before or after 1 December 2009, the only application for registration that can be made post 1 December 2009 would be an application for registration of the trustees as owners.

(b) The concept of a lien is not favoured, notwithstanding that *Kelaghan v Daly* [1913] 2 IR 328 stated that a right of residence, unless capable of being construed as a life estate, is a right 'in the nature of a lien for money's worth' which binds successors in title taking with notice of it. In the case of rights of residence, particularly under wills, they can be difficult to quantify in monetary terms especially if there are no clear directions as to support or maintenance. The concept of a lien would appear inconsistent with the intention of many testators providing for such a right of residence.

(c) Annuity: In relation to a general right of residence in *National Bank v Keegan* [1931] IR 344 the court was of the view that a right of residence may be an annuity or money charge. An annuity charged on land is usually for a definite sum and becomes a rent charge. Previously, by virtue of the Conveyancing Act, 1881, s 5, a landowner could sell the land free of such charge where the necessary amount of money required to discharge it (including interest) is lodged in court. The Conveyancing Act, 1881, s 5 was repealed by the 2009 Act. The 2009 Act, s 11(2), states that a 'freehold estate' means a fee simple in possession and includes a right of residence which is not an exclusive right over the whole land. Section 11(2)(c)(ii) includes in the definition of 'freehold estate' an annuity or other payment of capital or income for the advancement, maintenance or other benefit of any person.

(d) Trust: The Registration of Title Act, 1964, s 81 specifically states that a general right of residence in or on, or an exclusive right in or on, part of the land does not operate to create any equitable interest in the land. Courts are reluctant to accept that such a trust would exist.

(e) Licence: The view is that such a licence is personal to the licensee but the burden of the licence binds successors in title of the licensor.

Where such a right of residence is registered as a burden on a folio a purchaser will seek either to have the owner of the burden execute a Deed of Release prior to the Deed of Transfer to the purchaser or, alternatively, join as a party in the Deed of Transfer by the registered owner (vendor) to release the right of residence in the deed. The party entitled to the right of residence must obtain separate legal advice in such circumstances. If the party (or parties) in whose favour the right is registered is/are no longer living, then the purchaser must seek evidence. This is done by production of a death certificate. The Land Registry will remove the burden on application by the registered owner or, in the case of a purchaser, a party entitled to be registered as owner on production of the death certificate and the Land Registry form of application seeking the discharge. A lending institution will not advance monies to a purchaser where such a burden is on the folio unless it is released as, if they have to foreclose, they would not get vacant possession.

4.9   Caretaker

4.9.1   MEANING

A caretaker arrangement is widely used where an owner wishes to put someone else into occupation of his or her property as a temporary arrangement, often pending the finalisation of another agreement. A common example would be where the purchaser wishes to obtain possession of the property but the vendor, for some reason, is not able to complete the legal formalities by the due date. On signing a caretaker's agreement and paying over the balance of the purchase money to be held in the joint names of the solicitors acting for the purchaser and the vendor, the purchaser is allowed into possession. Such an agreement states specifically that the person has been put into possession of the property as a caretaker for the owner and will deliver up possession on demand. See the example at **4.9.2**.

A caretaker's agreement confers no estate or interest in land and, at most, it will be deemed a bare licence to occupy the premises. During the occupation no structural alterations or works are allowed to be carried out. In the case of *Davies v Hilliard* (1967) 101 ILTR 50, while a proposed tenancy agreement was being negotiated the future tenant went into occupation of two flats under a caretaker's agreement. The Circuit Court held that the future tenant held the premises as tenant but the Supreme Court did not agree. The future tenant had paid his future landlord for his occupation and the Supreme Court stated:

> 'it was intended that the nature of his occupation should remain that of a caretaker until the parties should agree upon the terms of an express contract of tenancy. The fact that the parties agreed on the rent to be reserved by such contract and that a sum described as rent was paid and received in anticipation of the conclusion of such an express contract does not per se create a contract of tenancy.'

Since he or she is not a tenant, a caretaker is not entitled to notice to quit and the standard caretaker's agreement provides that he or she is to give up possession on demand. If the caretaker refuses to do so, Deasy's Act, 1860, s 86 allows an owner to seek a summary order for possession from the District Court.

One of the most well-known cases involving a caretaker's agreement which arose under the Landlord and Tenant Act, 1931, is *Gatien Motor Co Ltd v Continental Oil Co of Ireland Ltd* [1979] IR 406, whereby the landlord of a service station refused to renew a tenant's three-year lease unless it was given back possession for a week. This was to prevent the tenant acquiring a statutory right to a new tenancy which would have arisen if the tenant or his predecessor in title was continuously in business for a period of three years or more. In this case it was agreed between the parties that the tenant would remain in possession for a week as a caretaker under a 'caretaker's agreement' after which a new lease for a further three years would be granted. In the Supreme Court Griffin J stated that to ascertain whether there was the intention to create the relationship of landlord and tenant the transaction had to be examined as a whole. Griffin J decided that on the facts of the case there was no inference that a tenancy was intended to be granted for the period which included the week under the caretaker's agreement.

For an examination of the likely effect of this decision in light of the provisions of the Landlord and Tenant (Amendment) Act, 1980, see the Practice Note in the April 1986 Law Society's *Gazette*. In this Practice Note Mr Eoghan P Fitzsimons SC states:

> 'I could not advise ... with confidence that the Supreme Court would give approval now to a scheme of the type reviewed in the *Gatien Motor Company* case in view of the changes in the law made by the 1980 Act.'

To date, there has been no case before the courts on similar facts. It should be noted that the parties were not allowed to contract out of the provisions of the 1980 Act which were in force at the time of this practice note. There was no similar provision in the 1931 Act.

Section 85 of the Landlord and Tenant (Amendment) Act, 1980, provides that any provision in an agreement between a landlord and tenant contracting out of the Act would be void. The purpose of such a provision in a lease would be to prevent tenants from acquiring statutory rights of renewal. Section 4 of the Landlord and Tenant (Amendment) Act, 1994, allows a tenant of premises used exclusively for office purposes to contract out of his/its right to a new tenancy after obtaining independent legal advice.

Section 47 of the Civil Law (Miscellaneous Provisions) Act 2008 extends the right to contract out of the 1980 Act to any type of business premises. This in effect gives a general right to contract out of the right to a new tenancy to all business tenants. In practice this is done by the tenant executing a deed of renunciation after obtaining independent legal advice on the effect of executing such a renunciation. See **chapter 10**.

4.9.2 EXAMPLE OF A CARETAKER'S AGREEMENT

A sample of a type of caretaker's agreement is set out below:

I,   of   in the County of   do hereby acknowledge that I have been this day put into possession of **ALL THAT**

situate in the Parish of   in the Barony of   and County of   ('the Property') and that I am in possession of the property solely as such Caretaker of and for [name of owner] ('the Owner') and not under any contract or tenancy. I hereby further acknowledge that I have undertaken and agreed with the Owner to take care of the Property for him/her/them/it, and to preserve same from trespass and injury, and to deliver up the possession thereof to the Owner his/her/their heirs or assigns [or its successors], when required so to do.

Dated this   day of   in the year Two Thousand and

Signed ....

Witness ....

CHAPTER 5

TAKING INSTRUCTIONS/ESSENTIAL CONTENTS OF A LEASE

5.1   Taking Instructions

The primary duty and function of a solicitor acting for a client, whether landlord or tenant, in relation to a business or residential lease, is to ensure that the agreement made between the parties is fully reflected in writing.

In the case of a business lease it is usual for the parties together with their respective letting agent or surveyor to set out Heads of Terms which incorporate the principle matters to be included in the lease. These would include matters such as the parties, description of the premises, terms to be granted, rent and rent reviews, repairs and insurance. The objective is to save time and money. If the main terms are agreed then less time is spent by solicitors on negotiating these terms and the final form of lease is agreed more quickly, resulting in costs savings for both parties.

Most firms of solicitors will have a standard Instruction Form, which in the case of business lettings will be comprehensive and will require more detailed information both on the Heads of Terms and other issues which need to be agreed between the parties. The standard type of form used by the firm for taking instructions may be adapted, improved and amended to the particular needs of the case and act as a comprehensive checklist. Such an instruction form can then be customised, depending on whether the solicitor is acting for a vendor, a purchaser, a landlord, a tenant or a lending institution.

There are several advantages in using such a form:

(a)   It lists the most essential questions and will enable a solicitor to take specific instructions to ensure the client has considered all the key issues, eg:

    (i)   the precise extent of the premises to be demised and whether a map/plan is required;

    (ii)   the rights to be granted to the tenant;

    (iii)   the exceptions and reservations in the demise;

    (iv)   the provisions regarding repair;

    (v)   planning, VAT, consents of third parties (bank/head landlord), alterations, authorised use, interest on late payments, service charge.

(b)   It saves time and the client can respond to specific questions with precise answers.

(c)   It allows more time to discuss and advise on the merits or otherwise of certain clauses with the client.

(d) It enables a solicitor to discuss with and advise a client who may be inexperienced in property matters, eg on the importance of a tenant having an architect survey the property, particularly if taking on a full repairing and insuring covenant in the lease.

Adopting the practice of preparing an agenda of steps to be taken and documents to be obtained prior to, and after execution of, the lease means it is unlikely any particular instruction or item will be overlooked at the relevant time.

It is important that the instruction sheet and agenda list are comprehensive but they can also be adapted according to the requirements of a particular case. The instruction sheet which follows is merely an example.

5.2   Instruction Sheet

As stated above, the following is a checklist which may be adapted for both short-term and long-term commercial leases. An abbreviated version of this form could also be used in the case of a residential lease.

(1) Client: whether landlord or tenant with address, correspondence address, if different, and contact details. If the party to the lease is a company, its registered office or obtain copy certificate of incorporation and constitution.

(2) If acting for a landlord obtain references, both bank and trade and audited accounts for the last three years of the proposed tenant.

(3) Existing client/introduced by . . . This is for the purpose of acknowledging the recommendation and building on the existing goodwill of that client.

(4) Name and address of solicitor acting for landlord/tenant.

(5) Estate agent.

(6) Address and specific description of property to be demised, especially if it forms a portion of the premises. Is there to be a map attached to the lease showing the demised area? If the premises are a unit in a shopping centre or an industrial estate or something similar is another map showing the entire of the development with the access roads etc also necessary?

(7) Is this an underlease? If so, check that its terms comply with those of the head lease.

(8) Is the consent of the head lessor or a third party required? Is there a mortgage? Check title, e.g. if the consent of a mortgagee is needed or if it is a requirement in the superior lease that the consent of the superior lessor be obtained.

(9) Is any right of way or use of common areas involved?

(10) Commencement date and term.

(11) Rent and gale days. Is it to be subject to review? Is the Law Society form of rent review clause to be used? Is interest to be charged if late payment?

(12) Details of landlord's bank, its address, bank code and account number for rent.

(13) Is there to be an arbitrator or an expert in the absence of agreement on a revised rent?

(14) Insurance provisions. Tenant reimburses premium. If multi-let premises what percentage of premium is paid by tenant? Obtain a waiver of subrogation rights from the insurer.

(15) Any special terms?

(16) Are any landlord's fixtures and fittings included in the letting? If so, inventory to be obtained.

(17) Is it to be a full repairing and insuring (FRI) lease? If not, what are the repairing obligations of the landlord?

If acting for a tenant of older premises, stress the importance of having a survey carried out on the condition of the building supported by photographic evidence. Warn the client that an FRI lease will mean that the tenant is liable if, for example, dry rot appears in the building, and that the survey should include the structure. Is a copy of the survey to form part of the agreement?

(18) If acting for a tenant of a newly constructed premises under an FRI lease ensure that the liability for structural defects excludes those arising as a result of defective design.

(19) In the case of a newly constructed property, if acting for the tenant, seek an assignment of collateral warranties given by the design team and the various parties involved in the construction, eg mechanical and electrical engineers, lift manufacturers, builders to the developer/landlord. These are the warranties and indemnities for defects which would have been given to the landlord. If the proposed lease is FRI, the tenant should have the benefit of these warranties.

(20) Is there a guarantor? If so, obtain:

   (a) full name and address and, if a company, address of registered office, copy certificate of incorporation and constitution to check it can give a guarantee and consider ss 238 and 239 of the Companies Act 2014;

   (b) trade and bank references.

(21) Are the premises separately rated or is there a notional rateable value to be agreed, pending a separate valuation of the premises by the rating authority?

(22) If the premises are multi-tenanted, what is the proportion of service charge that the tenant will contribute towards the maintenance and upkeep of the common areas maintained by the landlord?

(23) What are the limitations and requirements on assignment and sub-letting?

(24) Does the tenant have an option to purchase?

(25) Is there a break clause? If so, when and how is it to be exercised?

(26) What common services, if any, are to be shared?

(27) In a multi-let building has the lessor any rules and regulations to be observed and any security requirements?

(28) What exceptions and reservations are to be made by the landlord from the demise?

(29) What easements, privileges and rights are to be granted to the tenant?

(30) What is the proposed user? If acting for the tenant, is the user wide enough for the proposed business activities? Check the planning and user history of the building and that all necessary planning permissions, architect's opinions and fire certificates, if applicable, are available.

(31) Does the tenant need to carry out any fitting-out works or alterations? If so, details and plans to be furnished for landlord's written consent. Is planning permission required for such works? Will there be a rent-free period to fit out?

(32) Does VAT arise? If acting for a tenant, check if the tenant is registered for VAT. If acting for the landlord, raise with the landlord's accountant the standard Law Society VAT enquiries so that the VAT history of the premises and any queries arising therefrom can be dealt with in anticipation of the tenant's solicitor raising the same enquiries.

(33) If acting for a tenant, calculate stamp duty and registration fees due.

(34) Is an agreement for lease required if the landlord's premises are in the course of construction?

(35) If the lease is of business premises is the tenant required to sign a Form of Renunciation under the Landlord and Tenant (Amendment) Act, 1994, as amended by s 47 of the Civil Law (Miscellaneous Provisions) Act 2008, prior to commencement of the lease? If so, ensure that the steps advised by the Conveyancing Committee of the Law Society are followed (see **10.2.5.3**).

5.3   Pre-lease Enquiries

In the past it was standard practice for the tenant's solicitor to raise pre-lease enquiries including any issues regarding prima facie evidence of the lessor's title when acting for a tenant taking a lease of commercial premises for a period in excess of three years. A Practice Note issued January/February 1980 by the Conveyancing Committee advised that a solicitor acting for a lessee should take the ordinary conveyancing precautions before allowing his client to enter into the lease. That Practice Note also advised where a lease was for a period in excess of three years that VAT enquiries and Requisitions on Title should be raised.

Since *ICC Bank plc v Verling* [1995] 1 ILRM 123, pre-lease enquiries are raised for all leases of commercial premises irrespective of the term. In this case, the plaintiff recovered possession of the premises on the basis that the existence of the mortgage would have been revealed by a Registry of Deeds search. The lease was for a period of two years and nine months.

In the light of this decision, the Conveyancing Committee issued a Practice Note in May 2000 advising practitioners acting for tenants to make the same enquiries in relation to short-term leases of commercial property as for long-term leases. The committee advised that the Pre-Lease Enquiries or Checklist published in February 2001 and recommended by the Law Society be used. Many firms have adapted and updated this Checklist for use in different types of leasing transactions.

5.4   Covenants and Conditions in a Lease

The terms in a lease setting out the duties and obligations of the parties were classified as either covenants or conditions. Where there was a breach by the tenant of a term of the agreement it was relevant as to whether it was a breach of a condition or a covenant. Section 3 of the 2009 Act includes a condition in its definition of 'covenant'. Today, obligations in leases are generally stated to be covenants. Certain covenants are implied by statute, eg a covenant by the landlord that he/she/it has title to grant the lease and a covenant granting quiet enjoyment to the tenant.

By its nature, a condition has a more fundamental significance to the contractual relationship than a covenant and a lease may be forfeited for breach of a condition without any forfeiture proviso (commonly called a 're-entry clause'): see *Bashir v Commissioner of Lands* [1959] 3 WLR 996. If there is a breach of a covenant there must be a proviso in the lease that the landlord is entitled to re-enter upon breach of the specified covenant or covenants but the omission of the word 're-enter' may not be fatal provided there is a clear expression of the right to repossess for breach of covenant. This is examined further in **chapter 9**.

The Irish Times edition of 10 October 2005 reported on the case of *Manuel Jiminez v Daniel Morrissey & others*, which considered, inter alia, the construction of covenants to repair and whether there was a breach of the plaintiff's right to quiet and peaceful enjoyment. The judgment delivered 18 July 2005 held that for there to be a breach of covenant in regard to peaceful and quiet enjoyment the interference with the enjoyment of the lessee of the demise must be of a very substantial nature. Here the court held the first-named defendant was liable to the plaintiff in respect of the disrepair of the flat roof over the kitchen area of the demise (a restaurant). The roof had leaked.

The draft Landlord and Tenant Law Reform Bill 2011 ('the draft 2011 Bill') (see **1.4.4**) proposes to establish a new statutory scheme of obligations in relation to tenancies created after the Bill is passed and in force. An example would be a tenant's right to quiet enjoyment. Such statutory obligations will operate as if they were express covenants. It also provides for overriding obligations which the parties cannot contract out of and default obligations which would apply unless excluded or modified.

5.5   Essential Contents of a Lease

5.5.1   DATE OF COMMENCEMENT OF THE TERM

If there is no date specified for the commencement of the term a court can deduce evidence from any other date specified in the document, such as the date stated on the deed or the dates when payment of rent is to be made.

5.5.2   PARCELS

Parcels is the word used to describe the premises and it should be clear and exact. Where a map is attached or endorsed, it may be looked at in cases of doubt to determine what was demised (*Lyle v Richards* [1866] LR 1 HL 222) but the words will prevail unless they are ambiguous and the plan makes clear what the words fail to make clear. In *Horne v Struben* [1902] AC 454, where the words contained an error as to the measurements of the land demised but the map clearly described the boundaries, it was held that the land was as shown within the boundary and that the measurements should be ignored.

It is important the extent of the demise is identified accurately. The amount of detail in the description varies according to the nature of the premises to be demised. Obviously a lease of an entire building differs from a lease of part of a complex, such as offices on a particular floor of a building or a unit in a shopping centre. In these latter cases it is essential to describe exactly what is included in the letting. It is normal in such situations to have a map attached to the lease detailing the measurements and outlining the area to be demised. It is important to ensure there is no inconsistency between the parcels clause and any map attached and, in the event of conflict, which is to prevail.

Note that the air space goes with the lease of an entire premises unless it is expressly reserved by the landlord. This may occur where the landlord wants the right to put a mobile phone mast on top of the building or to add another floor to the building after granting the lease.

The definition of 'land' at s 3 of the 2009 Act has been given an extended meaning. It makes it clear that the land includes both the air space above and the substratum below the surface and layers of these, however the division is made (whether horizontally, vertically or in any other way). As the Explanatory Memorandum to the 2009 Act points out it 'has become increasingly common in modern times for transactions to be entered into with respect to such airspace before any buildings are erected to fill the airspace. The definition confirms that such transactions are valid (as was recognised by the common law in cases decided over a century ago)', ie that parts of the substratum and airspace can be owned and conveyed separately from the surface. Professor Wylie in his paper at the CPD seminar on the 2009 Act held on 25 September 2009 referred to the English case of *Star Energy UK Onshore Limited* v *Bocardo SA* [2009] EWCA Civ 579, which involved the invasion of the substratum by pipes for oil exploration and extraction. This case indicated that the only limitation is probably a practical one, ie the substratum or airspace claimed must be physically and commercially exploitable. Note that s 127 of the 2009 Act substitutes the new definition of 'land' in the 2009 Act for the definition in s 3 of the Registration of Title Act, 1964.

Under s 6(1) of the Conveyancing Act, 1881, a conveyance of land (which by definition included a lease) made after 31 December 1881 was deemed to include and operate to lease with the land all buildings, erections, fixtures, commons, hedges, ditches, fences, ways, waters, watercourses, liberties, privileges, easements, rights and advantages whatsoever appertaining or reputed to appertain to the land. Section 71 of the 2009 Act replaces and substantially re-enacts s 6 and specifies what features and rights are now included in a conveyance of land. Section 71 does not create any new rights or convert any quasi-right into a full one or extend the scope of an existing right or convert it into a greater one. This reflects the views of the Supreme Court in the case of *William Bennett Construction Ltd* v *Greene* [2004] 2 ILRM 96.

5.5.3 HABENDUM

The habendum states clearly the length of the term being granted and the date from which it is to commence. It should be expressed clearly and with certainty. Where there is apparent uncertainty, effect will be given to the demise if possible, eg where the tenant was not to be ejected as long as the rent was paid, it was held that the term created was equal to the landlord's: *Re King's Leasehold Estates* (1873) LR 16 EQ 521, but a lease for the duration of a war was held to be bad for uncertainty: *Lace* v *Chantler* [1944] KB 368.

5.5.4 REDDENDUM

The reddendum must be as clear as possible and must set out the rent reserved. If the rent stated is to include, for example, rates this must be specified. It is good practice nowadays to reserve payments such as service charges and contributions towards the insurance premium as additional rent and to include an express covenant to pay them. This enables a landlord to avail of the remedies for enforcement of payment of rent, eg enforcement actions under Deasy's Act, 1860. The draft 2011 Bill (see **1.4.4**) proposes to abolish the ancient remedy of distress under Deasy's Act and the action of ejectment but it does not affect other remedies for recovery of possession.

5.6 Practical Procedure when Drafting a New Lease

5.6.1 INTRODUCTION

The solicitor acting for the tenant should read the draft agreement critically and explain the implications of the main clauses as these would not be fully apparent to the average lay person. It is important to take the time to discuss the draft lease with the client, particularly if the client is inexperienced, and to advise, for example, on obtaining a survey of the property and what other costs may be involved over and above legal, stamping and registration charges, such as those where fitting-out works are required. These costs may vary from redecorating the premises to fitting out a shell unit in a shopping centre. The lessor's consent may be required for such works depending on the fitting-out works, as well as compliance with building regulations and possibly planning permission.

The importance of obtaining an architect's opinion on compliance with building regulations and, if necessary, planning permission must be stressed.

5.6.2 WHAT HAPPENS IN PRACTICE

5.6.2.1 Drafting the lease

The lease is drafted by the landlord's solicitor on the instructions of his or her client. All leases of registered land should be in the format set out in Form 31 of the Land Registration Rules 2012 (SI 483/2012) as follows:

Form 31

Lease of registered land (Rules 52 and 68)

Land Registry

County   Folio

Lease dated the   day of   20[ ]   .

A.B., the registered owner, in consideration of

(the receipt of which is hereby acknowledged *(if appropriate)*, hereby demises all the property described in   folio of the register County   (*or,* the part of the property described in folio   of the register County   specified in Schedule 1 hereto) to C.D. *(if more than one lessee, state whether taking as joint tenants or tenants in common and if taking as tenants in common, state the shares each lessee is taking)*

to hold for a term of   years from   at the   rent of payable on

(subject to the terms, clauses, appurtenances, ancillary rights, exceptions, reservations, covenants, conditions, provisos, and charges, set out in schedules 2, 3, 4 etc hereto).

The said A.B. hereby assents to the registration of the lease as a burden on the said property.

The address of C.D. in the State for service of notices and his/her description are: *(give address and description)*

Schedule (1)

(where necessary)

(to contain particulars of the part leased and a reference to the map thereof (Rule 56))

Signed (*or* Signed, sealed) and delivered

by A.B. in the presence of:

Signed (*or* Signed, sealed) and delivered

by C.D. in the presence of:

Note (1)—The standard terms, clauses, appurtenances, ancillary rights, exceptions, reservations, covenants, conditions, provisos, and charges may be included in separate schedules.

Note (2)—The relevant stamp certificate issued by the Revenue Commissioners should be attached to the deed or if an exemption from stamp duty is being claimed, evidence of such exemption should be lodged pursuant to Section 104 of the Registration of Title Act 1964, as substituted by Section 64 of the Registration of Deeds and Title Act 2006.

Note (3)—If there is more than one lessor/lessee, the form should be amended accordingly.

If it is a lease of part only of a building, of which the landlord has already let other parts, the same form of lease should be used. This would incorporate provisions covering the common areas and the service charge.

The landlord's surveyor will prepare the lease map where necessary and the Land Registry mapping requirements must be complied with.

The draft is sent to the tenant's solicitor for perusal, who takes instructions from the client. There may be several exchanges of correspondence and meetings before the final form is agreed and marked as approved by the tenant's solicitor.

5.6.2.2 Conveyancing aspects

The solicitor acting for a tenant must be satisfied on the following points:

(a) The landlord's title to grant the lease—the solicitor must insist on seeing prima facie evidence of the landlord's title before the lease is approved. Since the 2009 Act it is advisable to seek 15 years back title by way of certified copies, even if it is a short-term lease. If the lessor has owned the property less than 15 years then it is necessary to see his predecessor's title so as to make a total of 15 years back from the date of the proposed lease.

(b) Planning permission for the proposed user of the premises. A 20-year lease will usually contain a clause providing that the landlord does not warrant the existence of any planning permission for the user of the premises and it therefore rests with the tenant's solicitor to ensure that such matters are in order. Such a warranty is usually inserted by a landlord's solicitor to cover a situation where a former tenant may have carried out works or alterations to the premises which would have required compliance with either planning permission and/or building regulations or there was a material change of use. If all of this was done without the landlord's knowledge or consent the landlord requires protection from possible breaches of the planning legislation or fire safety requirements. A planning search should be done.

(c) Satisfactory searches against the landlord. There could be a mortgage registered which would require either the mortgagee to join as a party to the lease or release its charge or, if it were a floating debenture in the case of a company, a letter of non-crystallisation should be given by the debenture holder.

(d) The recommended standard form of pre-lease enquiries has been raised.

(e) The recommended standard form of Requisitions on VAT has been raised. This should be raised at the same time as the pre-lease enquiries. See **chapter 13**.

5.6.2.3 Executing the lease

When the final form of lease is agreed, the landlord's solicitor has it engrossed in duplicate and sends it to the tenant's solicitor with the approved draft for comparison. The tenant then executes the lease and counterpart and his or her solicitor returns them with a cheque usually for the first quarter's rent, service charge (if applicable), proportion of insurance premium (if applicable), stamp duty, registration fees, and security deposit (if payable). If future payments of rent are to be made by standing order, the completion of such a standing order is dealt with directly between the landlord and the tenant. If there is a guarantee, the guarantor also executes the guarantee.

Where there is a guarantor refer to **5.2** for the documentation to be obtained. If the guarantor is a company it is important to check the memorandum to ensure that the company has the power to give a guarantee. If the guarantor is incorporated outside the jurisdiction an opinion letter from the lawyers acting for the guarantor may be required to confirm its ability to give a guarantee.

The landlord executes the lease. The landlord's solicitor then has the lease and counterpart stamped and depending on the length of term, registered in the Registry of Deeds or Land Registry.

5.6.2.4   VAT and leases

The rules and regulations regarding VAT were radically changed with effect from 1 July 2008 and the Conveyancing Committee of the Law Society has issued several Practice Notes by way of guidance when dealing with this complex issue. See **chapter 13** and also the Revenue website for information: www.revenue.ie. The subject of VAT and leases is complex and should be approached with great care by the parties concerned. The legislation is very technical and, whether acting for a landlord or tenant, the solicitor should make careful enquiries about the VAT position at an early stage. The current VAT Requisitions recommended by the Law Society should be raised as part of the normal pre-contract enquiries a tenant's solicitor would make when negotiating a lease or purchasing a leasehold interest. These are available on the member's area of the Society's website

For further information see **chapter 13**.

5.6.2.5   Stamp duty

The Finance Act 2012 introduced a range of changes that came into force for instruments executed on or after 7 July 2012. One of these changes is that it is no longer necessary to include certificates in the deed as stamp duty is based on self-assessment with the liability for incorrect stamping lying with the lessee and/or his solicitor. Prior to 31 December 2009, duties were denoted by means of stamps affixed to or impressed on the documents. Following the introduction of the eStamping system, all instruments must be stamped by means of attaching the stamped certificate, obtained under the eStamping system, to the instrument.

A stamp duty return requires valid tax reference numbers for all parties to the instrument. Revenue recommends that the solicitor obtain valid tax reference numbers from all parties before the deed is executed. To ensure that the tax reference numbers are valid, the solicitor is recommended to request sight of official correspondence from Revenue or the Department of Social and Family Affairs. Such correspondence will always quote a valid tax reference or PPS number and show the name of the person registered against the number.

Stamp duty is a tax on documents. There are serious restrictions on the use that can be made of unstamped or incorrectly stamped documents. For example:

(a)   Such documents cannot be used as evidence in court proceedings other than criminal proceedings or proceedings brought by the Revenue to recover stamp duty.

(b)   Ownership of the property cannot be registered in the Land Registry or in the Registry of Deeds unless the document transferring title is correctly stamped.

The lessee is the party liable and accountable for stamp duty payable on the lease and counterpart. If there is a premium to be paid to the landlord on the creation of the lease, stamp duty is payable both on the premium and on the annual rent reserved by the lease. The rate of stamp duty applicable to a premium is calculated by reference to the consideration passing and not to the term of the lease. There is also a fixed stamp duty of €12.50 where there is a rent review clause. This is in addition to the stamp duty on the lease.

Stamp duty is not chargeable on any lease of land made, or agreed to be made, to bodies of persons or trustees of a trust established solely for charitable purposes and which will be used for charitable purposes in the State or Northern Ireland. Adjudication has been abolished for instruments executed on or after 7 July 2012 and a self-assessed stamp duty return must be filed under the e-stamping system in respect of which the relief is sought.

The rate of stamp duty to be paid is based on the average annual rent and any premium depending on the period of the lease and the type of property. Currently these are as shown in Tables 1 and 2.

The date of the lease is important for stamp duty purposes and there are penalties for late stamping. By law it must be stamped no later than 30 days after the date of first execution of the deed but Revenue practice is to accept returns filed up to 44 days after first execution.

In most cases 'first execution' is when it has been executed by all of the parties necessary to make it effective in law and that should be the date inserted in the instrument. In the case of an instrument held in escrow, the time for stamping only arises when the outstanding condition has been performed and the instrument released from escrow. The Revenue will always require evidence of the existence of escrow, which should include details as to the date the deed went into escrow, the reason it went into escrow and the date it came out of escrow.

In relation to filing of self-assessed returns under the e-stamping system see Stamp Duty (E-Stamping of Instruments and Self-Assessment) Regulations 2012 (S.I. 234 of 2012).

In the case of stamping a counterpart lease, a separate return is not required. Use the return for the original instrument to indicate the number of counterparts required. This

TABLE 1 Stamp Duty Rates on Average Annual Rent

Residential and Non-residential Property	Rate
Lease for a term not exceeding 35 years or for any indefinite term	1% of the average annual rent (if non-residential property) No stamp duty payable if residential property and the rent is €40,000 or less per year
Lease for a term exceeding 35 years but not exceeding 100 years	6% of the average annual rent
Lease for a term exceeding 100 years	12% of the average annual rent

TABLE 2 Stamp Duty Rates on Premium

Type of property	Consideration	Rate
Residential	First €1 million	1%
Residential	Excess over €1 million	2%
Non-residential		6%

results in separate stamp certificates being issued for each counterpart document. There is a fixed stamp duty rate of €12.50 per counterpart. As this fixed stamp duty is dependent on the original instrument being duly stamped the counterpart is impressed with a stamp denoting the original has been duly stamped.

For instruments executed on or after 7 July 2012 a new late filing surcharge applies, equal to 5 per cent of the unpaid duty where the delay in filing is less than two months, subject to a maximum surcharge of €12,695. The surcharge is 10 per cent if the delay is more than two months and is capped at €63,485. In the event of non-payment of the duty and penalties the Revenue may enforce payment through the courts or the Sheriff.

Where a person knowingly files an incorrect electronic or paper return there is a penalty of €3,000. There is a similar penalty for failure to file a return within 30 days of first execution (44 days in practice).

5.6.2.6 Registering the lease

The lease is then registered, usually by the landlord's solicitor. Very briefly, the rules regarding registration are as follows:

(a) *Unregistered land.* If the premises are unregistered land, the lease should be registered in the Registry of Deeds if it is for over 21 years where actual possession goes with the lease.

The application form is available at www.prai.ie. It is printed, signed by the lodging solicitor and lodged with the deed. Where the form is completed by a solicitor it need only be signed but if it is completed by a non-solicitor it must be sworn. A serial number is applied to the deed which will determine priority.

(b) *Where registration is compulsory.* If the lease is for more than 21 years it must be registered in the Land Registry even if it is carved out of an unregistered title.

(c) *Where the landlord's title is registered.* If the title out of which the lease has been carved is registered in the Land Registry and if the lease is for more than 21 years, it should be registered as a burden on the superior interest and a new leasehold folio will be opened by the Land Registry.

(d) *Non-registerable leases.* A tenancy for any term not exceeding 21 years, where there is an occupation under such tenancy, is a burden which affects registered land without being registered: Registration of Title Act, 1964, s 72. Therefore, it need not be registered in the Land Registry.

5.6.2.7 Commercial Rates

More often than not a tenant taking a lease of commercial property will undertake to discharge all rates due to the local authority.

Section 32 of the Local Government Reform Act 2014, which came into effect on 1 July 2014 (SI 146/14) and which applied to all sales/leases closing after that date, introduced some important changes to the treatment of rates liabilities. The section applies where a relevant property, or an interest in relevant property, is transferred from one person to another person in circumstances that render that other person liable for rates on the property so transferred.

Section 32 imposes a statutory obligation on a vendor to notify the rating authority that a sale has taken place and to discharge all arrears for which the vendor is liable, ie six years of arrears. Standard conveyancing practice is that the rating authority would be notified and all arrears of rates paid on completion in any event. Where such rates are due but not discharged they will be a charge on the property for a period of 12 years.

Section 32 also obliges a landlord to notify the rating authority that a tenant has transferred its interest within two weeks of the assignment. Also it provides that a landlord will be liable for a charge equivalent to no more than two years of the outstanding rates due by a previous tenant where

(a) the rating authority has not been notified by the landlord of an assignment, and

(b) the tenant did not discharge the arrears on the assignment.

Any such charge will affect the property for a period of 12 years. Hence there is the potential for arrears of rates owed by a tenant to become a charge on the landlord's interest consequent on an assignment where any rates arrears have not been discharged.

It is important that solicitors advise landlords of the risk of consenting to an assignment unless the tenant provides evidence that all rates have been paid up to date. The Law Society Conveyancing Committee issued a Practice Note in the August/September 2014 Gazette setting out the provisions of s 32 and its impact on transactions.

In a further updated Practice Note in the March 2016 *Gazette* the Committee clarified that the charge on a landlord's interest can be avoided so long as notice has been given within the two-week period following the assignment or subletting. This is a change to the previous position at law that, where there were arrears, landlords were automatically liable for up to two years' arrears as subsequent occupiers. There is no prescribed form of notice and a letter should suffice. The Committee pointed out that as the legislation does not clarify what is meant by 'transferred' a broad interpretation is preferred so as to include all circumstances, not just surrenders, in which the landlord obtains possession of the property, including lease expiry, the exercise of a break option or forfeiture.

5.7   Agreement for Lease

The parties may sometimes enter into an agreement for lease prior to the execution of the formal lease. This will be done where, for example, either the landlord or the tenant has to carry out extensive renovations or fitting-out works to the premises prior to the date of occupation by the tenant. It can also cover the situation where the landlord is in the course of constructing the premises and needs to tie in future tenants: see **Appendix 5**.

5.7.1   CONTENTS OF THE AGREEMENT

While it is only essential to specify the main terms of the lease in the agreement for lease, eg the description of the premises, the terms, the commencement date and probably certain covenants, it is standard practice that the entire draft lease duly approved by both parties is annexed to the agreement. In this way the agreement would be a very short and simple document where, perhaps, the only condition relates to the carrying out of building or fitting-out works by one or other of the parties. If the lease is due to commence on completion of construction of the building by the landlord, the agreement for lease will specify that 'completion' (as defined therein) is certified by the landlord's architect or engineer.

5.7.2   THE LIMITATIONS OF AN AGREEMENT FOR LEASE

(a) It operates only in equity.

(b) The legal rights of the parties will thus depend on an order for specific performance being available from the court for the execution and delivery of the lease.

(c) The agreement operates inter parties only, subject to the contractual doctrine of privity, whereas a lease gives rights and duties to the successors in title of both landlord and tenant.

(d) Statutory protections apply only to leases.

5.8 Residential Tenancy Agreements

The general outline of what has been said earlier in this chapter in relation to taking instructions and the essential contents also apply to a letting of a dwelling for residential purposes. The Instruction Sheet would be simpler on the following points:

(a) It is unusual for a tenant to contribute to the landlord's insurance of the property. In any case, s 12 of the Residential Tenancies Act 2004 requires the landlord to keep the structure insured against damage, loss and destruction and also have landlord's liability cover for at least €250,000. This obligation does not apply if during the tenancy insurance is either not obtainable or is only obtainable at an unreasonable cost.

(b) Generally, the tenant does not contribute to a service charge for any common areas whether it be part of a residential house or a purpose-built apartment. In the case of the latter the current practice is that the landlord charges a level of rent which is inclusive of any service charge.

(c) Section 12 of the Residential Tenancies Act 2004 requires a landlord to carry out all repairs to the structure of the building and to ensure the structure is kept in a proper state of structural repair. See **6.6.1** and **chapter 8**.

     The landlord must also carry out repairs to the interior of the dwelling and replace fittings, so the interior and those fittings are maintained in at least the condition in which they were at the commencement of the tenancy and in compliance with any prescribed standards.

(d) The liability to pay waste charges is usually stated in the agreement to be that of the tenant. There is a local property tax on residential property (LPT) and it is the owner's liability to discharge this, not the tenant's.

(e) There is no need for a waiver of subrogation rights or an architect's survey.

(f) VAT does not arise.

(g) It is normal practice for a landlord to seek a deposit. Section 12 of the Residential Tenancies Act 2004 requires the landlord to return or repay promptly any deposit paid by the tenant subject to the provisions therein. See also the note on the Residential Tenancies Board website: www.rtb.ie.

The Residential Tenancies Act 2004 does not apply to nine categories of dwelling, the most relevant in the normal situation being a dwelling let for holiday purposes only; a dwelling within which the landlord also resides and a dwelling within which the spouse, parent or child of the landlord resides and no lease or tenancy agreement in writing has been entered into by any person resident in the dwelling.

It is important that a landlord clearly understands his statutory obligations under the 2004 Act (as amended) in addition to obligations arising under any other enactment or Regulation, eg the Housing (Miscellaneous Provisions) Act, 1992. See **6.6.1** for details. The Landlord should also be aware of Part 5 of the 2004 Act (as amended), which contains detailed provisions governing the termination of tenancies, including the notice periods and important formalities for notice of termination. Landlords are obliged to register tenancies with the Residential Tenancies Board.

When acting for a residential tenant it is important to point out the statutory obligations of a tenant as set out in s 16 of the 2004 Act, particularly the obligation that there be no anti-social behaviour by the tenant or other occupiers or visitors. The definition of anti-social behaviour is set out at s 17 of the 2004 Act.

The tenant should also be advised of the security of tenure provisions and the existence of a user-friendly dispute resolution service. See **chapters 6** and **7**.

The Dublin Solicitors' Bar Association have updated their form of Residential Tenancy Agreement, which incorporates all the statutory requirements, and its use is recommended for all residential tenancies coming within the provisions of the 2004 Act (as amended).

CHAPTER 6

RESIDENTIAL TENANCIES ACTS 2004 TO 2016

6.1 Introduction

The Residential Tenancies Act 2004 ('the Act'), introduced significant changes in the law relating to the private rented residential sector. This chapter will examine Parts 1–5 of the Act in detail. **Chapter 7** will examine Parts 6–8 of the Act. Part 9, which contains miscellaneous provisions, will be dealt with where appropriate.

The Act has now been fully operational for well over a decade. In this time, certain problems with it have been identified. Amending legislation has been introduced, which has addressed and resolved issues identified in regard to the interpretation and operation of certain parts of the Act, some of which are discussed in this chapter.

Recent legislation has also introduced changes to the operation of the Act so that it now applies to certain non-private lettings, while also addressing market realities in the private rented sector, as will be seen below. Most of the amendments to the Act are contained in the Residential Tenancies (Amendment) Act 2015 ('the 2015 Act') and Part 3 (ss 30–50) of the Planning and Development (Housing) and Residential Tenancies Act 2016 ('the 2016 Act'). However, other legislation has affected the operation of the Act and is noted where appropriate. The legislation has not been consolidated and can be difficult to read through. This chapter deals with amendments as they arise rather than dealing with the amending legislation in self-contained sections.

6.2 Commencement

The Act was introduced in two phases in the latter half of 2004 by virtue of commencement orders SI 505/2004 and SI 750/2004. From today's viewpoint, the key starter date for the practitioner is 1 September 2004. This is the date on which Part 4 of the Act was commenced in full. The impact of Part 4 on tenancies which commenced on or before that date is discussed more fully below. Note also that a different date applies to Part 4 tenancies outside the private sector—see **6.3.2**.

6.3 Application of the Act

Section 3(1) states that, subject to the exceptions listed in subsection (2), the Act applies to every dwelling which is the subject of a tenancy. This includes a tenancy created before the passing of the Act. However, the scope of this section has been restricted by virtue of s 100 of the Housing (Miscellaneous Provisions) Act 2009. Tenancies the term of which exceed 35 years are now excluded from the provisions of the Act.

6.3.1 EXCEPTIONS TO THE APPLICATION OF THE ACT

The exceptions as originally listed in s 3(2) are:

(a) *a dwelling that is used wholly or partly for the purpose of carrying on a business, such that the occupier could, after the tenancy has lasted 5 years, make an application under section 13(1)(a) of the Landlord and Tenant (Amendment) Act 1980 in respect of it,*

(b) *a dwelling to which Part II of the Housing (Private Rented Dwellings) Act, 1982 applies,*

(c) *a dwelling let by or to—*

    (i) *a public authority, or*

    (ii) *a body standing approved for the purposes of section 6 of the Housing (Miscellaneous Provisions) Act, 1992 and which is occupied by a person referred to in section 9(2) of the Housing Act, 1988. See* **6.3.1.1**

(d) *a dwelling, the occupier of which is entitled to acquire, under Part II of the Landlord and Tenant (Ground Rents)(No. 2) Act, 1978, the fee simple in respect of it,*

(e) *a dwelling occupied under a shared ownership lease,*

(f) *a dwelling let to a person whose entitlement to occupation is for the purpose of a holiday only,*

(g) *a dwelling within which the landlord also resides,*

(h) *a dwelling within which the spouse, civil partner, parent or child of the landlord resides and no lease or tenancy agreement in writing has been entered into by any person resident in the dwelling,*

(i) *a dwelling the subject of a tenancy granted under Part II of the Landlord and Tenant (Amendment) Act, 1980 or under Part III of the Landlord and Tenant Act, 1931 or which is the subject of an application made under section 21 of the Landlord and Tenant (Amendment) Act, 1980 and the court has yet to make its determination in the matter.*

The High Court has examined the meaning of 'child' for the purposes of s 3(2)(h) above in the case of *Hyland v RTB* [2017] IEHC 557. This is one of a number of cases involving receivers appointed to dwellings which have come before the superior courts on appeal from the Residential Tenancies Board (RTB) in recent years. The receivers were named as notice parties.

The appellant was a stepchild of the original owner of the dwelling. She argued that 'child' as used in s 3(2)(h) includes a stepchild, so that the Act did not apply and that a notice of termination was thus invalid. The respondent found against her. Noonan J disallowed her appeal, agreeing with the respondent that the word 'child' does not include a stepchild. The court noted that, for example, s 39 makes explicit reference to 'a child, stepchild or foster child', but that no such reference was made at s 3(2)(h).

6.3.1.1 Amendments to s 3(2)

The Housing (Miscellaneous Provisions) Act 2009

The Housing (Miscellaneous Provisions) Act 2009 introduced some modifications to the foregoing list of exceptions. These are set out in s 100(2) as follows:

    (2) *Section 3 of the Act of 2004 is amended—*

(a) in subsection (2)(c)(ii), by substituting "a household within the meaning of the Housing (Miscellaneous Provisions) Act 2009 assessed under section 20 of that Act as being qualified for social housing support" for "a person referred to in section 9 (2) of the Housing Act 1988", and

(b) by inserting the following subsection:

"(3) Notwithstanding the definition of "tenancy" in section 5(1), in this section a reference to a tenancy does not include a tenancy the term of which is more than 35 years.".

Thus the Act does not apply to any tenancy which exceeds a term of 35 years, regardless of whether the tenant may or may not be able to acquire the fee simple to the property. The new subsection (3) was inserted following legal proceedings before Judge Linnane in Dublin Circuit Court. The owner-occupier of an apartment held under a long lease was not entitled to buy out the freehold. He argued that his dispute with the management company was a matter for the then-Private Residential Tenancies Board (PRTB) and not the courts because the basis on which he occupied the apartment did not fall under the list of exceptions to the operation of the 2004 Act, Part 6 of which had transferred jurisdiction of disputes in most cases to the PRTB. The learned judge agreed. The board sought a judicial review of her decision—see *PRTB v Judge Linnane* [2010] IEHC 476—but Budd J refused the reliefs claimed. The amending legislation addresses the decision of the Circuit Court judge by putting owner-occupiers on an equal footing regardless of the right to buy out the freehold. Thus any disputes relating to management and other charges in long leases are a matter for the courts, being outside the scope of the Act.

The Residential Tenancies (Amendment) Act 2015

This has been introduced in a somewhat piecemeal fashion and to date not all of its provisions have been commenced. However, s 3 of the 2015 Act, which fundamentally alters the scope of the original s 3 to bring certain non-private tenancies within the ambit of the legislation, was commenced by virtue of Commencement Order S.I. 151 of 2016 on 7 April 2016.

In effect this extends the provisions of the 2004 Act to approved housing bodies (AHBs) and their tenants. Approved housing bodies (also called housing associations or voluntary housing associations) are independent, not-for-profit organisations. They provide affordable rented housing for people who cannot afford to pay private sector rents or buy their own homes; or for particular groups, such as older people or homeless people.

AHBs also include housing co-operatives, which are housing organisations controlled by their members/tenants who actively participate in setting their policies and making decisions.

Section 3 of the 2015 Act substituted a new s 3(2)(c) for the 2004 version as follows:

(c) a dwelling that is let by or to a public authority and without prejudice to the generality of the foregoing, including a dwelling provided by a public authority to an approved housing body other than a dwelling referred to in subsection (2A).

Of course, the foregoing is an exception to the application of the 2004 Act. Thus it is important to be familiar with the provisions of the new subsection (2A), which applies the 2004 Act as follows:

(2A) Where—

(a) a public authority provides a dwelling, of which it is the owner, to an approved housing body under a contract or lease between the public authority and the approved housing body pursuant to paragraph (ea) of section 6(2) of the Housing (Miscellaneous Provisions) Act, 1992, and

(b) subsequent to such provision the dwelling concerned is the subject of a tenancy between the approved housing body concerned and a household within the meaning of section 20 of the

Housing (Miscellaneous Provisions) Act, 2009 that has been assessed under that section of that Act as being qualified for social housing support (within the meaning of that Act),

for the purposes of subsection (1) and without prejudice to paragraph (c) of subsection (2) —

(i)   *this Act applies to that dwelling (including any such dwelling that is the subject of a tenancy created before the coming into operation of this subsection),*

(ii)   *any such tenancy shall not, for the purposes of this Act, be treated as a sub-tenancy arising out of such lease or contract between the public authority and the approved housing body, and*

(iii) *references in this Act to a sub-tenancy shall not include a dwelling that is the subject of a tenancy between the approved housing body and the household within the meaning of section 20 of the Housing (Miscellaneous Provisions) Act 2009.*

It should be noted that s 3 of the 2015 Act goes on to insert new subsections (4)–(6) inclusive into s 3 of the 2004 Act. Section 4 of the 2015 Act, commenced on the same day, inserts new sections 3A and 3B into the 2004 Act. Regard must be had to the new subsection (2A) in the event that the practitioner is required to advise either the landlord or tenant of a dwelling let by or to a public authority.

6.3.2   EXCEPTIONS TO THE APPLICATION OF PART 4 ONLY

Regard should also be had to s 25 of the Act (in regard to security of tenure and the 'Part 4 Tenancy'—see **6.4.3**), which provides inter alia that Part 4 shall not apply to a dwelling which is one of two dwellings within a building that, as originally constructed, comprised a single dwelling, and the landlord resides in the other dwelling. However, in order for this aspect of s 25 to operate the landlord must, in accordance with subsection (3) thereof, opt in writing for Part 4 not to apply by means of a written notice to the tenant, such notice to be served before the commencement of the tenancy.

Section 9 of the 2015 Act amends s 25 by inserting new subsections (5)–(7) to disapply Part 4 in the case of some of the non-private lettings that now fall under the scope of the legislation. These tenancies concern 'transitional dwellings' as defined in the new subsection (6), leased by AHBs for periods not exceeding 18 months. Before leasing, the housing body must secure the consent of the public authority which provided the housing stock before designating the property in question to be a transitional dwelling. Notification of such designation must be sent to the Minister for the Environment, Community and Local Government (now the Minister for Housing, Planning, Community and Local Government) within six months of making that decision. However, in the case of tenancies predating the introduction of s 3 of the 2015 Act (being 7 April 2016), the approved body may make such a designation within 12 months thereafter and notify the Minister within three months of making that decision.

See also **6.10.6** for other instances in which Part 4 is disapplied.

Note also that s 25 does not operate to prevent the remaining Parts of the Act from applying to residential tenancies.

6.4   Interpretation of the Act

Definitions are contained in ss 4 and 5 of the Act. More recent legislation has amended the interpretation section. Perhaps the most notable example is that 'Board' is no longer the Private Residential Tenancies Board but rather, since 7 April 2016, the Residential Tenancies Board or An Bord um Thionóntachtaí Cónaithe (RTB). This change is required by virtue of the 2015 Act, which brings certain tenancies in the voluntary and co-operative housing sector within the scope of the 2004 Act.

The following is by no means an exhaustive list and the statute should be consulted in specific circumstances.

6.4.1   DEFINITION OF 'DWELLING'

Section 4(1) defines a dwelling to mean, subject to subsection (2) thereof, a property let for rent or valuable consideration as a self-contained residential unit and includes any building or part of a building used as a dwelling and any out office, yard, garden or other land appurtenant to it or usually enjoyed with it and includes a property available for letting but excludes a structure that is not permanently attached to the ground and a vehicle (whether mobile or not).

Subsection (2) sets out that the aforementioned definition shall not apply in relation to the construction of references to 'dwelling' to which it (ie subsection (2)) applies; each such reference shall be construed as a reference to any building or part of a building used as a dwelling (whether or not a dwelling let for rent or valuable consideration) and any out office, yard, garden or other land appurtenant to it or usually enjoyed with it.

6.4.2   DEFINITION OF 'TENANCY'

Section 5(1) defines tenancy to include a periodic tenancy and a tenancy for a fixed term, whether oral or in writing or implied and, where the context so admits, includes a sub-tenancy and a tenancy or sub-tenancy that has been terminated.

6.4.3   DEFINITION OF 'PART 4 TENANCY'

Part 4 of the Act covers security of tenure and is broken into seven chapters comprising ss 25–56 inclusive. Section 4(1) states that a Part 4 tenancy shall be construed in accordance with s 29 of the Act. This section, in turn, sets out that a tenancy continued in being by s 28 shall be known as a Part 4 tenancy.

Section 28 goes to the nub of the issue of security of tenure and sets out statutory relief for tenants of dwellings. Subsection (1) states that, where a person has, under a tenancy, been in occupation of a dwelling for a continuous period of six months then, provided that no notice of termination (*per* subsection (3), giving the required period of notice as set out in the Act) has been served in respect of the tenancy before the expiry of the period of the said six months, then (*per* subsection (2), and subject to Chapter 3 of Part 4), the tenancy shall continue in being for the period of four years from either the commencement of the tenancy or the relevant date, whichever is the later.

As has already been noted, Part 4 of the Act was commenced on 1 September 2004 by virtue of the Residential Tenancies Act 2004 (Commencement) Order 2004 (SI 505/2004). The 'relevant date' in question is therefore 1 September 2004.

For the purposes of the 2015 Act insofar as it relates to non-private lettings, s 4(1) thereof sets out the definition of 'relevant date' by reference to the commencement date of the new s 3(4) of the 2004 Act. The date is 7 April 2016. Note, however, that s 26 expressly provides that tenancies which may afford greater security of tenure will not be affected by the operation of Part 4. This will be examined later in this chapter.

Section 37(1) of the 2016 Act introduced a significant amendment to the concept of the Part 4 tenancy. This amends s 28 by substituting '6 years' for '4 years' wherever the reference occurs. Subsection (3) applies the new change to 'all tenancies created after the coming into operation of this section'. This date is 24 December 2016. Thus, any Part 4 or further Part 4 tenancies pre-dating the amendment continue for a total of four years; all other tenancies will subsist for six years.

6.4.4   DEFINITION OF 'PUBLIC AUTHORITY'

This is divided into eight paragraphs as follows:

(a)   *a Minister of the Government or a body under the aegis of a Minister of the Government,*

(b)   *the Commissioners of Public Works in Ireland,*

(c)   *a local authority,*

(d)   *a health board established under the Health Act, 1970,*

(e)   *the Eastern Regional Health Authority or an area health board established under the Health (Eastern Regional Health Authority) Act, 1999,*

(f)   *a voluntary body standing approved of by the Minister for Health and Children or by a health board or an authority or board mentioned in paragraph (e) of this definition for the purpose of providing accommodation for elderly persons or persons with a mental handicap or psychiatric disorder,*

(g)   *a recognised educational institution, namely, any university, technical college, regional technical college, secondary or technical college or other institution or body of persons approved of, for the purpose of providing an approved course of study, by the Minister for Education and Science, or*

(h)   *the Shannon Free Airport Development Company.*

Note that this last body was removed from the foregoing list by virtue of s 37 of the State Airports (Shannon Group) Act 2014, which was commenced under S.I. 396 of 2014 on 5 September 2014.

6.4.5   OTHER SECTION 4 DEFINITIONS

'Contract of tenancy' does not include an agreement to create a tenancy. 'Tenancy agreement' includes an oral tenancy agreement.

6.4.6   DEFINITION OF 'LANDLORD', 'TENANT' AND 'LEASE'

These are set out in s 5(1).

Landlord means:

. . . the person for the time being entitled to receive (otherwise than as agent for another person) the rent paid in respect of a dwelling by the tenant thereof and, where the context so admits, includes a person who has ceased to be so entitled by reason of the termination of the tenancy . . .

Tenant means:

. . . the person for the time being entitled to the occupation of a dwelling under a tenancy and, where the context so admits, includes a person who has ceased to be entitled to that occupation by reason of the termination of his or her tenancy . . .

Lease means:

. . . an instrument in writing, whether or not under seal, containing a contract of tenancy in respect of a dwelling . . .

Section 5(2) further sets out that a reference in the Act to either a landlord or a tenant is a reference to a landlord or a tenant under a tenancy of the dwelling.

6.5   Service of Notices

This is covered in detail by s 6 of the Act. All notices required to be served or given under the Act shall (subject to subsection (2)) be addressed to the person concerned by name and then served or given in one of the following ways:

A notice required or authorised to be served or given by or under this Act shall, subject to subsection (2), be addressed to the person concerned by name and may be served on or given to the person in one of the following ways:

(a)   *by delivering it to the person;*

(b)   *by leaving it at the address at which the person ordinarily resides or, in a case in which an address for service has been furnished, at that address;*

(c)   *by sending it by post in a prepaid letter to the address at which the person ordinarily resides or, in a case in which an address for service has been furnished, to that address;*

(d)   *where the notice relates to a dwelling and it appears that no person is in actual occupation of the dwelling, by affixing it in a conspicuous position on the outside of the dwelling or the property containing the dwelling.*

Subsection (2) provides that, in cases where the name of the notice party cannot be ascertained by reasonable enquiry, the notice may be addressed to 'the landlord/tenant/owner/occupier' as appropriate.

For service purposes, subsection (3) sets out that a company shall be deemed to be ordinarily resident at its registered office; every other body corporate or unincorporated body shall be deemed to be resident at its principal office or place of business.

Subsection (5) deems it an offence for the purpose of the Act if a person removes, damages or defaces a notice as affixed under subsection (1)(d) within three months and without lawful authority. The penalties for an offence are set out later in this chapter.

Subsection (6) places the onus of proof on the recipient, once it is shown that the notice was served or given in accordance with s 6, to prove that it was not received in sufficient time to enable compliance with the relevant time limit specified by or under the Act.

6.6   Tenancy Obligations of Landlords and Tenants—Part 2

Part 2 of the Act, comprising ss 12–18, is sub-divided into two chapters setting out the respective obligations of landlords and tenants. These provisions go into considerable detail. However, they exist alongside other legislative enactments; indeed, ss 12 and 16 expressly provide that the respective obligations of landlord and tenant are in addition to the obligations arising by or under 'any other enactment'. These cover not only certain Regulations already extant when s 12 was commenced but also Regulations which were introduced thereafter—see **6.6.1**. Section 18 expressly prohibits parties to any letting agreement from contracting out of the obligations imposed by ss 12 and 16. This applies equally to tenancies commenced before the operation of the Act. The section goes on to allow for the possibility that more favourable terms for the tenant than those that apply by virtue of s 12 may be incorporated into the agreement and that obligations additional to those imposed on tenants by virtue of s 16 may be imposed, but only if those obligations are consistent with the Act. Thus landlords are prevented from burdening tenants with any of their own obligations under the Act.

6.6.1   PART 2, CHAPTER 1—LANDLORD'S OBLIGATIONS

For details of the landlord's obligation to register particulars of the tenancy, as required by Part 7 of the Act, see **7.3.2**.

Section 12 sets out many (but not all) of the landlord's obligations to the tenant. Before going into the details of s 12, however, it should be noted that—prior to the commencement of the letting—all landlords are required to provide Building Energy Rating certification in accordance with the European Communities (Energy Performance of Buildings) Regulations 2012 (S.I. 243 of 2012) to their prospective tenants.

Moreover, s 23(10) of the Multi-Unit Developments Act 2011 requires landlords to incorporate a copy of the house rules for a managed development, where applicable, into the letting agreement of any dwelling within such a development.

In summary s 12 provides that the landlord shall:

(a)   allow the tenant peaceful and exclusive occupation of the dwelling (s 12(1)(a));

(b)   carry out to the structure of the dwelling all such repairs as are from time to time necessary and ensure that the structure complies with any standards for houses for the time being prescribed under s 18 of the Housing (Miscellaneous Provisions) Act, 1992 (s 12(1)(b)(i)). Thus landlords of most types of private dwelling will also need to be familiar with the provisions of the Housing (Standards for Rented Houses) Regulations 2017 (S.I. 17 of 2017)—'houses' being widely defined in the Regulations. The Regulations go into detail as regards minimum requirements relating to such matters as the structural condition of the dwelling as well as the provision and maintenance/replacement of sanitary facilities, food preparation, storage and laundry, availability of adequate heating, lighting and ventilation, safety of oil, electricity and gas installations, fire safety and refuse facilities—note that this list is not exhaustive;

(c)   carry out to the interior of the dwelling all such repairs and replacement of fittings as are from time to time necessary so that the interior and fittings are at least in the standard in which they were at the commencement of the tenancy and in compliance with any such standards for the time being prescribed (s 12(1)(b)(ii)). Section 13 provides for the possible introduction of regulations specifying that particular parts of a dwelling shall, for the purposes of s 12(1)(b), be regarded as parts of the interior or parts of the structure. Note that, by virtue of subsection (2), s 12(1)(b) does not apply to any repairs that are necessary due to the failure of the tenant to comply with s 16(f)—see **6.6.2.** Section 12(1)(ba) (as inserted by s 100 of the Housing (Miscellaneous Provisions) Act 2009) requires a landlord to provide receptacles suitable for the storage of refuse outside the dwelling;

(d)   keep the structure of the dwelling insured against loss, damage and destruction and take out liability cover for at least €250,000 (s 12(1)(c)); this does not apply if such a policy is either not obtainable or not obtainable at a reasonable cost (s 12(3));

(e)   return or repay promptly any deposit paid by the tenant (s 12(1)(d)); however, this does not apply in situations where, *per* s 12(4), either arrears of rent (including any taxes or other outgoings properly due by the tenant in accordance with the letting agreement) or the cost to the landlord of restoring the dwelling where the tenant is in breach of s 16(f) (see **6.6.2**) equal or exceed the amount of the deposit;

(f)   notify the tenant of the name of any person for the time being authorised to act on behalf of the landlord in relation to the tenancy for the time being (s 12(1)(e)), and provide particulars of the means by which the tenant may at all reasonable times contact the landlord or such agent (s 12(1)(f));

(g)   reimburse the tenant for all reasonable and vouched-for expenses incurred by the tenant for repairs to the structure or interior for which the landlord is liable under s 12(1)(b)(i)–(ii) aforementioned (s 12(1)(g)); however, this applies only where the landlord refuses to carry out such repairs when requested, and the postponement thereof poses either a significant risk to the health and safety of the tenant, or other lawful occupants, or a significant reduction in the quality of their living environment. Section 12(5) expressly deems s 12(1)(g) to apply where, after all reasonable attempts, the landlord or their agent could not be contacted to make the request;

(h)   if the dwelling is part of an apartment complex, forward to the management company (if any) any complaint in writing made by the tenant to the landlord of that company's functions and forward to the tenant any initial response by the company to that complaint and any written statement (*per* s 187(2)) made by them in relation to that complaint. (See s 187 generally with regard to the management company's obligations in relation to certain complaints.)

Section 33 of the 2016 Act, commenced on 24 December 2016, inserts a new obligation in the form of s 12(1)(i). This obligation applies to dwellings within a rent pressure zone and to tenancies commencing after that date. Landlords of such dwellings are henceforth required to furnish the tenant, in writing, with the following information at the commencement of a tenancy: (i) the amount of rent that was last set under a tenancy for the dwelling; (ii) the date the rent was last set under a tenancy for the dwelling; and (iii) a statement as to how the rent set under the tenancy of the dwelling has been calculated having regard to s 19(4) of the 2004 Act.

In addition to the obligations specified in s 12, the landlord is expressly prohibited under s 14 from penalising a tenant for:

(a)   referring any dispute between the parties to the RTB;

(b)   giving evidence in any proceedings under Part 6 to which the landlord is a party (whether or not the tenant is also a party);

(c)   making any complaint to a Garda, or any complaint or application to a public authority, in relation to any matter arising out of or in connection with the occupation of the dwelling; or

(d)   giving notice of their intention to do all or any of the foregoing matters.

Section 14(2) expressly states that a tenant is penalised if they are subjected to any action which adversely affects their peaceful enjoyment of the dwelling. Subsection (3) concerns a reasonable inference that certain otherwise lawful action on the part of the landlord in fact constitutes penalisation; and subsection (4) states that s 14 is without prejudice to any other civil or criminal liability to which a landlord may be subject for doing a thing prohibited by the section.

6.6.1.1   Third party complaints

An obligation on landlords in respect of third parties is imposed by s 15 of the Act. Under this section, landlords are stated to owe a duty of care to each person who would be directly and adversely affected by a failure to enforce an obligation of the tenant under the tenancy. Any such third party may refer a dispute under this section to the RTB using the Part 6 dispute resolution procedure, provided that they satisfy both of the conditions laid down in s 77(2), namely, that they are directly and adversely affected by the alleged breach, and that they took all reasonable steps (though not necessarily including litigation or the threat of it) to resolve the matter by communicating or attempting to communicate with the relevant parties or former parties to the tenancy.

Section 36 of the 2015 Act, commenced on 9 May 2016, makes additional provisions for the third party complaints procedure by adding a new subsection (4) to s 77. This new provision allows a complainant to require (a) an owners' management company as defined in the Multi-Unit Developments Act 2011, (b) a body corporate or (c) an unincorporated body such as a neighbourhood watch group or a residents' association to make the communication on their behalf and/or to refer the complaint to the RTB. The 2015 Act points out that any such body shall not be treated as a party to the dispute itself.

Landlords are therefore under a duty to ensure that the actions of all lawful occupiers of and visitors to the dwelling do not result in the peaceful enjoyment of their property by any third party (including co-tenants) being reduced. In effect this means that the neighbour of a tenant in breach of their obligations—say, by behaving in an anti-social manner—may seek redress against the landlord before the RTB.

6.6.1.2 Deposit retention by landlords

As noted above, s 12(4) clearly sets out only two instances in which it is permitted for landlords to retain some or all of a tenant's security deposit. However, in its annual reports to date the RTB has noted that almost one-half of all adjudications concern, in whole or in part, allegations of illegal deposit retention. This is one of the matters that the then Department of the Environment, Community and Local Government examined with a view to amending the Act, as noted in the introduction to this chapter.

Considerable new law in regard to deposits is contained in the 2015 Act. It is envisaged that the Board will take up and administer all deposits for tenancies of dwellings within its remit. Note however that this has not been commenced to date.

In the meantime, the RTB has published a website note on the issue of deposit refund. In effect the board notes a third instance where landlords might in their discretion retain some or all of a security deposit, namely, in cases where a tenant prematurely terminates a fixed-term letting in circumstances where the landlord is not in breach of their statutory or contractual obligations.

Adjudications and notes on this and other aspects of Chapter 1 obligations can be viewed on the RTB's website.

6.6.2 PART 2, CHAPTER 2—TENANT'S OBLIGATIONS

Section 16 sets out the tenant's obligations in detail. In summary these are:

(a) pay rent when due to the landlord or their agent (s 16(a)(i));

(b) pay charges or taxes imposed by the agreement, except where to do so is unlawful or in contravention of any other enactment (s 16(a)(ii));

(c) not to cause the landlord to be in breach of their statutory obligations under any enactment. This provision makes specific reference to '. . . regulations under s 18 of the Housing (Miscellaneous Provisions) Act, 1992'. These are the Housing (Standards for Rented Houses) Regulations 2017 (S.I. 17 of 2017), which set out minimum standards for rented dwellings, as well as the Housing (Rent Books) Regulations, 1993 (S.I. 146 of 1993) as amended (s 16(b));

(d) allow access to inspect the dwelling at reasonable intervals to the landlord or any person(s) acting on their behalf, on a time and date agreed in advance (s 16(c));

(e) notify the landlord or their agent of any defect requiring repair to enable them to comply with their obligations under any enactment in regard to the dwelling or tenancy (s 16(d));

(f) allow reasonable access to the landlord or any person(s) acting on their behalf for the purposes of carrying out any works for which the landlord is responsible (s 16(e));

(g) not to cause any deterioration in the condition of the dwelling. Normal wear and tear is expressly disregarded in determining whether the tenant is in compliance with this obligation. In this respect the length of time elapsed since the tenancy commenced, the extent of occupation that the landlord could have reasonably foreseen, and '. . . any other relevant matters' shall be taken into consideration (s 16(f)). While it is difficult to state in a given case precisely what will amount to 'normal' wear and tear, it may be noted that the RTB has published a website note on the topic of normal wear and tear as regards items of furniture. This note includes a reminder to landlords of their right to carry out regular inspections of the dwelling and its contents.

In the event of non-compliance with s 16(f), the tenant is obliged to take such steps as the landlord may reasonably require to restore the dwelling to the condition it was in at the commencement of the tenancy (subject to the matters to be disregarded in paragraph (f) and mentioned above) or to defray any costs incurred by the landlord as a result of their taking any reasonable steps for that purpose (s 16(g));

(h) not to behave or allow other occupiers of or visitors to the dwelling to behave in an anti-social manner (s 17 defines anti-social behaviour—see **6.6.2.1**) This paragraph refers expressly to behaviour not only within the dwelling but within the vicinity of it (s 16(h));

(i) not to act or allow other occupiers of or visitors to the dwelling to act in a way which would result in the invalidation of a policy of insurance in force in relation to the dwelling (s 16(i)). If any such act results in an increase in a policy premium, the tenant is obliged to pay the increased element to the landlord. This expressly includes each further premium falling due for payment that includes the increased element (s 16(j)). Section 17(4) clarifies the meaning of 'the increased element' to allow for a proportional increase or reduction in future policy premium payments due;

(j) not to assign or sub-let the tenancy without the written consent of the landlord, which consent may be withheld at their discretion. This discretion amounts to an absolute right on the part of the landlord; in such an event the tenant may simply terminate the tenancy in accordance with s 186 and having regard to notice provisions (s 16(k));

(k) Not to alter or improve the dwelling without the written consent of the landlord, which consent again may be withheld at their discretion except where such alteration or improvement consists only of repairing, painting and/or decorating, in which event consent may not be unreasonably withheld (s 16(l)). Section 17 defines 'alter and improve' to include changing the locks and adding to or altering the building or structure, including any building or structure that is subsidiary or ancillary to the dwelling;

(l) Not to use the dwelling or cause it to be used for any purpose other than as a dwelling without the written consent of the landlord; again, such consent may be withheld at the landlord's discretion (s 16(m));

(m) Notify in writing the landlord of the identity of each person (other than a multiple tenant) who, for the time being, resides ordinarily in the dwelling (s 16(n)).

In regard to s 16(k), (l) and (m), s 17(3) expressly provides that the landlord shall be entitled to any reasonable disbursements incurred by them in deciding upon the tenant's request, to include cases where consent is refused.

Section 4 of the 2015 Act (commenced on 7 April 2016) renders void the purported subletting and assignment of tenancies for those non-private dwellings that come under the new s 3(4). Moreover s 16(k) shall not apply in the case of any such letting.

The 2015 Act at s 24 envisages an additional subparagraph (o) to require tenants to communicate with the RTB in regard to the return of deposits to them, but this is yet to commence.

6.6.2.1   Anti-social behaviour

Section 17(1) defines 'behave in a way that is anti-social' to mean any of the following:

(a) *engage in behaviour that constitutes the commission of an offence, being an offence the commission of which is reasonably likely to affect directly the well-being or welfare of others,*

(b) *engage in behaviour that causes or could cause fear, danger, injury, damage or loss to any person living, working or otherwise lawfully in the dwelling concerned or its vicinity and, without prejudice to the generality of the foregoing, includes violence, intimidation, coercion, harassment or obstruction of, or threats to, any such person, or*

(c) *engage, persistently, in behaviour that prevents of interferes with the peaceful occupation—*

(i) *by any other person residing in the dwelling concerned, of that dwelling,*

(ii) *by any person residing in any other dwelling contained in the property containing the dwelling concerned, of that other dwelling, or*

(iii) *by any person residing in a dwelling ('neighbourhood dwelling') in the vicinity of the dwelling or the property containing the dwelling concerned, of that neighbourhood dwelling.*

6.7   Offences—Section 9

The penalty for an offence under the Act is a fine not exceeding €3,000 or a term not exceeding six months' imprisonment, or both. Any person convicted of an offence who continues in contravention of the Act thereafter shall be liable on summary conviction to a fine not exceeding €250 for every day on which the contravention continues.

Section 9(3) provides that the RTB may bring a prosecution for an offence under the Act. The limitation period is one year from the date of the offence (subsection (4)). Unless there are special and substantial reasons for not doing so, the court shall order a convicted person to pay the RTB's costs and expenses in relation to the matter (subsection (5)).

6.8   Redress under Part 6—Section 119

Chapter 8 of Part 6 generally deals with the redress that may be granted under the dispute resolution procedure. Section 119(1) provides that any amount of rent arrears stipulated to be paid following a determination shall be the gross amount of the arrears and other charges (if any), *less* any amount due by the landlord to the tenant under s 48 of Deasy's

Act, any set-off for repairs that the tenant could claim under s 87 of the Landlord and Tenant (Amendment) Act, 1980, any compensation due by the landlord to the tenant under s 61 of that Act, and any other amount which the adjudicator or Tenancy Tribunal (see Part 6) considers is warranted by the circumstances of the case. This amount may be increased by the landlord's reasonable costs incurred in pursuit of the rent arrears, damages and an amount in respect of the tenant's failure to comply with the obligation to repair set out in s 16(f).

6.9 Rent and Rent Reviews—Part 3

Part 3 of the Act, comprising ss 19–24 inclusive, sets out the provisions relating to rent and rent reviews. This Part of the Act has been considerably amended by both the 2015 and 2016 Acts. A couple of the amendments are intended to be of a temporary nature as set out below.

The original position is set out in s 19(1), which provides that rent may not be set at an amount greater than the market rent for the tenancy in question at that time. Section 24(1) defines 'market rent' to mean:

> the rent which a willing tenant not already in occupation would give and a willing landlord would take for the dwelling, in each case on the basis of vacant possession being given, and having regard to—
>
> (a)   the other terms of the tenancy,
>
> (b)   the letting values of dwellings of similar size, type and character to the dwelling and situated in a comparable area to that in which it is situated.

This definition may seem strictly legalistic, but it should be remembered that the Act requires detailed particulars of all residential tenancies to be registered with the RTB, whose statutory functions specifically include the collection and provision of information in regard to rent levels.

In regard to dispute resolution procedures under Part 6 of the Act, s 115(2)(b) accords the right to any Tenancy Tribunal set up thereunder to make a declaration as to whether or not an amount of rent complies with s 19(1); if it does not so comply, the Tribunal or its adjudicator shall indicate what amount would so comply.

Section 34 of the 2016 Act has amended s 19 in detail by adding new subsections (3)–(7) inclusive. This introduces the concept of the rent pressure zone and restricts rent increases in such areas to 4 per cent on every review according to a calculation that is set out in the new s 19(4). Rent pressure zones may be located in such areas as may be prescribed by the Minister for Housing, Planning, Community and Local Government. The 2016 Act itself introduced the first rent pressure zones, being all of the administrative parts of Dublin City and County together with Cork City. The zones were initially set to last for a period of three years from the commencement of s 33 of the 2016 Act, being 24 December 2016. Subsequent ministerial orders by way of statutory instrument have extended the concept of the rent pressure zone to Galway City as well as to many towns, particularly on the east coast as well as in Counties Kildare and Cork. In each case the designation is intended to have effect for three years from the date of the ministerial order. Full details can be found on www.housing.gov.ie and also by searching for 'Rent Pressure Zone' within the statutory instruments page on www.irishstatutebook.ie.

Section 20 covers the frequency of rent reviews. As originally enacted, it provided that a review may not occur for a period of 12 months after its initial setting or a subsequent review. This overrides any provision to the contrary contained in the letting agreement.

However, subsection (3) provides that s 20 shall not apply where there has been a substantial change in the nature of the accommodation provided under the tenancy.

Note that the wording of this subsection implies that the rent may be reduced or increased. The language used is not 'upwards only'. Damage, as much as an improvement to the dwelling, may be taken into account.

If there is no provision for a review in the agreement, or if the tenancy in question is an implied one, s 21 provides that either party may initiate the review procedure.

Section 25 of the 2015 Act inserts a new subsection (4) into s 20 with effect from 4 December 2015. This provision is intended to be temporary only, to have effect for a period of four years from that date before reverting to the 2004 position. The effect of the provision is to prevent a review from occurring less than 24 months either following the commencement of the tenancy or following the last review. This provision applies nationwide.

The effect of the 2016 Act is to disapply the two-year temporary rule to tenancies in rent pressure zones, provided they commence on or after 24 December 2016. On each review the maximum increase permitted is 4 per cent.

Thus the current position, in force up to 4 December 2019, is as follows:

(i)   If the dwelling is located outside a rent pressure zone, reviews are permitted every 24 months and there is no statutory cap on the increase, subject always to dispute resolution by the RTB, which is charged by the 2004 Act with taking account of current market rents.

(ii) If (a) the dwelling is located in a rent pressure zone and (b) the tenancy commenced prior to 24 December 2016, the first rent review is permitted after 24 months either since the tenancy commenced or since the last review; thereafter a review is permitted every 12 months. On every review, there is a statutory cap of 4 per cent on the rent increase.

(iii) If (a) the dwelling is located in a rent pressure zone and (b) the tenancy commenced on or after 24 December 2016, a review is permitted every 12 months and the statutory cap of 4 per cent applies.

Section 22(2) as enacted in 2004 provides that the landlord must notify the tenant in writing at least 28 days before the date from which the new rent is to take effect, setting out the amount and the date from which it is to have effect. Section 22(1) provides that if this notice is not served within the time stipulated then the new rent shall not have effect.

Section 26 of the 2015 Act amends the notification requirement. The notification period is currently 90 days. Section 26(1) requires landlords to give certain information to their tenants in the notice of rent review. S.I. 217 of 2016, in effect since 9 May 2016, sets out the form to be used. Besides setting out the new rent as well as the date from which it is intended to have effect, all notices are now required to include a statement by landlords that, in their view, the new rent is not greater than the market rent, having regard to (i) the other terms of the tenancy and (ii) letting values of dwellings (a) of a similar size, type and character and (b) situated in a comparable area. In this regard s 26 requires landlords to specify the amount of rent sought for three similar dwellings. Section 35 of the 2016 Act further amends s 22 insofar as the dwelling is located in a rent pressure zone. For such dwellings, the notice must state how the rent was calculated having regard to s 19(4) or, where s 19(4) does not apply, state why not.

In keeping with the requirements of s 22(3) of the Act, the notice must inform tenants of their right to refer a dispute to the RTB either (i) before the date that the new rent is intended to have effect or (ii) within 28 days, whichever is the later. This suggests that the amendment from 28 days' notice to 90 days may have temporary effect. However, a reading of the amending provision does not expressly indicate that the notice period will revert to 28 days at any future stage.

All notices must be dated and signed either by landlords or by their authorised agents. For provisions regarding service, see **6.5**.

As mentioned earlier, it is a specific function of the RTB to collate information in regard to rent levels. Landlords are therefore obliged by virtue of s 139 to notify the board of the new rent within one month of its alteration.

According to s 22(3), where notice has been served by the landlord within the time stipulated, upon receipt of this notice, the tenant may dispute the new rent by invoking the Part 6 procedure and referring the matter to the RTB under s 78(c) of the Act. This must take place before the date that the landlord has set out in the notice for the new rent to take effect, or within 28 days of receipt of the notice by the tenant, whichever is the later. Section 88 allows for a possible extension of time to refer a dispute if good reason is shown. Pending resolution thereof, s 86(1) as amended provides for payment of the existing rent; but s 86(2) provides that the rent may be suspended, or the new rent paid, should the parties so agree.

Section 23 deals with rent arrears. All persons who are entitled to payment of arrears of rent and other charges under a tenancy of a dwelling may, using the dispute resolution procedures under Part 6, recover the same from the person who occupied the dwelling as a tenant during the period when the arrears occurred or charges arose. For the purposes of this section, Part 6 expressly includes personal representatives of any party where appropriate—see s 75(4).

In relation to the foregoing, it should be noted that under the Part 6 dispute resolution procedure, the RTB is given express authority to deal with a dispute as to the amount of initial rent to be set under a tenancy, the time at which a rent review should take place or the amount of rent that should be set under that review—see s 78(1)(b) and (c). Note also that the list of complaints set out in s 78(1) is non-exhaustive. Moreover, it is one of the stated functions of the RTB to review the operation of the Act and in particular Part 3 thereof—see s 151(1)(g).

6.10 Security of Tenure—Part 4

Part 4 of the Act, divided into seven chapters and comprising ss 25–56 inclusive, represented a radical departure from the previous position with regard to the right of a tenant of residential premises to obtain a new tenancy. Previously such a tenant was entitled under s 13 of the Landlord and Tenant (Amendment) Act, 1980, subject to compliance with certain statutory definitions, to a new tenancy based either on 20 years' continuous occupation of the premises or on improvements carried out by the tenant which at least doubled the letting value thereof. Most landlords prefer to effect improvements themselves and as such tenants usually required a 'long possession equity' of 20 years or more to establish the right to a new tenancy. See **chapter 10**.

The Act encompassed almost entirely new thinking on this subject. Chapter 2 (ss 27–32) sets out the statement of essential protection currently enjoyed by residential tenants. Subject as always to statutory definitions and exceptions, Part 4 as enacted provides for tenancies of dwellings to be based on four-year cycles. Thus a tenant who is in continuous occupation for six months and who has not received a valid termination notice from the landlord shall be entitled to remain in the dwelling for a period of a further three and a half years (s 28). However, Chapter 2 Part 4 goes on to provide for the right of premature termination of the ensuing tenancy by either party. This is examined in detail at **6.10.1**.

In regard to the six-month continuous occupation requirement, the effect of s 27 may be summed up as follows. Firstly, where a tenant was in occupation of a dwelling for any period of time prior to 1 September 2004, no matter how short, that person became entitled to the security of tenure afforded by the Act by virtue of continuing in occupation thereof until 1 March 2005 (six months after the commencement of Part 4). Secondly, in cases where the tenancy commences on or after 1 September 2004, the tenant acquires such security once a period of six months' continuous occupation has elapsed. In each case it is assumed that no notice of termination has been served by either party. The four-year tenancy thus created shall commence either on 1 September 2004 or the date of commencement of the tenancy, whichever is the later.

A tenancy continued in being by virtue of s 28 is called a 'Part 4 tenancy' (s 29). Moreover, any further tenancy must be construed in accordance with the Act, so that any offending provisions of any pre-existing tenancy agreement no longer apply (s 30). This does not, *per* s 26, prevent tenants from enjoying any more beneficial rights by reason of that agreement. The parties are free to vary the terms of the agreement provided they comply with the Act. For an examination of the rights of both parties under fixed term letting agreements, see **6.10.3**.

Section 37 of the 2016 Act, commenced on 24 December 2016, contains a significant amendment to s 28. References to 'four years' shall be substituted by 'six years'. Subsection (3) makes clear that the new provision affects only tenancies that come into being after that date. Thus practitioners may find themselves advising clients in regard to s 28 as originally enacted for some time to come.

Section 31 of the Act extends the protection of Part 4 to tenants who have occupied the dwelling under a series of fixed term tenancies for a continuous period of at least six months.

Section 32 renders void any sub-tenancy purported to be created in respect of part only of a dwelling which is the subject of a Part 4 tenancy or a further Part 4 tenancy. The section does however provide for protection to be extended to sub-tenancies created out of Part 4 tenancies as set out in a detailed schedule to the Act.

Chapter 1 (ss 25–26) sets out instances in which Part 4 shall not apply. This has already been partly dealt with at **6.3**, including inter alia those provisions of the 2015 Act that disapply Part 4 in the case of certain non-private lettings. Section 25(4) also sets out that Part 4 does not apply to a tenancy—

(a) *if the landlord of the dwelling is entitled, in relation to expenditure incurred on the construction of, conversion into, or, as the case may be, refurbishment of, the dwelling, to a deduction of the kind referred to in section 380B(2), 380C(4) or 380D(2) (inserted by the Finance Act, 1999) of the Taxes Consolidation Act, 1997, or*

(b) *if the entitlement of the tenant to occupy the dwelling is connected with his or her continuance in any office, appointment or employment.*

6.10.1 TERMINATION OF RESIDENTIAL TENANCIES

It should always be remembered that there is nothing to prevent the parties from terminating either a Part 4 tenancy or a fixed term tenancy by mutual agreement: see s 69 of the Act.

By virtue of s 26, in order to advise the parties on the right to terminate, it is important to find out not only how long the tenant has been in occupation of the dwelling but also if there is a fixed term letting currently in operation. Particular care must be taken in all cases involving fixed term lettings, as they will afford tenants greater security of tenure than that which is put in place by virtue of Part 4. Tenants of fixed term tenancies enjoy security of tenure *ab initio* and not merely following the expiry of six months' uninterrupted occupation.

6.10.2 TERMINATION OF PART 4 TENANCIES

Chapter 3 (ss 33–39) and Chapter 4 (ss 40–42) of Part 4 deal with termination. The 2015 and 2016 Acts have introduced substantial amendments. These restrict landlords both as regards their right to terminate and as to the manner in which they go about termination of a letting. Once the tenant has been in occupation for a minimum of six months and no valid notice of termination has been served in accordance with the terms of the Act, then, in the absence of mutual agreement and assuming there is no fixed term letting currently in operation, the parties shall be entitled to terminate a Part 4 tenancy only in accordance with s 34 (landlords) or s 36 (tenants). Beyond s 36, tenants may also be deemed to have terminated a tenancy in certain circumstances. These are discussed **6.10.2.2**.

The parties must then comply with the notice and procedural requirements set out in detail in Part 5 of the Act—again, substantially amended, as will be discussed at **6.11**. Termination must take place by service of a valid notice of termination. The form of notice must comply with certain minimum requirements laid down in s 62—see **6.11.2**.

If neither party is in default of their obligations, the period of notice required will depend on the length of the tenancy; s 66 (as amended) requires a landlord to give the same or lengthier notice than a tenant, depending on the length of the tenancy involved. However, s 66 does not apply in cases involving default by either party or where termination takes place by mutual agreement. The appropriate notice periods are considered in detail at **6.11.3**.

6.10.2.1 Termination by the landlord

Section 34 provides for termination of a Part 4 tenancy by a landlord. This can be done in one of two ways. Section 34(a) provides for premature termination of a Part 4 tenancy only where one or more of the six grounds set out in the table, published in that section, applies; where the notice sets out the said ground(s); and when it has been served in accordance with the statutory notice provisions.

Section 34(b) permits the landlord to terminate by virtue of the fact that the tenancy (either four or six years as discussed at **6.10**) is coming to an end. A notice of termination must again be served giving the required period of notice and that period expires on or after the period of four or six years mentioned in s 28(2)(a) of the Act. Where s 34(b) applies, no ground for termination need be set out in the body of the notice.

Section 34 contains a table setting out the six grounds for termination pursuant to s 34(a). The six grounds as amended by the provisions of the 2015 Act are as follows:

1. *The tenant has failed to comply with any of his or her obligations in relation to the tenancy (whether arising under this Act or otherwise) and, unless the failure provides an excepted basis for termination—*

   (b) *the tenant has been notified in writing of the failure by the landlord and that notification states that the landlord is entitled to terminate the tenancy if the failure is not remedied within a reasonable time specified in that notification, and*

   (c) *the tenant does not remedy the failure within that specified time.*

2. *The dwelling is no longer suitable to the accommodation needs of the tenant and of any persons residing with him or her. Landlords relying on this ground are obliged by the 2015 Act to serve an accompanying statement in writing, confirming the number of bed spaces in the*

dwelling and setting out the reason why the dwelling is no longer suitable, having regard to the number of bed spaces contained in the dwelling and the size and composition of the occupying household.

3. *The landlord intends, within three months after the termination of the tenancy under this section, to enter into an enforceable agreement for the transfer to another, for full consideration, of the whole of his or her interest in the dwelling or the property containing the dwelling. The notice should be accompanied by a statutory declaration which includes an averment that the landlord intends to enter into such an agreement to transfer for full consideration their interest in the dwelling.*

4. *The landlord requires the dwelling or the property containing the dwelling for his or her own occupation or for occupation by a member of his or her family and the notice of termination (the 'notice') contains or is accompanied by a statutory declaration—*

   (a) *specifying:*

       (i) *the intended occupant's identity and (if not the landlord) his or her relationship to the landlord, and*

       (ii) *the expected duration of that occupation,*

   and

   (b) *that the landlord, by virtue of the notice, is required to offer to the tenant a tenancy of the dwelling if the contact details requirement is complied with and the following conditions are satisfied—*

       (i) *the dwelling is vacated by the person referred to in subparagraph (a) within the period of six months from expiry of the period of notice required to be given by the notice or, if a dispute in relation to the validity of the notice was referred to the Board under Part 6 for resolution, the final determination of the dispute, and*

       (ii) *the tenancy to which the notice related had not otherwise been validly terminated by virtue of the citation in the notice of the ground specified in paragraph 1, 2, 3, or 6 of this Table.*

5. *The landlord intends to substantially refurbish or renovate the dwelling or the property containing the dwelling in a way which requires the dwelling to be vacated for that purpose (and, where planning permission is required for the carrying out of that refurbishment or renovation, that permission has been obtained) and the notice of termination (the 'notice') contains or is accompanied, in writing, by a statement—*

   (a) *specifying the nature of the intended works*

   (aa) *that, in a case where planning permission has been obtained, a copy of the planning permission is attached to the notice or statement,*

   (ab) *that planning permission is not required and that the landlord has complied with the requirements of s 35(9)(b), and*

   (b) *that the landlord, by virtue of the notice, is required to offer to the tenant a tenancy of the dwelling if the contact details requirement is complied with and the following conditions are satisfied—*

       (i) *the dwelling becomes available for re-letting within the period of 6 months from the expiry of the period of notice required to be given by the notice, or if a dispute in relation to the validity of the notice was referred to the Board under Part 6 for resolution, the final determination of the dispute, and*

       (ii) *the tenancy to which the notice related had not otherwise been validly terminated by virtue of the citation in the notice of the ground specified in paragraph 1, 2, 3 or 6 of this Table.*

6. *The landlord intends to change the use of the dwelling or the property containing the dwelling to some other use (and, where planning permission is required for that change of use, that*

permission has been obtained) and the notice of termination (the 'notice') contains or is accompanied, in writing, by a statement—

(a)   specifying the nature of the intended use,

(aa) that, in a case where planning permission has been obtained, a copy of the planning permission is attached to the notice or statement,

(ab) as to whether any works are to be carried out in respect of the change of use and where such works are to be carried out, specifying-

(i) details of those works,

(ii) the name of the contractor, if any, employed to carry out such works, and

(iii)   the dates on which the intended works are to be carried out and the proposed duration of the period in which those works are to be carried out,

and

(b)   that the landlord, by virtue of the notice, is required to offer to the tenant a tenancy of the dwelling if the contact details requirement is complied with and the following conditions are satisfied—

(i)   the dwelling becomes available for re-letting within the period of six months from expiry of the period of notice required to be given by the notice or, if a dispute in relation to the validity of the notice was referred to the Board under Part 6 for resolution, the final determination of the dispute, and

(ii)   the tenancy to which the notice related had not otherwise been validly terminated by virtue of the citation in the notice of the ground specified in paragraph 1, 2 or 3 of this Table.

The High Court has considered some aspects of the s 34 table. The third ground—intended sale of the dwelling—was considered in the case of *Hennessy v RTB* [2016] IEHC 174. The receiver of the dwelling was a notice party. The respondent, through its Tenancy Tribunal, had rejected the appellant tenant's argument that a notice of termination which did not explicitly set out the notice party's intention to dispose of the property within three months of securing possession was invalid. Baker J however agreed with the appellant. The intention must be to sell within three months and not merely a general intention to sell; for example, to place the property on the market and wait a period of time until the appropriate price is achieved.

The fourth ground was considered in the case of *Duniyva v RTB* [2017] IEHC 578. It is notable that this ground does not define family members. The respondent had found against the appellant tenant and on appeal Barrett J upheld the validity of the termination notice. In this case the landlords wished to provide the dwelling to their grandson who was attending college and would otherwise face a lengthy commute. The case serves principally to remind litigants that an appeal lies to the High Court on a point of law and cannot proceed by way of a re-hearing on the merits. Barrett J saw no reason to interfere with the Tenancy Tribunal's application of the law. However, the decision is also authority for the view that a grandchild may be considered a family member for the purpose of s 34.

Section 35 deals with interpretation of the foregoing table and supplemental matters. It should be noted that, if a tenant takes up the offer mentioned in paragraphs 4(b), 5(b) or 6(b), within a reasonable period as specified in that offer, the resulting agreement is enforceable by either party, and the occupation by the tenant under the new tenancy thus created shall be regarded together with the former tenancy as continuous occupation by that tenant under one tenancy.

Section 40 of the 2016 Act effects a substantial amendment to s 35 in regard to developer landlords. It inserts a new s 35A, which in subsection (2) thereof imposes a ban on termination of a Part 4 tenancy using the third of the s 34 grounds (intended sale) in cases where the landlord intends to dispose of their interest in ten or more dwellings in a development (as defined), each of which is the subject of such a tenancy, and disposes of them within a six month period.

However, this will not apply in cases where the landlord can prove to the satisfaction of the Board (i) that the market value is more than 20 per cent below the market value that would be obtained for the dwelling with vacant possession and (ii) that the application of subsection (2) would either (I) be unduly onerous or (II) cause undue hardship on that landlord.

The new section 35A(3)(a) requires, in such an event, that the landlord accompany the notice of termination with a statutory declaration that subsection (2) does not apply as the price is more than 20 per cent below the market value that could be obtained with vacant possession and that the application thereof would be unduly onerous or would cause undue hardship on them.

6.10.2.2   Termination by the tenant

Actual, rather than deemed, termination of a Part 4 tenancy is covered by s 36. Without prejudice to Chapter 6 (ss 48–53, rules regarding multiple occupants) and assuming that no fixed term letting is in place, a tenant may terminate the tenancy by serving on the landlord a notice of termination giving the required notice period. See **6.11.3** for a consideration of the required notice periods pursuant to ss 66–69, as amended.

In contrast to the landlord's legal position, the tenant may terminate a Part 4 tenancy prematurely for no reason. However, if termination arises by virtue of the landlord's default, s 68 sets out that in certain instances the tenant should first give written notice to the landlord to remedy the failure within a reasonable time. Should no remedy be forthcoming, the tenant will rely on s 68 as regards the appropriate notice period. It follows that the notice of termination should clearly set out the reason for the same if the tenant is relying on s 68.

Section 37 provides for a deemed termination by a tenant. Provided that a Part 4 tenancy has not been assigned or sub-let, and subject to Chapter 6, there are two instances in which this arises.

Subsection (1) states that a Part 4 tenancy is deemed to have been terminated by the tenant on vacating the dwelling if: (a) before, on or about vacating they serve a notice which does not give the required notice period; and (b) before or on that vacating the rent has fallen into arrears.

Subsection (2) goes on to provide that a Part 4 tenancy is deemed to have been terminated by the tenant in circumstances where no notice of termination has been served if rent is owed for a period of 28 days or more and where, either before or after the end of that period, the tenant has vacated the dwelling.

Section 38 deals with assignments of tenancies. The assignment by a tenant of a Part 4 tenancy with the landlord's consent to a person other than a sub-tenant shall operate to convert the Part 4 tenancy into a periodic tenancy. The protection afforded under s 38 to the assignor ceases. The clock starts anew in respect of the assignee who may avail of s 28 only after six months' continuous occupation and only then if the landlord has not served a valid notice of termination (no reason needed) having regard to the notice provisions set out in Part 5.

If the tenant assigns to a sub-tenant, while the tenancy shall not be converted into a periodic tenancy, once again the protection afforded under s 38 to the assignor shall cease. The Part 4 tenancy shall continue in being in favour of the assignee for the period that it would have continued in being had the assignment not been made. The assignee becomes the tenant, the terms of the assignor's Part 4 tenancy continues in being and the sub-tenancy merges with the Part 4 tenancy. Such a merger does not affect any liabilities of either party to the other that may arise under the terms of the original sub-tenancy.

Finally, it should be noted that s 38(4) expressly prohibits the assignment of a Part 4 tenancy with regard to part only of the dwelling which is the subject of the tenancy.

Chapter 3 concludes with s 39 and termination on the death of a tenant. The position formerly was that a tenancy continued in being following the death of a tenant until such time as it was formally terminated, usually by service of a notice by one side on the other. The new position is set out in s 39(1) which provides that, subject to stated exceptions and to Chapter 6, a Part 4 tenancy shall terminate on the death of a tenant.

The exceptions are set out in subsection (3) as amended. This provides for any one of four classes of person to elect in writing to become a tenant or tenants of the dwelling. These are:

(i)   a spouse or civil partner of the tenant,

(ii)   a person who was not a spouse of the tenant but who was the tenant's cohabitant within the meaning of s 172 of the Civil Partnership and Certain Rights and Obligations of Cohabitants Act 2010 and lived with the tenant in the dwelling for a period of at least six months ending on the date of the tenant's death,

(iii) a child, stepchild or foster child of the tenant, or a person adopted by the tenant under the Adoption Acts, 1952 to 1998, being in each case aged 18 years or more, or

(iv)   a parent of the tenant.

As regards non-private lettings, s 10 of the 2015 Act amends s 39 to deal with applications to become tenants following the death of a tenant holding under s 3(4)(a) and (b) as inserted by that Act. In that event, the applicant must be a member of the household as defined by s 20 of the Housing (Miscellaneous Provisions) Act 2009.

Chapter 6 will clearly apply where a number of persons apply for a tenancy. Where a series of deaths of tenants occurs, subsection (5) provides that the Part 4 tenancy shall not continue in being any longer than it would otherwise have done had the first of those deaths not occurred.

6.10.2.3   Termination within the first six months

A tenancy may be validly terminated for no reason within its first six months, subject to the statutory notice period. However, this applies only where the tenancy is not for a fixed term. Part 4 would not apply to the termination as the tenant has not yet acquired any statutory rights, though, of course, regard should be had to Part 5 and the minimum notice period required by s 66. In the event that either party is in default of their obligations, however, the notice period will be governed by s 67 (termination by landlord) or s 68 (termination by tenant) as appropriate. See also **6.10.4** and the repeal of s 42, thereby in effect placing a ban on landlords terminating further Part 4 tenancies in their first six months without a reason. In practical terms, the scope for termination in the first six months is very limited.

6.10.3   TERMINATION OF FIXED TERM TENANCIES

Section 26 provides that nothing in Part 4 shall derogate from any greater security of tenure that a tenant may already enjoy by reason of the tenancy concerned. The parties typically will enter into a residential tenancy agreement for a fixed term of 12 months. Where the parties agree to this or indeed a fixed term of any length, regard should be had to the situation that arises, not only after six months have elapsed, but also where the question of termination may need addressing within the first six months of the tenancy.

The right to terminate a fixed term tenancy is limited to cases where either party is in default of their statutory obligations or the provisions of the lease. Assuming that the lease does not offend against the Act, and provided the tenant/landlord is not in default of any obligation thereunder, then quite simply the other party is not entitled to serve a notice of termination during the fixed term. A fixed term agreement thus affords the tenant and landlord extra protection over and above the scope of the Act.

It should be remembered that the law of landlord and tenant is founded in contract. Adherence to the provisions of fixed term tenancies applies to tenants as much as to landlords. Tenants have no entitlement to terminate a fixed term agreement prematurely except where landlords are in breach of their obligations.

It is, however, worth noting the provisions of s 186, which applies to a fixed term tenancy despite anything to the contrary that may be contained in the letting agreement. This section provides that where a landlord refuses consent to assign or sub-let a tenancy, the tenant may terminate it immediately, using the Part 5 termination procedure.

In conclusion, extra care must be taken where there is a fixed term letting, as it will generally afford a tenant greater security of tenure than that contained in Part 4. Tenants of fixed term tenancies enjoy security of tenure *ab initio* and not merely following the expiry of six months' uninterrupted occupation. In contrast the protection afforded to tenants in Part 4 only arises after the first six months. If no fixed term is agreed a landlord can terminate for no reason during the first six months of the initial letting or at the end of the four- or six-year period thereof.

6.10.4   FURTHER PART 4 TENANCIES

Chapter 4 (ss 40–42) sets out, under s 41, the right to a further Part 4 tenancy where a tenancy continues to the end of the four-year or six-year period without service of a notice of termination by either party. This is called a 'further Part 4 tenancy' and commences on the expiry of the four- or six-year period. It shall continue in being for four years (or, after 24 December 2016, six years) provided that the landlord does not serve a notice of termination under either s 34(a) or s 42 of the Act.

Section 34(a) has been dealt with at **6.10.2.1**. Section 42 as enacted provided that, no later than six months from the commencement of a further Part 4 tenancy, the landlord may serve a notice of termination in respect thereof. However, section 41 of the 2016 Act, commenced on 17 January 2017, has repealed this provision. It follows that the only occasion on which a landlord may now terminate a further Part 4 tenancy for no reason is by virtue of the fact that the four-year or six-year term is coming to an end.

Chapter 5 (sections 43–47) provides for the rolling nature of the Part 4 tenancy. Thus s 43 explicitly states that (unless the landlord uses the Part 4 termination procedure) on the expiry of a further Part 4 tenancy, after it has been in existence for four (or six) years, another such tenancy comes into being, and so on into the future. Section 45 provides that each such tenancy will continue to be referred to as a 'further Part 4 tenancy', commencing once again on the expiry of the preceding tenancy and continuing in being for four (or six) years provided that the landlord does not serve a notice of termination under s 34(b) of the Act.

According to s 46, the terms shall be those of the preceding tenancy, be it a Part 4 tenancy or a further Part 4 tenancy. Once again, the parties may agree to vary the terms provided that they are not inconsistent with the Act.

Section 47 explicitly applies Chapter 3 (termination) to every further Part 4 tenancy as it applies to a Part 4 tenancy. It goes on to clarify certain references in that chapter accordingly and to modify the application of certain provisions thereof so as to allow for instances where the tenancy in question is a further Part 4 tenancy. The 2016 Act amends s 47 both by virtue of the repeal of s 42 of the Act and the amendment of s 28 thereof as discussed at **6.10**.

6.10.5 PART 4 AND MULTIPLE OCCUPANTS

Chapter 6 (ss 48–53) sets out the rules governing the operation of Part 4 in cases of multiple occupants. Section 48 defines 'multiple tenants' to be two or more persons who hold, whether as joint tenants, tenants-in-common or under any other form of co-ownership, and 'multiple tenant' means any one of them. Section 49 states the general principle in regard to dwellings occupied by more than one person, namely, that the provisions of Part 4 apply not only to multiple tenants but also to one or more persons lawfully in occupation as licensees of the tenant or multiple tenants as the case may be.

Section 49 in particular states that Part 4 shall apply to a dwelling notwithstanding that the continuous period of occupation by any one or more of the multiple tenants is less than six months provided that another of the multiple tenants has been in occupation for six months and the landlord has not served a valid termination notice under s 28(3). Thus security of tenure applies to any dwelling occupied by multiple tenants and their lawful licensees from the earliest date at which any multiple tenant has been in occupation for six months.

From there, s 50 provides that, once a Part 4 tenancy has come into being, each multiple tenant who occupied the dwelling immediately before the coming into being thereof shall, on clocking up the requisite six months' continuous occupation themselves, benefit from the protection of that tenancy where it still subsists. Section 53 makes clear that this shall not be read as bringing into existence a separate Part 4 tenancy in favour of any such person in respect of that dwelling.

It follows from the foregoing, firstly, that in order for each individual tenant to benefit from the protection of Part 4, he or she must accrue six months' occupation; and, secondly, the Part 4 tenancy shall conclude and a further Part 4 tenancy shall commence, in respect of all of the co-tenants, on one and the same date, namely, four (or six) years after the longest-standing co-tenant took up occupation—provided, of course, that no notice of termination has been served. Further, the protection will remain in place for the aforementioned four or six years even where the original tenants have ceased to occupy the dwelling, provided that at least one of the current occupants has clocked up the requisite six months along the way.

Section 50 further envisages an application to the landlord by a lawful occupant, as a licensee of an existing tenant or multiple tenants, during the subsistence of a Part 4 tenancy to be allowed to become a tenant. The 2015 Act disapplies s 50(7) in the case of licensees of tenants or of multiple tenants in the non-private sector. The landlord may not unreasonably refuse such an application; if the request is acceded to, an acknowledgement in writing from the landlord to the requesting party will suffice as proof of their tenant's status. The same rights, restrictions and obligations of a tenant or multiple tenant shall apply to the requester, except that Part 4 protection shall not apply until six months' continuous occupation has accrued. Thus s 50(6) explicitly ensures that the distinction between licences and tenancies shall not operate to frustrate the objectives of Part 4. Moreover, the Act expressly provides for the licensee to refer the landlord's unreasonable refusal to accede to such a request to the RTB using the Part 6 dispute resolution procedure—see s 76(4).

Under s 51, the act of any one multiple tenant cannot prejudice the rights of the other multiple tenant(s) where such an act would have the effect of either terminating the tenancy or rendering it liable to be terminated by the landlord, provided that another multiple tenant provides an explanation or information from which a landlord acting reasonably would conclude that the act was done without that person's consent.

A landlord is deemed to be acting reasonably if the other multiple tenant fails to comply with a request for such information as the landlord may reasonably require for the purpose of finding out with whose consent (if any) the act was done, and the landlord concludes, on account of such non-compliance, that the act concerned was done with the tenant's consent (s 51(2)).

If it is shown that the act was done without the consent of one or more of the multiple tenants, then only the tenant responsible, including any tenant consenting to the act, shall lose the benefit of Part 4 protection.

Any dispute regarding this falls to be dealt with by the Part 6 procedure.

It is immaterial that the multiple tenant whose continuous occupation gave rise to the Part 4 tenancy in the first place may either vacate the dwelling or die. Section 52 expressly states that neither event shall of itself deprive the other multiple tenant(s) of the benefit of that tenancy's protection.

6.10.6   PART 4—MISCELLANEOUS MATTERS

These are contained in Chapter 7 (ss 54–56).

Section 54 expressly prohibits contracting out of Part 4. This includes agreements which pre-date the operation of the Act. This is of course without prejudice to s 26, which allows for terms that afford the tenant greater security of tenure than is provided for in Part 4.

Section 55 clarified the right of long-standing residential tenants to claim a long possession equity under the Landlord and Tenant (Amendment) Act, 1980. This right applied, however, only in cases where a notice of intention to claim relief as required under the 1980 Act was served by the tenant on or before 31 August 2009. Section 41 of the 2016 Act amends s 55(2) to remove references to a termination under s 42 in view of its repeal.

Section 56 sets out the grievance procedure for a tenant who has vacated possession of a dwelling on foot of a notice of termination served under s 34(a) where the stated ground is one or more of those set out at paragraphs 3 to 6 of the s 34 table. If the thing mentioned in such paragraph(s) should not take place within either the stated period (as required under paragraph 3) or a reasonable time and no offer of re-instatement was made (paragraphs 4–6)—in short, if the landlord's stated grounds turn out to be false—then the tenant may invoke the Part 6 grievance procedure before the RTB.

The adjudicator may order the landlord to pay compensation to the tenant, or direct that the tenant be entitled to resume possession of the dwelling concerned, or both. The upper limit of an award of damages is set out in s 182 and is currently €20,000.

For the avoidance of doubt, subsection (6) points out that this section applies, even where the tenant vacated only after a Part 6 dispute regarding the validity of the termination notice was determined in favour of the landlord; and that s 56 is without prejudice to the tenant's right to put in issue, in a dispute referred to the RTB under Part 6 regarding the validity of such a notice, the bona fides of the landlord in regard to their intention to do or permit to be done the thing(s) mentioned in the notice.

Regard should also be had to s 118 and the possibility that hardship may be caused to a third party who has in the intervening period taken up residence in the dwelling. Section 118(2) sets out the criteria to be taken into consideration in arriving at such a determination. These expressly include the length of that person's possession of the dwelling, any involvement they may have had in the original tenant's being deprived of possession thereof, and any knowledge they may have had, prior to taking such possession, of the existence of a dispute concerning the original tenant's right to possession.

6.11 Termination—Notice Periods and Other Procedural Requirements—Part 5

Part 5 of the Act is subdivided into five chapters comprising ss 57–74 inclusive. It complements the provisions of Part 4 and provides for termination to take place by way of notice in all cases (other than for tenancies deemed to have been terminated by a tenant *per* s 37; see **6.10.2.2**). This means that a notice must be served even in cases where the tenancy is being terminated in circumstances where no ground for doing so need be cited. This part of the Act contains statutory periods that now apply to the termination of residential tenancies, based on the duration of the tenancy in question.

The notice periods are set out in two tables, one for landlords and one for tenants. Landlords must give at least as much notice as tenants and, in the case of tenancies of three years and above, more so. This part of the Act further goes on to provide notice periods applicable to terminations arising where either the landlord or tenant is in default of their statutory obligations. It also provides for the parties to agree to a lesser period in certain circumstances.

Subject to such agreement, 28 days is the minimum notice period in respect of the termination of the tenancy of a dwelling other than a tenancy which is being terminated by reason of the default of one of the parties in regard to their statutory obligations. A maximum notice period of 28 days is required where the tenancy is terminated on a default basis.

6.11.1 SCOPE AND INTERPRETATION

Section 57 makes clear that Part 5 applies to the termination of all tenancies of dwellings—even those which are excluded from the operation of Part 4 *per* s 25. By the same token s 57(b) states that the procedural requirements set out under Part 5 for the valid termination of a tenancy are in addition to the requirements of Part 4 with regard to the termination of a Part 4 tenancy or of a further Part 4 tenancy. This gave rise to a procedural difficulty which Laffoy J identified in the case of *Canty v Private Residential Tenancies Board* [2007] IEHC 243 with regard to the use of s 67 in the case of termination by a landlord of a Part 4 tenancy where the matter complained of is non-payment of rent. The 2015 Act addressed this problem and clarified the necessary procedure for such terminations.

Section 58 provides that termination by either party must be done according to the procedures laid down in Part 5 only. This includes tenancies which, *per* s 26, contain terms more beneficial to the tenant than envisaged by the Act.

Moreover, s 59 expressly excludes from application any pre-existing rule of law or any enactment in relation to termination of the tenancy of a dwelling. This is subject to s 60, which provides that any lease or tenancy agreement containing a greater notice period than those set out in the tables will not be affected, so that the parties must proceed according to that agreement. This itself is subject to s 65(4), which applies a maximum notice period of 70 days where the duration of the tenancy in question is less than six months.

Section 61 reinforces the traditional position whereby so many clear days' notice must be given. It provides that any reference in Part 5 to a notice period in a termination notice is a reference to such a period commencing on the day after service of the notice. For provisions regarding service, see s 6 of the Act, which is dealt with at **6.5**. Further, any reference in Part 5 to the duration of a tenancy is a reference to the period beginning on the day the tenancy came into existence (or, if later, 1 September 2004) and ending on the date of service of the termination notice in question.

6.11.2 CONTENTS OF THE TERMINATION NOTICE

Chapter 2 (ss 62–64, as amended) deals with the new statutory requirements in regard to the contents of the notice. The Act does not provide any prescribed form as such. However, this may be introduced by regulations at any future time. In the meantime, further guidance on the essential contents of the notice can be found on the RTB's website: www.rtb.ie.

Section 62 sets out the essential contents. To be valid the notice must:

(a) *be in writing,*

(b) *be signed by the landlord or his or her authorised agent or, as appropriate, the tenant,*

(c) *specify the date of service of it,*

(d) *be in such form (if any) as may be prescribed,*

(e) *if the duration of the tenancy is a period of more than six months or the tenancy is a further Part 4 tenancy, state (where the termination is by the landlord) the reason for the termination,*

(f) *specify the termination date, that is to say, the day (stating the month and year in which it falls)—*

  (i) *on which the tenancy will terminate, and*

  (ii) *on or before which (in the case of a termination by the landlord) the tenant must vacate possession of the dwelling concerned, (and indicating that the tenant has the whole of the 24 hours of the termination date to vacate possession),*

  and

(g) *state that any issue as to the validity of the notice or the right of the landlord or tenant, as appropriate, to serve it must be referred to the Board under Part 6 within 28 days from the date of receipt of it.*

Note also s 81(3), which applies where the landlord of a head tenancy, in serving a notice of termination, requires the head tenant to terminate any sub-tenancy arising therefrom, and the head tenant intends to refer a dispute to the RTB for resolution regarding the validity of the notice. In such circumstances the head tenant, when serving the notice of termination on the sub-tenant, must require the sub-tenant, within a period of ten days' receipt of the notice, to inform the head tenant whether they, too, intend to refer a dispute regarding the validity of the notice to the RTB for resolution. This requirement must be stated in the notice that is served on the sub-tenant.

Section 63 provides that, for the purposes of s 62(1)(f), the day to be specified in the notice is the last day of either the period of notice required to be given under s 66 or such longer period as the party chooses, subject once again to s 65(4) and the rule that no more than 70 days' notice shall be given in respect of a tenancy the duration of which is less than six months.

Section 64 clarifies the question that may arise where a notice contains a reference to the date of its service as required by s 62(1)(c). The date specified in the notice will not be valid if any of the steps involved in the service thereof remains untaken on the said date.

In common with questions relating to withheld deposits and non-payment of rent, many complaints referred to the Board since the initiation of its dispute resolution procedure relate to the validity or otherwise of termination notices. Section 30 of the 2015 Act amends s 64 by introducing a 'slip' rule. It provides that, on the hearing of a complaint in respect of a notice of termination, the adjudicator or the Tenancy Tribunal may decide that a slip or omission contained in the notice, or which occurred in the service thereof, shall not of itself render the notice invalid if they are satisfied that (a) the slip or omission concerned does not materially prejudice the notice and (b) it is otherwise in compliance with the statutory requirements.

6.11.3 PERIOD OF NOTICE TO BE GIVEN

Chapter 3 (ss 65–69) sets out in detail the notice periods that apply to the parties based on the duration of the tenancy in question.

Section 65 clarifies s 62(1)(f) and states that that the period of notice itself need not be specified in the notice of termination. Either party may choose to give a greater notice period than is required under s 66, subject to the s 65(4) rule (see **6.11.2**).

Section 66 deals with terminations other than those provided for in ss 67 (tenant in default) and 68 (landlord in default). All three sections are subject to s 69, which provides that either party may agree to a lesser period of notice. However, it should be noted that this choice arises only at the time that the other party indicates that they are terminating the tenancy. As previously stated, there is no contracting out of the Act. Consequently, there is no question of providing for a lesser notice period at the time of entering into the lease or letting agreement.

It should be remembered that the tenancy shall terminate only on the completion of the notice period, not on the date that the notice is served. The s 66 tables should be consulted accordingly. Thus where one party serves notice after a period of, say, 11 months and two weeks, it is clear that the true length of the tenancy shall be between one year and two years, and not less than one year.

TABLE 3 Termination by Landlord

Duration of Tenancy (1)	Notice Period (2)
Less than six months	28 days
Six or more months but less than one year	35 days
One year or more but less than two years	42 days
Two years or more but less than three years	56 days
Three years or more but less than four years	84 days
Four years or more but less than five years	112 days
Five years or more but less than six years	140 days
Six years or more but less than seven years	168 days
Seven years or more but less than eight years	196 days
Eight or more years	224 days

TABLE 4 Termination by Tenant

Duration of Tenancy (1)	Notice Period (2)
Less than six months	28 days
Six or more months but less than one year	35 days
One year or more but less than two years	42 days
Two years or more but less than three years	56 days
Three years or more but less than four years	56 days
Four years or more but less than five years	84 days
Five years or more but less than six years	84 days
Six years or more but less than seven years	84 days
Seven years or more but less than eight years	84 days
Eight or more years	112 days

The notice periods have been significantly amended by virtue of s 31 of the 2015 Act. As originally enacted, the tables involved a sliding scale of notice requirements up to the fifth year of the tenancy and beyond. The old maximum notice to be given by landlords was 112 days and, by tenants, 56 days. Since December 2015 the notice periods now stretch out to the ninth year of the tenancy and beyond. For landlords, the maximum is now 224 days, or 32 weeks; for tenants, it is 112 days, being 16 weeks. The statutory minimum of 28 days continues to apply, to both parties, at the short end of the letting.

Under s 67, where the landlord terminates by reason of the tenant being in default of their statutory obligations, the notice period shall depend on the nature of the default complained of. In the case of anti-social behaviour falling within s 17(1)(a) or (b)—which is set out at **6.6.2.1**—or behaviour that is threatening to the fabric of the dwelling or of the property containing it, the period is seven days. For any other reason (except non-payment of rent), the period is 28 days. This period also applies to termination by reason of non-payment of rent, subject to the condition that the landlord must first notify the tenant in writing that an amount of rent is overdue. The termination notice may then be served once 14 days elapse from the date of service of the written notification if the amount remains unpaid. Section 67 was amended by s 32 of the 2015 Act to address the *Canty* problem. See **6.11.1**.

Under s 68, where the tenant terminates by reason of the landlord being in default of their statutory obligations, again the notice period shall depend on the nature of the default complained of. In the case of behaviour by the landlord that poses an imminent danger of death or serious injury or imminent danger to the fabric of the dwelling or of the property containing it, the period is seven days. In all other cases, the period is 28 days. This is subject to the condition that the tenant must first notify the landlord in writing of a failure to comply with their obligations. The termination notice may then be served in the event that the landlord does not remedy the failure within a reasonable time.

Subsection (4) defines 'remedy the failure' to mean the following:

(b) *in the case of a failure that does not result in financial loss or damage to the tenant or his or her property, to desist from the conduct that constitutes the failure, or if the failure consists of an omission to comply with an obligation, comply with that obligation, and*

(c)   *in the case of a failure that does result in financial loss or damage to the tenant or his or her property—*

    (i)   *to pay adequate compensation to the tenant or repair the damage fully, and*

    (ii) *unless the failure is not of a continuing nature, to desist from the conduct that constitutes the failure or comply with the obligation concerned, as the case may be.*

An overview of all the termination periods provided for in ss 66, 67 and 68 is set out at the end of this chapter at **6.11.8**.

6.11.4   ADDITIONAL REQUIREMENTS AND PROCEDURES WHERE THE TENANCY IS SUB-LET

Chapter 4 (ss 70–72) sets out the procedure to be followed in the event of a sub-tenancy and addresses contentious and non-contentious situations separately.

Section 70 provides that, where a landlord intends to terminate a head tenancy, the notice of termination in respect thereof must (in addition to complying with the requirements of s 62) state whether the landlord requires the head tenant to terminate the sub-tenancy. In such an event a copy of this notice 'must be served' on the sub-tenant. The 2004 Act employed passive terminology and accordingly it was not clear which party should arrange for service of such notice on the sub-tenant. Section 42 of the 2015 Act clarifies the matter: it is the landlord who should serve the sub-tenant in such an event.

Section 71 deals with cases where s 70 applies: the notice contains a requirement that the sub-tenancy be terminated and no dispute is referred to the RTB under Part 6. In such cases the head tenant must, within 28 days of receipt of the s 70 notice, serve a notice of termination in respect of the sub-tenancy on the sub-tenant.

Section 72 deals with procedures not arising under s 71. Under s 72(1), if s 70 applies, the s 70 notice does not require the termination of the sub-tenancy, and no dispute in respect of the termination of the head tenancy is referred under Part 6 to the RTB, the head tenant must, within 28 days of receipt of the s 70 notice, notify the sub-tenant of its contents. Subsection (2) stipulates that, where s 70 applies, the s 70 notice does not require the termination of the sub-tenancy, and a dispute in respect of the termination of the head tenancy is referred under Part 6 to the RTB, the head tenant must, within 28 days of receipt of the s 70 notice, notify the sub-tenant of its contents and of the fact that the dispute has been referred to the board. Where such referral results in a determination order by the board, the head tenant must notify the sub-tenant of the particulars of the order within 14 days of receipt thereof.

In circumstances where a head tenant does not refer a dispute to the RTB with regard to the notice of termination served in respect of the head tenancy, s 78(2) expressly sets out the right of the sub-tenant to do so; and s 78(3) notes the standing of the sub-tenant to do so even in cases where the head tenant may have done anything that estops them (ie the head tenant) from taking any such issue with the landlord. However, regard should be had to s 81, which limits this right in certain cases—see **6.11.6**.

Section 116 (Part 6 and dispute resolution procedures) deals with cases where the landlord, in serving the notice of termination of a head tenancy, requires the head tenant to terminate the sub-tenancy. If such a matter goes to the Tenancy Tribunal or an adjudicator, and their determination directs the head tenant to quit the dwelling by a specified date, then the determination may also include a direction requiring the sub-tenant to quit the dwelling by a specified date.

6.11.5   MISCELLANEOUS MATTERS

Chapter 5 comprises ss 73–74 inclusive. Section 73 provides that, where a tenancy is being terminated by all of the multiple tenants of a dwelling, the signature of one tenant will suffice for the purposes of compliance with s 62(1)(b) (signature of the termination notice) provided that the notice states that it is signed by that person on behalf of himself or herself and the other tenant(s), and that the other tenant(s) be named in that notice.

Section 74 makes it an offence knowingly to serve an invalid notice, and then to act in reliance on this notice that either affects adversely, or is calculated to affect adversely, the person on whom it is served. Such an act shall include making a statement, whether in writing or otherwise. An act is done in reliance on the notice either if its doing is preceded or accompanied by a statement by the server (whether in writing or otherwise) that it is being done, or will be done, in reliance on the notice, or where in all the circumstances it is reasonable to infer that it is done in reliance on the notice.

6.11.6   TIME LIMIT FOR DISPUTING A NOTICE OF TERMINATION

Section 80 states that a dispute relating to the validity of a notice of termination may not be referred to the RTB for resolution at any time after the period of 28 days has elapsed from the date of receipt thereof.

It is important also to note the separate time limits imposed on head tenants and sub-tenants by virtue of s 81 where (a) there is a sub-tenancy, (b) the landlord serves a notice of termination on the head tenant, (c) the notice expressly requires the head tenant to terminate the sub-tenancy and (d) the head tenant intends to refer a dispute to the RTB. In such circumstances, while the 28-day limit applies, it should also be noted that the head tenant must wait for at least 15 days following service of the notice of termination of the sub-tenancy before referring a dispute to the board. This notice should require the sub-tenant to notify the tenant, within ten days of receipt thereof, whether or not they (the sub-tenant) intend to refer any dispute to the RTB. As discussed at **6.11.4**, s 70(3) as amended now requires landlords to ensure service of the notice terminating the sub-tenancy on the sub-tenant; likewise the sub-tenant should waste little time in clarifying their position in correspondence with the head tenant. Indeed s 81 goes on to provide that if either the head tenant or the sub-tenant should fail to comply with the requirements of subsection (2), such party may not refer a dispute to the RTB.

6.11.7   PROHIBITIONS UNDER SECTION 184

Section 184 renders void any provision of a letting agreement from which it could reasonably be inferred that the sole or main purpose of that clause is to facilitate one of the parties being at all times in a position to terminate the tenancy on the grounds of non-compliance therewith by the other party. Such a provision would not reasonably be regarded as conferring any practical benefit on the putative terminating party in respect of their interest in the dwelling, compliance therewith is likely to be impractical, and/or it is framed in arbitrary terms.

Section 184 also renders void any tenancy or sub-tenancy where in the circumstances it may reasonably be inferred that it is not a bona fide arm's-length transaction but one created solely or mainly for the purpose of facilitating the termination through collusion of the sub-tenancy.

6.11.8 OVERVIEW OF TERMINATION PERIODS

Termination periods are summarised in Table 5.

TABLE 5 Termination Periods

Duration of tenancy	Notice by landlord	Notice by tenant	Reason
Less than six months	28 days	28 days	(s 66) None required by either party (only where the tenancy is for no fixed term exceeding six months); but note that a landlord can no longer terminate for no reason during the first six months of a further Part 4 tenancy
Six months or more but less than one year	35 days	35 days	(s 66) None required by tenant (s 36); Landlord must have grounds for termination (ss 33 and 34(a))
One year or more but less than two years	42 days	42 days	(s 66) None required by tenant (s 36); Landlord must have grounds for termination (ss 33 and 34(a))
Two years or more but less than three years	56 days	56 days	(s 66) None required by tenant (s 36); Landlord must have grounds for termination (ss 33 and 34(a))
Three years or more but less than four years	84 days	56 days	(s 66) None required by tenant (s 36); Landlord must have grounds for termination (ss 33 and 34(a), as amended)
Four years or more but less than five years	112 days	84 days	(s 66) None required by tenant (s 36), None required by landlord if terminating a Part 4 tenancy or a further Part 4 tenancy but notice must expire on or after end thereof (s 34(b))
Five years or more but less than six years	140 days	84 days	(s 66) None required by tenant (s 36); Landlord must have grounds for termination (ss 33 and 34(a), as amended)
Six years or more but less than seven years	168 days	84 days	(s 66) None required by tenant (s 36); None required by landlord if terminating a Part 4 tenancy of six years' duration (ie not before December 2022) but notice must expire on or after end of Part 4 tenancy (s 34(b))
Seven years or more but less than eight years	196 days	84 days	(s 66) None required by tenant (s 36); Landlord must have grounds for termination (ss 33 and 34(a), as amended)
Eight or more years	224 days	112 days	(s 66) None required by tenant (s 36); None required by landlord if terminating a Part 4 tenancy or a further Part 4 tenancy but notice must expire on or after end thereof (s 34(b))

Regardless of duration of tenancy		28 days	Termination by tenant. Landlord in default of obligations has been notified in writing and does not remedy within a reasonable time (s 68)
Regardless of duration of tenancy		7 days	Termination by tenant. Behaviour of landlord poses imminent danger of death or serious injury or imminent danger to the fabric of the dwelling or the property (s 68)
Regardless of duration of tenancy	28 days		Termination by landlord. Tenant in default of obligations. If failure to pay rent tenant must be notified in writing and 14 days must elapse from receipt of notice (s 67)
Regardless of duration of tenancy	7 days		Termination by landlord. Tenant behaves in a way that is anti-social or threatening to the fabric of the dwelling or the property (s 67)

CHAPTER 7

RESIDENTIAL TENANCIES BOARD

7.1   Introduction

As already noted at **chapter 6,** the Residential Tenancies Act 2004 ('the 2004 Act') governs the operation of residential tenancies. Its provisions included the establishment of a Private Residential Tenancies Board (PRTB) with three main areas of activity: the operation of a national registration system for all private residential tenancies; the operation of a dispute resolution service; and the provision of information, the carrying out of research and the provision of policy advice regarding the private rented sector.

Chapter 6 covers security of tenure and the rights and obligations of both parties under the Act and this chapter examines the functions of the PRTB now renamed the Residential Tenancy Board (RTB) under the Residential Tenancies (Amendment) Act 2015 (the '2015 Act').

To quote from the RTB website: 'The central role of the RTB is to support the rental housing market and to resolve cheaply and speedily disputes between landlords and tenants affording protection to both parties without having to resort to the courts'.

By 2011 it had become clear the PRTB had failed to live up to initial expectations. With a view to streamlining and simplifying the 2004 Act, the 2015 Act and the Planning and Development (Housing) and Residential Tenancies Act 2016 (the '2016 Act') were passed. They also reflected the changes necessary to deal with short-term pressures in the private rental market.

7.2   Establishment and Composition of the RTB

Part 8 (ss 149–181) of the 2004 Act deals with the establishment and principal functions of the RTB. The board came into existence as a statutory body on 1 September 2004, which was the establishment day for the purposes of s 149 of the 2004 Act. The Minister for the Environment, Heritage and Local Government (now the Minister for Housing, Planning, Community and Local Government) is the Minister referred to in the Act.

Sections 153–155 govern the composition of the RTB. Originally there was to be a minimum of nine and a maximum of 15 members. The 2015 Act reduced the maximum number of board members from 15 to 12. Under s 153(4), the Minister is required, so far as is practicable, to ensure an equitable gender balance is achieved. Under s 160 of the 2004 Act there is a chief officer of the RTB who is referred to as the 'Director'.

7.3   Functions of the RTB

These are set out at s 151 of the 2004 Act (as subsequently amended) and are as follows:

(a)   The resolution of disputes between tenants and landlords in accordance with the provisions of Part 6 of the 2004 Act.

(b)   The registration of particulars in respect of tenancies in accordance with the provisions of Part 7.

(c)   The provision to the Minister of advice concerning policy in relation to the private rented sector.

(d)   The development and publication of guidelines for good practice by those involved in the private rented sector.

(e)   The collection and provision of information relating to the private rented sector, including information concerning prevailing rent levels.

(f)   Where the board considers it appropriate, the conducting of research into the private rented sector and monitoring the operation of various aspects of the sector or arranging for such research and monitoring to be done.

(g)   The review of the operation of the 2004 Act (and in particular Part 3) and any related enactments and the making of recommendations to the Minister for the amendment of the 2004 Act or those enactments.

(h)   The performance of any additional functions conferred on the RTB under subsection (3).

Section 157 provides that the RTB may establish committees to assist it in any of its functions and must set up a Dispute Resolution Committee (DRC). Under the 2015 Act the DRC shall consist of not more than 45 members, which shall include the chairperson of the DRC including at least four board members who have at least three years of their term of membership left to run at the time of appointment to the DRC. From that committee three people will be selected to form Tenancy Tribunals for the purpose of holding hearings into disputes that are at the second stage of the dispute resolution process.

The Residential Tenancies (Amendment) Act 2009 validated the appointment of certain members of the DRC and each Tenancy Tribunal constituted under s 102 of the 2004 Act and provided that any act done by the DRC or a Tenancy Tribunal was deemed to have been valid and effectual for all purposes. This was to regularise the situation discovered in December 2008 that the appointment of board members to the DRC in December 2007 was technically invalid due to non-compliance with s 159(3), hence the 2009 Act was necessary to validate any decisions or determinations made.

Of the functions of the RTB set out above, the most important are (i) the resolution of disputes, (ii) the registration of tenancies and (iii) the provision of a data bank concerning prevailing rent levels.

7.3.1   RESOLUTION OF DISPUTES

The 2004 Act envisaged the principal function of the RTB was the resolution of all disputes to which the 2004 Act applied and this function was intended to replace that previously exercised by the courts in most disputes in the private rented sector (subject to the jurisdictional limits set down in s 182(1)). The RTB commenced its dispute resolution function on 6 December 2004 when it established the DRC but serious practical problems began to emerge as the dispute resolution procedures were multi-layered and in many cases did not facilitate timely outcomes. Even after a dispute had been determined by the RTB there was no guarantee of compliance and it might be necessary to bring Court proceedings to enforce the RTB determination order. This added further cost.

The RTB website publishes every quarter its decisions on dispute resolution. About two-thirds of disputes are referred by tenants. The majority of disputes referred by tenants include deposit retention, illegal evictions and invalid notices of termination. Rent arrears were the most frequent category referred by landlords to the RTB, followed by anti-social behaviour cases.

Statistics published for 2016 by the RTB show 31 per cent of disputes related to rent arrears and overholding, 43 per cent of termination notices were ruled invalid, there was a full or partial deposit refund in 68 per cent of cases and a record 130,000 calls (over 520 a day), 67 per cent of which were from a landlord and 20 per cent from a tenant.

Parties who can refer a dispute to the RTB include the following:

(a)   the parties to an existing or terminated tenancy—s 76.

(b)   in certain circumstances, licensees and sub-tenants. A licensee may complain that a landlord has unreasonably refused to allow him/her to become a tenant of the dwelling. A sub-tenant, by having complied with the requirements of s 81, may refer a dispute regarding notice of termination served in respect of the head tenancy regardless of whether or not the dispute is also referred by the head tenant.

(c)   the personal representative of the deceased landlord or tenant in respect of a claim to recover rent—s 75(4)(b). The personal representative may also refer a dispute in relation to a breach of some other tenancy obligation if the matter concerned were a cause of action that would have survived for the benefit of, or against, the estate of the landlord or the tenant, as the case may be.

(d)   a third party affected by a landlord's failure to enforce the obligations of a tenancy, but only if the conditions specified in s 77(2) have been satisfied.

(e)   a landlord when a person claims entitlement to the rights of a tenant, through a person who is or was a tenant—s 76.

A dispute may be referred to the RTB for the purpose of mediation, adjudication or a tribunal hearing. Disputes that are not resolved either by mediation or adjudication will be referred to a Tenancy Tribunal established by the RTB under s 102(1). A dispute may be referred directly by the board to a Tenancy Tribunal under s 94 without mediation or adjudication taking place in relation to it. If mediation takes place and is unsuccessful then the board must, at the request of either or both parties, refer the dispute to a Tenancy Tribunal (s 96(6)). One or more of the parties may appeal to the Tribunal against the determination of an adjudicator under s 100.

A dispute includes:

(a)   a disagreement between the parties; and

(b)   a complaint referred to in s 56(2); this involves:

(i)   a complaint that a landlord has abused the s 34 termination procedure;

(ii)   a complaint that a landlord has unreasonably refused to allow a licensee to become a tenant of the dwelling (s 76(4));

(iii)   a complaint by a neighbour regarding tenant behaviour (s 77);

(iv)   a complaint by a landlord that he or she has suffered loss or damage as a result of the tenant overholding under a fixed term tenancy (s 195(4)); and

(v)   a complaint by a sub-tenant that he or she has been unjustly deprived of possession of a dwelling by the head tenant (para 8(2) of the Schedule).

Disagreement will usually revolve around the compliance or otherwise of either landlord or tenant with their respective obligations under the tenancy, or whether or not the tenancy has been validly terminated. Section 75(3) includes a claim by the landlord for arrears of rent.

7.3.1.1 Time limits

The 2004 Act provides a time limit for referring particular types of dispute to the RTB. These time limits may be extended in certain circumstances if the applicant can show good grounds for the extension. Either the applicant or any other party to the dispute can appeal to the Circuit Court against a decision of the board to agree to or refuse an extension of time (s 88).

A dispute about a proposed rent increase must be referred to the RTB before the rent increase is due to take effect, or within 28 days of the tenant receiving a notice proposing the new rent, whichever is the later—s 22(3).

A dispute as to the amount of any rent that a former tenant agreed to or paid under a terminated tenancy must be referred by him/her to the RTB within 28 days of the termination of the tenancy—s 76(2).

A dispute relating to the validity of a Notice of Termination must be referred to the RTB within 28 days or receipt of that notice—s 80.

A dispute referred to the RTB may be withdrawn by the referring parties. Written notices must be served on the board and/or written notice given to the other parties involved, ie mediators/adjudicators/Tenancy Tribunal. Costs and expenses may be awarded against the party withdrawing the matter if the other party objects to the withdrawal—s 82.

Section 83 prohibits the RTB from dealing with any dispute until the appropriate referral fee has been paid and, if the dispute has been referred by the landlord, the tenancy has been registered in accordance with Part 7. The fee is €100 (€85 online) to appeal an adjudicator's or mediator's decision and refer a dispute to a Tenancy Tribunal.

7.3.1.2 Right of refusal

Section 84 gives the right to the RTB not to deal with certain references. These include the following:

(a) The dispute concerns a dwelling to which the 2004 Act does not apply.

(b) The dispute does not come within the board's jurisdiction for any other reason.

(c) The matter referred is vexatious or frivolous.

(d) The matter referred will be statute barred in the context of court proceedings.

The RTB must notify the referring party, who is then entitled to make a submission to the board as to why it should deal with the matter. If the board feels that its opinion was well founded and refuses to deal with the dispute, then either party to the dispute may appeal that decision to the Circuit Court.

There are similar provisions regarding the right of an adjudicator or the Tenancy Tribunal to refuse to deal with a particular reference—s 85.

The RTB will not deal with a dispute referred to it by a landlord in relation to a tenancy that is not registered under Part 7 of the Act. Should the landlord register within a reasonable time after the dispute has been referred to the RTB, the RTB is entitled to deal with it—s 83. As it is the landlord's responsibility to register the tenancy with the board a tenant is still entitled to refer a dispute to the RTB notwithstanding that the tenancy is unregistered. The party who initiates the dispute resolution procedure pays the fee prescribed by the rules made by the RTB.

It should be noted that if the tenancy is exempt from registration under the 2004 Act then the tenant cannot avail of the dispute resolution service. If a tenant is unsure whether their tenancy falls within the scope of the 2004 Act or not they can email the RTB for assistance. If the tenancy is exempt from registration, tenants can consider pursuing their case through the Small Claims Court.

7.3.1.3 Dispute procedure

Section 109 of the 2004 Act governs the dispute resolution procedure. The rules are available on its website and disputes referred to the RTB will be processed in accordance with it. There is no fee for mediation and there is a fee of €25 (€15 if submitted online) for adjudication. The referral of the dispute and the payments of the relevant fee must be made within the relevant time limits set out in the 2004 Act (as amended).

The initial steps the board may take after a dispute is referred to it are to see if the parties can resolve the matter between them and, if that fails, the board requests each of the parties to state whether they consent to the dispute being the subject of mediation. If both parties agree, the RTB appoints a person from its panel of mediators. If any of the parties either fail to respond or state that they do not consent to mediation the board arranges for the matter to be dealt with by adjudication, again by a person appointed from its panel of adjudicators.

The RTB operates a two-stage dispute resolution system. Stage one consists of either mediation or adjudication, both of which are confidential to the parties. Stage two is a public hearing by a Tenancy Tribunal if the matter is not resolved at stage one. The board refers some cases directly to stage two.

7.3.1.4 Mediation

This is the simplest and most efficient option. The aim of mediation is to have the dispute resolved by agreement between the parties themselves in a non-adversarial way, with the assistance and encouragement of a mediator, so that no further recourse to the procedures under Part 6 of the 2004 Act is required. Both parties must consent to the mediation process. The mediator is appointed from the panel of mediators set up by the RTB and his/her function is to enquire fully into each relevant aspect of the dispute concerned, provide to, and receive from, each party such information as is appropriate and generally make suggestions to each party and take such actions as he/she considers appropriate with a view to resolving the dispute. On the successful conclusion of mediation, a Determination Order is made by the board under s 121 of the 2004 Act.

Once mediation is completed, the mediator prepares a report. This is confidential to the parties and the Chief Officer of the RTB ('the Director'). The Director gives a summary of the issues agreed or, if applicable, a statement if the matter has not been resolved by mediation to the board. The board serves a notice on the parties asking them to confirm the agreement within 21 days—s 96. This has now been reduced to ten days by the 2015 Act. Unless notified within that period that the agreement no longer exists, the RTB must make a Determination Order within a further seven days. This contains the terms of the agreement reached by the parties. If the mediation has been unsuccessful or the agreement no longer exists, then the board at the request of either or both parties refers the dispute to the Tribunal for determination.

As the information leaflet issued by the RTB on its Dispute Resolution Service states, 'the mediation process is supportive and non-confrontational. It assists the parties to explore each other's respective positions and reach a resolution of the dispute to which both parties are agreed. Experience shows that a resolution or agreement freely reached by the parties is often preferable to a third-party decision being imposed.'

The 2015 Act revised the mediation rules:

(a) The board may not charge a fee for mediation services.

(b) Section 96 of the 2004 Act has been amended and sets out the procedures to be followed by the board following the report of the mediator.

(c) The cooling-off period is reduced for the purposes of s 97(4)(b) from 21 days to 10 days.

The RTB now offers telephone mediation as a convenient way to address disputes quickly and effectively. Telephone mediation is done at a time convenient to each party with whom the mediator will work separately from the other party to reach a mutually acceptable resolution, usually over a short period of time. If a satisfactory resolution cannot be reached either party may appeal to a Tenancy Tribunal. In 2015 the average processing time for telephone mediation was seven and a half weeks, compared to 14 weeks for adjudication. The service is free.

7.3.1.5   Adjudication

Subsections (2) to (7) of s 97 of the 2004 Act set out how an adjudication shall be conducted. An adjudication differs from mediation in that while an adjudicator may adopt an agreement reached by the parties in resolving the dispute, he/she is free to reach a decision himself/herself in the matter. This differs from mediation where it is the parties themselves who do or do not resolve the dispute while the mediator merely facilitates the process. If the adjudicator does adopt a decision reached by the parties themselves in the course of the adjudication then the adjudicator must allow a 21-day 'cooling off' period. Since 1 March 2016 this is now reduced to ten days. The adjudicator must also inform the parties that unless either party indicates within the time allowed that they no longer accept that decision, it will bind the parties once a Determination Order is made by the RTB and thereafter there will be no appeal to a Tenancy Tribunal. If neither party indicates that they have changed their mind, then their decision shall be binding. If, on the other hand, either or both parties indicate that they no longer accept that decision, then the adjudicator will proceed to reach a decision himself/herself in the matter.

On conclusion of the adjudication, the adjudicator prepares a report that includes a summary of the matters agreed by the parties, the adjudicator's determination and the reasons for it. This report is sent to the RTB, which then serves a copy of it on the parties together with a statement advising them that the adjudicator's decision will be the subject of a Determination Order unless a non-binding adjudication decision is appealed to the Tenancy Tribunal within 21 days (now ten working days under the 2015 Act) and that appeal is not subsequently abandoned. The adjudicator may award damages (max currently €20,000) and other costs and expenses and up to two years' arrears of rent (max currently €60,000).

Adjudication is a very different procedure from mediation. Mediation seeks a common ground on which the parties can agree to resolve the issues between them. In adjudication the process involves each party presenting their case and arguing that their particular viewpoint should be accepted over the other parties. In an adjudication there is a form of cross-examination but the process is more controlled than it might be in court. There are no rules of procedure and the adjudicator controls the process of giving or taking evidence. Legal separation is a matter for the adjudicator. In practical terms, the reality is often that the mediation process will fail because the parties have reached an impasse or their relationship has deteriorated to such an extent that mediation would not be a viable course of action.

7.3.1.6   Tenancy Tribunal

This is covered by ss 102 and 103 of the 2004 Act. Each tribunal will consist of three persons, one of whom is chairperson, who have relevant professional knowledge and experience and the tribunal holds its hearings in public. There is a majority rule on all matters. The three members are drawn from the board's DRC.

The tribunal deals with disputes:

(a)   that have been referred to it directly by the RTB without mediation or adjudication having taken place; or

(b)   where mediation has not resulted in the matter being resolved; or

(c)   where the dispute is the subject of an appeal from a determination of an adjudicator.

Parties to the dispute must be given at least 21 days' notice of one or more hearings to be held by the Tribunal. The only exception is where both parties agree to a shorter notice period or the dispute concerns alleged behaviour by the landlord or the tenant that poses an imminent danger of death or serious injury or imminent danger to the fabric of the dwelling concerned or the property containing that dwelling—s 104(5).

Each party is entitled to be heard, to be represented and to present evidence and witnesses at the hearing—s 104(6). It should be noted that the costs of witnesses or professional representation will not generally be awarded by the Tribunal. The Tribunal may require evidence to be given on oath, may summon and cross-examine witnesses and may require relevant documentation to be produced. It has similar features to High Court proceedings and is public. On completion of its hearing the Tribunal makes its determination in relation to the dispute and it notifies the board accordingly. There is an appeal to the High Court on a point of law only within 21 days after issue of the determination order.

The RTB website indicates that the procedures of the Tribunal are published in Latvian, Polish, Mandarin, Slovak, Russian and Lithuanian. This reflects the multi-cultural society Ireland has become since the Celtic Tiger years.

The Reports of the Tenancy Tribunal are published on the RTB website and provide an indication of the RTB's approach to particular categories of dispute.

Using an online account and the Tenancy Management System a tenant, landlord or involved parties can lodge an online dispute application or an appeal, and view disputes submitted online by that user or request access to online disputes.

7.3.1.7   Determination Orders

Section 121 of the 2004 Act obliges the RTB to make a Determination Order upon receipt of a report from a mediator under s 95(4), an adjudicator under s 99, a Tribunal under s 108 or a direction given by an adjudicator or the Tribunal under s 82(5) or s 117. It is a written record of every mediation agreement, adjudication determination, Tribunal determination or direction issued to the parties concerned and it simply states the conclusions reached. Determination Orders are brief and relatively uninformative documents often running to no more than two or three paragraphs. As no information by way of background or otherwise is given in these Orders it is not possible to use them as precedents. This makes it difficult to advise a client of the likely outcome of his particular case or to give any guidance on possible amounts of compensation that could be awarded. The Orders do, however, indicate the range of complaints that come before the RTB and, the most common ones relate to deposit retention, invalid notice of termination, rent arrears and breach of landlord's obligations.

Determination Orders issued by the RTB are published on a quarterly basis and are available at www.rtb.ie/dispute-resolution/prtb-dispute-outcomes.

RESIDENTIAL TENANCIES BOARD

A Determination Order embodying the terms of an agreement in a mediator's report or the determination of an adjudicator is binding when issued—s 123(1) and (2). A Determination Order resulting from a Tribunal determination may be appealed to the High Court within 21 days of the Order being issued on a point of law only—s 123(3). Failure to comply with a Determination Order is an offence and the RTB or the party affected by the non-compliance of the Order may apply to the Court for an Order. Initially under the 2004 Act such an application had to be made to the Circuit Court but under s 57 of the 2015 Amendment Act this has now been changed to the District Court (SI 37 of 2018).

Civil proceedings to enforce a Determination Order predominantly relate to rent arrears, deposit retention or vacant possession. In most cases where the RTB has initiated civil proceedings it has been awarded its costs. Court orders not complied with are registered as a judgment debt against the non-compliant party. This would have a negative impact on the future credit rating of the non-compliant party.

A criminal prosecution can also be initiated by the RTB or the party in whose favour the order is made under s 126 of the 2004 Act. These are brought in the District Court.

There is no obligation on the RTB to enforce its Orders. Under the Act enforcement is a discretionary power and the RTB exercises this power taking account of the circumstances pertaining to each case, and in the context of the more challenging financial situation within which the RTB has to operate. The RTB is a self-financing agency and must operate within its budget. The number of requests received by the RTB to enforce Orders remains high. Decisions on whether or not to pursue legal enforcement are made by the board on a case-by-case basis, taking into account the likely success of achieving a favourable outcome for the requester, a favourable outcome being that monies yet to be paid are discharged, or that vacant possession can be obtained. The criteria the board members refer to when making that decision are:

- dispute type;
- history of compliance with landlord/tenant legislation;
- technical strength of the case;
- what contact/steps, if any, the person seeking compliance has taken with the non-compliant party to obtain compliance of the Order;
- existing representations made by the RTB to the non-compliant party and relevant information obtained;
- geographical spread;
- particular circumstances of the case.

Section 124 of the 2004 Act as amended by s 57 of the 2015 Amendment Act permits the RTB to apply to the District Court at the request of one party to a Determination Order to enforce that Determination Order where the other party has failed to comply with one or more of the terms. Section 124 allowed the court to make ancillary or other orders but did not explicitly allow for the making of an order for possession. Section 49 of the 2016 Act amends s 124(7) of the 2004 Act to include the making of an order for possession of a dwelling. This came into effect on 19 December 2017 under SI 590 of 2017.

The cost to the RTB of making s 124 applications is very considerable in terms of time, money and the tying up of limited resources and staff, and due to the fact that it is open to the party in whose favour a Determination Order was issued to take such proceedings in his/her own right, the RTB has considered its other options in cases of non-compliance with Determination Orders. They can prosecute persons under s 9 of the 2004 Act for the offence and under s 126 for failing to comply with a Determination Order. Section 9 provides that a person found guilty of an offence under the 2004 Act shall be liable on summary conviction to a fine not exceeding €3,000 or imprisonment for a term not exceeding six months or both. Section 126(3) of the 2004 Act provides that a person convicted under that section shall not be sentenced to any term of imprisonment in respect of that offence if he/she shows that failure to comply with the terms of the Determination Order was due to his/her limited financial means.

Details of the RTB's efforts to ensure compliance with Determination Orders are in the RTB annual report, which also includes case studies.

7.3.2 REGISTRATION OF PARTICULARS

Sections 127–148 of the 2004 Act deal generally with registration.

The requirement for landlords to register details of their tenancies with the RTB is necessary for a number of reasons. The details are relevant to disputes relating to rents, rent reviews, terminations, security of tenure and also to provide reliable information and credible statistics. Where a landlord does not register a tenancy the RTB is precluded from dealing with any dispute relating to the tenancy that may be referred to it by the landlord. This does not affect a tenant who will have access to the dispute resolution service irrespective of whether the tenancy is registered.

Certain dwellings are excluded from the requirement to register. These include the following:

(a) business premises;

(b) a dwelling to which Part II of the Housing (Private Rented Dwellings) Act, 1982, applies (ie formerly rent-controlled dwellings); see **chapter 14**

(c) a dwelling let by a local authority or voluntary housing body;

(d) a dwelling occupied under a shared ownership lease;

(e) a holiday let;

(f) a dwelling in which the landlord is also resident;

(g) a dwelling in which the spouse, parent or child of the landlord is resident and there is no written lease or tenancy agreement.

See **6.3** for a comprehensive list of excluded dwellings *per* s 3(2) of the 2004 Act.

7.3.2.1 Registration under Part 7 of the 2004 Act

Part 7 of the 2004 Act established a new registration system whereby all private residential landlords are obliged to register tenancies with the RTB rather than the local housing authority (as was the case under legislation prior to the 2004 Act). Since 7 April 2016 approved housing bodies, which are not-for-profit housing providers, often referred to as housing associations, are also obliged to register their tenancies.

Section 127 of the 2004 Act required the RTB to establish and maintain a register to be known as the 'private residential tenancies register'.

Section 127 provides that the form of the register, the types of information to be contained in it and any other matters relevant to the maintenance of the register shall be determined by the board from time to time. Two types of register were envisaged. In addition to the internal register, under s 128, the RTB shall prepare a document to be known as the 'published register', which can be inspected. This consists of an extract of the information contained in the register and contains details from the registration form that is supplied by the landlord and the extent of that extract is such as the board determines is likely to make the published register useful to members of the public. It basically gives the address and description of the dwelling, the number of bedrooms and bed spaces and the floor area.

No information will be on the published register which could disclose or reasonably lead to the disclosure of the identity of the landlord or tenant or the amount of rent payable under the tenancy. The published register is updated on the RTB website on a weekly basis.

Each tenancy registered with the RTB is allocated a unique registration number. This, together with details of the registration entry, is issued to both the landlord and the tenant and the registration number is required in any dealings with the board.

Once a tenancy is registered, it remains a registered tenancy for as long as the tenancy remains in existence. Once the tenancy is terminated, any new tenancy must be registered with the RTB. If the dwelling ceases to be let, the board should be notified so that the record can be removed from the register. Registration lasts the length of the tenancy, which was up to a maximum of four years, now six years under the 2016 Act. If the tenant is in occupation after four/six years, the new tenancy that comes into existence must be registered with the RTB.

7.3.2.2 Procedure for registration

Chapter 2 (ss 134–148) sets out the procedure for registration. An application for registration must be lodged within one month from commencement of the tenancy. Only a landlord can register. Registration of a tenancy, and updating particulars of that tenancy, can now be done online under the Tenancy Management System set up by the RTB.

Section 137 sets out the fees payable. There is currently a registration fee of €90 per tenancy and the fee for late registration is an additional €90 (ie €180 in total). There is a fee of €375 to register multiple lettings in the same building but €180 on each property if late. The 2004 Act does not allow for any exemptions from the requirement to pay the late fee regardless of circumstances or reasons for the delay. There is an obligation under s 139 to update entries in the register within one month but there is no fee for doing so.

Section 136 states the particulars that are to be contained in the application form RTB1. The latest form as required under S.I. 150 of 2016 is included at **Appendix 1**.

7.3.2.3 Offences

Chapter 3 of Part 7 contains provisions for the updating of particulars entered in the register and also provisions for enforcement of the requirement to register. Within one month of an alteration of rent payable under a registered tenancy taking effect the landlord is required to furnish details in the prescribed form to the RTB. No fee is payable. Likewise, if a tenancy has ceased to be a dwelling to which the 2004 Act applies the landlord must notify the RTB in writing within one month of the occurrence and the board can delete the entry in the register.

It is an offence to furnish false or misleading information to the RTB—see ss 143–145. The board has power to serve a notice if they are of the opinion a tenancy should be registered and if the addressee of the notice does not respond he or she is guilty of an offence.

The RTB actively pursues landlords for non-registration. Failure to register tenancies can result in prosecution, with fines of up to €4,000 and/or six months' imprisonment. Enforcement activities undertaken by the RTB are in accordance with the provision of the 2004 Act, in particular, ss 144 and 145.

The RTB receives information from a number of sources including:

- Department of Social Protection (DSP)—rent supplement database;
- Local Authorities—standards for rented dwellings' inspections;
- general public—neighbours;
- TDs, councillors, Gardai;

• tenants;

• dispute/registration sections (internal RTB referrals).

New ICT systems were introduced in early 2011 to facilitate database comparisons with other state agencies and departments to identify unregistered landlords for compliance purposes.

Since 2013 the RTB intensified activity against unregistered landlords. A total of 33,968 enforcement notices/solicitor warning letters were issued in 2013.

Section 9 of the 2004 Act sets out the penalties for those found guilty of an offence under the 2004 Act. The RTB website published details of five criminal convictions obtained in 2012 for non-registration of tenancies. Sections 146–148 provide for an exchange of data between the RTB, local authorities, Revenue and the Minister for Social and Family Affairs.

Section 100(4) of the Housing (Miscellaneous Provisions) Act 2009 introduced important amendments to the 2004 Act. Section 100 came into force on 15 July 2009 and the main amendments can be summarised as follows:

(a) A tenancy 'the term of which is more than 35 years' is excluded from the scope of the 2004 Act.

(b) There is an additional obligation on the landlord to provide a receptacle suitable for the storage of refuse outside the dwelling, save where the provision of such receptacles is not within the power or control of the landlord in respect of the dwelling concerned.

(c) Section 100(3)(b) and (c) have substituted new provisions for s 12(4)(a)(i) and s 12(4)(b) of the 2004 Act. These amendments clarify the circumstances in which a landlord may retain all or part of the deposit where the tenant is in default.

(d) Section 100(4) provides that as from 15 July 2009 signatures are no longer required on the tenancy registration form. The purpose of this amendment is to facilitate online registration which is now available. Section 135(2) of the 2004 Act is deleted accordingly.

(e) Section 100(5) inserts a new section being s 147(A) in the 2004 Act to provide for disclosure by the RTB of certain information to the Revenue Commissioners which is contained in the register and which 'is reasonably necessary for the performance by the Revenue Commissioners of their functions'.

7.3.3 ADVICE TO THE MINISTER ON POLICY

A further role of the RTB is to provide advice to the Minister concerning policy in relation to the private rented sector.

Information obtained from the registration forms lodged by landlords is the main source of data about the private rented sector generally and provides information about prevailing rent levels. In 2013 the Rent Index was established. It is the most accurate and authoritative rent report of its kind on the private accommodation sector as it reflects the actual rents being paid.

Under the 2016 Act there is now a requirement for the RTB to publish quarterly statistical reports and timeline reports. This is produced in association with the Economic and Social Research Institute (ESRI). The latest Rent Index for 2017 shows a total of 29,528 new tenancies were registered in Q3, representing an increase of over 6,000 registrations since the last quarter. In percentage terms nationally, rents grew 9.5 per cent over the year to Q3. The latest RTB Rent Index also presents rental data on a regional basis.

The RTB has a specific function to monitor the operation of the 2004 Act in practice and it can make recommendations to the Minister for amending legislation where it is evident provisions in the 2004 Act are not operating in the manner intended. The Research Committee of the RTB has identified two areas of concern in relation to applications for dispute resolution. One is the high number of applications concerning deposit retention and the relatively high cost of processing these applications. Another is the concept of 'anti-social behaviour', which can be the subject of a complaint to the RTB under the 2004 Act in certain circumstances. Two reports by Candy Murphy and Associates entitled *Dispute Resolution Mechanisms in Relation to Deposit Retention* and *Third-Party Complaints of Anti-Social Behaviour in the Private Residential Tenancy Sector* have been published.

Research has also included papers on *Students in the Private Rented Sector; what are the issues* and *Analysis of Determination Orders and Disputes.*

The 2015 Act introduced a Deposit Protection Scheme (s 16(d)), but the section has not yet commenced. The tenant's security deposit has been a matter of concern for a number of years. The then Department of Environment, Community and Local Government has examined the issue as well as the Law Reform Commission, which has studied the practice in other countries. The RTB has a note on its website on the issue of deposit refunds as well as a note on deposit retention. In addition to s 16 other sections dealing with security deposits in the 2015 Act are ss 60(a) and (c) and 61, 64 and 65. None of these has yet commenced. When commenced, a landlord will be required to lodge the deposit with the RTB at the same time as he/she is registering the tenancy. The RTB will hold the deposit for the duration of the tenancy and will retain the interest generated on it towards the costs of funding the scheme. It was hoped the scheme would be in place in 2017 as soon as the necessary conditions were put in place to support it.

Section 36 of the 2015 Act amended s 77 of the 2004 Act in regard to anti-social behaviour and with effect from 8 May 2016 introduced changes in relation to third parties taking a case in regard to anti-social behavior. However, the changes have not really tackled this growing problem.

7.3.4 DEVELOPMENT AND PUBLICATION OF GUIDELINES FOR GOOD PRACTICE

A fourth role of the RTB lies in the development and publication of guidelines for good practice by those involved in the private rented sector.

Section 152 of the 2004 Act states that guidelines may include a precedent for a model lease of a dwelling.

The Dublin Solicitors Bar Association (DSBA) reviewed its precedent Tenancy Agreement in 2010 to incorporate the additional requirements of the 2009 Housing (Standards for Rented Houses) Regulations and has further updated it in 2017. Irishlandlord.com is an online resource for landlords and also provides a Lease Agreement to its members.

The RTB has published guidance for the public covering different aspects of the legislation. See also the Tenancy Registration Form RTB1 (**Appendix 1**), Approved Housing Bodies Tenancy Registration Form RTB2 (**Appendix 2**), landlords' and tenants' rights and obligations, the dispute resolution service and terminating a tenancy. There is a precedent notice to terminate a tenancy including one where arrears of rent are due. All of these together with the board's Determination Orders can be viewed at www.RTB.ie.

The RTB provides high-quality information and advice to the public, tenants and landlords as well as high-quality data on the rental sector such as the Rent Index, which allows it to monitor trends.

7.4 Overview of Changes to the 2004 Act

The Residential Tenancies (Amendment) Act 2015 and the Planning and Development (Housing) and Residential Tenancies Act 2016 made major changes and were in response to growing public concern over security of tenure and rent predictability. This section sets out the main changes introduced.

7.4.1 THE 2015 ACT

- notice of termination periods extended;
- restriction on rent reviews to once every 24 months (restriction is for four years from 4 December 2015);
- introduction of a security deposit retention scheme—not yet enacted;
- the expansion of the 2004 Act to include approved housing bodies and the PRTB re-named the RTB to reflect this.

7.4.2 THE 2016 ACT

- security of tenure—four-year tenancies becoming six-year tenancies,
- new rent review requirement in regard to notices and frequency;
- designation of Rent Pressure Zones;
- new rent predictability measures, formula and exclusions.

The private rental sector is currently volatile and it remains to be seen whether further measures will be required to stabilise the market. There is ongoing discussion about a further landlord and tenant law bill which would increase the minimum notice periods for tenants, give tenants access to details of rent paid by previous tenants and increase penalties under the 2004 Act.

CHAPTER 8

REPAIRS

8.1 Introduction

A glance at any modern lease indicates that the tenant tends to be bound by a great many more covenants than the landlord. This makes perfect sense; after all, the tenant is acquiring (or renewing) possession of the property and, having immediate control, will thus assume responsibility for a great many matters relating to the user of the property. The landlord will be concerned to make sure that the tenant uses the property in a responsible manner to protect and preserve a valuable investment.

Covenants relating to maintenance and repairs are a standard feature of modern leases. This is not to say that the onus to maintain and repair the premises will always fall on the tenant alone. Subject to statutory restrictions, the parties are entitled to conclude their own agreement and to spell out which of them will be liable in any given situation.

Nonetheless, broadly speaking, the tenant will usually be liable for repairs. The extent of the obligation varies depending on the length of the term granted, the type of property, whether the premises comprise a single or multi-tenanted property and whether the landlord prefers to carry out structural and exterior repairs at the tenant's expense.

The modern position is governed both by statute and by common law. The principal statutes are Deasy's Act, 1860, the Housing Acts, 1966 to 2004, the Landlord and Tenant (Amendment) Act, 1980, the Housing (Miscellaneous Provisions) Acts, 1992, 2002 and 2009, and the Residential Tenancies Act 2004 ('the 2004 Act'). Two sets of regulations made pursuant to the above Housing Acts are also considered in this chapter. They are firstly the regulations on rent books, ie the Housing (Rent Books) Regulations, 1993, as amended by the Housing (Rent Books) Regulations 1993 (Amendment) Regulations, 2004, as further amended by the Housing (Rent Books) (Amendment) Regulations 2010. The second set of regulations relate to the standards for rented houses and the current regulations are the Housing (Standards for Rented Houses) Regulations 2017.

A number of other statutes also govern particular types of letting agreement and consideration is given to these later in the chapter.

The obligation to repair imposed in respect of residential dwellings by the 2004 Act has been dealt with in **chapter 6**. However, it is worth noting in this chapter that the obligations imposed on the tenant by s 16 of the 2004 Act and on the landlord by s 12 of the 2004 Act are in addition to the obligations arising by or under any other enactment. Thus the statutory obligations imposed on the landlord and tenant of a dwelling (other than one which comes within the exceptions to the operation of the 2004 Act pursuant to s 3(2) thereof) are in addition to those imposed by other enactments such as the 1980 Act or the Housing (Standards for Rented Houses) Regulations (see **8.3.1.2**).

The 2004 Act, while introducing major changes in the private rented residential sector, did not consolidate all statutory provisions governing residential tenancies. A broad range of pre-existing measures continue in force and operate in parallel with the provisions of the 2004 Act. It should be borne in mind that it is necessary for cross-referencing to be done in respect of earlier provisions in order to be aware of all the current rules regulating residential lettings. Thus the statutory provisions examined in this chapter will need to be considered in conjunction with the 2004 Act when advising on the repairing obligations of landlords or tenants of residential dwellings which come within the 2004 Act.

It is perhaps easiest to approach the question of liability for repairs by examining the respective parties' positions both at common law and under statute. In general terms it should be remembered that a letting agreement or lease is a contract. The question of responsibility for repairs will be covered by a term of the contract, whether expressly by written covenant or implied by common law or statute. While the terms of any agreement or contract should always be considered the parties' freedom to contract as they wish may sometimes be restricted by statute.

8.1.1   2011 BILL

The draft Landlord and Tenant Law Reform Bill 2011 ('the draft 2011 Bill') (see **1.4.4**) proposes radical changes to the law on repairs. In particular it imposes a default obligation to repair on a landlord, thus displacing the common law and current statutory position (see **8.3.7** for further details). The Bill repeals Deasy's Act, 1860 in its entirety but replaces some of its provisions in a more modern form. For example, the part of s 40 of Deasy's Act dealing with surrender (see **8.5.2.5**) is repealed without replacement but parts of s 42 are recast into new provisions.

8.2   Common Law

Table 6 summarises the common law position regarding repairs. It should be read in conjunction with **8.3** as statute has amended the common law position.

TABLE 6   Common law principles concerning repairs

	ORAL TENANCIES	**WRITTEN AGREEMENTS**
	Oral tenancies are governed by common law. There are two well-established principles as set out below. The onus will be on the tenant to prove that the parties expressly agreed to the contrary in either case.	
LANDLORD	The landlord has no obligation to repair in the absence of an express agreement. Section 42 of Deasy's Act, 1860 governs the position.	Where the contract of tenancy is in writing then, in the absence of an express covenant or agreement to the contrary, there is no implied liability on the part of the landlord to repair: *Scales v Vandeleur* [1914] 48 ILTR 36.

		De facto repair on the part of the landlord does not create an obligation to repair where none had previously existed: *Cowan v Factor* [1948] IR 128.
		Where the premises comprise furnished accommodation the landlord is only obliged to ensure that they are fit for human habitation at the commencement of the tenancy: *Siney v Dublin Corporation* [1980] IR 400.
TENANT	The tenant must keep the premises 'wind and water-tight'—again in the absence of an express agreement. However, a weekly tenant is only obliged to keep the property in a tenant-like manner.	In the absence of an express covenant or agreement, a tenant from year to year is obliged to keep the premises 'wind and watertight, fair wear and tear excepted': *Warren v Keen [1954] 1 QB 15. A week-to-week tenant is obliged to keep the premises 'in tenant-like manner'*: *Mint v Good* [1951] 1 KB 517.

8.3   Statute

8.3.1   HOUSING (MISCELLANEOUS PROVISIONS) ACT, 1992

This important piece of legislation amended and extended no less than eight post-1937 statutes: the Housing Acts, 1966–1988, the Landlord and Tenant (Ground Rents) Act, 1978, the Landlord and Tenant (Amendment) Act, 1980, the Housing Finance Agency Acts, 1981–1988, the Housing (Private Rented Dwellings) Act, 1982 and the Building Societies Act, 1989. It went on to provide for certain other matters in relation to housing, many of which have impacted on the conduct of affairs between landlords and tenants. The 1992 Act has now been updated and amended by the Housing (Miscellaneous Provisions) Act 2009.

The Minister of the Environment (or the Minister of State at that Department) introduced a number of regulations under the provisions of the 1992 Act. The Housing (Standards for Rented Houses) Regulations are of particular interest in the context of repairs. However, it is not inappropriate to look briefly at the Housing (Rent Books) Regulations which were also introduced following the enactment of the 1992 Act.

8.3.1.1   Housing (Rent Books) Regulations, 1993 as amended by the Housing (Rent Books) Regulations 1993 (Amendment) Regulations 2004 as further amended by the Housing (Rent Book) (Amendment) Regulations 2010

Section 17(1) of the Housing (Miscellaneous Provisions) Act, 1992 reads as follows:

The Minister may make regulations requiring the landlord of a house let for rent or other valuable consideration to provide the tenant of such a house with a rent book or other documentation to the like effect (in this section referred to as 'other documentation').

The Housing (Rent Books) Regulations, 1993 (SI 146 of 1993) made pursuant to the provisions of the Housing (Miscellaneous Provisions) Act, 1992, came into operation for private rented dwellinghouses on 1 September 1993.

The regulations require a landlord (including a local authority) to provide each new tenant with a rent book (or other documentation serving the same purpose) at the commencement of the tenancy. Persons with tenancies which commenced before 1 September 1993 must have been given rent books before 1 November 1993. All rent and other payments under the tenancy must be acknowledged in writing by the landlord.

In addition, the rent book must contain specific particulars relating to the tenancy including, inter alia:

(a) the name and address of the landlord and of his agent (if any);

(b) the term of the tenancy;

(c) the amount of the rent and of any other payments to be made by the tenant to the landlord;

(d) details of any advance rent or deposit paid; and

(e) in the case of new tenancies, the date of commencement of the tenancy and particulars of furnishings and appliances provided by the landlord for the tenant's exclusive use.

The rent book must also include a basic statement of information for the tenant which is set out in the Schedule to the regulations. The information required in this statement of information has been amended by the Housing (Rent Books) Regulations, 1993 (Amendment) Regulations 2004 (SI 751 of 2004). These regulations provide that the statement of information must state that the tenant is entitled to enjoy peaceful and exclusive occupation of the house and that notice of termination of the tenancy must be in writing and must be made in accordance with the provisions of the 2004 Act. This makes the 1993 Regulations compatible with the provisions of the 2004 Act. The Housing (Rent Book) (Amendment) Regulations 2010 (SI 357 of 2010) make the 1993 Regulations compatible with the provisions of the Housing (Miscellaneous Provisions) Act 2009 and the Housing (Standards for Rented Houses) Regulations 2008 (though there are now new 2017 Standards Regulations).

Threshold has produced a rent book which complies with these regulations. The book is available from stationers nationwide or from any of Threshold's offices.

There is no exception for temporary convenience lettings.

8.3.1.2   Housing (Standards for Rented Houses) Regulations 2017

Section 18(1) of the Housing (Miscellaneous Provisions) Act, 1992 reads as follows:

The Minister may make regulations prescribing standards for houses (including any common areas, works and services appurtenant thereto and enjoyed therewith) let for rent or other valuable consideration and it shall be the duty of the landlord of such a house to ensure that the house complies with the requirements of such regulations.

There have been numerous sets of standards for rented houses regulations and amendment regulations ie 1984, 1993, 2008 and 2009, all made pursuant to the provisions of the Housing (Miscellaneous Provisions) Act, 1992. The current set of regulations are the Housing (Standards for Rented Houses) Regulations 2017 (SI 17 of 2017).

These regulations require landlords of rented houses (including flats and maisonettes) to ensure that such houses meet certain minimum standards. The standards relate to, inter alia, structural condition, fire safety, provision of sinks, waterclosets, fixed baths or showers, cooking and food storage facilities, safety of electricity and gas installations, availability of adequate heating, lighting and ventilation and maintenance of proper refuse facilities. One of the major effects of these regulations was to require landlords to provide self-contained sanitary facilities. These facilities had to be provided in a separate room and this resulted in the phasing-out of the traditional bedsit where sanitary facilities were shared between different rental units.

Houses must be maintained in a proper state of structural repair. Section 18 of the 1992 Act as amended by the 2009 Act provides that where, in the opinion of a housing authority a requirement of the regulations has not been complied with, then the authority may serve an improvement notice on the landlord requiring the landlord to carry out works to ensure the house complies with the regulations. The authority must copy the notice to the tenant at the same time. In the event of the failure of the landlord to comply with the improvement notice the housing authority can serve a prohibition notice directing the landlord not to re-let the house until the improvements have been carried out.

The statutory obligations imposed on the landlord of a dwelling (other than one which comes within the exceptions to the operation of the 2004 Act pursuant to s 3(2) thereof) are in addition to those imposed by the Housing (Standards for Rented Houses) Regulations 2017. Section 12(1)(b) requires the landlord to carry out such repairs necessary to ensure the structure of the dwelling complies with any standards prescribed by s 18 of the Housing (Miscellaneous Provisions) Act, 1992, save under s 12(2) those repairs necessary due to the failure of the tenant not to do any act that would cause a deterioration in the condition of the dwelling (disregarding normal wear and tear). Section 16(b) of the 2004 Act requires the tenant to ensure that no act or omission on his part results in the landlord not complying with his obligations under any enactment and in particular, the landlord's obligations under regulations under s 18 of the 1992 Act.

8.3.1.3   Enforcement of regulations

In its interim submission to the Commission on the Private Rented Residential Sector in October 1999, the Law Reform Committee of the Law Society of Ireland expressed concern at the lack of enforcement of the foregoing regulations by local housing authorities. There was little routine inspection of premises and the authorities were reluctant to bring legal proceedings in cases of non-compliance.

The committee noted that enforcement was largely dependent on the bringing of complaints by tenants but that this situation was unsatisfactory in the absence of provisions on security of tenure. There was nothing to prevent a landlord from taking retaliatory action, such as service of a notice to quit or imposing a significant rent increase on a tenant who attempted to assert the intended protection.

Prior to the 2004 Act it was difficult to escape the conclusion that the regulations were without teeth. Details of enforcement activity found in the Annual Housing Statistics Bulletin published by the then Department of the Environment and Local Government showed little action by the majority of local housing authorities.

Section 201 of the 2004 Act has now increased the penalties for contravention of regulations made under ss 17, 18 or 20 of the Housing (Miscellaneous Provisions Act), 1992. This brings the penalties for conviction for failure to comply with the Standards and Rent Books Regulations into line with those applying to convictions for offences under the 2004 Act. On summary conviction an offence carries a fine of €3,000 or imprisonment for a term not exceeding six months or both, and if the offence continues after conviction there is a maximum daily fine of €250.

While local authorities remain responsible for the enforcement of the Standards and Rent Books Regulations, as of 1 September 2004 responsibility for the registration of private residential tenancies passed to the Residential Tenancies Board.

8.3.2   DEASY'S ACT, 1860, SECTION 42

Section 42 of Deasy's Act, 1860, applies only if there is no express agreement and is precluded in toto by any such agreement. It goes on to state that, in the case of a lease made on or after 1 January 1861, the tenant is liable:

> to keep the premises in good and substantial repair and give up peaceful possession of the demised premises in good and substantial repair and condition on the determination of the lease.

The courts have considered the meaning of such statutory terminology as 'good and substantial repair', 'tenantable' and 'habitable'. The general conclusion is that, in any one written agreement, they amount to one and the same thing. See also *Proudfoot v Hart* (1890) 25 QB 42, which concluded that 'substantial' is not judicially defined as meaning anything different. This case also explored the significance of the word 'tenantable' as not requiring old, dilapidated premises to be made into new buildings but that the premises should be taken out of their dilapidated condition and delivered up fit to be occupied for the purposes they were used for. See also *Rabbitt v Grant* [1940] IR 323.

The standard set in *Proudfoot v Hart* (1890) 25 QB 42 was applied in *Anstruther-Gough-Calthorpe v McOscar* [1924] 1 KB 716 despite the absence of the word 'tenantable'. *Anstruther* was cited with approval in *Fleming v Brennan* [1941] IR 499.

By virtue of s 193(a) of the 2004 Act, s 42 does not apply to a dwelling to which the 2004 Act applies.

8.3.3   LANDLORD AND TENANT (AMENDMENT) ACT, 1980, SECTION 65

Part V (ss 64–69) of the Landlord and Tenant (Amendment) Act, 1980, repealed the former Part VI (ss 55–59) of the Landlord and Tenant Act, 1931. Of particular interest here is the new s 65—damages for breach of covenants to repair—which replaces s 55 of the 1931 Act. Section 65 places limitations on the landlord's remedy when the tenant is in breach of a covenant to repair under a lease of a tenement. The full text of s 65 reads as follows:

> (1)   Where a lease (whether made before or after the commencement of this Act) of a tenement contains a covenant (whether express or implied and whether general or specific) on the part of the lessee to put or to keep the tenement in repair during the currency of the lease or to leave or put the tenement in repair at the expiration of the lease and there has been a breach of the covenant, the subsequent provisions of this section shall have effect.

> (2)   The damages recoverable in any court for the breach shall not in any case exceed the amount (if any) by which the value of the reversion (whether mediate or immediate) in the tenement is diminished owing to the breach.

> (3)   Save where the want of repair is shown to be due, wholly or substantially, to wilful damage or wilful waste committed by the lessee no damages shall be recoverable in any court for the breach if it is shown:

>> (a)   that, having regard to the age and condition of the tenement, its repair in accordance with the covenant is physically impossible, or

>> (b)   that, having regard to the age, condition, character and situation of the tenement, its repair in accordance with the covenant would involve expenditure which is excessive in proportion to the value of the tenement, or

>> (c)   that, having regard to the character and situation of the tenement, the tenement could not when so repaired be profitably used or could not be profitably used unless it were rebuilt, reconstructed or structurally altered to a substantial extent.

Section 65 reflects in substance the provisions of s 55 of the Landlord and Tenant Act, 1931. In *Groome v Fodhla Printing Co* [1943] IR 380 Black J stated that the purpose of section 55(b) of the 1931 Act was:

> 'to free the covenanting tenant from having to provide his landlord with a white elephant, or, in the alternative, to pay what, from the tenant's point of view, would be a sheer penalty for his breach, and from the landlords point of view of pretended solatium for a loss that he had not suffered.'

8.3.3.1 Practical effect of section 65

In all cases, the tenant's liability in damages for repair will be restricted to the landlord's loss in value of the reversion. Take as an example a case where the landlord's interest in the premises immediately prior to the damage was worth €500,000. The premises were damaged to the extent that the landlord's interest is now valued at €400,000. The cost of repairs is €150,000. The tenant will be liable under s 65 for €100,000 and not €150,000.

8.3.3.2 Wilful waste

The Supreme Court, in the case of *Gilligan v Silke* [1963] IR 1, considered the meaning of 'wilful waste' as originally set out in the old s 5 of the Landlord and Tenant Act, 1931, since replaced (but in effect restated) by the Landlord and Tenant (Amendment) Act, 1980. The lease in question contained a covenant to 'preserve, uphold, support, maintain and keep . . . premises . . . in good and sufficient order, repair and condition'. The premises were surrendered in poor repair.

The court held in this particular case that the want of repair had not been shown to be wholly or substantially due to wilful waste on the part of the tenant, but the views of the judges are required reading when and if this question arises in practice.

In the earlier case of *O'Reilly v East Coast Cinemas Ltd* [1968] IR 56, again considered under the 1931 Act, it was held by the Supreme Court that the word 'wilful' was equivalent to 'deliberate and intentional', the word 'waste' included permissive waste, and the word 'committed' applied to an omission to act.

8.3.4 LANDLORD AND TENANT (AMENDMENT) ACT, 1980, SECTION 87

Note also the position under the Landlord and Tenant (Amendment) Act, 1980, s 87. At common law, the tenant was not entitled to carry out the necessary repairs and deduct the cost of the repairs from the rent, but s 87 now permits this, subject to the necessary notification. Section 87 sets out as follows:

> (1) *Where a landlord refuses or fails to execute repairs to a tenement which he is bound by covenant or otherwise by law to execute and has been called upon by the tenant to execute, and the tenant executes the repairs at his own expense, the tenant may set off the expenditure against any subsequent gale or gales of rent until it is recouped.*

> (2) *Where a set-off is made under this section against the whole or part of a gale of rent, the landlord entitled to receive the rent shall on receiving evidence of the expenditure of the amount so set off, be bound to give the like receipt for the gale of rent as he would be bound to give if the gale or part of the gale had been paid in money.*

However, this only applies to tenements as defined in s 5 of the 1980 Act (see **10.1.1.1**).

8.3.5 MISCELLANEOUS STATUTES

Various other statutes impose an obligation on the landlord as owner or on the tenant as occupier to carry out certain works. These may not be strictly in the nature of repairs, but work may need to be done to comply with these Acts. Various statutory bodies are responsible for the initiation of the procedure, and the overseeing of the completion of these works. Examples include legislation on planning, public health, safety at work, fire services etc.

8.3.6 LANDLORD MUST BE NOTIFIED

In all cases it is necessary for the tenant, or the appropriate statutory authority, to serve a notice on the landlord specifying the disrepair complained of and requesting the landlord to put the repair in hand before any liability can arise. This point was reiterated by Costello J in *Fetherstonhaugh v Smith* High Court 12 February 1979 (unreported).

8.3.7 CONCLUSION

As has already been stated, there is nothing to prevent the parties from concluding their own agreement and providing for liability to repair in any given situation. Broadly speaking, however, the tenant will usually be liable for repairs. Moreover, the tenant's obligations usually become more onerous as the length of the tenancy increases or the commercial value of the premises increases.

The draft 2011 Bill (see **1.4.4**) provides that where there is no obligation imposed on any party to repair any part of the premises, or it is unclear whether such an obligation is imposed on any party, then the landlord has a default obligation to repair. The Bill proposes to implement the recommendation in the Landlord & Tenant Consultation Paper (LRC CP 28–2003) that there should be a statutory provision to deal with cases where the tenancy agreement fails to deal exhaustively with repairs or to deal with the subject at all. If there are express provisions in the tenancy agreement or repairing obligations arising under the common law or other statutory provisions which cover the repairing obligation in respect of any particular part of the premises, then the Bill proposes that the default obligation will not apply. The Bill also provides that the tenant has default obligations to maintain the premises; carry out such repairs as are necessary to ensure compliance with the maintenance obligation and to notify the landlord of any defect or state of disrepair in the premises which the landlord is obliged to repair. There are overriding obligations on the part of the tenant to allow the landlord to inspect the premises and carry out such repairs which he is obliged to carry out and where the tenant is obliged to carry out repairs, but has failed to do so within a reasonable time, then to enable the landlord to carry out such repairs and reimburse to the landlord all reasonable costs and expenses in relation to the same.

8.4 Sample Covenants to Repair

8.4.1 RESIDENTIAL

Prior to the 2004 Act, many temporary convenience lettings were made orally or were in the form of written letting agreements available from stationers. It may be from these standard letting agreements that the common assumption arose that the landlord will take care of the external repairs and the tenant will be liable for the internal ones. A typical tenant's covenant might have been:

'To keep the interior of the premises including the glass in the windows all locks, sash-cords, electric, gas and other fittings and installations and all additions thereto and all drains, sanitary fittings, appliances and pipes in good and tenantable repair, order and condition (damage by fire only excepted) and keep the landlord effectually indemnified against all claims in respect thereof and to pay for any damage done to any drain, sewer or gulley trap caused by the negligence of the tenant, his guests, servants or agents.

'To keep the said furniture and fittings in good tenantable repair, order and condition (damage by fire excepted) and to replace such of the said furniture as may be broken, destroyed or damaged with other articles of equal value to the satisfaction and approval of the landlord and not to remove the said furniture or any part thereof from the premises nor to lend or part with the possession of same either directly or indirectly to any person whomsoever without the previous consent of the landlord.'

In return, the landlord will usually have covenanted 'to maintain and keep (the demised premises) in good order and repair'. The agreement would then address arrangements regarding insurance and other outgoings.

Subject to statutory restrictions, the parties are entitled to regulate the extent or otherwise of their respective liability for repairs. As the landlord's solicitor usually drafts the lease, the tenant (or the tenant's solicitor) will have to scrutinise the contents of the repairing covenants carefully and may need to clarify their scope and extent prior to execution.

Sections 12 and 16 of the 2004 Act now place specific obligations on both landlord and tenants in respect of the repair of dwellings to which the Act applies. See **6.6.** The 2004 Act includes virtually all residential dwellings. Section 18(1) also provides that no provision of any lease, tenancy agreement, contract or other agreement may operate to vary, modify or restrict in any way ss 12 or 16. Under s 18(2), this does not prevent the landlord giving more favourable terms to the tenant. Under s 18(3), the landlord can impose additional obligations on the tenant provided they are consistent with the Act.

8.4.2 COMMERCIAL

In the case of a commercial lease, it is far more usual for the tenant to bear responsibility for both the interior and exterior of the demised premises. A typical commercial tenant's covenant reads as follows:

'At all times during the said term to keep clean and tidy and to repair, renew, rebuild and to put and keep in good order, repair and condition and in good decorative condition from time to time and at all times during the said term the whole of the demised premises (both the interior and exterior) and every part thereof, and any additions, alterations and extensions thereto and to keep in good repair and condition and replace where necessary all sanitary and water apparatus, glass, conduits, utilities, electrical systems and the landlord's fixtures and fittings thereon belonging or which shall belong to the same with all necessary and usual reparations, dealings and amendments whatsoever (damage by any of the insured risks as hereinafter defined in clause hereof excepted if and so long only as the policy or policies of insurance shall not have been vitiated or payment of the policy monies withheld or refused in whole or in part by reason of any act, neglect or default of the tenant or the servants, agents or invitees of the tenant).'

Much of this terminology stems directly from statute.

8.4.3 INTERPRETATION OF COVENANTS TO REPAIR

8.4.3.1 *Groome v Fodhla Printing Co*

It is important to note the use of the phrase 'to put and keep' in a covenant. This term of expression does not derive from statute. It goes beyond the phrase 'to keep' in its scope. Commonly employed, it is not necessarily confined to commercial leases.

Moreover, if the premises are out of repair when the lease begins, the covenant 'to keep' them in repair implies that the tenant must put them in repair: *Groome v Fodhla Printing Co* [1943] IR 380. In that case, a covenant in a commercial lease read as follows:

> 'to keep the demised premises and all improvements and additions thereto in good and tenantable repair, order and condition, and to yield up the demised premises with the fixtures and additions thereto at the determination of the tenancy in good and tenantable repair'.

The trial judge (Hanna J) found that a sag in the roof of the demised premises, which developed during the term of the tenancy, had been caused by the removal of supporting tie-beams prior to the demise. No evidence was brought as to when, or by whom, the beams were removed, but Hanna J found that the removal was not made during this or the previous tenancy. He held that this want of repair should have been made good by the defendant tenants. Hanna J stated:

> 'The phrase "good and tenantable repair, order and condition" would in law mean such reasonable repair of such old premises as would make them reasonably fit for occupation as a store by a reasonably minded tenant who would be likely to take them. The tenant cannot avoid his responsibility by reason of the want of repair being of no importance to himself in his use of the premises.'

The Supreme Court upheld the judgment of Hanna J and dismissed their appeal. O'Byrne J stated:

> 'I accept, as established law, the principle that, in considering the obligations of a lessee under a general covenant to repair, regard must be had to the age and general condition of the premises at the date of the demise, and that, under such a covenant, the lessee is not bound to erect during the demise, or to give up at the expiration of his term, something different from that which he took when he entered into the covenant; but there is nothing in this principle to relieve the appellants of responsibility in this case.'

Black J noted:

> 'If the removal of the king-post trusses constituted disrepair, it existed at the date of the demise. But that would be no answer, since he who has to keep in repair, must put into repair.'

Noting that 'it would be no answer to say that repair would involve partial rebuilding', Black J went on to say:

> 'replacement of a thing is different from, and cannot reasonably be called "repair" of that thing, but it may properly be called "repair" of a larger entity of which that thing is a component part'.

Later in the judgment he stated:

> 'It has often been said that the covenanting lessee is not bound to give back a better house than the one demised to him. ... It is true in the sense that the lessee cannot be made do improvements in the guise of repairs. But if genuine repair involves, as it often does, inevitable improvement, that does not enable the covenantor to say he will not do the repair. He is often obliged in this way to give back a better house than the one he got.'

There may be serious consequences for the tenant where the demised property is in a poor state of repair at the commencement of the term and this phrase is employed in the appropriate covenant. The tenant will need confirmation that old premises need only be repaired as old premises and that no immediate repairs are envisaged at the outset.

In cases involving commercial premises, the tenant would be well advised to prepare a Schedule of Condition prior to execution. This may be supported by photographs showing the current state of the premises which then form part of the lease and will 'fix' the tenant's liability at the commencement date. In such a case the tenant will not be required to put the premises into a better state of repair than at the commencement of the lease unless this is specifically agreed between the parties.

8.4.3.2 Some general principles

Bearing in mind that leases, being written agreements, are governed generally by the principles of contract law, it is not surprising to note that the courts have been requested, with some frequency, to pronounce on the efficacy of certain express written covenants to repair. Each case turns on its own facts and the case law can seem contradictory. The following are some of the principles which have evolved quoting, where appropriate, the legal authority on which each principle is expressed or reiterated.

A covenant to repair shall be construed to have reference to the state of the premises when the covenant came into force: *Walker v Hatton* (1842) 10 M & W 249.

As noted at **8.4.3.1**, if the premises are out of repair when the lease begins, the covenant to keep them in repair implies that the tenant must put them in repair: *Groome v Fodhla Printing Co* [1943] IR 380.

The age of premises, their locality and the kind of tenant likely to take them are all relevant factors when determining the extent of the tenant's liability under an ordinary repairing covenant. The tenant will be liable for the cost of maintaining the premises as though they have been managed by a reasonable owner having regard to these matters and in such a way that only an average amount of annual repair will be necessary in the future; the age being the dominant factor and the other factors being taken into account only in relation to, or as a consequence of, the age: *Fleming v Brennan* [1941] IR 499.

Where premises are old they need only be maintained as old premises: *Lister v Lane* [1893] 2 QB 212. However, if the covenant is 'to put or keep in repair', the state of the premises when demised is not a basis for relief: *Groome v Fodhla Printing Co* [1943] IR 380. See also *Proudfoot v Hart* (1890) 25 QB 42.

Repair must be distinguished from rebuilding, renewal and improvement. This can be a difficult distinction to make in practice. There is no statutory definition of repair. In general terms, repair might be said to relate to the restoration by renewal or replacement of subsidiary parts of the premises whereas renewal relates to reconstruction of the premises in their entirety. This, in effect, means substantially the whole of the premises.

A repairing covenant does not call for the covenantor to rebuild the premises unless they were in such a condition at the date of the demise that repair necessarily involves rebuilding: *Chaloner v Broughton* (1865) 11 Ir Jur (NS) 84 or if, from an inherent defect therein they get into that condition during the term: *Sotheby v Grundy* [1947] 2 All ER 761. A repairing covenant does not, unless so expressed, require the covenantor to improve or renew the property by making it into something different from that demised.

Two English cases look at the distinction between repairs and improvements. *Ravenseft Properties Ltd v Davstone (Holdings) Ltd* [1980] QB 12 introduced a new test, asking whether the works required involved surrendering to the landlord a wholly different thing from that which was demised. In this case, the court contrasted the cost of the works with the replacement cost of the premises. *Post Office v Aquarius Properties Ltd* [1987] 1 All ER 1055 examined the distinction between repairs and renewals.

A tenant is generally free to choose the method of compliance with his covenant and need not replace old with new if a second-hand alternative can be obtained and he will not be criticised for choosing a cheaper but adequate method of compliance than the landlord would have chosen: *Riverside Automotive v Blackhawk Automotive* [2005] 1 EGLR 114 and *Ultraworth v General Accident Fire & Life Assurance Corporation* [2000] 2 EGLR 115.

Renewal of parts of a structure may be implicit in the duty to repair: *Lurcott v Wakely* [1911] 1 KB 905, where the tenant undertook to keep the water and sanitary apparatus in good and tenantable condition and was held liable to replace a cistern which collapsed from decay and was beyond repair.

Painting the premises, though not expressly mentioned in the written covenant, may be part of the duty to repair. See *Proudfoot v Hart* (1890) 25 QB 42, where it was held that mere decorative painting was not part of a covenantor's liability but that such painting would be part of the liability if the state of the premises was such that a reasonable tenant of the class likely to take them would not take them unless painted.

Exceptions for 'fair wear and tear' reduce liability considerably. This means damage or wearing out which comes from the agency of natural causes (time and weather) and the reasonable use by the tenant of the premises. Such defects need not be made good by the tenant unless the terms of the lease state otherwise. The general rule is that a fair wear and tear exception will not be implied in a commercial lease where it is not expressed, although in *McEvoy v O'Donnell* [1946] Ir Jur Rep 38 it was implied in the context of a residential letting.

The onus to prove the implication of a wear and tear exception is on the tenant: *Brown v Davies* [1958] 1 QB 117.

The tenant may remain liable for repairs for fair wear and tear where such repairs may be necessary to prevent further damage to the premises: *Regis Property Co Ltd v Dudley* [1959] AC 370. If there is a fair wear and tear exception, either express or implied, this does not permit the tenant to allow, through want of maintenance, damage to occur and thus, in that way, a duty to remedy what might be excepted as fair wear and tear can sometimes come within a repairing covenant.

8.4.3.3   *Whelan v Madigan*

The case of *Whelan v Madigan* [1978] ILRM 136 is useful in that Kenny J considered express covenants to repair in four separate leases for self-contained flats within one residential property. The plaintiff tenants, all overholding on the terms of their original leases, joined actions against the defendant landlord on a number of issues. The landlord counterclaimed, inter alia, for breach of the various covenants to repair.

The first-named plaintiff's lease contained a covenant to keep and maintain the interior of her flat in good and tenantable order, repair and condition, reasonable wear and tear excepted. The evidence pointed to plaster cracks and failure to paint the windows. Kenny J ruled that these came within the exception of reasonable wear and tear.

The second-named plaintiff covenanted to keep the interior of his premises in the same order, repair and condition as they were in when he took the lease in 1951, more than 20 years earlier. The landlord complained of a crack on the return of the premises. Damages against the tenant were not awarded as, in the opinion of the court, it was essential for the landlord to prove that the crack was not there when the lease was made.

The third-named plaintiff had covenanted in 1943 to keep his take in good repair. Evidence was adduced that the premises were full of dry rot. This was caused by the absence of a damp-proof course and proper ventilation into the sub-floor, and the absence of a concrete sub-floor. Applying *Lister v Lane, Lurcott v Wakely* and *Groome v Fodhla Printing Co* (see above), Kenny J stated that this case established that a covenant to repair did not extend to defects caused by a structural defect which was present in the premises when they were let to the tenant. No damages were thus recoverable against the tenant.

In the case of the fourth-named plaintiff, the original lease contained a covenant to keep the interior of her flat and the doors, windows, glass, sash cords, fittings and additions and the landlord's fixtures in good and tenantable order, repair and condition. Evidence of plaster cracks and a lack of proper maintenance of the windows and the decoration was adduced at the trial. Kenny J ruled that the tenant was in breach of the covenant but that the matters complained of in no way diminished the value of the reversion such that, as s 55 of the Landlord and Tenant Act, 1931 applied, nothing could be recovered. However, he ruled that s 55 was confined to covenants contained *in a lease*. The tenant was overholding and the section did not apply to a covenant imported into the monthly tenancy arising thereafter—a serious omission in the section, in the court's view. Had the landlord recovered possession or if the term of the tenancy was near completion then the full award of the cost of repair would normally be made. When, however, the tenancy is protected by the Rent Restrictions Acts and the tenant has no intention of giving up the tenancy, such an award would, in the judge's words, 'be unreal'. The landlord was thus awarded £25, being roughly one-quarter of the sum claimed, for breach of the covenant to repair by the fourth-named plaintiff.

8.5   Remedies

An examination of the remedies of termination and deemed termination under the 2004 Act is included elsewhere in the manual (see **chapter 6**).

8.5.1   THE LANDLORD'S POSITION

8.5.1.1   Forfeiture

This applies to premises outside the scope of the 2004 Act.

The remedy of forfeiture is available where the written lease contains a proviso for re-entry. If there is no such proviso it is unlikely that the tenant's repairing covenant(s) could be construed as having the effect of a condition such as would obviate the need for a re-entry proviso.

See **chapter 9** for a detailed consideration of the procedure. In brief, it should be noted that forfeiture is an equitable remedy and the courts tend to lean against it. A range of statutory and equitable reliefs may be afforded to the tenant. Moreover, the landlord is obliged in the first instance to serve a 'section 14 notice' (*per* the Conveyancing Act, 1881, s 14(1), as amended).

8.5.1.2   Damages

Most modern leases include a covenant by the tenant to make good all loss sustained by the landlord in consequence of any breach by the tenant (or any underlessee of the tenant) of any covenant or condition contained in the lease. The lease may also include a clause permitting the landlord to enter upon the premises and carry out the necessary repairs where the tenant is in breach.

In such an event, the landlord is entitled to sue for recovery of the losses sustained. See *Gooderham & Worts v Canadian Broadcasting Corp* [1947] AC 66 and also *Conquest v Ebbetts* [1896] AC 490 for a consideration of some of the issues.

As a repairing covenant is a continuing obligation which lasts for the entirety of the term the tenant will not be able to claim a limitation defence under the Statute of Limitations 1957.

Note the statutory restrictions imposed on landlords by virtue of the Landlord and Tenant (Amendment) Act, 1980, s 65. See **8.3.3**.

8.5.1.3 Specific performance/mandatory injunction

Neither specific performance nor mandatory injunction is codified in statute form, and the old English decision of *Hill v Barclay* (1810) 16 Ves 402 is authority for the view that the court will not compel a tenant to carry out a repairing covenant by granting a decree or declaration to such effect. But see also *Rainbow Estates Ltd v Tokenhold Ltd* [1998] 2 All ER 860 for a revised view, at least in principle.

Of course, a landlord who pursues the forfeiture procedure may succeed in securing specific performance in practice. The court may grant equitable or statutory relief but often this will be on the grounds that the tenant must carry out the repairs which are the subject of the landlord's complaint.

8.5.2 THE TENANT'S POSITION

8.5.2.1 Damages

A tenant may take matters in hand and effect the necessary repairs when the landlord is in breach of the covenant to repair. The tenant is then in a position to sue for damages. These may be divided between general and special damages. The tenant who keeps a record of the history of the complaint, notification to the landlord requiring the repair to be made and of the expenditure and inconvenience involved is in a strong position.

8.5.2.2 Equitable set-off against rent

A tenant will commonly avail of the remedy of set-off against rent as a defence by way of equitable set-off in proceedings brought by a landlord for non-payment of rent.

8.5.2.3 Specific performance/injunction

The remedy of specific performance is available to a tenant at common law where the landlord is in breach of a repairing obligation. In more urgent cases, and depending as always on the facts of the given case, a tenant may apply for injunctive relief where appropriate.

8.5.2.4 Termination

A landlord's failure to perform covenants in a lease may amount to a repudiatory breach of contract. The question was considered in a number of English decisions in the 1990s. *Hussein v Mehlman* [1992] 2 EGLR 87 concerned a short-term residential letting and directly involved a breach of repairing obligations. *Chartered Trust plc v Davies* [1997] 2 EGLR 83 and *Nynehead Developments Ltd v R H Fibreboard Containers Ltd* [1997] 2 EG 139; [1999] 1 EGLR 7 arose from commercial leases of multi-let properties and did not concern repairing obligations as such.

It is worth noting that the plaintiff in the first of these cases was the tenant; in the commercial cases it was the landlord who sued when the tenant withheld payment of the rent. Such a course of action on the part of the tenant is generally actionable—it is a brave tenant who will withhold the rent while not applying to court for relief.

8.5.2.5 Surrender under Deasy's Act, 1860, section 40

Section 40 of Deasy's Act, 1860 permits a tenant to surrender his tenancy on the destruction or rendering uninhabitable of the premises by fire or other inevitable accident. The fire or other accident must not have been due to the default of the tenant and there must be no express covenant by the tenant to repair in the lease. In modern commercial leases this right to surrender is usually expressly excluded by the terms of the lease. Deasy's Act, 1860, applies to all written agreements made on or after 1 January 1861.

CHAPTER 9

TERMINATION

9.1 Introduction

Tenancies may be terminated in over a dozen different ways. These are as follows:

(1) Notice to quit.

(2) Forfeiture.

(3) Effluxion of time.

(4) Merger with a freehold interest.

(5) Demand for possession pursuant to Deasy's Act, 1860, s 86.

(6) Decree or warrant for possession pursuant to Deasy's Act, 1860, s 78.

(7) Execution of a judgment or decree for possession pursuant to Deasy's Act, 1860, ss 52 and 66.

(8) Surrender.

(9) Occurrence of an event specified in the lease/letting agreement.

(10) Court order.

(11) Derelict sites and dangerous premises.

(12) Exercise of an option.

(13) Liquidator's disclaimer pursuant to the Companies Act, 2014, s 615.

(14) Termination or deemed termination of a residential tenancy under the provisions of the Residential Tenancies Act, 2004 ('the 2004 Act').

Prior to the 2004 Act, residential and commercial tenancies could be terminated by notice to quit or forfeiture. Since 1 September 2004, the 2004 Act has laid down specific provisions for termination of tenancies to which the Act applies. Thus notice to quit and forfeiture now apply only to commercial tenancies and a limited number of residential tenancies not coming within the provisions of the 2004 Act. Hence the focus of this chapter is primarily on commercial tenancies or residential tenancies not falling within the provisions of the 2004 Act.

Practitioners are most often instructed to deal with situations arising where the landlord urgently requires the tenant to quit the premises. It is commonly assumed that a notice to quit covers every situation where the landlord requires the tenant to deliver up possession. This is not the case. A notice to quit is required for periodic tenancies or in cases where the tenant remains in possession of premises after the expiration of the agreed term and continues to pay rent, again provided it is not a Part 4 tenancy or a further Part 4 tenancy under the 2004 Act. This is called overholding. In essence, a notice is required in any situation where a periodic tenancy arises, ie a tenancy from year to year or lesser period, provided it is not a Part 4 tenancy or a further Part 4 tenancy under the 2004 Act. However, practitioners will frequently take instructions when problems arise during the currency of the term. In such situations, and subject to any of the other methods listed above, forfeiture is the appropriate remedy, provided it is not a Part 4 tenancy or a further Part 4 tenancy under the 2004 Act.

This chapter focuses in detail on the first two procedures, the notice to quit and forfeiture, and then briefly examines the other procedures, save for point 14 of the above list. Termination or deemed termination of a Part 4 tenancy or a further Part 4 tenancy arising under the provisions of the 2004 Act is dealt with at **chapter 6**.

It should first be noted from the above list that tenancies are often determined by simple effluxion of time. Thus, where a written letting agreement sets out a specified term and the parties perform the covenants contained in the lease, the landlord will likely not be concerned with the notice to quit or forfeiture procedures. The practitioner may, however, be instructed to write and remind the tenant that the term is coming to an end and that possession should be given up. It is common to serve a notice of termination (Form No 2) pursuant to the Landlord and Tenant (Amendment) Act, 1980, s 20. As a result the time period within which the tenant will be entitled to serve a notice of intention to claim relief (Form No 1) will have started to run. Again, this only applies to tenancies outside the scope of the 2004 Act.

Many landlords communicate directly with their tenants in such an event. Matters will usually only go to law either if the tenant remains in possession beyond the expiration of the stated term or if the landlord wishes to determine the tenancy prior to the end of the stated term. A tenant who remains in possession beyond the expiration of the stated term is said to be overholding and a notice to quit will ensue. Where the landlord wishes to determine the tenancy prior to the end of the specified term, the appropriate procedure is forfeiture. However, once again it should be pointed out that notice to quit and forfeiture only apply to commercial tenancies and the limited number of residential tenancies not coming within the provisions of the 2004 Act.

9.1.1 FORTHCOMING REFORMS

The draft Landlord and Tenant Law Reform Bill 2011 ('the draft 2011 Bill') (see **1.4.4**) proposes an updated statutory redress scheme to replace the former old 'eviction' remedies, which will be abolished. The Bill proposes to replace the notice to quit procedure with a notice of termination and provides for new notice periods. The Bill also contains new provisions relating to surrender, forfeiture and re-entry. It contains provisions providing for possession proceedings to be taken by the landlord and for re-entry if premises have been abandoned. It also proposes to repeal Deasy's Act, 1860 in its entirety.

9.2 Notice to Quit

Notice to quit is the most common means used to recover possession of premises following the conclusion of the term of a given tenancy where the tenant is overholding. A notice to quit is the means by which a periodic tenancy—ie a tenancy from year to year or other, lesser, period—is brought to an end. It is important to note that the landlord is entitled to determine a periodic tenancy for no given reason. The tenant does not have to be in breach and the motive of the landlord is irrelevant. The landlord's right is absolute but the tenant may of course have certain rights to a new lease under the Landlord and Tenant

(Amendment) Act, 1980, as amended by the Landlord and Tenant (Amendment) Act, 1994, or to buy out the freehold under the ground rents legislation.

Notice to quit is no longer the appropriate procedure for the majority of residential tenancies since the enactment of the 2004 Act.

9.2.1 SITUATIONS WHERE A NOTICE IS NOT REQUIRED

A notice to quit is not required in the following situations:

(a) Where the demise is for a specific term of years or for a year certain. In such cases, if the landlord wishes to determine the tenancy prior to the date specified in the lease, the appropriate procedure is that of forfeiture. Otherwise, the tenancy expires automatically at the end of the term in question.

(b) Where the agreement is stated to terminate on the happening of a stated event.

(c) Where the contract expressly dispenses with the requirement for a notice to quit. Note, however, that if the letting is one to which the provisions of s 16 of the Housing (Miscellaneous Provisions) Act, 1992 apply a statutory minimum of four weeks' notice is required.

(d) Where a tenancy at will is determined by a demand for possession.

(e) Where a year's rent is in arrears under a lease, fee farm grant, etc and the landlord brings ejectment proceedings for non-payment of rent. This arises during the currency of the term and thus no notice to quit is required: Deasy's Act, 1860, s 52. The tenancy will determine upon the execution of the decree.

(f) Where the premises are deserted and a half-year's rent is in arrears, the landlord may commence ejectment proceedings without first having to serve a notice to quit: Deasy's Act, 1860, s 78. In such a case, the decree for possession determines the tenancy.

(g) Where the contract of tenancy is void by reason of illegality.

(h) Where an infant repudiates a tenancy upon reaching his or her majority.

9.2.2 WHO MAY SERVE THE NOTICE?

Any person who has received prior express (preferably written) authorisation may serve a notice to quit. Solicitors, rent collectors and estate agents do not have authority to serve the notice merely by virtue of their agents' status. Moreover, it is important to remember from the outset that any given case may end up in court. As such, unless the landlord serves the notice in person, it is wisest to arrange for prior written authority to be given to the server. Such authority cannot be given retrospectively.

Where the landlord is a company, a director, secretary, registered person or other authorised officer may sign the notice. The company is not required to seal the notice: Companies Act 2014, s 48.

Cases of implied authority may occur, but this will depend on the facts of the case in question.

9.2.3 FORM AND CONTENTS OF THE NOTICE

The Landlord and Tenant (Ireland) Act, 1870, and the Notices to Quit (Ireland) Act, 1876, applied only to agricultural property. Until relatively recently, therefore, only agricultural tenancies were covered by a strict statutory requirement that the notice be in writing. However, the Housing (Miscellaneous Provisions) Act, 1992, s 16 introduced a statutory requirement that (subject to certain exceptions set out in s 16(2)) the notice be in writing where a house is involved. 'House' is defined in the Act as including 'any building or part of a building used or suitable for use as a dwelling and out-office, yard, garden or other land appurtenant thereto or usually enjoyed therewith'.

Section 16 does not apply to a residential dwelling to which the 2004 Act applies by virtue of s 193(e) of the 2004 Act.

In a Practice Note published in the January/February 1993 Law Society *Gazette*, the Conveyancing Committee noted that s 16 introduced, for the first time, a minimum statutory notice period for a notice to quit relating to urban lands in Ireland. The committee further noted that the effect was to introduce a minimum mandatory period, but that a greater period may be provided for in the agreement or by operation of law, eg the 183 days required for yearly tenancies at common law. Today virtually all such residential tenancies will fall within the 2004 Act and hence the notice periods and requirements in relation to the form of notice of termination set out therein will apply; see **chapter 6**.

In practice, notices should always be in writing. If the tenant refuses to quit, a written notice will be required as proof in court. No particular form is necessary but, of course, the notice must contain a clear and unambiguous intention to determine the tenancy. As such, the notice must contain an explicit demand for possession of the premises on the expiry of the stated notice period.

A description of the premises must be given. If the original terms of the tenancy were reduced to writing, it is advisable to quote directly from the description of the premises as set out in the written agreement. In cases where part only of the premises as originally demised is required (eg where the premises were subsequently subdivided by virtue of a sub-letting or assignment) it is important to ensure that a specific description of that portion is given. The notice will be defective if the entire of the premises is described in such a case.

The notice must be clearly addressed to 'the tenant and all other persons in occupation'.

A notice to quit need not be signed unless it relates to an agricultural holding but, in practice, it should be signed to prove its origin and authenticity. The notice should be signed by the landlord or by an agent. An agent signing on behalf of a landlord must have prior authority to do so. This authority need not be in writing. However, bearing court proofs in mind, it is wiser to arrange for the landlord to give prior written authority.

Agents should expressly indicate their capacity to sign on the landlord's behalf. As already noted above, if the agent signs, prior written authority from the landlord should be on file as available proof if required in subsequent proceedings.

9.2.4   LENGTH OF NOTICE

The prior written agreement should be checked to see if provision was made for length of notice and any such provision should be followed accordingly, subject to the statutory minimum four weeks' notice.

If there is no such provision reasonable notice is required. The question of what is reasonable will depend on the nature of the tenancy.

Such notice must expire on a gale day, as there is a presumption that this day coincides with the commencement date of the tenancy. This gale day must be the point of recurrence when one period ends and another begins. If the notice expires after the gale day, ie after the point of recurrence, then another period begins before the notice becomes effective and that period will then run. The landlord will have lost the opportunity to end the tenancy for another week/month/quarter/year.

TERMINATION

9.2.4.1   Weekly tenancy

Where a house on a weekly tenancy is involved, four weeks' notice is required under the Housing (Miscellaneous Provisions) Act, 1992, s 16. The Act defines 'house' for this purpose. At common law, a week's notice expiring on a gale day will be required.

9.2.4.2   Monthly tenancy

At common law, a monthly tenancy requires one month's notice expiring on a gale day. A landlord may give a longer period than a month. This will be good so long as the expiry date is a gale day.

9.2.4.3   Quarterly tenancy

The general view is that three months' notice is sufficient to terminate a quarterly tenancy. Again, one should ensure that this expires on a gale day.

9.2.4.4   A tenancy from year to year

A tenancy from year to year requires a half-year's notice expiring on the anniversary of the tenancy. A half-year is calculated by reference not to six months but to a full 183 days. This is a very technical point and it will be necessary to consult the textbooks if it arises in practice. If the date of commencement of the tenancy is unknown, it shall be presumed to have begun on the last gale day of the year on which rent has become due by virtue of Deasy's Act, 1860, s 6. There is thus a presumption that the gale day coincides with the commencement date of the tenancy.

9.2.5   UPON WHOM AND HOW SHOULD THE NOTICE BE SERVED?

The notice must come into the possession of the tenant before the period of notice starts to run. In broad terms, therefore, personal service is best.

In the first instance, the contract should be checked to see if provision has been made for the mode of service and any such provision should be followed accordingly. If there is no such provision then the following rules apply.

9.2.5.1   Where the tenant is alive

Where the tenant is alive, personal service, and preferably on the premises in question, is the best course. Service may be effected by post but the landlord will have to prove that the notice came to the attention of the tenant prior to the commencement of the notice period. There may be a risk that, owing to absence from the premises on holidays, etc, the tenant may allege that the notice was not received before the period started to run.

9.2.5.2   Personal service on someone other than the tenant

When personal service is effected, any person on the premises may be served whose duty it would be to deliver the notice to the tenant, eg the tenant's spouse. The court determines this as a matter of fact. In such an event, the fact that the notice does not reach the tenant before the commencement of the notice period is irrelevant provided the notice was served on the spouse before the commencement of the notice period. Moreover, the notice need not necessarily be served at the premises in question. It will be a matter for proof in any given case.

9.2.5.3   Where the tenant is a limited liability company

If the tenant is a limited liability company service may be effected at its registered office pursuant to the Companies Act, 2014, s 51. It will therefore be necessary to conduct a Companies Office search at the outset in order to obtain the latest information on the whereabouts of the company's registered office. If such information has not been filed, service may be effected on the Registrar of Companies.

9.2.5.4   Where the premises comprise a family home

The family home status of the premises may be important. If one spouse is the tenant and the other is not, consideration should be given to serving the notice on the non-tenant spouse also. This is particularly important in cases where it is proved that the landlord was motivated by the tenant's non-payment of rent arrears. The Family Home Protection Act, 1976, s 7 provides as follows:

(1)   *Where a mortgagee or lessor of the family home brings an action against a spouse in which he claims possession or sale of the home by virtue of the mortgage or lease in relation to the non-payment by that spouse of sums due thereunder, and it appears to the court—*

    (a)   *that the other spouse is capable of paying to the mortgagee or lessor the arrears (other than arrears of principal or interest or rent that do not constitute part of the periodical payments due under the mortgage or lease) of money due under the mortgage or lease within a reasonable time, and future periodical payments falling due under the mortgage or lease, and that the other spouse desires to pay such arrears and periodical payments; and*

    (b)   *that it would in all the circumstances, having regard to the terms of the mortgage or lease, the interests of the mortgagee or lessor and the respective interests of the spouses, be just and equitable to do so, the court may adjourn the proceedings for such period and on such terms as appear to the court to be just and equitable.*

(2)   *In considering whether to adjourn the proceedings under this section and, if so, for what period and on what terms they should be adjourned, the court shall have regard in particular to whether the spouse of the mortgagor or lessee has been informed (by or on behalf of the mortgagee or lessor or otherwise) of the non-payment of the sums in question or of any of them.*

The court has discretionary jurisdiction in equity proceedings. Thus, in considering whether or not to adjourn the proceedings and in awarding costs if appropriate, the court will have regard to whether the non-tenant spouse was informed by, or on behalf of, the landlord of the non-payment of the sums in question. Service of the notice to quit on the non-tenant spouse is therefore recommended.

9.2.5.5   Service by post

Service by post is subject to the general principle that there must be reasonable proof that the notice came into the tenant's possession prior to the commencement of the notice period. Service is then deemed to take place on the date on which, in the ordinary course of postage, the notice would have been delivered.

9.2.5.6   Where the tenant has died

Where the tenant is dead, service should be on the legal personal representatives, if any, failing which the President of the High Court should be served. However, if someone else is in occupation of the premises that occupant should be served. Such a person is deemed to represent the estate for the purposes of determining the tenancy. Instead of referring to 'the tenant and all other persons in occupation' the notice should be addressed to 'the representative of AB Deceased and all persons claiming to represent his or her estate' or words to that effect.

9.2.6 WAIVER OF NOTICE

A notice may be waived expressly or by conduct. Waiver will cause the continuation of the tenancy: *Curoe v Gordon* (1892) 26 ILTR 95.

Waiver by conduct may be construed by any of the following:

(a) service of a subsequent notice to quit;

(b) a demand for rent which has accrued following the expiry of the notice period. This will depend on intention, which is a question of fact; or

(c) the acceptance of rent which has fallen due after the expiry of the notice period. Again, however, it must be shown that the landlord intended to waive the notice: *Lyons v Johnston* (1944) 78 ILTR 19.

9.2.6.1 Should a landlord accept payment of rent?

In practice, landlords are advised either not to accept rent in the circumstances outlined above or to mark the receipt as mesne rates only. 'Mesne rates' is the term given to compensation for trespass when the trespasser is a former tenant who is overholding. The amount is usually equal to the amount of rent and other sums reserved under the agreement during the period of overholding, and will be claimed as such in the event that the landlord issues equity civil proceedings against the former tenant.

Moreover, many practitioners advise landlords not to demand rent beyond the commencement of the notice period or at least not to incorporate any such written demand into the notice, in cases where the landlord genuinely requires possession. As stated earlier, the notice must contain an explicit demand for possession on expiry of the notice period and show a clear and unambiguous intention to determine the tenancy.

This is the position notwithstanding statutory provisions such as, for example, the Housing (Private Rented Dwellings) Act, 1982, s 20 which allows for all rent accepted (for 'dwellings' as defined in that Act) following the institution of legal proceedings and up to the date of judgment to be treated as mesne rates.

It should be remembered that there is no particular form of notice to quit. The court shall determine the intention of the landlord, which is a question of fact, from the wording of the notice if this is in written form. Care should therefore be taken to avoid any ambiguity when drafting the notice.

9.2.7 SAMPLE NOTICES TO QUIT

The following are examples of notices to quit.

9.2.7.1 Where the gale day is known

TAKE NOTICE that you are hereby required to quit and deliver up to me or my agent thereunto authorised possession of ALL THAT AND THOSE (describe the premises) which you hold as a yearly tenant on the 1st day of February 2019.

Dated this 19th day of June 2018.

Signed ....
Gerard Brady,
Landlord

To: Tara McGuire,
Tenant,
And all other persons in occupation.

It is assumed for the purposes of the foregoing that 1 February 2019 is the known gale day and that the tenant holds under a yearly tenancy. In this example, the landlord has personally signed the notice. See below for an example signed by an agent.

9.2.7.2 Where the gale day is not certain

If there is uncertainty as to the gale day, it is advisable to draft a notice to quit in the alternative:

> TAKE NOTICE that you are hereby required to quit and deliver up to me or my agent thereunto authorised possession of ALL THAT AND THOSE (describe the premises) which you hold as a yearly tenant on the 1st day of February 2019 or alternatively on the expiration of the year of your tenancy which shall occur after the expiration of 183 days after the service of this notice your tenancy being then terminated.
>
> Dated this 19th day of June 2018.
>
> Signed ....
> Veronica Matthews,
> Solicitor (as authorised agent previously authorised in writing),
> for and on behalf of Gerard Brady, Landlord
>
> To: Tara McGuire,
> Tenant,
> And all other persons in occupation.

The above indicates that the landlord has given prior written authority to the agent. It is not necessary for the prior authority to be in written form. In practice, however, it is impossible to predict whether a tenant will deliver up possession or force the landlord to resort to litigation. Given the latter possibility, agents are understandably reluctant to leave such matters to chance.

If the date of termination is not clear it is not necessary to specify the particular day on which the tenant must quit as long as it is clear which is the day. In other words, in the second example quoted above, the words 'or alternatively on the expiration of the year of your tenancy, etc' are quite sufficient to specify the day.

Care should be taken, as noted at **9.2.4** and **9.2.5**, to check the lease to see if provision has been made for a specific and exact method of terminating the tenancy. Leases commonly contain conditions setting out that, in the event of overholding, there shall be deemed to be a monthly tenancy which may be terminated by service of one month's written notice.

In the case of *Hynes v Walsh*, June 1994, Circuit Court (unreported), McGuinness J considered just such a clause in circumstances where the notice was issued in the alternative 'omnibus' form above. The clause stated:

> 'The tenancy hereby created may be determined by either the Landlord or the Tenant at any time after the 23rd July, 1975 by the service of one month's previous notice in writing expiring on any day of the month.'

The fixed term agreement between the parties expired on 23 July 1975.

The tenants contested the validity of the notice on two grounds. The second ground was that the alternative termination of the tenancy, ie the omnibus clause was not applicable in a situation where a clear and unambiguous period of notice was set out in the contract of tenancy. Counsel for the plaintiffs told the court that the omnibus clause was in very common use to cover any eventuality or mistake in the date given in the first part of the notice to quit.

McGuinness J found that, since the lease contained a clause specifying the precise method of termination, the exact requirements of that clause should be met. Where it was not met, the notice was invalid despite the use of the omnibus clause. She distinguished this case from the High Court case of *White v Mitchell* [1962] IR 348, which dealt with a tenancy arising under common law where there was a high degree of uncertainty as to the facts of the tenancy.

This appears to be the most authoritative statement to date on the effectiveness or otherwise of the omnibus clause. McGuinness J stated, however, that she would welcome a more authoritative reconsideration of the matter. This is a significant case as practitioners have tended to use the omnibus clause in all circumstances. This is now no longer advisable in circumstances where the precise date of termination can be established, subject of course, to the appropriate period of notice being given. In light of this judgment all notices to quit should be strictly scrutinised and construed.

9.3 Forfeiture

9.3.1 GENERAL

Forfeiture is appropriate only to terms certain where the term granted by the lease is still running. It is one of the ways of terminating a lease prematurely. It should be noted, however, that a landlord has no right whatsoever to forfeit the lease unless the tenant has been in breach of one or more of its terms. Moreover, a landlord loses the right to forfeit the lease by failing to follow certain statutory procedures designed to give the tenant a reasonable opportunity to remedy the breach.

If the court holds that the landlord was justified in forfeiting the lease the tenant will lose the benefit of any statutory protection that might otherwise have been available. However, forfeiture is an equitable remedy and the court has a wide discretion to grant relief to the tenant on such terms as it thinks just. All equity proceedings are subject to the equitable maxims. A tenant may thus avail of equitable as well as statutory relief. In practice, the courts tend to lean against forfeiture. It is extremely difficult to forfeit a lease successfully, particularly in cases where the parties' difficulties are being aired in court for the first time. However, relief from forfeiture may be denied where the parties are on equal terms.

Forfeiture no longer applies to the majority of residential tenancies since the enactment of the 2004 Act.

9.3.2 BASIS FOR FORFEITURE

Forfeiture may arise in one of three ways:

  (a)   disclaimer by the tenant of the landlord's title;

  (b)   re-entry or ejectment where there has been a breach of a condition in the lease; or

  (c)   re-entry or ejectment where there has been a breach of a covenant by the lessee if the lease contains a proviso or condition for re-entry for such breach.

9.3.2.1 Forfeiture by disclaimer

A tenant is estopped from disputing the landlord's title. Should a tenant so disclaim, the result is an immediate forfeiture and hence a determination of the tenancy. A mere oral disclaimer would not produce this result, but a positive act to that effect by the tenant may do so. For example, if the landlord brings ejectment civil proceedings against a tenant and the defence includes such a disclaimer, forfeiture will result.

9.3.2.2   Forfeiture for breach of condition

A lease may be forfeited for breach of a condition even if it does not contain a forfeiture proviso/proviso for re-entry. However, it is fundamental for the landlord to be able to distinguish between a condition and a covenant or other term of the lease. A condition is a more fundamental term of the contract. The right to forfeit is inherent in a condition.

The rules of contract law apply here. Whether a particular clause may be said to constitute a condition, as opposed to a 'mere' covenant (or other 'lesser' term) shall, in case of a dispute, be a matter for the court to consider. Each case shall turn on its own facts. The fact that a lease or letting agreement stipulates that any particular clause shall constitute a condition or covenant does not settle the matter.

9.3.2.3   Forfeiture for breach of covenant

A lease may not be forfeited for breach of a covenant unless it contains a forfeiture proviso/proviso for re-entry. It is the responsibility of the landlord's solicitor to draft the lease. Great care must be taken when drafting the proviso to ensure that the landlord is clearly entitled to re-enter upon the breach of the specified covenant or covenants.

The case of *Spencer v Godwin* (1815) 4 M & S 265 is instructive. In that case the court considered the impact of a proviso to the effect that if any covenants *thereinafter* contained were broken then forfeiture would lie. However, the lessee's covenants in their entirety preceded these words. Forfeiture was not granted.

Another common example is the proviso for re-entry if the lessee 'should do or cause to be done' something contrary to the covenants. Note that this will give no right of re-entry if the basis of the landlord's complaint is the lessee's omission to repair. Omission is not the doing or the causing to be done of anything contrary to the covenants.

Note also that covenants expressed in the negative form (ie that the lessee shall not do or not cause something to be done which is contrary to the covenants) may give rise to difficulty for the lessor if the proviso for re-entry is limited to circumstances where the tenant does or causes something to be done.

9.3.3   SAMPLE PROVISO FOR RE-ENTRY

Problems such as those outlined above can be avoided by clear drafting in the original agreement. The following is a commonly used modern proviso for re-entry:

> 'PROVIDED HOWEVER and it is hereby agreed that if the rent hereby reserved or any part thereof shall at any time be in arrears and unpaid for twenty-one days after the same shall have become due (whether any formal or legal demand therefor shall have been made or not) or if the tenant shall, at any time, fail or neglect to perform or observe or shall be in breach of any of the covenants, conditions or agreements herein contained and on the tenant's part to be performed or observed, or if the tenant be a company, shall enter into liquidation whether compulsory or voluntary (other than for the purpose of amalgamation or reconstruction) or being an individual or a firm shall become bankrupt or compound or arrange with his or its creditors, then and in any such case, it shall be

lawful for the landlord or any person or persons authorised by the landlord to enter upon the demised premises and to hold and enjoy the same as if the lease had not been made, but without prejudice to any right of action or remedy of the landlord in respect of any antecedent breach of any of the covenants by the tenant herein contained.'

This is a widely drafted clause. While it is the standard type you may encounter, the subject matter may be varied by agreement between the parties. It is not uncommon for the right to re-enter to be restricted to a particular type or types of breach. As such, the tenant's solicitor will always examine this clause closely.

An ambiguous proviso will be construed by the court as untenable and will not therefore effect a forfeiture. The contractual rule of *contra proferentum* will apply. This means that the court will interpret the clause against the party who drafted it.

9.3.4 SECTION 14 AND STATUTORY RESTRICTION ON RIGHT TO FORFEIT

Most practitioners will be familiar with the 'section 14 notice'. This arises by virtue of the Conveyancing Act, 1881, s 14(1), as amended by the Landlord and Tenant (Ground Rents) Act, 1967, s 35. This provision restricts the right of a landlord to re-enter on forfeiture in certain cases. It provides that, with certain exceptions, before forfeiture can take place a notice must be served by the landlord on the tenant. It should be noted that much of the Conveyancing Act, 1881, was repealed by the Land and Conveyancing Law Reform Act, 2009. However, s 14 is not included in the list of repeals.

Section 14(1) reads as follows:

> *A right of re-entry or forfeiture under any proviso or stipulation in a lease, for a breach of any covenant or condition in the lease, shall not be enforceable, by action or otherwise, unless and until the lessor serves on the lessee a notice specifying the particular breach complained of and, if the breach is capable of remedy, requiring the lessee to remedy the breach, and, in any case, requiring the lessee to make compensation in money for the breach, and the lessee fails, within a reasonable time thereafter, to remedy the breach, if it is capable of remedy, and to make reasonable compensation in money, to the satisfaction of the lessor, for the breach.*

Section 14 does not apply to a residential dwelling to which the 2004 Act applies by virtue of s 193(b) of the 2004 Act.

The exceptions to this general requirement are found in s 14(6) and s 14(8) of the 1881 Act, as amended by the Conveyancing Act, 1892, s 2(2).

The most notable exception is the non-payment of rent in s 14(8), ie a s 14 notice is not required. However, as has already been pointed out, forfeiture is an equitable remedy and the courts tend to lean against it. Thus, landlords should be advised to serve a demand for payment (often in the style of a s 14 notice) in such an event.

This contrasts with the situation pertaining to the service of a notice to quit where it is considered advisable not to demand the payment of any rent after the commencement of the notice period.

As with notices to quit there is no prescribed form of a s 14 notice.

9.3.5 FORFEITURE—THE PROCEDURE

9.3.5.1 Section 14 notice not required

If a s 14 notice is not required there must nonetheless be a clear and substantial breach on the part of the tenant. In such an event a demand is made for possession and, if applicable, for payment of the rent (a simple letter will suffice) and re-entry may then be effected if it can be done peaceably, ie where the exercise of the right of re-entry does not give rise to a breach of the peace.

In *FG Sweeney Ltd v Powerscourt Shopping Centre Ltd* [1985] ILRM 442, the defendant landlord sent a solicitor's letter, which was expressed to be a s 14 notice, in respect of arrears of rent and service charge payments to the defendant tenant. Negotiations ensued but no payment was made. The landlord effected re-entry on a Sunday, being a day when no one was in the shop and more than two weeks after service of the notice, using a master key for the purpose.

The tenant did not claim relief against forfeiture but sought, inter alia, an order restraining the landlord from obstructing its right to enter and occupy the premises, and obtained an interim injunction in those terms on the grounds that its interest in the lease had not been terminated.

At the interlocutory hearing to continue such restraint pending the trial of the action, Carroll J dismissed the application. Quoting s 14(1) which sets out that the right of re-entry on forfeiture shall not be enforceable 'by action or otherwise' unless and until a notice has been served, she observed that the words 'or otherwise' mean 'peaceable re-entry'. She found that a notice had been duly served in compliance with s 14 and that the lease had been lawfully terminated by peaceable re-entry.

Carroll J went on to comment on the commercial realities, noting that the commercial viability of a shopping centre may well depend on all the tenants paying rent and outgoings promptly. Why, she asked, should a lessee have a 'free ride' as far as rent and service charges are concerned for as long as it takes a lessor to bring a Circuit Court action and then wait for an appeal to the High Court?

It was noted that the tenant did not seek relief against forfeiture. Carroll J said she would not be surprised if the reason for this was because the court might enquire about the time when the lessee would be able to pay the arrears due.

9.3.5.2 Section 14 notice required

If a s 14 notice was required and has been served, and the time specified in the notice has elapsed without remedy of the breach, a demand is again made for possession and re-entry may be effected if this can be done peaceably.

9.3.5.3 Ejectment civil bill on title

If re-entry cannot be effected peaceably the landlord's remedy is to issue an ejectment civil bill on title based on forfeiture and seek an order for possession in court. The local sheriff or County Registrar executes this order.

9.3.5.4 Statutory prohibition on the use of force

If re-entry cannot be effected peaceably the landlord cannot use force. The Prohibition of Forcible Entry and Occupation Act, 1971, s 2 makes it a criminal offence to do so save in certain circumstances. It states:

A person who forcibly enters land or a vehicle should be guilty of an offence unless—

(a) *he is the owner of the land or vehicle, or*

(b) *if he is not the owner, he does not interfere with the use and enjoyment of the land or vehicle by the owner and, if requested to leave the land or vehicle by the owner or by a member of the Garda Síochána in uniform, he does so with all reasonable speed and in a peaceable manner, or*

(c) *he enters in pursuance of a bona fide claim of right.*

The definition of owner in relation to land in the Act is very wide and appears to include both tenant and landlord. It includes:

> *the lawful occupier, every person lawfully entitled to the immediate use and enjoyment of unoccupied land, any person having an estate or interest in land (including a person who remains in occupation of land after the determination of his tenancy therein), the owner of the servient tenement (in relation to an easement or profit à prendre), the owner of an easement or profit à prendre (in relation to the servient tenement) and in relation to land or a vehicle, any person acting on behalf of the owner and 'ownership' shall be construed accordingly.*

A tenant may hand over possession to the landlord or simply vacate the premises. However, if there is any doubt as to the tenant's intentions the landlord is better advised not to attempt re-entry. In *Harrisrange Limited v Duncan* [2002] IEHC 117 the court noted that both the plaintiff and defendant appeared to have at least on one, and probably on more than one, occasion changed the locks on the external doors of the demised premises and gained entry to it via this method. McKechnie J noted that:

> 'the unseemly events demonstrated by the landlords conduct . . . are to be seriously disapproved of. No re-entry is to take place unless it, and the method used, are lawful and in accordance with the law. The procedures available are quite adequate to vindicate any person's rights and access to the Court for that purpose is unlimited. Those who refuse to avail of such rights and such access can only intend to steal a march on the rule of law. This should not be allowed to happen.'

9.3.6 RELIEF AGAINST FORFEITURE

Relief comes in two forms: statutory and equitable. A tenant may be afforded statutory relief under the Conveyancing Act, 1881, s 14(2) by satisfying the landlord's demands at any time before the demand for possession is made. If the tenant is not so entitled, the court may afford equitable relief in the circumstances.

9.3.6.1 Statutory relief

Section 14(2) of the Conveyancing Act 1881 reads as follows:

> *Where a lessor is proceeding, by action or otherwise, to enforce such a right of re-entry of forfeiture, the lessee may, in the lessor's action, if any, or in any action brought by himself, apply to the Court for relief; and the Court may grant or refuse relief, as the Court, having regard to the proceedings and conduct of the parties under the foregoing provisions of this section, and to all the other circumstances, thinks fit; and in the case of relief may grant it on such terms, if any, as to costs, expenses, damages, compensation, penalty, or otherwise, including the granting of an injunction to restrain any like breach in the future, as the Court, in the circumstances of each case, thinks fit.*

In practice, the tenant may apply to the court for statutory relief only in some circumstances:

(a) If the landlord has brought ejectment proceedings arising from the forfeiture, the tenant is entitled to claim relief either by informal application to the court or by means of a formal counterclaim in the proceedings.

(b) Statutory relief is not available to a tenant if the landlord has entered into possession pursuant to a judgment in his favour.

(c) Statutory relief is available to the tenant provided re-entry has not occurred.

(d) Statutory relief is also available to the tenant after re-entry but only if the landlord re-entered other than on foot of an order for possession.

There are no fixed rules in regard to the exercise of the court's discretion. The court may grant or refuse relief and may impose such terms as it considers fit in the circumstances of the case. Moreover, it is in practice very difficult to overturn the exercise of judicial discretion on appeal.

In *Cue Club Ltd v Navaro Ltd* Supreme Court 23 October 1996 (unreported), the plaintiffs appealed to the Supreme Court a consent order made in the Circuit Court granting possession to the defendant along with judgment in respect of the arrears of rent. The respondents recovered possession on foot of that order. In the Supreme Court, the appellants contended that they had entered into the consent as a result of implied representations made by the respondent. Murphy J said that it was undisputed that rents payable under the lease remained unpaid and that the lease contained a proviso for re-entry for non-payment of rent. He went on to refer to the fact that in previous litigation and in the present action the appellants had pleaded and then withdrawn an allegation of forgery which on its own would suggest an abuse of the process of court.

Murphy J referred to the decision of Carroll J in *FG Sweeney Ltd v Powerscourt Shopping Centre Ltd*, (see **9.3.5.1**) a case which did not itself concern an application for statutory relief against forfeiture, for the recognition which it gave the commercial realities which might properly be taken into account by a judge in dealing with the question of forfeiture where that issue does arise. Murphy J ruled that the equitable discretion exercised by the courts in granting relief against forfeiture was hardly applicable or applicable to the same extent where the court was dealing with substantial commercial transactions in which the lessor and lessee are on equal terms.

9.3.6.2 Relief to under-lessees

Forfeiture of a lease does not necessarily determine all interests arising thereunder. Section 4 of the Conveyancing Act, 1892, reads as follows:

> *Where a lessor is proceeding by action or otherwise to enforce a right to re-entry or forfeiture under any covenant, proviso, or stipulation in a lease, the court may, on application by any person claiming as under-lessee any estate or interest in the property comprised in the lease or any part thereof, either in the lessor's action (if any) or in any action brought by such person for that purpose, make an order vesting for the whole term of the lease or any less term the property comprised in the lease or any part thereof in any person entitled as under-lessee to any estate or interest in such property upon such conditions, as to execution of any deed or other document, payment of rent, costs, expenses, damages, compensation, giving security, or otherwise, as the court in the circumstances of each case shall think fit, but in no case shall any under-lessee be entitled to require a lease to be granted to him for any longer term than he had under his original sub-lease.*

The position of a sub-lessee in such a situation has been altered by the Landlord and Tenant (Amendment) Act, 1980, s 78. This section provides that any sub-lease to which the Act applies does not automatically terminate under such circumstances but continues to exist as if the superior landlord were the immediate lessor. The rent may, however, be subject to an increase: see s 78(2). The scope of s 4 of the 1892 Act is, however, far wider as the term 'under-lessee' therein includes any person deriving title under or from an under-lessee: see 1892 Act, s 5.

If the 1892 Act is invoked, therefore, statutory relief will be afforded to the under-lessee. This will generally be effected by the execution of a new lease in favour of the sub-tenant the terms of which would be fixed by the court.

As with the relief available to a tenant under the terms of the 1881 Act, the sub-tenant must apply for statutory relief before the landlord has re-entered the premises. Thereafter, equitable relief only may be available.

Relief to sub-tenants is given sparingly and with caution. The court must be satisfied that the sub-tenant is blameless and has taken all reasonable precautions.

9.3.6.3 Landlord and Tenant (Ground Rents) (No 2) Act, 1978

The foregoing are the two principal reliefs available under statute to tenants and sub-tenants. The Landlord and Tenant (Ground Rents) (No 2) Act, 1978, s 27 should also be noted. This expressly provides that forfeiture will not lie by reason of failure to pay ground rent in the case of a 'dwellinghouse' as defined in the Act where the tenant is entitled to acquire the fee simple.

9.3.6.4 Equitable relief

There are two principal cases in which no statutory relief against forfeiture is available to a tenant. These are:

(a) Where the landlord has actually re-entered the premises prior in time to the tenant applying to the court for statutory relief, as noted at **9.3.6.1** above.

(b) Where the landlord has forfeited the lease by reason of non-payment of rent. Forfeiture on this basis is excluded from the statutory provisions referred to above. Note, however, that under-lessees are not so excluded.

In either of these cases, the court may exercise its equitable jurisdiction to grant relief where it would appear just to do so and on such terms as it thinks fit. A number of Irish decisions show that the courts tend to lean against forfeiture even where non-payment of rent is involved. In *Ennis v Rafferty* (1938) 72 ILTR 56, relief was granted on condition that the tenant paid all arrears of rent, together with costs, and undertook to the court to execute certain repairs. In *Blake v Hogan* (1933) 67 ILTR 237, relief was refused but the court took into account the fact that the rent was in arrears for the third time and the tenant had been relieved on the two previous occasions.

Whipp v Mackey [1927] IR 372 is an authority for the view that equitable relief will be afforded to a tenant where the forfeiture clause is really used for securing payment and the delay in paying has caused no injury, or only one which the payment of the arrears with interest and, if necessary, costs will cure. This may be distinguished from the English decision of *Public Trustee v Westbrook* [1965] 1 WLR 1160, where rent had not been paid for 22 years in respect of a sub-lease of demolished houses on a bombed site and everybody concerned had treated the sub-leases as gone. Relief was refused.

Relief may even be available in a case where the landlord has effected a peaceable re-entry: *Lovelock v Margo* [1963] 2 QB 786.

It should not be taken for granted that the court will grant equitable relief to a tenant when a dispute first comes to court. In a unanimous Supreme Court judgment in *Cue Club Ltd v Navaro Ltd* see **9.3.6.1**, relief was refused in the case of a commercial lease where the court considered that the parties were on equal terms. In the case of *Dickeson v Lipschitz* [1972] 106 ILTR 1, the Circuit Court refused equitable relief to a tenant who was in breach of a covenant to repair. This case is a reminder that the court will look to the conduct of the parties before deciding whether to grant relief.

9.4 Other Forms of Termination

9.4.1 EFFLUXION OF TIME

Effluxion of time applies in cases where the term specified by the lease is at an end. There is no need to serve a notice to quit. This has already been mentioned at the beginning of this chapter.

The 2004 Act is now the exception to this general rule. Prior to the 2004 Act, when the term of a fixed-term tenancy came to an end the tenancy expired. The landlord wrote to the tenant reminding him of this and the tenant gave up possession on the appropriate date. By virtue of the 2004 Act effluxion of time no longer applies to the majority of residential tenancies.

Section 41(1)–(3) provides:

(1) *If a Part 4 tenancy continues to the expiry of the four-year period without a notice of termination under sections 34 or 36 having been served in respect of it before that expiry, than a new tenancy shall, by virtue of this section, come into being between the landlord and the tenant on that expiry.*

(2) *Such a tenancy is referred to in this Act as a 'further Part 4 tenancy'.*

(3) *The commencement date of a further Part 4 tenancy is the expiry of the four-year period.*

In case there was any doubt about s 41 and the recurring nature of such tenancies, s 43 provides that the rights in the Act:

> are regarded as being of a rolling nature, that is to say, that (unless the landlord uses the means under this Part to stop the following happening)—
> (a) on the expiry of a further Part 4 tenancy, after it has been in existence for four years, another such tenancy comes into being, and
> (b) on the expiry of that tenancy, after it has been in existence for four years, a further such tenancy comes into being,
> and so on.

Section 37 of the Planning and Development (Housing) and Residential Tenancies Act 2016 amends the four years in the 2004 Act to six years for any tenancy created after 24 December 2016.

At the end of a Part 4 tenancy under the 2004 Act, a further Part 4 tenancy comes into being. At the end of a further Part 4 tenancy another further Part 4 tenancy comes into being. This continues indefinitely until the tenancy is terminated by one of the parties, or some other event brings the tenancy to an end. For example, s 39 of the 2004 Act provides that, in certain circumstances, the tenancy shall terminate on the death of the tenant.

9.4.2 MERGER

On the principle that a person cannot be both landlord and tenant of the same premises at the same time, a lease may determine when the interest of landlord and tenant becomes vested in the one person in the same right. If the rights differ, however, merger will be avoided as, for example, in the case of *Farrelly v Doughty* (1881) 15 ILTR 100. In that case the landlord took possession as mortgagee of the tenant's interest. It was held that the tenancy still subsisted.

Merger will not take place if the landlord acquires back part only of premises originally demised. There must be no intervening interest. A legal lease cannot merge in an equitable fee simple.

Merger is an equitable doctrine and is considered as a question of intention. In determining this question the court will look to the benefit of the person in whom the two estates have become vested. Unless it clearly appears that a merger was intended it will be presumed that none was intended if a merger would be against the interest of the party affected.

9.4.3 DEMAND FOR POSSESSION *PER* DEASY'S ACT, 1860, SECTION 86

A demand for possession of premises held under permission of the owner as servant, herdsman, caretaker, permissive occupant, tenant at will or by sufferance, ends such holdings. Modern legislation expressly excludes most of these arrangements from the modern definition of 'tenancy'.

9.4.4 DECREE OR WARRANT FOR POSSESSION *PER* DEASY'S ACT, 1860, SECTION 78

Section 78 of Deasy's Act is obsolete in practice. There does not appear to be any recorded case of it having been used in the last 50 years though, in theory, it could still be used as it remains on the statute books. It serves to terminate a tenancy where the tenant has deserted the premises and a half-year's rent is in arrears. Section 78 reads as follows:

In case it shall happen that a Half Year's Rent shall be in arrear of any Lands or Premises holden under any Lease or other Contract of Tenancy, or from Year to Year, and the Tenant thereof shall desert or otherwise abandon such Lands or Premises or the greater Portion of them uncultivated or unemployed, and without sufficient Distress, contrary to the Course of Husbandry, or carry off the Stock or Crop thereof, it shall be lawful for the Landlord thereof to proceed by Civil Bill Ejectment before the Chairman of the County in which the Lands or any Part of them shall be situate, to recover the Possession of them, and such Civil Bill may be according to the Form No 4 in the Schedule (A) to this Act annexed; such Landlord having first obtained a Certificate of Desertion in the Manner herein-after provided, and serving a Copy of the same, together with such Civil Bill Process, on the Tenant against whom such Proceedings shall be had, in the Manner herein-before provided in respect of Ejectments for Nonpayment of Rent, requiring such Tenant or other Person to appear to answer the Bill of the said Landlord, praying to be put into possession thereof; and it shall be lawful for the Chairman on Proof of the due Execution of such Certificate by any Person who may have witnessed the Execution of the same, and that One Half Year's Rent of the said Premises was due to the Landlord when such Certificate was granted, and that such Civil Bill Process and Copy of such Certificate were duly served in manner aforesaid, and upon hearing the Tenant, in case he shall appear, and such Evidence as he may offer, to decree the said Landlord to be put into possession of the said Premises.

Most landlords would take the view that it is not necessary to obtain a decree where the tenant has genuinely disappeared. Strictly speaking, however, it is a matter to be decided on the facts of the particular case in question. If consulted, the landlord's solicitor must be satisfied as to the landlord's reasons for believing that the tenant has indeed 'genuinely' disappeared.

9.4.5 EXECUTION OF A JUDGMENT OR DECREE FOR POSSESSION *PER* DEASY'S ACT, 1860, SECTIONS 52 AND 66

The execution of a judgment or decree for possession in ejectment for non-payment of rent under s 52 of Deasy's Act, 1860 determines the tenancy (see **9.5.2**). See also s 66 of Deasy's Act, 1860.

9.4.6 SURRENDER

Surrender cannot take place in futuro. It must operate as an immediate assignment of the tenant's interest. A contract to surrender in futuro is, however, valid and the tenant's failure to give up possession on the date agreed may entitle the landlord to damages. Such a contract must, of course, be in writing in order to satisfy the requirements of s 51 of the Land and Conveyancing Law Reform Act 2009.

9.4.6.1 Surrender by deed

In the case of surrender by deed the original and counterpart leases should be endorsed as to the fact. The disadvantage of this is that the deeds must be available. They may be held as security for a loan elsewhere or there may be some reason why either party does not wish to part with the deeds. It is therefore more common to execute a separate deed of surrender.

Details should be registered in the appropriate registry. Where the premises comprise unregistered land, the surrender should be noted in the Registry of Deeds. If the original lease was registered in the Registry of Deeds, registration of the deed of surrender will cancel it.

Where the lease has been registered in the Land Registry as a burden on a freehold folio Form 57A of the Land Registration Rules, 2012 (S.I. 483 of 2012) may be adapted to include the surrender. If the lease resulted in the creation of a new leasehold folio, the Registrar of Titles closes this folio and also cancels the registration of the lease as a burden on the freehold folio. The method used is a transfer of the leasehold folio to the landlord, which clearly shows the surrender and merger and extinguishes the lease in the reversion. The Land Registry cannot, however, accept this procedure for surrender by operation of law.

9.4.6.2   Surrender by operation of law

A lease may be surrendered by operation of law, that is in a physical way by handing over vacant possession. This is usually symbolised by the handing over of keys and the original documents of title, including the original lease. Note that this method is available where the entire demised premises is surrendered. Physical surrender must be accompanied by a statutory declaration of a competent independent person who was present at the surrender. Generally, the solicitors for each party will have been present. The statutory declaration should be kept with the title deeds. The provisions of the Family Home Protection Act, 1976, and associated legislation should also be observed.

9.4.7   OCCURRENCE OF A STATED EVENT

An example of a stated event would be the marriage or death of a named party. As with effluxion of time, above, there is no need to serve a notice to quit.

9.4.8   COURT ORDER

In addition to matters already discussed in this chapter the court has jurisdiction under certain legislation to make orders which would result in the termination of a tenancy. Section 60 of the Landlord and Tenant (Amendment) Act, 1980 provides that the court may terminate a tenancy if it considers it reasonable to do so if the building is situate in an obsolete area or, having regard to the age, condition or character of the building:

(a)   the repairing would involve expenditure excessive relative to the value of the tenement; or

(b)   the building could not profitably be used unless reconstructed or altered to a substantial extent or rebuilt; and

(c)   the landlord has a scheme for the development of the property which includes the tenement and planning permission for this has been granted.

Section 199(2) of the 2004 Act has now amended s 60 by substituting *obsolete area* for *area to which an integrated area plan relates*. Integrated area plan has the meaning assigned to it by s 7 of the Urban Renewal Act, 1998.

The court will, however, only make such an order where the lease or other contract of tenancy has an unexpired term of between three years and 25 years. If the tenancy is terminated the tenant is entitled to compensation for the termination.

9.4.9 DERELICT SITES AND DANGEROUS PREMISES

The Derelict Sites Act, 1990 enables a local authority to make a compulsory acquisition of any derelict site within its functional area. The acquisition is effected by means of a vesting order, the effect of which is to vest in the local authority the freehold title to the site in question. The Act provides for the procedure generally, and includes objections made by the owner or occupier of such premises as well as the payment of compensation to the holder of any interest therein. Under the Urban Regeneration and Housing Act 2015, each local authority is required from January 2017 to compile a vacant sites register. This is a register of lands in the local authority's area that are suitable for housing but are not coming forward for development. From January 2019 onwards, a vacant site levy will be charged on such sites.

9.4.10 EXERCISE OF AN OPTION

Commercial leases frequently contain a provision (commonly called a 'break clause') entitling either party to determine the lease prior to the expiry of the term, eg a lease for a term of 20 years determinable at the end of the first ten or 15 years by notice served in advance. The lease will provide for the notice period. It is usually six or 12 months but there is no mandatory period. The notice must conform exactly to the requirements for the exercise of the option set out in the lease: it has been held that an oral notice was bad where the lease required it to be in writing. Usually the option is given to the tenant only to exercise. The break clause is given as an inducement for the tenant to enter into the lease.

9.4.11 LIQUIDATOR'S DISCLAIMER *PER* THE COMPANIES ACT, 2014, SECTION 615

Section 615 of the Companies Act 2014 gives the liquidator of a tenant limited company the power to apply to the court, within 12 months from the date of commencement of its winding-up, or such extended period allowed by the court, to disclaim any onerous property. This is land of whatsoever kind burdened with onerous covenants or any other property which is unsaleable or not readily saleable due to it binding the possessor to the performance of any onerous act or to the payment of any sum of money.

Section 615(5) provides that the disclaimer shall operate as from the date thereof to determine the rights, interest and liabilities of the company and the property of the company in or in respect of the property disclaimed.

9.5 Legal Proceedings

Assuming the tenancy in question has been determined by one or other of the methods outlined above, it may still prove necessary for the landlord to go to court to obtain vacant possession of the premises. This will obviously arise where the tenant refuses to vacate. The principal reason for such refusal usually concerns a dispute over the landlord's entitlement to determine the tenancy. This may be based on, for example, a claim that the tenant has a statutory entitlement to a new tenancy. It is also common for a tenant to claim that there has been a technical deficiency in the relevant notice requirements. Moreover, given that there is equitable as much as legal jurisdiction in landlord and tenant proceedings, a tenant might reasonably expect the judge to lean against determining the tenancy. This, of course, will depend on the facts of the particular case.

Particular care should be taken in determining if jurisdiction is conferred on the Circuit Court or High Court; see *Meier and Anor v Lynch* [2017] IEHC 769.

While it is not proposed to examine the various procedures in detail, the following is a summary of four types of legal proceedings relating to the termination of tenancies.

9.5.1 EJECTMENT CIVIL BILL ON TITLE BASED ON FORFEITURE

In the case of an ejectment civil bill based on forfeiture, the landlord's claim for possession is based on the fact that the tenancy has been terminated by forfeiture and the tenant thus has no right to retain possession of the premises. This is not merely the obvious procedure for breaches of covenants generally, it is also the most common type of procedure where non-payment of rent occurs.

A well-drafted modern lease will provide for forfeiture in the event of non-payment of rent by the tenant on a stated gale day or a specific number of days thereafter. It is therefore open to a landlord in such a case to say to the tenant who renders payment out of time that the lease has been determined.

It is, however, unlikely that the landlord will succeed in gaining possession initially. The courts are reluctant to grant orders for possession based on non-payment of rent, and indeed forfeiture generally, until it is established that the tenant has a poor track record. An order may be granted, but it will usually impose a condition giving the tenant time to render payment, possibly to include interest and legal costs. Assuming the tenant can pay in the time set by the court, the order will lapse. Often the court will allow for payment to be made by instalments.

Many landlords will press ahead in the knowledge that establishing a poor track record on the part of the tenant in court will reap dividends eventually. Equity may swing in the landlord's favour on subsequent applications to the court. This is expensive and time consuming for the landlord, but reflects the historic Irish position where the courts tend to lean in favour of the tenant, at least in cases where the parties are not considered to be on equal terms at the outset.

9.5.2 EJECTMENT FOR NON-PAYMENT OF RENT

Ejectment for non-payment of rent is based on s 52 of Deasy's Act, 1860. The drawback of this procedure is that the landlord must wait until one year's rent is due. This is obviously not commercially acceptable to many landlords.

A rack rent lease usually provides for rent to be payable quarterly in advance and, more often than not, a landlord will be relying on these instalments of rent to discharge various outgoings, eg a mortgage on the premises.

Moreover, the landlord is not entitled to eject the tenant until six months have expired after the order is made. Again, the order will lapse if payment is made within that time.

As such, most landlords would prefer to avoid the s 52 procedure if at all possible and opt instead for the general forfeiture proceedings outlined above, assuming these are available. Section 52 ejectment proceedings may perhaps be used in cases involving non-payment of a non-domestic ground rent.

An order for ejectment under s 52 was considered in *Minister for Communications, Marine and Natural Resources v Figary Watersports Development Company Limited* [2015] IESC 74. Laffoy J, on appeal from the High Court, found that a procedure under s 52 is a separate procedure distinct from forfeiture and it is subject to equitable principles. She found that, in the interest of fairness and justice, for Figary to avail of a stay on the proceedings under s 60 it would need to pay all rent due, even arrears which the Minister was statute barred from seeking. The Minister had previously served a forfeiture notice but the court found that this ceased to exist from 2000 when the Minister confirmed that the lease was active. The court found, however, that the Minister had prima facie established an entitlement under s 52 of Deasy's Act, but, subject to compliance by Figary with the conditions stipulated, no order for possession would issue or be executed.

Section 60 of Deasy's Act, 1860 provides that proceedings will be stayed if the tenant pays the rent due plus the landlord's costs. Under s 71 the court may give such relief therein as a court of equity might have done.

9.5.3   EJECTMENT CIVIL BILL FOR OVERHOLDING

The procedure for an ejectment civil bill for overholding is invoked either following service of a notice to quit or where the original lease has expired by effluxion of time and the tenant remains in possession. It is based on s 72 of Deasy's Act, 1860.

Section 72 proceedings were commonly used prior to the Landlord and Tenant (Amendment) Act, 1980. Under the Landlord and Tenant Act, 1931, a tenant holding for a term certain was obliged to serve notice of intention to claim relief three months before the date of expiry of the lease. Failure to serve this notice resulted in the loss of renewal rights. The tenant could apply to court for an extension of time for service. However, the courts were reluctant to extend the time and so ejectment proceedings were likely to be successful. The case of *Wigoder & Co Ltd v Moran* [1977] IR 112 is an exception, time being extended in circumstances where the applicants proved that they had instructed their agents to serve the necessary notice in good time. See also *Linders Garage v Syme* [1975] IR 161.

The 1980 Act changed this. Pursuant to s 20 thereof, the tenant must now serve the notice of intention to claim relief (ie to seek a renewal of the lease) within a certain period following service of the notice to quit.

Section 21 of the 1980 Act provides that if, in the absence of an agreement between the parties, the tenant does not apply to the court to determine the tenant's right to relief within one month following service of the notice of intention to claim relief, then the landlord may make such application. However, the landlord does not acquire such right until three months following service of the (tenant's) notice.

9.5.4   EJECTMENT FOR DESERTED PREMISES

A decree or warrant for possession may be granted in a case where the premises have been deserted and a half-year's rent is overdue. The landlord's right to recover possession arises by virtue of s 78 of Deasy's Act, 1860. As mentioned at **9.4.4**, however, this section is practically obsolete. No specific form of ejectment civil bill exists for this type of proceeding. The ejectment civil bill for overholding could be adapted to cover the circumstances of a particular case.

Whether or not the landlord should seek a court order is a matter for consultation in every case between solicitor and client. The procedure itself is very cumbersome and it is by no means certain that the court will grant a certificate of desertion.

9.6   Summary of Practical Steps

The practical steps in regaining possession, whether on foot of forfeiture or a notice to quit, are broadly identical. These are:

(a)   Determine the tenancy as appropriate to the case.

(b)   Issue the appropriate legal proceedings.

(c)   Serve a motion for judgment or set the case down for a full hearing as the circumstances may require.

(d)   Obtain an order for possession. This may take a considerable amount of time particularly where the matter is being disputed by the tenant. The terms of the order will also cover arrears of rent and mesne rates (including rent from the date of issue of proceedings until the date of the order) and legal costs, if all or any of these items are claimed.

(e)   Serve a true copy of the order on the tenant and demand immediate possession.

(f)   If the tenant still does not leave lodge an Execution Order (Circuit Court) or Fi Fa (High Court) with the sheriff or County Registrar who will then eject the tenant.

CHAPTER 10

STATUTORY RELIEFS

10.1   Introduction

The Landlord and Tenant (Amendment) Act, 1980 ('the 1980 Act'), as amended by the Landlord and Tenant (Amendment) Act, 1994 ('the 1994 Act'), regulates the relationship between a landlord and tenant by providing a number of statutory reliefs to the parties to this relationship.

The general purpose of the 1980 Act is described as:

> to amend the law relating to the renewal of leases and tenancies and to compensation for improvements and for disturbance or loss of title and for these and other purposes to amend the law of landlord and tenant and to provide for other matters connected with the matters aforesaid.

This Act came into force on 8 September 1980.

The general purpose of the 1994 Act is described as:

> to amend the law relating to the renewal of leases and tenancies and to amend the laws of landlord and tenant.

This Act came into operation on 10 August 1994 and applies to all leases or other contracts for tenancies, the term of which commences after that date.

The 1980 Act is divided into six parts which deal with the following matters:

Part I (ss 1–12): Preliminary

Part II (ss 13–29): Right to a new tenancy

Part III (ss 30–44): Reversionary leases

Part IV (ss 45–63): Compensation for improvements and disturbance

Part V (ss 64–69): Covenants in leases of tenements

Part VI (ss 70–88): Miscellaneous

Part III is dealt with in **chapter 11**.

The 1994 Act amended ss 13, 17, 23 and 85 of the 1980 Act.

The Residential Tenancies Act 2004 ('the 2004 Act'), further amended ss 17 and 85 of the 1980 Act and also amended ss 58 and 60 of the 1980 Act. The 2004 Act also introduced the prospective abolition of entitlement to the long possession equity and improvements equity for dwellings to which the 2004 Act applies.

Sections 17 and 85 of the 1980 Act were again amended by ss 47 and 48 of the Civil Law (Miscellaneous Provisions) Act 2008 ('the 2008 Act'). Sections 47 and 48 came into operation on 20 July 2008. The draft Landlord and Tenant Law Reform Bill 2011 ('the draft 2011 Bill') (see **1.4.4**) proposes to replace s 17 of the 1980 Act.

This chapter examines the main reliefs provided for in the 1980 Act, as amended. These are the:

(a)   right of a tenant to a new tenancy;

(b)   right of a tenant to compensation for improvements;

(c)   right of a tenant to compensation for disturbance, and

(d)   provisions relating to covenants in leases of tenements.

References to sections of the legislation in this chapter are references to the 1980 Act unless stated otherwise.

The draft 2011 Bill proposes to repeal and replace substantial parts of the 1980 Act relating to statutory rights. Provisions relating to compensation for improvements are repealed without replacement. However, compensation for disturbance is retained in a new form (see **10.4**). Sections 13 and 16 of the 1980 Act are replaced. The long possession equity is removed (see **10.2.2**) so that the entitlement to a new tenancy only arises after five years' occupation of business premises or where the tenant has made improvements worth not less than one-half the letting value. Other provisions relate to the application for relief, the award of the new tenancy and terms including review of the rent.

10.1.1   TENEMENTS: SECTION 5

10.1.1.1   Meaning of tenement

Reliefs for tenants are available only in respect of tenements as defined in s 5. Section 5(1) states:

> In this Act 'tenement' means—
>
> (a)   premises complying with the following conditions:
>
> > (i)   they consist either of land covered wholly or partly by buildings or of a defined portion of a building;
> >
> > (ii)   if they consist of land covered in part only by buildings, the portion of the land not so covered is subsidiary and ancillary to the buildings;
> >
> > (iii) they are held by the occupier thereof under a lease or other contract of tenancy express or implied or arising by statute;
> >
> > (iv)   such contract of tenancy is not a letting which is made and expressed to be made for the temporary convenience of the lessor or lessee . . .; and
> >
> > (v)   such contract of tenancy is not a letting made for or dependent on the continuance in any office, employment or appointment of the person taking the letting;
>
> (b)   premises to which s 14 or 15 applies.

Section 5 includes not just land held under a lease but also express or implied tenancies, for example periodic tenancies. A lease is defined in s 3 of the 1980 Act as an instrument in writing, whether or not under seal, containing a contract of tenancy in respect of any land in consideration of a rent or return and includes a fee farm grant.

In *Like It Love It Productions v Dun Laoighre/Rathdown County Council* [2008] IEHC 26 Murphy J held that Blackrock Town Hall was not a tenement; the conduct of the plaintiff/appellant, the agreement and its renewal and the level of rent prevented the tenant from denying the temporary convenience of the agreement. In addition the principal of the appellant company had read and signed the agreement and had independent advice in doing so.

The main purpose/user of the property must be sought and this main purpose must attach to the buildings and not the land. The purpose/user of the land must then be subsidiary and ancillary to that main purpose/user. If the land is not subsidiary and ancillary it may be possible to change its purpose/user in order to bring the whole property within the definition of tenement.

Kenny Homes & Co Ltd v Leonard Supreme Court 18 June 1998 (unreported) involved a filling station with a substantial car parking business, with payment for the car parking made in a part of the filling station. Lynch J held that the car parking area was not subsidiary and ancillary to the buildings but that the reverse was the case.

It has been accepted that underground petrol storage tanks are 'buildings' within the meaning of the 1980 Act and that the area of land over the tanks is ancillary to the filling-station business.

In *Mason v Leavy* [1952] IR 40, 50-gallon oil storage tanks sunk in the ground surrounded by concrete foundations and walls were considered to be buildings.

In *Brendan Flynn v James McMahon* Circuit Court 3 May 2001 (unreported), the court held that the area in which cars were stored by a second-hand car dealer was subsidiary and ancillary to the shed in which the sales were processed. Buckley J was satisfied:

'[T]hat the business was carried on in the small shed and that the storage of the cars in the remainder of the yard primarily for display purposes was subsidiary and ancillary to the shed. There are a number of different businesses where goods for sale are, or perhaps, as in the case of a garden centre have to be, stored in the open air, while sales are concluded in the building related to that open air area. As long as the contracts are concluded in the buildings it seems to me that the storage or display areas are subsidiary and ancillary to the buildings.'

It was held in *Dursley v Watters and Castleblaney Plant Hire Ltd* [1993] 1 IR 224, that a self-assembled shed, holding tank, cage and small lock-up constituted buildings. Morris J stated:

'[T]hat the fact that the office in this case was capable of being removed from a site and placed or erected elsewhere is not of relevance. Nor do I consider the fact that the office was delivered on site in a semi-prefabricated state to be of relevance . . . The fact that it arrived "flat packed" . . . does not appear to me to deprive it of the essential quality of being a building when erected.'

However, Morris J held that the applicant was not entitled to relief as the shed and buildings were subsidiary and ancillary to the remainder of the premises because at most the buildings were a convenience to the carrying on of this business. None of the actual work associated with the main user was carried on in the buildings and the business could have been carried on without them. This contrasts with *Brendan Flynn v James McMahon*, where the contracts were concluded in the buildings.

The High Court held in *Michael Terry v Edward J Stokes* [1993] 1 IR 204 that sheds built without foundations and without planning permission were buildings. O'Hanlon J held that the definition of tenement in the 1980 Act referred to 'buildings simpliciter' as opposed to permanent buildings.

The requirement for buildings, no matter how broad the definition, means that vacant plots along with farm and agricultural land are excluded from the definition of tenement. Hence tenants holding these types of property do not have an entitlement to a new tenancy on the termination of a previous tenancy. However, the draft 2011 Bill (see **1.4.4**) proposes to remove the definition of tenement and thus bring such tenancies into this statutory framework for the first time. It is proposed that the concept of 'tenement' be dropped so that a tenant who runs a business on land without buildings (eg a car park or farming activities) would be entitled to statutory reliefs provided other conditions are met, eg holding under a tenancy and continuous occupation for the relevant period. This would be a significant policy shift that may not be welcomed by farmers who have not previously had to protect themselves against the possibility of renewal rights in respect of farm land.

10.1.1.2   Occupation

Section 5 provides, inter alia:

(2)   *For the purposes of subsection (1)(a)(iii), where a State authority holds premises under a lease or other contract of tenancy express or implied or arising by statute, the authority shall be deemed to be in exclusive occupation thereof notwithstanding that they may be occupied for the purposes of another State authority.*

(3)   *Where—*

(a)   *a person holds premises under a lease or other contract of tenancy express or implied or arising by statute, and*

(b)   *that person is entitled to the occupation of the premises, and*

(c)   *either—*

(i)   *the premises are used with that person's permission by a private company for the purpose of carrying on a business which that person himself carried on in the premises up to the time when it began to be carried on by the private company, or*

(ii)   *that person being a company which is another company's holding company, the premises are used for the purpose of carrying on a business by the other company, or*

(iii)   *that person being a company which is another company's subsidiary, the premises are used for the purpose of carrying on a business by the other company, or*

(iv)   *that person being a company which is another company's subsidiary, the premises are used for the purpose of carrying on a business by another subsidiary of the other company, the private company, the other company or the other subsidiary (as the case may be) shall be deemed for the purposes of subsection (1)(a)(iii) to be the tenant of the premises and to be in exclusive occupation thereof.*

(4)   *In subsection (3) 'company', 'private company', 'holding company' and 'subsidiary' have the same meanings respectively as in the Companies Act, 1963.*

This provision obviated inequitable anomalies which had developed in interpreting the Landlord and Tenant Act, 1931.

It deals with the position where a tenant sets up a company and transfers the business to the company but forgets to assign the lease to the company. Previously, under the 1931 Act, when the lease expired the tenant had no statutory right to renew his lease because he was not in continuous occupation prior to the expiry of the tenancy and the company had no rights because it was not the tenant. Under s 5(3) the company is now deemed to be the tenant and in exclusive occupation and it has all the rights of the tenant under the 1980 Act. Unfortunately this provision does not cover the alternative, ie where the individual remains in occupation and continues to trade but assigns the lease to a company.

A similar situation pertains where the named tenant is a holding company of an occupying subsidiary company or vice versa. The occupying party is deemed to be the tenant for the purposes of the definition of the 'tenement' under the Act.

10.1.1.3   Tenant

Tenant is defined in s 3 of the 1980 Act as:

the person for the time being entitled to the occupation of premises and, where the context so admits, includes a person who has ceased to be entitled to that occupation by reason of the termination of his tenancy.

10.1.1.4 Predecessors in title

Predecessors in title is also defined in s 3 as:

(a) *when used in relation to a tenant, means all previous tenants under the same tenancy as the tenant or any tenancy of which that tenancy is or is deemed to be a continuation or renewal, and*

(b) *when used in relation to a landlord, means all previous landlords.*

10.2 Right to a New Tenancy

Section 16 provides that where Part II applies to a tenement the tenant shall be entitled to a new tenancy in the tenement beginning on the termination of the previous tenancy. In order to establish this right the tenant must prove one of the following 'equities':

(a) business equity under s 13(1)(a); or

(b) long possession equity under s 13(1)(b); or

(c) improvements equity under s 13(1)(c).

10.2.1 BUSINESS EQUITY

10.2.1.1 Meaning of business equity

Under s 13(1)(a) a tenant has a business equity if:

the tenement was, during the whole of the period of five years (as inserted by s 3 of the 1994 Act) (formerly three years for tenancies the term of which commenced on or before the 10 August 1994, the date on which the 1994 Act came into force) ending at that time, continuously in the occupation of the person who was the tenant immediately before that time or of his predecessors in title and bona fide used wholly or partly for the purpose of carrying on a business.

The period of occupation previously required under the 1980 Act was three years.

In *Plant v Oakes* [1991] 1 IR 185, O'Hanlon J considered the genuineness of the use when considering whether or not the use was bona fide. In *M50 Motors Ltd v O'Byrne* Circuit Court 3 May 2001 (unreported), Buckley J took the view that where the tenancy agreement restricted the use to residential purposes only but there was business use, such use could not be a genuine use. It was not a bona fide use. Accordingly, the tenant was not entitled to a new tenancy and the landlord was entitled to possession. This was affirmed on appeal to the High Court; *O'Byrne v M50 Motors Ltd* [2001] IEHC 196.

In *Twil Ltd v Kearney* [2001] 4 IR 476 the proceedings in the form of a case stated centred on the interpretation of the phrase 'at any time' in s 13 of the 1980 Act. The applicant contended that once the tenant had at any stage during its occupancy of the premises satisfied the qualifying period of three years' business use, the relevant provisions of the 1980 Act applied and the tenant was entitled to renew. Fennelly J held that to allow a tenant to 'crystallise' his rights at any time would run counter to the nature and purpose of the Act. It was held that the expression 'at any time' referred to the date of the expiry of the lease. This was the relevant date for determining the tenant's entitlement to a new lease. The question was also raised as to whether continuous occupation by a sub-tenant would entitle the tenant to relief. The court held that the tenant seeking relief must occupy the property for the entire period and this did not include sub-tenants.

Thus, it is not sufficient for a tenant to stay in occupation for five years and then vacate the premises until he or she is ready to claim a new tenancy.

Business is defined in s 3 as:

> *any trade, profession or business, whether or not it is carried on for gain or reward, any activity for providing cultural, charitable, educational, social or sporting services, and also the public service and the carrying out by an authority being the council of a county, the corporation of a county or other borough, the council of an urban district, the commissioners of a town, a health board under the Health Act, 1970, or a harbour authority under the Harbours Act, 1946, of any of their functions.*

This is a very wide definition and it could, in fact, be argued that almost anything could be a business until the contrary is proven.

10.2.1.2 Occupation

Under s 13(2), for the purpose of determining the period of occupation for a business equity the court has power, if it considers it reasonable, to disregard a temporary break in the use of the tenement. In *Farrell v Wine* (1973) 107 ILT & SJ 222, no business was carried on in the premises for a period of four months. The landlord claimed that there had been no continuous user up to the date of termination of the lease and this contention was upheld in court. The fact that the tenant had left a number of items of furniture on the premises had no connection with the carrying on of a business. The tenant lost the entitlement to a new tenancy and thus a valuable interest in the property.

Section 85 provided that any provision contracting out of the Act would be void so landlords took other avoidance measures, the intent of which was to prevent tenants from acquiring statutory rights of renewal. (See *Gatien Motor Co Ltd v Continental Oil Co of Ireland Ltd* [1979] IR 406, which was decided under the Landlord and Tenant Act, 1931.) To prevent tenants acquiring renewal rights, many landlords were only prepared to enter into short-term letting agreements, usually for two years and nine months, or long-term leases, usually 35-year leases. For similar reasons, landowners entered into caretaker's agreements or licences, neither of which creates an interest in land. See Practice Note, Law Society *Gazette* (April 1986) in relation to the use of caretaker's agreements under the Landlord and Tenant Act, 1931. See **chapter 3** in relation to licences and the fact that the court will look at the true nature of the agreement rather than the label given to it by the parties.

When a short-term letting agreement was entered into, as the tenant did not acquire the right to a new lease at the end of the two years and nine months, there was a disincentive on the part of the tenant to invest money in the premises by way of repair or improvement because there was no guarantee that the landlord would agree to renew at the end of the term. Even if the lease was renewed the tenant would have to move temporarily to other premises to break the period of occupation and prevent renewal rights arising. Such a break would need to be a complete 'lock, stock and barrel' physical break of occupation for a trading period. Merely closing the premises for a period with the tenant's possessions remaining on the property for that period would not be sufficient to constitute a break in user, as we have noted that under s 13(2) the court has the power to disregard a temporary break in user such as the traditional two-week summer holiday period for that business or the landlord painting the premises.

These avoidance measures led to major problems in the property market. A letting agreement for two years and nine months was too short to cover the three- to five-year initial growth period of a new business and many businesses, both new and old, did not have the financial means to commit themselves to a 35-year lease with five-yearly rent reviews and onerous covenants. These 35-year leases are usually full repairing and insuring leases, which are dealt with in **chapter 12**. In addition, the provisions of the 1980 Act led to a climate which was not attractive to foreign businesses.

The 1994 Act attempted to remedy these problems by increasing the qualifying period to five years. As a result the standard short-term letting agreement is no longer two years and nine months. It is now for a period of four years and nine/eleven months. This has provided tenants with more certainty and a reasonable length of time to realise the benefits of any money invested by them in the premises, eg for repairs, improvements, fitting out and goodwill. It must be remembered, however, that the five-year period applies only to leases or other contracts of tenancy the terms of which commence after 10 August 1994. It does not apply to leases commencing before 10 August 1994. A question arises in relation to a lease created before that date which expired and was renewed after 10 August 1994. Does such a lease remain under the provisions of the 1980 Act or does it now come under the provisions of the 1994 Act?

Section 27 of the 1980 Act provides that:

> *where a tenancy is continued or renewed or a new tenancy is created under this Part, the continued, renewed or new tenancy shall for the purposes of this Act be or be deemed to be a continuation of the tenancy previously existing.*

This would indicate that such a lease remains under the provisions of the 1980 Act; however, the 1994 Act is stated to have effect in s 3(2) in relation to 'a lease or other contract of tenancy the term of which commences after the commencement of this Act'.

10.2.2 LONG POSSESSION EQUITY

Under s 13(1)(b) a tenant has a long possession equity if:

> *the tenement was, during the whole of the period of twenty years ending at that time, continuously in the occupation of the person who was the tenant immediately before that time or of his predecessors in title.*

Unlike the business equity, the long possession equity applies to both business and residential property. This equity may also be referred to as the long occupation equity.

Section 192(2) of the 2004 Act introduced the prospective abolition of entitlement to the long possession equity in relation to dwellings to which the 2004 Act applies. The margin only refers to the long occupation equity but this section also captures the improvements equity for dwellings to which the 2004 Act applies. It provides that on and from the fifth anniversary of the relevant date, Part II of the 1980 Act shall not apply to a dwelling to which the 2004 Act applies. The relevant date is defined in s 5 of the 2004 Act as the date on which Part 4 of the Act is commenced. This date is 1 September 2004 as set out in the Residential Tenancies Act 2004 (Commencement) Order, 2004 (S.I. 505 of 2004). The fifth anniversary is 1 September 2009.

On 1 September 2009, the entitlement to apply for an equity under the 1980 Act ceased to apply in relation to dwellings to which the 2004 Act applied. Thus tenants of such dwellings are no longer able to avail of the right to renew under the 1980 Act.

Section 192(3), however, sets out an exception. This arises where the tenant has served a notice of intention to claim relief under and in accordance with s 20 of the 1980 Act before 1 September 2009.

The Department of the Environment, Heritage and Local Government explanatory leaflet explains the rationale for the abolition as follows:

> 'The well-intentioned long occupation equity provision has proved counter-productive, prompting eviction of tenants approaching twenty years of occupancy. It has also discouraged institutional investment in private rental accommodation, particularly since the controversy surrounding the termination of tenancies in Mespil Estate in Ballsbridge in the early 1990s. A Working Group established in 1994 in the wake of the Mespil

Estate controversy recommended the amendment of the 1980 Act to provide an opt-out from the entitlement but this was not implemented. The Commission on the Private Rented Residential Sector recommended the abolition of the entitlement after a transitional period of five years and recommended the availability of an opt-out from the entitlement for that five-year period. The Government decided to implement the Commission's recommendations.'

The 2004 Act did not result in the complete abolition of long possession equity leases. Section 3(2) of the 2004 Act confirms that it does not apply to a dwelling which is the subject of a tenancy granted under Part II of the 1980 Act, Part III of the 1931 Act or which is the subject of an application made under s 21 of the 1980 Act and the court has yet to make its determination on the matter. Thus, the abolition of entitlement to a long possession equity only applies to those tenants who have never previously claimed the right to a new tenancy. Tenants who previously renewed their lease under the provisions of the 1931 or 1980 Acts are unaffected by s 192 and they will be able to keep renewing their lease under the 1931 or 1980 Acts as each one expires. As each such lease is renewable, the right of such tenants is potentially perpetual.

Section 55(1) of the 2004 Act provides that occupation under a Part 4 tenancy or a further Part 4 tenancy can be taken into account when determining the period of occupation for the purposes of a long possession equity. However, under s 55(2), the termination of a Part 4 tenancy or a further Part 4 tenancy is not a termination for the purposes of s 17(1)(a) of the 1980 Act save if that termination is on the ground specified in para 1 of the Table to s 34 of the 2004 Act (see **6.10.2**). If the tenant has failed to comply with their obligations and has been notified of the failure and the landlord's entitlement to terminate within a reasonable time, as specified in the notification, and the tenant does not remedy the failure within that specified time, the termination will be regarded as a termination for the purposes of s 17(1)(a) and the tenant will lose the entitlement to a new tenancy (see **10.2.5.6**).

10.2.3 IMPROVEMENTS EQUITY

Under s 13(1)(c) a tenant has an improvements equity if:

> *improvements have been made on the tenement and the tenant would, if this Part did not apply to the tenement, be entitled to compensation for those improvements under Part IV and not less than one-half of the letting value of the tenement at that time is attributable to those improvements.*

Improvement is defined in s 45 as:

> *any addition to or alteration of the buildings comprised in the tenement and includes any structure erected on the tenement which is ancillary or subsidiary to those buildings and also includes the installation in the tenement of conduits for the supply of water, gas or electricity but does not include work consisting only of repairing, painting and decorating, or any of them.*

Thus, if the tenant would be entitled to compensation for improvements and such improvements accounted for half or more than half of the letting value of the tenement when the notice of intention to claim relief is served, then the tenant has an improvements equity.

Unlike the business equity, the improvements equity applies to both business and residential property.

See **10.2.2** for the effect of s 192(2) of the 2004 Act on this equity.

10.2.4 TERMS OF A NEW TENANCY

Section 16 provides that when a tenant complies with Part II of the Act he is entitled to a new tenancy commencing on the termination of his previous tenancy, the terms of such new tenancy to be those as may be agreed between the landlord and the tenant or, in default of agreement, as fixed by the court. Section 18 states that, in the absence of agreement between the parties, the court shall fix the terms of the new tenancy commencing on the termination of the previous tenancy and the tenant shall not be entitled to compensation in respect of the termination of his previous tenancy.

The court in this instance is the Circuit Court by virtue of s 3(1) of the Act. See *Cuprum Properties Limited (Acting by its Joint Receivers and Managers Tom O'Brien and Simon Coyle) v Murray* [2017] IEHC 699, where an order for possession of leased premised was sought in the High Court but was dismissed for want of jurisdiction. The defendant had served notice of intention to claim relief but the claim for a new tenancy had yet to be determined by the Circuit Court.

10.2.4.1 Length of term

Under s 23 of the 1980 Act, the court is required to fix the duration of the tenancy at 35 years or such lesser term as the tenant may nominate.

If the tenant and landlord could not agree, the tenant could ask the court to grant a lease for any period up to a maximum of 35 years. This was unsatisfactory from the landlord's point of view as the tenant could seek a lease for as little as one month and there have been cases of tenants seeking a new lease for only a year. Renewals of this nature could continue for as long as the tenant wished to remain in occupation as at the end of the year he would presumably again be entitled to seek a further renewal from the court under s 13. There is no limit on the number of times a tenant can renew and as s 27 of the 1980 Act provides that the renewed tenancy is deemed to be a continuation of the previous tenancy, the tenant could exercise the right of renewal ad infinitum.

The landlord would have no way of knowing how long the tenant intended to continue this cycle. Such short-term renewals on a continuing basis led to difficulties in the management of investment properties. Landlords who entered the investment market to provide long leases and thus obtain a guaranteed return on their investment found themselves facing the uncertainty of short-term renewals. This damaged the value of their interest in the property both in terms of selling and raising security. Purchasers and lending institutions needed to know there was a certain rent roll which was not available with short-term renewals. This situation deprived the landlord of a secure and predictable income from the premises, with consequent financial implications.

The 1994 Act has attempted to remedy this uncertainty. Section 5 has substituted the following for s 23(2) of the 1980 Act:

> *The Court shall fix the duration of the tenancy at thirty-five years or such less term as the tenant may nominate save, where the right to a new tenancy arises in respect of a tenement referred to in section 13(1)(a)(as amended by section 3 of the Landlord and Tenant (Amendment) Act 1994), the duration of the tenancy shall be fixed at twenty years or such less term as the tenant may nominate provided that it shall not be fixed for a term of less than five years without the landlord's agreement.*

Thus, if the right to a new tenancy is based on a business equity, the duration of the new tenancy will be fixed at 20 years or such lesser term as the tenant may nominate, but it will not be fixed for a period of less than five years without the landlord's agreement. The landlord and tenant may agree to a lease of less than five years, but if the landlord does not agree the tenant will be entitled only to a lease of between five and 20 years as the tenant nominates.

If the right to a new tenancy is based on a long possession or improvements equity the term of the new tenancy is still 35 years or such lesser term as the tenant may nominate.

The standard long-term commercial lease has, in practice, been reduced from 35 years to 15–20 years and this move was intensified by s 5 of the 1994 Act. This change in the maximum term of a new tenancy granted to a business tenant by the courts was also to encourage overseas businesses to locate in Ireland as such businesses are more used to medium-term leases.

This was recognised by the Government in the case of mainly foreign businesses locating in the Custom House Docks area. The Landlord and Tenant (Amendment) Act, 1989, removed the renewal rights for leases granted in the period 1989 to 1994 for companies locating in the Irish Financial Services Centre, thereby allowing landlords to grant leases of medium-term length without giving the tenant companies any rights of renewal.

Many foreign businesses tend not to understand the value of the unexpired residue of the term of a lease or the value of a right to renew in this jurisdiction.

10.2.4.2 Rent

Under s 23(5), the rent set by the court for a new tenancy shall be the 'gross rent' reduced, where appropriate, by an allowance for improvements. Gross rent is defined as:

> *the rent which in the opinion of the Court a willing lessee not already in occupation would give and a willing lessor would take for the tenement, in each case on the basis of vacant possession being given, and having regard to the other terms of the tenancy and to the letting values of tenements of a similar character to the tenement and situate in a comparable area but without regard to any goodwill which may exist in respect of the tenement.*

In other words, the rent will be the rent the property would obtain if it was let on the open market.

Note that the court cannot fix a review clause in such a lease but both the landlord and tenant are entitled to apply to the court for a review of the rent at five-yearly intervals. Under the Landlord and Tenant (Amendment) Act, 1984, s 15, the party seeking the review must serve one month's notice on the other party for the first review and, for each subsequent review, the notice must be served no earlier than the fifth anniversary of the date of service of the notice for the preceding review. In default of agreement on the rent the person seeking the review may apply to court not earlier than one month after service of the notice. Thus, on a review there is an initial delay because the application cannot be brought until five years after the preceding review. Long delays might also arise before the matter is listed for hearing though the new rent, when set, does operate from the fifth anniversary.

It is clearly preferable for the landlord and tenant to agree the terms of the new lease as opposed to allowing the court to fix the terms—particularly on the landlord's part in relation to rent review.

Thus, it is preferable from the landlord's viewpoint for the tenant to be granted a modern commercial lease which provides for the reviewed rent, when agreed, to be backdated to the review date and also for interest to be paid for that period.

The Law Reform Commission Consultation Paper on General Law of Landlord and Tenant (LRC CP 28–2003) recommended in the case of non-residential tenancies a statutory model of rent review clause which should operate as a default provision that the parties would be free to amend. The draft 2011 Bill (see **1.4.4**) includes a schedule setting out rent review provisions and the basis on which the proposed assessor would determine the revised rent.

10.2.4.3 Conditions

Section 23(7) states that:

> *The Court may, as one of the terms of the new tenancy, require the intended tenant to expend, within such time as the Court thinks proper, a specified sum of money in the execution of specified repairs (including painting for purposes of preservation but not painting for purposes of mere decoration) to the tenement and authorise the postponement of the grant of the new tenancy until the requirement has been complied with.*

If the tenant refuses or fails to comply with this requirement the court has the power to declare the tenant to have forfeited his right to a new tenancy and to discharge any order granting it to him.

10.2.5 RESTRICTIONS ON RIGHT TO A NEW TENANCY

There are certain restrictions on the right to a new tenancy. These are contained in s 17 as amended by s 4 of the 1994 Act and s 191 of the 2004 Act.

10.2.5.1 Contracting out

Section 85 provided that any provision contracting out of the Act would be void. In representations made to the Law Reform Commission it was pointed out that s 85, coupled with reservations by lawyers about relying on the devices designed to prevent tenants from acquiring statutory rights of renewal, had led to a petrifaction of the business-letting market (Law Reform Commission Report 30–1989). The Law Reform Commission went on to state that there was no reason why two parties entering an agreement 'at arm's length' should not be allowed to contract out of the provisions of the 1980 Act.

In *Bank of Ireland v Fitzmaurice* [1989] ILRM 452, the court held that s 85 makes void direct and indirect attempts to contract out of the 1980 Act. In this instance it was a clause providing for a penal rent to be set on review thus pressurising the tenant to surrender the lease rather than be bound to such a prohibitive rent. The tenant had been assured that this clause would not be enforced against him. The clause also contained terminology referring to an index no longer in use.

Section 4 of the 1994 Act changed the position somewhat by allowing a tenant of office premises only to contract out of its right to a new tenancy after obtaining independent legal advice. Section 191 of the 2004 Act changed the position further by introducing a voluntary renunciation option where the long possession equity applies to the tenement. Section 47 of the 2008 Act amended the position again by providing that the section 4 renunciation would no longer be confined to tenants of office premises. Section 47 permits any tenant with a business equity to renounce his entitlement to a new tenancy and it made other significant changes to the terms of the renunciation.

10.2.5.2 Old section 4 renunciation

Section 4 of the 1994 Act inserted the following subparagraph in s 17 of the 1980 Act:

> *(iiia) if section 13(1)(a) applies to the tenement, the terms of the tenancy provided for the use of the tenement wholly and exclusively as an office and, prior to the commencement of the tenancy, the tenant had executed, whether for or without valuable consideration, a valid renunciation of his entitlement to a new tenancy in the tenement and had received independent legal advice in relation to the renunciation.*

Thus, a number of conditions were required to be met before the parties could contract out of the Act. These were:

(a) s 13(1)(a) must apply to the tenement, ie it must be a business premises;

(b) the terms of the tenancy must provide for the use of the premises, wholly and exclusively as an office;

(c) the tenant must execute prior to the commencement of the tenancy, whether for or without valuable consideration, a valid renunciation of his or her entitlement to a new tenancy; and

(d) the tenant must also receive independent legal advice in relation to the renunciation.

The Act was remiss in that there was no definition of what constituted 'an office'. It appeared from the wording of s 4 that a tenant of an office with ancillary non-office use was not in a position to contract out of the provisions of the 1980 Act unless the two parts of the premises were dealt with separately. This presented difficulties where a landlord wanted to grant a lease of, for example, an office and warehouse or an office and ancillary car parking. To avail of the protection offered by s 4, the landlord had to enter into a separate arrangement for the non-office premises. This was often dealt with by way of a licence which terminated when the lease of the office terminated.

The 2008 Act has now extended this renunciation to all business tenants and there is no requirement for this renunciation to be prior to the commencement of the tenancy.

10.2.5.3   New section 47 renunciation

Section 47 of the 2008 Act substituted a new (iiia) subparagraph into s 17 of the 1980 Act as follows:

> *(iiia) if section 13(1)(a) applies to the tenement, the tenant has renounced in writing, whether, for or without valuable consideration, his or her entitlement to a new tenancy in the tenement and has received independent legal advice in relation to the renunciation.*

Thus the premises need not be used wholly and exclusively as an office, the renunciation need no longer be executed prior to the commencement of the tenancy and the term 'valid renunciation' has been removed.

The conditions which must now be met before the parties can contract out of the 1980 Act are therefore as follows:

(a) s 13(1)(a) must apply to the tenement, ie it must be a business premises;

(b) the tenant must execute whether for or without valuable consideration, a renunciation of his or her entitlement to a new tenancy; and

(c) the tenant must also receive independent legal advice in relation to the renunciation.

This renunciation option has now been extended to all businesses and all commercial tenants including the retail and manufacturing sectors and this follows a recommendation of the Law Reform Commission.

Section 47 is also to be welcomed as it is no longer necessary for the tenant to execute the renunciation prior to the commencement of the tenancy. It can now be executed during the currency of the term if the parties so wish.

When acting for a landlord where the tenant agrees to 'contract out' a solicitor should:

(a) ensure that the renunciation states that the tenant renounces any entitlement to a new tenancy which he or she would otherwise have been entitled to under s 13 of the 1980 Act;

(b)   ensure that the renunciation states that the tenant has received independent legal advice; and

(c)   ensure that the solicitor giving independent legal advice has witnessed the tenant's signature or obtain confirmation from the tenant's solicitor that he or she did, in fact, advise the tenant in relation to the renunciation.

These new provisions came into operation on 20 July 2008 and appear to apply to new leases and also leases in existence at that date.

Form of renunciation

The Law Society recommended the following form of renunciation in the Law Society *Gazette* (June 2009):

THIS RENUNCIATION made the_____day of_____20___WHEREAS:

1.   I   (the Tenant) of

      (delete one of the following alternatives)

A.   have negotiated with   (*the Landlord*) of   to take a tenancy ('the Tenancy') of the premises ('the Premises') at to be granted by a lease or tenancy agreement in the form of the draft lease or tenancy agreement annexed hereto

B.   am the tenant under a tenancy ('the Tenancy') created by a lease or tenancy agreement made the   day of   between   of the one part and   of the other part of the premises ('the Premises') at   which are a tenement within the meaning of the Landlord and Tenant Acts and of which the said   is now the landlord.

2.   I have received independent legal advice in relation to this renunciation from

3.   I have been advised that under the existing legislation I would, subject to the terms of that legislation, be entitled to a new tenancy in the Premises on the termination of the Tenancy.

NOW I, (*the Tenant*),_____for the consideration hereinafter set forth under the provisions of Section 47 of the Civil Law (Miscellaneous Provisions) Act 2008 DO HEREBY RENOUNCE any entitlement which I may have under the provisions of the Landlord and Tenant Acts to a new tenancy in the Premises on the termination of the Tenancy AND DO HEREBY UNDERTAKE as set out hereunder.

UNDERTAKING

In consideration of

(i)   the landlord granting the Tenancy

      OR

(ii)   the payment by the landlord of the sum of €   in consideration of the premises

I,   (*the Tenant*), undertake:

(1)   To notify any proposed assignee of my interest of the existence of this renunciation

(2)   To notify any proposed sub-tenant of mine of this renunciation and to obtain from the proposed sub-tenant a renunciation in similar terms as a term of the sub-tenancy

(3)   To consent to the registration of an inhibition by the lessor on any leasehold folio opened in respect of the Tenancy

SIGNED by the said

in the presence of:

The practice note (Law Society *Gazette* June 2009) accompanying the precedent renunciation sets out the advice to be given to tenants and landlords and also provides some guidance about the operation of the renunciation in the event of a sub-tenancy or assignment. In particular solicitors acting for tenants should advise their client that by executing the renunciation they will automatically be waiving any rights to compensation for disturbance. See **10.4**.

10.2.5.4 Section 191 renunciation

Section 191 of the 2004 Act introduced a voluntary renunciation option where the long possession equity applies to the tenement. Section 191 inserted the following subparagraph in s 17:

> *(iiib) if section 13(1)(b) applies to the tenement (and the tenement is a dwelling to which the Residential Tenancies Act, 2004 applies), the tenant had completed and signed, whether for or without valuable consideration, a renunciation of his or her entitlement to a new tenancy in the tenement and had received independent legal advice in relation to such renunciation.*

Thus, as with a s 4 renunciation there are a number of conditions to be met before the parties can contract out of the Act. These are:

(a) Section 13(1)(b) must apply to the tenement, ie the long possession equity must apply;

(b) the tenement must be a dwelling to which the 2004 Act applies;

(c) the tenant must complete and sign the renunciation; and

(d) the tenant must receive independent legal advice in relation to the renunciation.

This provision applies on and from the *relevant date* which is defined in s 5 of the 2004 Act as the date on which Part 4 of the Act is commenced. This date is 1 September 2004 as set out in the Residential Tenancies Act 2004 (Commencement) Order, 2004 (S.I. 505 of 2004).

Where such a renunciation is properly entered into by the parties the tenant will have no entitlement to a new tenancy at the end of the 20 years' continuous occupation. This provision means that a tenant coming close to 20 years' occupancy where the landlord proposes to terminate the tenancy to prevent the right to renew arising, will be able to renounce that right in return for the landlord allowing the tenancy to continue.

Form of renunciation

The Law Society Conveyancing Committee recommended the following form of renunciation in the Law Society *Gazette* (May 2005):

Residential Tenancies Act, 2004—renunciation under section 191

THIS RENUNCIATION made the_____day of_____20_____ I,_____ AB_____, of_____ _____have, as of the date hereof, been in continuous occupation of the premises known as _____(hereinafter referred to as 'the said premises') for upwards of_____years.

The said premises is a 'tenement' within the meaning of the Landlord and Tenant Acts and is a 'dwelling' within the meaning of section 4 of the Residential Tenancies Act, 2004 ('the 2004 Act').

The landlord of the said premises is__CD____of_____(hereinafter called 'the landlord').

STATUTORY RELIEFS

I have received independent legal advice in relation to this renunciation from _____
_____.

I have been advised that under the terms of the Landlord and Tenant Acts, I would be entitled to a new tenancy in the said premises at the expiry of the period provided for in section 13(1)(b) of the Landlord and Tenant (Amendment) Act, 1980.

NOW I, in consideration of the landlord granting me a Part 4 tenancy (within the meaning of section 29 of the 2004 Act) in the said premises under the 2004 Act (*or set out such other consideration, if any, as may be applicable*) DO HEREBY, pursuant to section 191 of the 2004 Act, RENOUNCE any entitlement I may have under the provisions of the Landlord and Tenant Acts to a new tenancy on the expiry of the term provided for by section 13(1)(b) of the Landlord and Tenant (Amendment) Act, 1980.

SIGNED by the said

_____

in the presence of

_____

10.2.5.5   Restriction on application to State

The restriction on an application to the State is set out in s 4 of the 1980 Act, as amended by s 14 of the Landlord and Tenant (Amendment) Act, 1984. It provides that the 1980 Act does not bind a State authority in its capacity as lessor or immediate lessor of any premises. If the State authority acquires its interest after the commencement of the 1980 Act a lessee is, however, still entitled to compensation for improvements carried out before the State authority acquired its interest.

10.2.5.6   Other restrictions

Section 17(1) sets out the grounds for a tenant losing his entitlement to a new tenancy as a result of certain acts or defaults on his part. Section 17(1) states that:

(a)   *A tenant shall not be entitled to a new tenancy under this Part if—*

    (i)   *the tenancy has been terminated because of non-payment of rent, whether the proceedings were framed as an ejectment for non-payment of rent, an ejectment for overholding or an ejectment on the title based on a forfeiture, or*

    (ii)   *the tenancy has been terminated by ejectment, notice to quit or otherwise on account of a breach by the tenant of a covenant of the tenancy, or*

    (iii)   *the tenant has terminated the tenancy by notice of surrender or otherwise, or*

    (iv)   *the tenancy has been terminated by notice to quit given by the landlord for good and sufficient reason, or*

    (v)   *the tenancy terminated otherwise than by notice to quit and the landlord either refused for good and sufficient reason to renew it or would, if he had been asked to renew it, have had good and sufficient reason for refusing.*

(b)   *In this subsection 'good and sufficient reason' means a reason which emanates from or is the result of or is traceable to some action or conduct of the tenant and which, having regard to all the circumstances of the case, is in the opinion of the Court a good and sufficient reason for terminating or refusing to renew (as the case may be) the tenancy.*

In *McCarthy, Bolding and Cambridge v Larkin* [2009] IEHC 75 Clark J held that the plaintiffs had established good and sufficient reason in that the defendant tenant had failed to keep the premises in good repair. The plaintiffs were entitled to recover possession as the premises were in a deplorable state of repair.

If the tenant has terminated by notice of surrender then the entitlement to a new tenancy will be lost. In *Edward Lee & Co Ltd v N1 Property Developments Ltd* [2012] IEHC 494 Charleton J pointed out that surrender is ineffective unless the landlord consents to accept it and is therefore consensual in the fullest sense of the term. In this instance the notice given by the tenant to the landlord was that it did not wish to exercise the option of a new 36-year lease on the same terms as the previous 36-year lease and such a notice did not disentitle the tenant from statutory relief. See further analysis in relation to surrender in this context in *Stapleyside Company v Carraig Donn Retail Limited* [2015] IESC 60.

Section 17(2) provides grounds for a landlord to refuse to grant a new tenancy even though apart from s 17(2) the tenant would be entitled. It states:

(a)   *A tenant shall not be entitled to a new tenancy under this Part where it appears to the Court that—*

   (i)   *the landlord intends or has agreed to pull down and rebuild or to reconstruct the buildings or any part of the buildings included in the tenement and has planning permission for the work, or*

   (ii)   *the landlord requires vacant possession for the purpose of carrying out a scheme of development of property which includes the tenement and has planning permission for the scheme, or*

   (iii)   *the landlord being a planning authority, the tenement or any part thereof is situate in an area in respect of which the development plan indicates objectives for its development or renewal as being an obsolete area, or*

   (iv)   *the landlord, being a local authority for the purposes of the Local Government Act, 1941, will require possession, within a period of five years after the termination of the existing tenancy, for any purpose for which the local authority are entitled to acquire property compulsorily, or*

   (v)   *for any reason the creation of a new tenancy would not be consistent with good estate management.*

Section 3 defines planning permission as including outline permission.

The term 'good estate management' has given rise to a considerable amount of litigation. This term has been considered and defined in *Gallagher v Earl of Leitrim* [1948] Ir Jur Rep 23, *Ryan v Bradley* [1956] IR 31 and *Dolan v Corporation of the Corn Exchange Buildings Company of Dublin* [1973] IR 269.

In *Dolan v Corporation of the Corn Exchange Buildings Company of Dublin*, it was held by the Supreme Court that in deciding whether a tenant is disentitled to a new tenancy on the ground of the landlord's intention to develop the property, the court should determine that issue in the light of the circumstances prevailing at the time of the hearing of the tenant's application for a new tenancy and not on the basis of what the landlord hopes or expects in relation to, for example, obtaining planning permission. In this case there were conditions in the permission which had not been complied with.

See also *Johnston and Perrott Ltd v Cantrell*, 3 May 2001, Circuit Court (unreported). In this case the landlord invoked s 17(2)(a)(i). Planning permission had been granted but again it was subject to a number of conditions. The tenants argued that because there were outstanding conditions in the planning permission which had not been complied with at the date of the hearing there was no valid planning permission which could be implemented. The court adopted the course suggested by Henchy J in *Dolan v Corporation of the Corn Exchange Buildings Company of Dublin* and adjourned the matter for a period to enable the landlord to comply with the conditions in the planning permission.

Good estate management is particularly relevant where the landlord owns surrounding property and intends to incorporate the demised premises into them. This was the case in *Jones v Luke Gardiner Ltd* Circuit Court 17 May 1999 (unreported). A brief description of the facts and decision are recited in the *Conveyancing and Property Law Journal* Volume 4(3) 1999.

Under s 17(3), where the court is satisfied that the landlord will not require possession until after the expiration of a period of at least six months, the court may, if the tenant so requests, continue the existing tenancy until terminated by the landlord for those purposes by the service of six months' previous notice in writing. The court thus has the power to continue the tenancy temporarily.

Under s 17(4) where, in a case in which an application for a new tenancy has been refused, it appears to the court that the landlord has not, within a reasonable time, carried out the intention, agreement or purpose, as the case may be, on account of which such application was refused, the court may order the landlord to pay to the tenant such sum as it considers proper by way of punitive damages.

If a business tenant is entitled to a new tenancy and has been refused one on the basis of s 17(2), the tenant is entitled to compensation for disturbance under Part IV of the Act.

Section 60(2) of the 1980 Act as amended by s 199(2) of the 2004 Act also provides that the court may on application by the landlord terminate a tenancy provided it is reasonable to do so and provided the building is situate in an area to which an integrated area plan relates or having regard to the age, condition and character of the building the repair would involve excessive expenditure or the building could not be profitably used unless it was rebuilt or substantially altered or reconstructed. Certain other conditions must also be met for the court to make such an order and compensation is payable to the tenant (see **9.4.8**).

Section 199(2) of the 2004 Act has now amended s 60 by substituting *area to which an integrated area plan relates* for *obsolete area*. Integrated area plan has the meaning assigned to it by s 7 of the Urban Renewal Act, 1998.

10.2.6 PROCEDURE FOR CLAIMING A NEW TENANCY

The prescribed forms for claiming a new tenancy are set out in the Landlord and Tenant Regulations, 1980 (S.I. 272 of 1980). See **10.7**.

To claim a new tenancy the tenant must serve a notice of intention to claim relief in the prescribed form (Form No 1) on each person against whom the claim is intended to be made within the time limits set out in s 20. These time limits depend on the type of tenancy.

The notice must be served:

(a) in the case of a tenancy terminating by the expiration of a term of years or other certain period or by any other certain event—

   (i) before the termination of the tenancy, or

   (ii) at any time thereafter but before the expiration of three months after the service by the landlord of notice in the prescribed form (Form No 2) of the expiration of the term or period or the happening of the event (the landlord cannot serve this notice earlier than three months before the termination of the tenancy);

(b) in the case of a tenancy terminating by the fall of a life or any other uncertain event at any time but before the expiration of three months after the service on the claimant by the landlord of notice in the prescribed form (Form No 2) of the happening of the event;

(c) in the case of a tenancy which is terminable by notice to quit at any time but before the expiration of three months after the service of the notice to quit.

In *Baumann v Elgin Contractors Ltd* [1973] IR 169, the applicant had been in possession of a tenement under a lease for a term which ended on 30 November 1971. Before that date, he served on the lessor a notice of the applicant's intention to claim a new tenancy under the Landlord and Tenant Act, 1931. After the expiration of the term, the applicant continued in occupation of the tenement and paid rent to the lessor as if the term had not expired. Seventeen months after the expiration of the term, the applicant applied to the Circuit Court for an order declaring that he was entitled to a new tenancy under the 1931 Act. The application was refused and the applicant appealed to the High Court. Finlay J held, in allowing the appeal, that in the circumstances the creation of a tenancy could not be implied from the fact that the applicant continued in occupation and that the respondents received rent from him during such overholding, and that the applicant had a statutory right to a new tenancy under the provisions of the 1931 Act. The statutory right would not have been defeated if the creation of a tenancy could have been implied from the facts.

If the tenant fails to serve notice of intention to claim relief in circumstances where there is a right to renew, the landlord may force the issue by serving notice of termination of tenancy (Form No 2). The landlord cannot serve this notice earlier than three months before the termination of the tenancy. Once this notice is served the tenant then has three months to serve notice of intention to claim relief (Form No 1).

Under s 83 the court has discretion to extend the time limits set out in the Act where failure to observe the time limits was occasioned by disability, mistake, absence from the State, inability to obtain requisite information or any other reasonable cause unless the court is 'satisfied that injustice would be caused'. In *Londonderry and Lough Swilly Railway Co Ltd v Gillen* High Court 7 May 1984 (unreported), McCarthy J warned that extensions might not be granted automatically particularly to the careless tenant. In deciding whether to extend the time the fundamental consideration is whether the interests of justice in the circumstances of the case require that the relief sought be granted. See *Linders Garage Ltd v Syme* [1975] IR 161 and *Wigoder & Co Ltd v Moran* [1977] IR 112.

Under s 21, the person who serves the notice of intention to claim relief may at any time not less than one month after service of the notice, apply to the court to determine his right to relief and to fix the amount of the compensation for disturbance or the terms of the new tenancy to which he is found to be entitled.

If he does not apply within three months after service of the notice any person on whom the notice was served may apply to the court for determination of the matter. The landlord may use this provision in s 21(2) to have the matter resolved.

Under s 21(3), an application to court may be made, heard and determined either before and in anticipation of, or after the termination of the tenancy. However, practical difficulties will arise where the date of termination cannot be ascertained. Despite the provisions of s 21(3) in *Mealiffe v GN Walsh Ltd* [1986] IR 427, Carroll J held that an application could not be brought until the date of actual termination of the tenancy was ascertained. While a tenant could give notice of intention to claim relief in advance of service of a notice to quit, until notice to quit was actually served, thereby fixing a date for termination, the court could not hear and determine the matter. The court must be able to fix the new rent which could only be done by reference to the commencement date of the new tenancy.

It is important to note that the tenant's right to remain in occupation of the tenement only crystallises when a notice of application to the court issues. Where such an application is pending for a new tenancy or to fix the terms of a new tenancy the tenant may continue in occupation of the tenement under s 28 until the application is determined by the court and then during this period the tenant is subject to the terms, including the payment of rent, of such tenancy but without prejudice to such recoupments and readjustments as may be necessary in the event of a new tenancy being granted. This right is a personal right to continue in occupation and does not confer any estate or interest or other proprietary right in the land; see *Crofter Properties Ltd v Genport Ltd* [2007] IEHC 80, *Wintertide Ltd v CIE & Anor* [2010] IEHC 494 and *Harrisrange Ltd v Duncan* [2002] IEHC 14 and 117.

A tenant's position in the period between service of the notice of intention to claim relief and the issue of the notice of application is not clear.

10.3 Compensation for Improvements

10.3.1 GENERAL PRINCIPLES

Compensation for improvements is available to both business and residential tenants. Section 45 defines 'improvement' in relation to a tenement as:

> *any addition to or alteration of the buildings comprised in the tenement and includes any structure erected on the tenement which is ancillary or subsidiary to those buildings and also includes the installation in the tenement of conduits for the supply of water, gas or electricity but does not include work consisting only of repairing, painting and decorating, or any of them.*

Section 46 provides that where a tenant quits a tenement because of the termination of his tenancy, he or she is entitled to be paid, by the landlord, compensation for every improvement made on the tenement by him or her or any of his or her predecessors in title (whether before or after the commencement of the Act) which, at the termination of the tenancy, adds to the letting value and is suitable to the character of the tenement.

However, no compensation is payable if the tenant himself or herself has terminated the tenancy by notice of surrender or otherwise, or the tenancy is terminated because of non-payment of rent.

There are similar provisions entitling a landlord to compensation from his immediate superior landlord for every such improvement made by a sub-tenant where the landlord or any of his predecessors in title have given consideration to such sub-tenant, whether by reduction of rent or by a payment of compensation or in any other way.

This compensation is payable by the landlord on the expiration of one month from the date of the fixing, by agreement or by the court, of its amount, or the delivery to the landlord by the tenant of clear possession of the tenement, whichever is the later.

The amount of such compensation is set by s 47, as such sum as may be agreed between the landlord and the tenant or, in default of agreement, the capitalised value of such addition to the letting value of the tenement at the termination of the tenancy as the court determines to be attributable to the improvements. When determining the capitalised value of an addition to the letting value the court will have regard to the probable duration of such addition, the probable life of the improvement and all other relevant circumstances, but the capitalised value will not, in any case, exceed 15 times the annual amount of the addition.

10.3.2 IMPROVEMENT NOTICE

Under s 48, where a tenant proposes to make an improvement to his tenement he may serve on his landlord an improvement notice in the prescribed form (Form No 5). The notice must include:

(a) a statement of the works proposed for making the improvement;

(b) an estimate, verified by an architect, surveyor or building contractor, of the cost of making the improvement; and

(c) if the improvement is development for which planning permission is required, a copy of the permission.

Where an improvement notice is served, the landlord may, within one month, serve on the tenant any one of the following notices:

(a)   a notice in the prescribed form consenting to the making of the improvement (Form No 6);

(b)   a notice in the prescribed form undertaking to execute the improvement in consideration of either a specified increase of rent or an increase of rent to be fixed by the court (this must be stated in the undertaking) (Form No 7); or

(c)   a notice in the prescribed form objecting to the improvement on grounds specified in the notice (Form No 8).

Section 48(4) provides that where the landlord holds for a short term only he shall, within one week, serve the notice or a copy on his immediate superior landlord, endorsed with a statement of the date on which the notice was served on him, and the superior landlord may, within one month from the date of service of the improvement notice by the tenant on the landlord, serve on the landlord and on the tenant either an improvement consent or an improvement objection. There are similar provisions with regard to the next superior interest.

Section 50 provides that, if the landlord does not serve an improvement undertaking or an improvement objection within one month of service of the improvement notice, the tenant is entitled to execute the improvements specified within one year. In this circumstance, the tenant will be entitled to compensation.

Section 51(1) provides that when an improvement notice is served by the tenant, and the landlord agrees by notice to undertake the improvements, the tenant may, by notice in writing within 14 days, either accept the undertaking or withdraw his improvement notice or object to the increase in rent specified in the undertaking. Where the tenant does not serve a notice under s 51(1) or accepts the undertaking the landlord must complete the work within six months.

Section 52 provides that when an objection is served the tenant may, within one month, either withdraw his improvement notice or apply to the court. The court may authorise the tenant to make the improvement, or reject the application, if satisfied that the tenant holds the tenement otherwise than under a lease for a term of which at least five years were unexpired at the time when the improvement notice was served, and would, on any of the grounds specified in s 17(2)(a), not be entitled to a new tenancy. Thus the court can prevent the tenant carrying out the improvement if the tenant is not entitled to a new tenancy because of s 17(2)(a) or if the tenant's lease will expire within five years. As a result a landlord may only serve an improvement objection in these circumstances.

These procedures rarely work properly as in most instances the tenant cannot wait for the process to be completed and starts the work.

A professional landlord will generally prefer to undertake the work himself as this way he can ensure that the standard of work is to his satisfaction and he can rentalise the cost.

An improvement notice is not obligatory, but a tenant who fails to serve an improvement notice runs the risk of losing his entitlement to compensation in the circumstances specified in s 54(2), ie where the landlord can prove that he has been prejudiced by the notice not having been served, or where the improvement is in contravention of a covenant in the lease, or the improvement injures the amenity or convenience of the neighbourhood.

10.4   Compensation for Disturbance

Prior to the 2004 Act compensation for disturbance was only available to business tenants.

Section 58(1) of the 1980 Act provides that where the court is satisfied that a tenant would, but for s 17(2), be entitled to a new tenancy under Part II, and that s 13(1)(a) applies to the tenement, the tenant is, in lieu of a new tenancy, entitled, on quitting the tenement on the termination of the tenancy, to be paid by the landlord compensation for disturbance, eg the cost of moving. Section 199(1) of the 2004 Act amends s 58(1)(b) by the insertion of *or 13(1)(b)* after s 13(1)(a). This extends the right to compensation for disturbance to tenants holding a long possession equity whether of business or residential property.

Section 58(2) provides that the measure of the compensation is the monetary/pecuniary loss, damage or expense which the tenant sustains or incurs, or will sustain or incur, by reason of his quitting the tenement and which is the direct consequence of that quitting.

In *Aherne v Southern Metropole Hotel Co Ltd* [1989] ILRM 693, which was taken under the corresponding provisions of the 1931 Act, the court held that the availability to the tenant of other accommodation is a relevant factor in assessing compensation for disturbance.

This compensation must be paid (s 58(4)) on the expiration of one month from the date of the fixing, by agreement or by the court, of its amount, or the delivery to the landlord by the tenant of clear possession of the tenement, whichever is the later.

Under s 58(5), where compensation awarded under s 58 is not paid within that time, the tenant is entitled, after the expiration of that time and before the payment of the compensation, to renew his or her application for a new tenancy under Part II, and s 17(2)(a) and 17(3) shall not apply to that application and the granting of the application shall operate as a discharge of the award of compensation for disturbance. In other words, the tenant may apply for a new tenancy and the landlord will not be able to refuse him or her but the tenant will no longer be entitled to compensation for disturbance. The implications for a landlord are very serious. If the tenant is not paid the compensation within the time specified then he or she has an absolute entitlement to a new tenancy, unless the tenant loses the entitlement as a result of an act or default on his or her part as set out in s 17(1).

10.5   Practical Steps

If consulted by a tenant or landlord to advise as to whether the tenant is entitled to relief under the 1980 Act (as amended) the solicitor must consider:

(a)   Has the tenancy been terminated or has notice of termination been served?

(b)   Are the premises a tenement?

(c)   Are there buildings and is the land subsidiary and ancillary to those buildings?

(d)   Is there a lease or other contract of tenancy?

(e)   Is the contract of tenancy for temporary convenience?

(f)   Is the contract of tenancy due to the office, employment or appointment of the lessee?

(g)   Who is the lessee?

(h)   Is the lessee in occupation?

(i)   How long have the tenant and his predecessors in title been continuously in occupation?

(j)   Are the premises used for business or residential purposes?

(k)   Does the tenant have an equity under s 13?

(l)   Is there a valid renunciation?

(m)   Has the tenant lost his entitlement to a new tenancy under s 17(1)?

(n)   Is the landlord entitled to refuse a new tenancy under s 17(2)?

(o)   Has a notice of intention to claim relief been served within the time limit?

(p)   Is the tenant entitled to compensation for improvements?

(q)   Is the tenant entitled to compensation for disturbance and if so, has the compensation been paid within the time limit?

(r)   If a new tenancy was refused under s 17(2), has the landlord carried out the development within a reasonable time?

10.6   Provisions Relating to Covenants in Leases

In relation to s 65, refer to **8.3.3**.

10.6.1   COVENANTS AGAINST ALIENATION: SECTION 66

Section 66 provides that a covenant in a lease (whether made before or after the Act) of a tenement absolutely prohibiting or restricting the alienation of the tenement has effect as if it were a covenant prohibiting or restricting such alienation without the licence or consent of the lessor, and such licence or consent shall not be unreasonably withheld. Alienation includes assignment and sub-letting.

A provision absolutely prohibiting alienation is not unusual in a lease. Regardless of the fact that this term was agreed between the parties, s 66 provides that it will be interpreted as stating that alienation will be subject to the landlord's consent and such consent will not be unreasonably withheld.

This provision applies only to leases of tenements, and covenants in other leases are unaffected. In addition this provision relates to alienation of the tenement. Section 66 impacts on covenants relating to alienation of the whole tenement. Covenants prohibiting or restricting alienation of part of the tenement, ie partial assignment or sub-letting are unaffected.

What is or is not 'unreasonable' will depend upon the circumstances of each individual case. The onus of proving that consent has been unreasonably withheld lies on the tenant. See *Rice and Kenny v Dublin Corporation* [1947] IR 425.

In *Perfect Pies Ltd (In Receivership) v Chupn Ltd* [2015] IEHC 692 the court found that the refusal of the landlord to consider an application amounted to an unreasonable withholding of consent so that the application to the court for a declaration under s 66 was justified. The court granted a declaration that the landlord, in delaying and failing to consent to the request for consent to assignment, acted unreasonably. However, the court was unwilling to dispense with the landlord's consent to assignment on the basis that if it had given due and proper consideration to the application for consent to assignment, it would have been reasonable to refuse consent on a number of grounds related to shortcomings in the sureties offered and the financial references provided.

By virtue of s 193(d) of the 2004 Act, s 66 of the 1980 Act does not apply to a dwelling to which the 2004 Act applies.

Section 193(d) of the 2004 Act came into operation on 6 December 2004 by virtue of the Residential Tenancies Act 2004 (Commencement) (No 2) Order 2004 (S.I. 750 of 2004).

10.6.2   COVENANTS RESTRICTIVE OF USER: SECTION 67

Section 67 contains a similar provision in respect of covenants absolutely prohibiting the alteration of the user of the tenement.

In *OHS Ltd v Green Property Co Ltd* [1986] IR 39, the tenant of a unit in Northside Shopping Centre proposed to assign its interest subject to the landlord's consent for a change of user from a fruit and vegetable store to use by a building society. The landlord refused consent. The Circuit Court held that the withholding of consent was unreasonable; however, this decision was overturned on appeal to the High Court. The landlord pleaded that the centre had more financial institutions than any other shopping centre in Dublin and it withheld consent to avoid an excessive number of dead frontages. Lynch J held that the refusal of consent was based on valid estate management grounds and was not unreasonable. He stated:

> 'I do not think that a balancing of the positions of the landlord and tenant is quite the test . . . The real question is whether the landlord is unreasonably withholding its consent contrary to the term implied in the covenant restricting user by s 67 of the Landlord and Tenant (Amendment) Act, 1980. The onus is on the tenant to establish that the landlord is unreasonably withholding its consent.'

In *Wanze Properties (Ireland) Ltd v Mastertron Ltd* [1992] ILRM 746, Murphy J said:

> 'The lessor of a business centre does not unreasonably withhold consent to a change of user where he has reasonable grounds to believe that a more suitable tenant may be found who may better preserve the character and appearance of the demised business centre.'

In this case the landlord's refusal to consent to change of use from a retail shop to a Chinese takeaway was held to be reasonable.

In *Irish Glass Bottle Company Ltd v Dublin Port Co* [2005] IEHC 89 Carroll J found that the plaintiff failed to discharge the onus of proof that consent to a change of user was unreasonably withheld. It had failed to give the defendant all the details to which the defendant was entitled in order to enable it to reach a decision on the request.

By virtue of s 193(d) of the 2004 Act, s 67 of the 1980 Act does not apply to a dwelling to which the 2004 Act applies.

10.6.3   COVENANTS AGAINST MAKING IMPROVEMENTS: SECTION 68

Here again, under s 68, any covenant absolutely prohibiting the making of any improvement is deemed to be subject to a proviso that such improvements shall not be made without the licence or consent of the lessor which shall not be unreasonably withheld.

Under s 69, if the lessor cannot be found the tenant may apply to the court for permission to alienate, alter the user or make the improvement.

Section 29 of the Landlord and Tenant (Ground Rents) Act, 1967, is of relevance here. This section enables a tenant who is entitled to buy out the ground rent to breach a clause of the lease prohibiting change of user or the making of an improvement, provided planning permission has been obtained or the change of user or improvement is an exempted development. Effectively the tenant is deemed not to have breached the terms of the lease by changing the user or making the improvement. This, however, does not apply to covenants which would survive after acquisition of the fee simple (see **11.4.2.5**).

By virtue of s 193(d) of the 2004 Act, s 68 of the 1980 Act does not apply to a dwelling to which the 2004 Act applies.

10.6.4 FORTHCOMING CHANGES

The draft 2011 Bill (see **1.4.4**) proposes changes relating not just to assignment but also matters which a tenant may wish to do to the demised premises. It contains the basic principle that a landlord cannot unreasonably withhold or delay giving consent but reverses the onus of proof concerning reasonableness so that the landlord has to prove he has acted reasonably. The draft 2011 Bill also contains a time frame for dealing with the matter of consent.

10.7 Prescribed Forms

The prescribed forms are set out in the Landlord and Tenant Regulations, 1980 (S.I. 272 of 1980), which came into force on 8 September 1980.

10.7.1 FORM NO 1

Landlord and Tenant (Amendment) Act, 1980

NOTICE OF INTENTION TO CLAIM RELIEF

(Section 20) (See Note A)

Date: .... (Note B)

To: .... (Note C)

1.   Description of tenement to which this notice refers (Note D)

....

....

2.   Particulars of relevant lease or tenancy (Note E)

....

....

Take notice that I ....

(a)   intend to claim a new tenancy, under Part II of the Landlord and Tenant (Amendment) Act, 1980, in the above tenement

(b)   intend to claim in the alternative €   compensation for disturbance (Note F)

(c)   intend to claim €   compensation for improvements in respect of the improvements of which particulars are set out in the Schedule to this notice (Note G)

Signed by *the tenant/his authorised agent/his solicitor

....

Address: ....

(a), (b), (c)—Delete as appropriate. (Note J)

*Delete as appropriate

SCHEDULE

      Item

      Full description of the work comprising the improvement (Note H)

Probable life of the improvement

Addition to letting value of the tenement at termination of the tenancy due to the improvement and probable further duration of such addition

Capitalised value of addition to the letting value at termination of tenancy

Particulars of benefits (if any) received by the tenant or his predecessors in title from the landlord in consideration of the improvement.

Notes (for information only)

A. A person who proposes to claim a new tenancy (under Part II of the Act), compensation for disturbance or compensation for improvements should serve notice in this form of his intention so to claim (sections 20(1), (3), 56(1)).

B. Any claim mentioned in this notice may be made at any time up to three months after due notification made by the landlord (in Form No. 2 or, where appropriate, by notice to quit) to the claimant of the termination of the claimant's tenancy (sections 20(2), (3), 56(1)) although extension of time may be granted (section 83).

C. The notice should be served on each person against whom the claim is intended to be made (section 20(1)). Where the claim is for a new tenancy, that new tenancy (where the claimant is entitled thereto) must be granted not only by the landlord but by any superior landlord whose joined may be necessary (section 18). Section 84 provides for making necessary information available in such circumstances.

D. Particulars should be given sufficient to identify the premises.

E. State amount of rent, date of lease or tenancy, parties thereto and (if lease or tenancy has not terminated) tenure or length of term.

F. Compensation for disturbance (in lieu of a new tenancy) is payable by the landlord to a business tenant of three years' standing who would, but for section 17(2) of the Act, be entitled to that new tenancy (section 58).

G. Compensation for improvements (defined in section 45) made by a tenant to his tenement (defined in section 5) is payable by the landlord where the tenant quits because of the termination of his tenancy (section 46(1)(a)), subject to certain restrictions (sections 46(1)(b) and 54) and to claim within the time limit (Note B).

H. Where the improvements made are those specified in an improvement notice under the Town Tenants (Ireland) Act, 1906, an improvement notice or improvement order under the Landlord and Tenant Act, 1931, or this Act, or an order of a sanitary authority or housing authority, particulars of the relevant notice or order will suffice, together with particulars of any relevant improvement certificate or sanitary improvement certificate. Alternatively the description may be given in a statement of works herein or by reference to such statement in an accompanying document.

I. A notice of intention to claim relief may be limited to a claim for compensation for improvements (section 56(1)). Where the notice indicates an intention to claim a new tenancy, it may include a claim in the alternative for compensation (section 20(3)), that is, compensation for disturbance (section 58) or compensation for improvements (section 46).

10.7.2   FORM NO 2

Landlord and Tenant (Amendment) Act, 1980

NOTICE OF TERMINATION OF TENANCY

(Section 20) (See Note A)

Date: ....

To: .... (Note A)

1.   Description of tenement to which this notice refers (Note B)

....

....

2.   Particulars of relevant lease or tenancy (Note C)

....

....

Take notice that your tenancy in the above tenement *terminated/will terminate on
.... by reason of

....

(Note A)

Signed by *the landlord/his authorised agent/his solicitor

....

* Delete as appropriate.

Address:..

Notes (for information only)

    A.   Apart from cases where section 20(2)(c), (d) applies, such as tenancies that are terminable by notice to quit, a tenant may claim relief under the Act (i.e. a new tenancy, compensation for disturbance or compensation for improvements) at any time up to three months after service on him by the landlord of this notice (sections 20(2), 56). In the case of a tenancy that already has a fixed termination date this notice may be served not earlier than three months before that termination (section 20(2)(a)(ii)).

    B.   Particulars should be given sufficient to identify the premises.

    C.   State amount of rent, date of lease or tenancy, parties thereto and (if lease or tenancy has not terminated) tenure or length of term.

10.7.3   FORM NO 3

Landlord and Tenant (Amendment) Act, 1980

NOTICE OF OFFER OF NEW TENANCY

(Section 22) (See Note A)

Date: ....

To: .... (Note A)

1.   Description of tenement to which this notice refers (Note B)

....

....

2.   Terms of new tenancy in the tenement that is offered (Note C)

....

....

3.   Nature of the estate or interest in the tenement that is owned by each person offering
the new tenancy (Note D)

....

....

Take notice that I/We .... hereby offer you a new tenancy in the tenement
above-described (or above-mentioned) on the above terms.

Signed by ....

* his authorised agent/his solicitor

....

Address:.. * Delete as appropriate

Notes (for information only)

   A.   Where a tenant has served (in Form No. 1) notice of intention to claim relief by
        way only of compensation for improvements, notice in this form may within two
        months be served on him (section 22(1)).

   B.   Either particulars should be given sufficient to identify the premises, or the tene-
        ment may be identified by reference to its description in the notice in Form No. 1
        that was served by the tenant.

   C.   The new tenancy may be offered on terms specified in the notice or on terms to be
        fixed by the Circuit Court (section 22(1)).

   D.   The notice may be served by the landlord, any superior landlord or any two or
        more of such persons (section 22(1)).

10.7.4   FORM NO 4

Landlord and Tenant (Amendment) Act, 1980

NOTICE OF ACCEPTANCE OF NEW TENANCY

(Section 22) (See Note A)

Date: ....

To: .... (Note B)

1.   Description of tenement to which this notice refers (Note C)

....

....

2.   Name and address of tenant to whom new tenancy has been offered

....

....

Take notice that I, ... hereby accept the offer of a new tenancy in the above tenement that is made in your notice dated

....

Signed by *the above-named tenant/his authorised agent/his solicitor

....

Address: ....

* Delete as appropriate

Notes (for information only)

A.   Where notice in Form No. 3 has been served offering a new tenancy the tenant may, within one month, serve notice in this form accepting that new tenancy. Alternatively he may within one month serve notice refusing the new tenancy (section 22(2)(a), (c)).

B.   The notice in Form No. 3 may be served by the landlord, any superior landlord or any two or more of such persons (section 22(1)).

C.   Either particulars should be given sufficient to identify the premises, or the tenement may be identified by reference to its description either in the notice in Form No. 1 that was served by the tenant or in the notice in Form No. 3 that was served on him.

10.7.5   FORM NO 5

Landlord and Tenant (Amendment) Act, 1980

IMPROVEMENT NOTICE

(Section 48(1)) (See Note A)

To: .... (Note A) Date:...

1.   Description of tenement to which this notice refers (Note B)

....

....

2.   Particulars of relevant lease or tenancy (Note C)

....

....

Take Notice that I intend to make an improvement, in accordance with the accompanying statement of proposed works, to my tenement above described.

I annex an estimate verified by (state name and address of architect, surveyor or building contractor)

....

of the cost of making the improvement.

* I annex also a copy of the relevant permission granted under Part IV of the Local Government (Planning and Development) Act, 1963.

Signed by ** the tenant/his authorised agent/his solicitor ....

Address: ....

To

The above-named landlord.

* Delete if planning permission not required for the improvement.

** Delete as appropriate.

Notes (for information only)

   A.   A tenant who proposes to make an improvement (defined in section 45 of the Act) to his tenement (defined in section 5 of the Act) may serve on his landlord an improvement notice (section 48).

   B.   Particulars should be given sufficient to identify the premises.

   C.   State amount of rent, date of lease or tenancy, parties thereto and tenure or length of term.

   D.   Where an improvement notice is served the landlord may (within one month) serve on the tenant an improvement consent, an improvement undertaking or, in certain cases, an improvement objection (section 48(2), (3)).

   E.   A tenant who makes an improvement without having served an improvement notice may fail to qualify for compensation for the improvement (sections 46(1) and 54(2)).

   F.   Unless the landlord holds under a lease with at least twenty-five years certain to run (or under a tenure superior thereto) he must within one week serve this notice (or a copy) on his immediate superior landlord stating the date the notice was served on him (section 48(4)). Unless that superior landlord holds under a lease with at least twenty-five years to run (or under a tenure superior thereto) he must similarly notify his next superior landlord (section 48(5)).

10.7.6   FORM NO 6

Landlord and Tenant (Amendment) Act, 1980

IMPROVEMENT CONSENT

(Section 48(2)(a), (4), (5)) (See Notes A and B)

Date: ....

To:

....

....

*and to:

.... (Note B)

Take notice that I hereby consent to the making of the improvement to the tenement situate at (state full address of tenement)

....

....

in accordance with the statement of proposed works accompanying the Improvement Notice dated the

....

Signed by *the landlord/his authorised agent/his solicitor

....

Address

....

To
The above-named tenant.
OR
Signed by *the superior landlord/his authorised agent/his solicitor (Note B)

....

Address

....

To
The above-named landlord
and
To
The above-named tenant.
* Delete where appropriate.

Notes (for information only)

   A.   Where an improvement notice is served the landlord may (within one month) serve an improvement consent, an improvement undertaking or, in certain cases, an improvement objection (section 48(2), (3)).
   B.   In certain cases a superior landlord also may serve (on both the landlord and the tenant) an improvement consent or an improvement objection (section 48(4), (5)).
   C.   Where neither an improvement undertaking nor an improvement objection is served the tenant is entitled (whether or not an improvement consent is served) to execute his improvement within one year of service of his improvement notice (section 50).

10.7.7 FORM NO 7

Landlord and Tenant (Amendment) Act, 1980

IMPROVEMENT UNDERTAKING
(Section 48(2)(b)) (See Note A)

Date: ....

To:

....

....

Take Notice that I hereby undertake to execute the improvement to the tenement situate at (state full address of tenement)

....

.... in accordance with the statement of proposed works accompanying the Improvement Notice dated the

....

And Further Take Notice that this undertaking is in consideration of (a) an increase of (state the increase of rent demanded)

.... in the rent at present being paid by you for the said tenement; (b) an increase of rent to be fixed by the Circuit Court.

Signed by *the landlord/his authorised agent/his solicitor

....

Address:

....

To
The above-named tenant.
(a), (b) Delete whichever is inapplicable.
* Delete as appropriate.

Notes (for information only)

A. Where an improvement notice is served the landlord may (within one month) serve on the tenant an improvement consent, an improvement undertaking or, in certain cases, an improvement objection (section 48(2), (3)).

B. Where an improvement undertaking is served (and where no superior landlord serves an improvement objection) the tenant may by notice in writing served within fourteen days accept that improvement undertaking, withdraw his improvement notice or object to the amount of any increase in rent specified in the improvement undertaking (section 51(1)).

C. Unless the tenant either withdraws or objects in the manner mentioned in Note B the landlord must carry out the improvement within the six months following the fourteen days mentioned in Note B and has a right of reasonable entry on the tenement for that purpose (section 51(2)).

D. Where the tenant objects to the amount of an increase in rent specified in an improvement undertaking the amount of that increase falls to be settled between the parties or by the Circuit Court, or the Court may deal with the matter otherwise (section 51(4)).

10.7.8   FORM NO 8

Landlord and Tenant (Amendment) Act, 1980

IMPROVEMENT OBJECTION

(Section 48(2)(c)) (See Note A)

Date: .... (Note B)

To:

....

.... (tenant)

*and to

....

.... (landlord)

Take Notice that I do hereby object to the execution of the improvement the subject of the Improvement Notice dated the

.... on the tenement situate at

(state full address of tenement)

....

....

The grounds of objection are:—

....

....

Signed by *the landlord/his authorised agent/his solicitor

....

Address:

....

To

The above-named tenant.

OR

Signed by *the superior landlord/his authorised agent/his solicitor (Note C).

....

Address:

....

To
The above-named landlord
and

To

The above-named tenant.

* Delete where appropriate.

Notes (for information only)

STATUTORY RELIEFS

A. An improvement objection may be served only on certain grounds (section 48(3)).
B. Any improvement objection should be served within one month of the date of service of the tenant's improvement notice (section 48(2), (4), (5)).
C. A superior landlord may serve an improvement objection, on both the landlord and the tenant, but only where the relevant premises are held from him under a lesser tenure than a lease with at least twenty-five years certain to run (section 48(4)) and rather similar restrictions apply to the service of an improvement objection by any next superior landlord (section 48(5)).
D. Where an improvement objection is served the provisions of section 52 of the Act apply.

10.7.9 FORM NO 9

Landlord and Tenant (Amendment) Act, 1980

WORK UNDERTAKING
(Section 49(2)) (See Note A)

Date.. (Note A)

To:

....

Whereas you, the above-named tenant, have served on me, the landlord, a work notice dated .... stating that (a) the sanitary authority for the district of ....
.... (b) the housing authority for .... has served on you a notice requiring the execution by you on the tenement situate at (state full address of the tenement)

....

....

of work consisting of (material description of the work):

....

....

And Whereas that work is an improvement within the meaning of section 45 of the Landlord and Tenant (Amendment) Act, 1980.

Take Notice that I hereby undertake to execute that work in accordance with the notice of that authority.

And Further Take Notice that this undertaking is in consideration of (a) an increase of (state the increase of rent demanded)

....

in the rent at present being paid by you for the said tenement: (b) an increase of rent to be fixed by the Circuit Court.

Signed by *the landlord/his authorised agent/his solicitor

....

Address:

....

To
The above-named tenant.
(a), (b) Delete whichever is inapplicable.
* Delete as appropriate.

Notes (for information only)

   A.   Where a sanitary authority or a housing authority orders an improvement to a tenement, the tenant must notify the landlord within three days (by a 'work no-tice'—section 49(1)). The landlord may respond by serving on the tenant within three days a work undertaking in Form No. 9 (section 49(2)).
   B.   Service of a work undertaking has the same effect as service of an improvement undertaking (section 49(4)).
   C.   Where the tenant serves on the sanitary authority (or housing authority) con-cerned a copy of a work undertaking, the matter becomes one between that au-thority and the landlord (section 49(5)).

10.7.10 FORM NO 10

Landlord and Tenant (Amendment) Act, 1980

IMPROVEMENT CERTIFICATE
(Section 55(1)) (See Note A)

Date: .... (Note C)

To:

....

.... (tenant)

This is to certify that improvements have been duly completed upon the tenement situate at (state full address of tenement)

....

....

in accordance with (a) the Improvement Notice dated the

....

(b) the Improvement Order of the Court dated the

....

Signed by *the landlord/his authorised agent/his solicitor

....

Address:

....

To
The above-named tenant
(a), (b) Delete whichever is inapplicable.
* Delete as appropriate.

Notes (for information only)

A. A tenant who serves an improvement notice and who, being entitled under section 50 of the Act to do so or being authorised by the Circuit Court under section 52 of the Act to do so, duly completes the improvement, has the right to obtain an improvement certificate (in this form) if he applies to the landlord therefor within six months of that completion (section 55(1)).

B. An improvement certificate is (as against the landlord and his successors) conclusive evidence of the improvement (section 55(3)).

C. Where an improvement certificate is not given within one month of due application therefor the tenant may bring the matter before the Circuit Court (section 55(2)).

D. A landlord may require payment of his reasonable expenses as a condition of giving an improvement certificate (section 55(6)).

10.7.11 FORM NO 11

Landlord and Tenant (Amendment) Act, 1980

SANITARY IMPROVEMENT CERTIFICATE
(Section 55(4)) (See Note A)

Date: ....

To: (name of tenant and full address of tenement)

....

....

This is to certify that work consisting of (material description of the work)

....

....

....

executed upon the tenement situate at the above address has been so executed in pursuance of and completed in accordance with the Order dated

....

of (a) the sanitary authority for the district of

....

(b) the housing authority for

Signed for (a) the above-named sanitary authority:

(b) the above-named housing authority:

....

(an officer authorised in that behalf)

(a), (b) Delete whichever is inapplicable

Notes (for information only)

A. Where, on foot of an order of the sanitary authority (or the housing authority), a tenant duly completes an improvement to his tenement, he is entitled to obtain from the authority within the following six months a sanitary improvement certificate in this form (section 55(4)).

B. A sanitary improvement certificate is (as against the landlord) prima facie evidence of the matters which it purports to certify (section 55(5)).

C. A sanitary authority (or housing authority) may require payment of their reasonable expenses as a condition of giving a sanitary improvement certificate (section 55(6)).

10.7.12 FORM NO 12

Landlord and Tenant (Amendment) Act, 1980
NOTICE OF INTENTION TO APPLY FOR AN ORDER TERMINATING A TENANCY
(Section 60(2)) (See Note A)

Date: ....

To:

....

.... (tenant)

1. Description of tenement to which this notice refers (Note B)

....

....

2. Particulars of relevant lease or tenancy (Note C)

....

....

Take Notice that I intend to apply to the Circuit Court for an order under section 60 of the Landlord and Tenant (Amendment) Act, 1980 (No. 10 of 1980) terminating the above tenancy in the above tenement.

Signed by *the landlord/his authorised agent/his solicitor:

....

Address:

....

* Delete as appropriate.

Notes (for information only)

A. An order under section 60 terminating a tenancy in a tenement may be made only where—
    (i)   the relevant building is obsolete or is in an obsolete area, and
    (ii) the landlord has a development scheme which includes the tenement and for which planning permission has been granted, and
    (iii) the tenancy has, at the time of service of this notice, not less than three years and not more than twenty-five years to run, and
    (iv) the tenant has had at least six months' notice (in this form) of the application to the Court for a termination order, and
    (v)   the Court considers it reasonable to make the order (section 60(2)), and
    (vi) the tenancy is not a ground rent tenancy (section 60(6)).
B. Particulars should be given sufficient to identify the premises.
C. State amount of rent, date of lease or tenancy, length of term and parties to the lease or tenancy.
D. Where a termination order is made the tenant is entitled to compensation for the termination, comprising compensation for pecuniary loss, damage or expense directly sustained or incurred, to additional payment in respect of the pecuniary benefit accruing to the landlord and to further payment in respect of any further hardship sustained by the tenant (section 60(3),(5)).
E. Where a termination order is made the tenant may continue in occupation (on the same terms as under the terminated tenancy) for one year, or until compensation for the termination is paid, whichever is the later (section 60(4)).

10.7.13 FORM NO 13

Landlord and Tenant (Amendment) Act, 1980
NOTICE REQUIRING INFORMATION FROM A LESSOR (LANDLORD)
(Section 84(1)) (See Note A)

Date: ....

To:

....

.... (Note B)

1.   Description of premises to which this notice refers (Note C)

....

....

2.   Particulars of applicant's lease or tenancy (Note D)

....

....

Take Notice that I,............................... being a person seeking an estate or interest in the
above premises under the above Act, require you to give me, within one month after the
service of this notice on you, the following information—

   (a)   the nature and duration of your reversion in the premises, and

   (b)   the name and address of the person entitled to the next superior interest in the
         premises.

....

Signed by:

....

*his authorised agent/his solicitor

....

Address:

....

* Delete as appropriate.

Notes (for information only)

   A.   Section 84 of the Act provides for the service of this notice and for the duty to
        comply within one month.
   B.   The notice may be served on—
        (i)   the immediate lessor (landlord), and
        (ii)   each other person having a superior interest in the premises.
   C.   Particulars should be given sufficient to identify the premises.
   D.   State amount of rent, date of lease or tenancy, parties thereto and tenure or length
        of term.

10.7.14 FORM NO 14

Landlord and Tenant (Amendment) Act, 1980
NOTICE REQUIRING INFORMATION FROM A PERSON RECEIVING RENT
(Section 84(2)) (See Note A)

Date: .... (Note B)

To:

....

.... (person receiving rent)

1. Description of premises in respect of which the rent is received (Note C)

....

....

2. Particulars of lease or tenancy, the lessor or landlord under which cannot be found or ascertained (Note D)

....

....

Take Notice that I .... being a person seeking an estate or interest in the above premises under the above Act, require you to give me, within one month after the service of this notice on you, the following information:

   (i)   the name and address of the person to whom the rent under the lease or tenancy referred to in paragraph 2 is paid by you.

   (ii)

....

.... (Note E)

Signed by: ....

*his authorised agent/his solicitor ....

Address ....

* Delete as appropriate.

Notes (for information only)

   A.   This notice may be served where notice in Form No. 13 cannot be served because the lessor (landlord) or superior lessor, as the case may be, cannot be found or ascertained (section 84(2) of the Act).

   B.   Section 84(3) provides for the duty to comply (within one month) with this notice.

   C.   Particulars should be given sufficient to identify the property.

   D.   State amount of rent, date of lease or tenancy, parties thereto and tenure or length of term insofar as these particulars can reasonably be procured by the person serving the notice.

   E.   State here the nature of any other information sought which is reasonably necessary for the purpose of securing the joinder of all necessary parties in the grant of the estate or interest in question.

CHAPTER 11

GROUND RENTS

11.1   Historical Background

The term 'ground rent' has arisen from the manner in which Dublin and other urban centres, for example Limerick, developed. In the 18th and 19th centuries large tracts of Irish land were owned by landlords. To obtain a satisfactory income and create a pension fund from the land, the landlords entered into leases subject to the lessee building one or more dwellinghouses on the land. There was a proliferation of these types of lease which included fee farm grants. The leases became known as 'building leases'. The rent payable by the builder/lessee to the landlord became known as a 'ground rent' as it was payable for the ground only. Subsequent to the lease, and in compliance with the covenant therein to build, the builder/lessee built one or more dwellinghouses on the land. Afterwards the builder sold the dwellinghouses by assignment for the then market value, thus getting a one-off lump sum, or created sub-leases, reserving a fine or premium (ie payment of a capital sum) for granting the sub-lease, and also reserving an annual rent, which in practice was greater than the rent under his own lease, thus creating a profit rent for himself. These sub-leases became known as 'proprietary leases'.

The term 'ground rent' is not defined but it is intended to refer to a rent paid by a tenant where the tenant has built the buildings and the landlord has provided the ground only and the amount reserved reflects that, eg £12 per year; £25 per year. Ground rent leases are long-term leases for periods such as 99, 150, 500 or even 999 years. In many instances the landlord's successor in title can no longer be traced and the rent will not have been paid for many years. Dwellinghouses were built on the land by the lessee but some of these were subsequently converted to business use. Thus ground rent leases can relate to both residential and commercial property. The low rent and lack of rent review provisions makes these leases easy to distinguish from short-term letting agreements of residential property and commercial leases with a rack rent ie market rent for the premises.

When examining titles pertaining to properties registered in the Registry of Deeds, one will often come across building leases granted by landlords such as the Pembroke Estate. Such estates derived a substantial income from these leases, with the added benefit that at the end of the term of each lease the property, together with the dwellinghouse built by the lessee, reverted to the estate. Thus the lessee, who had built the house or who had paid consideration for it lost out. He was not entitled to compensation and had no guarantee that the landlord would renew the lease at the same rent.

This was felt to be inequitable and towards the end of the 19th century and beginning of the 20th century there was a move to improve the lot of urban tenants. This led to a series of statutes giving tenants the right to compensation for improvements and disturbance, the right to claim a new tenancy and the right to buy out the freehold. The aim of the legislation is to give rights to lessees who spent money on the land by paying them compensation or giving them a further interest in the land. The legislation is also designed to give lessors compensation for the loss of their interest in the property as a result of redemption of the rent, ie by the lessee buying the lessors' interest.

The draft Landlord and Tenant Law Reform Bill 2011 ('the draft 2011 Bill') (see **1.4.4**) does not amend the law relating to ground rents, save to provide that partial merger has always been possible (see **11.4.4**).

11.2   Right to Buy Out Freehold

11.2.1   INTRODUCTION

The right of a tenant to buy out the freehold was introduced by the Landlord and Tenant (Ground Rents) Act, 1967 ('the 1967 Act'), which came into operation on 1 March 1967.

This Act is entitled:

> *an Act to provide for the extinguishing of certain rents by enabling lessees and tenants liable to pay such rents in respect of land to purchase the fee simple in the land, to provide for the apportionment of certain rents, to make provision in relation to the waiver and relaxation of certain restrictive covenants in leases, to amend in other respects the law of landlord and tenant and to provide for other matters connected with the matters aforesaid.*

Section 3(1) of this Act states that:

> *A person who, as respects any land, is a person to whom this section applies, shall, subject to the provisions of this Act, have the right as incident to his existing interest in the land to enlarge that interest into a fee simple, and for that purpose to acquire by purchase the fee simple in the land and any intermediate interests therein.*

It should be noted that in addition to having the right to buy out the freehold a party may have the right to a new tenancy under the Landlord and Tenant (Amendment) Act, 1980, as amended. See **chapter 10**. While much of the terminology used in determining these two rights is the same there are two clear differences. First, there must be permanent buildings on the land to buy out the freehold. The right to renew only requires some form of buildings. Secondly, there is no occupancy requirement to buy out the freehold; however, the right to renew clearly requires occupation on the part of the tenant. If a tenant has both options available to him, it would obviously be preferable to buy out the freehold rather than take a commercial lease subject to a market rent.

If a tenant was entitled to purchase the freehold under the 1967 Act, the procedure to be used was a conveyance of the fee simple under s 6 or determination of the matter by arbitration by the County Registrar under s 17. This procedure applied for both residential and business premises.

While this procedure has been preserved and is dealt with later in this chapter the test for determining the right to buy out the freehold has changed.

11.2.2   TEST UNDER THE 1978 ACT

11.2.2.1   General

Section 7 of the Landlord and Tenant (Ground Rents) (No 2) Act, 1978, which came into operation on 1 August 1978 repealed s 3(1)–(3) of the 1967 Act. Sections 9–16 of the 1978

Act list the persons thereafter entitled to enlarge their interest into a fee simple instead of those listed in s 3 of the 1967 Act.

Unless otherwise stated, all references to the 1978 Act contained in this chapter are references to the No 2 Act, 1978. Part II of that Act sets out the types of leases which give the right to purchase the freehold.

The purchase scheme introduced by this Act was initially for a five-year period. It has now been extended indefinitely by the Landlord and Tenant (Ground Rents) (Amendment) Act, 1987.

It should be noted that a lease is defined in s 3 of the Act as:

> *an instrument in writing, whether under or not under seal, containing a contract of tenancy in respect of any land in consideration of a rent or return and includes a fee farm grant.*

In the case of a person holding under a fee farm grant what they would be buying out under the legislation is the fee farm rent.

Section 8 of the 1978 Act replaced s 3(1) of the 1967 Act and ss 9 and 10 laid down the new test for determining the right to buy out the freehold.

Before examining these new provisions it should be noted that s 73 of the Landlord and Tenant (Amendment) Act, 1980, provides that, if an applicant was a person to whom s 3 of the 1967 Act applied before the commencement of the 1978 Act, then Part II of the 1978 Act applies to that applicant. In other words, because that person was entitled to buy out the freehold under the 1967 Act, his or her right to buy out is preserved and he or she is now entitled to buy out under the 1978 Act.

Section 8 states the general right to acquire the fee simple:

> *A person to whom this Part applies shall, subject to the provisions of this Part, have the right as incident to his existing interest in land to enlarge that interest into a fee simple, and for that purpose to acquire by purchase the fee simple in the land and any intermediate interests in it and the Act of 1967 shall apply accordingly.*

11.2.2.2   Essential conditions: section 9

In order to have the right to buy out the freehold the lessee must comply with all of s 9 and one of the conditions laid down in s 10. This is the test for both residential and commercial property and it is based on rewarding a tenant who has added value to the land.

Section 9 is quoted in full. Emphasis has been added in bold.

*(1)   This Part applies to a person who holds **land** under a **lease**, if the following conditions are complied with:*

    *(a)   that there are **permanent buildings** on the land and that the portion of the land not covered by those buildings is **subsidiary and ancillary** to them;*

    *(b)   that the permanent buildings are **not an improvement** within the meaning of subsection (2);*

    (c)   that the permanent buildings were not erected in contravention of a covenant in the lease; and

    (d)   one of the alternative conditions set out in section 10.

(2)   In subsection (1)(b) 'improvement' in relation to buildings means any addition to or alteration of the buildings and includes any structure which is ancillary or subsidiary to those buildings, but does not include any alteration or reconstruction of the buildings so that they lose their original identity:

(3)   Where it is claimed that a lease complies with this Part on the ground that the permanent buildings were erected in pursuance of an agreement for the grant of the lease on their erection but express evidence of the agreement is not available, the following provisions shall have effect:

> (a) if it is proved that the buildings were erected by the person to whom the lease was subsequently made, it shall be **presumed**, until the contrary is proved, that the agreement was in fact made and that the buildings were erected in accordance with it;
>
> (b) in any other case, the arbitrator may, if he so thinks proper on hearing such evidence as is available and is adduced, **presume** that the agreement was in fact made and that the buildings were erected in accordance with it.
>
> (4) Permanent buildings erected by a lessee in pursuance of a covenant in his lease to reinstate the buildings comprised in the lease in the event of their destruction by fire or otherwise shall be **deemed** to have been erected by the person who erected the original buildings.
>
> (5) The arbitrator may declare a person to be a person to whom this Part applies notwithstanding that the buildings were, in whole or in part, erected in contravention of a covenant, if he is of opinion that it would be unreasonable to order otherwise.

The Interpretation Act 2005 provides that, in the absence of a contrary intention, land includes tenements, hereditaments, houses and buildings, land covered by water and any estate, right or interest in or over land. See *Metropolitan Properties Ltd v John O'Brien and the Commissioners of Public Works in Ireland* [1995] 2 ILRM 383, where O'Flaherty J leaned in favour of the view that the 1978 Act contains a contrary intention as it applies only to a person who holds permanent buildings on land. It was submitted that the lessee held buildings only. For a different viewpoint, see *A O'Gorman & Co Ltd v JES Holdings Ltd* High Court 31 May 2005 (unreported).

A very wide definition of 'land' is given in s 3 of the Land and Conveyancing Law Reform Act 2009, and it is much wider than that contained in the Interpretation Act 2005. It provides that land includes both buildings divided in any way, including horizontally (as in the case of apartments) and the airspace above the surface of land (or above a building) which is capable of being occupied by a building. It is of interest to note that the definition of 'land' in s 32 of the Registration of Deeds and Title Act 2006 differs somewhat from that contained in the 2009 Act.

Land is subsidiary and ancillary if it is used for the benefit of the buildings. As a rule it is generally accepted for residential property that the land is subsidiary and ancillary if it does not exceed one acre. If the land is over one acre it may be necessary to show that it is subsidiary and ancillary. This may be done by describing the use of the land. For an examination of the meaning of these words see *Killeen v Baron Talbot de Malahide* [1951] Ir Jur Rep 19.

An example of an improvement would be an extension. Improvement does not include any alteration or reconstruction of the buildings so that they lose their original identity, ie the building becomes something completely different as a result of the alteration or reconstruction. For example, a tenant who adds a kitchen extension will not be able to buy out the freehold solely on the basis of having built the extension. The tenant would need to have built the original house as well. However, a tenant who adds something which changes the fundamental character of the building will be entitled to purchase the freehold. It is as if the tenant has built a completely new building.

As a result of s 9(4), in *Fenlon v Keogh (Per Rep of Anna Keogh)* High Court 10 February 1997 (unreported), Mr Fenlon was held not to be entitled to buy out the freehold. In 1990 the premises were totally destroyed by fire. On foot of a covenant in the lease Mr Fenlon rebuilt the premises. As a result of planning difficulties the new premises were completely different from the old, but as a result of s 9(4) the new building was deemed to be the property of the lessor. See also *Keating v Carolin* [1968] IR 193.

The distinction to be made between a mere improvement as against an alteration or reconstruction of the buildings so that they lose their original identity was examined in detail in *A O'Gorman & Co Ltd v JES Holdings Ltd* High Court 31 May 2005 (unreported). In that case the history of the property was traced back as far as 1576 and each change to the structure of the buildings was traced up to the present day. Peart J found that the building had lost its original identity. In addition the character of the building was so completely altered from what it was that the original identity had been lost. In his view the meaning of identity embraced far more than the physical structure and therefore included a change of character. The works of construction carried out by the tenant were such that they caused the house to lose its original identity and this finding resulted in those works being classified as 'additions' rather than mere improvements. That finding in turn led to the unavoidable conclusion that the lessor had not erected all the permanent buildings on the property.

The arbitrator may dispense with the requirement that the buildings are not to be erected in contravention of a covenant in the lease.

11.2.2.3 Subsidiary and ancillary test: section 14

Where a difficulty arises with the subsidiary and ancillary test the lessee may find relief in s 14 of the 1978 Act.

Section 14 provides that where all the land is not subsidiary and ancillary to the buildings the land may be split into two separate leases; the built-on lease and the vacant lease. The built-on lease will comprise that portion of the land which is covered by the permanent buildings, together with so much of the land as is subsidiary and ancillary to those buildings, and the vacant lease will comprise the residue of the said land. The lessee will then be in a position to buy out the freehold for the built-on lease. No right will exist for the vacant lease and this will revert to the lessor at the end of the term of the lease unless the lessee had rights under the 1980 Act, as amended. The 1978 Act provides for the rent and the covenants to be apportioned between the two leases.

Section 14 was invoked in *Fitzgerald (Trustees of Castleknock Tennis Club) v John Corcoran* [1991] ILRM 545, with the result that the trustees were entitled to acquire the fee simple in the club house and the subsidiary and ancillary ground. The balance of the ground was deemed to be a vacant lease.

11.2.2.4 Alternative conditions: section 10

There are seven alternative conditions in s 10, one of which must be complied with. The Landlord and Tenant (Amendment) Act, 1980, also introduced an extension to condition 7 giving eight possible alternatives, only one of which must be complied with.

The eight alternatives could be grouped under the following headings:

Conditions 1 and 2: lessee built.

Conditions 3 and 4: involve a builder.

Condition 5: expired or surrendered lease.

Condition 6: reversionary lease.

Condition 7: lease of 50 years or more with a fine or expenditure.

Extension of condition 7: sub-lease of less than 50 years.

The following are alternative conditions one of which must also be complied with in a case to which s 9 relates. Each condition is recited in full. Emphasis has been added in bold.

Condition 1

> 1. *that the **permanent buildings were erected by the person who at the time of their erection was entitled to the lessee's interest** under the lease or **were erected in pursuance of an agreement for the grant of the lease upon the erection of the permanent buildings**;*

The permanent building must have been built by the lessee or future lessee.

Condition 2

> 2. *that the **lease is for a term of not less than fifty years** and the **yearly amount of the rent** or the greatest rent reserved thereunder (whether redeemed at any time or not) **is of an amount that is less than the amount of the rateable valuation** of the property at the **date** of service under section 4 of the Act of 1967 of notice of intention to acquire the fee simple or the date of an application under Part III of this Act, as the case may be, and that the **permanent buildings on the land demised by the lease were not erected by the lessor or any superior lessor or any of their predecessors in title**: provided that it shall be **presumed**, until the contrary is proved, that the buildings were not so erected;*

The lease must be for 50 years or more. The yearly rent must be less than the rateable valuation at the date of the application to purchase. The permanent buildings must not have been erected by the lessor and there is a presumption that they were not so erected.

It may not be necessary to rely on the presumption if it is clear from the terms of the lease that the lessee or the lessee's predecessors in title built the buildings; for example, if the lease contains a covenant to build. This presumption is commonly relied upon when it is not clear which party built the buildings. This presumption may, of course, be rebutted by the landlord and a lessee's solicitor should warn the lessee in writing that the lessor may produce proof to refute it. For this reason it is preferable to rely on one of the other conditions in s 10.

In *A O'Gorman & Co Ltd v JES Holdings Ltd* High Court 31 May 2005 (unreported) the court examined this presumption and a great deal of work went into trying to piece together the history of the house and property over a period of 200 years. The court found that the evidence did not go sufficiently far to rebut the presumption.

Condition 3

> 3. *that the **lease was granted by a lessor to the nominee of a person (in this paragraph referred to as the builder) to whom land was demised for the purpose of erecting buildings thereon in pursuance of an agreement between the lessor and the builder that the builder having contracted to sell the buildings would surrender his lease in consideration of the lessor granting new leases to the builder's nominees;***

This covers the situation where a builder takes a lease of land, builds a number of houses on it pursuant to an agreement with the lessor, and then surrenders the lease to the lessor. The lessor then grants a lease of each of the houses to nominees of the builder who will be the individual purchasers of the houses.

Condition 4

> 4. *that the **lease was granted by a lessor to the nominee of a person (in this paragraph referred to as the builder) in pursuance of an agreement between the lessor and the builder that the lessor, upon the erection of the buildings by the builder, would grant leases to the builder's nominees;***

This is similar to condition 3 but in this case there is no lease between the builder and lessor.

Condition 5

> 5. *that the **lease was granted, either at the time of the expiration or surrender of a previous lease** or subsequent to such expiration or surrender—*

> (a) *at a rent less than the rateable valuation of the property at the date of the grant of the lease, or*

> (b) *to the person entitled to the lessee's interest under the previous lease,*

> *provided that the **previous lease would have been a lease to which this Part would have applied had this Act then been in force** and provided that it shall be*

> **presumed,** *until the contrary is proved, that the person to whom the lease was granted was so entitled;*

The rent must be less than the rateable valuation at the date of the second lease or the lessee under the first lease and the second lease must be the same. The expired or surrendered lease must be obtained and checked to ensure that it comes within s 9 and one of the conditions in s 10.

This is condition 5 as amended by s 71 of the Landlord and Tenant (Amendment) Act, 1980.

Condition 6

> 6. *that the lease is a reversionary lease granted on or after the 31st day of March 1931, to a person entitled thereto under Part V of the Act of 1931 or the Act of 1958, whether granted on terms settled by the Court or negotiated between the parties;*

The Act of 1931 is the Landlord and Tenant Act, 1931, and the Act of 1958 is the Landlord and Tenant (Reversionary Leases) Act, 1958.

A reversionary lease is generally a lease for 99 years at one-eighth of the gross rent (see **11.3**).

Condition 7

> 7. *that **the lease**, being a lease for a **term of not less than fifty years**, was made—*
>
> **(a)** **partly in consideration of the payment of a sum of money** *(other than rent) by the lessee to the lessor at or immediately before the grant of the lease and, for this purpose, any money paid in redemption of any part of the rent reserved by the lease (whether the money was paid in pursuance of a covenant in the lease or in pursuance of an agreement made between the lessee and the lessor during the currency of the lease) shall be deemed to be part of the consideration, or*
>
> **(b)** **partly in consideration of the expenditure (otherwise than on decoration) of a sum of money** *by the lessee **on the premises** demised by the lease, or*
>
> (c) *partly in consideration of both that payment and that expenditure, where the sum so paid or expended or the total of those sums was **not less than fifteen times the yearly amount of the rent** or the greatest rent reserved by the lease, whichever is the less.*

The lease must be for 50 years or more and must have involved payment of a fine or expenditure on the premises such as improvements or repairs (decoration cannot be taken into account) or a combination of both a fine and expenditure of at least 15 times the yearly rent.

Section 12 of the 1978 Act extends condition 7 of s 10 by providing that a lease shall be deemed to comply with condition 7 if:

> (a) *the lease was granted partly in consideration of an undertaking by the lessee to carry out specified works on the premises demised by the lease,*
>
> (b) *the amount to be expended on the works was not specified,*
>
> (c) *the works were carried out by the lessee, and*
>
> (d) *it is proved that the reasonable cost of the works taken either alone or together with any fine or other payment mentioned in that condition was not less than fifteen times the yearly amount of the rent or the greatest rent reserved by the lease, whichever is the less.*

Condition 7 is extended even further by the Landlord and Tenant (Amendment) Act, 1980, s 72.

Section 72 extends condition 7 to a lease made for a term of **less than 50 years** if:

> (a) *the lease is a **sublease** (whether mediate or immediate) under a lease (in this section referred to as the **superior lease**) **to which Part II of that Act applies**,*

> *(b)   the land demised by the lease is the **whole or part of the land** comprised in the superior lease, and*
>
> *(c)   the lease is made for a **term which equals or exceeds the lesser of the following periods, namely twenty years or two-thirds of the term of the superior lease, and in any case expires at the same time as or not more than fifteen years before the expiration of the superior lease***

and the other requirements of the condition are fulfilled.

It extends condition 7 to a sub-lease of less than 50 years provided the superior lease comes within s 9 and one of the conditions in s 10. In addition, the land demised by the sub-lease and superior lease must be partly the same. The term of the sub-lease must equal or exceed the lesser of 20 years or two-thirds the term of the superior lease and the sub-lease must also expire at the same time as, or within 15 years of, the expiration of the term of the superior lease. The rest of condition 7 must also be complied with. Thus, there must also have been a fine or expenditure or a combination of both amounting to at least 15 times the yearly rent.

11.2.2.5   Yearly tenants: section 15

Sections 9 and 10 do not apply if the lessee is a yearly tenant. Section 15 provides that a yearly tenant is entitled to buy out the freehold if:

(a)   the land is covered wholly or partly by permanent buildings and any land not so covered is subsidiary and ancillary to those buildings;

(b)   the land is held under a contract of yearly tenancy or under a yearly tenancy arising by operation of law or by inference on the expiration of a lease, or under a statutory tenancy implied by holding over property on the expiration of a lease which reserves a yearly rent;

(c)   the land has been held continuously (including the term of any expired lease) by the person or his predecessors in title for a period of not less than 25 years prior to the date of application to purchase;

(d)   the yearly rent is less than the rateable valuation of the property at the date of application to purchase or it is proved that the permanent buildings were erected by the tenant or a predecessor in title (inserted by the Landlord and Tenant (Amendment) Act, 1984, s 9);

(e)   the permanent buildings were not erected by the immediate lessor or any superior lessor or any of their predecessors in title, provided, however, that it shall be presumed until the contrary is proved that the permanent buildings were not so erected;

(f)   that the contract of tenancy is not a letting which is made and expressed to be made for the temporary convenience of the immediate lessor or of the person holding under the contract; and

(g)   the contract of tenancy is not a letting which is made for or dependent on the continuance of the person holding under the contract in any office, employment or appointment.

The standard of proof to rebut the presumption in s 15(e) is on the balance of probabilities. See *Barry v Registrar of Titles and the Honourable Hemphill (ex tempore)* [1992] ILRM 62, which held that the onus is on the landlord to prove that the permanent buildings were built by the landlord or the landlord's predecessors in title.

It may be possible to bring a tenant within s 15 by having the property revalued by the Valuation Office so that the valuation would be greater than the rent. In *Kehoe and Kehoe v C J Louth & Son* [1992] ILRM 282, the Supreme Court held that the failure of the solicitors to advise the tenants that in order to purchase the freehold the property would have to be revalued, with consequent financial implications, was negligent.

The option of splitting the land into a built-on lease and a vacant lease is also available to a yearly tenant.

11.2.3 RESTRICTIONS ON THE RIGHT

Section 16 of the 1978 Act sets out various restrictions on the right to purchase the freehold. It provides that s 8 does not apply to a person who has been declared, by virtue of the Landlord and Tenant (Reversionary Leases) Act, 1958 (now Part III of the Landlord and Tenant (Amendment) Act, 1980), not to be entitled to a reversionary lease of the land. Section 16 has been amended by s 70 of the 1980 Act and also by s 76 of the Registration of Deeds and Title Act, 2006.

Thus under s 16(2) a person shall not be entitled to acquire the fee simple if the lease on which such right is based is:

(a)   a lease of land which is used for the purposes of business or includes a building divided into not less than four separate and self-contained flats being a lease which contains provisions enabling the amount of the rent reserved by the lease to be altered within 26 years from the commencement of the lease (not being provisions enabling such rent to be altered once only and within five years from such commencement or upon the erection after such commencement of any buildings upon the land or upon the breach of a covenant in the lease); or

(b)   a lease granted before the commencement of the 1967 Act of land which is used for the purposes of business, being a lease which contains provisions requiring the lessee to carry on business on the land which is restricted in whole or in part to dealing in commodities produced or supplied by the lessor; or

(c)   a lease of land containing a covenant by the lessee to erect a building or buildings or carry out development on the land if and so long as the covenant has not been substantially complied with; or

(d)   a lease made by the Commissioners of Irish Lights; or

(e)   a lease made by a harbour authority, within the meaning of the Harbours Act, 1946; or

(f)   subject to subsection (3), a sub-lease of land granted by a lessee who is not a person to whom this Part applies:

    (i)   on or after 27 February 2006, or

    (ii)   before that date, unless before that date—

    (I)   a notice of intention to acquire the fee simple in the land was served by the sub-lessee in accordance with section 4 of the Act of 1967, or

    (II)   an application was made by the sub-lessee to the Registrar of Titles under Part III of this Act.

In addition to introducing s 16(2)(f) above, the 2006 Act also introduced a new s 16(3). This provides that s 16(2)(f) above will not apply if, at the date of the sub-lease, the sole reason why the lessee is not entitled to buy out is because the covenant to erect permanent buildings on the land has not been substantially complied with and after that date the covenant is substantially complied with by the sub-lessee. Thus a sub-lessee who complies with this covenant is protected and can subsequently buy out the freehold. This is different to the rest of s 16(2) which provides that a lessee (as opposed to a sub-lessee) can buy out the freehold if he is in contravention of a covenant in the lease except where he is in breach of a covenant to build. See s 16(2)(c) above.

In all other cases a sub-lessee, unless an application has already been made or notice served before 27 February 2006, cannot buy out the freehold if the sub-lease was granted by a lessee who was not entitled to buy out the freehold.

Thus a sub-lessee cannot buy out the freehold unless:

(a) an application has already been made or notice served before 27 February 2006; or

(b) the lessee was entitled to buy out the freehold; or

(c) the covenant to erect permanent buildings on the land was not substantially complied with at the date of the sub-lease and after that date the covenant is substantially complied with by the sub-lessee.

This prevents 'unqualifying' lessees from creating a sub-lease which would qualify and thus allow the sub-lessee to have an advantage which the lessee itself did not have under the legislation.

Section 4 of the 1978 Act provides that the Act does not bind a government Minister, the Commissioners of Public Works in Ireland, or the Irish Land Commission. Section 4 has been amended by the Landlord and Tenant (Ground Rents) Act 2005, which removed the reference to the Irish Land Commission, which no longer exists, and added three other agencies to the list of bodies not bound by the 1978 Act. These are the Industrial Development Agency (Ireland), Shannon Free Airport Development Company and Údarás na Gaeltachta. For an examination of s 4 see *Digital Hub Development Agency v Keane & Ors* [2008] IEHC 22. In this instance the initial lease was found to be a building lease under the 1931 Act and a subsequent lease was by virtue of the entitlement of the lessee to a reversionary lease and that being so condition 6 of s 10 was satisfied.

Since 1980 the right to acquire the freehold from these state authorities, including the Commissioners of Irish Lights and the harbour authorities, is no longer automatically excluded as a result of s 70 of the Landlord and Tenant (Amendment) Act, 1980. Section 70 provides, in relation to dwellinghouses, that a lessee is entitled to acquire the fee simple save where the appropriate State authority or the Minister for Transport is satisfied that it would not be in the public interest and certifies this.

In *Metropolitan Properties Ltd v John O'Brien and the Commissioners of Public Works in Ireland*, it was held by the Supreme Court that, as the lessee was not entitled to buy out the freehold held by the Commissioners, then the lessee had no right to acquire the intermediate interests even though the lessee satisfied s 9 of the 1978 Act. O'Flaherty J stated 'the existence of such interest in the Commissioners precludes not merely the acquisition of the fee simple but also of any intermediate interests in the property'. Thus the right to purchase the intermediate interests exists only for the purpose of enlarging the interest held by the lessee into a fee simple interest. It is a case of all or nothing; either the applicant is entitled to buy out all interests or none.

It should be noted that, even though a lessee has the right to purchase the freehold, there is no requirement to exercise this right. A lessee would, however, be ill advised not to do so, particularly when the end of the term of the leasehold interest is approaching.

11.3 Right to a Reversionary Lease

A lessee entitled to purchase the freehold under s 9 and one of the conditions in s 10 of the 1978 Act is also entitled to a reversionary lease. This right is now governed by Part III of the Landlord and Tenant (Amendment) Act, 1980. Section 34 of the 1980 Act provides that where the terms of a reversionary lease are settled by the court the lease shall be for a term expiring 99 years after the expiration of the lease to which it is reversionary. The lessee shall be made liable to pay all rates and taxes in respect of the land and to insure against fire and keep the premises in repair.

In relation to rent, s 35 provides that the rent to be reserved by a reversionary lease, the terms of which are settled by the court, shall be one-eighth of the gross rent. A reduction will be made to take account of works of construction, reconstruction or alteration carried out by the lessee or any of the lessee's predecessors in title which add to the letting value of the land. No reduction will be made for works carried out in consideration of the granting of the lease or for repairs and maintenance carried out during the term of the lease.

Section 36 defines the gross rent as:

the rent which, in the opinion of the Court, a willing lessee not already in occupation would give and a willing lessor would take for the land comprised in the reversionary lease—

(a) *on the basis that vacant possession is given and that the lessee pays rates and taxes in respect of the land and is liable to insure against fire and to keep the premises in repair, and*

(b) *having regard to the other terms of the reversionary lease and to the letting values of land of a similar character to and situate in the vicinity of the land comprised in the lease or in a comparable area but without having regard to any goodwill which may exist in respect of the land.*

Where the terms of the reversionary lease are settled by the court either party may now seek a review of the rent every five years under the Landlord and Tenant (Amendment) Act, 1984, s 3.

In effect a reversionary lease is a 99-year lease at one-eighth of the market rent.

Under s 39, the new reversionary lease is deemed to be a continuation of the tenancy previously existing and is deemed to be a graft upon that tenancy and the lessee's interest under the reversionary lease is subject to any rights or equities arising from the old lease.

Thus, a lessee who holds under a lease giving the right to purchase the freehold may, in the alternative, claim a reversionary lease. In virtually every case, lessees would prefer to purchase the freehold rather than choose a reversionary lease as, in buying the freehold, they have enhanced their interest in the property to its maximum. The reversionary lease gives a lessee a leasehold term only, subject to rent reviews, albeit at a small rent. Thus the question arises as to why a lessee would seek a reversionary lease when he is entitled to the freehold. As there are few reasons to choose a reversionary lease, they are no longer common.

11.4   Procedure for Purchasing Fee Simple

There are two methods by which a lessee may purchase the freehold.

Even though the Landlord and Tenant (Ground Rents) (No 2) Act, 1978, s 7 repealed s 3(1)–(3) of the 1967 Act, the procedure thereunder remained. In *Heatons Wholesale Ltd v Anthony McCormack* [1994] 2 IR 400, Lynch J held that:

'the unrepealed provisions of the Act of 1967 are to apply to the persons listed in ss 9 to 16 of the Act of 1978 in the same way as they theretofore applied to the persons listed in s 3 of the Act of 1967. Included in the unrepealed provisions of the Act of 1967 is s 17 which provides for the determination by the County Registrar of disputes, questions and difficulties arising in regard to the acquisition of the fee simple . . . The Registrar of Titles is given jurisdiction only in cases coming within Part III of the Act of 1978. That part . . . provides a simplified way of vesting the fee simple estate in the case of applications relating to dwellinghouses only . . . The Registrar of Titles has however no jurisdiction in relation to applications regarding commercial premises which are not dwellinghouses.'

In short, if the premises comprise a dwellinghouse, a tenant may proceed under both the Landlord and Tenant (Ground Rents) Act, 1967, and the Landlord and Tenant (Ground Rents) (No 2) Act, 1978. If the premises comprise a business premises the tenant can only avail of the procedure under the 1967 Act.

Section 19 restricted the procedure in the 1978 Act to land where the permanent buildings were constructed for use wholly or principally as a dwelling and are so used and such land is referred to in the Act as a dwellinghouse.

Regardless of the procedure to be used by the lessee it must be remembered that for both residential and business premises, the test to be used for establishing the right to purchase the freehold is as set out in ss 9, 10 or 15 of the 1978 Act.

11.4.1 1967 ACT PROCEDURE—ALL PROPERTY

If the lessee is entitled to purchase the freehold by virtue of satisfying (complying with) s 9 and one of the conditions in s 10 of the 1978 Act and the premises comprise either a dwellinghouse or a business premises then the following procedure is laid down in the 1967 Act.

The Landlord and Tenant (Ground Rents) Act, 1967 (Forms) Regulations, 1967 (S.I. 43 of 1967) prescribed the forms for the purposes of the Landlord and Tenant (Ground Rents) Act, 1967 (see **11.8.1**).

Unders s 4, the lessee must serve a notice of intention to acquire the fee simple in the prescribed form (Form No 1) on the superior lessor and any person owning an incumbrance on the land, for example, a mortgagee. Under s 23 this notice should be served by registered post.

Section 7 provides that for the purpose of securing the joinder of all necessary parties in the conveyance of the fee simple in land to the lessee he may:

(a)   serve a notice in the prescribed form (Form No 2) upon his immediate lessor requiring information as to the nature and duration of his reversion in the land and the existence and nature of any incumbrance thereon, the name and address of the person for the time being entitled to the next superior interest in the land and of the owner of any such incumbrance and any other information reasonably necessary for the purpose aforesaid; and

(b)   serve a similar notice upon each other person having a superior interest in the land.

A person upon whom a notice is served under this section has one month to give to the lessee so much of the information required by the notice as is within his possession or procurement.

The information which must be furnished is:

(a)   nature and duration of his reversion in the land;

(b)   nature of any incumbrance thereon;

(c)   name and address of his superior lessor and the owner of the incumbrance; and

(d)   any other information which might be required to assist the lessee in tracing the freehold owner.

It is advisable to serve this notice requiring information unless it is evident that your client's landlord is the owner of the freehold free from incumbrances. This will rarely be evident and this notice should always be served with the notice of intention to acquire the fee simple.

11.4.1.1 Conveyance

Once a notice of intention to acquire the fee simple has been served, s 6(1) requires the lessee and the lessor upon whom the notice was served to take all necessary steps to effect a conveyance free from incumbrances of the fee simple and any intermediate interests in the land to the lessee without unreasonable delay.

If the acquisition of the fee simple is proceeding in this way the lessee will require the conveyance to be effected in the same manner as an arm's length transaction, eg with requisitions on title being raised and replied to, a deed being drafted and approved and completion occurring in the normal manner.

11.4.1.2 Arbitration by County Registrar

If, for some reason, it is not possible for a conveyance to be executed, the Act provides for application to be made to the County Registrar for the area in which the land is situate for the matter to be arbitrated. For example, the lessor may be of unsound mind, cannot be found or otherwise refuses or fails to execute the conveyance.

Common difficulties that arise in connection with the purchase of the freehold are:

(a) The right of the lessee to purchase is denied by the lessor.

(b) Agreement as to purchase price cannot be reached by the parties.

(c) A superior lessor cannot be found.

(d) Apportionment of purchase price cannot be agreed.

In these circumstances s 17 applies and any person concerned with these matters may apply to the County Registrar to have the matter determined by arbitration. Under this section, the County Registrar may make such award as justice requires.

Section 8 gives the County Registrar power to direct that the conveyance be executed or to appoint an officer of the court to execute the conveyance on behalf of the lessor. If an officer of the court is appointed to execute the conveyance s 8(4) provides for the purchase money to be paid into court.

Under s 17(2) and (3) the County Registrar has power to:

(2) . . . *make an award in relation to land—*
   (a) *determining the person (if any) entitled to acquire the fee simple therein under this Act,*
   (b) *determining the purchase price to be paid in respect of the acquisition,*
   (c) *determining the person or persons entitled to receive the purchase money in respect of the acquisition and the amount which each person is entitled to receive,*
   (d) *determining if a person is entitled to have a rent apportioned under section 5 or 11 of this Act, and*
   (e) *apportioning (whether under the said section 5 or 11 or otherwise for the purposes of this Act) any rent payable in respect of land part of which is land the fee simple in which is being acquired under this Act.*

(3) *A County Registrar shall have, for the purpose of and in relation to an arbitration under this Act, the same power of making orders in respect of—*
   (a) *security for costs,*
   (b) *discovery and inspection of documents and interrogatories,*

>   *(c)   the giving of evidence by affidavit,*
>   *(d)   examination on oath of any witness,*
>   *as the court has for the purpose of and in relation to any action or matter in that court.*

There is an appeal from the County Registrar's decision to the Circuit Court under s 22. See *Kenny Homes & Co Ltd v Leonard*, 11 December 1997, High Court (unreported).

11.4.1.3   Costs

Under s 9, the lessee is liable for the payment of the reasonable costs and expenses incurred by the lessor.

Lessees who change their mind about purchasing the freehold may serve a notice of discontinuance under s 10. On service of this notice a lessee's liability for costs and expenses will cease.

Under s 19(1) where an award or order is made on arbitration the County Registrar directs who is to pay the costs of the arbitration. In addition, s 19(2) provides that a County Registrar has the power to award costs against a person who has refused or failed or delayed in complying with the Act or in reaching agreement.

The County Registrar will not direct that fees of counsel incurred by one party be paid by the other party to the arbitration unless a question of law was involved such as, in the opinion of the County Registrar, rendered it necessary to retain counsel (s 19(3)).

11.4.1.4   Consideration

The consideration to be paid by the lessee for the freehold is determined as at the date of service of the notice of intention to acquire the fee simple. There are complicated statutory formulae laid down for assessing the consideration (Landlord and Tenant (Amendment) Act, 1984, s 7) and these are dealt with later in this chapter.

11.4.1.5   Apportionment of rent

Sections 11–16 deal with the apportionment of rent. The sections are similar to those setting out the procedure for buying out the freehold. Section 11 states the general right to apportionment. Section 12 provides for a notice of intention to be served. Section 13 states that, after service of the notice, the parties shall without unreasonable delay take all necessary steps to effect an apportionment of the rent. Section 14 provides for application to be made to the County Registrar in the event of a difficulty arising and s 15 makes the applicant liable for payment of the other parties' reasonable costs and expenses until a notice of discontinuance is served under s 16.

Apportionment of the rent will be necessary when the lessee is buying out the freehold in part of the lease only or in part of a superior lease or leases.

For example, X is purchasing the freehold in 5 Eyre Square. X holds under a lease dated 4 March 1860 and pays a rent of €5 to Y. The occupants of numbers 1, 2, 3 and 4 Eyre Square also hold under this lease and they each pay a rent of €5 to Y. Thus, in total Y receives a rent of €25. Y holds under a lease dated 7 May 1850 and under this lease pays a rent of €50 to Z. Z owns the freehold. On purchasing the freehold X will pay a purchase price for the freehold and this will be split between Y and Z to compensate them for the loss of their interests in the property. If the rent was not apportioned Y would, after the purchase, receive only €20 but he would still be liable to pay Z €50. The rent Y receives has been reduced but his obligation to Z has not changed even though Z received consideration for the loss of his interest in the property. In this situation Y will seek to have the rent of €50 apportioned as between 5 Eyre Square and numbers 1, 2, 3 and 4 Eyre Square so that Y will no longer have to pay rent to Z in respect of 5 Eyre Square.

Normally apportionment of the rent can be agreed between the parties.

Even where a lessee holds part only of the land comprised in a lease either indemnified against rent or subject to an apportioned part of the rent (ie the indemnity or apportionment was agreed when the land was divided into two and assigned to different lessees one of whom is now buying the freehold) the lessor is not bound to accept that indemnity or apportionment. This is because the lessor would not have been party to the agreement. The lessor can now seek an apportionment of the rent under s 11.

11.4.1.6 Record of awards

Under s 21, a County Registrar is obliged to keep a register of all awards made by him in arbitrations under the Act. This register is available for public inspection and copies of entries can be obtained. A copy of an entry signed by the County Registrar is, under s 21(3), evidence until the contrary is proved of the matters stated in the entry.

11.4.1.7 Covenants

Section 31 provided for the continuance of certain covenants even though the fee simple had been purchased. This section was repealed by s 28 of the 1978 Act, which is dealt with later in this chapter.

11.4.1.8 Contracting out of the Act

Under s 33, any clause providing for the variation, modification or restriction of the provisions of the Act is void. Thus a lessee cannot contract out of the provisions of the Act but the parties may agree among themselves that the lessee will take a lesser title than the freehold if the lessee so wishes.

11.4.2 1978 ACT PROCEDURE—DWELLINGHOUSES

The second procedure for purchasing the freehold is set out in the Landlord and Tenant (Ground Rents) (No 2) Act, 1978. Unlike the 1967 Act, the procedure under the 1978 Act applies only to residential premises.

Section 19 restricts the procedure in the 1978 Act to land where the permanent buildings were constructed for use wholly or principally as a dwelling and are so used and such land is referred to in the Act as a dwellinghouse.

Part III of the Act sets out the procedure, which is called the vesting certificate procedure as it provides for the issuing of two different types of certificate vesting the freehold in the lessee. These vesting certificates are issued by the Land Registry even when title to the property is unregistered.

Section 18 initially provided that the procedure would only be available for five years. However, this has been extended.

The two types of vesting certificate are:

    (a)   consent vesting certificate; and

    (b)   arbitration vesting certificate.

They are similar-looking documents, save for colour and the first paragraph. The consent vesting certificate has a green edge and the arbitration vesting certificate a red edge. Also the first paragraph of the consent vesting certificate refers to s 20 of the 1978 Act whereas the arbitration vesting certificate refers to s 21 of the 1978 Act.

GROUND RENTS

The Landlord and Tenant (Ground Rents) (No 2) Act 1978 Regulations, 1978 (S.I. 219 of 1978), set out prescribed forms for use when purchasing the freehold by way of vesting certificate. The forms are set out at **11.8.2**.

11.4.2.1   Vesting by consent

Section 20 states:

> *A person who is entitled to acquire the fee simple in a dwellinghouse by virtue of Part II may, with the consent of every person who would be a necessary party to the conveyance to him of the fee simple free from incumbrances, apply to the Registrar of Titles to vest the premises in him under section 22.*

Thus, as previously stated, the test for acquiring the freehold under the 1967 and 1978 Acts is the same. The lessee must satisfy s 9 of the 1978 Act and one of the conditions in s 10, regardless of the procedure to be followed.

Again, as previously noted, vesting by consent is available only for a dwellinghouse. Under s 19, this must be a building not only constructed as a dwelling but also used as a dwelling.

The lessee must, under s 20, obtain the consent of every person with an interest in the property and then apply to the Registrar of Titles to have the premises vested in him. The prescribed form for such consents is Form C. Form C should be lodged with an application for vesting by consent in Form A.

Section 22(1)(a) provides that where the Registrar of Titles is satisfied that an application under s 20 has been 'duly made' the Registrar will issue a vesting certificate (Form E) which will operate to convey free from incumbrances the fee simple and any intermediate interests in the dwellinghouse.

11.4.2.2   Vesting by arbitration

Section 21 provides for vesting by arbitration. Arbitration under the 1967 Act was by the County Registrar. Under the 1978 Act, arbitration is by the Registrar of Titles.

Section 21(1) provides that any person who claims to be entitled to acquire the fee simple in a dwellinghouse may, without the consents referred to in s 20, apply to the Registrar of Titles to have the premises vested in him under s 22. The lessee must serve a notice of application on the immediate lessor. Under s 23 of the 1967 Act this notice must be served by registered post.

The prescribed form of notice of intention to be served on the immediate lessor is Form D and this must be lodged with an application for vesting on arbitration in Form B.

Under s 21(2), the Registrar may, however, dispense with such service if it is not reasonably practicable.

The provisions in the 1967 Act pertaining to arbitration apply to arbitration under this Act with the references to the County Registrar replaced by references to the Registrar of Titles (s 21(4)).

Similarly, under s 21(5) there is an appeal to the Circuit Court against any award, order or other decision of the Registrar as arbitrator.

The test to be applied by the Registrar in determining whether or not to issue a vesting certificate on arbitration is different from that for the issuing of a consent vesting certificate.

Section 22(1)(b) provides that where the Registrar of Titles is satisfied that an applicant under s 21 'is entitled to acquire the fee simple' the Registrar will issue a vesting certificate

(Form F) which will operate to convey free from incumbrances the fee simple and any intermediate interests in the dwellinghouse.

11.4.2.3 Prior to issuing a vesting certificate

Under s 22(2), before issuing the certificate, the Registrar must be satisfied that:

    (a)   the purchase price has been paid or deposited with him;

    (b)   the prescribed fees have been discharged; and

    (c)   rent (other than that which is statute barred) has been paid up to date.

Section 22(5) provides for the Registrar to serve notice of the grant of the vesting certificate on every person owning an estate, interest or incumbrance extinguished by the vesting certificate.

Under s 22(6), any person with an interest in the property may apply to the Registrar for payment of the purchase money or any part of it which was deposited with the Registrar.

11.4.2.4 Costs

Section 23(4) provides that the applicant is liable for the prescribed fee for the issue of the vesting certificate. The prescribed fees are set out in the Landlord and Tenant (Ground Rents) (No 2) Act, 1978 (Fees) Order, 1984 (S.I. 194 of 1984), which came into operation on 1 August 1984. This order provided that the fees to be paid to the Land Registry for the purposes of Part III of the Landlord and Tenant (Ground Rents) (No 2) Act, 1978, are as follows:

    (a)   Application for consent vesting certificate:

        (i)   applicant in occupation of dwellinghouse €30

        (ii)   otherwise €65.

    (b)   Application for arbitration vesting certificate:

        (i)   applicant in occupation of dwellinghouse €105

        (ii)   otherwise €195.

In relation to additional costs s 23(5) provides that where the applicant is in occupation of the dwellinghouse neither the applicant nor any other party will be liable for additional costs save where any party has behaved unreasonably or delayed, refused or failed to comply with the Act, thereby causing costs to be incurred. If this arises the Registrar may direct that the costs incurred be paid by that party.

The provisions in the 1967 Act which provide for the costs of an arbitration do not apply under the 1978 Act when the applicant is in occupation of the dwellinghouse.

Thus, an applicant in occupation of the dwellinghouse will not have to pay any costs unless that person has behaved unreasonably or delayed, refused or failed to comply with the Act. This is unlikely. It is usually the lessor who behaves unreasonably; for example, by refusing to give a consent, thereby requiring the applicant to incur the additional cost of going to arbitration. The applicant will have to pay only the fee for issue of the vesting certificate. The applicant will not be liable to pay the lessor's legal costs.

11.4.2.5 Covenants

Section 28(2) of the 1978 Act provides for certain covenants to continue in full force and effect after acquisition of the fee simple. Those covenants are burdens which affect the lands without registration under the Registration of Title Act, 1964, s 72. They are:

(a) covenants which protect or enhance the amenity of any land occupied by the im-
     mediate lessor;

(b) covenants which relate to the performance of a duty imposed by statute on any
     person; and

(c) covenants which relate to a right of way over the acquired land or a right of drain-
     age or other right necessary to secure or assist the development of other land.

Section 28(2)(a) refers to covenants for the benefit of the lessor and s 28(2)(b) refers to
the performance of a duty imposed by statute. Only s 28(2)(c) preserves covenants in
favour of third parties. These are restricted to those which relate to a right of way over the
acquired land or a right of drainage or other right necessary to secure or assist the development of other land.

Previously all other covenants ceased to have effect and no new covenants could be created in conveying the fee simple. This position has been changed by s 77 of the Registration
of Deeds and Title Act 2006, which substituted a new s 28(1). This now provides that
where a lessee buys out the freehold only covenants affecting the land in the lease under
which the person held the land cease to have effect and no new covenants can be created
except with the person's agreement. Thus only the covenants in the lease cease to have
effect and new covenants can be created with the lessee's consent. This is a dramatic
change from the previous position as the previous s 28(1) did not refer to persons acquiring the fee simple under the Act and thus it could be argued that it applied to all cases
where the lessee acquired the fee simple. This new subsection applies where the fee simple
is acquired on or after 27 February 2006 unless the application was made or notice served
before that date.

11.4.2.6 Duty of Registrar

Section 24 imposes a duty on the Registrar to deal with applications for vesting certificates
in the order in which they are received. In exceptional circumstances the Registrar may
deal with an application other than in the order in which it was received. The Registrar is
afforded protection by s 24(3), which provides that no action lies against the Registrar in
relation to the duty imposed by this section.

11.4.2.7 Differences between vesting certificates

Under s 22, the test to be applied by the Registrar of Titles to the two types of application
is different. To issue a consent vesting certificate the Registrar must be satisfied that an
'application has been duly made'. To issue a vesting certificate by arbitration the Registrar
must be satisfied that the applicant 'is entitled to acquire the fee simple'.

Section 22 also states that, on the issue of both types of vesting certificate, they operate 'to
convey free from incumbrances the fee simple and any intermediate interests'.

The tenor of the Act is that either vesting certificate operates to vest the freehold and all
intermediate interests in the applicant. In other words, the intention of the Act is that a
vesting certificate of either type is conclusive evidence of the ownership of the freehold
despite any defects which might exist in the vesting certificate.

Unfortunately, the Act does not expressly state this and, as a result, practitioners have been
somewhat wary of relying on the consent vesting certificate.

The Landlord and Tenant (Ground Rents) (No 2) Act, 1978, came into operation on 1 July
1978. Because the consent vesting certificate procedure was designed to be consumer
friendly it has proved to be extremely popular. A solicitor is not required and many lessees
obtain the required consents and make the application themselves. This in itself has inevi-
tably led to a small number of problems. Examples include a vesting certificate being

issued when the premises is not a dwellinghouse or issued only in the name of one of the co-owners. The Land Registry guidance notes provide for vesting certificates to be modified if incorrect or, in some circumstances, cancelled.

Most practitioners would agree that a vesting certificate on arbitration is a good root of title. Many also accept a consent vesting certificate provided there is nothing to throw doubt on its validity. However, if a difficulty arises with a consent vesting certificate the safer option is to seek to have the certificate cancelled and re-issued and/or to seek first registration of the title in the Land Registry.

11.4.3 REGISTRATION

Regardless of whether the freehold is acquired by way of:

(a) conveyance;

(b) arbitration by the County Registrar;

(c) consent vesting certificate; or

(d) vesting certificate by arbitration

the deed/vesting certificate showing the lessee's new interest in the property (ie the freehold) requires to be registered.

Where it is registered depends on the nature of the freehold title. If the freehold title is registered in the Land Registry then the deed/vesting certificate must be lodged/relodged in the Land Registry for registration. If the freehold title is registered in the Registry of Deeds then the deed/vesting certificate must be lodged in the Registry of Deeds for registration. If there is a transaction subject to compulsory registration under s 24 of the Registration of Title Act, 1964, then the vesting certificate must be lodged in the Land Registry even if the freehold was previously unregistered. It is also advisable to register first in the Registry of Deeds to maintain priority as the application for first registration may take some time.

11.4.4 MERGER

Care should be taken when deciding whether or not to merge the freehold and leasehold interests. If merger occurs, the leasehold title ceases to exist and only the freehold title will be left. If the freehold title is not a good marketable title there might be difficulty on a sale or mortgage of the property.

If the title to the freehold is registered in the Land Registry it is guaranteed by the State and once the freehold has been acquired by the applicant he may register the transfer or vesting certificate in the Land Registry and become the registered owner. If the leasehold is unregistered it may be merged in the freehold and the applicant is then left with a registered freehold title. If the leasehold is registered the Land Registry automatically closes the leasehold folio when the applicant applies to be the registered owner of the freehold folio. Again the leasehold ceases to exist and the applicant is left with a registered freehold title.

If title to the freehold is registered in the Registry of Deeds the question of merger must be considered. As noted above it is advisable not to merge the interests unless the freehold title is a good marketable title ie title to the freehold:

(a) has been investigated and is a good marketable title;

(b) is based on a deed signed by an officer of the court;

(c)   is based on a vesting certificate by arbitration; or

(d)   is based on a consent vesting certificate where consent was furnished by the free-hold owner and the owner of any intermediate interests.

A first registration application lodged based on a consent vesting certificate, where consent was furnished only by the freehold owner, may disclose intermediate interests in the property that have not been acquired by the applicant. The Examiner of Titles will require these interests to be acquired before allowing the application to proceed.

If merger occurs then, in future transactions, the only interest to be passed is a conveyance or transfer of the freehold.

If merger has not occurred, then it is important that, in future transactions, the freehold is conveyed or transferred and the leasehold assigned.

11.5   Practical Steps

The following are some of the practical steps to be taken when consulted by a client who wants to buy out the freehold:

(a)   Examine the title to the property and determine whether the client is the lessee.

(b)   Determine if the lessee is entitled to buy out the freehold. In other words, are s 9 and one of the conditions in s 10 or, alternatively, s 15 of the 1978 Act satisfied?

(c)   Are the premises business or residential?

(d)   If the premises are residential were they constructed as a dwelling and are they being used as a dwelling? If the answer is yes then the lessee may proceed under either the 1967 Act or the 1978 Act. If the answer is no then the lessee may proceed only under the 1967 Act.

In either case, the lessee can seek to reach agreement with the landlord and proceed by way of deed of conveyance. If this is not possible then proceed under the 1967 Act or the 1978 Act.

11.5.1   1967 ACT PROCEDURE

Serve notice of intention to acquire the fee simple (Form No 1) by registered post on the superior lessor and any person owning an incumbrance on the land; for example, a mortgagee.

Serve a notice requiring information (Form No 2) upon the immediate lessor and any party with a superior interest in the land.

The parties are now required to take all necessary steps to effect a conveyance of the freehold.

If, for some reason, it is not possible for a conveyance to be executed make an application to the County Registrar for the matter to be arbitrated. There is no prescribed form of application.

Agree the purchase price with the landlord and parties holding superior interests. Alternatively obtain a valuation of the fee simple interest by a competent valuer.

If the client is not satisfied with the County Registrar's decision appeal the matter to the Circuit Court.

When the matter is completed have the deed registered in the Land Registry or Registry of Deeds.

11.5.2 1978 ACT PROCEDURE

Obtain the consent (Form C) of all necessary parties. Lodge with an application for vesting by consent (Form A), a copy of the lease, a copy of the deed by which the applicant acquired the tenancy and the appropriate fee.

Alternatively, serve notice of intention to acquire the fee simple (Form D) on the immediate lessor by registered post. Lodge with an application for vesting on arbitration (Form B) together with evidence of the service of Form D.

Agree the purchase price with the landlord and parties holding superior interests. Pay the agreed purchase price to the landlord and parties holding superior interests or lodge it in the Land Registry. (Note that on an application for a vesting certificate by arbitration the purchase money must be lodged in the Land Registry.) Alternatively, if the purchase price cannot be agreed, obtain a valuation of the fee simple interest by a reputable auctioneer or valuer.

Customer service leaflets, practice directions, explanatory leaflets and application forms are available at the public office of the Property Registration Authority, through the post and at the Land Registry web page located at www.prai.ie.

If the client is not happy with the decision of the Registrar of Titles appeal to the Circuit Court.

When the vesting certificate issues register it in the Land Registry or the Registry of Deeds.

11.6 Calculation of Purchase Price on Arbitration

The method by which the purchase price of the freehold is calculated is set down in s 7 of the Landlord and Tenant (Amendment) Act, 1984, which repealed s 17 of the 1978 Act.

This section states first that the relevant date for determining the purchase price on arbitration is the date of service of notice on the lessor under the 1967 Act and the date of the application under the 1978 Act.

Section 7(3) states that the purchase price is the sum which, in the opinion of the arbitrator, a willing purchaser would give and a willing vendor would accept for the fee simple or other interest at the relevant date having regard to the following:

(a)   the rent payable by the lessee;

(b)   where the land is held under a lease which provides for an increased rent within 15 years, the amount of that increase and the time when it becomes payable;

(c)   the current interest yields on securities of the Government issued for subscription in the State;

(d)   if the land is used for the purposes of business, or exceeds one acre in area and is not used for the purposes of business, the area and nature of the land, its location and user and the state of repair of any buildings or structures thereon;

(e)   the price paid for the fee simple or any other interest in the land on a sale taking place on or after 22 May 1964;

(f)   any mortgage or other charge on the interest in the land of any person from whom, mediately or immediately, the person acquiring the fee simple holds the land;

(g) the costs and expenses which, in the opinion of the arbitrator, would be reasonably incurred by the persons from whom, mediately or immediately, the person acquiring the fee simple holds the land, in investing the purchase money payable in respect of the acquisition of the fee simple;

(h) the costs and expenses which, in the opinion of the arbitrator, have been incurred by the lessee by reason of the failure of the lessor to maintain any amenities as required under a covenant in the lease;

(i) the current price of the immediate lessor's interest in land held under leases or yearly tenancies similar to the lease or yearly tenancy, as the case may be, under which the land is held by the person acquiring the fee simple; and

(j) such other matters as are, in the opinion of the arbitrator, relevant to the determination of the purchase price.

Thus the arbitrator has a wide discretion as to the matters which may be taken into account in determining the purchase price.

Where the lease is expired, or the premises is residential and does not exceed one acre, there are further statutory formulae laid down in s 7 for determining the purchase price.

11.6.1 EXPIRED LEASE

Section 7(4) provides that where the land is held under a lease that has expired or is held at a rent which, whether under the terms of the lease or by operation of a statute, is subject to a review which is due but has not been made, the purchase price of the fee simple shall, subject to the other provisions of the section, be a sum equal to one-eighth of the amount which, at that date, a willing purchaser would give and a willing vendor would accept for the land in fee simple free of all estates, interests and incumbrances, but having regard to any covenant which continues in force by virtue of s 28 of the (No 2) Act of 1978 and assuming that the lessee has complied with any other covenants or conditions in his or her lease that could affect the price. A deduction shall be made from that amount equal to the value of the goodwill, if any, in the premises of the person acquiring the fee simple. A deduction shall also be made for addition to the value of the premises resulting from such works of construction, reconstruction or alteration carried out by the lessee which add to the letting value of the land other than those in consideration of the lease or repairs or maintenance.

Thus, if the lease has expired or a rent review is outstanding, the purchase price will be one-eighth of the market price.

11.6.2 YEARLY TENANCY OR LEASE WITH MORE THAN 15 YEARS TO RUN OF RESIDENTIAL PREMISES LESS THAN ONE ACRE

If the land:

(a) is not used for the purposes of business;

(b) is held by the person acquiring the fee simple under a contract of yearly tenancy, or under a yearly tenancy arising by operation of law or by inference on the expiration of a lease or under a lease which will not expire within 15 years after the relevant date; and

(c) does not exceed one acre in area

then the purchase price shall not exceed the amount which, if invested on the date of the award in the security of the government which was issued last before that date for subscription in the State and is redeemable not less than 15 years after the date of issue, would produce annually in gross interest an amount equal to the amount of the rent payable under the lease or yearly tenancy, as the case may be, during the year immediately preceding the relevant date. This does not apply where an increased rent is or may become payable, or the rent is subject to review, within 15 years after the relevant date.

If there is a yearly tenancy, or a lease with more than 15 years to run, of residential premises less than one acre then the purchase price will be the amount if invested in government stock that would yield the amount of the yearly rent.

The logic behind this is that the owner of the freehold is entitled to such sum that, if invested in government stock, would yield the same return as the rent he previously received.

This will be the purchase price in most cases, ie more than 15 years to run on the lease or the tenancy is yearly and the land does not exceed one acre. The purchase price cannot exceed the amount which, if invested in government stock, would produce interest equal to the amount of the rent under the lease. This amount may be calculated by dividing the price of the government stock, as quoted on the stock exchange, by the interest rate on the stock and multiplying the resulting figure ('the multiplier') by the amount of the rent.

11.6.3 LEASE WITH LESS THAN 15 YEARS TO RUN OR RENT SUBJECT TO REVIEW WITHIN THE 15 YEARS OF RESIDENTIAL PREMISES LESS THAN ONE ACRE

If the land:

(a)   is not used for the purposes of business;

(b)   is held by the person acquiring the fee simple under a lease; and

     (i)   the lease will expire within 15 years after the relevant date; or

     (ii)   the rent is subject to review within that period, under the lease or by virtue of any statute; and

(c)   does not exceed one acre in area

the purchase price shall not exceed the amount which would be determined if it was a yearly tenancy or a lease with more than 15 years to run together with in respect of each year by which the unexpired term of the lease falls short of 15 years, one-fifteenth of the difference between that price and the price that would be determined if the lease had expired.

The purchase price will not exceed the price payable in the case of a yearly tenancy plus, for each year less than 15 years, one-fifteenth of the difference between that amount and the price if the lease had expired (ie one-eighth of the market price).

Example

Market value: €200,000

Rent: €20

'Multiplier' under s 7(5): 15

Price payable in the case of a yearly tenancy: €300 (ie €20 × 15)

Price payable if the lease has expired: €200,000 ÷ 8 = €25,000 (eighth of market value)

Price payable if the lease has only 4 years to run:

Purchase price is €300 plus (11 (15 years − 4 years) × €24,700 (difference between €25,000 and €300)) ie €300 + (11 × €24,700/15) = €18,413.33

11.6.4   GENERAL

When the lease has expired and a yearly tenancy has not arisen on expiry of the lease the calculation of the purchase price is relatively simple. It is one-eighth of the market price.

In determining the purchase price in other circumstances assistance may be sought from the Land Registry. The amount to be invested in government stock to give the lessor the same return is generally stated as a multiple of the annual rent. For example, eight to ten times the annual rent if it is a residential yearly tenancy, or 18 times the annual rent if the land is used for business. The Land Registry ground rents section is in a position to advise as to the multiple currently in use at any given time. This assists the calculation of the purchase price on arbitration and also provides assistance when negotiating an agreement with the lessor.

Due to the complicated nature of s 7 it may also be advisable to engage a professional valuer who will be able to offer evidence of the purchase price paid for similar properties in the same area.

For a detailed examination of s 7 see *A O'Gorman & Co Ltd v JES Holdings Ltd* High Court 31 May 2005 (unreported). This case also involved a constitutional challenge to the statutory scheme for buying out the freehold including the mechanism for calculating the purchase price provided for in s 7. Judgment in this matter was delivered by the High Court on 31 January 2006; *Shirley & Ors v A O'Gorman & Co Ltd & Ors* (2006) IEHC 27. In a detailed judgment Peart J found that there was nothing irrational, arbitrary or disproportionate about the manner in which the purchase price is arrived at. He found that the detailed provisions represent a balanced approach to valuation of the residual interest of the landlord and the figure arrived at ensures that fair, reasonable and appropriate compensation is paid to the landlord for that interest. He dismissed the plaintiff's claim. The Supreme Court dismissed an appeal and affirmed the High Court order; *Shirley & Ors v A O'Gorman & Co Ltd & Ors* [2012] IESC 5.

11.7   Abolition of Ground Rents: No 1 Act of 1978

The vesting certificate procedure was designed to provide a simplified procedure for buying out the freehold for owners of residential dwellinghouses. In conjunction with the setting up of this procedure the government of the time sought to prevent the future creation of ground rents for residential dwellinghouses.

The Landlord and Tenant (Ground Rents) Act, 1978 (No 1 Act of 1978), is entitled 'An Act to prevent the creation of new leases reserving ground rents on dwellings and to provide for related matters'. This Act came into force on 16 May 1978.

Section 2 of the No 1 Act of 1978 provides that a lease of land made after 16 May 1978 is void if the lessee would, apart from this section, have the right to enlarge his interest into a fee simple and the permanent buildings are constructed for use wholly or principally as a dwelling. Dwelling does not include a separate and self-contained flat in premises divided into two or more such flats.

This section does not apply to a reversionary lease granted under the Landlord and Tenant (Reversionary Leases) Act, 1958. It does, however, apply to fee farm grants. See Practice Note in the November 1978 Law Society *Gazette*.

Even if the buildings are not constructed until after the lease is granted the lease is still void if the lessee can buy out the freehold and the buildings are constructed for use wholly or principally as a dwelling.

Note the difference between this section and s 19 of the No 2 Act of 1978. Section 19 restricts the vesting certificate procedure to buildings constructed for use wholly or principally as a dwelling which are 'so used'. Under s 2 of the No 1 Act of 1978 a lease of buildings constructed for use wholly or principally as a dwelling is void if the lessee is entitled to buy out the freehold regardless of the actual use of buildings.

Section 2(4) of the No 1 Act of 1978 provides that a person who has given consideration for a lease that is void has the right to acquire the fee simple in the land and any intermediate interests at the expense, as to both purchase money and costs, of the person who purported to grant the lease. The freehold owners or the owners of an intermediate interest who inadvertently grant such a lease are required to buy out the freehold for the lessee at their own expense. Thus, s 2(4) protects the position of a purchaser of a leasehold interest deemed void under the act.

For the effect on lending institutions see the Practice Note in the Law Society *Gazette* of March 1978.

As it is no longer possible to grant leases of dwellings where the lessee would be entitled to buy out the freehold, any party selling residential property must pass his own interest in that property. However, s 2 does not apply to a separate and self-contained flat in premises divided into two or more such flats.

Thus a vendor who owns the freehold in a dwellinghouse must sell the freehold. A vendor who owns a leasehold interest must assign that interest to the purchaser. The vendor cannot create a new interest, eg a lease or sub-lease that would entitle the purchaser to buy out the freehold.

In addition there are various restrictions on the right to buy out the freehold as listed in s 16 of the No 2 Act of 1978 as set out at **11.2.3**. If any of these restrictions apply then the lease will not be void as the lessee is not entitled to buy out the freehold.

Examples are a lease of land used for business or a building divided into not less than four separate and self-contained flats which contains provisions enabling the amount of the rent reserved by the lease to be altered within 26 years from the commencement of the lease (not being provisions enabling such rent to be altered only once and within five years from such commencement or upon the erection after such commencement of any buildings upon the land or upon the breach of a covenant in the lease).

Thus, a lease of an apartment block containing four or more flats or a business premises where there are rent reviews in the first 26 years may be granted provided:

(a)   there is more than one rent review within the first five years;

(b)   the rent review is not due on the erection of a building, and

(c)   the rent review is not due to a breach of a covenant in the lease.

It is common to come across 500-year leases of apartments with a rent review every year for a number of years. The rent is usually nominal, for example €1 for the first year, €2 for the second year and €3 thereafter. It is also common to come across long leases of business premises such as shopping centres. As the lessees are not entitled to buy out the freehold, one does not need to be concerned with s 2 of the No 1 Act of 1978.

11.8   Prescribed Forms

11.8.1   1967 ACT PROCEDURE

The Landlord and Tenant (Ground Rents) Act, 1967 (Forms) Regulations, 1967 (S.I. 43 of 1967) which came into operation on 1 March 1967 prescribed the forms for the purposes of the Landlord and Tenant (Ground Rents) Act, 1967.

GROUND RENTS

11.8.1.1   Form No 1

Landlord and Tenant (Ground Rents) Act, 1967

Notice of intention to acquire fee simple (section 4) (see Note A)

Date: ....

To: ....

2.   Description of land to which this notice refers (Note B)

....

....

....

3.   Particulars of applicant's lease or tenancy (Note C)

....

....

....

4.   Part of lands excluded, if any (Note D)

....

....

Take notice that I, ..., being a person entitled under section 3 of the above Act, propose to purchase the fee simple in the land described in Paragraph 1.

Signature: ....

Address: ....

Notes

   A.   Section 4 of the Act provides that notice should be served by a person who proposes to acquire the fee simple on the person entitled to the next superior interest in the land, each superior lessor and any person who is the owner of an incumbrance.
   B.   Sufficient particulars should be given to identify the property.
   C.   State amount of rent and whether the land is held on a yearly tenancy or under a lease. If the land is held under a lease, state date of lease, length of term and parties to the lease.
   D.   This need only be completed when the applicant proposes to purchase the fee simple in part only of the land demised under the lease. He may exclude from this notice part of such land which he has subleased under a building or proprietary lease where he has not received the consent of the sublessee to his purchasing the fee simple in the subleased part (see section 5 of the Act).

N.B. The applicant will be liable for the payment of the reasonable costs and expenses actually and necessarily incurred in complying with the provisions of the Act by every person upon whom this notice is served. If the applicant subsequently decides to discontinue the acquisition of the fee simple he should serve Form No. 4 on the service of which his liability for the payment of any such costs and expenses subsequently incurred by such persons will cease.

11.8.1.2   Form No 2

Landlord and Tenant (Ground Rents) Act, 1967

Notice requiring information from a lessor (section 7(1)) (see Note A)

Date: ....

To .... (Note B)

1.   Description of land to which this notice refers (Note C)

....

....

....

2.   Particulars of applicant's lease (Note D)

....

....

....

Take notice that I, ... being a person entitled under the above Act to acquire the fee simple in the land described above, require you to give me, within one month after the service of this notice on you, the following information—

(a)   the nature and duration of your reversion in the land,

(b)   the nature of any incumbrance on your reversion in the land, and

(c)   the name and address of:—

(i)   the person entitled to the next superior interest in the land, and

(ii)   the owner of any such incumbrance,

(d)   .... (Note E)

Signature: ....

Address: ....

Notes

A.   Section 7 of the Act provides for the service of this notice and for the duty to comply within one month.

B.   The notice may be served on—

(i)   the immediate lessor, and

(ii)   each other person having a superior interest in the land.

C.   Sufficient particulars should be given to identify the property.

D.   State amount of rent, date of lease, length of term and parties to the lease.

E.   State here the nature of any other information reasonably necessary for the purpose of securing the joinder of all necessary parties in the conveyance of the fee simple.

GROUND RENTS

11.8.1.3   Form No 3

Landlord and Tenant (Ground Rents) Act, 1967

Notice requiring information from a person receiving rent (section 7(2)) (See Note A)

Date: ....

To ....

1.   Description of land in respect of which the rent is received (Note B)

....

....

....

2.   Particulars of lease, the lessor under which cannot be found or ascertained (Note C)

....

....

....

Take notice that I, ... being a person entitled to acquire the fee simple in the above land under the above Act, require you to give, within one month after the service of this notice on you, the following information—

   (i)   the name and address of the person to whom the rent under the lease referred to in paragraph 2 is paid by you,

   (ii) .... (Note D)

Signature: ....

Address: ....

Notes

   A.   This notice may be served when Notice No. 2 cannot be served because the lessor cannot be found or ascertained (section 7(2) of the Act).
   B.   Sufficient particulars should be given to identify the property.
   C.   State amount of rent, date of lease, length of term and parties to the lease.
   D.   State here the nature of any other information sought which is reasonably necessary for the purpose of securing the joinder of all necessary parties in the conveyance of the fee simple.

11.8.1.4   Form No 4

Landlord and Tenant (Ground Rents) Act, 1967

Notice of discontinuance of acquisition of fee simple (section 10) (see Note A)

Date: ....

To .... (Note B)

1.   Description of land to which this notice refers (Note C)

....

....

....

2.   Particulars of applicant's lease or tenancy (Note D)

....

....

Take notice that I,...................... hereby withdraw the notice of intention to acquire the fee simple in the above land previously served by me and do not now intend to acquire the fee simple in the land.

Signature: ....

Address: ....

Notes

A.   This notice may be served under section 10 of the Act: its effect is to discontinue the acquisition of the fee simple and to terminate the liability of the person serving it for costs and expenses incurred by the persons on whom it is served after service of the notice (section 9).

B.   This notice must be served on all the persons on whom notices of intention to acquire the fee simple were served.

C.   Sufficient particulars should be given to identify the property.

D.   State amount of rent and whether the land is held on a yearly tenancy or under a lease. If under a lease, state date of lease, length of term and parties to the lease.

GROUND RENTS

Form No 5

Landlord and Tenant (Ground Rents) Act, 1967

Notice of intention to have rent apportioned (section 12) (see Note A)

Date: ....

To.. (Note B)

Particulars of lease reserving the rent to which this notice refers (Note C)

....

....

Description of land demised by above lease (Note D)

....

....

....

Description of the parts of the above land between which it is proposed to apportion the rent (Note D)

....

....

(1) ....

(2) ....

(3) ....

(4) ....

(continue, if necessary, on back of form)

Take notice that I,............................. being a person entitled under section 11 of the above Act to have a rent apportioned, propose to have the rent reserved by the above lease apportioned between the parts of the land described above.

Signature: ....

Address: ....

Notes

    A.   Section 12 of the Act provides for the service of this notice.

    B.   This notice should be served on:
        (i)   the person to whom the rent is payable, and
        (ii)   any other person who holds any of the land as lessee under a building or proprietary lease, as assignee from any such lessee or as successor in title of any such assignee.

    C.   State amount of rent, date of lease, length of term and parties to the lease.

    D.   Sufficient particulars should be given to identify the particular property or properties.

11.8.1.6   Form No 6

Landlord and Tenant (Ground Rents) Act, 1967

Notice of discontinuance of apportionment (section 16) (see Note A)

Date: ....

To .... (Note B)

Particulars of lease reserving the rent to which this notice refers (Note C)

....

....

Take notice that I, ..., hereby withdraw the notice of intention to have the above rent apportioned and do not now intend to have the rent apportioned.

Signature: ....

Address: ....

Notes

    A.   This notice may be served under section 16 of the Act. Its effect is to terminate the liability of the person serving it for costs and expenses incurred by the person on whom it is served after the service of the notice (section 15).

    B.   This notice must be served on all the persons on whom notices of intention to have the rent apportioned were served.

    C.   State amount of rent, date of lease, length of term and parties to the lease.

11.8.2   1978 ACT PROCEDURE

The Landlord and Tenant (Ground Rents) (No 2) Act 1978 Regulations, 1978 (S.I. 219 of 1978), which came into operation on 1 August 1978, set out prescribed forms for use when purchasing the freehold by way of vesting certificate.

The first Schedule sets out the form of register to be kept by the County Registrar under s 21(1) of the 1967 Act. The second Schedule sets out the forms prescribed for the purposes of the 1978 Act.

The regulations also state that where the applicant relies on the consent of every person who would be a necessary party to the conveyance to him of the fee simple free from incumbrances, the agreed purchase price is deemed to include all arrears and apportionments of rent up to the date of such consent and, where the purchase money is lodged in the Land Registry, such agreed purchase price is deemed to include all such rent up to a date not exceeding one month after the date of such consent. Where the purchase money is deposited in the Land Registry with an application and consent forms, notice of the issue of the vesting certificate will be served on every party who signed a consent form. All money deposited in the Land Registry under s 22 of the 1978 Act may after a period of six months be lodged in the Circuit Court.

Where a title is not registered in the Land Registry, the arbitrator may accept, as evidence of such title, a certificate by a practising solicitor or barrister in Form G in the Second Schedule to these regulations.

Where the fee simple interest is not registered, the Registrar, for the purposes of registration in the Registry of Deeds, may accept a duplicate of the vesting certificate as a memorial.

Where, in the case of an application for a vesting certificate, a death, transmission or change of interest occurs before vesting is effected, the proceedings shall not abate, but may be continued by and in the name of any person who is the personal representative or successor in title of the applicant.

The second Schedule sets out the forms prescribed for the purposes of the 1978 Act.

11.8.2.1 Form A

LAND REGISTRY

LANDLORD AND TENANT (GROUND RENTS) (No. 2) ACT 1978

APPLICATION FOR VESTING BY CONSENT

Application to the Registrar of Titles under section 20 of the Landlord and Tenant (Ground Rents) (No. 2) Act 1978, for the vesting in fee simple, pursuant to section 22 of the said Act (with the consent of every person who would be a party to a conveyance of the fee simple free from incumbrances) of the property described in the Schedule hereto.

County:

I/We

of

declare:

1.   I/We am/are entitled under Part II of the above Act to acquire the fee simple in the property described in the Schedule hereto, the permanent buildings on which were constructed for use wholly or principally as a dwelling (not being a separate and self-contained flat in premises divided into two or more such flats) and are so used.
2.   I/We am/are in occupation of the said property. (Note (a)).
3.   I/We enclose herewith the consent(s) in Form C of the person(s) specified in section 20 of the above Act.
4.   The entire of the purchase money has been paid to the person(s) entitled thereto or authorised to give receipt therefor.

or

The agreed purchase price is lodged herewith.

5.   The fee simple title is registered on Folio of the Register County or

I/We refer to the certificate in Form G in relation to the fee simple title.

or

No evidence of the following consenting party's title is forthcoming: (Note (b)).

6.   I/We enclose herewith € being the fee payable for issue of the Vesting Certificate under section 22 of the said Act. (Note (c)).

SCHEDULE (Note (d))

To

The Registrar of Titles

Notes

(a)   Delete paragraph 2 if inapplicable.
(b)   Where an applicant has any doubt about the title to the property of the consenting party or parties the purchase price may be lodged in the Land Registry.
(c)   €30 if paragraph 2 applicable; €65 if paragraph 2 inapplicable.
(d)   Sufficient particulars should be given to identify the property including particulars of the tenancy under which it is held, e.g. location and whether the property is held under a yearly tenancy or a lease. The rent should also be stated and particulars of any lease given.

Where the property includes land which is not covered by the permanent buildings and which is not wholly subsidiary and ancillary to such buildings, such land must be excluded from the description and should if necessary be identified on a map.

11.8.2.2   Form B

LAND REGISTRY

LANDLORD AND TENANT (GROUND RENTS) (No. 2) ACT 1978

APPLICATION FOR VESTING ON ARBITRATION

Application to the Registrar of Titles under section 21(1) of the Landlord and Tenant (Ground Rents) (No. 2) Act, 1978, for the vesting in fee simple, pursuant to section 22 of the said Act, of the property described in the First Schedule hereto.

County:

I/We

of

declare:

1. I/We am/are entitled under Part II of the above Act to acquire the fee simple in the property described in the First Schedule hereto, the permanent buildings on which were constructed for use wholly or principally as a dwelling (not being a separate and self-contained flat in premises divided into two or more such flats) and are so used.

2. On the   I/we served notice on the immediate lessor of my/our intention to acquire the fee simple in the said property under section 21(1) of the said Act. A copy of the notice is enclosed herewith. (Note (a)).

or

I/We am/are unable to serve notice on the immediate lessor of my/our intention to acquire the fee simple in the said property under section 21(1) of the said Act for the following reason:

3. I/We have not received any reply to the notice. (Note (b)).

or

The lessor disputes my/our right to acquire the fee simple.

or

The lessor and I/we cannot agree on the purchase price.

4. I/We am/are in occupation of the property. (Note (a)).

5. I/We enclose herewith fee for arbitration and vesting certificate under the said Act.

6. I/We enclose herewith receipt for the rent due on the last gale day.

7. I/We enclose herewith the title documents specified in the Second Schedule hereto.

8. I/We hereby apply to the Registrar of Titles under section 21 of the Act of 1978 to have the fee simple in the property described in the First Schedule hereto vested in me/us under the said Act.

FIRST SCHEDULE (Note (c)).

The property known as   situate held by me/us   (under a Lease dated made between and for a term of years)

(Note (a)) at the yearly rent of   . (The said Lease is registered as a burden on Folio of the Register of Freehold land in the County of   . The title to the said Lease is registered on   Folio   of the Register of leasehold interests in the County of   ).

SECOND SCHEDULE

To

The Registrar of Titles

Notes

(a)   Delete if inapplicable.

(b)   Delete if inapplicable and insert reason for application for arbitration.

(c)   Sufficient particulars should be given to identify the property including particulars of the tenancy under which it is held e.g., location and whether the property is held under a yearly tenancy or a lease. The rent should also be stated and particulars of any lease given.

Where the property demised by the lease includes land which is not covered by the permanent buildings and which is not wholly subsidiary and ancillary to such buildings, such land must be excluded from the description and may if necessary be identified on a map.

11.8.2.3   Form C

LAND REGISTRY

LANDLORD AND TENANT (GROUND RENTS) (No. 2) ACT 1978

CONSENT

Consent by a person, who would be a necessary party to a conveyance of the fee simple free from incumbrances, to the vesting of the said fee simple by the Registrar of Titles under section 22 (1) of the above Act.

1.   I/We   of   (the owner(s) of the fee simple in the property specified in the First Schedule hereto)

or

(the owner(s) of the estate, interest or incumbrance specified in the Second Schedule hereto) hereby acknowledge that of is/are entitled under Part II of the Landlord and Tenant (Ground Rents) (No 2) Act, 1978, to acquire the fee simple in the property.

2.   The agreed purchase price is €   .
3.   I/We acknowledge receipt of €   , being the purchase money/my share of the purchase money (delete as inapplicable).
4.   I/We certify that the annual rent has been paid.
5.   I/We hereby consent to the vesting in said of the fee simple in the property specified in the First Schedule hereto by the Registrar of Titles.

Signed:

Witness:

FIRST SCHEDULE

SECOND SCHEDULE

FAILURE BY A PERSON TO GIVE A CONSENT MAY RESULT IN ARBITRATION COSTS BEING AWARDED AGAINST HIM. AN EXPLANATORY LEAFLET IS AVAILABLE ON REQUEST FROM LAND REGISTRY, NASSAU BUILDING, SETANTA CENTRE, NASSAU ST., DUBLIN, 2.

11.8.2.4 Form D

LAND REGISTRY

LANDLORD AND TENANT (GROUND RENTS) (No. 2) ACT 1978

NOTICE OF INTENTION

Notice to immediate lessor of intention to apply for the fee simple pursuant to section 21(1) of the Landlord and Tenant (Ground Rents) (No. 2) Act, 1978. (Note (a)).

To:

of:

1.   Description of land to which this notice refers: (Note (b))

2.   Particulars of applicant's lease or tenancy: (Note (c))

3.   Part of lands excluded (if any): (Note (d))

Take notice that I/we

of

being a person(s) entitled under Part II of the above Act propose to apply, after 21 days from the date hereof, to the Registrar of Titles to vest in me/us under section 22 of the said Act the fee simple in the property set out on paragraph 1 hereof.

Dated this   day of   20

(Name)

(Address)

Notes

(a)   Section 21(1) provides that a person who claims to be entitled to acquire the fee simple shall serve notice of his application upon the immediate lessor. Notice may be served upon the person to whom the applicant pays his rent at the place at or to which he pays or sends such rent. If notice is being served by post, same should be by registered post.

(b)   Sufficient particulars should be given to identify the property.

(c)   State amount of rent and whether the land is held on a yearly tenancy or under a lease. If the land is held under a lease, state the date of the lease, the duration of the term and the parties to the lease.

(d)   This need only be completed where the property includes land which is not covered by the permanent buildings and which is not wholly subsidiary and ancillary to such buildings. Such land must be excluded from the purchase under the Act (section 14) and should if necessary be identified on a map.

11.8.2.5 **Form E**

LAND REGISTRY

LANDLORD AND TENANT (GROUND RENTS) (No. 2) ACT 1978

VESTING CERTIFICATE

Whereas

of

has duly made an application under section 20 of the Landlord and Tenant (Ground Rents) (No. 2) Act, 1978, in respect of the property specified in Part I of the Schedule hereto:

Now therefore the Registrar of Titles in exercise of the powers conferred on him by section 22 of that Act hereby vests the fee simple in the said property in the applicant free from incumbrances and any intermediate interests.

The name and address of every party who prior to the making of this Certificate had a superior interest in the said property is set out in Part II of the Schedule hereto.

It is hereby certified that the transaction hereby effected does not form part of a larger transaction or of a series of transactions in respect of which the amount or value or the aggregate amount or value of the consideration exceeds   .

SCHEDULE

PART I

PART II

Dated this   day of

11.8.2.6 **Form F**

LAND REGISTRY

LANDLORD AND TENANT (GROUND RENTS) (No. 2) ACT 1978

VESTING CERTIFICATE

Whereas

of

has made an application under section 21 of the Landlord and Tenant (Ground Rents) (No. 2) Act, 1978, in respect of the property specified in Part I of the Schedule hereto and whereas the Registrar of Titles is satisfied that the applicant is entitled to acquire the fee simple in the said property:

Now therefore the Registrar of Titles in exercise of the powers conferred on him by section 22 of that Act hereby vests the fee simple in the said property in the applicant free from incumbrances and any intermediate interests.

The name and address of every party who prior to the making of this Certificate had a superior interest in the said property is set out in Part II of the Schedule hereto.

It is hereby certified that the transaction hereby effected does not form part of a larger transaction or of a series of transactions in respect of which the amount or value or the aggregate amount or value of the consideration exceeds

SCHEDULE

PART I

PART II

Dated this   day of

GROUND RENTS

11.8.2.7   Form G

LAND REGISTRY

LANDLORD AND TENANT (GROUND RENTS) (No. 2) ACT 1978

CERTIFICATE OF TITLE

1.   I,   Solicitor/Barrister of   hereby certify that I have investigated the title to the property set out in the First Schedule hereto, other than the title to the Lease specified therein.

2.   As a result of my investigations of the title, I certify that the fee simple (or superior leasehold interest) in the said property is/was vested in   of   free from any adverse rights, restrictive covenants or encumbrances, save the said Lease (or subject as set out in the Second Schedule hereto).

Dated this   day of

SIGNATURE:

FIRST SCHEDULE

The property known as

situate

demised by Lease dated   and made between   and   for a term of   years at the yearly rent of

SECOND SCHEDULE

11.9 Sample Notice of Application for Arbitration to the County Registrar

There is no prescribed notice of application for arbitration to the County Registrar under the 1967 Act. The following is a sample of such a notice of application.

THE CIRCUIT COURT   DUBLIN CIRCUIT

In the matter of the Landlord and Tenant (Ground Rents) Acts

SECTION 8

TONY MAHER   APPLICANT

JOHN TOMEY   RESPONDENT

WHEREAS the applicant has acquired and is now entitled to the lands comprised in an Indenture of Lease dated the 3 December 1965 and made between Ann Maher of the one part and Karen O'Neill of the other part for a term of 198 years from the 24 November 1965 at the yearly rent of Ten Pounds. The said lease is a lease to which Part II of the Landlord and Tenant (Ground Rents) (No. 2) Act 1978 applies.

The lands demised by the said lease are therein described as 'ALL THAT AND THOSE the dwellinghouse situate at 4 Marley Lawns in the Barony of Dun Laoghaire and County of Dublin'.

AND WHEREAS the said Respondent is the person now and at all relevant times entitled to the next superior interest in the lands which the applicant is informed are held under an Indenture of Conveyance the said title having been shown to the satisfaction of the applicant's solicitor.

AND WHEREAS on the 6 June 2018 the applicant being the person entitled under Sections 9 and 10 of the Landlord and Tenant (Ground Rents) (No. 2) Act 1978 to purchase the fee simple interest in the said premises served upon the said Respondent by registered post a Notice of Intention to Acquire Fee Simple under s 4 of the Landlord and Tenant (Ground Rents) Act 1967 and on the 6 June 2018 the applicant did serve on the said Respondent by registered post a Notice Requiring Information under s 7(1) of the Landlord and Tenant (Ground Rents) Act 1967.

AND WHEREAS the applicant has received no response to the said notices from the said Respondent and the applicant has now discovered that the said Respondent emigrated to England in 2001.

AND WHEREAS it would appear necessary to have someone appointed to represent the said Respondent and to convey his interest under Section 8 of the Landlord and Tenant (Ground Rents) Act 1967.

TAKE NOTICE that on the 7 November 2018 at the hour of 11 a.m. or at the first opportunity thereafter application will be made to the County Registrar for the City of Dublin sitting at his offices at the Four Courts, Dublin, for an Order:

1. Confirming that the applicant is entitled to acquire the fee simple interest in the said lands;

2. Determining the purchase price payable in respect of the said acquisition;

3. Determining the persons entitled to receive the said purchase money and the amount thereof that each is to receive;

4. Appointing a person to execute a conveyance to the applicant of the interest of the said Respondent in the said lands for and in the name of the said Respondent;

5. As to the costs payable by the parties in respect of this hearing; and

GROUND RENTS

For any further or other relief as may be necessary in the circumstances of the case.

Dated the   day of   2018.

Signed:

TO:

The County Registrar,

Circuit Court,

Four Courts,

Dublin 7.

John Tomey

of

11.10 Ground Rents—Guidelines for Ground Rents Purchase Scheme

Note	This information is designed to assist in the use of the ground rents purchase scheme. It is not a legal document and does not represent, in any way, an interpretation of the law relating to the purchase of ground rents.
Who can apply?	The owners of dwellings which are built wholly or principally as dwellinghouses; this does not include dwellings converted into flats.
What about local authority houses?	Owners of local authority housing can buy out their ground rents but they do not come under this scheme; they should get in touch with their local authority.
How do I apply?	By **CONSENT PROCEDURE** (see below), if you can contact your landlord/s and agree a purchase price for the Freehold Title. Once you have paid the purchase price to the landlord/s, he/they will complete a Consent Form/s. The onus of obtaining all of the necessary Consents lies with you as the applicant. If consent is not forthcoming, or if the identity of your Landlord/s is/are unknown, you may apply by **ARBITRATION PROCEDURE** (see below). Under Arbitration procedure a purchase price for the Freehold Title will be set by this office some time after the application has been lodged. You will be notified of the amount involved and requested to lodge the money in this office.
What do I get for my money?	You will receive a Vesting Certificate when your application has been completed. The Vesting Certificate is evidence that you have bought out your ground rents. **IT IS A NEW TITLE DEED TO YOUR PROPERTY AND, AS SUCH, IT IS A VERY IMPORTANT DOCUMENT**.
What do I do with the vesting certificate?	You are strongly advised to have your Vesting Certificate registered. Registration of the Vesting Certificate will mean that a permanent registry record of your freehold interest is available in the event of the document being lost or destroyed.
Where and how do I register?	This will depend on where your existing title deeds are registered and the date your Vesting Certificate issued. From 1 June 2011, compulsory registration in the Land Registry is extended to all counties (S.I. 516 of 2010) and all Vesting certificates issued on or after that date must be registered in the Land Registry. Previously compulsory registration dates varied according to county as follows:

1st January 1970 – Carlow, Meath & Laois,
1st April 2006 – Longford, Roscommon & Westmeath,
1st October 2008 – Clare, Kilkenny, Louth, Sligo, Wexford &
Wicklow,
1st January 2010 – Cavan, Donegal, Galway, Kerry, Kildare,
Leitrim, Limerick,
Mayo, Monaghan, Offaly, Tipperary & Waterford
With your Vesting Certificate,
you will receive more detailed information on registration.

Note You will be charged a separate fee for registration. The Registration Fee in the Land Registry is €40.

Additional Information on CONSENT APPLICATIONS

There are two Forms to be completed when applying for a Vesting Certificate under Consent procedure; these are Forms A and Form C.

Form A: is the application Form to be completed and signed by the owner/tenant of the premises. If you hold the premises jointly with a spouse or other relatives, Form A should also include their name/s and signature/s.

Form C: is the Consent Form to be completed by your Landlord/s when you have paid to him/them the purchase price for the freehold title.

Note: If there is more than one Landlord involved, it will be necessary to obtain a completed Consent Form from each Landlord. If you are unable to obtain a completed Consent Form from one or more of the Landlords you may buy out your ground rents through Arbitration procedure. Arbitration procedure requires that you lodge the purchase price for the Freehold Title with this office rather than paying it directly to the Landlord.

The onus of obtaining all of the necessary Consents rests with you as the applicant.

Your Consent application should consist of the following items:

1. Completed Form A

2. Completed Form/s C

3. A photocopy of your LEASE

4. A photocopy of your ASSIGNMENT (This document is required if you are not the original owner of the house; it is evidence of your ownership).

5. Application fee of €30 if you reside at the premises or €65 otherwise

   (Payment by cheque, postal order, bank draft or cash will be accepted; cheques, etc, should be made payable to "Property Registration Authority".

   To guard against fraud, the Property Registration Authority (the PRA) needs to confirm the identity of anyone, (other than by a practising solicitor acting for a third party client, financial institution, etc), making any application to the Land Registry, including a ground rents application.

Since the 1st of February 2013 *all personal* applicants are required to complete a **'Personal Applicant's Identification Form (ID Form)'**. If a joint application is being made each party must complete a separate form and produce evidence of their identity.

This form can found in the Forms Section of our website www.prai.ie.

Alternatively you can contact the Ground Rents section of the Property Registration Authority (PRA) at groundrents@prai.ie **and we can arrange to send a form by post**.

Note   Items 3 and 4 are two of the title deeds to your property. If you have a mortgage you may find that copies of the deeds are available from your Bank or Building Society. If your mortgage has been repaid in full, the deeds may be held by your solicitor.

Additional information on ARBITRATION APPLICATIONS

There are two Forms to be completed when applying for a Vesting Certificate under Arbitration procedure; these are Forms B and Form D.

Form B   is the application Form to be completed and signed by the owner/tenant of the premises. If you hold the premises jointly with a spouse or other relatives,
Form B should also include their name/s and signature/s.

Form D   is the Notice of your Intention to buy out the ground rents under Arbitration procedure. Form D should be sent, by REGISTERED POST to your Landlord (or his Agent/Solicitor).

Note   It is important that you retain a PHOTOCOPY of your completed and signed Form D AND a receipt for registered post as these items will form part of your application.

      You may hand the completed Form D to your Landlord instead of sending it by registered post; but if you do so, you must ask him/them for a letter acknowledging receipt of the Form D.

21 Days after you have served Form D you may lodge your application which should include the following items:

1. Completed and signed Form B

2. Photocopy of completed Form D

3. Receipt for registered post, or letter from your Landlord acknowledging receipt of same

4. Your latest ground rent receipt

5. A photocopy of your Lease

6. A photocopy of your Assignment (This document is required if you are not the original owner of the property; it is evidence of your ownership).

7. €105 application fee if you reside at the premises or €195 otherwise.

  (Payment by cheque, postal order, bank draft or cash will be accepted;

  cheques, etc. should be made payable to "Property Registration Authority".

GROUND RENTS

To guard against fraud, the Property Registration Authority (the PRA) needs to confirm the identity of anyone, (other than a practising solicitor acting for a third party client, financial institution, etc), making any application to the Land Registry, including a ground rents application.

Since the 1st of February 2013 *all personal* applicants are required to complete a **'Personal Applicant's Identification Form (ID Form)'**. If a joint application is being made each party must complete a separate form and produce evidence of their identity.

This form can found in the Forms section of our website www.prai.ie. **Alternatively** you can contact the Ground Rents section of the Property Registration Authority (PRA) at groundrents@prai.ie **and we can arrange to send a form by post**.

Note   (Items 5 and 6 are two of the title deeds to your property. If you have a mortgage you may find that copies of the deeds are available from your Bank or Building Society. If your mortgage has been repaid in full, the deeds may be held by your solicitor.

Applications may be delivered in person or posted to:
PROPERTY REGISTRATION AUTHORITY
GROUND RENTS SECTION
CHANCERY STREET
DUBLIN 7
PUBLIC HOURS ARE FROM 10.30 a.m. to 4.30 p.m.

CHAPTER 12

COMMERCIAL LEASES

12.1 Introduction

For the landlord, a commercial lease is a means of obtaining a return from the property it has acquired purely as an investment. For the tenant, a commercial lease is a means of obtaining a premises in which to carry on its business without tying up capital.

Commercial leases are commonly drafted to reflect the different types of letting involved: office, retail or industrial. They can relate to a single or multi-let building. There is also a distinction between short-term lettings, being for a term of less than five years, and leases for longer terms, being generally for 15–25 years. A short-term lease does not usually contain a rent review clause and the repairing covenant(s) will normally apply to the interior of the premises only. Leases for longer terms will contain rent review and (sometimes) 'break' clauses and the tenant will normally be obliged to repair both the interior and exterior of the demised premises including the structure.

12.1.1 'FRI' LEASE

Historically, commercial leases were relatively simple documents, but they have now evolved into a comprehensive form commonly known as 'FRI'—full repairing and insuring—leases, usually for a term of 20 years at open market rent subject to review every five years. In addition to the lease itself becoming more complicated it is not unusual for the parties to use a side letter to vary the terms of the standard lease. This may arise when a landlord of a multi-let building agrees more favourable terms with one tenant; for example, an anchor tenant in a shopping centre. The contents of a side letter are usually personal to the tenant but are binding on the landlord and his or her successors.

With a single letting of an entire building the tenant is liable for all repairs and outgoings. With a letting of part of a building the landlord usually covenants to maintain the structure and common areas but passes on the cost to the tenant through a service charge. In all cases the landlord should retain control of insurance of the building (to protect its investment), with the tenants covenanting to reimburse this cost.

In some cases the parties intend the lease to be temporary only. If so, it is vital to advise the landlord that, with rare exceptions (notoriously difficult to enforce), the tenant will acquire statutory rights under the Landlord and Tenant (Amendment) Act, 1980, ('the 1980 Act') as amended by the Landlord and Tenant (Amendment) Act, 1994, ('the 1994 Act') and the Civil Law (Miscellaneous Provisions) Act 2008 ('the 2008 Act') to a new lease after five years' occupation. The lease should therefore not exceed four years nine months (rent payable quarterly) or four years eleven months (rent payable monthly) and, if the tenant overholds, it is essential the landlord does not accept payment of any rent after expiry or otherwise tacitly allow the tenancy to continue.

Note that s 17(1)(a) of the 1980 Act as amended by the 1994 Act and the 2008 Act gives a right to contract out of the provisions of the 1980 Act in respect of premises used for business purposes.

12.1.2 SHOPPING CENTRES

Commercial leases affect any premises let for business purposes. This includes retail outlets, for example, units in shopping centres, or office blocks, business parks and industrial estates. While the detail of every lease differs, the basic format is essentially the same. With shopping centres, there are a number of specific covenants and provisions which are usually included in the lease in addition to obvious items, such as service charge, common areas, etc, for example:

(a) minimum trading hours;

(b) service areas/delivery hours;

(c) competition/use;

(d) window displays/shop fronts;

(e) common regulations/standards;

(f) additional services—crèche, restrooms, etc;

(g) 'broadcasting' music, etc;

(h) external walls.

12.1.3 PROCEDURE

See **chapter 5** on Taking Instructions/Essential Contents of a Lease. There are several key issues in every lease which require special consideration. These include the following:

(a) repairs;

(b) insurance;

(c) user and alienation;

(d) service charge;

(e) rent review.

Pre-Lease Enquiries should also be raised, both prima facie title and general, as well as the standard pre-lease VAT enquiries. Searches should also be carried out. The landlord is required to furnish a Building Energy Rating (BER) Certificate with Advisory Report attached.

12.2 Service Charge Clauses in Commercial Leases

12.2.1 GENERAL

Group occupation, whether it be of an industrial estate, business park, office block or a shopping centre, presupposes communal services. These services are provided by the landlord and charged back to the tenants on an apportionment which is usually based on area occupied so that the landlord receives rent free from the risk of incurring running costs.

The charge is on a non-profit basis, providing a pool of money out of which the manager of the building pays for heating, cleaning and lighting of communal areas, wages etc and reimburses any surplus or recoups any deficit at the end of each year. No element of the rent is attributable to the cost of providing such services. Each service charge clause must be carefully drawn having regard to the circumstances pertaining to the particular building. Modern leases involving multiple units commonly contain elaborately drafted service charge clauses and should be drafted to ensure they protect not only the landlord's interest but are also fair to the tenant. They are usually not negotiable.

Commercial buildings in single occupation do not normally require service charge clauses as a sole occupier provides its own services at its own direct cost. An exception would be a single let building in an industrial estate or business park where there is road maintenance, landscaping and estate upkeep.

The lease will usually detail the services in a separate schedule. These services can be quite extensive, particularly in the case of a very modern, high tech building. It is normal for a landlord to provide a 'catch-all' clause to the effect that he may introduce or discontinue services as appropriate. When drafting the service charge provisions and the schedule relating to it, do not 'cherry pick'. It is important to get specific instructions for the specific building and discuss the proposed lease in detail with the landlord client. The primary services are repairs and maintenance, including decoration and cleaning of the common areas of the building, together with lighting, heating, servicing and renewal and rebuilding of the retained parts. The provision of maintenance and renewing of plant and machinery which would normally include lifts and central heating/air conditioning plant would be included. The service charge should also include the cost of compliance with statutory requirements in relation to the building as a whole. It includes security and staff, if applicable, relating to security (and emergency systems). The list of services should also include management of the building and the fees for this (including VAT).

Increases in energy costs and the introduction of new legislation will focus both parties to consider 'green leases' and the issues likely to impact on the operation of many standard lease clauses and payment for waste and recycling. The European Commission's *Green Public Procurement Handbook* designed to assist public authorities implement green strategies including electricity usage has already resulted in regulations being brought in to some degree or other for all buildings.

Negotiation and agreement on any green clauses will be influenced by the age, use, size and location of the building as well as financial constraints and the degree of commitment of the parties. The issues will be more complex where the building or development is multi-occupied.

12.2.2 DETERMINING THE AMOUNT OF THE SERVICE CHARGE

There are five areas to consider in relation to problems which can arise with standard service charges: (a) method of payment; (b) items to be included; (c) apportionment between tenants; (d) sinking funds; and (e) certification.

The majority of modern commercial leases provide that the annual service charge is paid annually in advance generally in one payment. It is usual for the service charge to be reserved as rent as the landlord can forfeit the lease for non-payment. The payments for the first year of operation of the building are based on the landlord's estimate of the likely expenditure and must be notional. It is important that the landlord carefully costs out the projected expenses for the first year. When the actual costs are known, any overpayment is credited to the tenant or an underpayment charged on the next service charge demand. This is known as a balancing charge. For subsequent years, advance payments are normally made on the actual service charge calculated on the previous year's costs but increased proportionately according either to a specific percentage or, more likely, based on a budget for the year in question. Current practice is that the lease will provide for the expenditure to be certified by a surveyor or accountant employed by the landlord and the relevant clause in the lease states that this amount is to be conclusive evidence of the costs, save for manifest error. The lease will provide for a balancing charge in the case of an underpayment by the tenant, in which case the landlord has the facility to seek the extra sums due at the end of the financial year. Likewise, there is a provision for a balancing payment back to the tenant in the event of an overpayment. In practice, any overpayment by the tenant is shown as a credit against the following year's service charge. For certification of the charge see **12.2.5**.

Where there is a partial letting of a building it is important to spell out in the lease who bears the proportion of the service charge applicable to the voids, ie those portions of the building or parts of the shopping centre which are not currently let. This has often fallen to the landlord but if, for example, only the occupied floors of the building were being heated it would seem equitable that all of the heating charge should be borne by the occupiers.

The case of *Finchbourne Ltd v Rodrigues* [1976] 3 All ER 581 established that there are limitations at law on the landlord's right to recover service charge and that there is an implied term that the cost recoverable by the landlord from the tenant in respect of the provision of services should be fair and reasonable. This decision prevents the recovery by a landlord of unreasonably extravagant charges for the service items included in the lease.

In every case the tenant should be careful to check that the service charge does not include anything over and above the repair and maintenance of the common areas. It should not cover the landlord's initial capital cost, ie the cost of buying and fitting out the premises. In particular, care should be taken to ensure that the tenant does not bear responsibility for any extensions to the premises, to the benefit of the landlord and perhaps to the tenant's detriment; for example, where extra units are being added to a shopping centre and the potential tenants will provide extra competition for the tenant.

In determining the provision of services a tenant should seek to ensure that the landlord is obliged to procure services at a reasonable cost and likewise the landlord may only recoup from the tenant reasonable costs, fees and expenses. A well-drawn lease should include a clause obliging a landlord to submit certified accounts to all tenants—the cost of which should be included as service charge expenditure. As errors can occur a tenant should request a clause permitting an independent audit of the service charge accounts, the tenant to be responsible for the cost of same unless the audit discloses material errors and then the landlord should bear the cost. In *Concorde Graphics Limited v Andromeda Investments SA* (1983) 265 EG 386 a clause stating that the decision of a surveyor appointed by the landlord was final and binding in respect of any dispute as to the amount of the service charge was held to be unenforceable by the landlord.

As to the apportionment of the service charge between tenants, see **12.2.6**.

12.2.3 SERVICES TO BE INCLUDED IN THE LEASE

The landlord's obligation in relation to services should be clearly spelt out to avoid dispute.

The case of *Jacob Isbicki & Co Ltd v Goulding & Bird Ltd* [1989] 1 EGLR 236 concerned the interpretation to be placed on a service charge provision. The provision obliged the tenant to:

'pay to the landlord a proportionate part of the expenses and outgoings reasonably and properly incurred by the landlord in the repair, maintenance and renewal and insurance of the building and the provision of services therein and the other heads of expenditure as the same are set out in the fourth schedule'.

The fourth schedule detailed the expenses and outgoings in respect of which the tenant was to pay that service charge. While this referred to the costs incurred in the maintenance and repair of both specified internal common parts and drains, gutters and cables, there was no mention of the cost of repairing the structure or exterior of the building.

Difficulties arose when the landlord had the external walls sandblasted and sought to charge this work to the tenant. The landlord argued that the wording of the general obligation to pay the service charge, quoted above, was sufficient to render the tenant liable. However, the court accepted the tenant's contention that the general covenant only obliged the tenant to pay for the outgoings specifically listed in the fourth schedule. Accordingly, the court ruled that the tenant was not obliged to meet the cost of the work.

The court also declined to accept the suggestion made by the landlord that a clause in the lease under which the landlord could, in his or her absolute discretion, 'add to, extend, vary or make any alteration in the rendering of the said services' enabled it to extend the services so as to include external works. In the court's view this clause entitled the landlord only to vary the existing services, not to introduce new ones. The decision in this case clearly imposes an onus on the landlord to have the service charge covenant in the lease comprehensively drawn to include all possible items of service which may be required to be carried out and for which the landlord will seek reimbursement from the tenant.

The tenant will be liable to contribute towards any service specifically set out in a lease, usually in the Schedule of Services. The fact that such expenditure may not confer any benefit on a particular tenant is irrelevant if that tenant has agreed that the particular service is to be included in the service charge provisions. In *The Norwich Union Life Insurance Society v Gestetner Duplicators Ltd* High Court 14 February 1984 (unreported) the ground floor tenants of an office block were held to be liable to contribute to the replacement of two lifts—notwithstanding that they had no use or need for them. The lease provided that the cost of replacing 'any and every part of the building' was included in the service charge provisions.

There is no limit on the range of services which may be included in the lease. The more 'high tech' and high-class developments will include a very wide range of services but generally, most leases will include the following:

(a)   Conventional services—standard items such as heating, lighting, refuse collection and maintenance of common areas.

(b)   (i) Staff costs incurred by the landlord in retaining permanent staff to include national insurance, tax, training and Christmas bonuses; and (ii) management fees. The RICS Code recommends the fee should be fixed subject to annual review for indexation.

(c)   Structure of the building.

(d)   Any other expenditure—otherwise known as a 'mopping up clause'. By its nature, this clause is very open-ended and non-specific. In *Jacob Isbicki & Co Ltd v Goulding & Bird Ltd* [1989] 1 EGLR 236 the wording of the 'mopping up clause' was held to prevent the landlord from recovering the costs of external sand blasting on the basis that the particular clause was referable to the list of specified services listed in the Schedule of Services. Hence, from the landlord's point of view such a 'mopping up clause' must provide for the provision of services 'other than' those listed in the Schedule of Services to be provided.

Certain costs should not be included as they are of more benefit to a landlord than a tenant. Examples are:

(a) Initial costs incurred in relation to the original design and construction of the fabric, plant or equipment.

(b) Any setting-up costs reasonably considered part of the original development costs of the property.

(c) Improvement costs above the costs of normal maintenance, repair or replacement.

(d) Future redevelopment costs.

(e) Such costs as are matters between the owner and an individual occupier. Examples given are costs of letting units, enforcement of covenants for collection of rent, consents for assignments, alterations, rent review etc.

In *Staghold Ltd v Takeda* [2005] 3 EGLR 45 tenants of a multi-let building had challenged the amount of service charge levied by the landlord. The landlord sought to recover legal fees he had incurred in defending those challenges by incorporating them in the next year's service charge. This was on the basis that the lease provided the cost of employing legal or professional advisers for the collection of service charges was itself to be covered by the tenants through the service charge. The court held that the landlord was entitled to recover such legal costs—including the costs of the case hearing the issue.

The Royal Institution of Chartered Surveyors (RICS) publishes a Code of Practice which contains advice and recommendations. Its stated aims are to improve general standards and prompt best practice uniformity, fairness and transparency. Irish practitioners regularly consult this Code of Practice.

12.2.4 POTENTIAL AREAS OF DISPUTE

12.2.4.1 Staff costs

Where there is an obligation to provide staff, eg a caretaker or manager or security service, it is necessary to provide for payment of their wages including PAYE, cost of uniform, etc and incidental expenses such as accommodation, in the lease.

In *Regis Property Co Ltd v Dudley* [1959] AC 370 it was held that where a landlord manages a property without employing agents, a reasonable charge for any services may include an element of profit to the landlord. However, in the case of *Cleve House Properties v Schildof* [1980] CLY 1641 the court held that such management costs may only be recovered if they are specifically provided for in the lease and are in respect of a liability which the landlord has incurred.

12.2.4.2 Plant and machinery

The landlord would normally be obliged to maintain and repair mechanical equipment and plant such as lifts, boilers, central heating and air-conditioning equipment, and the lease should be drafted in such a way that the landlord is entitled to recover the renewal and replacement costs of such equipment from the tenants and not only the maintenance costs. The service charge provisions should also include the costs incurred by the landlord in entering into a fully comprehensive maintenance contract for the plant and machinery. In the absence of appropriate provisions, the landlord is not able to recover the full costs of a comprehensive maintenance contract allowing for complete renewal. Where there is a well-drawn clause there should be no need for a separate requirement of the tenant to contribute to a reserve fund for the renewal of the same equipment.

12.2.4.3 Extra services

The lease should provide that the landlord is entitled at his or her discretion to supply extra services and improvements which are reasonably required for the benefit of the tenants. However, see the limitations on such a provision as held in *Jacob Isbicki & Co Ltd v Goulding & Bird Ltd* (see **12.2.3**).

12.2.4.4 Sinking fund

The provision of a sinking or reserve fund to cover future capital expenditure put aside for the replacement at the end of the estimated life of equipment is commonly found in leases relating to shopping centres or purpose-built blocks. It is a fund built up over time to equalise expenditure for regularly recurring service items so as to avoid fluctuations in the amount of service charge payable each year.

This clause should include the following items:

(a) exact nature of the equipment for which the fund is to be used;

(b) exact cost of this equipment at the time of installation;

(c) estimate of the life of the equipment;

(d) provision for updating the replacement cost, say, every five years;

(e) how the fund is to be administered; is it to be a trust fund? How are the annual calculations as to contribution to be made? Is the landlord to account for interest (less tax) on the fund as trustee of the tenants?

(f) in what circumstances may the fund be drawn on?

The administration of a sinking fund is onerous on landlords and tenants alike and, as such, the question of whether a sinking fund is required needs to be considered. If the tenant's repairing covenant is extended to cover replacement of items of plant and machinery and this covenant may be effected either directly or through the service charge, a sinking fund may not be required, though it may result in heavy outgoings in any particular year.

To protect a tenant, a sinking fund clause should provide that the fund is to be kept separate from the landlord's own money to ensure that such fund does not form part of the landlord's assets on a bankruptcy or liquidation. The fund should be maintained in an interest-bearing account with the interest earned being applied to the fund. The lease should also provide that upon completion of any sale of the property, the vendor/landlord shall pass all sinking fund monies held, together with all accrued interest, to the purchaser.

The administration of a sinking fund can become extremely complicated. They are cumbersome and difficult to manage and there are financial implications involved. Essentially a sinking fund belongs to the tenants. If a building is destroyed and will not be rebuilt then the sinking fund will require to be distributed among the tenants. Likewise there is also a problem if a lease comes to an end or if a tenant exercises the break option and seeks repayment of the monies. In the case of *Secretary of State for the Environment v Possfund (North West) Limited* [1997] 2 EGLR 56 the tenant paid an element of the service charge described as a 'depreciation allowance' but which was effectively a contribution to a sinking fund. When the lease expired the tenant reclaimed the unexpended monies but the court held that the monies belonged to the landlord as they were intended to cover direct expenditure such as annual running costs and indirect costs such as annual depreciation of plant and machinery. In effect it was a form of indemnity paid by the tenant to the landlord.

12.2.4.5 Repairs and renewals

Repairs should be distinguished from renewals. This is a question of fact and degree as to whether work done or required to be done is a repair or a renewal. Any money collected by a landlord for repairs should be held in trust for the tenant and should not be accessible to the landlord other than to pay for the work in question. Otherwise the landlord may, for example, go into liquidation and the money would therefore be lost. Repair is restoration by renewal or replacement of subsidiary parts of a whole. Renewal as distinguished from repairs is the reconstruction of the entirety, meaning by the entirety not necessarily the whole but substantially the whole of the subject matter under discussion—*Lurcott v Wakely* [1911] 1 KB 905.

In practice a tenant will carry out a survey of the property before signing a lease and the report of that survey, often with photographs, will be included in a schedule to the lease. The draft 2011 Bill (see **1.4.4**) proposes to introduce default obligations to repair and overriding obligations, relating for example to inspection or notification. See **8.3.7** for further details.

12.2.4.6 Insurance

In general, it is preferable to recover the fire and other perils insurance separately from the service charge, but insurance in relation to employer's liability, plant and machinery and public liability for the common parts should properly form part of the service charge.

It is essential that a full definition of the risks against which the landlord is insuring is set out clearly in the lease. Such a clause will generally include a 'catch-all' phrase, including for example 'such other risks as the landlord may in its absolute discretion from time to time determine'. The clause recouping the cost of insuring the building/demised premises should reserve the insurance premiums as rent so that it attracts all the remedies for recovery of rent and thereby avoiding the notice required for forfeiture for breach of covenant. The landlord's covenant to insure the demised premises should be subject to the landlord being able to obtain cover, eg the building is in a bad area of the city. Insurance should be for the full reinstatement cost rather than reinstatement value as otherwise the liability of the insurance company is confined to the value of the landlord's interest. In *St Albans Investment Company v Sun Alliance and London Insurance Limited* [1983] IR 362 the policy provided for payment of the value of the property. There was no reinstatement clause and the question was raised whether the insurance company was obliged to pay up on a reinstatement basis. The court held this was not the case and payment should be based on the market value of the building less the site value. Clearly this could be very different from reinstatement cost and there could be a considerable shortfall in funds. Insurance should also cover loss of service charge, if applicable, and rent for a period, usually three years, and an obligation on the landlord to reinstate the premises within that period or the tenant can surrender the lease.

There should also be a provision for arbitration in the event of any dispute arising in relation to the suspension of rent or service charge during the period the tenant cannot use the premises. It is also normal for a tenant's solicitors to seek to have a non-invalidation clause included in the insurance policy along with a waiver of subrogation rights. Insurers generally have no problem in issuing such consents.

Another point is that the landlord should check that the definition of demised premises does not include any additions, alterations or improvements carried out by the tenant. This would relate to expensive fit-outs. It is up to the tenant to request such items be included but the tenant should pay the additional increase in the premium specifically relating to those items.

12.2.4.7 Costs of enforcing covenants

The landlord should be entitled to recover legal costs incurred in protecting his or her investment. An example of this is the expenses incurred by a landlord in preventing a tenant with a specific use from using the premises for other purposes which would not be in the overall interest of either the landlord or the tenant; for example, in a shopping centre where a 'mix' of goods and services is required (see *OHS Ltd v Green Property Co Ltd* [1986] IR 39 at **12.5.2**).

12.2.4.8   Reinstatement

A commercial lease will contain a clause providing for one of the parties to reinstate the premises in the event of it being destroyed by fire or some other insured event. More often than not the landlord is responsible as he or she will generally receive the insurance monies; the lease having provided that the landlord insures the premises and his fittings in his name and the tenant reimburses the premium or proportionate part in the case of a multi-let building.

The tenant should ensure that in case this arises the lease contains a rent and, if applicable, service charge suspension clause until the premises are rebuilt and ready for occupation. The tenant may also seek the right to surrender the lease if the demise is substantially damaged and cannot be reinstated within a reasonable period, generally three years.

Section 40 of Deasy's Act, 1860, permits a tenant to surrender his or her tenancy on the destruction or rendering uninhabitable of the premises by fire or other inevitable accident. The fire or other accident must not have been due to the default of the tenant and there must be no express covenant by the tenant to repair in the lease. In modern commercial leases this right to surrender is usually expressly excluded by the terms of the lease.

12.2.5   CERTIFICATION OF THE CHARGE

The lease should provide that the total cost to the landlord in providing the services be certified at the end of each year by an auditor appointed by the landlord. The certificate shall be final and binding. This clause should also provide that the person who certifies the charge is to act as an expert.

In the case of *Finchbourne Ltd v Rodrigues* [1976] 3 All ER 581, it was held that the issue of a valid certificate was a condition precedent to the recovery of the service charge.

12.2.6   APPORTIONMENT OF CHARGE AMONG TENANTS

The landlord will apportion a particular tenant's individual share of a service charge in one of the following ways:

(a)   A fixed amount—this is inflexible and should only be used in short-term leases. If acting for a landlord, agree a fixed amount for the first year and then have that amount linked to the Consumer Price Index thereafter.

(b)   A fixed percentage—this is simple and certain for both parties but is really only suitable for a smaller type of scheme. If acting for a tenant it would be important to insert a clause providing the percentage is reviewed at regular intervals in the event of the property being significantly altered or extended.

(c)   Rateable valuation—this is very rarely used.

(d)   Either:

(i)   Floor area—this is the most common method and is, in most circumstances, the fairest. Again if acting for a tenant ensure that the lease provides that any extensions to the floor area of the property will result in a revaluation of the tenant's proportion of the service charge; or

(ii) Weighted floor area—the tenant's share is based on the floor area method, discounted to reflect the tenant's size or location. It also covers a mezzanine level in a tenant's unit in a shopping centre.

The aim should be to seek an equitable distribution of the charge among the tenants. To do this, the specific proportions should be written into the lease, whether based on rate-able valuation or area of floor leased, together with a right of the landlord in the event of a change of circumstances, or at specified intervals, to reassess the proportions.

As mentioned, service charges are often calculated by reference to the ratio of the floor area of the premises to the total number of lettable units in the overall development. In this way, the tenant of a relatively small unit in, for example, a shopping centre will only pay in proportion to its take. This is important in cases where the prestige anchor tenants occupy a significantly greater proportion of the development.

In other cases there may be some 'weighting' of the service charge so that a particular tenant may pay either more or less than might be expected. In certain cases a smaller unit may pay a greater sum pro rata (or indeed in real terms) than a larger one depend-ing on the type of user involved. It is also well established that where a shopping centre is spread over several storeys, the highest proportion of visitors is concentrated on the ground floor—where the anchor tenants are most often located. In such a case it is common for the tenants of the smaller units in the upper levels to pay a lesser amount of the service charge than the tenants of similar units on the ground floor. Tenants on the top floor or mezzanine level may only pay service charge equivalent to half their take.

12.3 Rent Review Clauses in Commercial Leases

12.3.1 GENERAL

The normal occupational business lease in Ireland granted for more than five years con-tains a rent review clause which provides for the rent to be reviewed periodically to a figure agreed between the parties with procedures set out for determination by a third party if the landlord and tenant fail to agree. This is the best method as it is the most closely related to the value of the property itself.

Other methods which can be used to revise rents include:

(a) Index-Linked Rents: These can be linked to an official index, such as the Index of Retail Prices or an informal index such as the rent of a petrol station to be increased by reference to the rise in rents of other comparable filling stations (*British Railways Board v Mobil Oil Co Ltd* [1994] 1 EGLR 146 C.A.).

(b) Turnover Rents: These are increasingly popular in the lettings of hotels and restau-rants. VAT should be excluded in the definition of 'turnover'. It should as far as possible relate to the actual profit made by the tenant. Sometimes the rent reserved is a combination of a base rent and a turnover rent.

(c) Rent geared to sub-rents: The rent under the head lease is usually a basic rent plus a percentage of the rent due under the subleases granted by the tenant. This type of rent is mainly found in development leases where the landlord supplies the land, the tenants build and they both participate in the investment.

The objective of a rent review clause is twofold:

(a) to protect the value of the landlord's investment, and

(b) to reflect the changing value of the property during the term of the lease.

For leases entered into prior to 28 February 2010 it was common for the rent review to be an 'upwards only' clause. Whatever the economic climate at the time of the review, the rent could not fall below what was payable immediately before the review.

In a Practice Note in the Law Society *Gazette* (July 1997), the Conveyancing Committee had recommended that the following rent review clause be used and advised that appropriate amendments be made to leases to connect the clause to the reddendum:

'Yielding and paying therefor and thereout during each of the first years of the said term the yearly rent of € and thereafter during each of the successive periods of years of which the first shall begin on the   day of   20   a yearly rent equal to:

(a) The yearly rent payable hereunder during the preceding period, or

(b) Such revised yearly rent as may from time to time be ascertained in accordance with the provisions in that behalf contained . . . hereto

Whichever shall be the greater.'

The position changed with the enactment of s 132 of the Land and Conveyancing Law Reform Act 2009 ('the 2009 Act'). This was introduced by the Government as one of the remedial actions to save the economy after the Celtic Tiger collapse in 2008. It came into effect from 28 February 2010 (S.I. 471 of 2009).

Section 132 applies to a lease of land used wholly or partly for the purposes of carrying on a business and applies to any lease entered into after 28 February 2010. Section 132(3) states that notwithstanding any provision to the contrary contained in the lease or an agreement for lease and, only in respect of that part of the land demised by the lease in which business is permitted to be carried on under the terms of the lease, a provision which provides for the review of the rent payable under the lease shall be construed as providing that the rent payable following such review may be fixed at an amount which is less than, greater than, or the same as the amount of rent payable immediately prior to the date on which the rent falls to be reviewed. This in effect prevents the operation of an 'upwards only' rent review clause. The objective is that any reviewed rent is to reflect the market conditions prevailing at the time of the review.

The Law Reform Commission Consultation Paper on General Law of Landlord and Tenant (LRC CP 28–2003) recommended in the case of non-residential tenancies a statutory model of rent review clause which should operate as a default provision and which the parties would be free to amend. The draft 2011 Bill (see **1.4.4**) includes a Schedule setting out rent review provisions and the basis on which the proposed assessor would determine the revised rent.

The case of *Reox Holdings PLC v Cullen and Davidson* [2012] IEHC 299 deals with the matter of upwards only review. The issue before the court was to decide whether s 132 of the 2009 Act applies to a situation whereby a lease with a guarantee was entered into before the law commenced, but on the collapse of the business of the tenant after the law commenced, the guarantee provided that the landlord has the option to require the guarantor to step into the shoes of the tenant on the same terms, especially the term as to upwards only rent review. Briefly, the facts were that by a lease dated 16 April 2007 a retail unit was demised for a term of 25 years from 18 August 2006. The lease provided for the payment of a stepped rent for the first five years of the term with a provision for upwards only rent reviews every five years thereafter in accordance with the provisions of the lease. The guarantee provisions required the guarantor to accept a new lease of the demised premises subject to and with the benefit of the provisions of the existing lease if the landlord gave notice to the guarantor within 12 months after disclaimer or surrender of the lease. On 23 December 2010 the tenant passed a resolution for voluntary winding up and appointed a liquidator. On the same date the liquidator gave notice he was disclaiming the lease. On 11 January 2011 the landlord gave notice to the guarantor that he had elected to exercise the entitlement under the lease to require the guarantor to accept from and execute and deliver to him a new lease of the premises. The draft of the new lease contained an upwards only rent review clause and was for a term commencing 23 December 2010. The new lease stated explicitly that the agreement was not subject to the application of s 132 of the 2009 Act. The landlord claimed he was entitled to full indemnity for any loss on a downward rent review and argued that the 2009 Act had to be interpreted so as to avoid any retrospective effect.

The court held that the guarantor was entitled to a declaration that s 132 of the 2009 Act providing for upwards and downwards rent reviews applied to any new lease entered into by that guarantor with the landlord upon the exercise of the option to require the guarantor to step into the shoes of the tenant. The court could not extend the boundaries set by the legislator.

The Supreme Court decision in the case of *Ickendel Ltd v Bewley's Café Grafton Street Ltd* [2014] IESC 41 was a test case for upward only rent reviews. It concerned the interpretation of the term 'the preceding period' and its construction in the context of the determination of the rent for 'each of the successive periods of five years' after 31 December 1991. The facts briefly were Bewley's Café Grafton Street Limited entered into a 35-year lease from 1987 with rent reviews every five years. On each of the successive periods of five years the tenant was to pay a yearly rent which was equal to the greater of (a) the rent payable during the preceding period or (b) the revised rent ascertained in accordance with the rent review clause (ie open market rent). There was a rent review in 2007 at the height of the property boom but by 2012 some rents in Grafton Street had fallen as much as 52 per cent and the tenant sought a downwards revision of the rent. The High Court stated the parties had agreed the rent on a review would never fall below the initially agreed rent and they had agreed thereafter it would be a fair open market rent that could rise or fall. Following the decision an arbitrator reduced the original revised rent by 50 per cent approximately. The landlord appealed to the Supreme Court, which held unanimously that the expression 'the preceding period' was the period which immediately preceded the relevant review date. Accordingly, where the relevant review date was 2012 the preceding period was the five-year period immediately before the review date.

The judgment is of relevance for leases entered into prior to 28 February 2010. Leases after that date are subject to the provisions of s 132 of the 2009 Act.

12.3.2 TIME IS NOT OF THE ESSENCE

The first point to note in relation to a rent review clause is that time is not normally of the essence as regards the service of notices, unless there is a specific provision to this effect in the clause or there is an interrelation between the rent review clause and other clauses in the lease, eg where the tenant has an option to surrender at or around the time of the rent review date. In general, time should not be made of the essence as an oversight in the date of serving any notice under the rent review provisions could result in hardship for the party concerned.

12.3.3 PROVISION FOR INDEPENDENT REVIEW

Normally, the review of the rent is carried out, in default of agreement between the landlord and the tenant, by an independent person appointed, usually by the president of some well-recognised body, the said person appointed acting either as an expert or an arbitrator. Usually the landlord will have the choice.

Liability for an arbitrator's costs falls to be determined under the provisions of the Arbitration Acts, 1954 and 1998. An expert's costs are shared equally between the parties, either of whom may discharge them in full and then recover the other party's proportion on demand.

Note that the rent review clause set out in **Appendix 4** as drafted by the Law Society in 1993, whether for arbitrator or expert, allows for the appointment to be made in the first place by agreement between the parties and in default of agreement by the landlord. If the landlord fails to make the nomination within 28 days of being requested in writing by the tenant then the tenant may make the nomination. A tenant would be well advised to safeguard this provision. Aside from anything else it ensures that the tenant may take the initiative and prevent delay. This is particularly important if the tenant is thinking of assigning his or her interest. Prospective assignees are naturally reluctant to take on responsibility for performance of the covenants in a lease where a review is due but has not taken place.

In cases of delay, the tenant normally bears responsibility for any back-dated increase in rent together with interest which is normally calculated at a base rate. This is fair in that the tenant has had the use of the money during the period which can often be for several months.

12.3.4 BASIS FOR REVIEWING RENT

The vital element of the rent review clause is the basis on which the revised rent is to be determined. The rent to be reserved on the review date may be variously described but it is recommended that a phrase such as 'current market rent' or 'full open market yearly rent' be used, but any term such as 'fair' or 'reasonable' should be avoided as these are too vague.

12.3.5 INTERPRETATION OF RENT REVIEW CLAUSE

Close scrutiny must be paid to each part of the rent review provisions.

In particular it is important to note the provision of s 132 of the 2009 Act, which came into force on 28 February 2010. As noted this in effect prohibits rent review clauses operating as 'upwards only' in respect of leases created after 28 February 2010. There have been some attempts to lessen the impact of s 132 on the commercial property market. One method is to provide for a stepped rent. With Brexit approaching its effect is being felt in Ireland with increasing rental levels as UK companies seek a base in Ireland to access the EU market. What follows for the remainder of this part of **chapter 12** should be read bearing in mind that changes in this area are proposed in the draft 2011 Bill (see **1.4.4**). The Bill when passed will, however, only apply to leases granted after commencement.

For existing rent review clauses in leases granted before 28 February 2010 this section of the chapter remains relevant.

If using the standard Law Society rent review clause as set out at **Appendix 4**, care should be taken that it links in with the wording of the main part of the lease. It is drafted as a separate schedule and on the assumption that in the main body of the lease, in the reddendum, it is provided that on each of the rent review dates, the rent is to be the rent payable immediately preceding the rent review date or the revised rent determined in accordance with the rent review schedule, whichever is the greater.

12.3.6 SAMPLE CLAUSE RE BASIS FOR REVIEW

12.3.6.1 Basis on which reviewed rent is determined

Once having stated that the current market rent at the review date shall be the amount of rent payable for the period following the review date until the next following review date, the rent review clause should then go on to define precisely the basis on which the reviewed rent (whether called 'current market rent' or other) shall be determined. In a standard lease this is often defined as meaning:

> 'the gross full market rent without any deduction whatsoever at which the demised premises might reasonably be expected to be let as a whole at the nearest review date in the open market without a fine or premium as between a willing lessor and a willing lessee and with vacant possession for a term commencing on the review date, equal to the greater of fifteen years or the residue then unexpired of the term granted by the within written lease and on the same terms and conditions in all other respects as this present lease (including the provision for five-yearly rent reviews) and upon the supposition (if not a fact) that the tenant has complied with all the obligations as to repair and decoration herein imposed and that in the event of the demised premises having been destroyed or damaged the same shall then have been fully rebuilt, repaired or reinstated (as the case may be) in a good and substantial manner there being disregarded:
>
> (a) Any effect on rent of the fact that the tenant has been in occupation of the demised premises and any goodwill attached to the demised premises by reason of the carrying on therein of the business of the tenant.
>
> (b) Any effect on rent of any improvement (whether within the meaning of the Landlord & Tenant Acts 1931–1994 or any Acts amending or extending or reenacting same) of the demised premises or any part thereof or any alteration, addition or other work made or carried out by the tenant with the licence of the landlord at the tenant's own expense (otherwise than in pursuance of any obligation to the landlord whether pursuant to the provisions of this lease or otherwise) and carried out during the currency of this lease.'

Note, however, that even a seemingly minor alteration to the wording of a rent review clause could have a major, not to say catastrophic, effect. The foregoing example has evolved over time and takes relevant case law into account.

12.3.6.2 Parts of rent review clause

It is important to understand the reason why the various parts of the foregoing definition are necessary:

1. 'At which the demised premises might reasonably be expected to be let at the nearest review date in the open market'

    This ensures that the rent is reviewed on the basis of the demised premises being let as a whole—in other words, what a tenant would pay for taking a lease of the entire premises and not, for example, the aggregate rental which could be achieved by letting it in parts. Regard will be had to other open market rental values of similar premises.

2. 'Without a fine or premium'

    This prevents a landlord, on a rent review at a future date, seeking payment of a premium in circumstances where the then current practice might be for leases to be granted with rent reviews shorter than five years.

3.   'As between a willing lessor and a willing lessee'

Although not, if read literally, a very meaningful phrase it is the best definition that has yet been devised to express the intention of the parties that the rent should be reviewed on the basis of a 'free and open market'.

4.   'And with vacant possession'

The idea of the rent review clause is that each rent review date will, in effect, give rise to a situation similar to that which pertained at the beginning of the lease and it is therefore essential that the review of rent be carried out as if a lease of the premises was being granted in the open market to a tenant who was obtaining full vacant possession. Obviously, a tenant taking an assignment of a lease subject to occupational tenancies where the sub-tenants' rents are fixed will need to be advised to insist on an alteration to this phrase.

5.   'For a term commencing on the review date, equal to the greater of fifteen years or the residue then unexpired of the term granted by the within written lease'

This is an important clause as there has been a habit to use the phrase 'for the residue of the term of this lease' or 'for the term of this lease'. These phrases could cause the rent to be artificially higher or lower than the normal market rent—remember the intention of the rent review clause is to provide a situation on rent review whereby the rent will be determined as if it were the 'current market rent' which could be achieved if the property was then being freshly leased in the open market on the terms usual at the date of granting of the lease. The recommended clause provides that the term to be looked at is 15 years or the residue whichever is the greater.

6.   'And on the same terms and conditions in all other respects as this present lease (including the provision for five-yearly rent reviews)'

Again, the reason for this phrase is to ensure that the review reflects exactly the situation as at the beginning of the lease, except of course for the amount of the initial rent reserved.

See the Practice Note, Law Society *Gazette*, November 1984 which states:

'The letting value of property to be leased for a term of 20 years or upwards would almost certainly be substantially greater, if, in assessing that rent, the provisions for a review of rent were to be ignored. It is generally agreed by valuers and lawyers practising in this area that such provisions are not appropriate.' The Committee advised tenants' solicitors of the danger of such a provision in that it may result in a grossly inflated rent being set on review.

7.   'And upon the supposition (if not a fact) that the tenant has complied with all the obligations as to repair and decoration herein imposed and that in the event of the demised premises having been destroyed or damaged the same shall then have been fully rebuilt, repaired or reinstated (as the case may be) in a good and substantial manner'

This clause is clearly necessary to ensure that if the premises have not been maintained or repaired by the tenant, the landlord should not as a result suffer a lower rent on review.

It is assumed that the tenant has performed and observed his or her covenants and that, if the premises have been destroyed or damaged, they have been reinstated and fitted out and are thus ready for occupation. In some cases there will be an assumption that all the covenants on the part of the landlord have also been complied with. This would normally be resisted by a tenant as a landlord should not be able to benefit by getting a higher rent for a building where he has failed to comply with his covenant to keep the building in good repair or provide the services he was meant to under the service charge schedule.

8.   'There being disregarded ... etc'

This is a most important provision when acting for a tenant. Clearly, a tenant should not suffer on a rent review by reason of the fact that he or she is in occupation of the premises or that he or she has built up goodwill through the efficient running of his or her business. It is essential for tenants who carry out works to the property (provided of course that these are not works which they were bound by the lease or an agreement for lease to carry out) that they should not be subsequently penalised by having the rent reviewed on subsequent review dates to a level higher than would otherwise apply if the works which the tenants had thus carried out were disregarded. It is essential where acting for a tenant to discuss very carefully prior to the execution of a lease, any plans which he or she has for carrying out works to the demised property, whether at that time or in the future, and to ensure that the provisions for disregarding such works in a rent review are included. It is also of course necessary to explain to the tenant the need to obtain the landlord's consent to any works and the need to serve notices, etc under the 1980 Act.

If the tenant has carried out works which were required by the terms of the lease or agreement for lease then those works will not be disregarded. Those works will be rentalised on a rent review.

9.   Another assumption that may be found in a lease is that no work has been carried out to the premises that diminishes its rental value. Certain tenants may do work to premises which would suit their specific business purposes but which, for example, may reduce the floor area so this should be disregarded or assumed not to have happened. An example would be where stairs leading to the basement are installed in the prime zone A area at the front of the shop, which has the effect of reducing the valuable retail area and the increased rental value of the basement may not compensate the landlord for the loss in rental value of the prime zone A area.

12.3.7   RECORDING THE REVISED RENT

Where the revised rent has been settled by agreement or by arbitration, a memorandum recording the revised rent in duplicate executed by both parties should be put with the original lease and counterpart lease, but care should be taken that this is in a form which does not attract stamp duty. See Practice Note July 2006 for an example of such a Memorandum.

12.4   Alienation (Assignment and Sub-letting)

12.4.1   GENERAL

It is a rare lease that contains no restriction on a tenant's right to assign its interest. The main purpose of a restriction on alienation is to enable the landlord to control the quality/type of future tenant or sub-tenant especially in situations where such assignee or sub-tenant could obtain security of tenure. The overriding factor for a landlord in each case is the protection of its investment. If the assignee is not a good tenant, the landlord suffers the cost and inconvenience of enforcing the covenants and there is the possibility of an adverse effect on the value of the landlord's reversion. A landlord must consider the extent of the restrictions it places on alienation against the possible effect it may have both on rent and on a rent review. From a tenant's point of view, a tenant will consider its business, the actual premises and how restrictive the covenant is.

It is necessary firstly to summarise the general and the statutory/common law position and, secondly, to highlight the principal matters to be attended to on an assignment or sub-letting when acting for a landlord, a tenant, or an assignee or sub-tenant.

12.4.2 RESTRICTIONS

All modern commercial leases contain restrictions on alienation preventing the tenant from assigning, sub-letting, underletting or otherwise parting with possession of the premises without the landlord's prior consent, the purpose being to enable landlords to retain control over who occupies their property and thus protect their investment. Having entrusted possession of the property to a suitable tenant the last thing the landlord wants is for that tenant to unilaterally hand it over to someone undesirable or to fragment it by assigning or sub-letting parts of it, thereby creating a number of smaller and potentially less valuable units.

The restrictions are thus worded to create (with limited exceptions) an absolute prohibition on assignment, sub-letting or underletting of part and to provide that in the case of an assignment or sub-letting of the entirety the landlord will not unreasonably withhold consent. Limited exceptions may arise, for example, in the case of a building which naturally lends itself to economic division or which is intended to be let in several units and one tenant takes two of the units under one lease. In such instances the landlord may agree not to unreasonably withhold consent to the assignment or sub-letting of the entire of a 'natural division' or the entire of either of two units let.

Some leases are drafted to provide the landlord with a right of pre-emption (ie first refusal) on assignment. The landlord may also have the right to match any third party offer. In cases where the lease provides accordingly, the tenant should seek to exclude assignments between associated companies and where the tenant is selling more than one unit. Tenants who own a chain of similar properties will be keen to clarify the landlord's rights as they will be anxious to avoid seeing a deal for the sale of the chain collapse for want of consent from any one landlord.

A covenant against sharing possession or occupation or use of the premises should be resisted by the tenant where it is a member of a group of companies as such a covenant imposes unwarranted restrictions on the tenant's ability to use the premises by other companies which are part of the group. However, if the lease allows such right there should be a clause that the share capital of a company in occupation cannot be transferred without the landlord's consent otherwise the right could be used to circumvent restrictions on alienation.

Business needs to evolve constantly. A tenant concerned about the need for flexibility to take account of changed circumstances at a future point may seek a break clause. The landlord should, however, retain the right to pursue antecedent breaches by the tenant, ie breaches which occurred before the break.

Break clauses were common in leases granted at a time of economic depression or in a sluggish market. They were generally sought by tenants rather than offered by landlords. Such clauses normally provide that a tenant can terminate/surrender the lease on giving a stated period of notice at the end of the fifth or tenth year. This would coincide with the rent review. The operation of such a clause was subject to the tenant having complied with all its obligations under the lease. When a tenant proposes to exercise the break clause, it must carefully follow the provisions in the lease regarding it and particularly the time periods for the serving of notice. All rents as well as payments under the lease reserved as rent must be paid to date together with outgoings at the time the clause comes into effect and the tenant must not be in breach of any covenant unless it is specifically waived by the landlord. See *Avocet Industrial Estates LLP v Merol Ltd* [2011] EWHC 3422 (Ch).

If there is a guarantor ensure that the lease provides for it to be automatically released on exercise of the break option or else obtain a separate deed of release from the landlord. The same applies in the case of a surrender or assignment. Always check the provisions of the guarantee as some guarantees are very onerous.

Other issues a tenant's solicitor should check is if there is a prohibition in the lease on sub-letting save for units of a given size or for rent reviews to coincide with the review dates under the head lease or that the underlease contains covenants in the 'same' terms as the lease (*Allied Dunbar Assurance plc v Homebase Ltd* [2002] 2 EGLR 23). A lease may also place a limit on the number of permitted sub-lettings.

As an assignment is the primary method by which a tenant can transfer its liabilities under the lease the tenant's solicitor should check this can be done in as straightforward a way as possible.

12.4.3 STATUTORY/COMMON LAW

A lease is a personal contract and the common law position is therefore that the tenant prima facie remains personally liable on foot of the covenants in the lease for the entire term.

Section 66 of the 1980 Act (re-enacting earlier legislation) provides that any absolute prohibition on alienation has effect as if it were a prohibition restricting alienation without the licence or consent of the lessor, and further provides that notwithstanding any express provision to the contrary the licence or consent of the lessor shall not be unreasonably withheld. What is or is not a reasonable refusal is a question of fact, not of law, and depends entirely upon the particular facts and circumstances in each instance.

The remedy for a tenant who considers that a landlord has unreasonably refused consent is to apply to court for a declaration that consent has been unreasonably withheld and for an order permitting the tenant to proceed with the assignment or sub-letting without the consent. It is not always practical for a tenant to do this in view of the delay involved.

It would be a brave tenant who would assign or sub-let without consent or the protection of a court order, as the landlord may bring an action for damages for breach of covenant and, indeed, for forfeiture of the lease, which, if successful, would leave the tenant in an invidious position as regards the assignee.

Burns v Morelli [1953–54] Ir Jur Rep 50 concerned the question of costs following settlement of a dispute between the plaintiff tenant and defendant landlord while the plaintiff's appeal was pending before the High Court. The plaintiff had taken a lease for three years and continued in occupation after the term expired. Some time later the tenant sought the landlord's consent to an assignment to a third party. The landlord sought two guarantors together with evidence of the solvency of the proposed assignees. Guarantors came forward but the tenant did not comply with the latter request. The landlord refused consent. The tenant issued Circuit Court proceedings seeking, inter alia, a declaration that the landlord had unreasonably withheld consent and permitting the assignment to proceed. The claim was dismissed with costs.

Pending the appeal, the plaintiff produced the evidence of solvency and the landlord agreed to the assignment. The parties failed to agree the question of costs and so this aspect of the matter only was decided in the High Court, which awarded the landlord the costs of the Circuit Court and the tenant the costs of the High Court. Davitt P noted that, in his opinion, the landlord had acted reasonably in withholding consent pending receipt of the evidence sought. It was clear at the time of the application for consent the landlord did not have sufficient evidence with which to make a final decision as to whether or not it was reasonable to give consent.

The case of *International Drilling Fluids Ltd v Louisville Investments (Uxbridge) Ltd* [1986] 1 Ch 513 contained in the judgment of Balcombe LJ a summary of the principles to apply in determining whether or not the landlord's consent has been unreasonably withheld. Briefly, these can be summarised as follows:

(a) The purpose of the restriction against alienation is to protect the landlord from having its premises used or occupied in an undesirable way or by an undesirable tenant.

(b) A landlord cannot refuse consent on grounds which have nothing whatsoever to do with the relationship of landlord and tenant in regard to the subject matter of the lease so as to gain an advantage.

(c) The onus of proving that consent is unreasonably withheld is on the tenant.

(d) The landlord does not have to prove that his reasons for refusing consent were justified if they were such as might be reached by a reasonable man in the circumstances.

(e) It may be reasonable to refuse consent on the ground of the proposed use of the premises even if that use is not prohibited in the lease.

(f) The reasonableness or otherwise of a refusal is a question of fact in each case dependent on the circumstances.

All of the above related in the specific case to covenants against assignment but there is no reason why they cannot apply to a covenant against sub-letting or parting with possession.

In *Meagher & Anor v Luke J. Healy Pharmacy Ltd* [2010] IESC 40 the Supreme Court held that the terms of the covenant against assignment in the lease and s 66 of the 1980 Act gave the lessee no right of action for damages by reason of the lessors having unreasonably withheld consent to assign. It was, however, open to the parties to include a covenant by the lessor not to unreasonably withhold consent the breach of which covenant would give the lessee a right of action for damages.

12.4.4 ASSIGNMENT

12.4.4.1 The present tenant's position

The procedure for assignment is generally the same as for a conveyance on sale save that the title is the residue unexpired of an occupational lease. Contracts are prepared and evidence of title is furnished, etc.

The contract should contain additional special conditions:

(a) making the sale subject to the landlord's consent to assignment;

(b) providing that the purchaser, ie the assignee, should furnish all such references and other information as may reasonably be required by the landlord;

(c) providing that there should be no obligation on the vendor, ie the tenant, to issue court proceedings to obtain the landlord's consent; and

(d) providing that if the consent is not forthcoming within a reasonable time (generally four to six weeks) the contract may be rescinded and the deposit (if any) paid by the purchaser refunded.

If acting for the vendor, ensure appropriate references are obtained (trade and bank) and that the application for consent is submitted to the landlord (or the landlord's solicitor or agent) without delay.

Evidence should be requested from the client at the time of drafting the contract of payment of rent and rates. Details of the insurance premium and service charge may also be required.

Check whether any personal guarantees were given when the tenant took the lease or acquired the lessee's interest and, if so, arrange for these to be released.

Current practice is that a landlord executes a licence to assign which may incorporate consent to change of user if that is sought by the purchaser.

12.4.4.2 The proposed assignee's position

The proposed assignee's position is, again, generally the same as for a conveyance on sale save that he is taking on a lease for an unexpired term which requires him to observe covenants and take on liabilities. The solicitor investigates title, raises requisitions, makes searches, etc. Additionally:

(a) Send the client a copy of the lease and advise the assignee on the conditions and restrictions in the lease before contracts are signed.

(b) If relevant, make the contract conditional upon the landlord's consent to change of use as well as to assignment.

(c) If there is a service charge under the lease, ensure provision is made in the contract for readjustment of apportionment following certification of the charge—preferably by retention on joint deposit of a reasonable sum to cover any likely shortfall.

(d) Guarantors and references: the landlord may, and most likely will in the case of a company, require at least one guarantor. References will also be sought and in some cases where there is a non-Irish guarantor (eg where the parent company of the tenant is incorporated outside this jurisdiction) a letter of opinion will be required from lawyers in that jurisdiction confirming the company is properly constituted and has the power to enter into the contract.

12.4.4.3 The landlord's position

The principal concern is to ensure, so far as possible, that the proposed assignee is at least as satisfactory as the present tenant. Usually the lessee's agent will have obtained the references, audited accounts and prepared Heads of Terms which will cover matters such as change of use or the assignee seeking consent to carry out works and providing details of guarantors.

The tasks of the lessee's solicitors will include:

(a) Checking whether the terms of the lease provide for any assignee to enter into a direct covenant with the landlord.

(b) Preparing a draft consent or licence which should be limited to the particular assignment only and expressed not to be a waiver of the restrictions on alienation contained in the lease.

(c) If there are to be guarantors, preparing a draft guarantee.

(d) Ensuring the outgoing tenant pays the landlord's costs in relation to the application for consent.

(e)   Obtaining a certified copy of the assignment when completed.

In all cases of assignment, sub-letting or under-letting pre-contract VAT enquiries and pre-lease enquiries should be raised in advance as well as a BER Certificate with Advisory Report obtained and searches carried out. If the property is mortgaged, the consent of the mortgagee will be required.

12.4.5   SUB-LETTING

12.4.5.1   The current tenant's position

The procedure is generally the same as if acting for a landlord on a first letting as regards preparation of a draft lease, etc but in addition:

(a)   In preparing a draft sub-lease, include a covenant by the sub-tenant to perform and observe the covenants and conditions in the head lease (save the covenant to pay rent) where not inconsistent with the terms of the sub-lease.

(b)   Ensure satisfactory references for the sub-tenant are obtained

(c)   Apply for the head landlord's consent to the sub-letting and notify the solicitor for the sub-tenant of the conditions the landlord requires for the consent to be given.

12.4.5.2   The proposed sub-tenant's position

The procedure is essentially the same as if acting for a tenant on a first letting, ie one should endeavour to negotiate detailed conditions of the lease to the best advantage of the sub-tenant, ensure the sub-landlord has title to grant the sub-lease, make searches, etc. The only notable addition is to ensure the head landlord's consent to the sub-letting is granted.

12.4.5.3   The head landlord's position

The position is prima facie not affected in that the original tenant remains contractually liable to the head landlord. Nonetheless, reasonable care should be taken to ensure that the sub-tenant is likely to be satisfactory and to this extent much the same inquiries ought to be made as when acting for a landlord on an assignment by a present tenant. It is important also to obtain a copy of the proposed draft sub-lease to check that its terms and conditions do not vary significantly from the present tenant's lease.

12.4.6   PARTIAL ASSIGNMENT OR SUB-LETTING

Most present-day commercial leases contain an absolute prohibition on partial assignment or sub-letting. The main purpose of such a prohibition is to ensure that the landlord retains control over who his or her tenant (or sub-tenant) will be in the future and to protect his or her investment in the property. It is better to have one good tenant than multiple tenants in a building which increases the risk for the landlord in possible breaches of the tenancy, such as non-payment of rent. See **12.4.6.2**.

A well-drawn lease would contain an absolute prohibition against sub-letting of part only of the premises unless subject to stringent conditions.

When a landlord receives a request to sub-let part of the demise, the procedure is identical to that on assignment and sub-letting of the entire of a demise, with additional attention paid to the apportionment of outgoings and service charge and to the effect on the landlord's/sub-landlord's investment. It would also be a standard requirement of a land-lord's consent that the sub-lessee would not obtain statutory renewal rights.

12.4.6.1 Apportionment

It is not uncommon that one of the conditions subject to which landlords would allow a sub-letting is that the tenant cannot sub-let at a rent less than the rent (or proportion thereof in the case of part only) reserved (or if there has already been a rent review the rent then payable) under the lease. If there is a rent review of the lease during the term of the sub-lease the sub-lease should provide for the applicable proportion of the reviewed rent to be paid by the sub-lessee.

12.4.6.2 Effect on landlord

A significant matter for the landlord to consider is the possible effect on the value and marketability of its reversion, in that, while an investor may readily pay very good money indeed for a building with a 'natural' number of tenants the prospective purchaser may either not be interested in buying at all or, if so, at a reduced price if the same building has been fragmented by assignments or sub-lettings of small portions. In such cases the land-lord should always be advised to obtain professional advice from a valuer. If the valuer is of the opinion that either the value or marketability of the reversion would be prejudiced, then clearly the landlord should be advised not to consent to the division (or further divi-sion as the case may be) of the property.

12.5   Change of User

12.5.1   GENERAL

To preserve a good tenant mix, the landlord of a shopping centre will seek to restrict the nature of each tenant's user of its individual unit. This has advantages and disadvantages for both parties. Anchor tenants generally face fewer such restrictions, depending on the nature of their business and the size of their take. Moreover, an anchor tenant may secure user exclusivity and other prospective tenants will need to be alert to this.

In this context, the user may not necessarily have planning law connotations. In other words, after some time elapses the tenant may desire a switch to another type of retail which would not in itself amount to a change of user such as would require planning permission. However, the proposed change may offend against the narrow wording of the user clause in the lease. By the same token, a tenant may secure the necessary planning permission but may still be refused consent on the basis of the clause, as in *Wanze Properties (Ireland) Ltd v Mastertron Ltd* [1992] ILRM 746.

From the tenant's point of view it is desirable to have a wide user clause inserted into the lease; however, this will increase the rent on review as the lease is more attractive to a wider range of purchasers. A wide user clause would have the advantage of enabling the tenant to avail of future trends in its line of business without undue difficulty. For exam-ple, in recent years there has been a proliferation of coffee shops within retail units such as bookshops and fashion outlets. This may not have been foreseeable, say, 15 years ago.

12.5.2   STATUTE/COMMON LAW

Part V of the 1980 Act applies equally to restrictions on change of user as to proposed as-signments and sub-letting—see s 67 thereof. As such, the statute once again makes clear that the landlord's consent shall not be unreasonably withheld. As has already been noted at **12.4.3** above, the tenant's remedy is to seek a declaration to that effect in court, and permission to proceed accordingly. Once again, the facts of the case will be scrutinised and the result cannot be guaranteed to the tenant. Two cases which have been decided since 1980 are very instructive—to tenants, in particular.

In the case of *OHS Ltd v Green Property Co Ltd* [1986] IR 39, the plaintiff tenant took an assignment of a fruit and vegetable retail unit within a shopping centre subject to a covenant to use the premises 'for the purposes of business of victualler, fruit, fish and vegetable merchants'. Some time later a supermarket opened nearby and the tenant was unable to compete. This also placed the assignment value of the unit under pressure.

The tenant received an offer from a building society subject to consent. The defendant landlord refused on the grounds that this would be contrary to the principle of good estate management, as there were already a large number of financial institutions in the shopping centre and it did not want any more premises with dead frontages. The plaintiff sought a declaration of unreasonableness in the Circuit Court and was granted relief. The landlord appealed to the High Court.

Lynch J allowed the appeal. He ruled that the proper interpretation of s 67 of the 1980 Act is that the onus is on the tenant to prove that the landlord is acting unreasonably in withholding consent. Moreover, in this case, the landlord had correctly invoked the principle of good estate management in seeking to avoid an excessive number of dead frontages in one shopping centre.

Wanze Properties (Ireland) Ltd v Mastertron Ltd [1992] ILRM 746 further considered the question of reasonableness with regard to a proposed change of user. There were three plaintiffs: Wanze, who held the lessee's interest and a Mr and Mrs Lam, who purchased the sub-lessee's interest from Wanze in a unit located in a shopping centre which originally comprised one large unit and four smaller ones (including theirs). Wanze did not object to the Lams' application for planning permission and building by-law approval for a change of user of the unit to a Chinese takeaway, which was granted. The Lams carried out the conversion works at considerable expense and paid the agreed purchase price to Wanze.

The head lease contained a clause restricting user. The clause specifically prohibited a change of user under certain headings, including a fish and chip shop, although a Chinese takeaway was not specified. The clause emphasised the need to protect the standing, appearance and prosperity of the centre as a whole and, in its restrictive element, the importance of not causing a nuisance or annoyance to neighbouring units.

The head lessor refused consent to the change of user. Wanze and the Lams sought a declaration in the Circuit Court and were refused relief. They appealed to the High Court.

Murphy J dismissed the appeal. Quoting Lynch J in *OHS Ltd v Green Property Co Ltd* at length, he found that consent was not unreasonably withheld where the landlord had reasonable grounds to believe that it might find a more suitable tenant who might better preserve the character and appearance of the centre.

The court had no difficulty drawing a distinction between a fish and chip shop and a Chinese takeaway, but Murphy J also noted the wording, and thus the scope and purpose, of the clause as a whole. The takeaway proposed to operate between 12.00 noon and 12.00 midnight, whereas the other units traded from 9 am to 6 pm (9 pm Thursdays and Fridays). The centre was closed on Sundays.

Murphy J accepted that the owner of the defendant company had reasonable grounds to believe that he could find a more suitable tenant, being one which would, inter alia, keep to the opening hours for the centre, Murphy J stated, however, that the whole purpose of structuring things as he did enabled the landlord to create, maintain and control a relationship between himself and the tenants which would ensure the effective operation of the centre. As such, the reasonableness or otherwise of a landlord's conduct must be evaluated by reference to that consideration and not on the basis of his financial stake in the premises.

The current position is that the onus is on the tenant who seeks declaratory relief to prove that the landlord has acted unreasonably in refusing consent.

12.6 Insurance

12.6.1 WHO EFFECTS THE INSURANCE—AND WHY?

Normally the landlord effects insurance. This makes sense as it involves the protection of the landlord's capital investment. The policy issues in the landlord's name. The landlord then recovers the premium from the tenant.

Landlords are generally reluctant to have a tenant's interest noted on the insurance policy or for the tenant to be named jointly with the landlord on the policy. The main reason is that in the event of a successful claim, the cheque would be issued in the joint names of the landlord and the tenant. The tenant's signature would therefore be necessary to release funds to enable the landlord to carry out repairs and this could result in delays. A tenant should insist that the lease include a covenant by the landlord that the policy of insurance incorporates a non-invalidation clause and that the insurer waives its right of subrogation. A non-invalidation clause confirms that the insurance policy will not be vitiated by the insurance company without the tenant being informed. It is now standard practice for an insurance company to waive subrogation and confirm a non-invalidation clause.

Other factors to be considered in relation to insurance are:

(a) The amount of cover and the landlord's ability to reinstate.

(b) The landlord to make up any deficiency or shortfall in insurance monies paid out and their application.

(c) The landlord does not normally insure plate glass. Note that many modern commercial buildings incorporate glass in the structure of the building and not in the tenant's 'take'.

(d) The definition of 'Insured Risks' needs to be covered.

12.6.2 WHAT IS THE AMOUNT OF THE INSURANCE AND THE RATE?

The amount of insurance cover is the full reinstatement costs such as demolition and site clearance, professional fees and irrecoverable VAT (if any) plus an inflationary factor eg rising building costs. See *Gleniffer Finance Corporation Ltd v Bamar Wood & Products Ltd* [1978] 2 Lloyd's Rep 49; also *Argy Trading Development Co Ltd v Lapid Developments Ltd* [1977] 3 All ER 785.

It is important to provide that the premises are to be insured at the full reinstatement cost. If the premises are expressed to be insured for the full reinstatement value, then the liability of the insurance company is confined to the value of the landlord's interest. This was highlighted in *St Albans Investment Co v Sun Alliance & London Insurance Ltd* [1983] 1 IR 362. The building in question was insured against damage by fire and the policy provided for payment of the value of the property. There was no reinstatement clause in the insurance policies and an argument arose as to whether the insurance company was obliged to pay up on a reinstatement basis. McWilliam J held that this was not the case and that the payment should be based on the market value of the building less the site value. This was confirmed in the Supreme Court. Clearly, this could be very different from the actual cost of reinstating the building and hence there would be a considerable shortfall.

In addition to covering the cost of reinstatement of the building, the landlord should also insure against the loss of rent, which is usually for a period of three years or the period it takes to repair or reconstruct the building, whichever is the shorter. In addition, in a multi-tenanted building, where the lease incorporates a service charge, the insurance should cover loss of service charge as well, in a similar manner.

12.6.3 WHAT ARE THE INSURED RISKS?

It is important to set out a full definition of the risks which the landlord is insuring. The normal insured risks are fire, lightning, explosion, storm, tempest, bursting or overflowing of water tanks, apparatus and pipes, impact, aircraft, riot, civil commotion, labour disturbances and malicious injury except breakage of plate glass caused by storm, tempest or impact, boilers and pipes serving the demised premises against explosion and the cost of removal of debris and site clearance. The definition should include such other risks as the landlord may in its absolute discretion determine from time to time. This would enable the landlord to add such further risks as the market determines—an example being terrorism since the events of 9/11.

The obligation to insure against named risks should be qualified by a proviso that the obligation is subject to such limitations, exclusions and excesses as may be imposed by the insurers and subject to the availability of insurance in the market on reasonable terms and at a reasonable premium.

Where the landlord is required to reinstate, the tenant's repairing covenants should exclude liability to repair damage by insured risks (save where the insurance is voided by any act or omission of the tenant). The obligation to reinstate should be qualified that it is subject to all planning permissions and necessary consents being obtained and if not the tenant (or either party) has the right to terminate the lease. Reinstatement should be done to a specific timetable, usually three years.

If the demised premises form part of a building then the landlord's obligation to reinstate should extend to the common areas, particularly to ensure access to the demised premises.

The insurance provisions should include a clause providing for suspension of rent and service charge during the period the demised premises cannot be used by the tenant. In the event of partial destruction, it should provide for an abatement of rent and agreement on what percentage of these payments are to be suspended to be reached between the parties. This is a matter of fact in each case.

Aside from building insurance, the landlord will also need to take out public liability cover and, if services are provided, employer's liability insurance may be necessary. A policy may be 'loaded' depending on the nature of the tenant's business. This will arise where the tenant's business attracts a higher insurance premium. Needless to say, the tenant will be careful to check how the insurance premium is calculated and insist on copies of the up-to-date policy document and receipt for payment of the current premium.

The draft 2011 Bill (see **1.4.4**) provides for obligations on the part of the landlord in relation to insurance and contains a definition of 'insured risks' along the lines commonly adopted in leases. It provides that the landlord has default obligations to insure the buildings and the landlord's property against the insured risks and 'insured risks' are set out. The landlord can insure the buildings in the joint names of the landlord and tenant or with the tenant's interest noted on the insurance policy unless the insurer waives subrogation rights, for the full rebuilding cost together with incidental costs, expenses and fees, including loss of rent. The landlord can also increase the building's insurance cover where any review of cover reveals the need or, if the tenant requests it, where the tenant is liable to pay the premiums or reimburse the cost of the insurance. The landlord can also use the proceeds of the building's insurance to reinstate the building. There are also tenant's obligations including overriding obligations where the landlord insures the building. This is a corollary to the landlord's default obligations to insure the buildings.

12.6.4   SUBROGATION

In general commercial terms, the issue of subrogation arises following upon a successful claim by an insured party under a policy. Most insurance policies include a subrogation clause. Subrogation is where the insurer steps into the shoes of the insured party or policyholder and in the name of the policyholder pursues any right of action available.

Where a commercial lease is involved, as has been seen above, the landlord is usually named on the insurance policy. But what happens when the landlord recovers on foot of the policy when the premises have been destroyed owing to the negligence of the sitting tenant? Is the insurance company entitled to require their policyholder, the landlord, to sue the tenant?

This question fell for consideration by the English Court of Appeal in *Mark Rowlands Ltd v Berni Inns Ltd* [1985] 3 WLR 964. The relevant lease provided that the landlord should insure the whole building against fire and the tenant should contribute to the cost of the insurance. The tenant was to be relieved of its repairing obligation in the event of damage to the building by fire and the landlord was obliged in such circumstances to lay out the insurance money to rebuild the demised premises.

The premises were destroyed by fire and the landlord received full indemnification from its insurers and the building was duly reinstated.

The policy was in the landlord's name and contained no reference to the tenant.

The Court of Appeal upheld the High Court in agreeing that the policy was intended to fund the benefit of the tenant as well as the landlord, the tenant having an insurable interest. The real issue however, was whether the terms of the lease and the full indemnification of the landlord, by receipt of the insurance money, precluded the insurers from recovering damages for negligence from the tenant.

The Court of Appeal held that the intention of the parties to the lease was that in the event of damage by fire etc, whether due to accident or negligence, the landlord's loss was to be recouped from the insurance money and the landlord was to have no further claim against the tenant for negligence. Consequently, it was held that the landlord's insurers had no right of subrogation.

A tenant should seek to remove the right of subrogation by:

(a) being named as a joint insured on the policy; the landlord is unlikely to agree to this as any insurance monies would be paid out jointly; or

(b) obtaining a letter from the insurance company waiving its rights of subrogation. This is the usual method and generally there is no problem in a landlord obtaining this letter for the tenant.

12.7   Repair

12.7.1   ADVISING THE CLIENT

In a short-term lease the repairing covenant(s) will normally apply to the interior of the premises only. In long-term commercial leases, ie FRI leases, the tenant will normally be obliged to repair the structure, foundations and both the interior and exterior of the demised premises. The tenant may be liable to repair the interior directly and the exterior either directly or indirectly. In a single let, ie where the tenant takes the entire building under an FRI lease, the tenant will be responsible for all exterior repairs. In a multi-let such as a shopping centre, the tenant is likely to be indirectly responsible for a portion of the exterior repairs by way of a service charge. The landlord or management company will carry out repairs to the structure and common parts and recover the cost through the service charge.

When taking a lease of an old building the tenant should be advised to have a full survey of the premises carried out and have a schedule of condition with photographic evidence attached to the lease. This would involve a report by the surveyor setting out the condition of the premises. The lease would then contain a clause that the tenant is not liable to put the premises in a better state of repair than is evidenced by the schedule of condition. This fixes the obligation to repair to the state of the premises at the date of commencement of the lease.

The repairing clause should also exclude latent and inherent defects; for example, a shift in the foundations of new buildings as these defects may not become evident for a number of years. In relation to a newly constructed building the tenant should obtain an assignment of the collateral warranties from the engineer, architect, contractor etc involved in building the premises as there is no privity between the tenant and these professionals without these warranties. The tenant should also seek a structural defects indemnity from the landlord and contractor. It is advisable to check the insurance cover of those furnishing the warranties/indemnities. If a structural defects indemnity is not forthcoming, as an alternative the tenant could seek an insurance policy to cover major defects within a ten-year period.

For details of the obligation to repair see **chapter 8**.

12.8 Registers

In recent years attempts have been made to bring more transparency to the property market, both residential and commercial, with the establishment of several public registers.

The Property Services Regulatory Authority (PRSA) was established with the aim of achieving uniformity and transparency in licensing, regulation and provision of information to the public.

It established the following Public Registers under the below-mentioned sections of the Property Services (Regulation) Act 2011:

(a) Register of Licensed Property Services Providers (s 29). This comprises a list of all auctioneers, estate agents, letting agents and management agents licensed by the PRSA.

(b) Residential Property Price Register (s 86). This covers such properties purchased since 1 January 2010 as declared to the Revenue for stamp duty purposes.

(c) Commercial Leases Register (ss 87 and 88). This includes the address, rent, date, and term of all commercial leases entered into since 1 January 2010 as declared to Revenue for stamp duty purposes. Tenants who enter into a commercial lease with effect from 3 April 2012 must complete, within 30 days of receipt of the Stamp Certificate from the Revenue, a 'Commercial Leases Return' and furnish the PRSA with detailed particulars of their lease agreement. This return may be filed online.

COMMERCIAL LEASES

The Law Society Conveyancing Committee issued a Practice Note in October 2012 which sets out the risks to solicitors in completing these returns on behalf of their clients. The Practice Notice advises solicitors that they should inform clients of their obligations as tenants to make a return and the time limits that apply to submit the information. It advised that solicitors should not expose themselves to unnecessary and inappropriate risks by making submissions of particulars to the PRSA on behalf of their clients.

The Commercial Leases Register can be accessed at www.psr.ie/website/npsra/npsraweb.nsf/page/index-en.

Returns are now only conducted online through the PRSA website at www.propertypriceregister.ie/Website/NPSRA/pprweb-com.nsf/PSRA-CL117?OpenPage.

A reminder Practice Note was issued in January/February 2018 and this again recommended that solicitors should not routinely accept authorisations to make these submissions on behalf of clients.

It is difficult to know if the public availability of this information impacts on the granting of concessions by landlords such as rent reductions and break options. These statutory obligations override the confidentiality of the agreement between the parties and the details on the register do not reflect commercial pressures or the relative negotiating strength of the parties.

CHAPTER 13

VALUE ADDED TAX

13.1 General

13.1.1 BACKGROUND

Value Added Tax ('VAT') was introduced into Ireland on 1 November 1972 as one of the conditions of Ireland's accession to the European Economic Community. Irish VAT legislation is embodied primarily in the Value Added Tax Consolidation Act 2010 ('VCA') and various European Community regulations. (References to sections of the Act refer to the VCA.)

Many of the provisions of the VCA are supported or given effect by VAT Regulations.

VAT is a tax that all EU Member States must impose. All Member States, and all applicant States, must implement national VAT legislation in accordance with Council Directive 2006/112/EC (the recast of the Sixth VAT Directive).

An EU Member State's own national VAT legislation may only vary from obligations set out in EU VAT legislation where derogation is permitted and has been granted. In the absence of a derogation a person may seek to rely on EU legislation where he or she feels national legislation has not properly reflected the EU provision.

13.1.2 HOW VAT OPERATES

VAT is a transaction-based tax, its fundamental principle being that VAT is paid on the *value added* at each stage of the chain from production to consumption.

VAT is levied at each stage in the chain and that VAT (referred to as 'Output' VAT) is reported to the Revenue Commissioners on a periodic basis.

In order to tax the 'value added' by a supplier, the supplier can deduct from his or her output VAT, before payment, VAT charged to him or her on costs incurred for the purposes of his business (referred to as 'Input' VAT). Not all VAT incurred may be deductible, however. A deduction is prohibited for VAT incurred on certain specific costs (such as food and drink), on costs that relate to supplies that are exempt and on costs that do not relate to the person's business.

Each supplier must file regular VAT returns on which the supplier's output VAT and input VAT are declared. If output VAT exceeds input VAT, payment of the difference must be made to the Revenue. If input VAT exceeds output VAT the difference will be repaid by the Revenue.

An example of the operation of the system can be seen in Table 7.

TABLE 7 The VAT system in operation

Transaction	Price Exc VAT €	23% VAT €	Input Credit €	Pays to Revenue €
1 Manufacturer sells to wholesaler	300	69	(46) (say)	23
2 Wholesaler sells to retailer	400	92	(69)	23
3 Retailer sells to consumer	500	115	(92)	23
Total VAT paid				69

13.1.3 WHAT IS SUBJECT TO VAT?

Irish VAT arises on the supply of VATable goods or VATable services:

(a)   made within the State;

(b)   by a taxable person acting as such;

(c)   in the course or furtherance of business;

(d)   for consideration.

Where any of these elements is missing the transaction is not subject to Irish VAT.

Irish VAT also arises on the arrival of goods from jurisdictions outside the EU on their importation into Ireland (VAT in this instance is levied by Customs and Excise when the goods arrive in Ireland).

VAT also arises on the acquisition of goods from other EU Member States and on services received from both other EU Member States and non EU territories (in these instances the trader must self-account for that VAT, referred to commonly as 'reverse charge' VAT).

13.1.3.1 Taxable goods and taxable services

Supplies of goods and/or services meeting the conditions mentioned above are subject to VAT unless the supplies are specifically exempted from VAT. The exemptions are listed in Schedule 1 to the VCA and include medical care services, public transport services, education, admission to sporting and live theatrical and musical performances, insurance and banking services together with related agency services and the supply of stocks and shares and related agency activities.

13.1.3.2 Supply of goods and services—VCA Part 3 Chapters 1 and 3

In general, a supply of goods takes place where there has been a transfer of ownership of goods by agreement. Goods are defined (s 2) as all movable and immovable objects, but this does not include things in action, or money. References to goods include references to both new and used goods. The legislation also contains specific provisions which hold that certain transactions are regarded as being a supply of goods, eg electricity, gas, heat, refrigeration and ventilation.

Conversely certain transactions are specifically deemed not to be a supply of goods. These include the transfer of ownership of goods as security for a loan (particularly relevant when mortgaging a property) and the transfer of ownership of goods in connection with the transfer of a business or part of a business.

A self-supply of goods takes place when a person either appropriates goods from his or her business for a non-business use (eg takes goods from his or her shop for his or her own house) or, in the case of movable goods, applies the goods from a taxable to an exempt activity. A self-supply is also liable to VAT and the trader must charge himself or herself VAT based on the tax exclusive cost of acquiring or manufacturing the goods that have been self-supplied.

A supply in relation to a service means:

> *the performance or omission of any act or the toleration of any situation other than(a) the supply of goods and, (b) other than a transaction specified in Section 20 or 22(c)).*

This provision is sufficiently wide so as to encompass all VATable transactions which are not treated as a supply of goods for VAT purposes.

13.1.3.3 Place of supply of goods and services—VCA Part 4 Chapters 1 and 3

As stated earlier, only supplies of goods and services effected within the State can be subject to Irish VAT. It is essential, therefore, to determine the place where the supply of goods or the supply of services has taken place. The legislation provides a complex series of rules for determining the place of supply and these rules include that the place of supply of immovable goods and of services connected to supplies of immovable goods is where that property is situated.

13.1.3.4 Rates of VAT—VCA Part 6 Chapter 1 and Schedules 2 and 3

Currently the rates applicable are:

(a) Zero—most food and drink, children's clothing and footwear, oral medicine and exports of goods (VCA s 46(1)(b) and Schedule 2);

(b) 4.8 per cent—supply of livestock (s 46(1)(d));

(c) 13.5 per cent—sale, maintenance and repair of property; tour guide services; short-term hire of cars, boats and caravans; general repair and maintenance services; certain personal services and certain flour-based bakery products (s 46(1)(c) and Schedule 3);

(d) 23 per cent—all goods and services not listed in the Schedules to VCA s 46(1)(a) and including VAT on rental income.

(e) 9 per cent—since 1 July 2011 this temporary rate applies to restaurant and catering services; hotel and holiday accommodation; cinema, certain theatre and musical tickets; museum tickets; use of sporting facilities; hairdressing services; and certain printed matter.

Certain activities are specifically exempt from VAT. These are set out in Schedule 1 of the VCA.

13.1.4 ACCOUNTING FOR VAT

13.1.4.1 Basis of accounting for output VAT

When a trader is completing his periodic VAT return he or she must calculate the amount of output tax arising in the period. There are two bases under which output VAT may be calculated: the invoice basis and the cash receipts basis.

Invoice basis

Under the invoice basis, a trader must pay output VAT to the Revenue based on the sales invoices issued (or which should have issued) in the VAT period, irrespective of whether the invoice has been paid or not. For supplies which do not require an invoice to be issued, VAT is due at the time the goods or services are supplied.

Cash receipts basis

Under the cash receipts basis, VAT is only payable to Revenue when the cash is received by the trader.

The cash basis is only available to traders whose turnover from the supply of goods or services to customers not registered for VAT exceeds 90 per cent of total turnover, or to traders whose turnover in a continuous 12-month period does not exceed €2m.

The main advantage of the cash receipts basis is that the trader only accounts for the output VAT when he himself has been paid, whereas a trader on the invoice basis must pay over VAT at the due date whether or not he himself has been paid.

13.1.4.2 Issuing VAT invoices—VCA Part 9 Chapter 2

When a taxable person supplies taxable goods or services to a person who is in business in the EU (or to the State or a Local Authority or a body established by statute) a VAT invoice must be issued by the 15th of the month following the month in which those goods or services are supplied. The invoice must contain specified details including:

    (a)   the name, address and registration number of the supplier;

    (b)   the name and address of the person to whom the supply is made;

    (c)   the date of issue of the invoice;

    (d)   a sequential number;

    (e)   the date on which the goods or services were supplied;

    (f)   a description of the goods or services supplied;

    (g)   the quantity or volume of goods supplied;

    (h)   the consideration exclusive of VAT for the supply; and

    (i)   the rate of VAT applicable to the supply.

Other details are required on specific transactions, for example, when supplying most legal services to businesses based within the EU but outside Ireland, the customer's non-Irish VAT number must be included on the fee note and an indication that the recipient must account for the VAT arising on the supply.

There is generally no requirement to issue an invoice for supplies to a private individual (ie a person not acting in a business capacity) but the supplier may issue an invoice if they so wish.

As mentioned, the requirement to issue an invoice is normally triggered by the completion of the supply of the goods or services in question. By way of special rules the receipt of a payment (for example a deposit, pre-payment or a retainer) in advance of completion of the supply is deemed to be a supply in itself in that amount therefore triggering an obligation to issue an invoice and account for VAT in relation to the amount received.

Example

ABC Limited agrees to sell the freehold to a new store to Retail Ltd for €1.5m. Under the sale agreement a deposit of €150,000 is payable in March 2010 (deposit paid to ABC Ltd, ie not held in escrow) and the sale will close in May 2010.

- The deposit is deemed to create a supply and so the invoice relating to the payment must be raised by 15 April 2010 at the latest.

The invoice in respect of the balance is triggered when the sale closes in May 2010 and so must be issued by 15 June at the latest.

13.1.4.3 VAT returns

The majority of traders are required to file VAT returns for each two-month taxable period, those periods being based on a calendar year (ie January–February, March–April and so on).

Certain traders may be granted permission by the Collector General to file an annual return, a biannual return, a quarterly return or a thrice annual return instead depending on the size of their annual VAT liability.

Returns must be completed and filed online through the Revenue's ROS portal with a filing deadline of the 23rd of the month following the end of the filing period in question.

The VAT charged by a person on the supply of goods or services (together with any VAT deemed to arise and any VAT he or she must report under reverse charge) is known as 'output' tax. The VAT payable by a person on goods and services supplied to him is known as 'input' tax. When filing a VAT return, a person may claim credit for 'input tax' against 'output tax' arising, paying the excess only to the Revenue. If allowable 'input tax' in the period exceeds the 'output tax', the person is entitled to a refund of the difference from Revenue.

Example

A solicitor bills fees of €5,000 (excl VAT @ 23 per cent) in the period March/April 2010. During that period he purchased a dictaphone costing €200 (excl VAT @ 23 per cent). The VAT return will show the following:

		Price €	VAT €
Output VAT	Supplies—fees	5,000	1,150
Less: Input VAT	Purchases—dictaphone	(200)	(46)
Net VAT payable			(1,104)

13.1.5 INPUT CREDIT—VCA PART 8 CHAPTER 1

Generally, a taxable person can obtain an input credit for any VAT borne on purchases of goods for resale and most business expenses when they relate to VATable supplies. However, an input credit is not allowed for the following:

(a) the provision of food, drink, accommodation or other personal services supplied to the taxable person, his or her agent or employee, eg VAT on hotel bills incurred while a solicitor is on circuit is not recoverable;

(b) entertainment expenses;

(c) the purchase, lease or hire of cars and petrol otherwise than as stock in trade (except car hire firms and driving schools). (A proportion of the VAT incurred on new cars purchased after 1 January 2009 with a CO_2 emission of less than 156g/km may also be reclaimed.)

Generally a trader is prohibited from claiming input tax on costs associated with exempt sales. Therefore a trader who makes an exempt sale of property or an exempt letting will be prohibited from taking a deduction for VAT incurred on costs such as estate agent fees, legal fees and any costs incurred in preparing the property for sale.

13.1.6 RECORDS

A taxable person must keep records in such form and containing such information as is necessary so that his liability to VAT (output VAT) and the credits (input VAT) to which he is entitled for taxable purchases can be checked. Records must be maintained for six years from the date of the transaction to which they relate.

Records relating to property transactions must be retained for the entire period that the person holds an interest plus six years thereafter.

Revenue officials have powers enabling them to:

(a) enter premises;

(b) seek production of the relevant business records and inspect them;

(c) make extracts or remove them for a reasonable period, and

(d) seek assistance from any person on the premises.

Generally notice of any intention to inspect records is given.

13.2 Lettings

13.2.1 INTRODUCTION

The VCA uses the term 'letting'. That term is not specifically defined, though its meaning has been considered by various courts. A common thread running through the various judgments is that the characteristics of a letting are as follows:

1. There is a defined area of the property.

2. The owner of that property assigns the right to occupy that space to the tenant or licensee.

3. There is an agreement for a fixed term.

4. There is a payment by the tenant or licensee in return for the rights of occupation.

5. The agreement is for the passive provision of space.

6. The owner of the property assigns to the tenant/licensee the right to exclude other persons from that part of the property.

From a VAT perspective it is the characteristics of the agreement that are important rather than whether, for example, the agreement is titled a licence, a lease or whether or not there is any written document in place.

A transaction that does not amount to a letting (eg a licence which does not satisfy all of the conditions to amount to a letting) would be regarded as a service and is simply subject to VAT at the standard rate, currently 23 per cent.

Certain transactions are excluded from the specific VAT provisions relating to lettings. These include hotel and holiday accommodation (subject to VAT at the second reduced rate, currently 9 per cent), operator-run car parks and road/bridge toll charges (subject to VAT at the standard rate, currently 23 per cent).

With effect from 1 July 2008 the manner in which VAT is levied on property transactions (including sales and lettings) was fundamentally changed.

The following is a brief summary of the manner in which VAT was applied to lettings *prior* to 1 July 2008:

- Lettings for periods of less than ten years were exempt from VAT. A landlord could choose to waive this exemption in which case VAT at the standard rate applied to the rents as they fell due.

Care was needed when waiving as, in general, when a landlord waived the waiver applied to all his lettings which were for periods of less than ten years.

A landlord could cancel his waiver; however, on cancellation a look-back had to be undertaken. Under this look-back if the VAT the landlord had claimed on an input deduction relating to the acquisition/development etc of the property(or properties) was greater than the VAT he charged on the rents then he must pay an amount equal to the excess (if he had paid more on rents than he had claimed on inputs there is no refund permitted).

- Lettings for periods of ten years or more were subject to VAT only when a number of conditions were met. Where any of the conditions were not met VAT did not arise. The conditions in question were: the property must have been developed or redeveloped on or after 1 November 1972, the vendor must have been entitled to recover at least some of the VAT incurred on the acquisition or development of the property, the letting must have been in the course of business and the letting must have met the Economic Value Test ('EVT').

When the conditions were met and the letting was taxable then VAT was levied on a capitalised value which was placed on the lease (there were three permitted methods to arrive at this capital value). VAT was then levied on this capital value up front at the commencement of the lease. The subsequent rents paid under the lease were then outside the scope of VAT.

In certain instances the parties could apply for a 4A authorisation. If granted the landlord was relieved from actually charging and collecting the VAT on the capitalised value and instead the tenant self-accounted for VAT. *NOTE:* a 4A did not exempt a transaction from VAT, it merely shifted responsibility for accounting for the VAT to the tenant.

- When leases that were for ten years or more when granted were surrendered or assigned special rules applied. Essentially the existing tenant was treated as if he were creating a new interest in the property equal to the remaining life of the lease being surrendered or assigned and VAT was then levied or not depending on whether or not the conditions mentioned above were met afresh. In the majority of such transactions responsibility automatically shifted to the landlord in the case of a surrender and the new tenant in the case of an assignment to self-account for any VAT due.

- For completeness there were also special rules which governed the taxation of a new lease granted by a landlord following the surrender of a lease which when created was for ten years or more and where there had been no redevelopment of that property since the original lease was granted.

A brief summary of the rules which apply to lettings created on or *after* 1 July 2008 is as follows:

- Lettings which amount to a 'Freehold Equivalent' are treated as a sale and the rules applicable to freehold sales apply (Freehold Equivalents are considered in the publication *Conveyancing*, 5th edition, 2010, published by OUP and the Law Society).

- All lettings other than freehold equivalents are exempt from VAT (*NOTE:* there is no longer any distinction between lettings of less than ten years and those for ten years or more).

- A landlord may 'Opt to Tax' any individual lease (*NOTE:* unlike a waiver each individual lease can be opted on a case-by-case basis). Where a landlord does opt to tax the lease then VAT arises on the rents at the standard rate (currently 23 per cent) as they fall due.

- Where parties (being the landlord and the tenant or occupier of the property) are 're-lated', they may only opt to tax the letting if the tenant has greater than 90 per cent VAT recovery (*NOTE:* the definition of related is extremely broad so care is required);

- No option to tax may be exercised in respect of residential lettings.

13.2.2 GENERAL APPROACH

While the new provisions came into effect on 1 July 2008 clearly there were many lettings taxed under the old rules still in existence at that time. As a consequence it has been necessary to implement a number of 'transitional measures' to deal with transactions in certain leases which have been in place prior to 1 July 2008.

Given the number and complexity of the rules now in place it is first necessary to determine in which category the transaction falls, as shown in Table 8 below.

TABLE 8 Categories of transaction

Category	Transaction Type	Comment
Category 1	**Freehold Equivalents**	These are taxed in the same manner as freehold sales and the rules applicable to lettings do not apply. This category is not considered here—see *Conveyancing*, 5th edition, 2010, Oxford University Press, published in conjunction with the Law Society.
Category 2	**' "New" Lettings'**	Lettings since 1 July 2008 *not falling within either Category 3 or 4 below.*
Category 3	**'Legacy Leases'**	Surrender/assignment of +10-year leases first granted before 1 July 2008.
Category 4	**Waiver Lettings**	Leases granted by a landlord who has a waiver of exemption in place on 1 July 2008.

The category into which the transaction falls will then determine how the transaction is to be taxed, what amount is to be taxed and the impact of issues such as tenant works and the Capital Goods Scheme (CGS). In order to assist practitioners in establishing the correct VAT treatment, the Taxation Committee and the Conveyancing Committee of the Law Society jointly issued Pre-Contract Enquiries. While these are primarily aimed at transactions involving Freehold and Freehold Equivalent properties, they also address the position regarding properties which are being sold subject to existing leases and assignments or surrenders of certain leases. As the Pre-Contract Enquiries are subject to change, practitioners are urged that they use the most up-to-date edition in respect of each transaction. The Enquiries may be accessed by logging onto the Member's Area of the Law Society's website at www.lawsociety.ie. The Pre-Contract Enquiries are essential in order to determine the appropriate VAT clause to be included in the documents (see **Appendices 7** to **10** which include the Law Society's Special Condition 3 standard VAT clauses).

13.2.3 'NEW' LETTINGS AFTER 1 JULY 2008 (CATEGORIES 1 AND 2)

13.2.3.1 Lettings and landlord's Opt to Tax ('Opt')

A 'freehold equivalent' is defined as:

> *An interest in immovable goods other than a freehold interest the transfer of which constitutes a supply of immovable goods in accordance with VCA Part 3 Chapter 1.*

VCA Part 3 Chapter 1 specifies that a supply in relation to immovable goods shall be regarded as including:

> *the transfer in substance of (a) the right to dispose of immovable goods as owner or (b) the right to dispose of immovable goods.*

Essentially therefore a letting which amounts to a freehold equivalent is regarded as a sale and is subject to the VAT provisions relating to property sales (see *Conveyancing*, 5th edition, 2010, OUP and Law Society) rather than the rules examined here in relation to lettings.

From 1 July 2008 all lettings created, other than 'Freehold Equivalents', are exempt from VAT (paragraph 11 Schedule 1).

A landlord may, however, exercise the 'Landlord's Option to Tax' the lease (an 'Opt'). The detailed provisions relating to the Opt are contained in s 97 VCA. In summary:

- The Opt is exercised on a letting-by-letting basis (the decision to opt or not must therefore be made each time there is a letting and only applies to that specific letting).

- The Opt can be exercised by either including an appropriate provision in writing within the letting agreement or by issuing a document to the tenant notifying him that VAT is chargeable on the rents.

- There is no requirement to notify Revenue of the Opt.

- An Opt cannot be exercised in respect of a letting of residential accommodation.

- An Opt cannot be exercised where the tenant is connected to the landlord UNLESS the tenant is entitled to claim an input VAT credit of at least 90 per cent of the VAT that would arise on the rents.

- The landlord can end an Opt at any time. An Opt is terminated by a written agreement between landlord and tenant that the Opt is terminated or by the delivery by the landlord of a document notifying the tenant that the Opt is terminated.

- An Opt is automatically terminated when the landlord and the tenant become connected, unless the tenant is entitled to claim an input VAT credit of at least 90 per cent of the VAT that would arise on the rents.

- An Opt is automatically terminated where the landlord or a person connected with the landlord occupies the property, unless the person connected is entitled to claim an input VAT credit of at least 90 per cent of the VAT that would arise on the rents.

- A trader in the process of developing a property with a view to letting is deemed to Opt upon claiming an input deduction for VAT incurred on the development. Should the trader (landlord) subsequently make a letting and does not actually Opt then the deemed Opt is terminated.

When a landlord opts and the tenant is a VAT-registered person, Department of State or local authority body established by statute, or a person engaged in VAT-exempt activities, he is required to issue a VAT invoice in respect of the rents. Alternatively, he can issue a one-off statement stating the dates the rent falls due and the VAT thereon.

13.2.3.2 Why would a landlord opt?

Why would someone choose to tax a transaction when it could be regarded as exempt? The answer is that the decision to opt or not will dictate the landlord's input VAT deduction entitlement.

A trader is prohibited from recovering VAT incurred on costs that relate directly to an exempt transaction. Where a landlord grants a VAT-exempt letting (ie where he does not opt) the landlord cannot recover any of the VAT incurred on the costs associated thereto such as legal fees, tax advice and estate agent's fees.

More importantly, however, he also loses the right to a deduction entitlement in relation to the cost of acquiring and/or developing the property (or if he has already deducted such input VAT on the basis of 'intention' he is obliged to repay such VAT). The amount of this deduction entitlement loss is dictated by the Capital Goods Scheme (CGS).

13.2.3.3 Capital Goods Scheme

The detailed provisions relating to the CGS are contained in VCA Part 8 Chapter 2.

The CGS generally attributes a 20-interval life to a property. See Table 9 below for an illustration.

TABLE 9 Property intervals

Initial Interval	The 12 months immediately following the completion or supply of the property is known as the 'initial interval'.
Second Interval	The period from the end of the initial interval to the trader's financial year-end.
Third and subsequent Intervals	Trader's next accounting year which follows the second and each subsequent interval.

In the initial interval the use (or intended use) of the property is examined and if it is taxable, then all VAT is recoverable. If it is exempt, no VAT is recoverable and if it has a 'mixed use' then an element of the VAT incurred is deductible. At the end of the initial interval an adjustment is performed to take account of any change in deductibility which occurred within 12 months of the acquisition of the property.

In each of the following intervals an adjustment is made *if* the use of the property varies from the use in the initial interval (as adjusted).

Example 1

In June 2009 Trated Ltd purchases the freehold in a new building for €10m plus €1.35m VAT. This VAT is recoverable in full in 2009 if the building is used wholly for taxable purposes in that initial interval. For the second and subsequent intervals for the remaining VAT life of the property, the VAT deduction entitlement of Trated Ltd must be reviewed under the CGS.

The VAT life of a freehold interest is deemed to be 20 intervals. Therefore every year the CGS will consider one-twentieth of the VAT initially recovered, ie €1.35m ÷ 20 (€67,500).

In 2010 etc if Trated Ltd continues to use the property fully for taxable purposes no adjustment needs to be made in these years.

However, let us assume that in 2015 Trated Ltd lets 30 per cent of the property for a five-year period and does not opt to tax the lease. Trated Ltd will have to pay a claw-back under the

CGS of €20,250 to Revenue ((€1.35m ÷ 20) × 30%)) for that interval. For each subsequent interval that the letting continues without an Opt, Trated Ltd will have to repay €20,250.

Example 2

Edition Limited is engaged in VAT-exempt education services. In June 2009 it purchases the freehold in a new building for €10m plus €1.35m VAT. None of this VAT is recoverable in 2009 as the building is used wholly for VAT-exempt purposes in that initial interval.

As in example 1 the VAT life of a freehold interest is deemed to be 20 intervals; therefore every year the CGS will consider one-twentieth of the VAT initially incurred, ie €1.35m ÷ 20 (€67,500).

Let us assume that in 2015 Edition Ltd grants a five-year lease of 30 per cent of the building to Retail Limited. If Edition Ltd opts to tax the lease and charge VAT on the rent then Edition Ltd has moved that part of the property from an exempt to a taxable use. Under the CGS, Edition Ltd is therefore entitled to a deduction of VAT it previously was prohibited from deducting. The deduction will be €20,250 ((€1.35m ÷ 20) × 30%) for the tax year 2015. For each subsequent interval that the letting continues with an Opt, Edition Ltd will have an input VAT deduction of €20,250.

From these examples it can be seen that the decision to opt or not is fundamentally linked to the landlord's CGS position in relation to the property in question.

The CGS works, in general, on the basis that VAT is reclaimed in year one and an annual adjustment is made in each succeeding year to the extent that the recovery varies from the proportion deductible in the initial interval. An exception, however, arises where in any interval other than the initial interval the proportion of tax deductible differs by more than 50 per cent from the initial interval proportion of tax deductible then the owner of the Capital Good must perform a single recalculation covering all of the remaining intervals.

Refurbishment/development

The development/refurbishment of an existing property creates its own Capital Good and so there can be two or more Capital Goods relating to the same property, for example the acquisition/development of the building and the monies spent on refurbishing that building would be two separate CGSs. 'Refurbishment' is defined as 'development on a previously completed building, structure or engineering work'.

It is possible for a landlord to own a Capital Good (the building itself) and the tenant to own a Capital Good (the refurbishment if carried out by the tenant), both relating to the same property.

The CGS adjustment period for Refurbishment is ten intervals.

Keeping records

Section 64(12) of the VCA requires Capital Goods owners to create and maintain a record in respect of each Capital Good and s 85(1) provides an obligation to retain these records together with the taxpayer's existing records. This document is referred to in the legislation as a 'Capital Good record' and is a form of 'VAT passport'.

This document is essential in order to allow traders to calculate the amount of any annual adjustment and, as we will see later, compute the amount on which VAT is chargeable on certain assignments or surrenders.

Tenant's VAT status

While it is the landlord's prerogative to opt, the ability of the tenant to recover VAT arising on the rents has an impact on the decision.

Commercially, it may make sense for the tenant to agree to pay a premium to the landlord to cover any CGS (and other tax) adjustment the landlord will incur should he not opt rather than incurring VAT at the standard rate on all the rents payable under the lease for the duration of the lease.

13.2.3.4 Premium

Where the tenant pays a lump sum to the landlord at the commencement of one of these lettings the treatment of that payment follows the treatment of the rents, ie where the landlord has opted to tax then the payment is subject to VAT; where the landlord has not opted the payment is exempt.

Where the landlord makes a payment to the tenant the matter is more complex. Revenue accepts that where the tenant does not make any supply in relation to obtaining the payment (ie does not give any rights or undertakings) then the payment is not subject to VAT. Where a supply is made then VAT will arise. The nature of the agreement will determine the VAT treatment in each individual instance.

A bona fide rent-free period does not give rise to a VAT event; however, the landlord should ensure the Opt is in place and not terminated during that period, otherwise a CGS adjustment may arise.

13.2.3.5 Subsequent surrender and assignments

The surrender or assignment of leases created since 1 July 2008 does not trigger a VAT event in relation to the letting itself (note this is very different to the treatment of a surrender or assignment of a legacy lease, which is examined later). However, see **13.2.3.6** regarding any tenant works.

Where the tenant pays a lump sum to the landlord to take the surrender, the treatment of that payment will follow that of the rents, ie where the landlord has opted to tax then the payment is subject to VAT, where the landlord has not opted the payment is exempt.

Where the lease is surrendered, however, the landlord will need to consider any CGS impact in relation to any subsequent use of the property including any re-lettings.

Where the lease is assigned the landlord needs to consider whether or not he and the new tenant are 'connected' and if so if this will cause the termination of any Opt he has in place.

13.2.3.6 Tenant works

There will be instances where a tenant undertakes works on a property and where those works will constitute refurbishment.

From the tenant's perspective he will have created a Capital Good with a ten-interval life. The same general rules as outlined earlier will similarly apply to the tenant's Capital Good.

An issue will arise for the tenant where he surrenders or assigns a lease in respect of which the VAT life has not expired at the time of surrender/assignment. Unless the tenant can get the agreement of the landlord (in the case of a surrender) or the new tenant (in the case of an assignment) to 'step into his shoes' and take on the tenant's CGS obligations in relation to the refurbishment for the remainder of the VAT life then at the time of surrender/assignment the tenant will incur a VAT liability in accordance with the formula:

$$\frac{B \times N}{T}$$

Where B = the total reviewed deductible amount in relation to the Capital Good (the refurbishment)

N = the number of full intervals remaining in the VAT life of the Capital Good plus one.

T = the total number of intervals (ie ten)

Where the tenant works are destroyed then no claw-back arises.

13.2.4 SURRENDERS AND ASSIGNMENTS OF TEN-YEAR+ LEASES GRANTED PRE-1 JULY 2008 (CATEGORY 3—'LEGACY LEASES')

Section 95 of the VCA contains transitional measures relating to a post-1 July 2008 surrender or assignment of 10-year+ leases granted pre-1 July 2008.

13.2.4.1 Capital Goods Scheme

Specific CGS rules apply to legacy leases. Section 95 provides that these leases are to be regarded as Capital Goods; however, the landlord is relieved from conducting the annual look-back and adjustment generally required under the CGS.

Should the landlord (or tenant) undertake any refurbishment works on the property then those works are subject to all the normal CGS rules (see above).

The CGS adjustment period (ie standard number of intervals) for a legacy lease is 20 years or the number of full years remaining in that interest from the date when it was created or last assigned pre-1 July 2008, whichever is the shorter. However, if the property has been developed (which according to Revenue is to be regarded as meaning developed to completion, ie it does not apply to development that is refurbishment) since it was acquired then the 20-year life runs from the date of the most recent development.

In the case of the first assignment or surrender of a legacy lease after 1 July 2008 then the CGS adjustment period is *the number of full years remaining in the adjustment period plus one*:

- The adjustment period where the lease was not previously surrendered or assigned is 20 years from its creation or the number of full years if the lease is for a period of less than 20 years.

- The adjustment period where the lease had been assigned prior to 1 July 2008 is 20 years from that date of assignment or the period remaining in the lease when the assigned occurred if shorter.

In the case of the second or subsequent assignment of a legacy lease after 1 July 2008 the adjustment period is *the number of full years remaining in the adjustment period plus one* as obtained under the rule above.

VAT treatment

Where the person surrendering or assigning a legacy lease was entitled to deduct input VAT on the acquisition of their interest or development of that property then the assignment or surrender will be subject to VAT.

Where the person surrendering or assigning a legacy lease was not entitled to deduct input VAT on the acquisition of their interest or development of that property then the assignment or surrender is not subject to VAT. In these instances, however, both the vendor and the purchaser can jointly exercise an option for taxation in relation to the surrender or assignment. *NOTE:* this differs from a landlord's option to tax a letting in that *both* the existing tenant and the landlord/new tenant as the case may be must jointly agree to exercise the option for taxation. Also the landlord's option to tax relates to a supply of a service whereas the joint option for taxation relates to a supply of goods.

VALUE ADDED TAX

Section 95(8)(a) of the VCA dictates the amount on which VAT must be levied in relation to surrenders or assignments of legacy leases that are subject to VAT including those where a joint option for taxation has been exercised. The taxable amount is based on a formula as follows:

$$\frac{T \times N}{Y}$$

Where T = the total tax incurred on his acquisition of the lease by the existing tenant making the surrender/assignment

N = the number of full intervals plus one remaining in the adjustment period (see comments above)

Y = the total number of intervals in the adjustment period

Example

Berga Limited took a 25-year lease in a warehouse unit on 1 July 2003. VAT of €450,000 was incurred on the lease. On 1 October 2009 Berga Limited agreed to assign the lease to Bria Limited.

T = €450,000

N = Number of full intervals plus *one* = 13 + 1 = 14 (the adjustment period is 20 years, there are 6 years and 3 months expired leaving 13 years and 9 months in the adjustment period)

Y = 20 (note while the lease is a 25-year lease the adjustment period is capped at 20 years).

VAT arising on the assignment = 450,000 × 14/20 = €315,000

Accounting for the VAT on the surrender/assignment

The provisions of VCA s 95(8) apply to these surrenders and assignments. As a consequence, where the recipient (landlord or new tenant as the case may be) is an accountable person, a Department of State or a local authority or a person engaged in exempt lettings then a reverse charge applies in relation to the VAT arising on the supply. This means the existing tenant does not levy the VAT, instead the recipient is obliged to self-account for the VAT. If the recipient is not already registered for VAT he would be obliged to register for VAT and report the reverse charge. In terms of potential VAT clauses this is an important point as it is essential to be aware of who has the responsibility to report the VAT and to provide accordingly.

Where VCA s 95(8) applies there is also a requirement to hand over a document (this is not a VAT invoice). The document must stipulate the VAT value of the interest being surrendered or assigned and the amount of VAT arising and the number of intervals remaining in the adjustment period (VAT life).

Taking the example above and assuming a VAT rate of 13.5 per cent this would be

Value = €2,333,334 and

VAT = €315,000 and

Adjustment Period = 14

NOTE: The landlord or new tenant as the case may be is regarded as taking on a Capital Good. Their initial interval will be a 12-month period commencing on the date of the surrender or assignment.

Tenant Works

A tenant may have undertaken works on a property which constitutes refurbishment. As a consequence the tenant will have created a Capital Good with a ten-interval VAT life. The same general rules as outlined earlier will similarly apply to the tenant's Capital Good.

Where the tenant surrenders or assigns a lease in respect of which he holds an unexpired Tenant Works Capital Good then unless the tenant can get the agreement of the landlord (in the case of a surrender) or the new tenant (in the case of an assignment) to step into his shoes and take on the remainder of the Capital Good then at the time of surrender/assignment an additional VAT liability of the remaining CGS value is triggered. This liability cannot be passed on to the landlord or new tenant.

Where the Tenant Works are destroyed then no claw-back arises.

NOTE: The assignment/surrender of the lease and the taking on of a CGS relating to Tenant Works are two separate matters and should be addressed separately.

Premium

Where the existing tenant pays a premium to the landlord (in the case of a surrender) or new tenant (in the case of an assignment) it is outside the scope of VAT; any VAT arising is based on the CGS-based formula outlined earlier.

Where the landlord (in the case of a surrender) or the new tenant (in the case of an assignment) pays a premium to the existing tenant it is subject to VAT at the standard rate, currently 23 per cent (as it is regarded as a payment in respect of the tenant giving up his entitlement to the lease).

Reversionary Interest

Where a taxable legacy lease was created the interest in the property which was retained by the landlord is referred to as the reversion on that legacy lease. Where a landlord sells a reversion on a legacy lease on or after 1 July 2008, the sale of the reversion is not subject to VAT unless the property was developed by, on behalf of and to the benefit of the landlord subsequent to the creation of the legacy lease, in which case the supply of the reversion would be taxable if it occurs while the property is considered new.

13.2.5 LEASE GRANTED BY A PERSON WHO HAS A WAIVER OF EXEMPTION IN PLACE ON 1 JULY 2008 (CATEGORY 4)

While no new waivers are permitted after 1 July 2008 a trader with a waiver in respect of a short-term letting in place prior to 1 July 2008 will, subject to the rules in relation to connected persons, be permitted to keep that waiver in place.

Where a landlord has a waiver in place it cannot extend to any letting of a property acquired or developed on or after 1 July 2008 (though a waiver can cover a property where the waiver was in place on 18 February 2008 and the property was undergoing development on that date even if completion did not take place until after 1 July 2008).

All new lettings of properties not precluded from falling within the waiver will be treated under the waiver rules, irrespective of their duration (ie the old ten-year rule does not apply, but of course excluding freehold equivalents).

Where a letting is subject to the Waiver of Exemption the Opt to tax regime and the CGS regime do not apply to that letting.

Where a landlord who has a waiver in place grants a new letting which is not covered by the waiver rules then the 'normal' rules apply, ie the lease will be exempt and the landlord may opt to tax the letting.

VALUE ADDED TAX

Where a waiver is in place VAT at the standard rate is applied to the rents as they fall due.

As a general rule a waiver cannot be extended to a residential letting (the exception being situations where the landlord had a waiver in place at 2 February 2007 and the property has not been developed since that date).

A landlord can cancel his waiver should he wish. On cancellation a look-back takes place. Under the look-back any excess VAT recovered by the landlord on the acquisition/development relating to properties to which the waiver relates exceeds the VAT paid to Revenue arising from the waiver on the letting must be repaid to Revenue.

An important point to note is that when a general waiver cancellation adjustment is made then any subsequent sale of that property is not subject to VAT (provided of course it hasn't been redeveloped in the interim and subject to the exercise of a joint option for taxation).

NOTE: The waiver regime is a very different regime to the CGS. The waiver regime considers VAT reclaimed and VAT paid. When the VAT paid equals the amount of VAT reclaimed the waiver can be cancelled without any further cost. The CGS focuses only on the VAT deducted, adjusting the amount recovered up or down in line with the use of the property, interval by interval; there is no credit for VAT charged on the rents.

Specific measures ensure that the CGS shall not also apply where this waiver cancellation look-back applies.

In certain instances a waiver will be cancelled automatically. Section 96(8) of the VCA provides that where a person has a letting in respect of which a waiver is in place, that waiver will be cancelled with immediate effect if the parties are/become connected and the tenant does not have over 90 per cent VAT recovery. However, by way of exception, if the parties can establish that on the basis of the VAT already charged to the tenant, and the VAT to be charged in the future, an amount equivalent to the VAT recovered by the landlord would be charged to the tenant within the first 12 years of the letting then the waiver can remain in place. In addition, to benefit from this exception, the waiver must have been in place prior to 18 February 2008 or the property was owned by the landlord on 18 February 2008 and was 'in the course of development' on that day, or the landlord himself held a long lease (ie a lease of ten years or more) granted to him between 18 February 2008 and 30 June 2008 by an unrelated person.

Example

Alba Ltd acquires a building and incurs VAT of €1 million. In January 2004 Alba Ltd puts a six-year short-term letting in place with Bineva Ltd (a related company with only 35 per cent VAT recovery). Between January 2004 and June 2008 Alba Ltd has charged VAT of €300,000 to the tenant.

In July 2008 this waiver of exemption terminates unless the annual VAT charged by Alba Ltd to Bineva Ltd exceeds €77,778:

$$\frac{€1,000,000 - €300,000}{12 - 3}$$

If the annual VAT charged exceeds €77,778 then the waiver may stay in place but if not, it will terminate triggering an immediate repayment of the difference between the VAT recovered and VAT paid (here €700,000) to Revenue.

Where a particular letting no longer qualifies for the waiver (eg it no longer meets the 12-year test) then there is a deemed cancellation of the waiver in relation to that property and a look-back specific to that particular property takes place. Where the VAT reclaimed exceeds the VAT paid on that property then a payment of the difference must be made to Revenue.

Specific measures were introduced by the Finance Act (No 2) 2008 to address situations where a landlord with a waiver in place and a tenant become members of a VAT group. Essentially a waiver cancellation claw-back is triggered when they become members of a VAT group unless the group enjoys at least 90 per cent VAT input deduction entitlement.

13.3   Summary

The new regime in respect of lettings (other than freehold equivalents) is deceptively simple: all lettings are exempt and the landlord may opt to tax on a letting-by-letting basis. However because of the stock of legacy leases and landlords with waivers of exemptions in place on 1 July 2008 specific transitional rules have had to be implemented.

In tackling a letting from a VAT perspective it is first necessary to categorise the transaction:

* freehold equivalent,

* new lease,

* legacy lease surrender or assignment,

* new lease falling within the old waiver regime.

Once the transaction has been categorised see Tables 10, 11 and 12 for the matters to be considered to determine the VAT consequences:

TABLE 10 New Lettings

Option To Tax	If the landlord is opting to tax he/she is required to notify tenant in writing.
Who accounts?	Landlord will levy VAT on the rents.
	Lease should provide that the VAT will be paid (generally on presentation of a VAT invoice).
	Lease needs to be clear as to whether the agreed rent is inclusive or exclusive of VAT.
Other issues	Landlord may wish to restrict the tenant from assigning the lease to a person connected with the landlord or restrict the right of the tenant to undertake works.
	Tenant may wish to have an obligation included that the landlord will take on a CGS relating to tenant works.
Premium	Tenant pays landlord—treatment follows that of the rents.
	Landlord pays tenant—not subject to VAT unless tenant is regarded as providing some form of service for that payment.

TABLE 11 Legacy Lease Surrenders and Assignments

Taxable	Where the surrender or assignment is taxable, VAT will arise on the remaining CGS value.
Joint Option	Joint option for taxation should be documented.

Who accounts?	Where reverse charge applies the landlord or the new tenant as the case may be must self-account for the VAT. Lease needs to stipulate this responsibility and should also require the landlord/ new tenant to confirm their status such that the reverse charge does actually apply. Lease also needs to stipulate the landlord will provide the required document.
	Where the reverse charge does not apply existing tenant must levy the VAT and the lease should provide accordingly.
Tenant works	Where the tenant has a Tenant Works CGS then he/she may seek to have the landlord in the case of a surrender, or the new tenant in the case of an assignment, step into his/her shoes. If this is agreed then the agreement needs to reflect this.
Premium	Where the landlord or the new tenant as the case may be pays a premium to the existing tenant it is subject to VAT at the standard rate, currently 23 per cent. Agreement needs to reflect this and provide that the VAT be paid on presentation of a valid VAT invoice issued by the existing tenant.

TABLE 12 New Lease by Person with a Waiver of Exemption

Who accounts?	The landlord must levy the VAT.
	Lease should provide that the VAT will be paid (generally on presentation of a VAT invoice).
	Lease needs to be clear as to whether the agreed rent is inclusive or exclusive of VAT.
Cancellation of waiver	Landlord may issue a statement covering the life of the lease rather than consecutive invoices.
	Landlord may wish to ensure no rent revision creates a situation where a cancellation of the waiver occurs.
	Landlord may wish to require a connected tenant to advise immediately if their VAT recovery entitlement is/will fall under 90 per cent—landlord also likely to oblige the tenant in such instances to make a payment equivalent to any claw-back incurred by the landlord as a consequence of the waiver cancellation.
Premium	A payment by tenant will follow the rents and will therefore be taxable. Agreement needs to reflect this.
	A payment made by the landlord to the tenant will not be taxable unless the tenant provides a service in return. The tenant is responsible for determining whether or not VAT arises and for levying any VAT arising.

13.3.1 TRANSFER OF BUSINESS

The VCA contains specific measures that stipulate the transfer of intangible assets in connection with the transfer of a business or part thereof is not a supply from a VAT perspective and is therefore not subject to VAT. Where an interest in property including a leasehold interest transfers as part of a transfer of business it will not be subject to VAT. Specific rules apply to the transferee as to the VAT obligations he or she takes on as a consequence of taking on the business.

13.4 Miscellaneous

13.4.1 RENT TO BUY

These are schemes whereby potential purchasers are attracted by initial periods of renting. It should be noted that as the conditions of these schemes can vary significantly, each should be examined on their own merits. Commonly, however, they feature:

- an upfront payment,
- the prospective purchaser renting the property for a defined period of time,
- at the end of the rental period an option to purchase the property at an agreed price or walk away,
- a final price paid that will generally be net of the upfront payment and some or all of the rental payments.

Revenue eBrief 40/09 announced Revenue's general position regarding Rent to Buy schemes. Essentially, Revenue view these agreements as being a multiple supply, ie two supplies being (1) the granting of an option to purchase the property at an agreed price and (2) the granting of a lease. The consideration for these supplies must therefore be apportioned between these two supplies and are taxed accordingly.

With regard to the option to purchase, the VAT treatment will follow that of the underlying supply (ie if the option is granted on undeveloped land it is exempt from VAT/if the sale of the property would be subject to VAT then the option is also taxable).

With regard to the letting of the property, the letting of property is exempt from VAT in accordance with paragraph II Schedule 1 to the VAT Act, 1972 (as amended) (now paragraph 11 Schedule 1 VCA). The landlord's option to tax cannot apply to the letting of residential property as per s 97(4) VCA.

Revenue regards any upfront payment as a payment in respect of the granting of an option to purchase the property, unless refunded at the end of the scheme. The monthly payments made are regarded as consideration for the letting of the property but where the amount paid exceeds the market rent then any excess is regarded as being in respect of the option. In such cases it is then necessary to split the payment between the rent element (exempt) and the option element (taxable or exempt as mentioned above).

If the purchaser does not exercise the option to buy there are no further VAT implications in relation to the transaction. If the option to purchase is exercised then generally, as the vendor is the person who developed the property, the sale will be subject to VAT.

13.4.2 COMPLETION OF RESIDENTIAL PROPERTIES—REVENUE CONCESSION

Where, subsequent to 1 July 2008, a landlord develops residential properties with the intention to sell the same but where, for whatever reason, subsequent to completion of the development decides to let them (ie an exempt letting) then he must make a CGS adjustment on a yearly basis from the second interval and for each subsequent interval during which the property is let by way of repaying one-twentieth of the input VAT recovered for each of the years in which an adjustment is required. The eventual sale of the property will always be subject to VAT and no CGS adjustment will be made upon sale. This is of cash-flow benefit to the developer.

Where residential properties, built with the intention of sale, were completed prior to 1 July 2008 and let before or after 1 July 2008, then a deductibility adjustment (equal to a full claw-back of input VAT) would arise upon first letting. The subsequent sale would be liable to VAT and an adjustment made whereby a proportion of the input VAT previously clawed back would become available to the vendor. By way of concession, Revenue has indicated that where properties have been developed for sale and were completed prior to 1 July 2008 and where it is first let subsequent to 1 July 2008 it is prepared to accept that completion occurred after 1 July 2008 (and so the benefit of the annual CGS adjustment as opposed to a full deductibility adjustment arises upon first letting).

13.4.3 LETTINGS BY MORTGAGEE IN POSSESSION, LIQUIDATOR OR RECEIVER

Specific provisions apply to mortgagees in possession (MIPs), liquidators and receivers. These provisions confirm that where an MIP, liquidator or receiver lets a property they can exercise the landlord's option to tax in respect of the letting. Where an MIP, liquidator or receiver takes possession of a property which is subject to lettings, the MIP, liquidator or receiver is entitled to the rents and is obliged to account for VAT on the rents if the letting is taxable.

Once an MIP, liquidator or receiver is appointed, the defaulter must furnish the MIP, liquidator or receiver with the Capital Goods Record for the property. The MIP, liquidator or receiver is treated as the Capital Goods Owner and is responsible for all obligations of the defaulter under the CGS. Therefore, if for example the property is sold by the MIP, liquidator or receiver and the sale gives rise to a claw-back of VAT under the CGS, the MIP, liquidator or receiver must pay the amount due to Revenue.

CHAPTER 14

HOUSING (PRIVATE RENTED DWELLINGS) ACT, 1982

14.1. 'Controlled Dwellings'

The Rent Restrictions Acts, 1960–1981, placed a statutory restriction on the rents payable by tenants of dwellinghouses with rateable valuations which did not exceed specified sums. These dwellinghouses were commonly called 'controlled dwellings'.

In *Madigan v Attorney-General* [1982] IR 117 and *Dorothy Blake v Attorney-General* [1982] IR 117, the courts held that parts of the Rent Restrictions Act, 1960 were an unconstitutional interference with the property rights of landlords as the Act restricted the exercise of these rights without providing for compensation and did so for the benefit of tenants without taking into account the financial means of either landlords or tenants.

14.2 Housing (Private Rented Dwellings) Act, 1982

As a result of these cases the Housing (Private Rented Dwellings) Act, 1982 was enacted giving the District Court the power to fix the rent for formerly 'controlled dwellings' save where the dwelling was held under a contract of tenancy greater than a yearly tenancy. Section 13 of the Act provides that the gross rent should be fixed with regard to certain criteria. These include:

(a) the nature, character and location of the dwelling;

(b) the terms of the tenancy;

(c) the date of purchase of the dwelling by the landlord;

(d) the amount paid for it;

(e) the length of the tenant's occupancy of the dwelling;

(f) the number and ages of the tenant's family residing in the dwelling; and

(g) the means of the landlord and tenant.

These criteria were considered by the Supreme Court in *Quirke v Folio Homes Ltd* [1988] ILRM 496.

14.3 Jurisdiction

The jurisdiction for determining the terms of such tenancies was passed to a statutory Rent Tribunal on 2 August 1983 under the Housing (Private Rented Dwellings) (Amendment) Act, 1983. Part 4 of the Residential Tenancies (Amendment) Act 2015 ('the 2015 Act') dissolved the Rent Tribunal and its functions were transferred to the Residential Tenancies Board. See **chapter 7** for further details.

14.4 Statutory Protection

Section 2(1) of the 1982 Act defines 'dwelling' as:

a house let as a separate dwelling, or a part so let, of any house, whether or not the tenant shares with any other persons any portion thereof or any accommodation, amenity or facility in connection therewith.

It should be noted that such 'dwellings' may have partial business use. The Act does not apply to contracts of tenancy greater than a yearly tenancy, lettings bona fide for temporary convenience or tenancies dependent on the tenant's continuance in any office, appointment or employment. The Act also excludes dwellings built on or after 7 May 1941.

In addition to providing for the fixing of the rent of formerly 'controlled dwellings', the Act provided for the eventual cessation of the right of tenants in these premises to retain possession. The Act included provisions whereby the prior absolute statutory protection enjoyed by these tenants would be phased out.

Most importantly, the tenants of formerly controlled dwellings have the right to remain in the dwelling for life. Any spouse living in the dwelling at the date of the tenant's death may also remain there for life. Thus, the protection for tenants and their spouses will continue until their death.

However, any member of the family bona fide residing in the dwelling at the date of death of the tenant and/or his or her spouse was only entitled to remain in the dwelling until 26 July 2002 (20 years after the passing of the Act) or for a period of five years from the date of death of the tenant and/or his or her spouse, whichever is the greater.

'Family member' is broadly defined in s 7(2) of the Act and includes, inter alia, parents, grandparents, children, father-in-law, mother-in-law, step-parents, son-in-law, daughter-in-law, nephew, niece, grandchildren, brother, sister, step-children, adopted persons, 'illegitimate' offspring and any person bona fide in residence with the tenant for not less than six years and to whom the tenant was in loco parentis. These family members are often called successor tenants.

Thus, from 26 July 2002 many family members occupying formerly controlled dwellings ceased to enjoy the statutory protection previously afforded to them. If the tenant and/or his or her spouse died within the five years prior to that date, then the protection afforded to the family member continued for a five-year period from the death and did not cease on 26 July 2002. However, if the death occurred on or prior to 26 July 1997 the statutory protection ceased on 26 July 2002.

14.5 Practical Concerns

This issue was one of grave concern to legal practitioners as many of the people occupying these properties are elderly and frequently live on their own. They may have occupied the property for the majority of their lifetime and be unable to cope with the prospect of leaving their home and entering the private rented residential sector where there is less security of tenure and where they would be required to pay a market rent.

The Report of the Commission on the Private Rented Residential Sector answer to this problem was to provide a five-year period within which these tenants could claim the right to a new lease under the provisions of the Landlord and Tenant (Amendment) Act, 1980, as amended. This recommendation was partially adopted in s 192 of the Residential Tenancies Act 2004 ('the 2004 Act').

However, it is by no means certain that all of these tenants come within the requirements of the 1980 Act as amended.

14.6   Entitlement under the 1980 Act (as amended)

Many of these properties are in disrepair as noted in the Commission's report so there may be few tenants or successor tenants who could claim an improvements equity (see **10.2.3**). However, most if not all would be able to claim a long possession equity (see **10.2.2**). Section 192(2) of the 2004 Act introduced the prospective abolition of entitlement to the long possession equity in relation to dwellings to which the 2004 Act applies. On 1 September 2009, the entitlement to apply for an equity under the 1980 Act ceased to apply in relation to dwellings to which the 2004 Act applied. The margin only refers to the long occupation equity but this section also captures the improvements equity. However, the 2004 Act does not apply to a dwelling to which Part II of the Housing (Private Rented Dwellings) Act, 1982 applies. Thus it appears that these tenants still have an entitlement to claim an improvements or long possession equity.

They may also be able to claim a business equity (see **10.2.1**). Section 13(1)(a) requires that the premises are bona fide used wholly or partly for the purpose of carrying on a business.

While there is no doubt that these tenants would satisfy one of more of the equities required under the 1980 Act it must be remembered that relief is only available for tenements as defined in s 5 of the 1980 Act (see **10.1.1**). In examining the component parts of s 5, it appears that these properties would consist of land covered wholly or partly by buildings. As most are residential, it is likely that the land not so covered is subsidiary and ancillary to the buildings. They are not for temporary convenience and not dependent on the tenants' continuance in some office, employment or appointment, as these are expressly excluded by s 8 of the 1982 Act.

The real difficulty lies with s 5(1)(a)(iii), which requires that:

> *(iii)   they are held by the occupier thereof under a lease or other contract of tenancy express or implied or arising by statute;*

When their statutory protection expires what is the status of successor tenants of formerly controlled dwellings?

Are they holding under a lease or other contract of tenancy express or implied? It appears unlikely unless they overhold, ie remain in occupation and continue to pay rent which is accepted by the landlord. In that instance there is an argument that they are in much the same position as a tenant who overholds at the end of a fixed-term lease, ie an implied periodic tenancy would arise (see **2.3**). Would residential premises then be subject to the the 2004 Act? Tenancy is defined in s 5(1) as including a periodic tenancy, even though s 3(2) provides that the 2004 Act does not apply to a dwelling to which Part II of the Housing (Private Rented Dwellings) Act, 1982 applies.

Perhaps such tenants are holding under a lease or other contract of tenancy arising by statute? This appears to be the most likely option but the matter will not be definitively decided until it comes before the courts. Even then, each case may be decided on its own merits. In the interim, the occupiers are left in a precarious position. If they remain in occupation until the matter is decided, the courts may find that there is no right to a new lease. Even if the courts do decide that these properties are tenements and there is a right to a new lease under the 1980 Act, the occupiers are faced with a market rent which many of them may not be able to afford.

The Department of the Environment, Heritage and Local Government explanatory leaflet on the changes to the 1980 Act brought about by the 2004 Act takes it for granted that successor tenants are entitled to apply for a long possession equity. The explanatory leaflet states:

> 'Successor tenants are entitled to apply for long occupation equity lease tenancies since they have all completed the 20-year occupation requirement by virtue of their own tenancies and that of the rent controlled tenants from whom they succeeded to the tenancy. Any successor tenant who has not yet applied for one of these leases may do so only until 1 September 2009. After that date the entitlement to apply will be gone. A successor tenant who has not applied for a long occupation equity lease before 1 September 2009 will be no different to tenants in the general private rented sector and the provisions of the Residential Tenancies Act will apply.'

Thus it appears that original tenants may still be entitled to claim a long possession equity but successor tenants may not. Successor tenants, ie family members occupying formerly controlled dwellings, could have applied for a long possession/occupation equity under the 1980 Act prior to 1 September 2009. If they did not do so they are the same as other tenants in the marketplace. However, even if such tenants apply for an equity under the 1980 Act they may not be entitled to one as a result of failure to comply with s 5 of the Act. In that instance it appears that residential premises would be subject to the 2004 Act despite the exclusion in s 3(2) of the Act. But what about business premises? If they are held not to be tenements and thus cannot avail of the 1980 Act, can they find statutory protection elsewhere?

14.7   Entitlement under the Ground Rents Legislation

The ground rents legislation provides no protection. Section 9 of the Landlord and Tenant (Ground Rents) (No. 2) Act, 1978 requires that the land must be held under a lease (see **11.2.2.2**). A lease is defined in the Act as an instrument in writing, whether or not under seal, containing a contract of tenancy for any land in consideration of a rent or return and includes a fee farm grant (see **11.2.2.1**). Section 15 of the Act may apply, however, if the occupier overholds and a yearly tenancy arises. Unfortunately, such occupiers are likely to fall foul of the requirement that the permanent buildings were not erected by the immediate lessor or any superior lessor (see **11.2.2.5**).

14.8   Implications

As of 26 July 2002, those family members who occupied formerly controlled dwellings began to face the full rigours of the private rented sector. For such successor tenants, the end of the statutory protection meant a period of uncertainly and insecurity as they were faced with the prospect of eviction from their homes.

For a landlord this opened up the possibility of disposing of or developing property which had up to now been unprofitable. Many landlords bought these properties as investments knowing the statutory protection would soon expire and were waiting to regain possession. Many of these properties are in disrepair as the rents did not cover the cost of keeping them in good condition.

While it appears that the changes of 26 July 2002 affected an extremely small percentage of the population, a number of cases of extreme hardship may have arisen. At a Law Society public seminar on 22 February 2002 entitled 'July 2002—The end of Rent Control: Mespil Flats revisited' the Department of the Environment estimated that from a survey it recently carried out 1,700 of these dwellings remained and a significant number (1,300) remained occupied by the original tenant or spouse. This indicates that there might have been fewer than 400 family members affected by the 26 July deadline.

In light of the insignificant numbers there has been little political will to address the situation. However, without new legislation or a decision by the courts on the exact status of family members after their statutory protection expired, these successor tenants faced a legal quagmire. It is questionable how many of these tenancies remain in existence. It is notable that no onslaught of case law has arisen though see *Beatty v The Rent Tribunal* [2005] IESC 66, which related to a claim in damages for negligence against the Rent Tribunal arising out of the tribunal's manner of determining a rent.

APPENDIX 1

TENANCY REGISTRATION FORM RTB1

© PRTB. This material is reproduced with the kind permission of the PRTB.

Tenancy Registration
Application Form RTB1

Important:
To ensure a more satisfactory customer experience, please take care to **complete the form in full and correctly.** Ensure to include the correct payment. Incomplete forms may lead to multiple communications from the RTB. Details of the fees are on page 7 and guidance notes are on page 8 of the form.

Section 1 - Application Type (See Note 1)

1. Registration   New ☐   Renewal of existing tenancy after four years ☐
                                                   (Further Part 4)

    If you have selected "Renewal of existing tenancy after four years" above, please insert previous registration number

2. Previous RT No. ☐☐☐☐☐☐☐☐☐☐☐☐☐☐☐☐☐

Section 2 - Details of the Rented Dwelling (See Note 2)

3. Address of Rented Dwelling

    Apt./House No.   ☐☐☐☐☐☐☐☐☐☐☐☐☐☐☐☐☐☐☐☐☐☐☐

    Address Line 1   ☐☐☐☐☐☐☐☐☐☐☐☐☐☐☐☐☐☐☐☐☐☐☐

    Address Line 2   ☐☐☐☐☐☐☐☐☐☐☐☐☐☐☐☐☐☐☐☐☐☐☐

    Address Line 3   ☐☐☐☐☐☐☐☐☐☐☐☐☐☐☐☐☐☐☐☐☐☐☐

    Address Line 4   ☐☐☐☐☐☐☐☐☐☐☐☐☐☐☐☐☐☐☐☐☐☐☐

    County   ☐☐☐☐☐☐☐☐☐☐☐☐☐☐☐☐☐☐☐☐☐☐☐

    Eircode   ☐☐☐   ☐☐☐☐   (Please ensure to include Eircode)

4. Dwelling Type

    House ☐   Apartment ☐   Flat ☐   Part of House ☐   Maisonette ☐   Bedsit ☐

5. Property Type (if the dwelling type selected above is House, Part of House or Maisonette, place an X in the relevant box below to indicate the property type)

                      Semi Detached ☐   Detached House ☐   Terraced ☐

6. No. of Bedrooms ☐☐

7. No. of Occupants ☐☐

8. BER Rating (if any) ☐☐

9. Local Authority in which rented dwelling is located
    ☐☐☐☐☐☐☐☐☐☐☐☐☐☐☐☐☐☐☐☐☐☐☐☐☐☐☐☐

RPC008848_EN_PR_L_1

278

Section 3 - Details of Tenancy (See Note 3)

10. If the tenancy is for a fixed term, please indicate the duration of the term   Years ☐☐   Months ☐☐

11. (a) Tenancy commencement date   ☐☐ / ☐☐ / ☐☐☐☐

    (b) Date tenancy ended
       (only relevant if registering a tenancy that has ended)   ☐☐ / ☐☐ / ☐☐☐☐

12. Sub-letting - if this tenancy is a sub-letting, place x in the box   ☐

13. Rental Amount   € ☐☐☐☐☐☐ . ☐☐   14. Deposit Amount   € ☐☐☐☐☐ . ☐☐

15. Frequency of Payment   Weekly ☐   Monthly ☐   Annually ☐

16. Charges (incurred by tenant)

Electricity ☐   Oil ☐   TV Licence ☐   Waste ☐   Gas ☐   Other ☐

Details of
"Other" charges

Section 4A - Landlord Details (See Note 4A)

If you wish to enter a company name, please do so using the First Name and Surname fields.

17. **Landlord** - Name and Contact Details   Are You: Individual ☐   Company ☐

First Name

Surname

PPSN
(if Individual)   **CRO Reg. No.**
     (if Company)

Address

County

Eircode   ☐☐☐   ☐☐☐☐   (Please ensure to include Eircode)

Country

Telephone No.

Mobile No.

Email

If you wish to opt out of receiving tenancy information from the RTB by email, please insert X in the box   ☐

Section 4A - Landlord Details continued (See Note 4A)

18. **Landlord** - Name and Contact Details   Are You: Individual ☐   Company ☐

First Name

Surname

PPSN
(if Individual)   **CRO Reg. No.**
(if Company)

Address

County

Eircode   (Please ensure to include Eircode)

Country

Telephone No.

Mobile No.

Email

If you wish to opt out of receiving tenancy information from the RTB by email, please insert X in the box ☐

19. **Landlord** - Name and Contact Details   Are You: Individual ☐   Company ☐

First Name

Surname

PPSN
(if Individual)   **CRO Reg. No.**
(if Company)

Address

County

Eircode   (Please ensure to include Eircode)

Country

Telephone No.

Mobile No.

Email

If you wish to opt out of receiving tenancy information from the RTB by email, please insert X in the box ☐

280

Section 4B - Tenants (See Note 4B)

20. Tenant

First Name

Surname

Mobile No.

PPSN — If tenant has no PPSN or you have made a reasonable effort to obtain it but it has not been provided, place X in the box

21. Tenant

First Name

Surname

Mobile No.

PPSN — If tenant has no PPSN or you have made a reasonable effort to obtain it but it has not been provided, place X in the box

22. Tenant

First Name

Surname

Mobile No.

PPSN — If tenant has no PPSN or you have made a reasonable effort to obtain it but it has not been provided, place X in the box

23. Tenant

First Name

Surname

Mobile No.

PPSN — If tenant has no PPSN or you have made a reasonable effort to obtain it but it has not been provided, place X in the box

24. Tenant

First Name

Surname

Mobile No.

PPSN — If tenant has no PPSN or you have made a reasonable effort to obtain it but it has not been provided, place X in the box

Section 5 - Details of the Landlord's Authorised Agent (See Note 5)

If you wish to enter a company name, please do so using the First Name and Surname fields.

25. Landlord Authorised Agent   Individual ☐   Company ☐

First Name

Surname

PPSN
(if Individual)   **CRO Reg. No.**
                                                 (if Company)

Address

County

Eircode   (Please ensure to include Eircode)

Country

Telephone No.

Licence No.

If you wish to opt out of receiving tenancy information from the RTB by email, please insert X in the box ☐

Section 6 - Management Company (See Note 6)

THIS SECTION IS ONLY FOR USE WHERE THE RENTED DWELLING IS AN APARTMENT IN AN APARTMENT COMPLEX

26. Apartment Blocks / Complexes Only

Name

Address

County

Eircode   (Please ensure to include Eircode)

Country

Telephone No.

CRO Reg. No.

Section 7 - Declaration of Undertaking for Deduction for Interest on Borrowings

To register an undertaking by a landlord to make a dwelling available for a period of three years to a tenant in receipt of rent supplement, or to a tenant whose rent is payable by a local authority, in order that the landlord may apply to the Revenue Commissioners, after the end of the three year period, for a 100% rather than a 75% deduction for interest on borrowings under Section 97(2K) Taxes Consolidation Act 1997.

I [INSERT NAME] _____ undertake to make, or continue to make, the dwelling the subject of the above registered tenancy available under a qualifying lease for a period of three years commencing on [DD/MM/YYYY] _____/_____/_____ to a qualifying tenant in order to qualify for 100% interest relief as provided for in Section 97(2K) Taxes Consolidation Act 1997.

Signature:

Date:

Section 8 - Declaration by Applicant (See Note 8)

Please note that it is an offence to knowingly or recklessly furnish false or misleading information in a material respect when submitting an application to register a tenancy or submitting updated information in respect of a registered tenancy.

If found guilty, a person shall be liable on summary conviction to a fine of up to €4,000 or a term of imprisonment of up to six months or both.

Before submitting this form, please ensure you have read the notes on page 8 of this form.

Please proceed to Section 9 for payment.

I declare that, to the best of my knowledge and belief, all the information I have given on this form is correct.

Applicant Signature

Date

Registration Data collected by the Residential Tenancies Board (RTB) will be used in accordance with the provisions of the Residential Tenancies Act 2004 and any other relevant legislation and for statistical and policy research purposes.

The RTB will treat all information and personal data you supply as confidential. However, it should be noted that information may be exchanged with various Government Bodies as set out in Section 146 of the Residential Tenancies Act 2004.

Please keep a copy of the form as submitted & proof of postage to the RTB for your own records.

Please return this RTB registration form with fee by post to -

Residential Tenancies Board,
Registration Section,
PO Box 47,
Clonakilty,
Co. Cork.

TENANCY REGISTRATION FORM RTB1

	Type of Application	Fee
Standard Fee	Application received by RTB within one month of tenancy commencement date	€90
Late Fee (1)	Application received by RTB more than one month after tenancy commencement date where the tenancy commenced on or after 01/01/2011	€180
Late Fee (2)	Application received by the RTB more than one month after the tenancy commencement date where the tenancy commencement date was before 01/01/2011	€140
Composite Fee	A reduced fee subject to a **maximum of 10 Tenancies** in one building being registered by the same Landlord at same time and all received by the RTB within one month of the earliest tenancy commencement date	€375
3rd Registration or subsequent in a 12 month period	Where in respect of the same dwelling, a change of tenancy occurs within a 12 month period a maximum of two registration fees apply. 3rd and subsequent no fee applies providing they are received on time	No Fee

Payment Type

Please indicate the method of payment you wish to use

Credit Card ☐   Debit Card ☐   Cheque ☐   Postal Order ☐   Bank Draft ☐

If you have selected Credit Card or Debit Card above complete mandate below, otherwise attach payment to this form.

MANDATE

Cardholder

Address

County

Eircode   (Please ensure to include Eircode)

Mobile No.

Card No.

Expiry Date ☐☐ / ☐☐ (M M / Y Y)

CVV/CVS ☐☐☐ (last 3 numbers on the back of card)

Please debit my account by € ☐☐☐☐☐

Cardholder Signature

Date ☐☐ / ☐☐ / ☐☐☐☐

Please note that all fields must be completed in order to submit a valid application for the registration of a tenancy. An incomplete application cannot be processed through to registration.

Note 1 (Section 1 – Application Type)

There are two options for the application type:

(1) A "New' Tenancy registration means a new tenancy with new tenants has commenced.

(2) A "Renewal" (Further Part 4 Tenancy) refers to a tenancy that has existed for four years (or longer). When a tenancy has been in existence for four years (i.e. same tenants remain) it must be re-registered with the RTB. Tenancies which commenced prior to 24 December 2016 can last for a maximum of four years before having to be renewed (re-registered) with the RTB. Tenancies which commenced on or after 24 December 2016 can last for a maximum of six years before having to be renewed (re-registered) with the RTB.

The tenancy commencement date for a "Renewal" registration is the expiry of a four year period. For example: the commencement date for a renewal where the original tenancy began on the 1 May 2013 will be the 1 May 2017. If you are registering a Renewal tenancy please indicate the previous RT number. You can locate this number on the confirmation letter that would have issued to you by the RTB when the tenancy was originally registered. If you are unable to locate the number you can contact RTB on 0818 30 30 37.

Each application to register a tenancy must be completed on a separate form. If more than one tenancy is included on a single form it will be an incomplete application and cannot be processed through to registration. This will result in a delay in the processing of your application.

Note 2 (Section 2 - Details of the Rented Dwelling)

The full address of the rented dwelling must be given. If the rented dwelling is an Apartment or Flat then the Apartment number or Flat number must be given.

Only complete question 5 (Property Type) if Dwelling Type selected at question 4 is House, Part of House or Maisonette.

Number of bedrooms must be provided; this is not the same as number of bed spaces.

Note 3 (Section 3 – Details of Tenancy)

If the tenancy is for a fixed term, the length of that term must be provided.

Tenancy commencement date **must** be provided. Your registration fee will be calculated on the basis of this date, make sure the full date is given, e.g. DAY/MONTH/YEAR. From the 15 July 2009 please note that the definition of "tenancy" under the Residential Tenancies Act 2004 does not include a tenancy the term of which is more than 35 years.

The tenancy commencement date depends on the circumstances of each individual tenancy. For example, if there is a written lease/tenancy agreement the tenancy commencement date will usually be clearly stated within the lease/tenancy agreement. However, it may also be the date on which it is agreed verbally that the tenant:

- is entitled to take up occupation of the dwelling in question

or

- actually takes up occupation of the dwelling.

Please note there does not have to be a written lease/tenancy agreement in place for the tenancy to be registered with the RTB.

If a sub-tenancy is being registered you must tick the box to indicate this.

Rental Amount must be completed. This amount must be the total amount received by the landlord each week/month/year.

All charges paid by the tenant must be ticked in boxes provided. If not specified then other charges box must be ticked and these listed in space provided.

The Local Authority area in which the rented dwelling is situated must be provided. Please see www.rtb.ie if you require a list of the local authorities.

Note 4A (Section 4A – Landlord Details)

Please note that the address provided here is the address which will be used for correspondence purposes by the RTB in respect of this registration.

Landlord's Personal Public Service Number (PPSN) **must** be provided if the landlord has a PPSN. A PPSN is unique to each individual. It is used to distinguish between individuals with similar names or addresses. The PPSN is usually identified on tax certificates and welfare statements. If you do not have a PPSN please contact your local Department of Social Protection office. Use of the PPSN is governed by law. The PPSN Code of Practice is available from the Department of Social Protection and on their website www.welfare.ie

If a landlord is a company then the registered number of that company (CRO) must be provided.

Please include the details of any additional landlords. Please note that the address of the landlord given on this form will be used by the RTB for corresponding with the landlord in relation to this tenancy.

Note 4B (Section 4B – Tenants)

Please use Section 4B of this form to list all tenants in the rented dwelling. Minors (persons under the age of 18) are not required to be registered.

The PPSN of the tenant(s) should be provided. If tenant(s) has no PPSN or you have made a reasonable effort to obtain it but it has not been provided please tick space provided. Please note that the tenant's PPSN is required in the event of a subsequent dispute between the landlord and tenant. If a landlord does not have a correspondence address for a former tenant, it may be possible in limited circumstances for the RTB to trace the tenant, using their PPSN, to serve dispute case papers on them.

Note 5 (Section 5 – Details of the Landlord's Authorised Agent)

Give the details of the person/company who is authorised to act on behalf of the landlord in relation to the tenancy of the rented dwelling.

Note 6 (Section 6 – Management Company)

Only complete this section if the dwelling is an apartment in an apartment complex under the operation of a management company.

Note 7 (Section 7 - Declaration of Undertaking)

Complete this section if you are entitled to and wish to avail of a 100% deduction of interest on borrowings for tax purposes.

Note 8 (Section 8 - Declaration)

In this part you confirm that all information provided is true and accurate to the best of your knowledge.

Note 9 (Section 9 – Fees & Payment Details)

Ensure that you have included the correct fee. There are no exceptions to the late fee. Since the Residential Tenancies Act 2004 prescribes that a late fee shall apply the RTB has no discretion to waive the late fee regardless of the reasons or circumstances for the delay.

Fees paid by cheque, postal order or bank draft should be made payable to the RTB. The cheque should be crossed. You may pay by credit/debit card by completing the mandate in Section 8. If more than one application is submitted in the same envelope, credit/debit card details for each application must be completed. For security reasons, the RTB is unable to accept cash as payment for fees.

The fees set out in the table in Section 8 are the current fees at the time of printing. As fees could be subject to change in the future, you are advised to check up-to-date fees payable at the time of registration the tenancy. Details are available at www.rtb.ie

APPENDIX 2

APPROVED HOUSING BODIES TENANCY REGISTRATION FORM RTB2

Approved Housing Bodies Tenancy Registration Application Form RTB2

Important:

To ensure a more satisfactory customer experience, please take care to **complete the form in full and correctly**. Ensure to include the correct payment. Incomplete forms may lead to multiple communications from the RTB. Details of the fees are on page 6 and guidance notes are on page 8 of the form.

Section 1 - Details of the Rented Dwelling (See Note 1)

1. Address of Rented Dwelling

   Apt./House No.

   Address Line 1

   Address Line 2

   Address Line 3

   Address Line 4

   County

   Eircode ____ _____ (Please ensure to include Eircode)

2. Dwelling Type

   House ☐   Apartment ☐   Flat ☐   Part of House ☐   Maisonette ☐   Bedsit ☐

3. Property Type (if the Dwelling Type selected above is House, Part of House or Maisonette, place an X in the relevant box below to indicate the Property Type)

   Semi Detached ☐   Detached House ☐   Terraced ☐

4. No. of Bedrooms

5. No. of Occupants

6. BER Rating (if any)

7. Local Authority in which rented dwelling is located

APPROVED HOUSING BODIES TENANCY REGISTRATION FORM RTB2

Section 2 - Details of Tenancy (See Note 2)

8. If the tenancy is for a fixed term, please indicate the duration of the term   Years ☐☐   Months ☐☐

9. Tenancy commencement date   ☐☐ / ☐☐ / ☐☐☐☐

10. Rental Amount   € ☐☐☐☐☐ . ☐☐

11. Deposit Amount   € ☐☐☐☐☐ . ☐☐

12. Frequency of Payment   Weekly ☐   Monthly ☐   Annually ☐

13. Charges (incurred by tenant)

Electricity ☐   Oil ☐   TV Licence ☐   Waste ☐   Gas ☐   Other ☐

Details of "Other" charges ☐☐☐☐☐☐☐☐☐☐☐☐☐☐☐☐☐☐☐☐☐☐☐☐☐☐☐☐☐☐☐☐☐

☐☐☐☐☐☐☐☐☐☐☐☐☐☐☐☐☐☐☐☐☐☐☐☐☐☐☐☐☐☐☐☐☐

Section 3A - Landlord Details (See Note 3A)

14. **Landlord** - Name and Contact Details

AHB Name

AHB Ref. No. ☐☐☐☐☐☐☐☐   CRO Reg. No. ☐☐☐☐☐☐☐☐☐

AHB Ref. Number as provided by RTB   CRO must be provided if applicable

Address

County

Eircode ☐☐☐   ☐☐☐☐   (Please ensure to include Eircode)

Country

Telephone No.

Mobile No.

Email

If you wish to opt out of receiving tenancy information from the RTB by email, please insert X in the box ☐

287

APPROVED HOUSING BODIES TENANCY REGISTRATION FORM RTB2

Section 3B - Tenants (See Note 3B)

15. Tenant

First Name

Surname

Mobile No.

PPSN — If tenant has no PPSN or you have made a reasonable effort to obtain it but it has not been provided, place X in the box

16. Tenant

First Name

Surname

Mobile No.

PPSN — If tenant has no PPSN or you have made a reasonable effort to obtain it but it has not been provided, place X in the box

17. Tenant

First Name

Surname

Mobile No.

PPSN — If tenant has no PPSN or you have made a reasonable effort to obtain it but it has not been provided, place X in the box

18. Tenant

First Name

Surname

Mobile No.

PPSN — If tenant has no PPSN or you have made a reasonable effort to obtain it but it has not been provided, place X in the box

19. Tenant

First Name

Surname

Mobile No.

PPSN — If tenant has no PPSN or you have made a reasonable effort to obtain it but it has not been provided, place X in the box

Section 4 - Details of the Landlord's Authorised Agent (See Note 4)

20. **Landlord Authorised Agent**   Individual ☐   Company ☐

First Name

Surname

PPSN   CRO Reg. No.

Address

County

Eircode   (Please ensure to include Eircode)

Country

Telephone No.

Licence No.

Section 5 - Management Company (See Note 5)

THIS SECTION IS ONLY FOR USE WHERE THE RENTED DWELLING IS AN APARTMENT IN AN APARTMENT COMPLEX

21. **Apartment Blocks / Complexes Only**

Name

Address

County

Eircode   (Please ensure to include Eircode)

Country

Telephone No.

CRO Reg. No.

Section 6 - Declaration by Applicant (See Note 6)

Please note that it is an offence to knowingly or recklessly furnish false or misleading information in a material respect when submitting an application to register a tenancy or submitting updated information in respect of a registered tenancy.

If found guilty, a person shall be liable on summary conviction to a fine of up to €4,000 or a term of imprisonment of up to six months or both.

Before submitting this form, please ensure you have read the notes on page 8 of this form.

Please proceed to Section 7B for payment.

I declare that, to the best of my knowledge and belief, all the information I have given on this form is correct.

Applicant's Signature

Date ☐☐ / ☐☐ / ☐☐☐☐

Registration Data collected by the Residential Tenancies Board (RTB) will be used in accordance with the provisions of the Residential Tenancies Act 2004 and any other relevant legislation and for statistical and policy research purposes.

The RTB will treat all information and personal data you supply as confidential. However, it should be noted that information may be exchanged with various Government Bodies as set out in Section 146 of the Residential Tenancies Act 2004.

Please keep a copy of the form as submitted & proof of postage to the RTB for your own records.

Please return this RTB registration form with fee by post to -

Residential Tenancies Board,
Registration Section,
PO Box 47,
Clonakilty,
Co. Cork.

Type of Application		Fee
Standard Fee	Application received by the RTB **within one month** of the Tenancy Commencement Date	€90
Late Fee	Application received by the RTB **more than one month** after the Tenancy Commencement Date	€20 per month or part thereof to a max. penalty of €240 + €90. Total of €330
Composite Fee	A reduced fee subject to a maximum of 10 Tenancies in one building being registered by the same Landlord at the same time and all received by the RTB within one month of the earliest Tenancy Commencement Date	€375
3rd Registration or Subsequent in a 12 month period	No fee applies to the 3rd and subsequent registration in a 12 month period in respect of the same dwelling, providing they are received within one month of the Tenancy Commencement Date of the new tenancy	No Fee

Section 7B - Payment Details (See Note 7B)

Payment Type - please indicate the method of payment you wish to use

Credit Card ☐   Debit Card ☐   Cheque ☐   Postal Order ☐   Bank Draft ☐

If you have selected Credit Card or Debit Card above complete mandate below, otherwise attach payment to this form

MANDATE

Cardholder

Address

County

Eircode   (Please ensure to include Eircode)

Mobile No.

Card No.

Expiry Date   ☐☐ / ☐☐   (M M / Y Y)

CVV/CVS   ☐☐☐   (last three numbers on the back of card)

Please debit my account by € ☐☐☐☐☐

Cardholder Signature

Date   ☐☐ / ☐☐ / ☐☐☐☐

APPROVED HOUSING BODIES TENANCY REGISTRATION FORM RTB2

Please note that all fields must be completed in order to submit a valid application for the registration of a tenancy. An incomplete application cannot be processed through to registration.

Note 1 (Section 1 – Details of the Rented Dwelling)

The full address of the rented dwelling must be given. If the rented dwelling is an Apartment or Flat then the Apartment number or Flat number must be given.

Only complete question 3 (Property Type) if Dwelling Type selected at question 2 is House, Part of House or Maisonette.

Number of bedrooms must be provided.

Note 2 (Section 2 – Details of Tenancy)

If the tenancy is for a fixed term, the length of that term must be provided. If the tenancy has no fixed term, please leave the years/ months option blank.

Any Approved Housing Body (AHB) Tenancies in existence prior to the Commencement order date of the legislation which was the 6 April 2016 should be given a "Tenancy Commencement Date" of 6 April 2016. From the 15 July 2009 please note that the definition of a "tenancy" under the Residential Tenancies Act 2004 does not include a tenancy the term of which is more than 35 years.

For AHB Tenancies that commenced after the 6 April 2017, the tenancy commencement date depends on the circumstances of each individual tenancy. For example, if there is a written lease/tenancy agreement the tenancy commencement date will usually be clearly stated within the lease/tenancy agreement. However, it may also be the date on which it was agreed verbally that the tenant:
 -is entitled to take up occupation of the dwelling in question
 or
 -actually takes up occupation of the dwelling.

Please note there does not have to be a written lease/tenancy agreement in place for the tenancy to be registered with the RTB.

Rental amount must be completed. This amount must be the total amount received by the landlord each week/month/year.

Tenancies which commenced prior to 24 December 2016 can last for a maximum of four years before having to be renewed (re-registered) with the RTB. Tenancies which commenced on or after 24 December 2016 can last for a maximum of six years before having to be renewed (re-registered) with the RTB.

All charges paid by the tenant must be ticked in the boxes provided. If the charge is not specified then list the charge in the space provided titled "Other Charges".

The Local Authority area in which the rented dwelling is situated must be provided. Please see www.rtb.ie if you require a list of the local authorities.

Note 3A (Section 3A – Landlord Details)

AHB Name must be provided. This name must be the same name which was supplied to the Department of Environment, Community and Local Government (now known as Department of Housing, Planning, Community & Local Government) when seeking approved housing body approval.

Please note that the address provided here should be the address which you have supplied to the Department of Environment, Community and Local Government when seeking approved housing body approval. If your address has changed since then you may enter your new correspondence address. You may be asked to verify this address at some point.

You must also enter your unique AHB Reference number as provided by the RTB. If you have mislaid this number please contact the RTB at 0818 30 30 37 to obtain same.

If you are a company, then the registered number of that company (CRO) must be provided.

Note 3B (Section 3B – Tenants)

Please use Section 3B. of this form to list all tenants in the rented dwelling. Minors (persons under the age of 18) are not required to be registered.

The PPSN of the tenant(s) should be provided. If tenant(s) has no PPSN or you have made a reasonable effort to obtain it but it has not been provided please tick space provided. Please note that the tenant's PPSN is required in the event of a subsequent dispute between the landlord and tenant. If a landlord does not have a correspondence address for a former tenant, it may be possible in limited circumstances for the RTB to trace the tenant, using their PPSN, to serve dispute case papers on them.

Note 4 (Section 4 – Details of the Landlord's Authorised Agent)

Give the details of the person/company who is authorised to act on behalf of the landlord in relation to the tenancy of the rented dwelling.

Note 5 (Section 5 – Management Company)

Only complete this section if the dwelling is an apartment in an apartment complex under the operation of a management company.

Note 6 (Section 6 – Declaration)

In this part you confirm that all information is true and accurate.

Note 7A (Section 7A – Fees)

The fees set out in the table in Section 7A are the current fees at the time of printing. There are no exceptions to the late fee. Since Residential Tenancies Act 2004 prescribes that a late fee shall apply the RTB has no discretion to waive the late fee regardless of the reasons or circumstances for the delay.

Note 7B (Section 7B – Payment Details)

Ensure that you have included the correct fee as an incorrect fee will cause a delay in processing your application. Fees paid by cheque, postal order or bank draft should be made payable to the RTB. The cheque should be crossed. You may pay by credit / debit card by completing the mandate in Section 7B. If more than one application is submitted in the same envelope, credit/debit card details for each application must be completed. For security reasons, the RTB is unable to accept cash as payment for fees

Page 8

APPENDIX 3

NOTES ON SERVICE CHARGE CLAUSES IN COMMERCIAL LEASES

These notes were produced by a working party of the Republic of Ireland Branch of The Royal Institution of Chartered Surveyors and the Incorporated Law Society, and are intended for the guidance of surveyors and solicitors concerned with the leasing of commercial property.

Some of the practical problems encountered in this relatively new field are discussed and a checklist of services appropriate to each type of property has been prepared. This is intended only as a guideline, and as circumstances are likely to vary from case to case careful consideration should be given to the particular items to be included in each lease.

INTRODUCTION

Group occupation, whether it be in an industrial estate, an office block or a shopping centre, presupposes communal services. These services are provided by the landlord and charged back to the tenants on an apportionment which is usually based on area occupied.

The need for service charges springs from group occupation of single buildings which due to modern construction techniques tend to be larger and more complicated than heretofore. Buildings in single occupation do not normally require service charge clauses as the tenant or occupier provides his own services at his own direct cost.

The charge is on a non-profit basis providing a pool of money out of which the manager pays for heating, cleaning, wages etc. reimbursing any surplus or recouping any deficit at each year end. At this point we would emphasize the distinction between the rent in respect of the premises and the service charge in respect of the services provided by the landlord, in that no element of the premises rent is attributable to the cost of providing such services. Each service charge clause must be carefully drawn having regard to the circumstances pertaining to the particular building and in relation to other lettings, e.g. joint fire-escapes etc.

GENERAL

It is usual for service charges to be estimated for the first year of operation with each tenant paying quarterly in advance. Thereafter each year is based on the foregoing with each year's differential (if any) being collected in a lump sum at the end of the year.

On the whole leases have followed this pattern, itemising services to be charged and usually drawing a wide general over-rider in case any service has been omitted from the detailed list.

NOTES ON SERVICE CHARGE CLAUSES IN COMMERCIAL LEASES

We set out below some considerations which we as a profession would like to become standard. In addition we list a representation of the services which may be required by the different types of property.

1. When setting out the proportion of service charge payable, such proportion should be quantified either as a fraction or as a percentage and not left open for negotiation. Do allow for flexibility over the years particularly in phased developments.

2. A realistic estimate for the first year's costs having been obtained, this figure should be apportioned on the basis in (1) above and provision made either to hand back any surplus at the end of the year or alternatively, to collect any shortfall.

3. It is important in the event of a partial letting only to spell out who bears the percentage of service to be levied on the voids. This has often fallen to the landlord, but if, for example, only the occupied floors were being heated there might be a case where all the heating charge should be borne by the occupiers.

4. In times of inflation it can be seen from the method of collection outlined above that the landlord basing his advance contributions on the previous year's expenditure is short a considerable sum by the year end. A provision therefore to add a percentage to the previous year's figures in an effort to maintain parity is only prudent.

5. Service charges do not include housekeeping services within the demise, nor rates nor insurances.

6. Sinking Fund—the creation of a fund for future capital expenditure is frequently included. For further details see Appendix A.

7. A clause should be incorporated referring to the auditing of accounts and should in our view specify that an accountant be used but no time limit should be stated for the provision of account, or time should not be of the essence, as such time limit can be exceeded causing more problems.

8. In any development there should be no onus on the landlord to provide the services in the event of strikes, shortage of supplies etc; the landlord should, of course, use his best endeavours to obtain supplies.

SERVICE CHARGE COMPONENTS

(1) Office Blocks

A. Central heating or air-conditioning to a statutory level between 15 October and 15 May and at other times as deemed necessary, including the provision of fuel, maintenance, repair, replacement, supervision of the central heating, plant and installation and purchase of spare parts.

B. Cleaning of the common parts including cost of labour and materials if necessary by a firm on contract.

C. Supply of electricity to the common parts including light, power, motive power and water heating, also replacement and repair of bulbs, fittings etc.

D. Cleaning of glass on both sides in the common parts including entrance doors, windows and glass partitions and all fixed external glass as often as considered necessary.

E. Supply of hot and cold water and drinking water to lavatory accommodation, tea stations and drinking fountains.

F. Supply and maintenance of fire-fighting equipment including extinguishers, dry risers, hose reels and sprinklers and maintenance of fire exits, signs and an alarm system.

G. Cost of fitting and maintaining internal telephone or Tannoy system, porter's telephone and house telephone.

H. Operation and upkeep and replacement of lift service, lift plant and equipment including electricity and maintenance contract, and purchase of spare parts (if any).

I. Maintenance and installation of emergency lights.

J. Insurance of central heating/air-conditioning plant, lift plant and mechanical equipment generally.

K. Repair, maintenance and decoration of interior and exterior of building, including where necessary the replacement or renewal of a section.

L. Removal of refuse.

M. Wages, uniform, insurance and pension premium for commissionaires and/or porters, car park attendants and all such service staff and including rent and rates for a flat in the building occupied by a resident caretaker if any.

N. Reasonable professional fees for the management of the building by whomsoever carried out.

O. Provision of internal and external shrubs and flowers and maintenance thereof.

P. Reasonable accountants' fees incurred in the auditing of service charge figures.

Q. Provision and maintenance of sanitary towel disposal systems within the women's toilet accommodation.

S. Provision of working clothes, tools and appliances and other equipment to porter staff.

T. Rates, if levied on the common areas.

U. Provision and maintenance of such security arrangements as shall be considered necessary by the lessor including guards, alarms and mechanical services as are agreed.

V. VAT on fees or service provided in the course of management of the building.

W. Provision of all such further or other services or amenities as the lessor shall consider ought properly and reasonably be provided for.

(2) Shopping Centres

Some provision should be made in the service charge (or elsewhere in the lease) for the collection of promotional moneys for the centre.

(2–1) Covered Shopping Centres

A. Central heating, air-conditioning or mechanical ventilation including the provision of fuel, maintenance, repair, replacement, supervision of the central heating plant and installation and purchase of spare parts.

B. Cleaning of the common parts including cost of labour and materials if necessary by a firm on contract.

C. Supply of electricity to the common parts including light, power, motive power and water heating, also replacement and repair of bulbs, fittings etc.

D. Cleaning of general glass throughout the shopping centre including shop fronts if any.

E. Supply of hot and cold water to lavatory accommodation (if any).

F. Supply and maintenance of fire-fighting equipment including extinguishers, dry risers, hose reels and sprinklers and maintenance of fire exits, signs and an alarm system.

G. Cost of fitting and maintaining internal telephone system, Tannoy, piped music and close circuit television.

H. Operation and upkeep and replacement of lift/escalator service, lift plant and equipment including electricity and maintenance contract, and purchase of spare parts (if any).

I. Maintenance and installation of emergency lights.

J. Insurance of central heating/air-conditioning plant, lift and escalator plant and mechanical equipment generally.

K. Repair, maintenance and decoration of interior and exterior of building, including where necessary the replacement or renewal of a section.

L. Removal of refuse and the cost of any equipment for treating or packaging of same.

M. Wages, uniform, insurance and pension premium for centre manager, commissionaires and/or porters, car park attendants and all such service staff and including rent and rates for a flat in the building occupied by a resident caretaker if any.

N. Reasonable professional fees for the management of the building by whomsoever carried out.

O. Provision of internal and external shrubs and flowers and maintenance thereof.

P. Reasonable accountants' fees incurred in the auditing of the service charge figures.

Q. Provision of towels, soap, deodorisers etc. in the toilet accommodation (if any).

R. Provision and maintenance of sanitary towel disposal system within the women's toilet accommodation.

S. Provision of working clothes, tools and appliances and other equipment to porter staff.

T. Rates, if levied on the common areas.

U. Provision and maintenance of such security arrangements as shall be considered necessary by the lessor including guards, alarms and mechanical services as are agreed.

V. VAT on fees or services provided in the course of management of the building.

W. Providing traffic control to and from within the centre including the maintaining and replacing of signs and signals and other equipment.

X. Maintenance and repair and cleaning of service area, access roads and perimeter walls and where necessary rebuilding or renewal.

Y. Provision of all such further or other services or amenities as the lessor shall consider ought properly and reasonably be provided for.

(2–2) Uncovered Shopping Centres

A. Cleaning of the common parts including cost of labour and materials if necessary by a firm on contract.

B. Supply of electricity to the common parts including light, power and water heating, also replacement and repairs of bulbs, fittings, etc.

C. Cleaning of glass within the centre including shop fronts.

D. Supply of hot and cold water and drinking water to lavatory accommodation.

E. Repair, maintenance and decoration of exterior of building, including where necessary the replacement or renewal of a section and also including downpipes, drains etc.

F.   Removal of refuse and the cost of any equipment for treating or packaging of same.

G.   Wages, uniform, insurance and pension premium for centre manager, commissionaires and/or porters, car park attendants and all such service staff and including rent and rates for a flat in the building occupied by a resident caretaker if any.

H.   Reasonable professional fees for the management of the building by whomsoever carried out.

I.   Provision of external shrubs and flowers and maintenance thereof.

J.   Reasonable accountants' fees incurred in the auditing of the service charge figures.

K.   Provision of towels, soap, deodorisers etc. in the toilet accommodation (if any).

L.   Provision and maintenance of sanitary towel disposal system within the women's toilet accommodation.

M.   Provision of working clothes, tools and appliances and other equipment to porter staff.

N.   Rates if levied on the common areas.

O.   Provision and maintenance of such security arrangements as shall be considered necessary by the lessor including guards, alarms and mechanical services as are agreed.

P.   VAT on fees or service provided in the course of management of the building.

Q.   Maintaining and repair and cleaning of service area access roads and perimeter walls and where necessary to rebuild or renew.

R.   Providing traffic control to and from within the centre including the maintaining and replacing of signs and signals and other equipment.

S.   Provision of all such further or other services or amenities as the lessor shall consider ought properly and reasonably be provided for.

(3)   Industrial Estates

A.   Provision of fuel to central oil tank and maintenance, repair and replacement of oil tank and pipes.

B.   Cleaning of the common parts including cost of labour and materials if necessary by a firm on contract.

C.   Supply of electricity to the common parts including light and power, also replacement and repair of bulbs, fittings etc.

D.   Insurance of heating plant.

E.   Repair, maintenance and decoration of exterior of building, including where necessary the replacement or renewal of a section.

F.   Removal of refuse.

G.   Wages, uniform, insurance and pension premium for commissionaires and/or porters, car park attendants and all such service staff.

H.   Reasonable professional fees for the management of the building by whomsoever carried out.

I.   Provision of internal and external shrubs and flowers and maintenance thereof.

J.   Reasonable accountants' fees incurred in the auditing of the service charge figures.

K. Provision of work clothes, tools and appliances and other equipment to porter staff.

L. Rates if levied on the common areas.

M. Provision and maintenance of such security arrangements as shall be considered necessary by the lessor including guards, alarms and mechanical services as are agreed.

N. Maintenance and repair and cleaning of the service area, access roads and perimeter walls and where necessary to build or renew.

O. Providing traffic control to and from within the centre including the maintaining and replacing of signs and signals and other equipment.

P. VAT on fees or services provided in the course of management of the building.

Q. Provision of all such further or other services or amenities as the lessor shall consider ought properly and reasonably be provided for.

APPENDIX A

Sinking Fund

A major source of discussion is the construction of the sinking fund clause. At present, where included, this sub-clause is frequently drawn in very general terms leaving its implementation totally in the hands of the lessor.

1. It is our view that if such a fund is to be set up the following should be itemised:

    (a) The exact nature of the equipment for which the fund is to be used, for example, in the Plant account the boilers, fans, cooling tower, compressor, refrigeration machine but NOT the ducting or the electric wiring.

    (b) The exact cost of this equipment at installation.

    (c) An estimate of the plant's life.

    (d) A provision for updating the replacement cost say, every five years.

    (e) How the fund is to be administered, i.e. where it is to be invested, how the annual calculations as to contributions are to be made, whether the fund is to be in the joint names of landlord and tenants.

    (f) In what circumstances may the fund be drawn on.

2. It is our view that with the increase in the rate of inflation the administration and collection of such a fund is onerous on landlord and tenant alike.

3. As items of plant are insurable and as the tenant is responsible for replacement and repair it is recommended that a sinking fund contribution be omitted, but if this is so, the repairing covenant must be reinforced to include replacement of items of plant etc. either directly or through the service charge.

Short-term Reserve Fund

Fund Provision may be made for a short-term reserve fund for the completion of ongoing repetitive maintenance works like painting on a three-yearly or five-yearly basis.

Published by the Incorporated Law Society of Ireland/Royal Institution of Chartered Surveyors (Republic of Ireland branch) 1981.

STANDARD RENT REVIEW CLAUSES

> These rent review clauses should be read in light of the provisions of s 132 of the Land and Conveyancing Law Reform Act, 2009 for leases entered into after the 28 February 2010. Relevant case law should also be consulted. See 12.3 for a detailed explanation.

EXPLANATORY MEMORANDUM

Some twelve years ago, standard forms of rent review clauses were produced by a joint working party established by the Incorporated Law Society of Ireland and the Society of Chartered Surveyors. Generally speaking, these clauses have operated very well over that period. However, in order to broaden the scope of the rent review clauses and to bring them up to date taking into account current market forces, a wider working party of members of the Law Society, the Irish Auctioneers and Valuers Institute and the Society of Chartered Surveyors assembled to produce updated versions of rent review clauses which are set out herein. The explanatory memorandum from March, 1981 is set out hereunder as a reminder of various considerations to be borne in mind when using these clauses. The following additions should likewise be noted:

1. Prior to publication of these clauses, the Society of Chartered Surveyors expressed a wish to be disassociated from these on the basis that they would not accept that anyone other than the Chairman of that Society could act in the nomination of either an arbitrator or an expert. The clauses provide that in the first instance the landlord, in the event of a dispute over settlement of rent, may apply to the President of the Law Society, the President of the IAVI, or the Chairman of the Society of Chartered Surveyors to nominate the arbitrator or the expert. The choice is the landlord's. This point appears to have been overlooked in a recent newspaper article when the reservations of the chartered surveyors were expressed. There is a general trend against anti-competitive arrangements and the Law Society feels that these clauses are in line with such trends and, accordingly, strongly encourages their use when drafting commercial leases.

2. In the former rent review clauses, the assumed term of a hypothetical lease when assessing a rent at rent review dates was 35 years whatever the actual residue of the term of the subject lease would be. It was felt that this could possibly lead to a distortion in the assessment of rent when the residue of the actual term was greatly reduced, and, as a compromise, it has been provided that the assumed term should be the actual residue or 15 years, whichever is the greater.

3.   When disregarding works carried out by the tenant, save those works (required works) carried out by the tenant pursuant to an obligation imposed on the tenant by the subject lease or any agreement for such lease, excluded from such 'required works' are works which the tenant may be obliged to carry out of a statutory nature e.g. works subsequently required to be carried out by the Fire Officer, and it is important to note that the relevant clause number must be inserted Paragraph 1 (D) (c) when preparing the lease.

4.   Some other small administrative amendments have also been added so as to avoid any problems of implementation of the rent review procedures and reference in particular is made to paragraph 4 of the 'Arbitration' clause and paragraph 3 (v) of the 'Expert' clause.

Conveyancing Committee
Incorporated Law Society of Ireland
March, 1993.

EXPLANATORY MEMORANDUM, 1981 REVISED RENT REVIEW CLAUSES

1.   These rent review provisions are the product of a joint working committee established by the Society and the Republic of Ireland Branch of the Royal Institute of Chartered Surveyors. The task was beset with all the normal difficulties encountered in the preparation of standard documentation and members are urged to bear in mind that the provisions now submitted are in general terms and may need to be amended to suit special cases.

2.   After detailed consideration, the working party has decided not to make any recommendation as to a preference between (a) arbitration or (b) determination by an expert in the event of the parties failing to agree on a revised rent. Under ordinary conditions, the question is very much open to choice and alternative sets of provisions are accordingly published. The circumstances of each case should be examined in conjunction with the texts of the drafts before deciding whether to adopt or perhaps adapt either of the standard provisions.

3.   It will be noted that the working party has deliberately omitted, for the most part, formalities as to time limits and notices. The provisions have been so worded as to reflect market conditions prevailing at the commencement of each review period.

4.   The bulk of the provisions has been arranged to comprise a separate schedule to the subject lease.

5.   The wording of the provision covering the appointment of the arbitrator or expert (as the case may be) is regrettably very detailed. It should be borne in mind, however, that the provision is one which may well have to be operated in 30 years time, if not longer, and an effort was made to try to ensure that an appropriate appointor would at all times be available.

6.   Considerable difficulty was experienced in dealing with matters which might have an effect upon rent and which could, in certain circumstances, fairly be disregarded for review purposes. In this connection particular attention is drawn to the question of works executed by the lessee to the demised premises. Members will be aware that some recently decided cases have evidenced some serious inequities in this area. The draft endeavours to cater for the situation but before adopting the draft the circumstances of each case should be carefully considered. Where it is intended that the review should reflect the state and condition of the premises as demised in the first instance, and indeed in other instances where the facts so

warrant, it is suggested that the lease could embrace an additional schedule containing descriptive particulars of the subject property.

7. The working committee has no doubt that future developments in the law and practice will render changes in the draft necessary. It is felt by both institutions, however, that a standard form will be of great assistance to both professions in their day to day work.

March, 1981

STANDARD RENT REVIEW CLAUSES

ARBITRATOR

... TO HOLD the same UNTO the tenant for the term of   years commencing on the   day of   20   YIELDING AND PAYING therefor and thereout during each of the first   years of the said term the yearly rent of £   and thereafter during each of the successive periods of   years of which the first shall begin on the   day of   20   a yearly rent equal to (a) the yearly rent payable hereunder during the preceding period or (b) such revised yearly rent as may from time to time be ascertained in accordance with the provisions in that behalf contained in the   schedule hereto (whichever shall be the greater) AND the rent in respect of each year of the said term is to be paid by ...

SCHEDULE

(Provisions as to Rent Revisions)

1. The revised rent referred to in the within lease in respect of any of the periods therein mentioned may be agreed at any time between the landlord and the tenant or (in the absence of agreement) be determined not earlier than the date of commencement of such period ('the review date') by an arbitrator to be nominated (in the absence of agreement between the parties) upon the application (made not more than two calendar months before or at any time after the review date) of the landlord (or if the landlord fails to make such application, within twenty-eight days of being requested in writing so to do by the tenant then on the application of the tenant) by either the President of the Incorporated Law Society of Ireland or the President of the Irish Auctioneers and Valuers Institute or the Chairman of the Society of Chartered Surveyors in the Republic of Ireland at the discretion of the party entitled to make the application.

and

the revised rent so to be determined by the arbitrator shall be such as in his opinion represents at the review date the full open market yearly rent for the demised premises let as a whole without fine or premium:

    (A) ON THE BASIS of a letting with vacant possession thereof by a willing landlord to a willing tenant for a term (commencing on the review date) equal to the greater of fifteen years or the residue then unexpired of the term granted by the within-written lease and subject to the provisions therein set forth (other than as to the amount of the initial rent thereby reserved but including such of said provisions as pertain to the review of rent).

    (B) ON THE ASSUMPTIONS that:

        (i) at and until the review date all the covenants on the part of the tenant and the conditions contained in the within lease have been fully performed and observed

(ii) in the event of the demised premises having been damaged or destroyed and not having been fully repaired reinstated or rebuilt (as the case may be) such damage or destruction had not occurred

and

(C) HAVING REGARD to other open market rental values current at the review date insofar as the arbitrator may deem same to be pertinent to the determination.

(D) BUT DISREGARDING any effect on letting value of:

(a) the fact that the tenant is or has been in occupation of the demised premises or any part thereof

(b) the goodwill which shall have attached to the demised premises by reason of the business carried on thereat

(c) any works executed by and at the expense of the tenant in, on, to or in respect of the demised premises other than required works PROVIDED that in the interpretation of this sub-paragraph (c):

the expression 'the tenant' shall extend to include the tenant or any predecessor in title of the tenant or any party lawfully occupying the demised premises or any part thereof under the tenant.

and

the expression 'required works' shall mean works executed by the tenant in pursuance of an obligation imposed on the tenant (i) by the within lease or by any lease of which the within is a renewal (other than works which may be required pursuant to clause(s) of such lease) OR (ii) by an agreement for the granting of the within lease or of any lease of which the within is a renewal or by virtue of any licence or deed of variation relating to the demised premises.

2. All arbitrations hereunder shall be conducted in accordance with the provisions set forth in the Arbitration Act, 1954 or in any Act or statutory rule or order extending, amending, modifying or replacing the same and for the time being in force.

3. In the event of the President or Chairman or other officer endowed with the functions of the President or Chairman of such Society or Institute as shall be relevant for the purposes of Paragraph 1 of this Schedule being unable or unwilling to make the nomination therein mentioned the same may be made by the next senior officer of that Society or Institute who shall be so able and willing.

4. If the arbitrator shall relinquish his appointment or die, or if it shall become apparent that for any reason he shall be unable or shall have become unfit or unsuited (whether because of bias or otherwise) to complete his duties, or if he shall be removed from office by court order, a substitute may be nominated in his place and in relation to any such nomination the procedures herein before set forth shall be deemed to apply as though the substitution were a nomination de novo which said procedures may be repeated as many times as may be necessary.

5. If the revised rent in respect of any period ('the current period') shall not have been ascertained on or before the review date referable thereto, rent shall continue to be payable up to the gale day next succeeding the ascertainment of the revised rent at the rate payable during the preceding period AND on such gale day the tenant shall pay to the landlord the appropriate instalment of the revised rent together with any shortfall between (i) the aggregate of rents (including such instalment if payable in arrear) actually paid for any part of the Current Period and (ii) rent at the rate of the revised rent attributable to the interval between that review date and such gale day and together also with interest on said shortfall such interest to be computed on a day to day basis and to be assessed at such a rate as shall be

equivalent to the yield (at issue and before deduction of tax if any) on the security of the Government last issued before the commencement of the current period (allowance having been made in the calculation of the said yield for any profit or loss which may occur on the redemption of the security). For the purpose of this paragraph the revised rent shall be deemed to have been ascertained on the date when the same shall have been agreed between the parties or as the case may be on the date of the notification to the tenant of the award of the arbitrator.

6. If there should be in force at the commencement or during the currency of any particular relevant period any Statute or Order (directly or indirectly) prohibiting or restricting an increase of rent in respect of the demised premises the provisions of this Schedule and of the within lease may nevertheless be invoked or reinvoked to determine the rent which would but for the said prohibition or restriction be payable during such relevant period but (if appropriate) the further implementation thereof shall be suspended in effect for such period as may be required by law.

7. When and so often as the revised rent shall have been ascertained pursuant to the provisions herein set forth memoranda recording the same shall thereupon be signed by or on behalf of the landlord and the tenant and shall be annexed to the within lease and its counterpart and the parties shall bear their own costs in relation to the preparation and completion of such memoranda.

EXPERT

... TO HOLD the same UNTO the tenant for the term of   years commencing on the   day of   20   YIELDING AND PAYING therefor and thereout during each of the first   years of the said term the yearly rent of £   and thereafter during each of the successive periods of   years of which the first shall begin on the   day of   20   a yearly rent equal to (a) the yearly rent payable hereunder during the preceding period or (b) such revised yearly rent as may from time to time be ascertained in accordance with the provisions in that behalf contained in the   schedule hereto (whichever shall be the greater) AND the rent in respect of each year of the said term is to be paid by ...

SCHEDULE

(Provisions as to Rent Revisions)

1. The revised rent referred to in the within lease in respect of any of the periods therein mentioned may be agreed at any time between the landlord and the tenant or (in the absence of agreement) be determined not earlier than the date of commencement of such period ('the review date') by an independent valuer (being a member of the Irish Auctioneers and Valuers Institute or of the Society of Chartered Surveyors in the Republic of Ireland or of such body of professional Valuers or Surveyors as shall for the time being have undertaken in Ireland the functions in the activity of property valuation currently performed by said Institute or Society) such independent valuer to be nominated (in the absence of agreement between the parties) upon the application (made not more than two calendar months before or at any time after the review date) of the landlord (or, if the landlord fails to make such application, within twenty-eight days of being requested in writing so to do by the tenant then on the application of the tenant) by either the President of the Incorporated Law Society of Ireland or the President of the Irish Auctioneers and Valuers Institute or the Chairman of the Society of Chartered Surveyors in the Republic of Ireland at the discretion of the party entitled to make the application.

and

the revised rent so to be determined by the independent valuer shall be such as in his opinion represents at the review date the full open market yearly rent for the demised premises let as a whole without fine or premium:

(A) ON THE BASIS of a letting with vacant possession thereof by a willing landlord to a willing tenant for a term (commencing on the review date) equal to the greater of fifteen years or the residue then unexpired of the term granted by the within-written lease and subject to the provisions therein set forth (other than as to the amount of the initial rent thereby reserved but including such of said provisions as pertain to the review of rent).

(B) ON THE ASSUMPTIONS that:

(i) at and until the review date all the covenants on the part of the tenant and the conditions contained in the within lease have been fully performed and observed

(ii) in the event of the demised premises having been damaged or destroyed and not having been fully repaired reinstated or rebuilt (as the case may be) such damage or destruction had not occurred

and

(C) HAVING REGARD to other open market rental values current at the review date insofar as the independent valuer may deem same to be pertinent to the determination.

(D) BUT DISREGARDING any effect on letting value of:

(a) the fact that the tenant is or has been in occupation of the demised premises or any part thereof

(b) the goodwill which shall have attached to the demised premises by reason of the business carried on thereat

(c) any works executed by and at the expense of the tenant in, on, to or in respect of the demised premises other than required works PROVIDED that in the interpretation of this sub-paragraph (c):

the expression 'the tenant' shall extend to include the tenant or any predecessor in title of the tenant or any party lawfully occupying the demised premises or any part thereof under the tenant.

and

the expression 'required works' shall mean works executed by the tenant in pursuance of an obligation imposed on the tenant (i) by the within lease or by any lease of which the within is a renewal (other than works which may be required pursuant to clause[s] of such lease) OR (ii) by an agreement for the granting of the within lease or of any lease of which the within is a renewal or by virtue of any licence or deed of variation relating to the demised premises.

2. In the event of the President or Chairman or other officer endowed with the functions of the President or Chairman of such Society or Institute as shall be relevant for the purposes of paragraph 1 of this schedule being unable or unwilling to make the nomination therein mentioned the same may be made by the next senior officer of that Society or Institute who shall be so able and willing.

3. An independent valuer in relation to any matter so to be determined by him shall:

(i) give notice of his nomination to the landlord and the tenant

(ii) be entitled to enter the demised premises as often as he may reasonably require for the purpose of inspection and examination

(iii) afford to each of the parties concerned a reasonable opportunity of stating (whether in writing or otherwise as may be decided by him and within such time as he may stipulate in that behalf) reasons in support of such contentions as each party may wish to make relative to the matter or matters under consideration

(iv) act as an expert and not as an arbitrator and so that his determination or determinations shall be final and conclusive between the parties

(v) be entitled to seek and pay for advice on any matter which he reasonably considers pertinent to the reference or to his determination thereof

(vi) be empowered to fix his reasonable fees in relation to any such reference and determination and matters incidental thereto which said fees and any reasonable expenses incurred by the independent valuer in or about the said reference and determination shall be shared equally between the landlord and the tenant

(vii) give notice in writing of his determination to the landlord and the tenant within such time as may be stipulated by the terms of his appointment or in the event of there being no such stipulation within six calendar months of the acceptance by him of the nomination to act in the matter PROVIDED ALWAYS that the independent valuer may defer the giving of such notice until such time as his fees and expenses as aforesaid shall have been discharged.

4. Either party shall be at liberty to pay the entire of the fees and expenses as aforesaid of the independent valuer in which event the party so paying shall be entitled to be reimbursed by and to recover from the other on demand any proportion so paid on behalf of such other.

5. If an independent valuer in relation to any matter for determination by him shall fail to conclude such determination and give notice thereof within such time as may be relevant or if he shall relinquish his appointment or die or if it shall become apparent that for any reason he shall be unable or shall have become unfit or unsuited (whether because of bias or otherwise) to complete the duties of his nomination a substitute may be nominated in his place and in relation to any such nomination the procedures hereinbefore set forth shall be deemed to apply as though the substitution were a nomination *de novo* which said procedures may be repeated as many times as may be necessary.

6. If the revised rent in respect of any period ('the current period') shall not have been ascertained on or before the review date referable thereto rent shall continue to be payable up to the gale day next succeeding the ascertainment of the revised rent at the rate payable during the preceding period AND on such gale day the tenant shall pay to the landlord the appropriate instalment of the revised rent together with any shortfall between (i) the aggregate of rents (including such instalment if payable in arrear) actually paid for any part of the current period and (ii) rent at the rate of the revised rent attributable to the interval between that review date and such gale day and together also with interest on said shortfall such interest to be computed on a day to day basis and to be assessed at such a rate as shall be equivalent to the yield (at issue and before deduction of tax if any) on the security of the Government last issued before the commencement of the current period (allowance having been made in the calculation of the said yield for any profit or loss which may occur on the redemption of the security). For the purpose of this paragraph the revised rent shall be deemed to have been ascertained on the date when the same shall have been agreed between the parties or as the case may be on the date of the notification to the tenant of the determination of the independent valuer.

7. If there should be in force at the commencement or during the currency of any particular relevant period any Statute or Order (directly or indirectly) prohibiting

or restricting an increase of rent in respect of the demised premises the provisions of this schedule and of the within lease may nevertheless be invoked or reinvoked to determine the rent which would but for the said prohibition or restriction be payable during such relevant period but (if appropriate) the further implementation thereof shall be suspended in effect for such period as may be required by law.

8. When and so often as the revised rent shall have been ascertained pursuant to the provisions herein set forth memoranda recording the same shall thereupon be signed by or on behalf of the landlord and the tenant and shall be annexed to the within lease and its counterpart and the parties shall bear their own costs in relation to the preparation and completion of such memoranda.

Published by the Law Society of Ireland 1993

APPENDIX 5

AGREEMENT FOR LEASE

NOTE:

This precedent has been prepared for guidance of students of the Law School of the Law Society of Ireland. It assumes that, if utilised in practice, practitioners will take due care in adapting it to incorporate the particular terms and conditions of the subject transaction and that the general terms and conditions of this precedent will be the subject of prudent negotiation. Accordingly, no responsibility can be accepted for its individual content and utilisation in any transaction whether in whole or in part.

This precedent relates to an office unit in a multi-let building which has either yet to be constructed and/or where both landlord's works and tenant's works are being carried out. Accordingly, it may require amendment for use in connection with premises in an existing building or where no landlord's works or tenant's works are being carried out. It is assumed that the landlord will be exercising the option to tax under the Value Added Tax Consolidation Act 2010 when the Lease is granted. This precedent is drafted from a landlord's perspective.

March 2018

© Arthur Cox. This precedent is reproduced with the kind permission of Arthur Cox.

[SUBJECT TO CONTRACT]

Draft [1]: [date]

Dated   20 •

(1)   **Landlord**:   •

(2)   **Tenant:**   •

(3)   **Guarantor:**   •

AGREEMENT FOR LEASE

ADDRESS OF PREMISES TO BE DEMISED   •

ARTHUR COX

•

TABLE OF CONTENTS

1.   DEFINITIONS 3

2.   INTERPRETATION 7

4.   CONSTRUCTION AND LANDLORD WORKS 9

5.   COLLATERAL WARRANTIES 10

7.   PRACTICAL COMPLETION 11

8.   DEFECTS LIABILITY 13

9.   RENT CALCULATION AND MEASUREMENT 14

10.   GRANT OF LEASE 15

11.   VAT 16

12.   PAYMENTS...16

13.   DOCUMENTS TO BE DELIVERED...................................17

14.   FITTING OUT OBLIGATION 19

15.   POSSESSION..24

16.   NO ASSIGNMENT..24

17.   NO DAMAGE...24

18.   NOTICE TO FUNDERS 25

19.   TITLE..25

23.   AGREEMENT TO REMAIN IN FORCE..............................28

24.   SEVERANCE...28

25.   GUARANTOR 28

26.   NOTICES..28

APPENDIX 1
COLLATERAL WARRANTIES...30

APPENDIX 2
LEASE...31

APPENDIX 3
LICENCE FOR WORKS 32

APPENDIX 4
DRAWINGS LIST/SPECIFICATION/PLANS 33

AGREEMENT FOR LEASE

APPENDIX 5
MEASUREMENT PLANS...34

APPENDIX 6
TENANT'S VARIATIONS/CREDITS 35

THIS AGREEMENT made the   day of   20●

BETWEEN:

(1)   ● a company incorporated under the laws of Ireland (registration number ●) having its registered office at ● (hereinafter called the **"Landlord"**);

(2)   [● a company incorporated under the laws of Ireland (registration number ●) having its registered office at ● (hereinafter called the **"Management Company"**);]

(3)   ● a company incorporated under the laws of Ireland (registration number ●) having its registered office at ● (the **"Tenant"**);

(4)   [● a company incorporated under the laws of Ireland (registration number ●) having its registered office at ● (hereinafter called the **"Guarantor"**).]

BACKGROUND:

A.   [The Landlord is the owner of the [Building] / [Estate]] / [The Landlord is in the course of procuring the design, construction and development of the [Building] / [Estate] / [certain elements of the [Building] / [Estate]].

B.   Subject to the terms hereinafter appearing the Landlord shall grant and the Tenant shall take the Lease of the Demised Premises [and the Guarantor shall guarantee the Tenant's obligations under this Agreement subject to the terms and conditions hereinafter appearing].

C.   The Demised Premises form part of the [Building] / [Estate].

THIS AGREEMENT PROVIDES as follows:

1.   **DEFINITIONS**

In this Agreement the following expressions shall be deemed to have the following meanings:-

"**Assigned Certifier**" has the meaning ascribed to it in the BCR Code;

"**BCR Code**" means the Code of Practice for Inspecting and Certifying Buildings and Works issued by the Minister for the Environment, Community and Local Government pursuant to Article 20G of the Building Control (Amendment) Regulations 2014;

"**Building**" means the building located at • and more particularly shown coloured • on plan • annexed to the Lease and shall be deemed to include any extensions or alterations to or any reductions or variations of it now or in the future respectively made within the term of the Lease;

"**Building Contract**" means the building contract entered into between the Landlord and the Contractor substantially in the form of the RIAI standard form with amendments in respect of the Landlord's Works;

"**Building Control Acts**" means the Building Control Acts 1990 to 2014;

"**Building Control Authority**" means a local authority to which Section 2 of the Building Control Act 1990 applies;

"**Building Control Legislation**" means the Building Control Acts and the Building Control Regulations;

"**Building Control Regulations**" means the Building Control Regulations 1997 to 2015;

"**Certificate of Compliance on Completion**" means a certificate of compliance in respect of the Landlord's Works to be submitted to the Building Control Authority for registration and validation in accordance with the Building Control Regulations;

"**Certificate of Practical Completion**" means the certificate of the Landlord's Architect that the Landlord's Works have been practically completed in accordance with the Specification and the Building Contract (insofar as it relates thereto);

"**Collateral Warranties**" means the collateral warranties from the Contractor and the Design Team substantially in the forms annexed hereto in Appendix • .

"**Contractor**" means • or such other contractor as the Landlord shall appoint from time to time in connection with the Landlord's Works;

"**Date of Practical Completion**" means the date which the Landlord's Architect certifies as being the date on which, in his opinion, the Demised Premises has been practically completed in accordance with the Specification and the Building Contract or such later date as may be determined in accordance with Clause 7 hereof;

"**Demised Premises**" means the premises more particularly described in the [First] Schedule to the Lease;

"**Design Team**" means the Landlord's Architect, the Landlord's Structural Engineer, the Landlord's Mechanical and Electrical Engineer and the Landlord's Assigned Certifier;

"**Disability Access Certificate**" means the disability access certificate(s) to be obtained by the Landlord in relation to the Demised Premises;

"**Estate**" means the development known or intended to be known as • and more particularly shown [outlined/coloured] in • on plan • annexed to the Lease and the extent of which Estate may be expanded or reduced from time to time by the Landlord and / or the Management Company, and for the avoidance of doubt, the Estate may from time to time include areas which are not immediately contiguous in location to one another;

"**Estimated Floor Area**" means • square [feet/meters];

"**Family Law Acts**" means the Family Home Protection Act 1976, the Family Law Act 1981, the Judicial Separation and Family Law Reform Act 1989, the Family Law Act

1995, the Family Law (Divorce) Act l996 and the Civil Partnership and Certain Rights and Obligations of Cohabitants Act 2010;

"**Fire Safety Certificate**" means the fire safety certificate(s) to be obtained by the Landlord in relation to the Demised Premises;

"**Floor Area**" means the total floor area of the Demised Premises expressed in square [feet/metres] measured in accordance with the Measuring Code;

"**Funder**" means any person, entity or body providing financial assistance to the Landlord in relation to the Landlord's Works or the Landlord's interest in the Building or the Estate or any part thereof holding a charge over the Demised Premises and/or the Estate;

"**Guarantor**" means the party (if any) named as "Guarantor" and in the case of an individual includes the personal representatives of such Guarantor;

"**Independent Architect**" means • or in the event of him being unwilling or unable to act such other architect (who shall have at least ten (10) years standing as an architect in Ireland) as may be agreed between the parties and in default of agreement to be nominated upon the application of either party by the President for the time being of the RIAI;

"**Independent Chartered Surveyor**" means a chartered surveyor of more than ten (10) years standing and experience in projects in Ireland similar to the construction of the Building or in the event of him/her being unwilling or unable to act such other chartered surveyor (who shall have at least ten (10) years standing as a chartered surveyor in Ireland) as may be agreed between the parties and in default of agreement to be nominated upon the application of either party by the President for the time being of the Society of Chartered Surveyors Ireland;

"**Landlord**" includes its successors and assigns;

"**Landlord's Architect**" means • or such other suitably qualified Architect as the Landlord may appoint from time to time in connection with the Landlord's Works following notice to the Tenant;

"**Landlord's Mechanical and Electrical Engineer**" means • or such firm (if any) of mechanical and electrical engineers as the Landlord may appoint from time to time in connection with the Landlord's Works but without being obliged to do so;

"**Landlord's Structural Engineer**" means • or such firm (if any) of structural engineers as the Landlord may appoint from time to time in connection with the Landlord's Works but without being obliged to do so;

"**Landlord's Works**" means the construction of the Demised Premises substantially in accordance with the Specification;

"**Landlord's Solicitor**" means • ;

"**Law**" means every Act of Parliament and of the Oireachtas, law of the European Union and every instrument, directive, regulation, requirement, action and bye law made by any government department, competent authority, officer or court which now or may hereafter have force of law in Ireland;

"**Lease**" means the lease of the Demised Premises in the form annexed hereto in Appendix 2;

"**Licence for Works**" means the form of licence for works annexed hereto at Appendix 3;

"**Measuring Code**" means the International Property Measurement Standards: Office Buildings published by the International Property Measurement Standards Coalition (or if there is no such code, such code as may reasonably be determined by the Landlord);

"**Measurement Plans**" means the plans annexed hereto in Appendix 5;

"**Necessary Consents**" means the Planning Permission, the Fire Safety Certificate, the Disability Access Certificate and any regulations or requirements under the Building

Control Regulations and all other consents, approvals or licences of and from all competent and statutory authorities in relation to the Landlord's Works;

"Opinion on Compliance" means a certificate or opinion from the Landlord's Architect in the usual RIAI or Law Society recommended form as of the date it is given confirming substantial compliance with the Planning Permission;

"Outgoings" means any rates, taxes, duties, charges, assessments, impositions and outgoings whatsoever whether parliamentary, parochial, local or of any other description and whether or not of a capital or non-recurring nature or of a wholly novel character;

"Planning Permission(s)" means the [the final grant of planning permission obtained in connection with the Landlord's Works in accordance with Clause 3] / [the final grant of planning permission register reference • applicable to the Demised Premises to be referenced in the Opinion on Compliance];

"Planning Acts" mean the Local Government (Planning and Development) Acts 1963 to 1999 and the Planning and Development Acts 2000 to 2017;

"Plans" means the plans of the Demised Premises referred to in the Specification;

"Practical Completion" means the practical completion of the Demised Premises and associated works (excluding Snag Items) in accordance with the Specification as certified by the Landlord's Architect pursuant to the Building Contract which, for the avoidance of doubt, excludes practical completion of the Building;

"Prescribed Rate" means on each occasion when the same falls to be calculated the rate of interest which is 7% above EURIBOR or if there shall be no such rate then such rate as the Landlord's accountants or auditors shall certify to be the nearest equivalent then existing;

"Public Health Acts" mean the Local Government (Sanitary Services) Act, 1878 to 2001;

"RIAI" means the Royal Institute of the Architects of Ireland;

"Safety Act" means the Safety, Health and Welfare at Work Acts 2005 to 2014;

"Safety Regulations" means the Safety Act and any and all legislation pursuant thereto (including but not limited to the Safety, Health and Welfare at Work (Construction) Regulations 2013) as may be modified, amended or extended from time to time;

"Snag Items" includes items which are normally dealt with in a snagging list (which term shall have the meaning understood by custom in the building trade in Ireland);

"Specification" means the plans referred to in Appendix 4 with the specification annexed thereto;

"Tenant" includes its successors and permitted assigns;

"Tenant's Approvals" means any approvals, consents, permissions and licences of any competent authority that may from time to time be required by any Law to enable the Tenant to commence and carry out the Tenant's Works;

"Tenant's Architect" means • or such other suitably qualified Architect as the Tenant shall appoint in substitution therefor following notice to the Landlord;

"Tenant's Plans" means the detailed plans, drawings and specifications setting out the Tenant's proposals for the Tenant's Works and any other documents and information the Landlord reasonably requires in order to satisfy himself as to the nature and extent of the Tenant's Works;

"Tenant's Specification" means the plans and specifications to be furnished by the Tenant's Architect to the Landlord's Architect in accordance with Clause 14 (*Fitting Out Obligation*) of this Agreement;

"Tenant's Works" means the Tenant's works in accordance with the Tenant's Specification as may approved by the Landlord pursuant to Clause 14 (*Fitting Out Obligation*);

"**Term Commencement Date**" means the Date of Practical Completion;

"**VAT**" means Value Added Tax;

"**VAT Act**" means Value-Added Tax Consolidation Act, 2010;

"**Working Day**" or "**Days**" means a day other than a Saturday or Sunday or Good Friday or public holiday in Ireland on which clearing banks are generally open for business in Ireland.

2.   INTERPRETATION

Save as otherwise provided herein:-

2.1   any reference to a clause, paragraph or sub-paragraph shall be a reference to a Clause, paragraph or sub-paragraph (as the case may be) of this Agreement and any reference in a Clause to a paragraph or subparagraph shall be a reference to a paragraph or sub-paragraph of the Clause or paragraph in which the reference is contained unless it appears from the context that a reference to some other provision is intended;

2.2   any reference to the masculine gender shall include reference to the feminine gender and any reference to the neuter gender shall include the masculine and feminine gender and reference to the singular shall include reference to the plural;

2.3   any reference herein to any statute or section of any statute include a reference to any statutory amendment, modification, replacement or re-enactment thereof for the time being in force and to every instrument, order, direction, regulation, bye-law, permission, licence, consent, condition, scheme and matter made in pursuance of any such statute;

2.4   words such as "hereunder", "hereto", "hereof", and "herein" and other words commencing with "here" shall unless the context clearly indicates to the contrary refer to the whole of this Agreement and not to any particular Clause or paragraph thereof;

2.5   clause headings, captions and headings are for reference only and shall not affect the construction or interpretation of this Agreement;

2.6   any reference to a clause, sub-clause or schedule shall mean a clause, sub-clause or schedule of this Agreement and a reference in a schedule to a paragraph is to a paragraph of that schedule;

2.7   "Week" shall mean calendar week;

2.8   "Month" shall mean calendar month;

2.9   "Person" includes a firm or a body corporate or unincorporated;

1.1   any covenant by the Tenant not to do any act or thing shall include an obligation not to permit or suffer such act or thing to be done and any references to any act, neglect, default or omission of the Tenant shall be deemed to include any act, neglect, default or omission of the Tenant or the under-lessees, servants, agents, licensees or invitees of the Tenant or any person under its or their control;

2.10   any reference to any right of the Landlord to have access to or entry upon the Demised Premises shall be construed as extending to all persons authorised by the Landlord and any person holding an interest in the Demised Premises superior to the Landlord;

2.11 any reference to a Law (whether specifically named or not) or to any sections or sub-sections in a Law shall include any statutory modifications, extensions, amendments or re-enactments thereof for the time being in force and all statutory instruments, orders, notices, regulations, directions, bye-laws or other subordinate legislation, certificates, permissions and plans for the time being made, issued or given thereunder or deriving validity from it;

2.12 any reference to "this Agreement" shall where the context so requires include this Agreement as supplemented, amended, modified or varied from time to time;

2.13 the Schedules shall be read and construed as if they formed part of the body of this Agreement and the term "this Agreement" shall be construed as including the Schedules hereto;

2.14 any reference to any society, institute or other professional body shall include any other body established from time to time in succession to or in substitution for or carrying out the function formerly carried out by such society, institute or other professional body; and

2.15 where two or more persons are included in the expression "Landlord" "Tenant" or "Guarantor" the covenants which are expressed to be made by the Landlord, the Tenant or the Guarantor shall be deemed to be made by such persons jointly and severally.

3. [PLANNING PRE-CONDITION

3.1 The Landlord shall at its own expense submit an application for the Planning Permission and shall use reasonable endeavours to progress the said application and to obtain on foot thereof the Planning Permission for the Landlord's Works.

3.2 The Landlord shall keep the Tenant apprised of the Landlord's progress in obtaining the Planning Permission.

3.3 This Agreement is conditional on the Landlord obtaining the Planning Permission [within • months of the date of this Agreement / by •] (the "**Planning Long-Stop Date**").

3.4 If the Planning Permission in a form acceptable to the Landlord (acting reasonably) is not obtained by the Planning Long-Stop Date, then either party may determine this Agreement by notice in writing to the other whereupon this Agreement shall cease and be of no further effect without any interest, costs or compensation being payable by either party to the other.]

4. CONSTRUCTION AND LANDLORD WORKS

4.1 The Landlord shall [as soon as reasonably practicable after the fulfilment of the pre-condition in Clause 3 (*Planning Pre-Condition*)] use reasonable endeavours to procure that the Contractor proceeds diligently with the construction of the Demised Premises substantially in accordance with the Specification and with a view to completion of same as soon as reasonably practicable but so that the Landlord shall not have any liability to the Tenant for delay for any reason other than default of the Landlord in the completion of same.

4.2 The Landlord shall use reasonable endeavours to procure that the Contractor undertakes the construction of the Landlord's Works in a good and workmanlike manner in accordance with good building practice and the Specification and in substantial compliance with the Necessary Consents.

4.3   The Landlord shall be liable for payment of all financial contributions pursuant to the Planning Permission in respect of the Demised Premises.

4.4   If the Landlord is unable to obtain any of the materials referred to in the Specification on reasonable terms, the Landlord may substitute for them alternative materials as nearly as may be of the same quality.

4.5   In complying with its obligations to deliver the Demised Premises substantially in accordance with the Specification, it is agreed and confirmed that the Landlord may make any modifications to the details contained in the Specification that are required by any competent authority as a condition of the grant or continuance in force of any Necessary Consents, or that are reasonably required by the Landlord provided that no modification may be made pursuant to this clause that would substantially alter the location, layout or extent of the Demised Premises as provided for in the Specification or substantially prejudice the use of the Demised Premises for the purpose specified in the Lease, save as may be agreed with the Tenant.

5.   COLLATERAL WARRANTIES

5.1   The Landlord shall procure that the Contractor and the Design Team shall furnish the Collateral Warranties to the Tenant on the grant of the Lease pursuant to this Agreement.

5.2   The Landlord shall exercise the due skill and care reasonably expected of an experienced and prudent landlord in procuring the construction and completion of the Demised Premises. Subject to compliance by the Landlord with its obligations herein contained it is agreed that the Landlord shall not otherwise have any liability to the Tenant in relation to the construction and completion of the Demised Premises or the Building.

6.   ADDITIONAL ITEMS AND EXCLUSIONS

6.1   The Landlord shall, at the request and cost of the Tenant, act reasonably in seeking to procure the provision as part of the Landlord's Works, and over and above the items listed in the Building Contract, such additional items to the Demised Premises as shall be reasonably requested by the Tenant and agreed by the Landlord (the "**Additional Items**") PROVIDED THAT:

(a)   the inclusion of the Additional Items as part of the Landlord's Works shall be solely at the Landlord's discretion and shall not impact upon or cause a delay in the Date of Practical Completion; and

(b)   such request(s) must be received by the Landlord on or before l.

6.2   Where the Landlord agrees to carry out and complete the Additional Items, any and all costs and expenses which will be incurred by the Landlord shall be payable by the Tenant to the Landlord in instalments against certificates furnished by the Landlord's Architect under the Building Contract which certificates shall state that they are in respect of the Additional Items and the amount payable in respect of this Agreement. All payments shall be made within ten (10) Working Days from the issue of a certificate.

6.3 [Notwithstanding the Specification, the Landlord and the Tenant have agreed a schedule of exclusions from the Specification and which are more particularly detailed at Appendix 6 hereto (the "**Tenant's Variations**"). The Landlord and the Tenant have agreed that in lieu of the Landlord including the Tenant's Variations in the Landlord's Works, the Landlord shall pay to the Tenant on completion of the Tenant's Works in accordance with Clause 14 (*Fitting Out Obligation*) hereof the credits for each element of the Tenant's Variations, details of which are set out at Appendix 6. Notwithstanding that the Landlord's Works shall not include the Tenant's Variations, the Specification shall remain the deemed specification and condition of the Demised Premises for the purposes of the rent review and yield up provisions of the Lease and the installation of the Tenant's Variations by the Tenant shall not constitute or be deemed to constitute an improvement for the purposes of the Landlord and Tenant Acts.]

7. PRACTICAL COMPLETION

7.1 The Landlord shall keep the Tenant generally informed of the progress of the Landlord's Works towards Practical Completion.

7.2 The Landlord's Architect shall:

(a) notify the Tenant's Architect in writing not less than ten (10) Working Days before the date on which the Landlord's Architect anticipates that he will issue the Certificate of Practical Completion and

(b) invite the Tenant's Architect to arrange a joint inspection with the Landlord's Architect of the Demised Premises not less than five (5) Working Days prior to the date that it is anticipated the Certificate of Practical Completion will issue.

7.3 The Tenant shall co-operate in arranging such a joint inspection, and if the Tenant fails to respond to the Landlord's Architect's invitation within five (5) Working Days, then the Landlord's Architect may finalise the Certificate of Practical Completion without the Tenant's input.

7.4 The Tenant's Architect shall notify the Landlord's Architect in writing within three (3) Working Days of such inspection of any matters which in the view of the Tenant's Architect should have attention prior to the issue of the Certificate of Practical Completion. The Landlord's Architect shall take due regard of same but nothing herein shall limit the right of the Landlord's Architect to issue the Certificate of Practical Completion.

7.5 The Landlord's Architect will furnish a copy of the Certificate of Practical Completion together with a list of the Snag Items to the Tenant within five (5) Working Days following its issue.

7.6 If the Certificate of Practical Completion is issued with a list of Snag Items remaining to be completed or remedied, the Landlord shall use reasonable endeavours to procure that those Snag Items are completed or remedied (as the case may be) as soon as reasonably practicable following the date of issue of the Certificate of Practical Completion but the existence of any remaining Snag Items shall not affect the Date of Practical Completion

7.7 If the Tenant's Architect shall object to the issue of the Certificate of Practical Completion he shall do so in writing to the Landlord's Architect such notice to be received by the Landlord's Architect within five (5) Working Days of receipt by the Tenant's Architect of a copy of the Certificate of Practical Completion specifying his objections which shall not include Snag Items.

7.8 In the event of a dispute between the Landlord's Architect and the Tenant's Architect as to whether the Certificate of Practical Completion should have issued having regard to the objections of the Tenant's Architect then the items in dispute shall be referred forthwith to the Independent Architect who shall be required to give a decision as to the Date of Practical Completion within ten (10) Working Days of being requested to resolve such dispute.

7.9 The Independent Architect shall act as an expert and not as an Arbitrator and his fees shall be borne by the party against whom he holds.

7.10 Where the Independent Architect finds in favour of the Tenant that the Certificate of Practical Completion should not have issued, the Landlord shall procure that the items of works identified by the Independent Architect required to be completed to achieve Practical Completion shall be remedied forthwith and the provisions of Clauses 7.3 – 7.12 hereof shall be repeated mutatis mutandis.

7.11 Where the Independent Architect finds in favour of the Landlord, the Date of Practical Completion shall remain as certified and all appropriate provisions shall apply thereto.

7.12 If there is any dispute between the Landlord and the Tenant as to whether any items properly constitute Snag Items, either party shall have the right to refer the determination of such matter in dispute to the Independent Architect. The Independent Architect shall be requested to give his decision within twenty (20) Working Days of his/her appointment and shall be entitled to receive oral and/or written submissions from the parties. The Independent Architect shall act as an expert and not as an arbitrator and his fees shall be borne equally between the parties.

7.13 Subject to Clause 7.7 (*Objections by Tenant's Architect*) the Landlord will use reasonable endeavours to procure that the Certificate of Compliance on Completion and all necessary ancillary documentation is submitted to the Building Control Authority for registration and validation on or before the Date of Practical Completion or, in any event, as soon as practicable thereafter.

8. DEFECTS LIABILITY

8.1 The Landlord will use reasonable endeavours to enforce all provisions available to it to procure the making good by the Contractor at its cost as soon as practicable of any defects appearing in the Demised Premises within twelve (12) months from the Date of Practical Completion which the Contractor is obliged to make good under the Building Contract PROVIDED ALWAYS that such defects shall be notified in writing to the Landlord at least twenty (20) Working Days before the expiration of the said twelve (12) month period.

8.2 The Tenant shall permit the Landlord and the Contractor together with their respective servants, agents and advisers at reasonable times and on giving reasonable prior notice to enter the Demised Premises with all such equipment and machinery as is reasonably required, notwithstanding and following the grant of the Lease, in order to:

(a) examine the state and condition of the Demised Premises in connection with the enforcement of the defects liability provisions of the Building Contract and shall have due regard to any reasonable observations or representations made by the Tenant's Architect; or

(b) comply with the Landlord's obligations under Clause 8.1 and otherwise execute outstanding or remedial works (if any) in the Demised Premises having first agreed a method statement, phasing and programme of works with the Tenant (both parties acting reasonably) which will allow the making good of defects or faults but with minimum disruption to the Tenant's Works or (if the Tenant has already commenced trading from the Demised Premises) to the operation of the Tenant's business; or

(c) procure that any making good of defects or faults is carried out in accordance with the method statement and programme of works agreed between the Landlord and Tenant;

and any persons so entering causing as little damage to the Demised Premises as reasonably possible and making good as reasonably practicable and to the reasonable satisfaction of the Tenant any damage caused to the Demised Premises and the Tenant's fixtures and fittings, furnishings, equipment and stock in the exercise of those rights.

8.3 The Tenant acknowledges that the Landlord's obligation in relation to the design and construction of the Demised Premises, without prejudice to the obligations under Clause 8.1, will cease forthwith upon receipt by the Tenant of the Collateral Warranties.

9. RENT CALCULATION AND MEASUREMENT

9.1 The rent to be reserved by Clause • of the Lease (for the first five (5) years thereof) shall be € • per square [foot/metre] of the Floor Area of the Demised Premises calculated in accordance with the Measuring Code [together with € • in respect of each of the car parking spaces]. [For the avoidance of doubt the area to be so measured is outlined in • on the Measurement Plans.] The Floor Area of the Demised Premises shall be measured and ascertained by the Landlord and the Tenant on such date as the Landlord shall notify to the Tenant and in the event of there being a dispute as to the Floor Area the matter shall be determined by an Independent Chartered Surveyor as set out hereunder:

(a) The Landlord and the Tenant shall endeavour to agree the Floor Area of the Demised Premises;

(b) If they cannot do so the Floor Area shall be determined by such Independent Chartered Surveyor as the parties may agree or in default of agreement by such Independent Chartered Surveyor as may be nominated upon the application of either party by the President (or other acting senior officer) of the Society of Chartered Surveyors Ireland;

(c) The Independent Chartered Surveyor so appointed shall act as an expert and shall afford to the Landlord and the Tenant a reasonable opportunity of stating (whether in writing or otherwise as may be decided by him and within such time as he may stipulate in that behalf) reasons in support of such contentions as each party may wish to make relative to the matter or matters under consideration;

(d) The Independent Chartered Surveyor shall be required to give a decision within five (5) Working Days of being requested to resolve such dispute.

9.2 The determination of the Surveyor shall be binding on the parties and his costs shall be borne by the parties [as he shall decide / by the party against whom he holds].

9.3 In the event of the Floor Area not having been agreed by the Date of Practical Completion, the Tenant shall pay to the Landlord rent of € • per annum based on the Estimated Floor Area [together with € • in respect of each of the car parking spaces] and within ten (10) Working Days of agreement on or determination of the Floor Area there shall be paid by the Landlord to the Tenant (or vice versa) any excess or underpayment (as the case may be) in respect of the period for which rent has been paid. The rent in the Lease shall be initially calculated by reference to the Estimated Floor Area and the Landlord and the Tenant shall enter into a memorandum supplemental to the Lease according to the adjusted yearly rent calculated by reference to the Floor Area agreed or determined in accordance with the provisions of this Agreement.

10. GRANT OF LEASE

10.1 At the time of the execution of this Agreement, the Tenant [and the Guarantor] shall execute the Lease [and •] (and any ancillary documents) (the "**Lease Documents**") in [duplicate/triplicate] and they shall be held by the Landlord's Solicitor in escrow pending the later of (i) the Date of Practical Completion and (ii) the issue of the Tenant's Certificate PROVIDED ALWAYS that nothing herein shall prevent the Landlord from delivering the Lease Documents at any time after the Date of Practical Completion.

10.2 The Tenant shall become liable to comply with all the covenants on the part of the Tenant and conditions contained in the Lease with effect from the Date of Practical Completion so certified or (if applicable) such later date as the Independent Architect certifies as being the date on which Practical Completion of the Demised Premises has been achieved.

10.3 The Landlord shall, subject to receipt of the relevant stamp duty, stamp the original and counterpart of this Agreement (and in due course the original and counterpart of the Lease) and shall return the original of this Agreement, duly stamped, to the Tenant upon the later of the dates specified in Clause 10.1 hereof.

10.4 The term of the Lease held in escrow, the rent, the service charge and the insurance premium (as defined in the Lease) shall commence upon the Date of Practical Completion as certified by the Landlord's Architect (or as determined by the Independent Architect if appointed) and the Tenant [with the consent of the Guarantor] hereby irrevocably authorises the Landlord to insert these dates in the relevant parts of the Lease and counterpart thereof and also to insert the Floor Area (calculated pursuant to Clause 9.1 hereof) of the Demised Premises in the rent review schedule of the Lease.

10.5 This Agreement is not intended nor shall it operate or be deemed to operate either at law or in equity as a demise of the Demised Premises notwithstanding that the Landlord could deliver or that either the Landlord or the Tenant or either of them could specifically enforce the delivery of the Lease nor shall the Tenant have or be entitled to any estate, right or interest in the Demised Premises or any part thereof or in any materials in or upon the same or any part thereof nor shall the relationship of Landlord and Tenant exist or arise or be deemed to exist or arise between the parties hereto.

10.6 As and from the Date of Practical Completion, the Tenant shall pay to the Landlord by way of licence fee but not by way of rent the same sums as would have been payable by it or him by way of rent or otherwise under the Lease had same then been delivered and been in full force and effect such sums to be paid at the time or times and in the manner and in all respects as to rent and other monies which would have been payable under the said Lease and as and from the Date of Practical Completion the Tenant shall observe and perform the covenants on the part of the Tenant and conditions contained in the Lease insofar as the same may be applicable as though the same were herein contained and set forth in full but until the Lease has been delivered the Tenant shall not be entitled to the exclusive occupation of the Demised Premises, and shall not trade or do business from the Demised Premises prior to delivery of the Lease and shall as aforesaid be a bare licensee only of the Landlord.

11. VAT

11.1 The Landlord confirms to the Tenant that the Landlord will be exercising its option to tax the rents payable under the Lease pursuant to Section 97(1) of the VAT Act (the "**Landlord's Option to Tax**"). The Tenant shall, in addition to any other amounts payable under the Lease, pay to the Landlord the amount of VAT arising in relation to any rent or other payments due under this Lease and the Tenant shall keep the Landlord indemnified against such VAT.

11.2 At any time during the Term the Landlord may terminate the Landlord's Option to Tax in respect of the Lease by giving written notice to this effect to the Tenant.

11.3 Where at any time during the Term the Landlord has terminated the Landlord's Option to Tax, the Landlord may thereafter from time to time during the Term exercise the Landlord's Option to Tax the rents payable under the Lease by giving notice to the Tenant pursuant to Section 97(1)(c)(ii) of the VAT Act and where such notice is given, the Tenant shall, in addition to any other amount payable under this Lease, pay to the Landlord the amount of VAT arising in relation to any rent or other payments due under the Lease and the Tenant shall keep the Landlord indemnified against such VAT.

11.4 Where during the Term the Landlord's Option to Tax is at any time terminated pursuant to Section 97(1)(d)(iii), (iv) or (v) or Section 97(2) of the VAT Act (with the exception of any termination caused solely by the actions of the Landlord) the Tenant hereby covenants to reimburse the Landlord on demand on a net of tax basis for the Landlord the amount of any VAT clawback or VAT payment obligations suffered by the Landlord as a result of such termination (hereinafter referred to in this Lease as a "**VAT Adjustment**"). If the VAT Adjustment payable under this sub-clause is subject to tax in the hands of the Landlord the Tenant shall also pay in addition to the VAT Adjustment such further sum which will leave the Landlord in the same position as if such amount had not been subject to tax.

12. PAYMENTS

12.1 The Tenant shall pay on the signing hereof:

(a) the stamp duty payable on this Agreement and its counterparts;

(b) the stamp duty payable on the Lease and its counterparts; and

(c) [VAT (if any) payable on this Agreement subject to receipt by the Tenant of a VAT invoice].

12.2 The Tenant shall pay prior to the Date of Practical Completion and prior to entering the Demised Premises to carry out any works:-

(a) an amount equal to one quarter of the annual rent as provided in the Lease;

(b) such sum as the Landlord shall advise the Tenant as being the advance payment of service charge payable pursuant to the Lease; and

(c)   such sum as the Landlord shall advise the Tenant on account of the first year's insurance premium payable by the Tenant under the Lease.

13.   DOCUMENTS TO BE DELIVERED

13.1   Subject to the Tenant complying with its obligations under this Agreement, the Landlord will furnish the following to the Tenant within ten (10) Working Days (or such other time frame as the parties may agree) of the registration and validation of the Certificate of Compliance on Completion:

(a)   the original Lease duly stamped;

(b)   a declaration pursuant to the Family Law Acts;

(c)   [the original Side Letter(s) fully executed and in the form attached hereto;]

(d)   [the original Licence for Works fully executed and in the form attached hereto with the Tenant's Plans appended thereto (if applicable);]

(e)   the Opinion on Compliance;

(f)   evidence of compliance with any relevant financial conditions in the Planning Permission;

(g)   a letter consenting to the creation of the Lease (and this Agreement) from any Funder [/ confirmation that lender consent is not required];

(h)   a letter from the holder of any floating charge over the Demised Premises confirming that any such charge has not crystallised;

(i)   a certificate from the company secretary of the Landlord that:

    (i)   the Landlord has not executed any charges of any description which are not shown as registered in the Companies Registration Office; and

    (ii)   that no resolution to wind up the Landlord has been passed and that no notice of a meeting at which it is proposed to wind up the Landlord has issued or been published and that no petition has been presented or is pending to wind up the Landlord and no steps have been taken to place the Landlord in receivership or to have a receiver or an examiner appointed;

(j)   copy of the BER Certificate;

(k)   [copies of any LEED Gold accreditation certificates received;]

(l)   Land Registry compliant map (if required);

(m)   evidence of the Landlord's insurances carried in accordance with the Lease in the form of a broker's certificate;

(n)   [an undertaking to furnish within • months of the Date of Practical Completion a copy of the safety file in respect of the Landlord's Works pursuant to the Safety, Health and Welfare at Work (Construction) Regulations 2013 (to include "as built" drawings in respect of the Demised Premises) PROVIDED ALWAYS that in the event of the Tenant surrendering the Lease it shall return the said safety file to the Landlord within ten (10) Working Days of that surrender taking effect / a letter from the Landlord or the Management Company confirming the location of the original safety file and arrangements for the inspection of same by the Tenant];

(o)   original signed replies to pre-lease enquiries together with written confirmation that the replies and any additional replies to such pre-lease enquiries and any rejoinders remain true and correct;

(p)   all documents that the Landlord has agreed to furnish to the Tenant in accordance with the replies given by the Landlord's Solicitor;

(q) completion searches duly certified and explained (subject to the Tenant's solicitor furnishing searches to the Landlord's Solicitor);

(r) evidence that the Certificate of Compliance on Completion has been registered and validated by the Building Control Authority;

(s) [copies of all keys/access/swipe cards in the Landlords possession in relation to the Demised Premises;] and

(t) the Collateral Warranties.

13.2 It is agreed and confirmed that the Landlord shall have no further liability in respect of the Landlord's Works once the Collateral Warranties are delivered to the Tenant.

14. FITTING OUT OBLIGATION

14.1 The Tenant shall be solely responsible at its own expense for the Tenant's Works so as to enable the Tenant to occupy and trade from the Demised Premises in accordance with the Tenant's Specification which must be provided to the Landlord in triplicate and which must be approved in writing by the Landlord prior to the carrying out of any such works (such approval not to be unreasonably withheld or delayed).

14.2 Not later than twenty (20) Working Days after the execution of this Agreement the Tenant shall submit to the Landlord for approval the Tenant's Specification in such format (electronic or otherwise) as the Landlord may reasonably require.

14.3 The Landlord reserves the right to require the Tenant to enter into the Licence for Works which form may be amended to include the Landlord's reasonable requirements in particular in relation to reinstatement of the Demised Premises on the expiry or sooner determination of the Lease and the provision of collateral warranties to the Landlord.

14.4 Immediately the Landlord's approval of the Tenant's Plans is obtained, the Tenant must apply for all Tenant's Approvals, use all reasonable endeavours to obtain them without delay, and furnish copies of the Tenant's Approvals to the Landlord once they are obtained and for the avoidance of doubt the Tenant shall not be entitled to commence the Tenant's Works until it has obtained all necessary Tenant's Approvals and furnished copies to the Landlord.

14.5 Subject to approval of the Tenant's Works, the Landlord shall hand over to the Tenant possession of the Demised Premises on the later of (i) the Date of Practical Completion and (ii) receipt by the Landlord of the payments to be made by the Tenant in accordance with Clause 12 (*Payments*) whereupon the Tenant shall carry out and complete the fitting out of the Demised Premises in accordance with the Tenant's Specification as soon as practicable in all material respects substantially in accordance with the Tenant's Approvals.

14.6 For the avoidance of any doubt, the details and specifications which the Landlord might reasonably require in order to approve the Tenant's Specification include:

(a) full details of the Tenant's contractor and the Tenant's professional team;

(b) if any of the Tenant's Works are to be carried out by way of sub-contract, a copy of the sub-contract and details of the sub-contractor, the insurance obligations imposed on the sub-contractor and the requirements in relation to providing a performance bond imposed on the sub-contractor;

(c) full details of the insurances carried by such agents or contractors which insurances must be satisfactory to the Landlord (acting prudently but reasonably). In this respect, the relevant contractor shall be obliged to effect contractors all risks, public liability and employer's liability insurances, professional indemnity insurance, to a level and extent acceptable to the Landlord and such insurances shall, if required, by the Landlord, be extended to include the Landlord either as Joint Insured or with an indemnity to principals clause. (In the event of the Landlord within ten (10) Working Days of receipt of the said notification, notifying the Tenant that such fit-out contractor is not suitable to the Landlord, it shall not be lawful for the Tenant to permit or authorise such contractor to enter upon the Estate or the Demised Premises but such notice shall not be given otherwise than for good or substantial reasons which shall be advised to the Tenant in writing by the Landlord at the time of notification.);

(d) confirmation of the existence of the insurances required by the Landlord together with receipts in respect of payment of the premium;

(e) such other reasonable evidence of insurances as may be required by the Landlord from time to time, including evidence of renewals;

(f) evidence of payment of any additional insurance premium payable by the Landlord as a result of the Tenant's Works provided that the Tenant's Works shall be carried out at the sole risk of the Tenant;

(g) copies of such permissions, approvals, certificates, licences and consents including without limitation a copy of the commencement notice and any fire safety certificate required by Building Control Legislation;

(h) full details of collateral warranties (the form of which shall be subject to the Landlord's approval) in relation to the Tenant's Works addressed to the Landlord which the Tenant's contractor, sub-contractors and Tenant's professional team will provide on completion of the Tenant's Works; and

(i) the method statements and such other information and documentation as the Landlord might require.

14.7 The Landlord shall not be liable for completion of the Tenant's Works.

14.8 Subject to the Landlord consenting to the Tenant's Works, and in addition to any Licence for Works that may be entered into:

(a) The Tenant covenants with the Landlord to carry out the Tenant's Works in a good and workmanlike manner in accordance with the Tenant's Specification, subject to approval of same by the Landlord and to complete same for use as an office;

(b) To the extent that the Tenant has possession of the Demised Premises at any time before the Lease is delivered to the Tenant, it is to hold the Demised Premises as a licensee of the Landlord and not under any contract of tenancy; and

(c) Before carrying out any fitting out of the Demised Premises the Tenant shall obtain all Tenant's Approvals and the Tenant shall further ensure that all such fitting out works shall comply therewith and shall comply with the Planning Permission, the Fire Safety Certificate and the Disability Access Certificate granted to the Landlord in respect of the Demised Premises and shall furnish copies of the Tenant's Approvals to the Landlord for approval prior to such works commencing.

(d) On completion of the Tenant's Works the Tenant shall furnish to the Landlord:

(i) an unqualified certificate or opinion from the Tenant's Architect in the usual RIAI or Law Society recommended form as of the date it is given confirming either (i) that the Works are in compliance with any planning permission required or (ii) that the Works are exempt from the requirements of the Planning Acts;

(ii) evidence of compliance with any financial conditions contained in any planning permission;

(iii) a copy (or certified copy if the certificate on the Building Control Authority register is not accessible to the public) of the Certificate of Compliance on Completion (if applicable) together with satisfactory evidence that the Certificate of Compliance on Completion has been lodged with, validated and registered by the relevant Building Control Authority or (as appropriate) written confirmation from the Tenant's Architect that the Tenant's Works are exempt from the requirements of the Building Control Legislation and/or that the Tenant's Works do not require a fire safety certificate;

(iv) a certified copy of the safety file for the Tenant's Works required by the Safety Regulations, (the original of which the Tenant shall furnish to the Landlord upon the expiration or earlier termination of the Lease). Pending delivery of the safety file, the Tenant shall upon request make the up to date working draft thereof available to the Landlord for review;

(v) as constructed drawings;

(vi) copy operating manuals;

(vii) all collateral warranties required by the Landlord in relation to the Tenant's Works;

(viii) certified copy letters of appointment in relation to the Tenant's professional team; and

(ix) certified copy building contract and any sub-contract in respect of the Tenant's Works.

(e) [Two (2) printed copies and two (2) electronic (scanned) copies on two (2) compact discs of each of the documents referred to in sub-clause (d).]

(f) The Tenant shall:

(i) give the Landlord twenty-four (24) hours' prior notice of the commencement of the Tenant's Works;

(ii) carry out the Tenant's Works with all due expedition and in accordance with the plans and specifications approved by the Landlord with good quality materials and in a proper and workmanlike manner to the satisfaction of the Landlord's Architect in such a way as to cause no obstruction to or interference with the carrying out of any outstanding Snag Items;

(iii) make good any damage caused by the Tenant, its servants, agents and any other party involved in carrying out of the Tenant's Works;

(iv) comply with all rules and regulations imposed by the Landlord and the Contractor and observe and perform all proper precautions in executing the Tenant's Works and in particular not to endanger the safety of the Demised Premises or the Building or any part thereof;

(v) comply with the requirements and recommendations (whether notified or directed to the Landlord and then to the Tenant or directly to the Tenant) of the appropriate local authority, the insurers of the Building and the Landlord in relation to the fire security and safety precautions affecting the Demised Premises;

(vi) permit the Landlord and its agents to enter upon the Demised Premises at any time while the Tenant's Works are being carried out (subject only to the reasonable safety requirements of the Tenant or its contractors) for the purposes of carrying out any outstanding Snag Items, inspecting the manner of execution of the Tenant's Works and compliance with provisions of this Agreement provided that the Tenant receives reasonable written notice of such inspection and the inspection does not delay the carrying out of the Tenant's Works;

(vii) not cause or allow to be caused a nuisance or damage or disturbance to the Landlord, the occupiers for the time being of any adjoining property, the users of the Building and/or the safe and orderly operation of the Building and not to infringe the rights of any aforementioned persons;

(viii) not to acquire or entitle any person to acquire by prescription any right which would interfere with the free use of any neighbouring or adjoining property;

(ix) remove from the Demised Premises upon completion of the Tenant's Works all debris arising from and equipment used in connection with the carrying out of the Tenant's Works;

(x) comply with all obligations under or by virtue of any Law and obtain and comply with such permissions, approvals, certificates, licences and consents as may be required to comply with all such Laws (and in particular with the provisions of the Planning Acts, Building Control Legislation and Safety Regulations) so far as the same relate to or affect the Tenant's Works and any operations, acts or things carried out, executed, done or omitted on the Demised Premises in connection with the Tenant's Works.

14.9 It is hereby expressly agreed that the Certificate of Compliance on Completion in respect of the Landlord's Works and the Tenant's Works must be registered and validated by the Building Control Authority before the Demised Premises may be opened, used or occupied by the Tenant.

14.10 In the event of the Tenant's Works not conforming to the Tenant's Approvals or not satisfying the requirements of the fire officer or the competent person or authority in relation to the application for a fire safety certificate, to carry out such alterations or amendments as necessary to the Tenant's Works that they comply with such planning permissions and fire safety requirements PROVIDED HOWEVER that in the event of it becoming impossible for the Tenant's Works to comply with the planning permissions procured and/or the requirements of the fire officer or other competent person or authority to restore, at the Tenant's own cost, the Demised Premises to the condition prevailing prior to the Tenant's Works being carried out and to the reasonable satisfaction of the Landlord or the Landlord's Architect.

14.11 The Tenant hereby keeps the Landlord fully indemnified from and against all actions, proceedings, claims, demands, losses, costs, expenses, damages and liability (including without limitation those in respect of personal injury to or the death of any person or any injury or damage to any property, real or personal) arising in any way directly or indirectly out of any act omission or negligence of the Tenant or any persons in on or about the Demised Premises expressly or impliedly with the Tenant's authority in connection with the carrying out of the Tenant's Works or arising from the failure or omission by the Tenant, its servants, agents or any other party involved in the carrying out of the Tenant's Works to comply with any of the terms and provisions of this Agreement or relating to any claim made by any adjoining owner or occupier or member of the public or other person in connection with the carrying out of the Tenant's Works.

14.12 **The Tenant shall pay, and indemnify the Landlord against:**

    (a)   all fees, charges and other payments whatever payable to any local or other competent authority at any time in respect of the Tenant's Works and the Tenant's Approvals;

    (b)   the Landlord's surveyors', architects' and engineers' reasonable and proper fees in connection with the application for approval of the Tenant's Works;

    (c)   the Landlord's legal costs in connection with the preparation of any licence for works; and

    (d)   all rates, taxes, assessments, duties, charges, impositions and Outgoings from time to time charged on the Demised Premises or the owner or occupier of them with effect from the Date of Practical Completion.

14.13 Without prejudice to the completion deliverables in any Licence for Works or those set out in Clause 14.8(d) above, upon completion of the Tenant's Works, the Tenant shall forthwith notify the Landlord, and the Landlord's Architect shall be at liberty to inspect the same and if the work has been carried out to the satisfaction of the Landlords Architect, the Tenant's Architect shall forthwith issue to the Landlord and the Tenant a certificate that the Tenant has executed the works in accordance with the Tenant's Specification and the Tenant's Approvals.

14.14 All Tenant's Works undertaken by or on behalf of the Tenant shall be under the management of the Landlord or the Landlord's Architect and the Tenant hereby agrees not to damage or cause to be damaged the Demised Premises or any part of the Estate or any adjoining premises or to obstruct the Landlord or its tenants or its nominated agents or contractors in the course of executing any works on the Building or the Estate, or the use or occupation of the Building or any part thereof.

14.15 The Tenant shall provide method statements and such other information and documentation as the Contractor may require to carry out its duties as project supervisor (construction stage) for the Landlord's Works and shall fully co-operate with the Contractor in all respects.

14.16 The Tenant shall procure the appointment of competent persons to act as project supervisor (construction stage) and project supervisor (design stage) required by the Safety Regulations for the purposes of the Tenant's Works.

14.17 The Tenant's Works shall not be deemed to be improvements for the purposes of the Landlord and Tenant (Amendment) Act 1980.

15. POSSESSION

Upon taking possession of the Demised Premises the Tenant shall be deemed to take possession of the Demised Premises with full knowledge of the actual state and condition of the Demised Premises as to repair, finishes, means of access, enjoyment of light and air, party walls and otherwise, and subject to the terms hereof shall take the same as it stands.

16. NO ASSIGNMENT

16.1 The benefit of this Agreement is personal to the Tenant and the Tenant shall not assign, under-let, charge, share, part with or otherwise dispose of or in any way whatsoever (either directly or indirectly) deal with its interest under this Agreement or any part thereof [without the prior written consent of the Landlord].

16.2   This Agreement enures for the benefit of the successors and assigns of the Landlord's interest in the site of the Demised Premises without the necessity for any assignment of it. The Landlord shall not require the prior consent of the Tenant to charge, pledge or assign by way of security its interest under the within Agreement to any Funder.

17.   NO DAMAGE

The Tenant on behalf of itself, its servants and agents hereby further specifically agrees not to damage the Demised Premises or any part of the Building or the Estate or any adjoining premises in the course of executing any works on the Demised Premises and if the Tenant, its servants or agents shall cause any damage as aforesaid, the Landlord in addition to any other remedy may make good all such damage and the Tenant hereby agrees to pay to the Landlord the sum equal to the costs and expenses of making good all such damage within ten (10) Working Days of such written demand having been made and if such sum is not paid within that period, the Tenant shall pay interest on such sum at the Prescribed Rate from the expiration of the said ten (10) Working Day period until payment is made.

18.   [NOTICE TO FUNDERS

18.1   The Tenant warrants and undertakes that it will not exercise or seek to exercise any right of termination of this Agreement by reason of breach on the part of the Landlord without giving to a Funder not less than 60 days' notice of its intention to do so and specifying the grounds for the proposed determination or discontinuance.

18.2   The right of the Tenant to determine this Agreement shall cease within the period of 60 days referred to in Clause 18.1 if a Funder shall give notice to the Tenant requiring it to continue its obligations under this Agreement; and

(a)   the Funder confirms that it is assuming all the obligations of the Landlord under this Agreement; or

(b)   a third party confirms that it is assuming all the obligations of the Landlord under this Agreement and provides reasonably satisfactory evidence that it has adequate resources to do so.

18.3   Upon compliance by a Funder or a third party with the requirements of clause 18.2 this Agreement shall continue in full force and effect as if the right of determination on the part of the Tenant had not arisen and in all respects as if this Agreement had been made between the Tenant and the Funder or third party as the case may be.]

19.   TITLE

19.1   Landlord's title

The Tenant confirms that it has received prima facie evidence of the Landlord's title to the Demised Premises, has been afforded a reasonable opportunity to raise all such pre-lease enquiries as it may have wished in relation to the Landlord's title, is satisfied with the evidence of Landlord's title furnished and shall not make any further objections or requisitions in respect of the Landlord's title to the Demised Premises.

19.2 **No implied easements**

Nothing in this Agreement shall impliedly confer upon or grant to the Tenant any easement, right or privilege other than those expressly granted by this Agreement or the Lease.

19.3 **No warranty as to user**

Nothing contained in this Agreement shall imply or warrant that the Demised Premises may be used under the Planning Acts and the Public Health Acts for the purpose herein authorised or any purpose subsequently authorised and the Tenant hereby acknowledges and admits that the Landlord has not given or made at any time any representation or warranty that any such use is or will be or will remain a permitted use under the Planning Acts.

19.4 **Representations**

(a) The Tenant acknowledges that this Agreement has not been entered into in reliance wholly or partly on any statement or representation made by or on behalf of the Landlord except any such statement or representation that is expressly set out in this Agreement.

(b) This Agreement embodies the entire understanding of the parties and there are no other arrangements between the parties relating to the subject matter of this Agreement.

(c) No amendment or modification of this Agreement is to be valid or binding on any party unless it is made in writing, refers expressly to this Agreement and is signed by or on behalf of all parties.

20. TERMINATION

20.1 This Agreement may be terminated with immediate effect by the Landlord (upon notification to the Tenant) in the following circumstances if at any time before completion of the Lease:

(a) an event of substantial loss or damage occurs to the Building such that the Landlord cannot deliver the Demised Premises in accordance with the Specification;

(b) any of the events described in the forfeiture provisions of the Lease occurs to the Tenant [or the Guarantor]; or

(c) if the Tenant [or the Guarantor] commits a material breach of the terms of this Agreement.

20.2 In the event that the Landlord terminates this Agreement pursuant to Clause 20.1, this Agreement shall for all purposes other than the purposes of this clause be deemed to be absolutely rescinded but without prejudice to any remedy of the Landlord for any breach of this Agreement prior to such rescission:

(a) the Tenant must immediately release or cancel any registration against the Landlord's title in respect of this Agreement;

(b) the Tenant must, if in occupation, immediately vacate the Demised Premises and deliver it to the Landlord, who in the event of the Tenant failing to vacate and deliver up the same shall be entitled to recover possession of the Demised Premises from the Tenant by action or otherwise;

(c) the Tenant must remove from the Demised Premises all building and other materials and equipment on the Demised Premises in connection with the Tenant's Works;

(d) the Landlord may, immediately or at any time subsequently, take and retain possession of all completed or partially completed Tenant's Works on the Demised Premises, which are to be forfeited and become the property of the Landlord without the Landlord being liable to make to the Tenant any compensation or allowance in respect of them;

(e) the Landlord shall be entitled to recover from the Tenant and the Tenant shall pay to the Landlord in addition to all damages, costs and expenses which the Landlord may have suffered by reason of the rescission of this Agreement, a licence fee in respect of the Demised Premises from the Date of Practical Completion up to the date on which the Tenant shall actually vacate the Demised Premises at the rate per day or part thereof which would have been payable by the Tenant under the Lease by way of rent, service charge and insurance premium from the said date had the Lease been delivered by the Tenant on the Date of Practical Completion and had the rent and additional sums payable under the Lease been payable as from such date.

20.3 The Tenant hereby agrees to indemnify and keep the Landlord indemnified against all and any expenses, costs, claims, demands, damages and other liabilities whatsoever arising as a result of any breach by the Tenant of any of the terms of this Agreement.

20.4 In the event of the rescission of this Agreement for any reason whatsoever the amounts paid by the Tenant as prepaid rent in accordance with Clause 12 (*Payments*) hereof together with any interest payable thereon shall be applied in the following order of priority:

(a) in payment of the licence fee which may be due or payable in accordance with Clause 20.2(e);

(b) in payment of any damages to which the Landlord may be entitled as against the Tenant for any breach of the terms or provisions hereto; and

(c) in payment of any costs or expenses which the Landlord may have incurred as a result of any such breach of the terms or provisions hereof and for the payment of which the Tenant is responsible.

21. STAMP DUTY

The Tenant shall be responsible for and discharge to the Landlord on demand all stamp duty arising in respect of this Agreement, the Lease and counterparts thereof.

22. [CAPITAL ALLOWANCES

22.1 The Tenant shall be entitled to claim capital allowances in relation to expenditure on items of plant and machinery comprised in the Tenant's Works and the Landlord shall not claim capital allowances in respect of such expenditure. The Landlord agrees to co-operate with the Tenant insofar as may be reasonably possible to enable the Tenant or any party that is associated with the Tenant to secure capital allowances in relation to the Tenant's Works.

22.2 The Landlord shall be entitled to claim capital allowances in relation to expenditure which it incurs on items of plant and machinery comprised in the Landlord's

Works and the Tenant shall not claim capital allowances in respect of such expenditure. The Tenant agrees to co-operate with the Landlord insofar as may be reasonably possible to enable the Landlord or any party that is associated with the Landlord to secure capital allowances in relation to the works set out in the Specification.]

23.   AGREEMENT TO REMAIN IN FORCE

The terms and conditions of this Agreement shall remain in full force and effect notwithstanding the grant of the Lease insofar as they remain to be observed and performed.

24.   SEVERANCE

If any term or provision of this Agreement shall be held to be invalid or unenforceable in whole or in part for any reason then such term or provision shall to that extent be deemed not to form part of this Agreement and the validity and enforceability of the remainder of this Agreement shall not be affected.

25.   [GUARANTOR

25.1   The Guarantor jointly and severally covenants with the Landlord as a primary obligation that:

(a)   the Tenant or the Guarantor shall perform and observe the covenants and conditions on the part of the Tenant herein contained and that the Guarantor shall be a party to the Lease in the manner therein provided;

(b)   the Guarantor indemnifies the Landlord against all claims, demands, losses, damages, liability, costs, fees and expenses whatsoever sustained by the Landlord by reason of or arising in any way directly or indirectly out of any default by the Tenant in the performance and observance of any of its obligations to the Landlord under this Agreement;

(c)   that the Guarantor is jointly and severally liable with the Tenant (whether before or after any disclaimer by a liquidator, official assignee, trustee in bankruptcy or other persons administering the assets of the Tenant or whether before or after any repudiation by an examiner or other persons administering the assets of the Tenant) for the fulfilment of all the obligations of the Tenant under this Agreement and agrees that the Landlord in the enforcement of its rights hereunder, may proceed against the Guarantor as if the Guarantor was named as the Tenant in this Agreement; and

(d)   the Guarantee provisions of the Lease are to apply to the Guarantor's obligations under this clause in respect of the Tenant's obligations to the Landlord under this Agreement mutatis mutandis as if same were set out in full in this Agreement.

25.2   In the event that the Guarantor as named in this Agreement enters into liquidation, whether compulsory or voluntary, or passes a resolution for winding-up while solvent, except where the liquidation or winding-up resolution is for the purposes of reconstruction or amalgamation while the Tenant or the Guarantor (as the case may be) remains solvent, the Tenant will ensure that the Guarantor as named in this Agreement is replaced with another entity acceptable to the Landlord (acting reasonably) as being capable of complying with its obligations under this Agreement and the Lease.]

26. NOTICES

26.1 Any notice under this Agreement shall be effectively given if sent by post or delivered to the intended recipient or its solicitors at its, his or their last known address. Where sent by post the notice shall be deemed to be served on the second day after posting.

26.2 Where the last day for taking any step would but for this provision be Christmas Day, Good Friday, a Saturday or Sunday or a public holiday such last day shall be the next following working day instead.

27. JURISDICTION

This Agreement shall be construed in accordance with the Laws of Ireland.

APPENDIX 1
Collateral Warranties

APPENDIX 2
Lease

APPENDIX 3
Licence for Works

AGREEMENT FOR LEASE

APPENDIX 4
Drawings List/Specification/Plans

APPENDIX 5
Measurement Plans

APPENDIX 6
Tenant's Variations/Credits

IN WITNESS whereof the parties hereto have executed this Agreement in the manner following and on the day and year first herein written.

GIVEN under the common seal of
[•] [*insert name of company*]
and **DELIVERED** as a **DEED:**

GIVEN under the common seal of
[•] [*insert name of company*]
and **DELIVERED** as a **DEED:**

AGREEMENT FOR LEASE

GIVEN under the common seal of
[•] [*insert name of company*]
and DELIVERED as a DEED:

[GIVEN under the common seal of
[•] [*insert name of company*]
and DELIVERED as a DEED:]

340

APPENDIX 6

LEASE

This precedent has been prepared for guidance of students of the Law School of the Law Society of Ireland. It assumes that, if utilised in practice, practitioners will take due care in adapting it to incorporate the particular terms and conditions of the subject transaction and that the general terms and conditions of this precedent will be the subject of prudent negotiation. Accordingly, no responsibility can be accepted for its individual content and utilisation in any transaction whether in whole or in part.

This precedent relates to an entire office building so it contains no service charge provisions. It is assumed that the landlord is exercising the option to tax under the Value Added Tax Consolidation Act 2010. It is assumed that there is at least one rent review during the term. This precedent is drafted from a landlord's perspective.

March 2018

© Arthur Cox. This precedent is reproduced with the kind permission of Arthur Cox.

[SUBJECT TO CONTRACT]

Draft [1]: [date]

Dated   20 •

(1) **Landlord:**   •

(2) **Tenant:**   •

[(3) **Guarantor:**   •]

LEASE OF •

Term Commences: •

Length of Term: • years

Rent Review: Every • years

Initial Rent: € • p.a. exclusive [(subject to review as herein provided)]

ARTHUR COX

LEASE

TABLE OF CONTENTS

1   **DEFINITIONS** 1

2   **INTERPRETATION** 4

3   **DEMISED PREMISES AND RENTS** 5

4   **TENANT'S COVENANTS** 5

    4.1   Payments 5

    4.2   Interest...6

    4.3   Outgoings...6

    4.4   Utilities..6

    4.5   Repairs 6

    4.6   Cleaning and Decoration 7

    4.7   Yield Up 8

    4.8   Landlord's Right to Enter...9

    4.9   To Comply With Notices 10

    4.10 Nuisance and Dangerous Materials 10

    4.11 Structure..11

    4.12 Services...11

    4.13 Use Restrictions..11

    4.14 Use 12

    4.15 Alterations 13

    4.16 Alienation 14

    4.17 Disclosure Of Information 17

    4.18 Costs..18

    4.19 Compliance with Laws...18

    4.20 Safety File 19

    4.21 Planning Acts, Public Health Acts and Building Control Act......................19

    4.22 Statutory Notices 21

    4.23 Fire and Security Systems..21

    4.24 Encroachments and Easements 21

    4.25 Disposal of Refuse...22

    4.26 Signs and Advertisements...22

    4.27 Insurance and Indemnity 22

    4.28 VAT..23

    4.29 [Company Registration..24

5   **LANDLORD'S COVENANTS** 24

    5.1   Quiet Enjoyment 24

	5.2	Insurance	24
	5.3	Reinstatement	25
6		**PROVISOS AND AGREEMENTS**	**26**
	6.1	Forfeiture	26
	6.2	Suspension of Rent	27
	6.3	Waiver of 1860 Act Surrender	27
	6.4	No Implied Easements	28
	6.5	Release of Landlord	28
	6.6	No Warranty as to User	28
	6.7	Representations	28
	6.8	Covenants Relating to Adjoining Property	28
	6.9	Effect of Waiver	28
	6.10	Notices	29
	6.11	No Liability	29
	6.12	Applicable Law	29
	6.13	[Assent to Registration	30
7		**GUARANTOR COVENANTS**	**30**
8		**SECTION 238 COMPANIES ACT, 2014**	**30**
9		**TENANT'S ADDRESS AND DESCRIPTION**	**30**

SCHEDULE 1
THE DEMISED PREMISES 31

SCHEDULE 2
EASEMENT RIGHTS AND PRIVILEGES GRANTED 32

SCHEDULE 3
EXCEPTIONS AND RESERVATIONS 33

SCHEDULE 4
RENT REVIEWS 35

SCHEDULE 5
GUARANTOR COVENANTS 41

THIS LEASE dated 20 •

BETWEEN:

(1) l a company incorporated under the laws of Ireland (registration number •) having its registered office at • (the "**Landlord**");

(2) l a company incorporated under the laws of Ireland (registration number •) having its registered office at • (the "**Tenant**"); and

[(3) l a company incorporated under the laws of Ireland (registration number l) having its registered office at • (the "**Guarantor**").]

THIS LEASE PROVIDES as follows:

LEASE

1. **DEFINITIONS**

In this Lease unless the context otherwise requires the following expressions shall have the following meanings:

"**1860 Act**" and "**1881 Act**" mean respectively the Landlord and Tenant Law, Amendment Act, Ireland, 1860, and the Conveyancing Act, 1881;

"**Adjoining Property**" means any land or buildings adjoining or neighbouring the Demised Premises and any other premises in the vicinity which the Landlord or any person connected to the Landlord now owns or acquires during the Term and for the avoidance of doubt does not include the Demised Premises;

"**Base Rate**" means on each occasion when the same falls to be calculated the Prescribed Rate less five (5) percent;

"**Building Control Acts**" means the Building Control Acts 1990 to 2014;

"**Building Control Regulations**" means the Building Control Regulations 1997 to 2015;

"**Building Control Legislation**" means the Building Control Acts and the Building Control Regulations;

["**Car Park Spaces**" means the • car park spaces referred to in paragraph 5 of Schedule 2 which shall be included in the definition of "Demised Premises" for the purposes of Schedule 4;]

"**Conduits**" means each of the following of whatsoever nature: all sewers, drains, soakaways, pipes, gullies, gutters, ducts, mains, watercourses, tanks, attenuation tanks and systems, interceptors, channels, subways, wires, shafts, cables, valves, flues and other transmission or conducting media, installations and equipment (including all fixings, covers, cowls, louvres and other ancillary apparatus) of whatsoever nature or kind or any of them;

"**Demised Premises**" means the premises described in Schedule 1 and for the avoidance of doubt includes only for the purposes of rent review the rights described in Schedule 2;

"**External Decoration Year**" means the fifth year of the Term and thereafter in every subsequent fifth year of the Term;

"**EURIBOR**" means (a) the percentage rate per annum equal to the offered quotation which appears on the page of the Reuters Screen which displays an average rate of the European Banking Federation for the euro (currently pages 248-249) for three months at 11.00am (Brussels time) on the quotation date or, if such page or service ceases to be available, such other page or other service for the purpose of displaying an average rate of the European Banking Federation agreed by the parties; or (b) if no quotation for the relevant period is displayed and the parties have not agreed an alternative service on which a quotation is displayed, the arithmetic mean (rounded upwards to four decimal places) of the rates at which each of the Panel Banks was offering to prime banks in the European interbank market for term deposits in the euro of an equivalent amount for such period at 11.00am (Brussels time) on the quotation date;

"**euro**" or "**EUR**" or "**€**"means the lawful currency of Ireland;

"**Gale Days**" means 1 January, 1 April, 1 July and 1 October in every year of the Term;

"**Guarantor**" means the party (if any) named as "Guarantor";

"**Initial Rent**" means € • (• euro) per annum [subject to review at the Review Dates in accordance with the terms set out in Schedule 4];

"**Insurance Premium**" means the aggregate of the total premiums and other costs and expenses paid or to be paid by the Landlord in complying with its obligations under clause 5.2 (including the cost of periodic valuations for insurance purposes);

"**Insured Risks**" means, subject always to such insurance as may ordinarily and reasonably be available to the Landlord and to such exclusions, excesses and limitations as may be imposed by the Landlord's insurers for the time being in respect of any or all of the following risks:

fire, storm, tempest, flood, earthquake, [subsidence,] [land slip,] lightning, explosion, [terrorist damage], impact by any road vehicle, aircraft and other aerial devices and articles dropped therefrom, riot, civil commotion and malicious damage, bursting or overflowing of water tanks, apparatus or pipes, property owner's liability and, if appropriate, public liability, fire brigade charges (if available on reasonably commercial terms) and such other risks as the Landlord may in its absolute discretion from time to time determine;

"**Internal Decoration Year**" means the third year of the Term and thereafter in every subsequent third year of the Term;

"**Landlord**" includes the person for the time being entitled to the reversion immediately expectant on the determination of the Term;

"**Law**" means every Act of Parliament and of the Oireachtas, law of the European Union and every instrument, directive, regulation, requirement, action and bye law made by any government department, competent authority, officer or court which now or may hereafter have force of law in Ireland;

"**Lease**" means this lease, any document which is made supplemental to it, or which is entered into pursuant to or in accordance with it;

"**Outgoings**" means any rates, taxes, duties, charges, assessments, impositions and outgoings whatsoever whether parliamentary, parochial, local or of any other description and whether or not of a capital or non-recurring nature or of a wholly novel character which may at any time during the Term be payable in respect of the Demised Premises and the Utilities enjoyed in connection with them including any insurance excesses or other sums not recoverable by the Landlord;

"**Permitted Use**" means use of the Demised Premises [for/as] l;

"**Plan**" means the plan(s) (if any) annexed to this Lease;

"**Planning Acts**" means the Local Government (Planning and Development) Acts 1963 to 1999, the Planning and Development Acts 2000 to 2017, the Building Control Acts and the Building Control Regulations;

"**Prescribed Rate**" means on each occasion when the same falls to be calculated the rate of interest which is 7% above EURIBOR or if there shall be no such rate then such rate as the Landlord's accountants or auditors shall certify to be the nearest equivalent then existing;

"**Public Health Acts**" mean the Local Government (Sanitary Services) Act, 1878 to 2001;

"**Review Dates**" means • in the year • and every fifth anniversary of that date during the Term and Relevant Review Date shall be construed accordingly;

"**Review Period**" means the period starting on any Review Date up to the next Review Date or starting with the last Review Date up to the end of the Term;

"**Safety Act**" means the Safety, Health and Welfare at Work Acts 2005 to 2014;

"**Surveyor**" shall have the meaning given to that term in Schedule 4;

"**Term**" means • ;

"**Term Commencement Date**" means • ;

"**Utilities**" means each of the following of whatsoever nature: water, soils and wastes of all kinds, steam, gas, air, electricity, telephone and other communications systems, fire-fighting and fire prevention systems and equipment, radio and television transmissions, telecommunications, data transmission lines, computer linking, electronic and optical communications, oil and heating fuels and other services and supplies (including any plant, machinery, apparatus and equipment required to operate the same) and "Utility" means any of them; and

"**VAT**" means Value Added Tax pursuant to the VAT Act or any similar or other tax from time to time substituted for it;

"**VAT Act**" means the Value Added Tax Consolidation Act 2010, as amended from time to time, regulations made thereunder and any enactment for the time being extending, amending, repealing, replacing or continuing same;

"**Working Day**" or "**Days**" means a day other than a Saturday or Sunday or Good Friday or public holiday in Ireland on which clearing banks are generally open for business in Ireland.

2. **INTERPRETATION**

Unless there is something in the subject or context inconsistent therewith, in interpreting this Lease:

2.1 words importing the singular number include the plural number and vice versa and reference to any party includes its successors in title, personal representatives and permitted assigns;

2.2 where two or more persons are included in the expression "Landlord", "Tenant" or "Guarantor" the covenants which are expressed to be made by the Landlord, the Tenant or the Guarantor shall be deemed to be made by such persons jointly and severally.

2.3 A "company" shall be construed so as to include any company, corporation or body corporate, wherever and however incorporated or established;

2.4 any covenant by the Tenant not to do any act or thing shall include an obligation not to permit or suffer such act or thing to be done and any references to any act, neglect, default or omission of the Tenant shall be deemed to include any act, neglect, default or omission of the Tenant or the under-lessees, servants, agents, licensees or invitees of the Tenant or any person under its or their control;

2.5 references to any right of the Landlord to have access to or entry upon the Demised Premises shall be construed as extending to all persons authorised by the Landlord [and any person holding an interest in the Demised Premises superior to the Landlord] and each of their agents, professional advisors, prospective purchasers of any interest of the Landlord [or superior landlord] in the Demised Premises or Adjoining Property, contractors, workmen and others;

2.6 unless the context otherwise requires, a reference to the Demised Premises is to the whole and any part of it;

2.7 the conclusiveness (expressed in this Lease) of determinations, findings or certificates of any auditor or surveyor of the Landlord shall not extend to questions of Law;

2.8 any reference to a Law (whether specifically named or not) or to any sections or sub-sections in a Law shall include any amendments or re-enactments thereof for the time being in force and all statutory instruments, orders, notices, regulations, directions, bye-laws, certificates permissions and plans for the time being made, issued or given thereunder or deriving validity from it;

2.9 if any term or provision shall be held to be illegal or unenforceable in whole or in part, then that term shall be deemed not to form part of this Lease and the enforceability of the remainder of this Lease shall not be affected;

2.10   clause, paragraph or schedule headings are for reference only and shall not affect the construction or interpretation of this Lease;

2.11   any reference to a clause, sub-clause or schedule shall mean a clause, sub-clause or schedule of this Lease and a reference in a schedule to a paragraph is to a paragraph of that schedule;

2.12   any reference to "day" shall mean a period of twenty-four (24) hours running from midnight to midnight;

2.13   any reference to a "month" shall mean a calendar month; and

2.14   any reference to "times" are to time in Ireland.

3.   DEMISED PREMISES AND RENTS

In consideration of the rents herein reserved (including the revisions thereof following any rent review as hereinafter provided) and the covenants on the part of the Tenant and the conditions contained in this Lease the Landlord **HEREBY DEMISES** unto the Tenant **ALL THAT** the Demised Premises **TOGETHER** with the easements, rights and privileges specified in Schedule 2 **EXCEPTING AND RESERVING** at all times during the Term unto the Landlord the easements, quasi easements, rights and privileges specified in Schedule 3 **SUBJECT TO** all easements, quasi easements, rights, privileges, covenants, restrictions and stipulations of whatsoever nature affecting the Demised Premises **TO HOLD** the same (excepted and reserved as aforesaid) unto the Tenant from and including the Term Commencement Date for the Term **YIELDING AND PAYING** unto the Landlord during the Term by way of rent:

3.1   yearly and proportionately for any fraction of a year the Initial Rent and from and including the Rent Review Date such yearly rent as shall become payable under and in accordance with the provisions of Schedule 4 by equal quarterly payments in advance on the Gale Days (the first payment to be made on the execution of this Lease); and

3.2   the Insurance Premium to be paid [annually in advance] within seven (7) days of demand.

in each case to be paid (at the option of the Landlord, which option may be exercised on any number of occasions) either by standing order, direct debit, credit transfer or cheque without any deduction, set-off or counterclaim whatsoever.

4.   TENANT'S COVENANTS

The Tenant to the intent that the obligations may continue throughout the Term **HEREBY COVENANTS** with the Landlord as follows:

4.1   Payments

To pay to the Landlord:

(a)   the rents or revised rents reserved by this Lease reserved at clause 3.1;

(b)   the Insurance Premium reserved at clause 3.2;

(c)   interest covenanted to be paid at clause 4.2;

(d)   any additional sums payable under the terms of this Lease;

(e)   the stamp duty payable on this Lease and its counterpart; and

(f)   any VAT payable on the delivery of this Lease and on any rents reserved by this Lease and on any other payments to be made under this Lease in each case at the times and in the manner prescribed for the payment of each of them or if no manner is prescribed then within seven (7) days of demand.

4.2 Interest

Without prejudice to any other right, remedy or power contained in this Lease or otherwise available to the Landlord, to pay interest to the Landlord on any sum of money payable by the Tenant to the Landlord which remains unpaid (whether formally demanded or not) (including any sum of rent the acceptance of which may be refused bona fide by the Landlord in order not to waive any right of forfeiture of this Lease arising by virtue of the breach of any of the Tenant's covenants contained in this Lease) for more than seven (7) days after the date when payment was due at the Prescribed Rate from and including the date on which payment was due to the date of payment to the Landlord (both before and after any judgment).

4.3 Outgoings

To pay and indemnify the Landlord against all Outgoings which time during the Term be charged, levied, assessed or imposed upon or payable in respect of the Demised Premises or upon the owner or occupier of the Demised Premises but excluding any taxes referable to the receipt of rent by the Landlord or to a dealing by the Landlord with the reversion expectant upon the determination of the Term.

4.4 Utilities

(a) To pay all charges for Utilities consumed in or on the Demised Premises, including any connection and hiring charges and meter rents and to perform and observe all present and future regulations and requirements of each of the Utility supply authorities in respect of the supply and consumption of Utilities in or on the Demised Premises and to keep the Landlord indemnified against any breach thereof;

(b) To pay to the Local Authority or such other statutory body on demand the cost from time to time of water supply to or consumed in the Demised Premises in accordance with meter reading.

4.5 Repairs

From time to time and at all times during the Term:

(a) to keep clean and tidy and to maintain, repair, replace and reinstate and to put into and keep in good order repair and condition from time to time and at all times during the Term, the interior and exterior of the Demised Premises and every part of it and any additions, alterations and extensions to it including, without derogating from the generality of the foregoing, the roof, structure, drains, foundations, walls (including external and load bearing walls), timbers, joists and beams of the floors and ceilings, chimney stacks, gutters, doors, locks, plate glass and other windows, fixtures, fittings, fastenings, wires, waste water drains and other pipes and sanitary and water apparatus in or on the Demised Premises; and

(b) to keep clean and tidy and to maintain, repair and keep in good working order and condition and (where necessary) renew and replace with articles of a similar kind and quality all plant and machinery in or forming part of the Demised Premises including the Conduits and the central heating and air conditioning plant (if any), the sprinkler system and all lifts, lift shafts and lift machinery, all boilers and all electrical and mechanical plant, machinery, equipment and apparatus;

(damage by any of the Insured Risks excepted if and so long only as the policy or policies of insurance shall not have been vitiated or payment of the policy monies withheld or refused in whole or in part by reason of any act, neglect, default or omission of the Tenant or the under-lessees, servants, agents, licensees or invitees of the Tenant or any person under its or their control).

(c)   To keep all parts of the Demised Premises which are not built upon (if any) in a good and clean condition, adequately surfaced and free from weeds, and all landscaped areas properly cultivated and maintained and all trees (if any) preserved.

4.6   Cleaning and Decoration

(a)   In every External Decoration Year and also in the last six (6) months of the Term (whether determined by effluxion of time or otherwise) in a good and workmanlike manner to prepare and decorate (with two (2) coats at least of good quality paint) or otherwise treat as appropriate all external wood, metal, stucco, cement work and other exterior parts of the Demised Premises required to be so treated in colours to be approved by the Landlord (such approval not to be unreasonably withheld) and as often as may be reasonably necessary to properly wash down, clean, restore, repoint and make good and, wherever appropriate, treat with suitable preservative all stonework, brickwork, concrete and other finishes to the reasonable satisfaction of the Landlord.

(b)   In every Internal Decoration Year and also in the last three (3) months of the Term (whether determined by effluxion of time or otherwise) in a good and workmanlike manner to prepare and decorate (with two (2) coats at least of good quality paint) or otherwise treat as appropriate all interior parts of the Demised Premises required to be so treated and as often as may be reasonably necessary to wash down all tiles, glazed bricks and similar washable surfaces to the reasonable satisfaction of the Landlord and to comply with the Landlord's requirements as to colours and materials in respect of decoration in the last year of the Term (whether determined by effluxion of time or otherwise).

(c)   To keep the Demised Premises in a clean and tidy condition and at least once a month to properly clean both sides of all windows and window frames and all other glass in the Demised Premises.

4.7   Yield Up

(a)   At the expiration or sooner determination of the Term to quietly yield up the Demised Premises to the Landlord in such good and substantial repair and condition as shall be in accordance with the covenants on the part of the Tenant in this Lease and in any licence or consent granted by the Landlord and if any of the Landlord's fixtures and fittings are missing, broken damaged or destroyed to forthwith replace them with others of a similar kind and of equal value and to give up all keys and to remove from the Demised Premises any moulding, sign, writing or painting of the name or business of the Tenant or occupiers and unless stipulated to the contrary by the Landlord (including in any licences for works or other document consenting to any works carried out by the Tenant), to remove and make good to the original prevailing condition all the alterations or additions made to the Demised Premises by the Tenant (or such of them as the Landlord shall require) including the making good of any damage caused to the Demised Premises by the removal of the Tenant's fixtures, fittings, furniture and effects.

(b) Should the Tenant fail to have remedied any breaches of the Tenant's repair or yield up covenants under this Lease, or under any documents supplemental hereto and / or under any licences for works granted hereunder and as may be entered into from time to time, on or prior to the expiry of the Term (whether terminated by effluxion of time or otherwise) (the "**End Date**"), then the Tenant will pay to the Landlord within twenty-one (21) days of demand (or from when determined by the Expert (as hereinafter defined) as the case may be):

(i) the cost of remedying such breaches, and in the event that the parties cannot agree on the cost of remedying such breaches the matter shall be determined by the Expert; and

(ii) an amount equal to the Outgoings for the Works Period (the "**Works Period Outgoings**").

(c) **In this clause:**

(i) "**Works Period Outgoings**" means the aggregate of each of the following, calculated at the rate payable as if the Lease had not terminated:-

(A) rent;

(B) the Insurance Premium payable by the Tenant in accordance with clause 3.2;

(C) the outgoings payable by the Tenant in accordance with clause 4.4; and

(D) all other sums which would be payable by the Tenant under the Lease.

(ii) "**Works Period**" means the period of time which it would reasonably be expected to undertake the dilapidation/repair obligations (to include the time taken to determine the condition of the Demised Premises, time to appoint a design team, time for pricing of works (i.e. tendering etc.), and the appointment/mobilisation of a contractor as well as the time to undertake the works themselves and also the time taken for the appointment of the Expert (if so required) and time for him to deliver his award), as may be agreed between the parties or, in default of agreement as shall be determined by the Expert.

(d) In the case of a dispute under clause 4.7(a) and 4.7(b) the matter shall be determined by the Expert who shall:

(i) be an independent chartered surveyor (with not less than fifteen (15) years' relevant experience) agreed between the parties or appointed if requested by either party by the President (or the next most senior available officer) of Society of Chartered Surveyors Ireland or any successor body failing which the appointment shall be made by the President (or the next available officer) of the Law Society of Ireland) (the "**Expert**");

(ii) act as an expert and not as an arbitrator and his fees shall be borne by the party against whom he holds or in default of such holding by the parties equally;

(iii) afford to the Landlord and the Tenant a reasonable opportunity of stating (whether in writing or otherwise as may be decided by him and within the time as he may stipulate in that behalf) reasons in support of such contentions as each party may wish to make relative to the matter or matters under consideration;

(iv) be required to give a decision without delay and in any event within ten days of being requested to resolve such dispute.

(e)   The determination of the Expert shall be binding on the parties.

(f)   If at such time as the Tenant has vacated the Demised Premises at the ex-piration or sooner determination of the Term any property of the Tenant shall remain in or on the Demised Premises and the Tenant shall fail to remove the property within seven (7) days after being requested in writing by the Landlord to do so, then and in such case the Landlord (without being obliged to do so and in any event without prejudice to such other rights as the Landlord may have in that behalf) may, as agent of the Tenant (and the Landlord is hereby appointed by the Tenant to act as such agent), sell such property and shall then hold the proceeds of sale after deducting the costs and expenses of removal storage and sale reasonably incurred by it to the order of the Tenant **PROVIDED THAT** the Tenant shall indem-nify the Landlord against any liability incurred by the Landlord to any third party whose property shall have been sold by the Landlord in the bona fide mistaken belief (which shall be presumed unless the contrary be proved) that such property belonged to the Tenant and was liable to be dealt with as such pursuant to this clause 4.7(f).

4.8   **Landlord's Right to Enter**

(a)   To permit the Landlord with all necessary materials and appliances at all reasonable times upon reasonable prior notice (except in cases of emer-gency in which cases no notice shall be required) to enter and remain upon the Demised Premises to exercise any of the rights excepted and reserved by this Lease or for any other purposes connected with this Lease.

(b)   To permit the Landlord at all reasonable times to enter and remain upon the Demised Premises and (but not so as to materially affect the access of light and air to the Demised Premises) to affix and retain without interfer-ence upon any suitable parts of the Demised Premises notices for re-let-ting the same and not to remove or obscure the said notices and to permit the Landlord, its agents and potential tenants or owners of the Demised Premises or their agents to view the Demised Premises at all reasonable hours.

(c)   To permit the Landlord at all reasonable times to enter and remain upon the Demised Premises to view the state and repair of the Demised Premises and to take schedules and inventories of the Landlord's fixtures.

(d)   To permit the Landlord at all reasonable times to enter and remain upon the Demised Premises for any other purpose connected with the interest of the Landlord in the Demised Premises including but not limited to valuing or disposing of any interest of the Landlord.

4.9   **To Comply With Notices**

(a)   If the Landlord gives written notice to the Tenant of any defects, wants of repair or breaches of covenant then the Tenant shall within thirty (30) days of such notices or sooner if requisite make good and remedy the de-fect, want of repair or breach of covenant to the satisfaction of the Landlord.

(b)   If the Tenant fails within seven (7) days of such notice or, as soon as pos-sible in the case of emergency, to commence and then diligently and expe-ditiously to continue to comply with such notice, the Landlord may enter the Demised Premises and carry out or cause to be carried out all or any of the works referred to in such notice, and all costs and expenses thereby incurred shall be paid by the Tenant to the Landlord on demand and in default of payment shall be recoverable as rent in arrears.

4.10 **Nuisance and Dangerous Materials**

(a) Not to do anything in or about the Demised Premises which may be or become a nuisance, pollutant, or contaminant or which may cause damage, annoyance, inconvenience or disturbance to the Landlord or the other owners, tenants or occupiers of the Adjoining Property or which may be injurious to the value, tone or amenity or character of the Demised Premises.

(b) Not to bring into or on or keep in or on the Demised Premises any article or thing which is or might become deleterious, dangerous, offensive, unduly combustible or inflammable, radioactive or explosive or which might unduly increase the risk of fire or explosion or which might interfere with any fire and safety equipment or appliances installed in or on the Demised Premises.

(c) Not to do anything in or about the Demised Premises or bring into or on or keep in or on the Demised Premises any article or thing which may interfere with or obstruct any of the rights, easements and privileges excepted and reserved and specified in Schedule 3.

(d) Not to keep or operate in the Demised Premises any machinery which shall be unduly noisy or cause vibration or which may annoy or disturb the other owners, tenants or occupiers of the Adjoining Property.

(e) Not [without the prior written consent of the Landlord,] to cook or prepare any food in or on the Demised Premises and to take all necessary steps to ensure that all smells caused by cooking, refuse or food shall not cause any nuisance or annoyance to the Landlord or any of the owners, tenants or occupiers of the Adjoining Property.

4.11 **Structure**

(a) Not to overload the floors of the Demised Premises or suspend any excessive weight from the roofs, ceilings, walls, stanchions or structure of the Demised Premises and not to overload the Utilities and Conduits in or serving the Demised Premises.

(b) Not to do anything which may subject the Demised Premises or any parts of it to any strain beyond that which they are designed to bear with due margin for safety, and to pay to the Landlord on demand all costs reasonably incurred by the Landlord in obtaining the opinion of a qualified structural engineer as to whether the structure of the Demised Premises is being or is about to be overloaded.

(c) To observe the weight limits and capacity prescribed for all lifts in the Demised Premises.

4.12 **Services**

Not to discharge into any Conduits any oil or grease or any noxious or deleterious effluent or substance whatsoever which may cause an obstruction or might be or become a source of danger or which might injure the Conduits in the Demised Premises or the Adjoining Property.

4.13 **Use Restrictions**

(a) Without prejudice to the provisions of clause 4.14 not to use the Demised Premises or any part of it for or as:

(i) public or political meetings, public exhibitions or public entertainments shows or spectacles;

(ii) dangerous, noisy, noxious or offensive trades or businesses;

(iii) illegal or immoral purposes including the sale hire, distribution, viewing or display of any books, magazines, films, video or other recordings or other material when the keeping of such material or materials on the Demised Premises or the sale hire, distribution, viewing or display of such material or materials on or from the Demised Premises is unlawful or renders the same liable to forfeiture or seizure;

(iv) residential or sleeping purposes;

(v) a restaurant or café;

(vi) for the sale of food or food products or grocery products for consumption off the premises;

(vii) a pharmacy or chemist;

(viii) gambling, betting, gaming or wagering (including gambling machines);

(ix) a betting office;

(x) banking purposes or for the provision of financial services;

(xi) gymnasium;

(xii) cinema;

(xiii) an amusement shop or arcade; or

(xiv) for the sale or supply of intoxicating liquor whether for consumption on or off the Demised Premises.

(b) Not to use the Demised Premises for any purpose or in a manner that would cause loss, damage, injury, nuisance or inconvenience to the Landlord and any tenants and occupiers of the Adjoining Property.

(c) Not to play or use any live or recorded music, musical instrument, record player, loudspeaker or similar apparatus in such a manner as to be audible outside the Demised Premises.

(d) Not to hold any auction on the Demised Premises.

(e) Not to use the Demised Premises or any part of it as a club where intoxicating liquor is supplied to members and their guests.

(f) Not to keep any live animal, fish, reptile or bird on the Demised Premises.

(g) Not to burn any rubbish or refuse on or in any part of the Demised Premises.

(h) Not to place outside the Demised Premises nor expose from the windows of the Demised Premises any articles, goods or things of any kind.

4.14 **Use**

(a) Not without the prior written consent of the Landlord (which consent shall not be unreasonably withheld) to use the Demised Premises or any part thereof except for the Permitted Use.

(b) Not to make any application for planning permission or fire safety certificate or other relevant consents with regard to any change of user without the prior written consent of the Landlord (which consent shall not be unreasonably withheld).

(c) To ensure that at all times the Landlord has written notice of the name, home address and home telephone number of at least two keyholders of the Demised Premises and to notify the Landlord of any changes in the persons so authorised as keyholders of the Demised Premises.

(d) To provide such caretaking or security arrangements as the Landlord or the insurers of the Demised Premises shall reasonably require in order to protect the Demised Premises from vandalism, theft or unlawful occupation and not to leave the Demised Premises unoccupied (other than for normal holiday periods) without notifying the Landlord and providing such care-taking or security arrangements as so required.

(e) At all times to comply with all the requirements of the relevant local authority in connection with the Permitted Use.

4.15 Alterations

(a) Not to alter, divide, cut, maim, injure or remove any of the principal or load bearing walls, floors, beams or columns of or enclosing the Demised Premises nor to make any other alterations or additions of a structural nature to any part of the Demised Premises (either internally or externally).

(b) Not to erect any new building or structure (including any mezzanine or similar structure) on the Demised Premises or any part of it nor to add to or change the height elevation or external architectural or decorative design or appearance of the Demised Premises nor to unite the Demised Premises or any part of it with any other property nor to demolish the Demised Premises or any part of it.

(c) Not to make any change in the existing design or appearance (whether internal or external) of the Demised Premises.

(d) Not to make any alterations or additions to the Landlord's fixtures and fittings nor to any of the Conduits without obtaining the prior written consent of the Landlord.

(e) Not to make any alterations or additions of a non-structural nature to the Demised Premises without obtaining the prior written consent of the Landlord, such consent not to be unreasonably withheld.

(f) Not to affix to the outside of the Demised Premises any bracket, aerial, fixture, wire or other apparatus for radio-diffusion, wireless television or telephone without obtaining the Landlord's written consent and its written approval of the location and method of affixing.

(g) The Landlord may, as a condition of giving any such consent under this clause, require the Tenant to enter into such covenants as the Landlord shall require regarding the execution of any such works and the reinstatement of the Demised Premises at the end or sooner determination of the Term.

(h) The Tenant agrees with the Landlord may refuse an application for consent to alterations on the basis that any consent, certificate or approval required under any Law contains or omits terms or conditions which would in the opinion of the Landlord, be or be likely to be prejudicial to the Landlord's interest in the Demised Premises whether during or following the expiration or soon determination of the Term.

(i) If any alterations or additions to or within the Demised Premises result in a variation of the reinstatement cost of the Demised Premises from the said cost prior to such alterations or additions then the Tenant shall:

(i) give notice in writing to the Landlord forthwith of the variation in value so caused to enable the Landlord to alter the insurance cover in respect of the Demised Premises; and

(ii) pay or reimburse to the Landlord any shortfall of insurance cover caused by a failure to comply with the requirements in clause 4.15(i)(i).

The Tenant agrees that notice under clause 4.15(i)(i) notifying the variation of the reinstatement cost shall only be sufficient notice if it refers to clause 4.15(i)(i) and the Landlord shall not otherwise be deemed to have received such notice or to be responsible for the varying of the said insurance cover.

4.16 **Alienation**

(a) Not to assign, transfer, underlet, charge (including lodgement of this Lease with anyone as security) or share or part with the possession or occupation of the Demised Premises or any part of it or suffer any person to occupy the Demised Premises or any part of it as a licensee, franchisee or concessionaire.

(b) Notwithstanding the provisions of clause 4.16(a) the Landlord shall not unreasonably withhold its consent to the charging (including lodging this Lease with anyone as security) of the entire of the Demised Premises with a recognised financial institution or to an assignment of the entire or to an under-letting of the entire of the Demised Premises to an assignee or under-lessee acceptable to the Landlord and of financial standing satisfactory to the Landlord and otherwise subject to the following provisions or such of them as may be appropriate.

   (i) The Tenant shall prior to any such alienation apply to the Landlord in writing and give all reasonable information as the Landlord may require concerning the proposed transaction and concerning the proposed assignee, under-lessee or disponee.

   (ii) Prior to any permitted transfer, assignment or underletting of the whole or part of the Demised Premises the Tenant shall notify the Landlord in writing prior to such proposed transfer, assignment or underletting indicating the name and address of the proposed transferee, assignee or underlessee in order that the Landlord can establish and confirm to the Tenant whether the proposed transferee, assignee or underlessee is or is not connected with the Landlord within the meaning of Section 97(3) of the VAT Act **AND** in the event of the proposed transferee, assignee or underlessee being so connected and the transfer, assignment or underletting would result in the termination of the Option to Tax (as hereinafter defined) the Tenant shall prior to such transfer, assignment or underletting pay to the Landlord on a net of tax basis for the Landlord the amount equivalent to the VAT liability quantified by the Landlord arising as a result of such assignment, transfer or underletting. For the avoidance of doubt, the Landlord's and the Tenant's tax advisors shall endeavour to agree the level of such liability in advance of any assignment, transfer or underletting but in the event of failure to do so, the written opinion including relevant computations of the Landlord's tax advisors shall save in the case of manifest error be taken as conclusive evidence for these purposes as to the amount so payable.

   (iii) The Landlord's consent to any such alienation shall be in writing and shall be given in such manner as the Landlord shall decide and the Tenant shall pay the reasonable costs of the Landlord in connection with the consideration of each such application and (where applicable) the furnishing of such consent.

   (iv) Without prejudice to any other grounds on which the Landlord may be entitled to withhold its consent to any such alienation, it shall be deemed a reasonable ground for the withholding of Landlord's consent that:

      (A) the Tenant is in breach of any of the Tenant's covenants and conditions contained in this Lease; or

(B)   the proposed assignee, under-lessee or disponee intends to alter the Permitted Use or any part thereof in a manner which would be prohibited under the provisions of clause 4.14; or

(C)   the proposed assignee, under-lessee or disponee has or may have immunity from legal proceedings in relation to any breach of any covenant or condition in this Lease or any under-lease; or

(D)   such alienation causes a VAT cost for the Landlord, either as a VAT clawback or as a VAT liability; or

(E)   the proposed assignee, under-lessee or disponee does not intend to occupy the Demised Premises.

(v)   In the case of an assignment to a limited liability company, if it shall be deemed reasonable, the Landlord may require that a surety (or sureties) of standing satisfactory to the Landlord join in the relevant consent as surety for such a company in order jointly and severally to covenant with the Landlord in the manner described in the guarantee contained in Schedule 5 (mutatis mutandis) or in such other form as the Landlord may from time to time require.

(vi) In the case of an under-lease, the same shall be of the entire of the Demised Premises and be made without taking a fine or premium and reserving the then current market rent or the rent payable hereunder at the time of the granting of such under-lease (whichever is the higher) and be in a form approved by the Landlord (such approval not to be unreasonably withheld). The under-lessee shall if required by the Landlord enter into a direct covenant with the Landlord to perform and observe all the covenants (other than that for payment of the rents hereby reserved) and conditions contained in this Lease. Every such under-lease shall also contain:

(A)   provisions for the review of the rent thereby reserved (which the Tenant hereby covenants to operate and enforce) corresponding both as to terms and dates and in all other respects (mutatis mutandis) with the rent review provisions contained in this Lease [unless the term of the under-lease does not extend beyond the next Review Date];

(B)   a covenant condition or proviso under which the rent from time to time payable under such under-lease shall not be less than the rent from time to time payable under this Lease;

(C)   a covenant by the under-tenant (which the Tenant hereby covenants to enforce) prohibiting the under-tenant from doing or suffering any act or thing upon or in relation to the Demised Premises inconsistent with or in breach of the provisions of this Lease;

(D)   a provision giving the Landlord right of re-entry on breach of any covenant by the under-tenant; and

(E)   the same restrictions as to alienation, assignment, under-letting, mortgaging, charging (including lodging the under-lease with anyone as security) and parting with or sharing the possession or occupation of the premises underlet as this Lease.

(vii) To enforce at the Tenant's own expense the performance and observance by every such under-tenant of the covenants conditions and provisions of the under-lease and not at any time either expressly or by implication to waive any breach of the same.

(viii) Not to agree any reviewed rent with the under-tenant nor any rent payable on any renewal of an under-lease without the prior written consent of the Landlord (such consent not to be unreasonably withheld).

(ix) Not to vary the terms or consent to alienation of or accept any surrender of any permitted under-lease without the prior written consent of the Landlord, such consent not to be unreasonably withheld.

(x) Within seven (7) days of every alienation, assignment, transfer, assent, under-lease, assignment of under-lease, mortgage, charge (including lodgement of the relevant document or instrument as security) or any other disposition whether mediate or immediate of or relating to the Demised Premises or any part of it, to deliver to the Landlord or its solicitors a solicitor's certified copy of the deed instrument or other document evidencing or effecting such disposition duly stamped and shall pay the Landlord's reasonable costs and expenses in connection with such alienation including, for the avoidance of doubt, the Landlord's reasonable professional costs and expenses.

(xi) The Tenant covenants to indemnify and keep indemnified the Landlord in respect of any and all tax liabilities (including any VAT clawback or VAT liability) which the Landlord may suffer in the event the Tenant breaches the conditions of clause 4.16(a) or 4.16(b). All sums payable by the Tenant to the Landlord under this clause 4.16(b)(xi) shall be paid free and clear of all deductions or withholdings save only as may be required by law. If any such deductions or withholdings are required by law, the Tenant shall pay to the Landlord such sum as will, after such deduction or withholding has been made, leave the Landlord with the same amount as it would have been entitled to receive, in the absence of such requirement to make a deduction or withholding. If any sum payable by the Tenant to the Landlord under this clause 4.16(b)(xi) shall otherwise be subject to tax in the hands of the Landlord, the same obligation to make an increased payment shall apply in relation to such tax as if it were a deduction or withholding required by law, as referred to above.

(xii) For the avoidance of doubt, the Tenant shall pay the Landlord's reasonable costs and expenses (including the Landlord's reasonable professional costs and expenses) in connection with the Landlord's consideration of any application made under this clause 4.16(b) irrespective of whether or not the application is ultimately refused or withdrawn.

4.17 Disclosure Of Information

Upon making any application or request in connection with the Demised Premises or this Lease, to disclose to the Landlord such information it may reasonably require and, whenever the Landlord shall reasonably request to supply full particulars of:

(a) all persons in actual occupation or possession of the Demised Premises and the basis on which they are in such occupation or possession;

(b) the entire agreement between the Tenant and another party relevant to the application or request; and

(c) all persons having an interest in the Demised Premises (other than in the reversion to the Term).

4.18 **Costs**

To pay and indemnify the Landlord against all costs, fees, charges, disbursements and expenses incurred by the Landlord, including, but not limited to, those payable to solicitors, counsel, architects, surveyors and sheriffs:

(a) in relation to or in contemplation of the preparation and service of a notice under Section 14 of the 1881 Act and of any proceedings under the 1881 Act and/or the 1860 Act (whether or not any right of re-entry or forfeiture has been waived or a notice served under Section 14 of the 1881 Act has been complied with by the Tenant and notwithstanding that forfeiture has been avoided otherwise than by relief granted by the Court);

(b) in relation to [or in contemplation of] the preparation and service of all notices and schedules relating to wants of repair, whether served during or after the expiration of the Term (but relating in all cases only to such wants of repair that accrued not later than the expiration or sooner determination of the Term);

(c) in connection with the recovery or attempted recovery by the Landlord of arrears of rent or other sums due from the Tenant to the Landlord (such expenses being in addition to and not in substitution for any interest payable to the Landlord pursuant to the provisions of clause 4.2 of this Lease) or in procuring the remedying of the breach of any covenant by the Tenant;

(d) in relation to any application for consent required or made necessary by this Lease whether or not the same is granted or has been withdrawn;

(e) in relation to any application made by the Landlord at the request of the Tenant and whether or not such application is accepted, refused or withdrawn; or

(f) in the clearance or repair of the Utilities and Conduits in or serving the Demised Premises where they have been blocked or damaged by any act, neglect, default or omission of the Tenant.

4.19 **Compliance with Laws**

(a) At the Tenant's own expense to comply in all respects with the provisions of all Laws relating to the Demised Premises or its use.

(b) To execute all works and provide and maintain all arrangements upon or in respect of the Demised Premises or any part of it or the use of the Demised Premises which are directed or required (whether of the Landlord, Tenant or occupier) by any Law and to indemnify and keep the Landlord indemnified against all costs, charges, fees and expenses of or incidental to the execution of any works or the provision or maintenance of any arrangements so directed or required.

(c) Not to do anything in or about the Demised Premises by reason of which the Landlord may under any Law incur or have imposed upon it or become liable to pay any penalty, damages, compensation, costs, charges or expenses.

(d) To comply at all times with the provision of the Safety Act and where applicable to furnish the Landlord with a copy of the safety file prepared pursuant thereto.

4.20 **Safety File**

(a) To maintain and keep and to hand over to the Landlord all relevant information for updating the safety file of the Landlord (the "**Landlord's Safety File**") in respect of any construction work as defined in the Safety Act including fit-out works carried out by the Tenant (or its under-tenant(s) where appropriate) to the Demised Premises

(b)   In respect of any construction work carried out or to be carried out by the Tenant (or its under-tenant(s) where appropriate) to the Demised Premises which obliges the Tenant or such other party to keep a safety file (the "**Tenant's Safety File**") the Tenant shall retain or procure that there is retained therein all relevant information in relation to such construction work and on completion of such construction work shall expeditiously hand a duplicate copy of the Tenant's Safety File to the Landlord or his authorised agent or nominee.

(c)   To maintain, keep and update as and when required the Tenant's Safety File and when requested to do so to make same available for inspection by the Landlord or its authorised agent or nominee.

(d)   To supply the Landlord or his authorised agent or nominee with all necessary information and updates relating to the Tenant's Safety File to enable the Landlord to update any copy thereof maintained by the Landlord.

(e)   On the permitted assignment of this Lease to hand over the Tenant's Safety File to the assignee and on the expiration or sooner determination of the Term to hand over the original Tenant's Safety File to the Landlord or his authorised agent or nominee.

(f)   In the event that the Landlord makes available the Landlord's Safety File to the Tenant, to hold the Landlord's Safety File in trust and to the order of the Landlord and to return it as soon as possible and in any event at the request of the Landlord or his authorised agent or nominee.

(g)   To comply with the requirements of the Safety Act and any regulations made thereunder and/or under any legislation repealed by it including provisions for the appointment of a project supervisor for the design stage and the construction stage of any works carried out by or on behalf of the Tenant or any other occupier of the Demised Premises and to indemnify and keep indemnified the Landlord against any loss incurred by the Landlord as a result of the breach by the Tenant of its obligations under this clause.

4.21   **Planning Acts, Public Health Acts and Building Control Legislation**

Without prejudice to the generality of clause 4.19:

(a)   Not to do anything on or in connection with the Demised Premises the doing or omission of which shall be a contravention of the Planning Acts, the Public Health Acts or Building Control Legislation or of any notices, orders, licences, consents, permissions and conditions (if any) served, made, granted or imposed thereunder and to indemnify (after the expiration of the Term as well as before whether by effluxion of time or otherwise as during its continuance) and keep indemnified the Landlord against all actions, proceedings, damages, penalties, costs, charges, claims and demands in respect of such acts and omissions or any of them and against the costs of remedying such a contravention;

(b)   In the event of the Landlord giving written consent to any of the matters in respect of which Landlord's consent shall be required under the provisions of this Lease or otherwise and in the event of permission, consent or approval from any local or other authority under the Planning Acts, the Public Health Acts or Building Control Legislation being necessary for any addition, alteration or change in or to the Demised Premises or for the change of its use to apply, at the Tenant's own expense, to the local or other authority for all such permissions, certificates, consents or approvals required therewith and to give notice to the Landlord of the granting or refusal (as the case may be) together with copies of all such approvals, certificates, consents and permissions on receipt thereof and to comply with all Laws either generally or specifically in respect thereof and carry out such works at the Tenant's own expense in a good and workmanlike manner to the satisfaction of the Landlord;

(c) To produce to the Landlord on demand all plans, documents and other evidence as the Landlord may reasonably require (including certificates or opinions on compliance from duly qualified professionals) in order to satisfy itself that any works carried out to the Demised Premises by the Tenant have been carried out in substantial compliance with the requirements of the Planning Acts, the Public Health Acts and Building Control Legislation and with any consents required thereunder;

(d) To give notice forthwith to the Landlord of any notice, order or proposal for same served on the Tenant under the Planning Acts, the Public Health Acts or Building Control Legislation or any other statutory provision and if so required by the Landlord to produce a true copy thereof and any further particulars or information reasonably required by the Landlord and, at the request of the Landlord but at the cost of the Tenant, to make or join in making such objections or representations in respect of any proposal as the Landlord may require; and

(e) To comply at its own expense with any notice or order served on the Tenant under the provisions of the Planning Acts, the Public Health Acts or Building Control Legislation.

(f) Not to implement any planning permission before it and any necessary fire safety certificates or other certificates or consents have been produced to and approved in writing by the Landlord (such approval not to be unreasonably withheld) **PROVIDED THAT** the Landlord may refuse to approve such planning permission or fire safety certificate or other certificates or consents on the grounds that any condition contained in it or anything omitted from it or the period referred to in it would, in the reasonable opinion of the Landlord, be or be likely to be, prejudicial to the Landlord's interest in the Demised Premises.

4.22 Statutory Notices

If a notice under any Law relevant to the Demised Premises or a proposal for such a notice is given to the Tenant or the occupier of the Demised Premises by any competent authority, then:

(a) To produce to the Landlord a true copy of the notice or proposal and any further particulars required by the Landlord within fourteen (14) days (or sooner if requisite having regard to the requirements of the notice or proposal in question or the time limits stated therein) of receipt by the Tenant or the occupier of the Demised Premises of the notice or proposal; and

(b) To immediately take all necessary steps to comply with the notice or proposal and at the request of the Landlord but at the cost of the Tenant, to make or join with the Landlord in making such objection or representation against or in respect of any such notice or proposal as the Landlord shall require.

4.23 Fire and Security Systems

(a) To comply with the requirements [and recommendations] (whether notified or directed to the Landlord and then to the Tenant or directly to the Tenant) of the appropriate local authority, the insurers of the Demised Premises and the Landlord in relation to fire and safety precautions affecting the Demised Premises.

(b) To keep the Demised Premises supplied and equipped with such fire fighting and extinguishing appliances as shall be required by Law, any appropriate local authority or the insurers of the Demised Premises or as shall be reasonably required by the Landlord.

(c) Not to obstruct the access to or means of working any fire fighting, extinguishing and other safety appliances for the time being installed in the Demised Premises or the means of escape from the Demised Premises in case of fire or other emergency.

4.24 Encroachments and Easements

Not to stop up, darken or obstruct any windows or openings of the Demised Premises rights of light or rights of way belonging to the Demised Premises nor to permit any new window, light, opening, doorway, passage, Conduit or other encroachment, right of way or easement to be made or acquired into upon or over the Demised Premises or any part of it and in case any person shall attempt to make or acquire any encroachment, right of way or easement whatsoever to give written notice of such attempt or acquisition to the Landlord immediately the same comes to the notice of the Tenant and, at the request of the Landlord but at the cost of the Tenant, to adopt such means as may be reasonably required by the Landlord for preventing any such encroachment, right of way or the acquisition of any such easement.

4.25 Disposal of Refuse

To observe (and procure the observance by the Tenant's employees (if any) of) the Landlord's and any relevant local authority's recommendations and requirements in relation to the collection, storage and disposal of all waste matter and refuse from the Demised Premises and to provide and maintain sufficient and appropriate containers of an approved design to the requirements of the Landlord and the local authority as may be necessary for the disposal of such waste matter and refuse and not to burn any such waste matter or refuse on the Demised Premises.

4.26 Signs and Advertisements

(a) Not to place affix or display any sign, advertisement, notice, banner, poster or other notification whatsoever on the outside of the Demised Premises except a sign bearing the name of the Tenant and the nature of the trade and business carried on at the Demised Premises by the Tenant which may be erected only in a manner, location, size, colour design, form and character approved in writing by the Landlord in its absolute discretion and not to place affix or display any sign, advertisement, notice, poster or other notification whatsoever on the inside of the Demised Premises so as to be visible from outside the Demised Premises unless first approved in writing by the Landlord (such approval not to be unreasonably withheld).

(b) At the expiration or sooner determination of the Term to remove any such sign, advertisement, notice, banner, poster or other notifications and make good all damage caused to the reasonable satisfaction of the Landlord.

4.27 Insurance and Indemnity

(a) To keep the Landlord fully indemnified from and against all actions, proceedings, claims, demands, losses, costs, expenses, damages, and liability arising in any way directly or indirectly out of any act omission or negligence of the Tenant or any persons in on or about the Demised Premises expressly or impliedly with the Tenant's authority or the user of the Demised Premises (which, for the avoidance of doubt, shall include any plant or machinery the Tenant may be permitted to install in the Demised

Premises) or any breach of the Tenant's covenants or the conditions or other provisions contained in this Lease.

(b) To effect and keep in force during the Term such public liability, employer's liability and other policies of insurance (to the extent that such insurance cover is available) as may be necessary to cover the Tenant against any claim arising under this covenant or under this Lease and to extend such policies of insurance so that the Landlord is indemnified by the insurers in the same manner as the Tenant and whenever required to do so by the Landlord to produce to the Landlord the said policy or policies together with satisfactory evidence that the same is or are valid and subsisting and that all premiums due thereon have been paid.

(c) To indemnify the Landlord in respect of any excess applicable in relation to its policies of insurance in place.

(d) Not do anything that could cause any policy of insurance in respect of or covering the Demised Premises to become void or voidable wholly or in part nor (unless the Tenant has previously notified the Landlord and agreed to pay the increased premium) do anything whereby any abnormal or loaded premium may become payable and the Tenant shall, on demand, pay to the Landlord all expenses incurred by the Landlord in renewing any such policy.

(e) To comply with all of the [recommendations and] requirements of the Landlord's insurers in respect of the Demised Premises.

(f) To insure and keep insured any glass forming part of the Demised Premises against breakage in an amount not less than the full replacement value thereof and to extend such policies of insurance so that the Landlord is indemnified by the insurers in the same manner as the Tenant and whenever required to do so by the Landlord to produce to the Landlord the said policy or policies together with satisfactory evidence that the same is or are valid and subsisting and that all premiums due thereon have been paid.

(g) To notify the Landlord forthwith upon the happening of any event or thing that might affect any insurance policy relating to the Demised Premises.

(h) To pay to the Landlord an amount equal to any insurance monies that the Landlord's insurers of the Demised Premises refuse to pay by reason of any act, neglect, default or omission of the Tenant the under-lessees, servants, agents, licensees or invitees of the Tenant or any person under its or their control.

4.28 VAT

(a) The Landlord notifies and confirms to the Tenant that the Landlord has exercised its option to tax in accordance with the provisions of Section 97(1)(c) of the VAT Act ("Option to Tax").

(b) In addition to the rent, Insurance Premium and other payments payable by the Tenant under this Lease, the Tenant shall pay to the Landlord any VAT which is now or may become payable in respect of such sums and the Tenant shall indemnify the Landlord against same.

(c) The Landlord may at any time during the Term terminate the Landlord's Option to Tax in respect of this Lease and where the Landlord does so, the Landlord may thereafter from time to time at all times during the Term again exercise the Option to Tax the rent and other monies payable by the Tenant under this Lease by giving notice to the Tenant pursuant to Section 97(1)(c)(ii) of the VAT Act and where such notice (and as often as the same may be given) is given to the Tenant the Tenant shall thereafter pay to the Landlord in addition to the rent and other monies payable under this Lease any VAT payable in respect of the rent and other monies payable under this Lease and shall indemnify the Landlord against same.

(d) Where during the Term the Option to Tax is at any time terminated pursuant to Section 97(1)(d)(iii), (iv) or (v) of the VAT Act, the Tenant hereby covenants to reimburse the Landlord on demand on a net of tax basis for the Landlord the amount equivalent to the VAT liabilities suffered by the Landlord as a result of any such termination and shall indemnify the Landlord in respect of same.

(e) The Tenant shall notify the Landlord in writing of any development, within the meaning of Section 2 of the VAT Act, of the Demised Premises and shall provide to the Landlord all relevant details necessary to enable the Landlord to keep accurate VAT records for the purpose of any transaction relating to the Demised Premises, and the Tenant shall generally facilitate the Landlord by providing the Landlord on demand with such information as the Landlord may request which is of significance for VAT purposes to the Landlord for the good management of the Demised Premises and to enable the Landlord to comply with the VAT Act in relation to any transaction affecting the Demised Premises.

4.29 Company Registration

Where applicable, to comply with all statutory requirements necessary to ensure that the Tenant remains on the register of companies.

5. LANDLORD'S COVENANTS

Subject to the Tenant paying the rents reserved by this Lease and due to the Landlord and performing and observing the covenants on the part of the Tenant herein contained the Landlord **HEREBY COVENANTS** with the Tenant as follows:

5.1 Quiet Enjoyment

That the Tenant shall and may except where otherwise provided in this Lease peaceably hold and enjoy the Demised Premises during the Term without any interruption by the Landlord or any person lawfully claiming through under or in trust for it.

5.2 Insurance

(a) Subject to the Landlord being able to effect on reasonable commercial terms and with substantial and reputable insurers insurance against any one or more of the items referred to in this clause and subject to payment by the Tenant of the Insurance Premium, the Landlord covenants with the Tenant to insure the following in the name of the Landlord:

(i) the Demised Premises and all Landlord's fixtures and fittings therein or thereon in their full reinstatement cost (to be determined from time to time by the Landlord) against loss or damage by the Insured Risks including:

(A) architects', surveyors', consultants' and other professional fees (including VAT on those fees);

(B) the costs of shoring up, demolishing, site clearing and similar expenses;

(C) all stamp duty and other taxes or duties exigible on any building or like contract as may be entered into and all other incidental expenses relative to the reconstruction, reinstatement or repair of the Demised Premises;

(D) such provision for inflation as the Landlord in its reasonable discretion shall deem appropriate; and

(E) fire brigade and other emergency service charges.

(ii) the Landlord against public, property owners, employer's and any other legal liability of the Landlord arising out of or in relation to the Demised Premises; and

(iii) the Landlord against such other risks as the Landlord may in its discretion from time to time deem necessary to effect including but without prejudice to the generality of the foregoing engineering insurances in respect of breakdown and/or replacement of plant and equipment.

(b) Subject to the Landlord being able to effect on reasonable commercial terms and with substantial and reputable insurers insurance against any one or more of the items referred to in this clause and subject to payment by the Tenant of the Insurance Premium, the Landlord covenants with the Tenant to insure the prospective loss of rent from time to time payable or reasonably estimated to be payable under this Lease (taking account of any review of the rent which may become due under this Lease) following loss or damage to the Demised Premises by the Insured Risks for three (3) years or such longer period as the Landlord may, from time to time, reasonably deem to be necessary having regard to the likely period required for rebuilding and for obtaining planning permission, fire safety certificates and any other necessary consents, certificates and approvals for reinstating the Demised Premises.

(c) If requested by the Tenant, the Landlord shall produce to the Tenant reasonable evidence of the terms of the policy or policies of insurance maintained under this clause and the fact that the premium has been paid.

(d) If requested by the Tenant the Landlord shall use reasonable endeavours to ensure that the insurance policy or policies in respect of the Insured Risks include either or both a non-invalidation clause and waiver of subrogation rights in favour of the Tenant in respect of the Demised Premises if available from substantial and reputable insurers and the Tenant shall pay any additional premium arising from such a request.

(e) For the purposes of clause 5.2 reference to the "Demised Premises" in so far as it includes the Demised Premises shall not include (unless otherwise agreed in writing by the Landlord and the Tenant) any additions, alterations and improvements made to the Demised Premises by the Tenant (including, for the avoidance of doubt, any of the Tenant's fixtures, fittings, furniture and effects).

5.3 **Reinstatement**

(a) If the Demised Premises or any part or parts of it is destroyed or damaged by any of the Insured Risks so as to render the Demised Premises unfit for use and occupation then:

(i) unless payment of the insurance moneys shall be refused in whole or in part by reason of any act neglect or default of the Tenant the under-lessees, servants, agents, licensees or invitees of the Tenant or any person under its or their control; and

(ii) subject to the Landlord being able to obtain any necessary planning permission, fire safety certificates and all other necessary licences, approvals, certificates and consents (in respect of which the Landlord shall use its reasonable endeavours to obtain); and

    (iii) subject to the necessary labour and materials being and remaining available (in respect of which the Landlord shall use its reasonable endeavours to obtain);

the Landlord shall lay out the proceeds of such insurance (other than any in respect of the loss of rent) in the rebuilding and reinstating of the Demised Premises or the part or parts of it so destroyed or damaged substantially as the same were prior to any such destruction or damage (but not so as to provide accommodation identical in layout and manner or method of construction if it would not be reasonable or practical to do so).

(b)   If the Landlord is prevented (for whatever reason) from reinstating as aforesaid the Demised Premises or any part or parts of it so destroyed or damaged the Landlord shall be relieved from the obligations of clause 5.3(a) and shall be solely entitled to all the insurance monies and if such rebuilding or reinstating shall continue to be so prevented for three (3) years after the date of the destruction or damage the Landlord of the Tenant may at any time after the expiry of such three (3) years by notice in writing to the other determine this Lease and, if requested by the Landlord at such time, the Tenant hereby agrees to enter into a deed of surrender or execute such other document as the Landlord may reasonably require to record that this Lease shall have determined but such determination shall be without prejudice to any claim by either party against the other in respect of any antecedent breach of the covenants and conditions of this Lease.

6.   PROVISOS AND AGREEMENTS

PROVIDED ALWAYS AND IT IS HEREBY AGREED AND DECLARED as follows:

6.1   Forfeiture

Without prejudice to any other right, remedy or power herein contained or otherwise available to the Landlord:

(a)   if the rents or any other sums reserved by this Lease shall be unpaid for fourteen (14) days after becoming payable (whether formally demanded or not); or

(b)   if any of the covenants by the Tenant contained in this Lease shall not be performed or observed; or

(c)   if the Tenant or the Guarantor (either or both being a body corporate) has a winding-up petition presented against it or passes a winding-up resolution (other than in connection with a members voluntary winding up for the purposes of an amalgamation or reconstruction which has the prior written approval of the Landlord) or resolves to present its own winding-up petition or is wound up (whether in Ireland or elsewhere) or a receiver or liquidator (provisional or otherwise) is appointed in respect of the Demised Premises or any part of it or of the Tenant or the Guarantor or if the Tenant or the Guarantor has a petition for the appointment of an examiner presented against it (or the Tenant or the Guarantor present the petition for the appointment of an examiner) or if either the Tenant or the Guarantor enters into a scheme of arrangement or composition with or for the benefit of creditors generally or suffers any distress, execution, sequestration, attachment or similar process to be levied on the Demised Premises; or (d)　if the Tenant or the Guarantor (either or both being an individual, or if more than one individual, then any one of them) commits an act of bankruptcy or has a bankruptcy summons or a bankruptcy petition presented against him or is adjudged bankrupt (whether in Ireland or elsewhere) or suffers any distress, execution, sequestration, attachment or similar process to be levied on the Demised Premises or enters into a scheme of arrangement or composition with or for the benefit of his creditors or shall have a receiving order made against him or makes an application to any court for an order under Section 87 of the Bankruptcy Act, 1988; or

(e)　if the Tenant or the Guarantor otherwise cease to exist;

THEN and in any such case the Landlord may at any time thereafter re-enter the Demised Premises or any part of it in the name of the whole and thereupon the Term shall absolutely cease and determine but without prejudice to any rights or remedies which may then have accrued to the Landlord against the Tenant in respect of any antecedent breach of any of the covenants or conditions contained in this Lease.

For the purposes of this provision, the Tenant acknowledges that the Landlord may take such reasonable steps as may be necessary to effect such re-entry so as to minimise such losses as may be incurred by the Landlord.

6.2　Suspension of Rent

(a)　If during the Term the Demised Premises or any part or parts of it shall be destroyed or damaged by any of the Insured Risks so as to render same unfit for use and occupation and the Landlord's insurances shall not have been vitiated or payment of the policy monies refused in whole or in part as a result of some act or default of the Tenant or the under-lessees, servants, agents, licensees or invitees of the Tenant or any person under its or their control, then the rent or a fair proportion of the rent according to the nature and extent of the damage sustained shall be suspended until the Demised Premises or the part or parts of it destroyed or damaged shall be again rendered fit for use and occupation or until the expiration of three (3) years from the date of such destruction or damage (or such longer period as the Landlord may have insured against and notified the Tenant in writing of) whichever is the shorter.

(b)　Any dispute regarding the suspension of the rent shall in default of agreement be referred to a single arbitrator to be appointed upon the application of either party to the President (or other officer endowed with the functions of President) for the time being of the Society of Chartered Surveyors Ireland in accordance with the provisions of the Arbitration Act 2010.

6.3　Waiver of 1860 Act Surrender

In case the Demised Premises or any part of it is destroyed or become ruinous and uninhabitable or incapable of beneficial occupation or enjoyment the Tenant hereby absolutely waives and abandons its rights (if any) to surrender this Lease under the provisions of Section 40 of the 1860 Act or otherwise.

6.4　No Implied Easements

(a)　Nothing herein contained shall impliedly confer upon or grant to the Tenant any easement, right or privilege other than those expressly granted by this Lease.

(b)　The Tenant shall not by virtue of this demise be deemed to have acquired nor shall the Tenant during the Term acquire by prescription or any other means in the Demised Premises any right of air or light or any right of way or other easement from or over or affecting any, land or hereditaments belonging to the Landlord and not included in this demise.

6.5 **Release of Landlord**

If the person comprising the Landlord from time to time disposes by way of conveyance, transfer, assignment or lease of its interest in the reversion expectant on the determination of the Term, the person so disposing shall be released from its obligations under this Lease on notice of such disposal being given to the Tenant.

6.6 **No Warranty as to User**

Nothing contained in this Lease (or in any consent granted by the Landlord under this Lease) shall imply or warrant that the Demised Premises or any part of it may be used under the Planning Acts or the Public Health Acts for the purpose herein authorised or any purpose subsequently authorised and the Tenant hereby acknowledges and admits that the Landlord has not given or made at any time any representation or warranty that any such use is or will be or will remain a permitted use under the Planning Acts.

6.7 **Representations**

The Tenant acknowledges that this Lease has not been entered into in reliance wholly or partly on any statement or representation made by or on behalf of the Landlord except any such statement or representation that is expressly set out in this Lease.

6.8 **Covenants Relating to Adjoining Property**

(a) Nothing contained in or implied by this Lease shall give to the Tenant the benefit of or the right to enforce or to prevent the release or modification of any covenant, agreement or condition entered into by any tenant of the Landlord in respect of the Adjoining Property.

(b) Any dispute arising between the Tenant and other tenants or occupiers of such of the Adjoining Property as may be owned by the Landlord relating to any easement, quasi-easement, right, privilege or Conduit in connection with the Demised Premises or the Adjoining Property or as to party or other walls shall be fairly and reasonably determined by the Landlord.

6.9 **Effect of Waiver**

Each of the Tenant's covenants shall remain in full force both at law and in equity notwithstanding that the Landlord shall have waived or released temporarily any such covenant whether through the demand for and the acceptance of the rent reserved under this Lease by the Landlord or its agents or otherwise, or waived or released temporarily or permanently, revocably or irrevocably a similar covenant or similar covenants affecting other property belonging to the Landlord.

6.10 **Notices**

(a) Any demand or notice required to be made given to or served on the Tenant or the Guarantor under this Lease shall be duly and validly made given or served if addressed to the Tenant or the Guarantor respectively (and, if there shall in either case be more than one of them, then to any one of them) and delivered personally or sent by pre-paid registered or recorded delivery post addressed:

(i) in the case of a company to its registered office, or

(ii) in the case of a company or individual to its last known address; or

(iii) to the Demised Premises;

and unless it is returned through the post office undelivered a notice sent by pre-paid registered or recorded delivery post is to be treated as served on the second working day (being a day other than a Saturday or Sunday or public holiday in Ireland on which clearing banks are generally open for business in Ireland) after posting whenever and whether or not it is received.

(b) Any notice required to be given to or served on the Landlord shall be duly and validly given or served if sent by pre-paid registered or recorded delivery post addressed to the Landlord (if an individual) at his principal address or (if a company) at its registered office.

6.11 No Liability

The Landlord shall not be responsible to the Tenant, or the under-lessees, servants, agents, licensees or invitees of the Tenant or any person under its or their control for any injury, death, damage, destruction or financial or consequential loss whether to persons or property due to the state and condition of the Demised Premises or any part of it or due to any act or default of any agent, servant, workman or other person authorised by the Landlord to enter on the Demised Premises save to the extent to which the same may be insured against by the Landlord pursuant to the terms of this Lease.

6.12 Applicable Law

(a) This Lease shall in all respect be governed by and interpreted in accordance with the Laws of Ireland.

(b) Both the Tenant and the Guarantor hereby submit to the exclusive jurisdiction of the Courts of Ireland to settle any disputes which may arise out of or in connection with this Lease and that accordingly any suit, action or proceedings (together in this clause 6.12 referred to as "proceedings") arising out of or in connection with this Lease may be brought in such Courts.

(c) The Tenant and the Guarantor hereby irrevocably waive any objection which they or either of them may have now or hereafter to the taking of any proceedings in any such Court as is referred to in this clause and any claim that any such proceedings have been brought in an inconvenient forum and further irrevocably agree that any judgment in any proceedings brought in the Courts of Ireland shall be conclusive and binding upon them and may be enforced in the courts of any other jurisdiction;

(d) Nothing contained in this clause shall limit the right of the Landlord to take proceedings against the Tenant and/or the Guarantor in any other Court of competent jurisdiction nor shall the taking of proceedings in one or more jurisdictions preclude the taking of proceedings in any other jurisdiction whether concurrently or not.

6.13 [Assent to Registration

The Landlord hereby assents to the registration of this Lease as a burden on the property comprised in folio • of the Register County l.]

7. GUARANTOR COVENANTS

In consideration of this demise having been made at its request, the Guarantor **HEREBY COVENANTS** with the Landlord, as a primary obligation, in the terms contained in Schedule 5.

8. **SECTION 238 COMPANIES ACT, 2014**

    IT IS HEREBY CERTIFIED for the purposes of Section 238 of the Companies Act 2014 that the Landlord and the Tenant are not bodies corporate connected with one another in a manner which would require this transaction to be ratified by resolution of either.

9. **TENANT'S ADDRESS AND DESCRIPTION**

    The address of the Tenant in the State for service of notices and its description are as appear at the commencement of this Lease.

    IN WITNESS whereof the parties have executed this Lease in the manner following and on the day and year first herein **WRITTEN**.

Schedule 1
The Demised Premises

[**ALL THAT** the entire of the lands and premises together with the buildings erected thereon [shown for the purposes of identification only outlined in • on the Plan] and each and every part of them and all the appurtenances belonging to them and known as • and situate at • in the County/City of • [comprising • acres] and including without prejudice to the generality of the foregoing:

1. all the Conduits and plant in, upon, over or under and exclusively serving the same;

2. all Landlord's fixtures and fittings now or afterwards in or upon the same;

3. all additions, alterations and improvements to them;

4. [the car spaces and loading bay areas and landscaped areas within the Demised Premises]

but excluding the airspace above and the ground below the Demised Premises.]

Schedule 2
Easement rights and privileges granted

The following rights and privileges (to the extent only that the Landlord is entitled to make such a grant) are to be enjoyed by the Tenant in conjunction with the Landlord and the tenants and occupiers of the Adjoining Property and all other parties or persons nominated or authorised by the Landlord or having like rights and easements:

1. Subject to temporary interruption for repair, alteration or replacement or interruptions outside the control of the Landlord, the free passage and running of the Utilities to and from the Demised Premises through the Conduits which are now, or may at any time during the Term be, in, under or passing through or over the Demised Premises;

2. The right to enter the airspace above the roof of the Demised Premises temporarily and for the sole purpose of carrying out any works or repairs required for which the Tenant is liable under this Lease;

3. [The right at convenient times and upon reasonable notice (except in cases of emergency) to enter upon the Adjoining Property temporarily and for the sole purpose of viewing the state and condition of and executing works and repairs to the Demised Premises for which the Tenant is liable under this Lease and which would not otherwise be reasonably practicable subject to the Tenant making good and damage and minimising any disturbance caused;]

4. [The right to pass and repass at all times at day and at night and for all purposes in connection with the use and enjoyment of the Demised Premises on foot or with vehicles over and along the route shown coloured [yellow] on the Plan [such right to extend to the Tenant's staff]] ;

5. [The [exclusive] right to use [during business hours] [the/ •] Car Park Space[s] shown coloured • on the Plan or such other car park space[s] as the Landlord may designate from time to time during the Term] ; and

6. • .

Schedule 3
Exceptions and Reservations

The following rights and easements are excepted and reserved out of the Demised Premises to the Landlord, [the tenants and occupiers of the Adjoining Property] and all other persons having the like rights and easements:

1. The free and uninterrupted passage and running of the Utilities to and from the Demised Premises through the Conduits which are now, or may at any time during the Term be, in, under or passing through or over the Demised Premises;

2. The right, at all reasonable times upon reasonable prior notice except in cases of emergency to enter (or, in cases of emergency or after the giving of reasonable notice during the Tenant's absence, to forcibly enter) the Demised Premises in order to:

    (a) view and examine the state and condition of the Demised Premises and to take schedules or inventories of the Landlord's fixtures and fittings;

    (b) inspect, cleanse, maintain, repair, connect, remove, lay, renew, relay, reroute, replace, alter or execute any works whatever to or in connection with the Conduits and any other services;

    (c) execute repairs, decorations, alterations and any other works and to make installations to the Adjoining Property or to do anything whatsoever which the Landlord may or must do under this Lease;

    (d) see that no unauthorised erections, additions or alterations have been made and that authorised erections, additions and alterations are being carried out in accordance with any consent given herein and any permission or approval granted by the relevant local authority;

    (e) build on or into any dividing boundary or party walls or fences on the Demised Premises and for such purpose to excavate (if deemed necessary by the Landlord) the Demised Premises along the line of the junction between the Demised Premises and the Adjoining Property;

    (f) for any other purpose connected with the interest of the Landlord in the Demised Premises, including but not limited to, valuing or disposing of any interest of the Landlord;

    (g) and the person exercising the foregoing rights shall cause as little inconvenience as reasonably practicable to the Demised Premises and shall make good as soon as reasonably practicable any damage thereby caused to the Demised Premises;

3. The right to erect scaffolding for the purpose of repairing or cleaning any building now or hereafter erected on the Adjoining Property or in connection with the exercise of any of the rights mentioned in this Schedule notwithstanding that such scaffolding may temporarily interfere with proper access to or the enjoyment and use of the Demised Premises;

4. The rights of light, air, support, protection and shelter and all other easements, quasi-easements, rights and privileges now or hereafter belonging to or enjoyed or required by the Adjoining Property together with the benefit of such rights for any works carried out by the Landlord pursuant to the exceptions and reservations herein contained;

5. The air space over and the ground below the Demised Premises;

6. Full right and liberty at any time hereafter to raise the height of, or make any alterations or additions or execute any other works to any buildings on the Adjoining Property, or to erect any new buildings of any height on the Adjoining Property in such a manner as the Landlord or the person exercising the right shall think fit notwithstanding the fact that the same may obstruct, affect or interfere with the amenity of, or access to, the Demised Premises or the passage of light and air to the Demised Premises but not so that the Tenant's use and occupation of the Demised Premises is materially affected;

7.   All mines and minerals in or under the Demised Premises with full power of working and getting to the same provided reasonable compensation in paid to the Tenant for any damage thereby occasioned to the Demised Premises;

8.   The right to affix to the outside walls of the Demised Premises (but not so as to hinder access to the Demised Premises) any such items which may be considered by the Landlord to be requisite or desirable, including, but not limited to, advertising and promotional displays and panels, building block names, notices for selling or re-letting the Demised Premises or for the purposes of a planning or other application, fire escapes, information panels and signs, kiosks or other articles or structures of a like nature, television aerials and connections, lighting brackets, seats, plant holders, street names, clocks, vending machines and litter receptacles; and

9.   •.

Schedule 4
Rent Reviews

1. **Definitions**

In this Schedule, the following expressions shall have the following meanings:

(a)   **"Open Market Rent"** means the yearly open market rent without any deductions whatsoever at which the Demised Premises might reasonably be expected to be let as a whole on the open market with vacant possession at the Relevant Review Date by a willing landlord to a willing tenant (which expression "willing tenant" shall for the avoidance of doubt include the Tenant) and without any premium or any other consideration for the grant of it for a term equal to the length of the Term remaining unexpired at the Relevant Review Date or a period of fifteen (15) years from the Relevant Review Date whichever is the longer and otherwise on the same terms and conditions and subject to the same covenants and provisions contained in this Lease (other than the amount of the rent payable hereunder but including these provisions for the review of rent in the same form as this Lease at similar intervals):

    (i)   assuming:

        (A)   that the Demised Premises is at the Relevant Review Date fit, ready and available for immediate occupation by the willing tenant so that they are immediately capable of being used by the willing tenant for all purposes required by the willing tenant that would be permitted under this Lease and in calculating the Open Market Rent it shall be assumed that the willing tenant has enjoyed whatever rent concessions are being offered in the open market for fitting out purposes and that all Utilities and other facilities necessary for such occupation are connected to and immediately available for use at the Demised Premises;

        (B)   that no work has been carried out to the Demised Premises by the Tenant, any under-lessee or their respective predecessors in title during the Term, which has diminished the rental value of the Demised Premises;

        (C)   that if the Demised Premises or any part of it has been destroyed or damaged it has been fully rebuilt and reinstated;

        (D)   that the Demised Premises is in a good state of repair and decorative condition;

(E)   that all the covenants on the part of the Tenant contained in this Lease have been fully performed and observed;

(F)   that the Demised Premises may be used for [any of the purposes permitted by this Lease or any licence granted pursuant to it] ;

(G)   • ;

(ii)   but disregarding:

(A)   any effect on rent of the fact that the Tenant, any permitted under-lessee or their respective predecessors in title have been in occupation of the Demised Premises or any part of it;

(B)   any goodwill attaching to the Demised Premises by reason of the business then carried on at the Demised Premises by the Tenant, any permitted under-lessee or their respective predecessors in title;

(C)   any effect on the rental value of the Demised Premises attributable to the existence at the Relevant Review Date of any works executed by and at the expense of the Tenant (or any party lawfully occupying the Demised Premises under the Tenant) with the consent of all relevant persons where required in on or to the Demised Premises otherwise than in pursuance of an obligation under this Lease or any agreement therefor ;

(D)   • ;

(b)   the "**Presi**dent" means the President for the time being of the Society of Chartered Surveyors Ireland or any successor professional body and includes any duly appointed deputy of the President or any person authorised by the President to make appointments on his behalf;

(c)   "Rent Restrictions" means restrictions imposed by any statute in force on a Review Date or on the date on which any revised rent is ascertained in accordance with this Schedule which operate to impose any limitation, whether in time or amount, on the collection, review or increase in the rent reserved by this Lease;

(d)   the "Surveyor" means an independent chartered surveyor who is experienced in the valuation or leasing of property similar to the Demised Premises and is acquainted with the market in the area in which the Demised Premises are located, appointed from time to time to determine the Open Market Rent pursuant to the provisions of this Schedule.

2.   **Rent Review**

The rent reserved by this Lease shall be reviewed at each Review Date in accordance with the provisions of this Schedule and during each successive Review Period the rent shall equal the Open Market Rent on the Relevant Review Date, as agreed or determined pursuant to the provisions of this Schedule.

3.   **Agreement or determination of the reviewed rent**

(a)   The Open Market Rent at any Review Date may be agreed in writing at any time between the Landlord and the Tenant but if, for any reason, they have not so agreed by the Relevant Review Date then the Landlord may by notice in writing to the Tenant require the Open Market Rent to be determined by the Surveyor.

(b)   The Surveyor shall, at the option of the Landlord, act either as an arbitrator in accordance with the Arbitration Act 2010 or as an expert, such option to be exercised by the Landlord by giving written notice to the President at the time of the Landlord's written application to the President but if no written notice is given by the Landlord as aforesaid, then the Surveyor shall act as an arbitrator. If the Surveyor is to act as arbitrator, then this clause shall be deemed to be a submission to arbitration within the meaning of the Arbitration Act 2010 and to the jurisdiction of the courts of the State for the enforcement of any award of the said arbitrator.

4. **Appointment of Surveyor**

If the Landlord has required the Open Market Rent to be determined by the Surveyor, then in default of agreement between the Landlord and the Tenant on the appointment of the Surveyor, the Surveyor shall be appointed by the President on the written application of the Landlord to the President.

5. **Functions of the Surveyor**

The Surveyor shall:

(a) determine the Open Market Rent in accordance with the terms of this Schedule;

(b) if acting as an expert, invite the Landlord and the Tenant to submit to him, within such time limits (not being less than fifteen (15) days) as he shall consider appropriate, a valuation accompanied if desired, by a statement of reasons and such representations as to the amount of the Open Market Rent with such supporting evidence as they may respectively wish;

(c) be entitled to have access to the Demised Premises for the purposes of inspecting and examining it as often as he may require; and

(d) within sixty (60) days of his appointment, or within such extended period as the Landlord and the Tenant shall jointly agree in writing, give to each of them written notice of the amount of the Open Market Rent as determined by him.

6. **Fees of Surveyor**

The fees and expenses of the Surveyor (if acting as an expert) and the party responsible for paying him shall be determined by the Surveyor (but this shall not preclude the Surveyor from notifying both parties of his total fees and expenses notwithstanding the non-publication at that time of his decision) and, failing such determination of the party responsible for paying him, such fees and expenses of the Surveyor together with costs of his nomination shall be payable by the Landlord and the Tenant in equal shares who shall each bear their own costs, fees and expenses. Without prejudice to the foregoing, both the Landlord and the Tenant shall each be entitled to pay the entire fees and expenses due to the Surveyor and thereafter recover as a simple contract debt the amount (if any) due from the party who failed or refused to pay same.

7. **Appointment of new Surveyor**

If the Surveyor fails to give notice of his determination within the time aforesaid or if he relinquishes his appointment or dies, is unwilling to act or becomes incapable of acting or if he is removed from office by court order, or if, for any other reason, he is unable or unsuited (whether because of bias or otherwise) to act, then either party may request the President to discharge the Surveyor (if necessary) and appoint another surveyor as substitute to act in the same capacity. The procedures set out in this Schedule shall apply as though the substitute were an appointment de novo, and such procedures may be repeated as many times as necessary.

8.   **Interim payments pending determination**

If by the Relevant Review Date the amount of the reviewed rent has not been agreed or determined as aforesaid (the date of agreement or determination being the "Determination Date"), then:

(a)   in respect of the period (the "Interim Period") beginning with the Relevant Review Date and ending on the day before the Gale Day following the Determination Date, the Tenant shall pay to the Landlord rent at the yearly rate payable immediately before the Relevant Review Date, and

(b)   within seven (7) days of the Determination Date either:-

   (i)   the Tenant shall pay to the Landlord as arrears of rent:

      (A)   the amount (if any) by which the Open Market Rent reviewed in accordance with this Schedule exceeds the rent actually paid during the Interim Period (apportioned on a daily basis);

      (B)   interest on that amount at the Base Rate from the Relevant Review Date to the due date for payment of that amount; and thereafter;

      (C)   interest on that amount at the Prescribed Rate until the date of actual payment; or

   (ii)   the Landlord shall pay to the Tenant:

      (A)   the amount (if any) by which the Open Market Rent revised in accordance with this Schedule is less than the rent actually paid during the Interim Period (apportioned on a daily basis);

      (B)   interest on that amount at the Base Rate from the Relevant Review Date to the due date for payment of that amount; and thereafter

      (C)   interest on that amount at the Prescribed Rate until the date of actual payment

      less any sums due by the Tenant to the Landlord under the terms of this Lease at the Determination Date.

9.   **Rent Restrictions**

On each and every occasion during the Term that Rent Restrictions shall be in force, then and in each and every case:

(a)   the operation of the provisions herein for review of the rent shall be postponed to take effect on the first date or dates thereafter upon which such operation may occur, and

(b)   the collection of any increase or decrease in the rent shall be postponed to take effect on the first date or dates thereafter that such increase or decrease may be collected and/or retained in whole or in part and on as many occasions as shall be required to ensure the collection of the whole increase or decrease;

AND until the Rent Restrictions shall be relaxed either partially or wholly the rent reserved by this Lease (which if previously reviewed shall be the rent payable under this Lease immediately prior to the imposition of the Rent Restrictions) shall (subject always to any provision to the contrary appearing in the Rent Restrictions) be the rent from time to time payable hereunder.

10. **Memoranda of reviewed rent**

    5.2   As soon as the amount of any reviewed rent has been agreed or determined, a memorandum of such reviewed rent shall be prepared by the Landlord or its solicitors and shall be signed by or on behalf of the Landlord and the Tenant;

    5.3   The Tenant shall be responsible for and shall pay to the Landlord the stamp duty (if any) payable on such memoranda and any counterparts but the parties shall each bear their own costs in respect of their preparation and execution of such memoranda and any counterpart.

11. **Time not of the essence**

For the purpose of this Schedule, time shall not be of the essence.

Schedule 5
Guarantor covenants

The Guarantor, if any, named herein, in consideration of this Lease being validly granted to the Tenant at the Guarantor's request hereby jointly and severally, irrevocably and unconditionally covenants and guarantees to the Landlord, as a primary obligation, as follows:

1. **Covenant and Indemnity**

That the Tenant or the Guarantor shall at all times during the Term (including any continuation or renewal of this Lease and whether before or after the expiration or termination of the Term) duly and promptly perform and observe each and all duties, obligations, covenants, conditions, warranties and undertakings on the part of the Tenant contained in this Lease, including for the avoidance of doubt the prompt payment of the rents, insurance premia and all other sums payable under this Lease (or any continuation or renewal of it) in the manner and at the times herein specified and all sums which may be due to the Landlord for mesne rates or as payment for the use and occupation of the Demised Premises, and the Guarantor hereby jointly and severally indemnifies the Landlord immediately on demand against all claims, demands, losses, damages, liability, costs, fees and expenses whatsoever sustained by the Landlord by reason of or arising in any way directly or indirectly out of or in connection with:

    1.1   any default by the Tenant in the performance and observance of any of its obligations, covenants, conditions, warranties and undertakings and/or the payment of any rent, insurance premia and other sums arising before or after the expiration of termination or this Lease or any continuation or renewal of it; and

    1.2   any obligation guaranteed by the Guarantor being or becoming unenforceable, illegal or invalid for any reason whatsoever irrespective of whether such reason was or ought to have been known to the Landlord or its officers, employees, agents or professional advisors, with the amount of the loss being equal to the amount that the Landlord would otherwise have been entitled to recover.

2. **Principal Obligor**

    2.1   That as between the Guarantor and the Landlord (but without affecting the duties, obligations, covenants, warranties and undertakings of the Tenant under and pursuant to this Lease) the Guarantor's liability under this Lease shall be as sole principal and primary obligor and not merely as surety and shall not be impaired or discharged by reason of any matter, act or omission whereby the liability of the Guarantor would not have been discharged if it had been the principal debtor and the Guarantor hereby waives all and any of its rights as surety which may at any time be inconsistent with any of the provisions of this Lease.

2.2 For the avoidance of doubt, that if any purported obligation or liability of the Tenant to the Landlord which, if valid, would have been subject to this guarantee, is not or ceases to be valid or enforceable against the Tenant, the Guarantor shall nevertheless be liable to the Landlord in respect of that purported obligation or liability as if the same were fully valid and enforceable and the Guarantor were the primary obligor in respect thereof.

3. Joint and Several Liability

That the Guarantor is jointly and severally liable with the Tenant (whether before or after any disclaimer by a liquidator, official assignee, trustee in bankruptcy or other persons administering the assets of the Tenant or whether before or after any repudiation in the context of examinership or other persons administering the assets of the Tenant) for the fulfilment of all the obligations of the Tenant under this Lease and agrees that the Landlord, in the enforcement of its rights hereunder, may proceed against the Guarantor as if the Guarantor was named as the Tenant in this Lease (notwithstanding that this Lease does not confer on the Guarantor any benefit or rights as tenant under this Lease).

4. Waiver

That the Guarantor hereby waives any right to require the Landlord to proceed against the Tenant or to pursue any other remedy whatsoever which may be available to the Landlord before proceeding against the Guarantor and the Guarantor further acknowledges that these provisions are in addition to and not in substitution for any other rights which the Landlord may have and which may be enforced against the Guarantor whether or not recourse has been had to any such rights and whether or not any steps or proceedings have been taken against the Tenant.

5. Postponement of Claims

That the Guarantor will not claim in any liquidation, examinership, bankruptcy, composition or arrangement of the Tenant in competition with the Landlord and will not claim or recover by the institution of proceedings or the threat of proceedings or otherwise any sum from the Tenant, or claim any set-off, counterclaim or proof against or dividend, composition or payment by the Landlord and will remit to the Landlord the proceeds of all judgments and all distributions it may receive from any liquidator, examiner, official assignee, trustee in bankruptcy, supervisor or other persons administering the assets of the Tenant and will hold for the benefit of the Landlord all security and rights the Guarantor may have over assets of the Tenant whilst any liabilities of the Tenant or the Guarantor (whether actual or contingent) to the Landlord remain outstanding.

6. Postponement of Participation

That the Guarantor is not entitled to participate in any security held by the Landlord in respect of the Tenant's obligations to the Landlord under this Lease or to stand in the place of the Landlord in respect of any such security until all the obligations (actual or contingent) of the Tenant or the Guarantor to the Landlord under this Lease have been performed or discharged and in case the Guarantor receives any sums from the Tenant in respect of any payment hereunder the Guarantor shall hold such monies in trust for the Landlord so long as any sums are payable (contingently or otherwise) under this Lease.

7. **Additional Security**

The obligations of the Guarantor herein contained shall be in addition to and shall be independent of and shall not merge with or otherwise prejudice or affect any contractual or other right or remedy or any other guarantee or security which the Landlord may now or at any time hereafter hold whether from the Tenant, the Guarantor or otherwise in respect of the performance of any of the obligations of the Tenant under this Lease and this guarantee may be enforced without the Landlord first taking steps or proceedings against the Tenant.

8. **Release**

The Guarantor shall not be exonerated, released, determined or discharged from its liability hereunder nor shall such liability nor the rights, powers and remedies conferred upon the Landlord be lessened, impaired, discharged or otherwise affected by any act, omission, matter or thing which but for this provision might operate to release or otherwise exonerate the Guarantor in whole or in part from its obligations as principal obligor under this Lease, including without limitation and whether or not known to the Guarantor or the Landlord:-

8.1 any concession arrangement waiver or indulgence and/or any neglect, delay or forbearance of the Landlord or any additional time given by the Landlord in endeavouring to obtain payment of any part of the rent, Insurance Premium or the other amounts required to be paid by the Tenant (or any part or parts of them) or in enforcing the performance or observance of any of the obligations of the Tenant under the Lease;

8.2 any refusal by the Landlord to accept any money tendered as rent by or on behalf of the Tenant at a time when the Landlord was entitled (or would after the service of a notice under Section 14 of the Conveyancing Act 1881 have been entitled) to re-enter the Demised Premises;

8.3 any extension of time given by the Landlord to the Tenant;

8.4 any amendment to or variation of this Lease (including any reviews of rent payable hereunder) (and in this regard the Guarantor hereby authorises the Landlord jointly upon agreement in writing with the Tenant to agree (or accept the determination of) any rent review and to make any amendments or variations to the Lease) whether or not such amendment or variation shall increase the liabilities of the Tenant or the Guarantor hereunder;

8.5 the transfer of the Landlord's reversion or the assignment of the Lease or the interposing of an intermediate lease;

8.6 the extent to which it may be or become illegal, invalid or unenforceable for the Tenant to fulfil any duty, obligation, covenant, warranty or undertaking under this Lease;

8.7 the bankruptcy, insolvency, liquidation, examination, reorganisation, receivership, dissolution, amalgamation, reconstruction, winding up or any analogous proceeding relating to the Tenant;

8.8 any licence, consent or approval granted by the Landlord;

8.9 any judgment against the Tenant;

8.10 any assignment by the Tenant of the Lease, unless it is an express condition of the Landlord's consent to assignment that the Guarantor shall be released from its obligations hereunder;

8.11 without prejudice to clause 14, any change in the constitution, status, function, control, ownership, structure or powers of either the Tenant, the

Guarantor or the Landlord or the liquidation, administration, examination or bankruptcy (as the case may be) of either the Tenant or the Guarantor, or the appointment of a receiver over all or some of its or their assets;

8.12 any legal limitation, or any immunity, disability or incapacity of the Tenant (whether or not known to the Landlord) or the fact that any dealings with the Landlord by the Tenant may be outside or in excess of the powers of the Tenant; and

8.13 any other act, omission, event, fact, circumstance, matter, thing, provision of statute or rule of law which but for this clause might operate to release, determine or discharge or otherwise affect any of the obligations of the Guarantor hereunder or any of the rights, powers or remedies conferred upon the Landlord by this Lease or by operation of law (other than a release under seal given by the Landlord).

9.   **Disclaimer, Repudiation, Forfeiture or Other Event**

Without prejudice to the Landlord's right to rely and to continue to rely on any other provisions of this Schedule or other right that may be available to the Landlord (which the Tenant and the Guarantor hereby confirm) and not by way of limitation of the obligations on the part of the Guarantor contained in this Schedule, the Guarantor hereby further covenants with the Landlord that:

9.1   If:

(a)   a liquidator, official assignee or trustee in bankruptcy or other person administering the assets of the Tenant shall disclaim or surrender this Lease; or

(b)   the Tenant shall repudiate this Lease in the case of examinership; or

(c)   this Lease shall be forfeited or otherwise terminated; or

(d)   the Tenant shall cease to exist;

THEN the Guarantor shall, if the Landlord by notice in writing given to the Guarantor within twelve (12) months after such disclaimer or other event so requires, accept from and execute and deliver to the Landlord a new lease of the Demised Premises subject to and with the benefit of this Lease (if the same shall still be deemed to be extant at such time) for a term commencing on the date of the disclaimer or other event and continuing for the residue then remaining unexpired of the Term, such new lease to be at the cost of the Guarantor (which, for the avoidance of doubt, shall include the Landlord's costs of granting such new lease) and to be at the same rents in this Lease and subject to the same covenants, conditions and provisions as are contained in this Lease; and

9.2   If the Landlord does not require the Guarantor to take a new lease, the Guarantor shall nevertheless upon demand pay to the Landlord a sum equal to the rents, insurance premia and other sums (as mesne rates or for the use and occupation of the Demised Premises or as legal costs and expenses) that would have been payable under this Lease (or for any continuation or renewal of it) but for the disclaimer, repudiation, forfeiture or other event in respect of the period from and including the date of such disclaimer, forfeiture or other event, such sums to be paid on the same dates and in the same manner as they would have been payable by the Tenant in respect of the period from and including the date of such disclaimer, repudiation, forfeiture or other event until the Landlord has granted a lease of the Demised Premises to a third party (but without being under any obligation to do so) with the Landlord's costs of such a grant and/or any attempted grant of a new lease being discharged by the Guarantor.

LEASE

10. Replacement Guarantor

That if any of the events referred to in clause 6.1 of the Lease (*forfeiture*) occur in relation to the Guarantor, the Tenant will give written notice to the Landlord of such occurrence and if the Landlord so requires in writing at any time afterwards (without prejudice and in addition to the Landlord's rights hereunder) the Tenant will within twenty eight (28) days of receipt of the Landlord's requirement procure some other person or persons of standing satisfactory to the Landlord to covenant with the Landlord in a deed in the terms set out in this Lease.

11. Benefit of Guarantee

11.1 That this guarantee shall apply for the entire of the Term, and any continuation or renewal of the Lease. It shall apply to all Landlord claims whether before or after the expiration or termination of the Term and whether arising pursuant to this Lease, or to any overholding or continued occupation by the Tenant following its termination.

11.2 That this guarantee enures for the benefit of the successors and assigns of the Landlord under this Lease (notwithstanding the fact that same may automatically pass with the reversion) without the necessity for any assignment of this guarantee and references to the Landlord in this Lease include the landlord for the time being under this Lease.

12. Litigation

That in any claim relating to this Lease, the Guarantor irrevocably waives the right to interpose any defence based upon any statute of limitations or any claim of laches or set-off or counter-claim of any nature or description.

13. [Jurisdiction

That the Guarantor will submit to the jurisdiction of the Irish courts in relation to any proceedings taken against the Guarantor or in relation to any new lease granted as aforesaid.]

14. Registration or Control of Company

14.1 That the Guarantor will comply with all statutory requirements necessary to ensure that the Tenant and the Guarantor remain on the register of companies and the Guarantor shall not permit such registration to lapse, or to be struck off;

14.2 That the Guarantor will not permit any transaction or arrangement which would result in a change in effective control of the Guarantor PROVIDED THAT where not inconsistent with the principles of good estate management the Landlord shall not unreasonably withhold its consent to an application for a change in the effective control of the Guarantor in any case in which the new owner is financially and otherwise acceptable to the Landlord and any such application for consent shall be accompanied by all accounts and information concerning the proposed owner and the proposed transaction as the Landlord may require.

15. Process Agent

Without prejudice to any other mode of service allowed under any relevant law, the Guarantor:

15.1 irrevocably appoints • having its registered office at • (the "Agent") as its agent for service of process in relation to any proceedings in connection with this Lease;

15.2 agrees to procure that the Agent executes a letter confirming its appointment on or about the date of this Lease; and

15.3 agrees that failure by a process agent to notify the Guarantor of the process will not invalidate the proceedings concerned.

If any person appointed as an agent for service of process is unable for any reason to act as agent for service of process, the Guarantor must immediately (and in any event within ten (10) days of such event taking place) appoint another agent on terms acceptable to the Landlord. Failing this, the Landlord may appoint another agent for this purpose.

GIVEN UNDER the Common Seal of
[INSERT NAME OF LANDLORD COMPANY]
AND delivered as a **DEED**:

_____
Director

_____
Director/Secretary

GIVEN UNDER the Common Seal of
[INSERT NAME OF TENANT COMPANY]
AND delivered as a **DEED**:

_____
Director

_____
Director/Secretary

GIVEN UNDER the Common Seal of
[INSERT NAME OF GUARANTOR COMPANY]
AND delivered as a **DEED**:

_____
Director

_____
Director/Secretary

APPENDIX 7

SEPTEMBER 2011 PRACTICE NOTE REVISED VAT SPECIAL CONDITION 3 AND PRE-CONTRACT VAT ENQUIRIES

02.09.2011
Conveyancing Taxation

The current VAT on property system came into operation on 1 July 2008 (see 'VAT on property guide' on the Revenue website, www.revenue.ie). Since the introduction of this system, the Law Society has issued two revisions of the VAT Special Condition 3 to be used in contracts dealing with property. In addition, the Law Society has issued Pre-Contract VAT Enquiries. The Society's Conveyancing and Taxation Committees continuously monitor the effect of the VAT system on conveyancing practice and, on foot of this, have now issued a revised version (August 2011 edition) of the VAT Special Condition 3, together with a revised version (August 2011 edition) of the Pre-Contract VAT Enquiries.

These new documents can be downloaded from the Law Society's website, www.lawsociety.ie, by logging into the members' area and following links to either the precedents section or to the two committees' pages.

In addition to making amendments necessitated by the VAT Consolidation Act 2010, the following major amendments have been made to the documents. Previous versions of the VAT Special Condition 3 and the Pre-Contract VAT Enquiries should no longer be used.

Both the revised VAT Special Condition 3 and the new Pre-Contract VAT Enquiries have been reviewed by the Revenue Commissioners on a 'without prejudice' basis, and the Revenue Commissioners did not have any comments in respect of the documents.

Pre-Contract VAT Enquiries (PCVE) (August 2011 edition)

- The first page of the PCVE lists circumstances in which it is not necessary to raise the PCVE, either because VAT does not arise on the transaction, or because the Vendor is not charging VAT, notwithstanding the fact that the transaction is otherwise subject to VAT. In these circumstances, it is not appropriate for the Purchaser to raise the PCVE.

- The first and second pages of the PCVE set out instructions and guidelines as to the completion of the PCVE. A new process to be followed in the case of a sale at auction has now been introduced.

- The enquiries raised in the PCVE are now divided into seven sections, at the end of which a 'Guide to Completing VAT Special Condition 3 (August 2011 edition)' has been added. This guide is intended to assist practitioners in correctly selecting the sub-clauses of VAT Special Condition 3 that are appropriate in each transaction. The guide also contains a helpful note in respect of the joint option to tax, and illustrates the operation of the joint option to tax with two examples.

VAT Special Condition 3 (August 2011 edition)

Practitioners are reminded that, unlike the version of VAT Special Condition 3 that existed prior to the introduction of the current VAT on property system, the VAT Special Condition 3 that has been drafted to address the various permutations arising out the of the current VAT on property system contains sub-clauses that are, in some cases, mutually exclusive. Great care must therefore be taken to select the appropriate sub-clauses and to delete those that do not apply. The latest version of the VAT Special Condition 3 has been further subdivided in order to give greater clarity to the application of each sub-clause.

Practitioners should bear in mind that it is possible that further alterations may require to be made to the VAT Special Condition 3 and the PCVE. While the VAT Special Condition 3 and PCVE are intended to cover most VAT situations, they do not necessarily cover all situations. In particular, as a result of the lack of activity in the commercial property market, there has been limited opportunity to test the effectiveness of the documents in that context. It is therefore recommended that the documents be used with caution in commercial transactions, particularly those involving a combination of varying VAT situations.

APPENDIX 8

VAT ON PROPERTY: AMENDMENTS TO PRE-CONTRACT VAT ENQUIRIES AND SPECIAL CONDITION 3 (AUGUST 2011)

CONVEYANCING, TAXATION 07/02/2014

Last year, practitioners were invited to make submissions regarding amendments or re-finements to Law Society's Pre-Contract VAT Enquiries (PCVE) and Special Condition 3 of its standard contract for sale in relation to VAT on property in order to improve their ef-ficiency and fitness for purpose. The Law Society Taxation and Conveyancing Committees have decided to make the following amendments.

SPECIAL CONDITION 3

1. Clause 3.2.2, 3.3.1, 3.5 and 3.6.2 includes a reference to section 94(7) of the VAT Consolidation Act 2010 to ensure that the provisions for the exercise of the joint option to tax includes liquidators/receivers/MIP type sales,

2. Clause 3.7 is amended to include the words 'of the Subject Property' after 'Sale' for clarity purposes,

3. Clause 3.9, 3.10 and footnote 11 have been amended for greater clarity regarding legacy leases. They now read as follows:

   • "3.9 On the Assignment or Surrender of an interest in an occupational lease (which is not a legacy lease) for a premium…",

   • "3.10 On the Assignment or Surrender of an interest in an occupational lease (legacy or otherwise), the Vendor….",

   • Footnote "11 Required only if Special Condition 3.7 or 3.10 are used…"

PCVE

1. "and enquiries 2.2 and 2.3" are deleted from Clause 1.2 for clarity purposes.

   The updated PCVE and Special Condition 3 are now available on both the Convey-ancing and Taxation Committees' web pages in the members' area of the Society's website.

APPENDIX 9

VAT SPECIAL CONDITION 3 FEBRUARY 2014 EDITION

Law Society of Ireland

SPECIAL CONDITION 3 (February 2014 Edition)

(INSERT (AMENDED AS APPROPRIATE) INTO THE LAW SOCIETY CONDITIONS OF SALE)

For use in sale of property where VAT is relevant to the sale[1]
It is recommended that where this special condition is to be used, prior to settling it, the current
Pre-Contract VAT Enquiries should be answered.
© Law Society of Ireland

---

3. DEFINITIONS

3.1 In this Special Condition:

"Adjustment Period", in respect of Capital Goods, is the period attributed under Section 63(1) of the VAT Act but, where appropriate, is the period attributed to that term under Section 95(12)(c) of the VAT Act;

"Accountable Person", *"Assignment"*, *"Immovable Goods"*, *"Surrender"* and *"Taxable Person"* have the meanings attributed to those terms by Section 2(1) of the VAT Act;

"Capital Goods" has the meaning attributed to that term under Section 2 and Section 63(2) of the VAT Act;

"Capital Goods Adjustment", a liability to repay an amount of VAT to Revenue which arises on a supply of a capital good under Section 64 of the VAT Act;

"Capital Goods Record" has the meaning attributed to that term under Section 64(12) of the VAT Act;

"Freehold Equivalent Interest" has the meaning attributed to that term under Section 2 and Section 19(2) of the VAT Act;

"Interest" has the meaning attributed to that term in Section 93(1)(a) of the VAT Act;

"Interval" and *"Refurbishment"* have the meanings attributed to those terms under Section 63(1) of the VAT Act;

"Tenant's Refurbishment", means capital goods as described in Section 64(7) of the VAT Act;

"VAT" means Value Added Tax; and

"VAT Act" means Value-Added Tax Consolidation Act 2010 and related VAT regulations.

---

[1] This special condition is not appropriate for use:
- on the sale of secondhand residential property sold in a private capacity;
- on the sale of new residential property to a Purchaser as a private person for a VAT inclusive consideration;
- on the grant of an occupational lease; or
- where VAT is otherwise not relevant to the sale.
In any such case Special Condition 3 will be deleted entirely

3.2   Vendor charges VAT at the Appropriate Reduced Rate

3.2.1 In addition to the Purchase Price, the Purchaser shall pay to the Vendor the amount of any VAT as shall be exigible in relation to the Sale, same to be calculated in accordance with the provisions of the VAT Act and the Purchaser shall pay this amount to the Vendor on the later of the completion of the Sale or when an invoice is required to be issued by the Vendor in accordance with the provisions of the VAT Act on delivery of such invoice to the Purchaser.

3.2.2 If the completion of the Sale, being of a Freehold and/or a Freehold Equivalent Interest, is delayed beyond the Closing Date to the extent that the Sale becomes an exempt sale under the VAT Act and the Subject Property comprises Capital Goods, as soon as practicable after such situation arises, the Vendor shall notify the Purchaser in writing accordingly. In such situation, no VAT shall be payable by the Purchaser to the Vendor under Special Condition 3.2.1 but on completion, in addition to the Purchase Price, the Purchaser shall pay to the Vendor the amount which prior to completion the Vendor notifies the Purchaser in writing is equal to the amount for which, as a consequence of the Sale, the Vendor is liable to account for to the Revenue under Section 64(6)(b)(i) of the VAT Act, unless not less than three days prior to the closing date:

- the Purchaser demonstrates to the reasonable satisfaction of the Vendor that the Purchaser is a Taxable Person who independently carries on business in the State; and

- the Purchaser notifies the Vendor in writing that the Purchaser irrevocably joins with the Vendor in the exercise of the joint option to tax the Sale under Section 94(5) or Section 94(7)(b) as appropriate of the VAT Act;

   in which case, the joint option to tax the Sale under Section 94(5) or Section 94(7)(b) as appropriate shall be treated as duly exercised and the Purchaser shall account to the Revenue for VAT arising on the Sale on a reverse charge basis in accordance with the provisions of Section 94(6) or Section 94(7)(c) as appropriate of the VAT Act.

3.2.3 The Purchaser is not a person of a kind specified in Section 95(8)(c) of the VAT Act.

   The sale of the Subject Property is by private treaty by a Taxable Person and by way of Assignment or Surrender of a lease described in Section 95(1)(b) of the VAT Act (a "Legacy Lease") in respect of which the Adjustment Period will not have expired at the Closing Date.

3.2.4 The Sale is by way of Assignment or Surrender of a lease described in Section 95(1)(b) of the VAT Act (a "Legacy Lease") in respect of which the Adjustment Period will not have expired at the Closing Date and in respect of which the right to exercise the joint option to tax under Section 94(5) of the VAT Act is conferred by Section 95(7)(b) of the VAT Act. Such joint option to tax is hereby exercised. The Purchaser is a Taxable Person for the purpose of the VAT Act which status the Purchaser warrants to the Vendor.

3.3   The Purchaser self-accounts for VAT at the appropriate Reduced Rate in a Private Treaty Sale.

3.3.1 The Sale of the Subject Property is of a Freehold/Freehold Equivalent Interest in the Subject Property, which is otherwise exempt. The Purchaser is a Taxable Person which status the Purchaser warrants to the Vendor. The joint option to tax the Sale under Section 94(5) or Section 94(7)(b) as appropriate of the VAT Act is hereby exercised by the Vendor and the Purchaser. The Purchaser shall account to Revenue for any VAT arising on the Sale upon a reverse charge basis in accordance with Section 94(6) or Section 94(7)(c) as appropriate of the VAT [2]Act.

3.3.2 The Sale is by private treaty by way of Assignment or Surrender of a lease described in Section 95(1)(b) of the VAT Act (a "Legacy Lease") in respect of which the Adjustment Period will not have expired at the Closing Date. The Purchaser is a person described in Section 95(8)(c) of the VAT Act, which status the Purchaser hereby warrants to the Vendor. Accordingly, the Purchaser shall account to Revenue for any VAT arising on the sale in accordance with Section 95(8)(c) of the VAT Act.

3.3.3 The Sale is by way of Assignment or Surrender of a lease described in Section 95(1)(b) of the VAT Act (a "Legacy Lease") in respect of which the Adjustment Period will not have expired at the Closing Date and in respect of which the right to exercise the joint option to tax under Section 94(5) of the VAT Act is conferred by Section 95(7)(b) of the VAT Act. Such joint option to tax is hereby exercised. The Purchaser is a Taxable Person for the purpose of the VAT Act which status the Purchaser warrants to the Vendor. Accordingly, the Purchaser shall account to Revenue for any VAT arising on the Sale upon a reverse charge basis in accordance with of Section 95(8)(c) of the VAT Act[3].

3.4 The Purchaser pays the Vendor an amount to compensate the Vendor for the Vendor's liability to pay the Vendor's Capital Goods Adjustment which arises on the Sale of a Freehold/Freehold Equivalent Interest which is exempt.

3.4.1 In addition to the Purchase Price, the Purchaser shall pay the Vendor the sum of € _____ being the amount for which, as a consequence of the Sale being exempt, the Vendor is liable to account to Revenue under Section 64(6)(b)(i) of the VAT Act [and € _____ being the amount which as a consequence of the Sale not being taxable, the Vendor is unable to reclaim from Revenue under Section 64(6)(a) of the VAT Act][4], such amount [or amounts][5] to be reduced as appropriate on the date of completion in the event of the passing of any Interval or Intervals after the Closing Date and on or before the date of completion. Where appropriate, the Vendor shall notify the Purchaser in writing of the amount of any reduction in a timely manner prior to the completion of the Sale.

3.4.2 The Purchaser is not a Taxable Person which status the Purchaser warrants to the Vendor. In addition to the Purchase Price, the Purchaser shall pay the Vendor the sum of € _____ being the amount which, as a consequence of the joint option to tax the Sale not being exercisable or exercised, the Vendor is unable to reclaim from Revenue under Section 64(6)(b)(i) of the VAT Act. Such amount is to be reduced as appropriate on the date of completion in the event of the passing of any Interval or Intervals after the Closing Date and on or before the date of completion. Where appropriate, the Vendor shall notify the Purchaser in writing of the amount of any reduction in a timely manner prior to the completion of the Sale.

---

[2] The difference between the situation covered in clause 3.3.2 and the situation covered in clause 3.3.3 is that, in the latter, the joint option to tax is exercised.
[3] Ibid.
[4] Delete words in square brackets unless the Vendor was only entitled to partial deductibility on the acquisition or development of the Subject Property.
[5] Ibid.

3.5 Sale by auction of a Freehold/Freehold Equivalent Interest which is an exempt sale where, unless the joint option to tax the sale is exercised, the Purchaser pays the Vendor the amount of the Vendor's Capital Goods Adjustment or adjustments which arise on the sale.

The Vendor warrants that the Sale of the Subject Property is exempt subject to the joint option to tax provided that the Purchaser is a Taxable Person for the purpose of the VAT Act.

On completion, in addition to the Purchase Price, the Purchaser shall pay to the Vendor the sum of € _____ being the amount, which as a consequence of the Sale, the Vendor is liable to account for to the Revenue under Section 64(6)(b) of the VAT Act [and € _____ being the amount which, as a consequence of the Sale not being taxable, the Vendor is unable to reclaim from Revenue under Section 64(6)(a) of the VAT Act][6], such amount [or amounts][7] to be reduced as appropriate on the date of completion in the event of the passing of any Interval or Intervals after the Closing Date and on or before the date of completion, unless, not less than three days prior to the Closing Date:

- the Purchaser demonstrates to the reasonable satisfaction of the Vendor that the Purchaser is a Taxable Person; and

- the Purchaser notifies the Vendor in writing that the Purchaser irrevocably joins with the Vendor in the exercise of the joint option to tax the Sale under Section 94(5) or Section 94(7)(b) as appropriate of the VAT Act;

in which case, the joint option to tax the Sale under Section 94(5) or Section 94(7)(b) as appropriate shall be treated as duly exercised and the Purchaser shall account to the Revenue for VAT arising on the Sale on a reverse charge basis in accordance with the provisions of Section 94(6) or Section 94(7)(c) as appropriate of the VAT Act.

3.6 Sale by Auction of a Legacy Lease[8]

3.6.1 The Sale of the Subject Property is by way of Assignment or Surrender of a Lease described in Section 95(1)(b) of the VAT Act (a "Legacy Lease") in respect of which the Adjustment Period will not have expired at the Closing Date.

Unless, not less than three days prior to the Closing Date, the Purchaser demonstrates to the reasonable satisfaction of the Vendor that the Purchaser is a person of a kind specified in Section 95(8)(c) of the VAT Act, in addition to the Purchase Price, the Purchaser shall pay to the Vendor the amount of any VAT as shall be exigible in relation to the Sale on the assumption, whether or not true, that the Purchaser is not a person of a kind specified in Section 95(8)(c) of the VAT Act, same to be calculated in accordance with the provisions of the VAT Act and the Purchaser shall pay this amount to the Vendor on the later of the completion of the Sale or when an invoice is required to be issued by the Vendor in accordance with the provisions of the VAT Act on delivery of such invoice to the Purchaser.

3.6.2 The Sale is by way of Assignment or Surrender of a Lease described in Section 95(1)(b) of the VAT Act (a "Legacy Lease") in respect of which the Adjustment Period referred to in Section 95(12) of the VAT Act will not have expired at the Closing Date.

---

[6] Delete words in square brackets unless the Vendor was only entitled to partial deductibility on the acquisition or development of the Subject Property
[7] Ibid
[8] See footnote 4 of the Pre-Contract VAT Enquiries (February 2014 Edition)

The Sale is of an Interest in respect of which the right to exercise the joint option to tax under Section 94(5) or Section 94(7)(b) as appropriate of the VAT Act is conferred by Section 95(7)(b) provided the Purchaser is a Taxable Person.

On completion, in addition to the Purchase Price, the Purchaser shall pay to the Vendor the sum of € _____ being the amount, which as a consequence of the Sale not being taxable, the Vendor is unable to reclaim from Revenue under Section 64(6)(a) of the VAT Act, such amount to be reduced as appropriate on the date of completion in the event of the passing of any Interval or Intervals after the Closing Date and on or before the date of completion, unless, not less than three days prior to the Closing Date that either:

- the Purchaser demonstrates to the reasonable satisfaction of the Vendor that the Purchaser is both a Taxable Person of a kind described in Section 95(8)(c) of the VAT Act; and

- the Purchaser notifies the Vendor in writing that the Purchaser irrevocably joins with the Vendor in the exercise of the joint option to tax the Sale under Section 94(5) or Section 94(7)(b) as appropriate of the VAT Act;

    in which case, the joint option to tax the Sale under Section 94(5) or Section 94(7)(b) as appropriate of the VAT Act shall be treated as duly exercised and

- if the Purchaser is a person not described in Section 95(8)(c) of the VAT Act then, in addition to the Purchase Price, the Purchaser shall pay to the Vendor the amount of any VAT as shall be exigible in relation to the Sale, same to be calculated in accordance with the provisions of the VAT Act and the Purchaser shall pay this amount to the Vendor on the later of the completion of the Sale or when an invoice is required to be issued by the Vendor in accordance with the provisions of the VAT Act on delivery of such invoice to the Purchaser; and

- if the Purchaser is a person described in Section 95(8)(c) of the VAT Act, the Purchaser shall account to the Revenue for VAT arising on the Sale on a reverse charge basis in accordance with the provisions of Section 94(6) or Section 94(7)(c) as appropriate of the VAT Act.

3.7 **On the sale of a property constituting the transfer of a business or part of a business[9], no VAT applies but the Vendor is required to provide certain information to the Purchaser relating to any Capital Goods comprised in the Subject Property.**

The Sale is by way of a transfer of a business.

The Purchaser warrants to the Vendor that the Purchaser is an Accountable Person for the purposes of Section 20(2)(c) the VAT Act and the Purchaser has taken or will take all steps[10] necessary to be taken on the Purchaser's part so that the Sale of the subject property will qualify for relief from VAT under Section 20(2)(c) of the VAT Act, and that the Sale shall not be a supply of goods for the purposes of the VAT Act. The Purchaser shall indemnify and keep the Vendor indemnified against any loss, cost or liability which arises as a result of such warranty being or becoming untrue or incorrect in any respect due to the act, neglect or default of the Purchaser.

---

[9] A supply to which Section 20(2)(c) of the VAT Act applies.
[10] For example, in the case of the sale of a let property, Revenue require the Purchaser to exercise the Landlord's joint option to tax in respect a letting to which the Subject Property is subject.

3.8 **On the Assignment or Surrender of an Interest in an occupational lease (which is not a Legacy Lease) for a premium paid by the Purchaser to the Vendor where the Purchaser pays the Vendor VAT at the Standard Rate.**

The Sale is the supply of a taxable service by the Vendor to the Purchaser for the purposes of the VAT Act. In addition to the Purchase Price, the Purchaser shall pay to the Vendor the amount of any VAT as shall be exigible in relation to the Sale, same to be calculated in accordance with the VAT Act. The Purchaser shall pay this amount to the Vendor on the later of the completion of the Sale or, where an invoice is required to be issued by the Vendor in accordance with the provisions of the VAT Act, on delivery of such an invoice to the Purchaser.

3.9 **On the Assignment or Surrender of an interest in an occupational lease (not being a legacy lease) for a premium (reverse premium) paid by the Vendor to the Purchaser, the Vendor pays the Purchaser VAT at the Standard Rate.**

The Sale is the supply of a taxable service by the Purchaser to the Vendor for the purpose of the VAT Act.

On the later of the completion of the Sale or where an invoice is required to be issued by the Purchaser in accordance with the provisions of the VAT Act, on delivery of such an invoice to the Vendor, the Vendor shall pay to the Purchaser the amount of any VAT as shall be exigible in relation to the supply in question, same to be calculated in accordance with the provisions of the VAT Act.

3.10 **On the Assignment or Surrender of an interest in an occupational lease (legacy or otherwise), the Vendor requires the Purchaser to become responsible for a Tenant's Refurbishment.**

The Purchaser undertakes to be responsible for all of the obligations of the Vendor under Section 64(7) of the VAT Act which arise in respect of the Refurbishment of the Subject Property comprising the following works:

[Insert details of works]

The Vendor warrants to the Purchaser that he was entitled to deduct all of the VAT incurred by the Vendor on the acquisition and development of this Refurbishment.

3.11 **VAT Information Warranties and Confirmations**

Unless previously supplied at or prior to the signing hereof, the Vendor shall supply to the Purchaser:

- copies of the Capital Goods Records for the period up to the latest date prior to the date hereof for the filing of returns in relation to any Capital Goods comprised in the Subject Property[11];

- if applicable, a draft of any statement[12] required to be supplied by the Vendor to the Purchaser, under the VAT Act as the Purchaser may reasonably require to enable the Purchaser, on becoming the owner of the Subject Property to comply with the Purchaser's obligations in respect of the Subject Property under the VAT Act;

- answers to any pre-contract VAT enquiries raised by the Purchaser; and

---

[11] Required only if Special Condition 3.7 or 3.10 is used (Transfer of a Business). Delete if not applicable.
[12] Required only if the Subject Property sold is a Legacy Lease. Delete if not applicable.

- such other information in relation to the VAT history of the Subject Property as the Purchaser, acting reasonably, shall in writing require in order to comply with the Purchaser's obligations in respect of the Subject Property under the VAT Act.

The Vendor warrants that all such information and records and, if relevant, any such statement are materially correct and up to date at the date of furnishing thereof and will remain correct and up-to-date on completion save for such adjustment as may be necessary as a result of the passing of any Interval or Intervals, in which case revised information and copy records and if relevant, a revised draft statement to reflect such passing, will be furnished by the Vendor to the Purchaser on or prior to completion.

The certificate of the Vendor's tax advisor shall in the absence of manifest error be conclusive evidence of the amount of any Capital Goods Adjustment relevant to the Subject Property.

The obligations imposed on the Parties under this Agreement shall be in addition to the obligations imposed in relation to the Sale by the VAT Act.

APPENDIX 10

PRE-CONTRACT VAT ENQUIRIES
FEBRUARY 2014 EDITION

Law Society of Ireland

PRE-CONTRACT VAT ENQUIRIES (February 2014 Edition)

Subject to Contract / Contract Denied

To be answered prior to settling the conditions of sale where VAT is relevant[1] © Law Society of Ireland

---

Vendor:

Vendor's VAT Registration No:

Purchaser:

Subject Property:

"Occupational Lease" means a lease which is not a freehold equivalent interest as defined in Section 2(1) the VAT Act.

"PCVE" means these Enquiries.

"Tenant's Refurbishment" means capital goods as described in Section 64(7) of the VAT Act.

"VAT Act" means the Value-Added Tax Consolidation Act 2010 as amended from time to time and related VAT regulations.

"TOB" means transfer of a business or part of a business under Section 20(2)(c) the VAT Act.

Reference to "VAT Special Condition 3" means the recommended format of VAT special condition current at the time of sale as referred to in Special Condition 3 of the Law Society's standard General Conditions of Sale.

Private Treaty Sale

Prior to the presentation of the draft Conditions of Sale by Private Treaty, the Purchaser shall complete the Purchaser Statement on the Purchaser's VAT status on Page 3 and issue these PCVE in duplicate to the Vendor. After completing the answers, the Vendor shall complete the drafting of Special Condition 3. The Vendor shall then send the draft Conditions of Sale together with one completed form of these PCVE to the Purchaser.

Auction Sale

When furnishing the Conditions of Sale for an auction sale, the Vendor shall answer these PCVE purely for the purposes of providing VAT information to a prospective Purchaser in relation to the sale of the Subject Property, including a sale which would otherwise be exempt,[2] on the assumption that the prospective Purchaser is a taxable person who will exercise the joint option to tax the sale but without prejudice to the Purchaser's right to opt, or not to opt, as provided in Special Condition 3.

The enquiry part of these PCVE is divided into 7 Sections:

Section 1: Is VAT chargeable on the sale.
Section 2: Vendor charges VAT at the appropriate reduced rate.
Section 3: Purchaser self accounts for VAT at the appropriate reduced rate.
Section 4: Transfer of Business.
Section 5: Vendor charges VAT at the standard rate.
Section 6: Sale of Let Property.
Section 7: Tenant's Refurbishment.

---

1   This form is not appropriate for use:
   • on the sale of secondhand residential property sold in a private capacity;
   • on the sale of new residential property to a Purchaser as a private person for a VAT inclusive consideration;
   • on the grant of an Occupational Lease; or
   • on a sale where VAT Special Condition 3 will be deleted entirely and the Purchaser does not require to know the VAT history of the Subject Property.
   In any such case Special Condition 3 will be deleted entirely
2   "Exempt" includes the situation where the property is not mandatorily taxable but the joint option to tax may be exercised where both parties are taxable persons.

1

Where appropriate the terms "vendor"/"landlord" and "purchaser"/"tenant" are used interchangeably.

The Vendor should answer these PCVE in the section(s) which are relevant to the sale of the Subject Property.

Where there is insufficient space, the Vendor should provide the answer on an attached sheet or attached sheets.

For each part of the Subject Property which has a separate VAT status, a separate set of answers will be required.

The purposes of these PCVE are to enable the Purchaser's Solicitor to obtain the information necessary to advise the Purchaser on VAT issues relating to the Subject Property and to assist in the drafting of Special Condition 3. These purposes are stressed as in certain situations these PCVE may require more information to be furnished than is necessary and in other situations more information may actually be required.

To avoid serious difficulties, it is important that Special Condition 3 is drafted to suit the VAT status of the sale and paragraphs which are not relevant are struck out or omitted. A guide (the "Guide") as to how, using the answers to these PCVE, the Vendor shall settle VAT Special Condition 3 is set out on pages 19 to 25. If VAT Special Condition 3 is to be struck out in its entirety and the Purchaser does not require to know the VAT history of the Subject Property, it is not necessary to use these PCVE.

These PCVE, the Guide and VAT Special Condition 3 are general in nature and may not cover all situations. If in doubt, the advice of a tax expert should be sought.

These PCVE shall be furnished in its entirety without amendment.

Warning: Before answering the PCVE, the Vendor should be satisfied as to the VAT status of the Subject Property and the sale. The answers will be relied upon by the Purchaser.

_____

We certify that these PCVE are those as issued by the Law Society of Ireland (February 2014 Edition) without alteration or omission and that the numbering is unchanged.

_____

Signature of Issuing Solicitor

_____

Date

SUBJECT TO CONTRACT/CONTRACT DENIED

Purchaser Statement on Purchaser's VAT Status

	Please mark as appropriate	Yes	No
1.	The Purchaser is a taxable person as defined in Section 2 of the VAT Act who carries on a business in the State.[3]	☐	☐
2.	On the assignment or surrender of a "legacy lease"[4] (see VAT Special Conditions 3.2 and 3.6 and enquiries 2.4 and 3.3) the Vendor will require the Purchaser to confirm whether the Vendor or the Purchaser will account for VAT on the assignment or surrender. If the Purchaser answers "No" to this item 2, the Vendor must account for VAT on the assignment or surrender. The Purchaser is a person described in Section 95(8)(c) of the VAT Act.[5]	☐	☐
3.	The Purchaser is an accountable person[6] as defined in Section 5 of the VAT Act.[7]	☐	☐
4.	Purchaser's VAT registration number:		

_____

Signature of Purchaser (or Purchaser's Agent)

_____

Date

_____

Capacity of Signatory

---

3   In the case of a sale where the joint option to tax (see VAT Special Condition 3.3.1 first paragraph) is to be exercised, the Vendor will require the Purchaser to confirm that the Purchaser is a "taxable person" who carries on a business in the State. Section 1 of the VAT Act defines a "taxable person" as "a person who independently carries on a business in the Community or elsewhere". Where the joint option to tax is exercised, the Purchaser, if a taxable person not already registered for VAT, should register for VAT and account accordingly.

4   Legacy leases (see Section 95(1)(b) of the VAT Act) are interests in leasehold property (so called because they are a legacy from the old system of VAT on property) that were treated as a supply of goods under the old rules. For a definition of "Legacy Lease" see section 3.7 of the Revenue VAT on Property Guide.

5   The following is a <u>non-exhaustive</u> list of purchasers described in Section 95(8)(c) of the VAT Act who should "self-account":
      (a) an accountable person;
      (b) a Department of State or Local Authority;
      (c) a landlord;
      (d) a bank;
      (e) an insurance company or insurance broker;
      (f) An Post;
      (g) the operator of a national broadcasting or television service; or
      (h) a transport operation
    and the following is a non exhaustive list of persons who do not "self account":
      (i) a bookmaker;
      (j) a doctor;
      (k) a dentist;
      (l) a private individual;
      (m) a university, training college or other educational establishment;
      (n) an undertaker.
    When in doubt, a direction should be sought from the Inspector of Taxes.

6   An accountable person is a taxable person who engages in the supply within the State of taxable goods or services.

7   Required only if the transaction is a transfer of a business under Section 20(2)(c) of the VAT Act.

SECTION 1: IS VAT CHARGEABLE ON THE SALE

		Yes	No
	Please mark as appropriate		
1.	**IS VAT CHARGEABLE ON THE SALE?**	☐	☐
	If the answer to enquiry 1 is "Yes", confirm that the Vendor is a taxable person under Section 2 of the VAT Act for the purposes of the sale of the Subject Property.	☐	☐
	If "Yes", please state Vendor's VAT Number and proceed to Section 2.		
1.1	If the answer to enquiry 1. is "No", please indicate by a "Yes" or "No" answer which of the following categories of sale applies:		
(a)	The sale of a freehold/freehold equivalent interest which: (i) is not a sale as part of a TOB; and (ii) is not a sale where the Vendor is requesting the Purchaser to exercise the joint option to tax.	☐	☐
(b)	The assignment or surrender of an Occupational Lease: (i) which is not a sale as part of a TOB; and (ii) which is not a supply of a good or a service where VAT is chargeable on the sale.	☐	☐
(c)	The sale as part of a TOB qualifying for non application of VAT under the VAT Act Section 20(2)(c).	☐	☐
(d)	Other category of sale on which VAT will not be chargeable either as the supply of a good or a service.	☐	☐
1.2	If the answer to either of enquiries 1.1(a) or (d) is "Yes", confirm that VAT Special Condition 3 will be deleted in its entirety. (If Vendor has answered "Yes" to either of such enquiries and agrees that VAT Special Condition 3 is to be deleted, answer enquiry 1.6 and related enquiries. No further answers are required in these PCVE but the right is reserved to make further enquiries to investigate the VAT history of the Subject Property.		
1.3	If the answer to enquiry 1.2 is "No", answer enquiry 1.6 and related enquiries and enquiries 2.2 and 2.3 and explain in writing on an **attached sheet** how the Vendor proposes to deal with VAT Special Condition 3 of the Law Society General Conditions of Sale.[8] No further answers to these PCVE are required but the right is reserved to make further enquires to investigate the VAT history of the Subject Property.		
1.4	If the answer to enquiry 1.1(b) is "Yes", answer enquiry 1.6 and related enquiries and Section 7 and give details on an **attached sheet** to satisfy the Purchaser as to why VAT is not chargeable. No further answers to these PCVE are required but the right is reserved to make further enquires to investigate the VAT history of the Subject Property.		
1.5	If the answer to enquiry 1.1(c) is "Yes", answer enquiry 1.6 and related enquiries and proceed to Section 4 (Transfer of Business).		
1.6	**Let (or previously let within 20 years) Subject Property**		
1.6.1	Is any part of the Subject Property let or sublet?	☐	☐
1.6.2	Within the last 20 years was any part of the Subject Property let or sublet and the subject of a waiver of exemption under Section 96 of the VAT Act?	☐	☐
1.6.3	If the answer to either enquiry 1.6.1 or 1.6.2 is "Yes", please also answer Section 6.		

---

8   If it is the case that in addition to the purchase price, under VAT Special Condition 3.4 the Vendor will charge the Purchaser an amount equal to the capital goods adjustment which the Vendor will suffer as a result of the sale of the Subject Property, give details to satisfy the Purchaser as to how this amount is calculated together with copies of relevant capital goods records.

SECTION 2: VENDOR CHARGES VAT AT THE APPROPRIATE REDUCED RATE

		Please mark as appropriate	Yes	No
2.	**WILL THE VENDOR CHARGE VAT AT THE APPROPRIATE REDUCED RATE?**[9]		☐	☐
	If the answer to enquiry 2 is "No", proceed to Section 3.			
2.1	If the answer to enquiry 2 is "Yes" indicate by a "Yes" or "No" answer which one of the following categories of sale at (a) to (d) applies:			
(a)	Sale of partially developed property.[10]		☐	☐
(b)	Sale of property coupled with building.[11]		☐	☐
(c)	Sale of a completed "new or nearly new" freehold/freehold equivalent interest.[12]		☐	☐
(d)	Assignment or surrender of a legacy lease to a person not specified in Section 95(8)(c) of the VAT Act.[13]		☐	☐
	If the answer to either of enquiries 2.1 (a) or (c) is "Yes", answer enquiries 2.2, 2.3 and 2.5. No further answers are required.			
	If the answer to enquiry 2.1(b) is "Yes", answer enquiries 2.2 and 2.5. No further answers are required.			
	If the answer to enquiry 2.1(d) is "Yes", answer enquires 2.4 and 2.5. No further answers are required.			
2.2	Please furnish now a draft VAT invoice showing the amount of VAT chargeable on the sale of the Subject Property.			
2.3	**Development**[14]			
2.3.1	Please state the date (irrespective of whether or not such date was before, on or after 1 July 2008) when the Subject Property was last developed to such an extent that such development renders the sale of the Subject Property a taxable supply of immovable goods in respect of which the development has been completed.[15]			
2.3.2	Please provide a description of such development on an **attached sheet**. Please also state: (i) the cost of the development (ii) the total tax incurred; and (iii) the non deductible amount[16] and furnish copies of the development contract or contracts		€ _____ € _____ € _____	

---

9   Sections 3(1)(a), 94(5) and 95(3) or (6) of the VAT Act. Note if the Vendor will not charge VAT but either the Purchaser will be chargeable to VAT or the Vendor intends that the Purchaser will be so chargeable, the appropriate answer is "No".

10   Partially developed property refers to property which has been developed but has not been completed within the meaning of Section 94(1) of the VAT Act and is not excluded by Section 94(2)(d) of the VAT Act (20 year look back period). See Note 14 below for definition of "development".

11   Section 94(3) of the VAT Act.

12   This includes transitional properties held on 1 July 2008 by a taxable person where the Vendor had the right to deduct VAT on the acquisition or development. The supply of these properties can be taxable under the VAT Act as a supply of immovable goods without reference to the exercise of any joint option. This enquiry can only be answered in the affirmative where development (other than minor development) to a non residential property has been completed within 5 years prior to completion of the sale and the property has not been occupied for at least 2 years.

13   See footnote 5.

14   Section 2(1) of the VAT Act defines "development" as the construction, demolition, extension, alteration or reconstruction of any building on the land, or the carrying out of any engineering or other operation in, on, over or under the land to adapt it for a materially altered use. This does not include minor development to a building which does not adapt the building for a materially altered use and the value of the works do not exceed 25% of the value of the property at the time of sale.

15   Section 94(1) of the VAT Act.

16   Section 63(1) of the VAT Act.

		Please mark as appropriate	Yes	No
2.3.3	If more than one such development has taken place which renders the sale of the Subject Property taxable, answer enquiry 2.3.2 for each such development on **attached sheet.**			
2.3.4	2.3.4 Was any such development a refurbishment[17]? If the answer is "Yes", please provide details on an **attached sheet.**		☐	☐
	Completed[18]			
2.3.5	If such development of the Subject Property was completed in stages please describe on an **attached sheet** the stages, and specify the date of completion for each stage and the relevant costs.			
2.3.6	Produce documentary evidence of the date(s) of completion of such development(s) and if relevant, the stages.			
	Occupied[19]			
2.3.7	Has the Subject Property been occupied in its entirety in accordance with appropriate planning permission since the date of such development?		☐	☐
2.3.8	If the answer to enquiry 2.3.7 is "No", give particulars on an **attached sheet** of: (a) dates, periods and other details of occupation of the Subject Property since such completion; and (b) the authorised use under any planning permission in respect of the Subject Property.			
2.3.9	Since completion of the most recent development which for the purposes of the VAT Act causes the sale of the Subject Property to be taxable as the supply of immovable goods, was every part of the Subject Property occupied for the purposes of the VAT Act?		☐	☐
2.3.10	If the answer to enquiry 2.3.9 is "Yes", please provide details on an **attached sheet**.			
	Sales Since Completion of Development[20]			
2.3.11	Since the completion of the most recent development of the Subject Property which for the purposes of the VAT Act causes the sale to be taxable as the supply of immovable goods, has there been a sale or sales of the Subject Property?		☐	☐
2.3.12	If the answer to enquiry 2.3.11 is "Yes", give details on an **attached sheet** of all sales for the period since the later of the most recent development or 5 years last past and include information on: (a) The VAT charged on each such sale; and (b) Whether the parties were "connected persons" within the meaning of Section 97(3) of the VAT Act.			
2.4	**Legacy Lease[21] – Vendor Accountable for VAT**			
2.4.1	Please identify by a "Yes" or "No" answer the type of sale of the Subject Property by reference to the following:			
	(a) assignment/surrender of a legacy lease held by the original lessee.		☐	☐
	(b) assignment/surrender of a legacy lease acquired by the Vendor by assignment prior to 1 July 2008.		☐	☐
	(c) assignment/surrender of a legacy lease acquired by the Vendor by the first assignment made after 1 July 2008.		☐	☐

17   Section 63(1) of the VAT Act.
18   Section 94(1) of the VAT Act.
19   "Occupied" means occupied and fully in use following completion where that use is one for which planning permission for the development of the property was granted and where the Subject Property is let, occupied and fully in use by the tenant.
20   "Sale" or, in the term used in the VAT Act, "supply", means "the transfer in substance of (a) the right to dispose of immovable property as owner or (b) the right to transfer immovable goods". (See the VAT Act Section 19(2)).
21   See footnote 4.

		Please mark as appropriate	Yes	No
(d)	assignment/surrender of a lease acquired by the Vendor as the successor in title of a person who acquired the legacy lease in the manner described in (c) above.		☐	☐
2.4.2	Was the Vendor entitled or deemed to have been entitled to deduct any VAT on the acquisition or development of the Subject Property?		☐	☐
2.4.3	If the answer to enquiry 2.4.2 is "Yes", please provide now:			
(a)	draft document specified by Section 95(9)(a) of the VAT Act containing details of the VAT due on the sale of the Subject Property and the number of intervals remaining in the adjustment period;			
(b)	evidence to verify the "total tax incurred"; and			
(c)	evidence to confirm the number of intervals in the adjustment period.			
2.4.4	If the answer to enquiry 2.4.2 is "No", is the Vendor requesting the Purchaser to co-operate in exercising the joint option to tax the sale in accordance with Section 94(5) as authorised by Section 95(7)(b) of the VAT Act?		☐	☐
2.4.5	If the answer to enquiry 2.4.4 is "Yes", please set out the quantum of the VAT that may be recovered by the Vendor as a result of the exercise of such joint option	€_____		
2.4.6	Without prejudice to the Purchaser's position in respect of the response to enquiry 2.4.4 would the Vendor agree not to exercise the joint option to tax and on what terms?		☐	☐
2.4.7	If the answer to enquiry 2.4.4 is "Yes", the Vendor is a taxable person but is not registered for VAT and the Purchaser is willing to co-operate in exercising the joint option to tax, please confirm that the Vendor will be so registered before completion and will on or prior to completion supply evidence of such registration.		☐	☐
2.5	**Let (or previously let within 20 years) Subject Property**			
2.5.1	Is any part of the Subject Property let or sublet?		☐	☐
2.5.2	Within the last 20 years was any part of the Subject Property let or sublet and the subject of a waiver of exemption under Section 96 of the VAT Act?		☐	☐
2.5.3	If the answer to either enquiry 2.5.1 or 2.5.2 is "Yes", please also answer Section 6.			

SECTION 3: PURCHASER SELF ACCOUNTS FOR VAT AT THE APPROPRIATE REDUCED RATE

		Please mark as appropriate	Yes	No
3.	**DOES THE VENDOR INTEND THAT THE PURCHASER WILL SELF ACCOUNT FOR VAT AT THE APPROPRIATE REDUCED RATE[22]?** **If the answer to enquiry 3 is "No", proceed to Section 4.**		☐	☐
3.1	If the answer to enquiry 3 is "Yes", indicate by a "Yes" or "No" answer which of the categories of sale at (a) or (b) applies:			
(a)	Sale of freehold/freehold equivalent interest where the Vendor is requesting that the joint option to tax the Subject Property shall be exercised.[23]		☐	☐
(b)	Assignment or surrender of legacy lease[24] to a Purchaser who is a person specified in Section 95(8)(c) of the VAT Act.[25]		☐	☐
	If the answer to enquiry 3.1(a) is "Yes", answer enquiries 3.2 and 3.4. No further answers in these PCVE are required but the right is reserved to make further enquiries to investigate the VAT history of the Subject Property.			
	If the answer to enquiry 3.1(b) is "Yes", answer enquiries 3.3 and 3.4. No further answers are required in these PCVE but the right is reserved to make further enquiries to investigate the VAT history of the Subject Property.			
3.2	**Development[26]/Completion[27]**			
3.2.1	Please:			
(a)	state the date (irrespective of whether or not such date was before, on or after 1 July 2008) when the Subject Property was last developed to such an extent that any supply of the Subject Property immediately following the completion of that development was or would have been treated under the VAT Act as in force on 1 July 2008 as a taxable supply of immovable goods in respect of which the development had been completed (as defined in Section 94(1)) of the VAT Act);			
(b)	provide a description of such development on an **attached sheet** giving the following information: (i) the cost of the development; (ii) the total tax incurred; and (iii) the non-deductible amount,[28] and	€_____ €_____ €_____		
(c)	furnish copies of the development contract or contracts			

---

22 Sections 94(5), 95(5) or 95(7)(b) of the VAT Act.
23 This includes:
(a) transitional freehold/freehold equivalent property held prior to 1 July 2008 which is not new or nearly new and where the Vendor had the right to deduct VAT; and
(b) transitional freehold/freehold equivalent property held prior to 1 July 2008 where the Vendor had no right to deduct VAT regardless of whether the property is new or nearly new but the Vendor requires the joint option to tax to be exercised in a sale to a taxable person.
24 See footnote 4.
25 See reply 2 of the Purchaser Statement on Purchaser's VAT status at page 3. See also footnote 5.
26 Section 2(1) of the VAT Act defines "development" as the construction, demolition, extension, alteration or reconstruction of any building on the land, or the carrying out of any engineering or other operation in, on, over or under the land to adapt it for a materially altered use. This does not include minor development to a building which does not adapt the building for a materially altered use and the value of the works do not exceed 25% of the value of the property at the time of sale.
27 Section 94(1) of the VAT Act.
28 Section 63(1) of the VAT Act.

			Yes	No
		Please mark as appropriate		
	Joint Option to Tax[29]			
3.2.2	If the Vendor is requesting that the Purchaser shall agree to jointly opt to have the sale chargeable to VAT in accordance with Section 94(5) of the VAT Act, please set out the quantum of the VAT that may be recovered by the Vendor as a result of the exercise of such option if the sale of the Subject Property is completed on the closing date.[30]		€ _____	
3.2.3	If the Vendor is requesting that the Purchaser shall agree to jointly opt to have the sale chargeable to VAT in accordance with Section 94(5) of the VAT Act, please state the amount of the VAT repayment under the Capital Goods Scheme which the Vendor will be obliged to repay and, if applicable, the amount of any VAT reclaim which the Vendor will forego, if the sale of the Subject Property is completed on the closing date and the joint option to tax the sale is not exercised.		€ _____ VAT repayable € _____ Reclaim foregone	
3.2.4	Without prejudice to the Purchaser's right not to participate in the exercise of the joint option to tax, will the Vendor agree not to request the exercise of the joint option to tax?		☐	☐
	If so, specify the amount (with breakdown for each capital good on an **attached sheet** if necessary) required to compensate the Vendor for any capital goods adjustment which will apply for the Vendor and state the additional consideration which the Vendor would propose charging the Purchaser for not exercising such joint option.		€ _____ Additional consideration	
3.2.5	If the Vendor intends that the joint option will be exercised, state how the Vendor proposes that this exercise will be documented for record purposes?			
3.3	**Assignment/Surrender of Legacy Lease[31] – Purchaser Self Accounts for VAT**			
	Vendor should only answer this enquiry if the Purchaser answered "Yes" to the Purchaser Statement on VAT status number 2 at page 3.[32]			
3.3.1	Please identify by a "Yes" or "No" answer the type of sale by reference to the following:			
(a)	assignment/surrender of a legacy lease held by the original lessee.		☐	☐
(b)	assignment/surrender of a legacy lease acquired by the Vendor by assignment prior to 1 July 2008.		☐	☐
(c)	assignment/surrender of a legacy lease acquired by the Vendor by the first assignment made after 1 July 2008		☐	☐
(d)	assignment/surrender of a lease acquired by the Vendor as the successor in title of a person who acquired the legacy lease in the manner described in (c) above.		☐	☐
3.3.2	Was the Vendor entitled or deemed to have been entitled to deduct any VAT on the acquisition or development of the Subject Property?		☐	☐
3.3.3	If the answer to enquiry 3.3.2 is "Yes", please provide now:			
(a)	draft document specified by Section 95(9)(a) of the VAT Act containing details of the VAT due on the sale of the Subject Property and the number of intervals remaining in the adjustment period;			
(b)	evidence to verify the "total tax incurred"; and			
(c)	evidence to confirm the number of intervals in the adjustment period.			
3.3.4	If the answer to enquiry 3.3.2 is "No", is the Vendor requesting the Purchaser to co-operate in exercising the joint option to tax the sale in accordance with Section 94(5) as conferred by Section 95(7)(b) of the VAT Act?		☐	☐

---

29 The joint option to tax under Section 94(5) of the VAT Act can only be exercised where the Vendor and the Purchaser are taxable persons.
30 This is only exercisable where the Vendor is a taxable person.
31 See footnote 4.
32 Sale of legacy lease. Vendor not entitled to deduct VAT on acquisition or development of the Subject Property.

		Please mark as appropriate	Yes	No
3.3.5	If the answer to enquiry 3.3.4 is "Yes", please set out the quantum of the VAT that may be recovered by the Vendor as a result of the exercise of such option.		€ _____	
3.3.6	Without prejudice to the Purchaser's position in respect of the response to enquiry 3.3.4, would the Vendor agree not to exercise the joint option to tax? If the answer is "yes", please set out the terms on an **attached sheet.**		☐	☐
3.3.7	If the answer to enquiry 3.3.4 is "Yes", the Vendor is a taxable person but is not registered for VAT and the Purchaser is willing to exercise the joint option to tax, please confirm that the Vendor will be so registered before completion and will on or prior to completion supply evidence of such registration.		☐	☐
3.4	**Let (or previously let within 20 years) Subject Property**			
3.4.1	Is any part of the Subject Property let or sublet?		☐	☐
3.4.2	Within the last 20 years was any part of the Subject Property let or sublet and the subject of a waiver of exemption under Section 96 of the VAT Act?		☐	☐
3.4.2	If the answer to either enquiry 3.4.1 or 3.4.2 is "Yes", please also answer Section 6.			

SECTION 4: TRANSFER OF BUSINESS (TOB)[33]

		Please mark as appropriate	Yes	No
4.	**IS THE SALE PART OF A TOB?**		☐	☐
4.1	If the answer to enquiry 4 is "Yes", indicate by a "Yes" or "No" answer which of the following categories of sale at (a) to (d) applies:			
(a)	Sale of partially developed property. If the answer to (a) is "Yes", please answer enquiries 4.2 and 4.6.		☐	☐
(b)	Sale of new or nearly new freehold/freehold equivalent interest.[34] If the answer to (b) is "Yes", please answer enquiries 4.3 and 4.6.		☐	☐
(c)	Sale of freehold/freehold equivalent interest in the Subject Property under TOB rules which would otherwise be exempt with a joint option to tax the Subject Property.[35] If the answer to (c) is "Yes", please answer enquiries 4.4 and 4.6.		☐	☐
(d)	Assignment or surrender of legacy lease. If the answer to (d) is "Yes", please answer enquiries 4.5 and 4.6.		☐	☐
4.2	**Partially Developed Property**			
4.2.1	Describe on an **attached sheet** the development or, if there is more than one development, each of the developments of the Subject Property relevant for VAT on the sale.			
4.2.2	Please state the amount on which VAT would be chargeable on the sale of the Subject Property in the absence of TOB relief.	€ _____		
4.3	**New or Nearly New Property**			
	(a) Development[36]			
4.3.1	Please state the date (irrespective of whether or not such date was before, on or after 1 July 2008) when the Subject Property was last developed to such an extent that in the absence of TOB Relief such development renders the sale of the Subject Property a taxable supply of immovable goods in respect of which the development has been completed.[37]			
4.3.2	Please provide a description of such development on an **attached sheet**. Please also state: (i) the cost of the development; (ii) the total tax incurred; and (iii) the non-deductible amount.[38] and furnish copies of the development contract or contracts.	€ _____ € _____ € _____		
4.3.3	If more than one such development has taken place which renders the sale of the Subject Property taxable, answer enquiry 4.3.2 for each such development on an **attached sheet.**			

---

33 Section 20(2)(c) of the VAT Act.
34 This includes transitional properties held on 1 July 2008 by a taxable person where the Vendor had the right to deduct VAT on the acquisition or development. The supply of these properties is taxable under the VAT Act as a supply of immovable goods without reference to the exercise of any joint option. This enquiry can only be answered in the affirmative where development (other than minor development) to a non residential property has been completed within 5 years prior to completion of the sale and the property has not been occupied for at least 2 years.
35 This includes:
(a) a transitional freehold/freehold equivalent property held from prior to 1 July 2008 which is not new or nearly new and where the Vendor had the right to deduct VAT; and
(b) a transitional freehold/freehold equivalent property held prior to 1 July 2008 where the Vendor is a taxable person and had no right to deduct VAT on the acquisition or development regardless of whether the property is new or nearly new.
36 Section 2(1) of the VAT Act defines "development" as the construction, demolition, extension, alteration or reconstruction of any building on the land, or the carrying out of any engineering or other operation in, on, over or under the land to adapt it for a materially altered use. This does not include minor development to a building which does not adapt the building for a materially altered use and the value of the works do not exceed 25% of the value of the property at the time of the sale.
37 Section 94(1) of the VAT Act.
38 Section 63(1) of the VAT Act.

		Please mark as appropriate	Yes	No
4.3.4	Was any such development a refurbishment[39]? If the answer is "Yes", please provide details on an **attached sheet.**		☐	☐
	(b) Completed[40]			
4.3.5	If such development of the Subject Property was completed in stages please describe on an **attached sheet** the stages, and specify the date of completion for each stage and the relevant costs.			
4.3.6	Produce documentary evidence of the date(s) of completion of such development(s) and if relevant, the stages.			
	(c) Occupied[41]			
4.3.7	Has the Subject Property been occupied in its entirety in accordance with appropriate planning permission since the date of such development?		☐	☐
4.3.8	If the answer to enquiry 4.3.7 is "No", give particulars on an **attached sheet** of: (a) dates, periods and other details of occupation and vacancy of the Subject Property since such completion; and (b) the authorised use under any planning permission in respect of the Subject Property.			
4.3.9	Since completion of the most recent development which for the purposes of the VAT Act causes the sale of the Subject Property (in the absence of TOB relief) to be taxable as the supply of immovable goods, was every part of the Subject Property occupied for the purposes of the VAT Act?		☐	☐
4.3.10	Please provide details on an **attached sheet** of all occupations and non-occupations of the subject property relevant for the purposes of enquiry 4.3.9.			
	(d) Sales[42]			
4.3.11	Since the completion of the most recent development of the Subject Property which for the purposes of the VAT Act causes the sale to be taxable as the supply of immovable goods, has there been a sale or sales of the Subject Property?		☐	☐
4.3.12	If the answer to enquiry 4.3.11 is "Yes", please provide details on an **attached sheet** of each sale.			
4.3.13	Since the date of such development(s), has there been a sale or sales of the Subject Property to a "connected person" or "connected persons" within the meaning of Section 97(3) of the VAT Act?		☐	☐
4.3.14	If the answer to enquiry 4.3.13 is "Yes", please provide details on an **attached sheet** of each such sale.			

---

39 Section 63(1) of the VAT Act.
40 Section 94(1) of the VAT Act.
41 "Occupied" means occupied and fully in use following completion where that use is one for which planning permission for the development of the property was granted and where the Subject Property is let, occupied and fully in use by the tenant.
42 "Sale" in this section means "the transfer in substance of the right to dispose of immovable property as owner or the transfer in substance of the right to transfer immovable goods". (See VAT Act Section 19(2)).

		Please mark as appropriate	Yes	No
4.4	**Freehold/Freehold Equivalent Interest which is no longer new or nearly new**			
4.4.1	Please state the date (irrespective of whether or not such date was before, on or after 1 July 2008) when the Subject Property was last developed to such an extent that any supply of the Subject Property immediately following that development was or would have been treated under the VAT Act as in force on 1 July 2008 as a taxable supply of immovable goods in respect of which the development had been completed (as defined in Section 94(1)) of the VAT Act.			
4.4.2	Please provide a description of such development on an **attached sheet**. Please also state: (i) the cost of the development; (ii) the total tax incurred; and (iii) the non-deductible amount[43], and furnish copies of the development contract or contracts.	€ _____ € _____ € _____		
4.4.3	If more than one such development has taken place which renders the sale of the Subject Property taxable, give details of each of them on an **attached sheet**.			
4.4.4	Was any such development a refurbishment[44]? If the answer is "Yes", please provide details on an **attached sheet**.		☐	☐
4.4.5	If such development of the Subject Property was completed in stages, please describe the stages on an **attached sheet**, and specify the date of completion for each stage and the relevant costs.			
4.4.6	Since the date given in the answer to enquiry 4.4.1 above, has the Subject Property or any part of it been developed or undergone works to effect or materially alter the use? If so, please provide details on an **attached sheet**.		☐	☐
	Other Capital Goods			
4.4.7	Please produce now a copy of the capital goods record written up to date for each development of the Subject Property and confirm that capital goods records for the Subject Property written up to date of completion will be handed over on completion.			

---

43   Section 63(1) of the VAT Act.
44   Section 63(1) of the VAT Act.

		Please mark as appropriate	Yes	No
4.5	**Assignment/Surrender of Legacy Lease**[45]			
4.5.1	Was the Vendor entitled to deduct any of the VAT incurred on the acquisition or development of the lease?		☐	☐
4.5.2	State the amount on which VAT would be chargeable on the sale of the Subject Property in the absence of TOB relief.	€ _____		
4.5.3	Produce a copy of the capital goods record written up to date for the Subject Property and confirm that a capital goods record for the Subject Property written up to date of completion will be handed over on completion.			
4.6	**Let (or previously let within 20 years) Property**			
4.6.1	Is any part of the Subject Property let or sublet?		☐	☐
4.6.2	Within the last 20 years was any part of the Subject Property let or sublet and the subject of a waiver of exemption under Section 96 of the VAT Act?		☐	☐
4.6.3	If the answer to either enquiry 4.6.1 or 4.6.2 is "Yes", please also answer Section 6.			

---

45   See footnote 4.

SECTION 5: VENDOR CHARGES VAT AT THE STANDARD RATE

			Yes	No
		Please mark as appropriate		
5	**WILL THE VENDOR CHARGE VAT AT THE STANDARD RATE?**		☐	☐
5.1	If the answer to enquiry 5.1 is "Yes", please indicate by a "Yes" answer which one of the following categories of transaction (a) to (d) applies:-			
(a)	The sale is a surrender for a premium payable by the purchaser of an occupational lease created prior to 1 July 2008 for a term of less than 10 years where the landlord's waiver of exemption under section 7 of the VAT Act 1972 applies; or		☐	☐
(b)	The sale is a surrender for a premium payable by the purchaser of an occupational lease created after 30 June 2008 where the landlord's option to tax is in place; or		☐	☐
(c)	The sale is an assignment for a premium payable by the purchaser of an occupational lease created prior to 1 July 2008 for a term of less than 10 years where the landlord's waiver of exemption from VAT applies; or		☐	☐
(d)	The sale is an assignment for a premium payable by the purchaser of an occupational lease created after 30 June 2008 whether or not the landlord's option to tax is in place.		☐	☐
5.2	Please furnish now a draft VAT invoice showing the amount of VAT chargeable.			
5.3	Is the Subject Property assigned or surrendered the subject of a Tenant's Refurbishment?		☐	☐
5.4	If the answer to enquiry 5.3 is "Yes", please also answer Section 7.			
5.5	**Let (or previously let within 20 years) Property**			
5.5.1	Is any part of the Subject Property let or sublet?		☐	☐
5.5.2	Within the last 20 years was any part of the Subject Property let or sublet and the subject of a waiver of exemption under Section 96 of the VAT Act?		☐	☐
5.5.3	If the answer to either enquiry 5.5.1 or 5.5.2 is "Yes" please answer Section 6.			

SECTION 6[46] : SALE OF LET OR SUBLET PROPERTY (INCLUDES A PROPERTY WHICH WAS WITHIN THE LAST 20 YEARS LET OR SUBLET AND THE SUBJECT OF A WAIVER OF EXEMPTION UNDER SECTION 96 OF THE VAT ACT)

For each lease or sublease please complete a separate answer sheet for the following section.

		Please mark as appropriate	Yes	No
6.	**IS THE SUBJECT PROPERTY ITSELF THE SUBJECT OF ANY LEASE OR SUBLEASE OR SINCE ITS ACQUISITION, WAS IT LET AT ANY TIME WITHIN THE LAST 20 YEARS?**		☐	☐
	If the answer to enquiry 6 is "No", proceed to Section 7.			
6.1	If the answer to enquiry 6 is "Yes", please confirm in respect of the lease or sublease:-			
(a)	the name and address of the [current] lessee/sublessee;			
(b)	the business carried on by the [current] lessee/sublessee;			
(c)	the date of creation of the lease or sublease;			
(d)	the date of expiry of the leasehold term.			
6.2.1 (a)	Was VAT charged or deemed to have been charged on the grant of the lease?;		☐	☐
(b)	Was VAT charged on the rent?		☐	☐
	If the answer to both of these enquiries is "No", proceed to Section 7.			
6.2.2	If the answer to either of enquiries 6.2.1 (a) or (b) is "Yes", please confirm by a "Yes" or "No" answer which one of the three following descriptions applies to the lease or the sublease			
	The lease or sublease in question is:-			
(a)	A legacy lease[47]; If the answer is "Yes" please answer enquiries 6.3 and 6.6.		☐	☐
(b)	A lease subject to Vendor's waiver of exemption; If the answer is "Yes" please answer enquiries 6.4 and 6.6.		☐	☐
(c)	A lease subject to Vendor's option to tax. If the answer is "Yes" please answer enquiries 6.5 and 6.6		☐	☐
6.3	**Legacy Lease**			
6.3.1	State the VAT charged (if any) or which would have been charged except for the operation of Section 4A of the Value Added Tax Act 1972 on the creation of the lease.	€ _____		
6.3.2	State the expiration date in respect of the lease of the period specified in Section 95(5) of the VAT Act.			
6.3.3	Please provide now a copy of the relevant Section 4B Certificate issued under Section 4A of the Value Added Tax Act 1972.			

---

46   The purpose of this section is to clarify the application of VAT to a let or previously let or sublet subject property.
47   See footnote 4.

		Please mark as appropriate	Yes	No
6.4	**Waiver of Exemption**			
6.4.1	Please provide now copy documents to show that the tenant is liable to pay VAT in addition to the rent under the terms of the lease.			
6.4.2	Does the sale of the Subject Property result in a cancellation of a waiver of exemption made by the Vendor under Section 96 of the VAT Act?[48]		☐	☐
6.4.3	Was any such waiver of exemption previously cancelled in respect of any letting of the Subject Property?		☐	☐
6.4.4	Does the fact that any such cancellation of a waiver has occurred or will occur impact on the sale?		☐	☐
6.4.5	If the answer to enquiry 6.4.2, 6.4.3 or 6.4.4 is "Yes", please give details on an **attached sheet.**			
6.5	**Option to Tax**			
6.5.1	Is the tenant liable to pay VAT in addition to the rent under the terms of the lease?		☐	☐
6.5.2	Is the landlord's option to tax still in place in accordance with Section 97 of the VAT Act?		☐	☐
6.5.3	Please provide copy documentation showing that the landlord for the time being is entitled to exercise the landlord's option to tax in respect of the lease and that the landlord's option to tax has been exercised.			
6.6	**Refurbishment**			
6.6.1	Has any tenant of any such let property carried out any refurbishment on the let property?		☐	☐
6.6.2	If the answer to enquiry 6.6.1 is "Yes", has the landlord agreed to accept responsibility on any surrender of the Lease for any Tenant's Refurbishment?		☐	☐
	If so please give details of such 'tenant's' refurbishment on an **attached sheet.**			

---

48   Vendor should be aware that the cancellation of a waiver under Section 96 of the VAT Act may have an impact on the Vendor's VAT position in relation to the Subject Property.

SECTION 7: TENANT'S REFURBISHMENT[49]

		Please mark as appropriate	Yes	No
7	**HAS THE VENDOR OR PREDECESSOR IN TITLE, BEING A TENANT OF THE SUBJECT PROPERTY UNDER AN OCCUPATIONAL LEASE, CARRIED OUT A TENANT'S REFURBISHMENT OF THE SUBJECT PROPERTY OR TAKEN RESPONSIBILITY FOR A TENANT'S REFURBISHMENT?**		☐	☐
7.1	If the answer to enquiry 7 is "Yes", confirm that the Vendor was entitled to deduct all VAT incurred in relation to the/each Tenant's Refurbishment			
7.2	Is the Vendor requesting that the Purchaser agree to be responsible for all obligations in respect of each Tenant's Refurbishment?		☐	☐
7.2.1	If the Vendor is requesting that the Purchaser agree to be responsible for all obligations in respect of each Tenant's Refurbishment, please set out the quantum of the VAT which would otherwise have been payable to Revenue by the Vendor pursuant to Section 64(7)(a) of the VAT Act in the absence of the Purchaser so agreeing.	€_____		
7.2.2	If the answer to enquiry 7.2 above is "Yes", without prejudice to the Purchaser's position on an **attached sheet** please:- (a) describe each Tenant's Refurbishment; (b) specify the adjustment period of each Tenant's Refurbishment; and in respect of each Tenant's Refurbishment, provide a copy of the capital goods record and state the form of the written agreement to be entered into by the Purchaser to enable Section 64(7) of the VAT Act to apply on the sale.			

Dated _____ 20_____   Dated _____ 20_____

_____   _____
Vendor/Solicitors for Vendor   **Purchaser/Solicitors for Purchaser**

---

49   This Section need only be completed where the Subject Property is an interest under an Occupational Lease. A tenant under an occupational lease who was not entitled to deduct all of the VAT incurred on the acquisition or development of a refurbishment is NOT entitled to transfer responsibility to an Assignee or Surrenderee.

GUIDE TO COMPLETING VAT SPECIAL CONDITION 3 (FEBRUARY 2014 EDITION)

PLEASE NOTE THAT WHEN COMPLETING A CONTRACT FOR SALE IT IS NECESSARY TO INSERT THE CURRENT RECOMMENDED FORMAT OF VAT SPECIAL CONDITION 3 (available at www.lawsociety.ie in the precedents section of the members' area) AMENDED AS APPROPRIATE.

1. **VAT Inclusive Selling Price/ Vendor Charges no VAT/ VAT not Relevant to the Sale**

   Where the sale of the Subject Property is by auction or private treaty:
   (a) of second-hand residential property sold by the Vendor in a private capacity;

   (b) of a new residential property sold to a private Purchaser and the selling price is VAT inclusive;

   (c) of a freehold/freehold equivalent interest which:
   (i) is not sold as a TOB where the subject property comprises capital goods; and
   (ii) is a VAT exempt sale in which the Vendor is neither requesting the Purchaser to exercise the joint option to tax nor requiring the Purchaser to pay the Vendor the amount of the Vendor's capital goods adjustment on the sale;

   (d) by the assignment or surrender of an Occupational Lease which is not:
   (i) a TOB comprising a legacy lease; and
   (ii) a supply of a good or a service where VAT is chargeable on the sale; or

   (e) of any other category of sale, not being a TOB referred to in (c)(i) or (d)(i) above, in which VAT will not be chargeable either as the supply of a good or a service;

   delete Special Condition 3 entirely.

2. **The Vendor Charges VAT at the Appropriate Reduced Rate (Special Condition 3.2)**

   Special Condition 3.2 is intended for use where the sale of the Subject Property, not being a TOB, is:

   (a) by private treaty or auction of a partially developed freehold/freehold equivalent interest;

   (b) by private treaty or auction of a freehold/freehold equivalent interest coupled with a building agreement;

   (c) by private treaty or auction of a completed "new or nearly new" freehold/freehold equivalent interest;

   (d) by private treaty only, by way of the assignment or surrender of a legacy lease to a person not specified in Section 95(8)(c) of the VAT Act[50] and which is not covered in (e) below; or

   (e) by private treaty only, by way of the assignment or surrender of a legacy lease to a person

---

50   In other words, the Purchaser has answered "No" to Item 2 of the Purchaser's Statement on Purchaser's VAT Status. See footnote 5.

not specified in Section 95(8)(c) of the VAT Act[51] where the Vendor is a person described in Section 95(7)(b) of the VAT Act who requires the option to tax to be exercised.

In situation (a) or (b), use Special Condition 3.1, 3.2.1 and 3.11 only.

In situation (c), use Special Condition 3.1, 3.2.1, 3.2.2 and 3.11 only.

In situation (d), use Special Condition 3.1, 3.2.1, 3.2.3 and 3.11 only.

In situation (e), use Special Condition 3.1, 3.2.1, 3.2.4 and 3.11 only.

In each case, delete all other clauses in Special Condition 3.

3. **The Purchaser Self Accounts for VAT at the Appropriate Reduced Rate (Special Condition 3.3) in a Private Treaty Sale**

Special Condition 3.3 is intended for use where the sale of the Subject Property, not being a TOB or an auction sale, is:

(a) of a freehold/freehold equivalent interest in property, the sale of which is exempt where the Vendor (including a Vendor who is a person described in Section 95(3) of the VAT Act exercising an option under Section 94(5) of the VAT Act) requires that the Purchaser shall cooperate in the exercise of the joint option to tax the sale of the Subject Property[52];

(b) by way of the assignment or surrender of a legacy lease to a Purchaser who is a person specified in Section 95(8)(c) of the VAT Act which is not covered in (c) below;

(c) by private treaty only, by way of the assignment or surrender of a legacy lease, where the Vendor is a person described in Section 95(7)(b) of the VAT Act[53] who requires that the Purchaser, who is also a taxable person, agrees to cooperate in the exercise of the joint option to tax the sale.

In situation (a), use Special Condition 3.1, 3.3.1 and 3.11 only.

In situation (b), use Special Condition 3.1, 3.3.2 and 3.11 only, except where in addition to the sale, the Vendor requires the Purchaser to take responsibility for a Tenant's Refurbishment[54], in which case use 3.10 also.

In situation (c), use Special Condition 3.1, 3.3.3 and 3.11 only.

In each case, delete all other clauses in Special Condition 3.

4. **The Purchaser pays the Vendor an amount to compensate the Vendor for the Vendor's liability to pay a Capital Goods Adjustment or to receive a Capital Goods Adjustment which arises on the sale of a Freehold/Freehold Equivalent Interest which is exempt (Special Condition 3.4)**

Special Condition 3.4 is intended for use where the sale, being of a freehold/freehold equivalent interest in property, is not chargeable to VAT, but where as a result of the sale, the Vendor will

---

51 Ibid.
52 Refer to paragraph 11 of this guide (below) for commentary on the exercise of the joint option.
53 The Vendor was not entitled to deduct VAT on the acquisition or development prior to 1 July 2008 of the Subject Property.
54 "Tenant's Refurbishment" means capital goods as described in Section 64(7) of the VAT Act.

suffer a capital goods adjustment and if the Vendor was only entitled to partial deductibility on the acquisition or development of the Subject Property, will be unable to reclaim a capital goods adjustment from Revenue by reason of the sale being exempt and requires the Purchaser to pay the Vendor a sum in addition to the selling price to compensate the Vendor for the amount of such capital goods adjustment or adjustments. This condition can be used in either a private treaty sale or an auction sale of an exempt property where the Vendor does not intend to exercise the joint option to tax.

After every interval in the adjustment period until the adjustment period has expired, the amount of the Vendor's liability and, if applicable, reclaim entitlement on the sale of a property comprising capital goods will reduce. The Special Condition has been drafted to provide that where there is a delay in the completion of the sale and an interval[55] passes or intervals pass, the amount payable by the Purchaser in respect of the Vendor's capital goods adjustment or adjustments will be reduced so as to conform with the Vendor's actual liability.

Use Special Condition 3.1, 3.4 and 3.11. Delete all other clauses in Special Condition 3.

Rather than use 3.1, 3.4 and 3.11 a Vendor may find it convenient to omit special condition 3 entirely and simply specify a composite selling price.

5. Sale by Auction of a Freehold/Freehold Equivalent Interest which is a Capital Good where, to preserve a VAT neutral position on the sale, the Vendor requires either to be paid an amount to cover the Vendor's Capital Goods Adjustment(s) on the sale or to have the joint option to tax exercised (Special Condition 3.5)

Special Condition 3.5 is intended for use where the sale of the Subject Property being of a freehold/freehold equivalent interest is exempt, but still comprises capital goods. Unless the joint option to tax the sale is exercised, the Vendor must account to Revenue for the capital goods adjustment which will arise for Vendor on the sale and if the Vendor was only entitled to partial deductibility on the acquisition or development of the Subject Property, the Vendor will lose the right to claim a capital goods adjustment from Revenue on the sale.

If the Purchaser is not a taxable person or does not agree to exercise the joint option to tax, the Vendor will generally wish to be compensated by the Purchaser (by way of an additional payment on completion) for the Vendor's liability to pay and if appropriate forego any capital goods adjustment. When a Vendor's solicitor is settling the conditions in an auction sale of this particular type of sale, the VAT status of the Purchaser will be uncertain. Therefore, the Vendor will generally require the Purchaser either to pay the Vendor the amount of any Vendor's capital goods adjustment or adjustments which arises on the sale or, if the Purchaser is a taxable person, to co-operate in the exercise of the joint option to tax the sale.

This condition provides that the default position is that in addition to the Purchase Price, the Purchaser will pay the Vendor the amount of the Vendor's capital goods adjustment but if the Purchaser is a taxable person, the Purchaser has the right, by notifying the Vendor prior to the closing date, to cause the joint option to tax to be exercised whereupon the Purchaser will self account for VAT on the sale.

Use Special Conditions 3.1, 3.5 and 3.11. Delete all other clauses in Special Condition 3.

---

55   See definition of "interval" in Section 63 (1) of the VAT Act

Special Condition 3.5 is only appropriate for an auction sale of a freehold equivalent interest in the circumstances described above. For an auction of other classes of property see paragraphs 2 and 6.

6. **Sale by Auction of Legacy Lease (Special Condition 3.6)**

   Special Condition 3.6 is intended for use where the sale is by auction of a legacy lease where:

   (a) the Vendor is a taxable person selling to:

      (i) a Purchaser who is a person who is obliged to self-account for any VAT on sale; or

      (iii) a Purchaser who is not a person described in Section 95(8)(c) of the VAT Act in which case the Vendor must account for the VAT on the sale and will wish to pass on this VAT cost to the Purchaser; or

   (b) the Vendor is a person described in Section 95(7)(b) of the VAT Act[56] who requires the sale to be made taxable or to be compensated in lieu for loss of a capital goods adjustment.

   In situation (a) above, use Special Condition 3.1, 3.6.1 and 3.11 except where as part of the sale the Vendor requires the Purchaser to take responsibility for a Tenant's Refurbishment[57] in which case use 3.10 also.

   In situation (b) above use Special Condition 3.1, 3.6.2 and 3.11.

   In each case delete all other clauses in Special Condition 3.

7. **On the sale of a Subject Property constituting a TOB, no VAT applies but the Vendor is required to provide certain information to the Purchaser relating to capital goods (Special Condition 3.7)**

   Special Condition 3.7 is intended for use in the case of a TOB. If the answer to PCVE 1 is "No" and PCVE 1.1d and PCVE 4 is "Yes", use Special Condition 3.1, 3.7 and 3.11.

8. **On the assignment or surrender of an Occupational Lease (other than a Legacy Lease) for a premium paid by the Purchaser to the Vendor, the Purchaser pays the Vendor VAT at the standard rate (Special Condition 3.8)**

   The assignment or surrender by a Vendor, being a taxable person, of an occupational lease for a premium paid by the Purchaser is regarded not as the supply of immovable goods but rather as the supply of a service which is generally taxable at the standard rate.

   VAT is chargeable on a premium paid for:

   (i) the assignment of an occupational lease created on or after 1 July 2008;

   (ii) the surrender of an occupational lease created on or after 1 July 2008 where the landlord's option to tax the rent was not exercised; or

   (iii) the assignment of an occupational lease created prior to 1 July 2008 for a term of less

---

56   See footnote 50.
57   See footnote 54.

than 10 years where a waiver of exemption from VAT on letting services was exercised and is in place at the date of the assignment.

However where the occupational lease:

(a) assigned or surrendered is a legacy lease which is still in the adjustment period, the sale is taxed at the appropriate reduced rate and any premium paid is ignored;

(b) assigned or surrendered was created prior to 1 July 2008 for a term of less than 10 years and is not subject to a waiver of exemption by the landlord in respect of the rent or other consideration payable thereunder, the sale is exempt and any premium paid is ignored;

(c) assigned or surrendered is a legacy lease but the adjustment period has expired or another class of occupational lease created prior to 1 July 2008 which was not in the VAT net on 1 July 2008, the sale is exempt and any premium paid is ignored; or

(d) surrendered only, was created on or after 1 July 2008 where the landlord's option to tax has not been exercised, the sale is exempt and any premium paid is ignored.

If the answer to PCVE 1 is "Yes", the answer to PCVE 2, PCVE 3 and PCVE 4 is "No" and the answer to PCVE 5 is "Yes", use Special Condition 3.1, 3.8, 3.10 (if relevant) and 3.11. Delete all other clauses in Special Condition 3.

9. **On the assignment or surrender of certain Occupational Leases (other than Legacy Leases) for a premium (reverse premium) paid by the Vendor to the Purchaser, the Vendor pays the Purchaser VAT at the standard rate (Special Condition 3.9)**

The Law Society Taxation Committee understands that Revenue regard the following supplies as taxable at the standard rate:

(a) the surrender for a reverse premium by a taxable person of an occupational lease created on or after 1 July 2008 where the landlord's option to tax the lease is in place;

(b) the surrender by a taxable person for a reverse premium of an occupational lease created prior to 1 July 2008 for a term of less than 10 years where the landlord's waiver of exemption has been exercised in respect of the let property and is in place; and

(c) the assignment for a reverse premium by a taxable person of an occupational lease created on or after 1 July 2008.

In each of situations (a), (b) and (c) above use Special Condition 3.1, 3.9 and 3.11 and if, in addition to the assignment or surrender, the Vendor requires the Purchaser to accept responsibility for a Tenant's Refurbishment[58], use Special Condition 3.10 also. Delete all other clauses in Special Condition 3.

According to the best information available to the Law Society Taxation Committee, Revenue regard the following supplies as exempt:

(i) the assignment or surrender by a taxable person for a reverse premium of an occupational

---

58   See footnote 54.

lease for a term of 10 years or more created prior to 1 July 2008 which is not a Legacy Lease or which was such a Lease but in respect of which the adjustment period has expired.

(ii) The assignment or surrender by a taxable person of an occupational lease for a term of less than 10 years created prior to 1 July 2008 where the landlord did not waive his exemption from VAT on rent.

10. On the assignment or surrender of an Occupational Lease, the Vendor requires the Purchaser to become responsible for the tenant's capital goods (Tenant's Refurbishment[59]) of the Vendor (Special Condition 3.10)

Special Condition 3.10 is intended for use where a Vendor who was entitled to deduct all VAT incurred on the installation of a Tenant's Refurbishment wishes to oblige the Purchaser to assume responsibility for it after completion.

If the answer to PCVE 7 is "Yes", use Special Condition 3.10 in addition to the relevant Special Condition for the sale of an occupational lease.

11. Note on the Joint Option to Tax

It should be noted that a contract for sale is a Vendor's document, and in this context draft Special Condition 3.3 represents the best position for a Vendor. However, the same cannot be said as regards the position of a Purchaser.

Thus, in this context it is important that a practitioner acting for a Purchaser, on receipt from the Vendor of the draft Conditions of Sale where Special Condition 3.3 is used, also receives responses to the Pre-Contract VAT Enquiries to satisfy him/herself of the correct or best VAT treatment for his or her client.

This is illustrated in two situations.

Situation 1

VAT Special Condition 3.3 as drafted ensures that a property sale that is prima facie exempt from VAT but which is capable of being made subject to VAT by the way of a joint option to tax, is so jointly opted by agreement of both the Vendor and Purchaser, or the Purchaser agrees to pay a compensatory amount to the Vendor to cover any VAT costs. Generally speaking the option to tax will be utilised to ensure the Vendor avoids a VAT liability to Revenue, or alternatively to increase VAT recovery for the Vendor where VAT in relation to the Subject Property was previously disallowed, both being to the benefit of the Vendor.

This may well not be in the best interests of a Purchaser, and a Purchaser should be made aware that in agreeing to such a joint option there are the following implications:-

i. The Vendor may secure the advantage of avoiding a VAT liability or increasing VAT recovery;

ii. It brings an otherwise VAT exempt property into the VAT net;

---

59   See footnote 54.

iii. The Purchaser must monitor the use of the Subject Property for the next 20 years or until sold;

iv. The Purchaser will have an exposure to VAT costs for any VAT exempt use of the Subject Property over the next 20 years, such exposure to be met from the Purchaser's own resources;

v. If the Purchaser wants to sell at anytime in the next 20 years, in the absence of major development by him, he will have to get the purchaser from him to agree to a joint option, otherwise he will incur VAT costs; and

vi. The Purchaser has effectively created a capital good for which he must continue to maintain capital goods records.

Situation 2

This relates to the takeover of a refurbishment capital good by a landlord/assignee on surrender/assignment of an occupational lease. VAT Special Condition 3.10 as drafted provides that, where such a capital good has been created by a Vendor (tenant), the Purchaser (landlord/assignee) agrees to take same over for the purposes of the VAT Act. This mechanism will be utilised to ensure the Vendor (tenant) avoids a VAT liability to Revenue, thus it being to the benefit of the Vendor (tenant).

A refurbishment is defined as development of an existing building, etc. Development means the construction, demolition, extension, alteration or reconstruction of any building on the land, or the carrying out of any engineering or other operation in, on, over or under the land to adapt it for materially altered use, which is very wide. A tenant fit out or other works may very well fall into the definition.

This may well not be in the best interests of a Purchaser, and a Purchaser should be made aware that in agreeing to such a take over there are the following implications:-

i. The Vendor (tenant) may secure the advantage of avoiding a VAT liability;

ii. The Purchaser (landlord/assignee) must monitor the use of the refurbishment for the remainder of its Adjustment Period (possibly up to 10 years);

iii. The Purchaser (landlord/assignee) will have an exposure to VAT costs for any VAT exempt use of the Subject Property over its Adjustment Period (possibly up to 10 years), such exposure to be met from the Purchaser's own resources; and

iv. The Purchaser (landlord/assignee) steps into the Vendor's (tenant's) shoes for the remainder of the Adjustment Period, and any VAT costs due to exempt use would be in effect a claw back of VAT recovered by the Vendor (tenant).

Index

absentee landlords 6
access for works, allowing 69
Act of Union, 1800 6
adjudication by Residential
  Tenancies Board
  (RTB) 10, 93–9
adverse possession 24
affordability of rents 276
age, condition and character
  of building, termination
  due to 135
agents 120–1
agistment holders 2, 6, 39–40
agreements see contract/
  agreements
agreements for leases 2, 8,
  56–7, App 5
agriculture
  agistment holders 2, 6, 39–40
  agrarian disturbances 6
  conacre 2, 6, 37–8
  farmhouses and farm
    holdings 41
  fee farm grants 2, 14–15, 179,
    181
  herdsmen, demands for
    possession from 133–4
  notice to quit 120–1
  small tenant farmers, economic
    and social conditions of 6
airspace 50, 182
alienation see also assignment;
  sub-tenancies
  break clauses 241–2
  commercial leases 240–6
  common law 242–3
  consent 69, 161–3, 241–3,
    246–7
  covenants 56, 159, 241–5
  damages 242
  declarations that consent
    has been unreasonably
    withheld 242
  definition of alienation 2
  flexibility 241
  guarantees 242

improvements 161
Landlord and Tenant
  (Amendment) Act,
  1980 160, 242
licences 161, 242
purpose of restrictions 241–2
reasonable refusal 160–1
rent, effect on 241
Residential Tenancies Act,
  2004 57–8, 161
restrictions 241–2
security of tenur 240
statutory framework 242–3
tenements 161
withholding consent,
  unreasonably 241–2
alterations of premises 43, 52,
  69, 112, 147, 182–3, 232
anchor tenants 225, 234, 246
annuities 10, 41–2
anti-social behaviour 67–70
  definition 58, 70
  notice of termination 85–6
  Residential Tenancies Act,
    2004 58, 68, 85–6, 93
  Residential Tenancies Board
    (RTB), dispute resolution
    by 67–8, 93, 94, 102–3
  tenant's obligations 70
apportionment
  purchase price 191
  rent 183, 192–3, 208–9
  service charges 226–7, 228,
    233–4
approved housing bodies
  (AHBs) 61–2
appurtenants 2, 63
arbitration 191–2, 199–202,
  212–13, 219–20, 236
arrears and non-payment of
  rent
  deposits 66
  ejectment 120, 137, 154
  family homes 123
  forfeiture 127–8, 132, 137
  forms and precedents 101–2

freehold, right to purchase 210
new tenancy, right to a 143
notice to quit 120
rack rent 137
repairs 117
Residential Tenancies Act,
  2004 70–1, 73, 85–6
Residential Tenancies Board
  (RTB) 93, 102
set-off 110, 117
termination 78, 85–6, 102, 120,
  131, 134, 137–8
assignment 243–6
  commercial leases 242–6
  companies 143
  consent 69, 78, 79, 161–3,
    241–7
  contracts 243–5
  costs 242–3
  covenants 161
  definition 2
  deposits, refund of 243–4
  enquiries 245
  guarantees 244
  insurance 244
  landlord's position 244–5, 246
  legacy leases 260, 264, 265–7
  licences 25
  original tenant liability on
    covenants 245
  partial assignment 245–6
  periodic tenancies 78
  pre-emption, right of 241
  present tenant's position 243–4
  proposed assignee's position 244
  purpose of restrictions 241–2
  references 244
  rent, apportionment of 246
  rent review clauses 236, 246
  restrictions 241–2
  reversionary interests, damage
    to 246
  security of tenure 240
  service charges 244–6
  sub-tenancies 78–9, 80, 245–6
  surrender 134–5

assignment (*cont.*)
tenements 143
terms and conditions 243–6
VAT 245, 258, 259, 264–7,
269–70, 289–90
withholding consent,
unreasonably 69, 161–3,
241–3, 246–7

bare licences 2, 20, 24, 43
break clauses 20, 136, 225,
241–2
Brehon law 5
build, covenants to 184, 187
**Building Energy Rating (BER)
certification** 66
building leases 179
built-on leases 183, 187
business equity 144–6, 275
business tenancies *see*
commercial leases

**Capital Goods Scheme
(CGS)** 260–70
car parking 26–8, 37, 142
caretakers 42–4, 145
**categorisation of
tenancies** 14–18
certificates
Building Energy Rating
certification 66
improvements 174–5
sanitary improvement
certificates 175
service charges 227–8
stamp duty 53–5
title 218
vesting certificates 193–7, 199,
202, 209, 211–13, 216–17
change of user 52, 162, 244,
246–8
charities 54
Church of Ireland, tithes to 6
civil bills
ejectment, of 129, 137, 138
overholding 138
cohabitants, succession of 78
**commencement of leases, date
of** 49, 74, 106, 122, 251
commercial leases 1, 225–52
agreements for a lease 8
alienation 240–6
assignment 242–6
break clauses 136, 225, 242
business, definition of 144–5
business equity 144–6, 275
change of user 246–8
construction, developments
under 8
controlled dwellings 273–7

disturbances, compensation
for 156
drafts 8, 225
forfeiture 118–19, 132
franchises 40–1
freehold, right to buy out 179,
187, 190, 198, 200
FRI (full repairing and
insurance) leases 225–6
ground rents 179
instructions, taking 48–9
insurance 248–50
investment 225
Landlord and Tenant Law
Reform Bill 2011
(draft) 232, 235, 237, 249
Law Reform Commission
reports 11
long possession equity 141
notice to quit 118–19
occupation 145–6
options, exercise of 136
partial business use 274
planning permission 246
procedure 226
registers 251–2
renewals 232
rent review clauses 136, 225–6,
234–40
repairs 112, 117, 225, 232,
250–1
service charge clauses 226–34
shops 226–8, 231, 233
short-term lettings 225
sub-tenancies 245–6
surrender 117
surveys 232, 251
temporary convenience
lettings 17–18
termination 118–19, 136
transfer of businesses 271
**Commission on the Private
Rented Residential
Sector** 10, 91, 108, 147,
274–5
**Commissioners of Irish Lights
(CIL)** 187, 188
**Commissioners of Public Works
in Ireland** (OPW) 188
common law 5–6, 8, 12, 104–6,
110–11, 242–3
companies 60, 67–8, 120, 123,
143, 250–1
compensation *see also*
**damages; disturbance,
compensation for**
Deasy's Act 70–1
derelict sites and dangerous
premises, compulsory
acquisition of 136

Determination Orders 97–9
forfeiture 128, 130
goodwill 9
ground rents 179–80, 202
improvements 7, 9, 19, 69, 147,
154, 158–9, 179–80
Landlord and Tenant Law
Reform Bill 2011 (draft) 12
removal expenses 9
termination 135
trespass 124
**compulsory acquisition of
dangerous sites and
derelict sites** 136
conacre 2, 6, 37–8, 39
concessions in shops 24, 29–35
conditions *see* **terms and
conditions**
confidentiality 95
consent
agreements for leases 241–2
alienation 69, 161–3, 241–3,
246–7
assignment 69, 78, 80, 161–3,
241–3, 246–7
change of user 246–8
costs 242–3
covenants 162
declarations 242
freehold, right to buy out 194,
210, 211, 214
improvements 159, 162
mediation 95
sub-tenancies 78–9, 241–2,
244–5
sufferance, tenancies at 16
vesting certificate
procedure 193–7, 211
withholding consent
unreasonably 69, 161–3,
241–3, 246–7
**construction, premises
under** 8, 48, 56
contents of leases 49–50
continuous occupation 5,
17–18, 37, 63, 74, 78, 81–2,
142–8, 186
contract/agreements *see
also* **contracting out;
covenants; terms and
conditions**
agistment holders 39
agreements for leases 2, 8, 56–7,
App 5
assignment 249–52
caretakers 42–4, 145
categorisation of tenancies 14
conacre 38
Deasy's Act 6–7, 12
deposits 8

drafting leases 56–8
grant of lease and contract for lease, difference between 8
Landlord and Tenant Law Reform Bill 2011 (draft) 12
licences 20–1
lodgers/guests 36–7
oral agreements 7
possession, agreements to enter into 9
privity 57
purchase price 191
residential tenancy agreements 56–8
Residential Tenancies Act, 2004 58
Statute of Frauds (Ireland) 1695 8
writing 7–8, 9, 14–15, 105–6

contracting out
freehold, right to buy out 193, 198
ground rents 193
Landlord and Tenant (Amendment) Act, 1980 43–4, 145, 150–4
Landlord and Tenant (Amendment) Act, 1994 10
new tenancy, right to a 150
Residential Tenancies Act, 2004 65, 82, 85
terms and conditions 10, 44, 170–4

controlled dwellings 273–7
conveyancing 2, 3, 6, 10–11, 50, 52
correspondence in writing 7
costs and expenses *see also* **fees and charges**
arbitration 191–2, 195, 199, 236
assignment 242–3
covenants, enforcement of 232–3
drafting leases 51
forfeiture 130–1, 137–8
freehold, right to buy out 191–2, 195, 199–200
insurance 248–9
landlord's obligation 67
removal expenses 9
repairs 111
Residential Tenancies Board (RTB) 70, 92–3, 98, 100, 113, 114
service charges 227–30
service of notice to quit 123
termination 123, 130–1, 138
County Registrar 191–2, 193, 198, 210, 219–20

covenants
alienation 161, 241–5
breach 3, 48, 115–16, 126
build, covenants to 184, 187
change of user 247–8
conditions 48
costs of enforcement 232–3
damages 109
enforcement 232–3
estoppel 17
express covenants 49
fair wear and tear 106
forfeiture 3, 48–9, 126, 137
forms and precedents 111–16
freehold, right to buy out 195–6, 200
implied by statute 48
improvements 162
instructions, taking 45
insurance 50, 248
interpretation 112–16
Landlord and Tenant (Amendment) Act, 1980 161–2
Landlord and Tenant Law Reform Bill 2011 (draft) 49
original tenant liability 245
overriding obligations 49
painting 115
quiet enjoyment 49
re-entry 49
remedies 116–17
repairs 104–6, 109, 110–16
restrictive of user 162
rights of way 196
service charges 229–30
shops 162, 226, 233
sub-tenancies 244–5
tenements 109–10
water and sanitary apparatus 112, 115
creation of tenancies 12
criminal offences *see* **offences**
crops, liens on 38
Crown 5
custom 37

damages *see also* **compensation**
alienation 242
covenants, breach of 109–10
insurance 250
negligence 250
new tenancy, right to a 156
punitive damages 156
repairs 87, 109–10, 116, 117
Residential Tenancies Act, 2004 82–3
surrender 134–5

dangerous sites and derelict sites, compulsory acquisition of 136
date of commencement of leases 49, 74, 106, 122, 251
Deasy's Act
caretakers 43
common law 8
compensation 70–1
consolidation 6–7
contract, relationship of landlord and tenant based on 6–7, 12, 19
covenants 49
creation of tenancies 12
decrees or warrants for possession 134–5
demands for possession 133–4
distress, abolition of 50
duration of leases 14–15
fee farm grants 14–15
fixed term tenancies 15
formalities 7–9, 12, 14–15
historical background 6–7
intention 7, 12
Landlord and Tenant Law Reform Bill 2011 (draft) 9, 12, 14–15, 50, 105, 119
licences 19, 26
oral agreements 7, 12
periodic tenancies 14–15, 16
rent 6, 50, 70–1
repairs 104, 109, 117
repeal, proposal for 12, 14–15, 50, 105, 119
surrender 105, 117, 134–5
termination 137
written agreements 7–8, 12, 14–15
death of tenants 79, 123, 133, 274
decrees or warrants for possession per Deasy's Act 134–5
deeds
agistment holders 39
habendum 3
interest, licences coupled with an 20
profits à prendre 38–9
registration of deeds 6
Registry of Deeds 11, 135, 179, 197, 199, 210
release or transfer, of 42
stamp duty 53–4
surrender 134–5
definition of a tenancy/lease 3, 7, 12, 16, 17, 63–4, 181, 275
definitions 2–5

demolition or destruction of premises 34, 117, 233, 248

deposits
arrears 66
assignment 243–4
contracts 8
execution of leases 52–3
offences 101
protection schemes 102
repayment 57, 66, 68, 97–8, 101, 243–4
Residential Tenancies (Amendment) Act 2015 98
Residential Tenancies Board (RTB), dispute resolution by 68, 93, 97–101
VAT 256

derelict sites, compulsory acquisition of 136
deserted premises 134, 138
destruction or demolition of premises 34, 117, 233, 248
deterioration, tenant's duty not to cause 69, 108
determination *see* **termination**
Determination Orders 95–9, 102
development
contracts/agreements 8
freehold, right to buy 187, 196
improvements 158, 162
new lease, right to a 9, 154
planning permission 158
refurbishment and redevelopment 74, 76, 259, 263, 265, 267
service charges 229, 234
termination 135
VAT 259, 281, 263, 265, 267, 271–2
way, rights of 196
disappeared, where tenant has 134, 138
disbursements 70
disclaimers 118, 126–7, 136
discontinuance, notice of 192, 207
dispute resolution by Residential Tenancies Board (RTB) 91–103
adjudication 10, 91–103
anti-social behaviour 67–8, 93, 94, 102–3
cooling off period 96
confidentiality 95
costs of withdrawal 94
definition of dispute 93
deposit retention 68, 93, 97–101

Determination Orders 95–102
Dispute Resolution Committee (DRC) 92
enforcement 93, 98
exemption from registration 95
extension of time limits 94
fees and expenses 94, 96
hearings 92, 95–7
holding over 93
imprisonment 98–9
information 92–3, 95, 97–102
licences 93–4
mediation 10, 93–9
Murphy Report 102
notices of termination 93, 103
offences 98–100
overholding 93
personal representatives 93
policy, advice to the minister on 101–2
procedure 95, 103
public hearings 95
refer disputes, who can 93
refusal of Residential Tenancies Board (RTB), right of 94–5
registration 10, 94–5, 99–101
rent increases 94
reports 95–6
Residential Tenancies Act, 2004 91–103
Residential Tenancies (Amendment) Act, 2009 92
Residential Tenancies (Amendment) Act 2015 96, 98, 103
stages 95
students 102
sub-tenants 93, 94
Tenancy Tribunal 92–3, 95, 97
termination 93–100, 102–3
third parties 92
time limits 94, 95
vexatious or frivolous applications 94
website 93, 101–2
withdrawal 94
distress, abolition of 50
disturbance, compensation for
Landlord and Tenant (Amendment) Act, 1980 141, 160
long possession equity 160
new tenancy, right to a 156
removal expenses 9
Residential Tenancies Act, 2004 159–60
time limits 160
drafting leases 8, 21, 50–6, 112, 225, 244

Dublin Solicitors' Bar Association's draft agreement 58
duration of tenancies 14–15, 17–18, 50, 59, 60, 73–4, 104, 147–50
dwelling, definition of 63, 274

economic and social conditions 10, 12, 235, 241
effluxion of time, termination by 119, 132–3, 138
ejectment
arrears 120, 137, 154
civil bills for overholding 138
civil bills on title 129, 137, 138
Deasy's Act 6, 137
decrees or warrants for possession 138
deserted premises 138
forfeiture 126, 129, 130, 137
Landlord and Tenant Law Reform Bill (draft) 50
notice to quit 120, 138
rack rent 137
rent, non-payment of 120, 137
election, right of 16
electronic conveyancing 10–11
employees/servants 30, 36
engrossments 43, 52
enquiries 48, 245, 260, App 7, App 8, App 10
entry, right of 24, 39
equity
agreements for leases 56
forfeiture 116, 126, 128, 132
improvements equity 140, 144, 146–9, 274
Land and Conveyancing Law Reform Act, 2009 11
merger 133
Statute of Frauds (Ireland), 1695 8
eStamping 53–4
estoppel 8, 17, 21–2, 126–7
European Union and VAT 253
eviction
controlled dwellings 276
Landlord and Tenant Law Reform Bill 2011 (draft) 12, 119
redress scheme 11, 119
Examiner of Titles 198
exclusive possession 12, 19, 22–6, 36, 38, 258
execution of judgments 14, 134
execution of leases 52–3
expenses *see* **costs and expenses; fees and charges**

experts, costs of 237
extension of time limits 73, 94, 138, 157, 164
extensions, building of 182
exterior 104, 112, 251

fair wear and tear 106, 115
false or misleading information, offence of furnishing 100
family homes, service of notice to quit concerning 123
family members and controlled dwellings 274–6
family settlements 41
famine 6
farming *see* **agriculture**
fee farm grants 2, 14–15, 179, 181
fee simple 2–3, 19–20
fees and charges
  freehold, right to buy out 195
  insurance 248–9
  legal fees, recovery of 230
  registration 100
  Residential Tenancies Board (RTB), dispute resolution by 94, 96
  service charges 230
  Tenancy Tribunal 94
fences, maintenance and repair of 39
feudal system 5, 6
fieri facias, **writs of** 14
filling stations 24–5, 142
Finance Act 2012 53
fines 14, 70, 98–9
fire, destruction by 117, 182, 233
fittings 3, 57, 66, 111–12, 115–16
fixed term/term certain tenancies 14–15, 74, 79–80, 258
fixtures 3, 50, 112, 115–16
flats 182, 187, 202–3
foreign businesses, encouragement of 145, 149
forfeiture 126–32
  basis 126–7
  breach of conditions 127
  breach of covenant 3, 127
  commercial leases 118–19, 131–2
  costs and expenses 130–1, 137–8
  covenants and conditions 49, 127, 136–7
  disclaimers 127

disturbance, compensation for 140–1
ejectment 127, 129, 130, 137–8
ejectment civil bill on title 129, 137, 138
equitable remedy, as 116, 126, 132
estoppel 126–7
ground rents 132
injunctions 129–30
Landlord and Tenant Law Reform Bill (draft) 119
notices 116–17, 120, 128–9
peaceable re-entry 129–30
procedure 128–30
re-entry 127–32
relief from forfeiture 130–2, 130–2
rent, non-payment of 128, 132, 137–8
repairs 116, 117
Residential Tenancies Act 2004 126
section 14 notices 116, 128–9
statutory relief 130–2
statutory restrictions 128
sub-tenants 131, 132
termination 118–19
terms and conditions 127–8, 137
use of force, statutory prohibition on 129–30
formalities 7–9, 12, 14–15, 24 *see also* **writing**
forms and precedents
  agreement for lease App 5
  arrears 102
  certificates of title 218
  covenants to repair 111–16
  drafting leases 50–1
  Dublin Solicitors' Bar Association's draft agreement 58
  freehold, right to buy out 190, 193–4, 198–9, 203–18
  improvements, compensation for 158
  improvements 168–72, 174–5
  information, notice requiring 177–8
  instructions, taking 45–9
  Landlord and Tenant (Amendment) Act, 1980 162–3
  lease App 6
  new tenancy, right to a 151–4, 156–8, 166–7
  notice of intention to claim relief 156, 164–5, 176
  notice of termination 165

notice to quit 120–1, 124–6
re-entry 128
rent, notice requiring information on 178
rent review clauses 235, 237–40, App 4
repairs 111–16
Residential Tenancies Board (RTB) 99–101
  tenancy registration form (RTB1) 100, 102, App 1, App 2
  notes for completion App 2
vesting certificates 193–7, 209, 211, 216–17
franchise (elections) 37
franchises 40–1
freehold *see also* **freehold, right to buy out**
  definition 3
  fee simple 2–3, 19–20
  leasehold and freehold, difference between 14
  VAT and freehold equivalents 260
freehold, right to buy out 180–8
  abolition of ground rents 202–3
  airspace 182
  arbitration 191–2, 199–202, 212–13, 219–20
  arrears 210
  built-on leases 183, 187
  certificates of title 218
  change of mind 192
  commercial leases 180, 187, 190, 198, 200
  Commissioners of Irish Lights 187, 188
  Commissioners of Public Works in Ireland 188
  conditions 181–7
  consent 194, 210, 211, 214
  consideration 192
  contracting out 193, 198
  conveyance 190–1
  costs and expenses 191–2, 195, 199–202
  County Registrar 191–2, 193, 198, 210, 219–20
  covenants 184–5, 187, 195–6, 200
  definition of a lease 181
  development land 187
  discontinuance, notice of 192, 207
  Examiner of Titles 198
  expired leases 200
  explanatory leaflet 221–4
  extensions 182

freehold, right to buy out (*cont.*)
  fee farm grants 181
  fees 195
  flats 182, 187, 202–3
  forms 190, 193–4, 198, 203–18
  harbour authorities 187, 188
  historical background 179–80
  improvements 181–3, 185
  information, notice
        requiring 190–1, 205–6
  intention 182, 190–1, 196, 198
  Irish Land Commission 188
  joinder 190
  land, definition of 182
  Land Registry 193, 195–200,
        202, 210
  Landlord and Tenant (Ground
        Rents) Act, 1967 180, 184,
        187, 190–5, 198–9, 203–10
  Landlord and Tenant (Ground
        Rents) Act, 1978 180–7,
        193–203, 210–18
  merger 197–8
  new tenancy, right to a 179–80
  nominees, leases granted to 184
  notice
    arbitration, form for 219–20
    discontinuance of
        apportionment of rent,
        of 208–9
    intention, of 190–2, 194, 204,
        215
    quit, to 119
    rent, apportionment of 208–9
    service 190–1, 199, 204
  occupancy 180
  overholding 186
  permanent buildings built
        by lessees of future
        lessees 178–85, 186, 190,
        193, 202
  personal representatives 210
  practical steps 198–9
  prescribed forms 203–18
  procedure 190–9, 210–18
  purchase price 191, 195,
        198–202, 210
  rebuilding 182–3
  record of awards 193
  registration 195–8
  Registrar of Titles 187, 190,
        194–6, 199
  Registry of Deeds 180, 197, 199,
        211
  rent 183–6, 188–9, 200–3,
        205–6, 208–9
  repairs and maintenance 185,
        189
  residential property 179–83,
        190, 193, 198, 200–1

restrictions on right 187–8
reversionary leases 185, 187,
        188–9, 202
sub-leases 185–8, 203
subsidiary and ancillary
        test 181–3
terms and conditions 181–6,
        188–9, 190, 194, 198, 200
vacant leases 181, 187
vesting certificate
        procedure 193–7, 199,
        202–3
    arbitration 193–4, 196–7,
        212–13
    consent, by 193–6, 211
    forms 193–7, 209, 211,
        216–17
    prior to issuing a
        certificate 195
    yearly tenants 186–7, 200–2
**FRI (full repairing and
    insurance) leases** 225–6,
    250–1
**future leases where tenant
    has entered into
    possession** 8

gale days 3, 121–2, 124–6, 137
gardens 121
glass, insurance of 248
**good estate management,
    definition of** 155
goodwill 9, 40, 238
**graze animals, right to
    (agistment)** 2, 6, 39–40
ground rents 179–224
    see also **freehold, right to
        buy out**
    abolition 202–3
    building leases 179
    commercial leases 179
    compensation 179–80, 202
    controlled dwellings 276
    definition 3, 179
    fee farm grants 179
    fixed term tenancies 15
    forfeiture 132
    historical background 179–80
    improvements 179–80
    Landlord and Tenant Law
        Reform Bill 2011
        (draft) 180
    lease, definition of 276
    long leases 179
    proprietary leases 179
    sub-leases 179
    urban tenants 179–80
guarantees 53, 235–6, 241–2,
    244
guests/lodgers 36–7

habendum 3, 50
harbour authorities 187, 188
hardship 82–3, 277
health and safety 67
**herdsmen, demands for
    possession from** 133
hirers 37
historical background 1, 5–13
    17th century 6
    18th century 6
    19th century 6–9
    20th century, legislation in
        the 9–10
    21st century 10–12
    absentee landlords 6
    Act of Union, 1800 6
    agrarian disturbances 6
    Brehon laws 5
    centralised administration 5
    conacre 37
    confiscation and resettlement of
        land 6
    Deasy's Act 6–7
    feudal system 5, 6
    freehold, right to buy
        out 179–80
    ground rents 179–80
    Pale of Dublin 5
    Registration of Deeds Act
        (Ireland), 1707 6
    small tenant farmers, economic
        and social conditions of 6–7
    sources of law 5, 12
    Statute of Frauds (Ireland) Act
        1695 6
holding over *see* **overholding**
Home Rule 6
house, definition of 121
housing co-operatives 61
**Housing (Miscellaneous
    Provisions) Act, 1992,
    repairs under** 104, 106–8
**Housing (Private Rented
    Dwellings) Act, 1982,
    rent under** 273–7
    affordability issue 276
    business equity 275
    commercial premises 275–6
    Commission on the Private
        Rented Residential Sector,
        report of 274–5
    controlled dwellings 273–7
    criteria for fixing rent 273
    definition of lease 276
    dwelling, definition of 274
    entitlement under Act 275–6
    explanatory leaflet 276
    family members 274–6
    grounds rents legislation,
        entitlement under 276

hardship 277
improvements equity 275
Landlord and Tenant
    (Amendment) Act,
    1980 276–7
long possession equity 275
overholders 275–6
partial business use 274
phasing out 274
practical concerns 276–7
Rent Restrictions Acts 273
Rent Tribunal, role of 273–4
Residential Tenancies Act,
    2004 275–7
Residential Tenancies Board
    (RTB) 274
spouses 274–7
successor tenants 274–7
temporary convenience
    lettings 274, 275
tenements, definition of 275
yearly tenants 276
Housing (Rent Book)
    Regulations 1993 68, 104,
    106
Housing (Standards for Rented
    Houses) Regulations,
    2008 106–7

identity, loss of premises'
    original 181–3
identity of persons resident,
    notification of 69
illegality 2, 4, 68, 120 *see also*
    offences
imprisonment 70, 98–9, 108
improvements
    18th century, small farms in 6
    agreements for leases 56–7
    alienation 162
    amenity or convenience of
        neighbourhood, injury
        to 159
    arrears 158
    certificates 174–5
    change of user 162
    compensation 6, 9, 71, 19,
        140–1, 146, 154, 158–9,
        179–80
    consent 159, 161, 168
    controlled dwellings 275
    covenants 161–2
    definition of improvement 158
    equity 140, 144, 146–9, 274
    extensions 182
    forms and precedents 159,
        168–72, 174–5
    freehold, right to buy out 181–
        3, 185
    ground rents 162, 179–80

Landlord and Tenant
    (Amendment) Act,
    1980 141–2, 146, 160–1,
    168–72, 174–5
licences 161
long possession equity 146–7
new tenancy, right to a 146, 154
notices 3, 108, 158–9, 168
objections 159, 171–2
planning permission 158, 162
prohibition notices 108
rebuilding and renewal,
    distinguished from 114
rent review 238
repairs 108, 114
Residential Tenancies Act,
    2004 162
sanitary improvement
    certificates 175
security of tenure 73
service charges 230
statements of works 164
sub-tenants 158
tenements 158
termination 158
time limits 159
undertakings 170
indemnities 32–3, 112, 193, 231,
    250–1
indenture, definition of 3
industrial estates 225–7
information
    freehold, right to buy out 190–1,
        205–6
    Landlord and Tenant
        (Amendment) Act,
        1980 177–8
    rent
        notice requiring information
            on 177–8, 190–1, 205–6
        previous tenants, rent paid
            by 103
    Residential Tenancies Board
        (RTB) 91–3, 95–6, 97–102
    Revenue Commissioners 101
inherent defects 114
injunctions 20, 25, 117, 129–30
inspection 108, 111, 258
instructions 1, 45–9
    covenants and conditions 45
    forms 45–9
    instruction sheet, example of
        contents of 46–8
    pre-lease enquiries 48
    commercial leases 48–9
    residential leases 57–8
    taking instructions 45–9
    terms and conditions 1, 49,
        57–8
    writing 45

insurance 248–50
    amount 248–9
    assignment 244
    commercial leases 244
    covenants 50, 248
    damages 250
    deficiency, landlord's obligation
        to make up 248
    destruction of premises 248
    FRI (full repairing and insurance)
        leases 225–6, 250–1
    insurable interests 250
    insured risks 249–50
    intention 250
    invalidating insurance 69
    Landlord and Tenant Law Reform
        Bill 2011 (draft) 249–50
    landlord's obligations 66
    negligence of tenant, damages
        for 250
    non-invalidation clauses 248
    plate glass 248
    premiums 248, 249
    professional fees 248
    public liability cover 249
    rate 248–9
    reinstatement 248, 248–9
    repairs 251
    residential leases 57
    service charges 249
    subrogation 248, 250
    tenant's interests noted on
        policy 248, 249
    tenant's obligations 69, 76
    who effects the insurance 248
integrated area plans,
    termination where
    building is in area
    with 135, 156
intention
    Deasy's Act 7, 12
    freehold, right to buy out 182,
        190–1, 196, 198
    insurance 250
    licences 22, 23–5
    new tenancy, right to a 156
    notice of intention 190–3, 194,
        204, 215
    notice to quit 119
interest, licence coupled with
    an 4, 20
interior 66, 104, 112, 250–1
interpretation 59, 62–5, 83–4,
    112–16, 143–4, 237
investment properties,
    problems with
    management of 148
Irish Financial Services Centre
    (IFSC) 149
Irish Land Commission 188

INDEX

joinder 190
judgments, execution of 14, 134

keys, handing over 135

Land Act, 2005 10
Land and Conveyancing Law
    Reform Act, 2009 5, 7–8,
    11, 12–13, 235
Landlord and Tenant Act,
    1931 9
land, definition of 50
Land Registry 11, 193, 195–200,
    202, 210
Landlord and Tenant
    (Amendment) Act, 1980
  alienation 161–2, 242
  change of user 246–7
  contracting out 43–4, 145,
    150–4
  controlled dwellings 275–7
  covenants 161–2
  disturbance, compensation
    for 141, 159–60
  entry into force 140
  forms 162–78
  improvements 140–1, 146, 162,
    168–72, 174–5
  information, forms for notice
    requiring 177–8
  Landlord and Tenant
    (Amendment) Act,
    1931 9
  Landlord and Tenant
    (Amendment) Act,
    1994 140
  Landlord and Tenant Law
    Reform Bill (draft)
    2011 141, 163
  long possession equity 141,
    146–7, 160
  new tenancy, right to a 17, 141,
    144–58, 166–7
  notice of intention to claim
    relief, form for 164
  purpose of Act 140–1
  renewal of leases 140–1
  rent, form for notice requiring
    information from person
    receiving 178
  repairs 109–10
  Residential Tenancies Act,
    2004 140–1
  restrictive of user, covenants
    which are 162
  statutory relief 140–78
  tenements 141–4
  work undertakings, form
    for 173
Landlord and Tenant Law
    Amendment Act

(Ireland), 1860 see Deasy's
    Act
Landlord and Tenant
    (Amendment) Act,
    1994 10, 140
Landlord and Tenant Law
    Reform Bill 2011 (draft)
  arbitration, vesting by 194–5
  commercial leases 232, 235,
    237, 249
  compensation 12
  contents 11–12
  consultation 11, 12
  contract, relationship based on 12
  covenants 49
  creation of tenancies 12
  Deasy's Act, replacement of 9,
    12, 14–15, 50, 105, 119
  definition of tenancy 12
  distress, abolition of 50
  ejectment 50
  eviction remedies, replacement
    of 12, 119
  fixed term tenancies 15
  fixtures and fittings 3
  forfeiture 119
  ground rents 180
  insurance 249–50
  Land and Conveyancing Law
    Reform Act, 2009 12–13
  Landlord and Tenant
    (Amendment) Act,
    1980 140–1, 162
  licences 20
  new tenancy, right to a 10, 12,
    150
  notice of termination 119
  notice to quit 119
  oral agreements 12
  overriding obligations 11–12
  pre-legislative scrutiny 12
  redress scheme 11, 119
  re-entry 119
  renewal, right to 12, 15, 140–1
  repairs 105, 111
  rights and obligations of
    parties 11–12
  surrender 105, 119
  tenements 142
  termination 12, 119
  writing 12, 14–15
landlord's obligations
  anti-social behaviour 67–8
  Building Energy Rating
    certification 66
  complaints 67–8
  deposits, repayment or return
    of 66, 68
  evidence, penalties for giving 67
  exclusive occupation 66
  expenses, reimbursement of 67

fittings, replacement of 66
health and safety 67
insurance 66
interior 66
management companies,
    complaints to 67
name of persons entitled to act
    for landlord, providing 67
peaceful and exclusive
    occupation 66, 67
penalties against tenant 67
registration of particulars 66
repairs 66, 67, 104–5, 108, 110,
    116–17, 225
Residential Tenancies Act, 2004
    65–8, 82, 85–6, 91
Residential Tenancies Board
    (RTB) 67
standards 66, 68
statutory obligations, tenant's
    obligation not to cause
    breach of 68
third party complaints 67–8
latent and inherent
    defects 251
Law Reform Commission
    (LRC) 11, 12, 23, 26, 111,
    150, 235
Law Society 235, 237, 252, 260,
    App 3, App 7, App 8, App
    10
lease, precedent for a App 6
leases for lives renewable
    forever 14–15
legacy leases 260, 265–7, 269
length of tenancies see duration
    of tenancies
licences 19–35
  adverse possession 24
  agreements 20–1
  alienation 161–2, 242
  assignment 25
  bare licences 2, 20, 24, 43
  car parking licences 26–8
  caretakers 43
  certainty 21
  characteristics of a licence 22–6
  conacre 38
  concession areas 24, 29–35
  contractual licences 20–1
  contract 19
  Deasy's Act 19, 26
  definition 4, 19–20
  distinguished from leases 19, 26
  entry, right to 24
  estoppel licences 21–2
  evasion of rights 19–20, 22–4
  example licences 26–35
  exclusive possession 19, 22–6
  fee simple, right to buy out 19–20
  filling stations 24–5

formalities 24
franchises 40
hirers 37
improvements 162
intention 22, 23–5
interest, licence coupled with
    an 4, 20
Landlord and Tenant Law
    Reform Bill 2011 (draft) 20
Law Reform Commission 23, 26
lease, distinguished from 12
new licence, no right to 19–20,
    22, 145, 150
payments 22–6
renewal rights 20, 22
rent 19
repairing obligations 24
residence, right of 42
Residential Tenancies Board
    (RTB), dispute resolution
    by 93–4
reversion, no right to 19–20
servants/employees 36
shams 19–20, 22–4
shops 24, 26, 29–35
special relationships 24
statutory rights 19–20
terms and conditions 21, 26, 31
trespass 19, 20–1
undue influence 25
liens 38, 42
life estate, definition of 4
life or lives, tenancies for 14–15
life tenants 41–2
lives renewable forever, leases
    for 3–4
liquidators
    disclaimers 118, 136
    VAT on lettings by
        liquidators 272
livestock, grazing 2, 6, 39–40
lodgers/guests 36–7
long leases
    fixed term/term certain
        tenancies 15
    ground rents 179
long possession equity
    commercial tenancies, 5 year
        occupation of 141
    controlled dwellings 275
    disturbance, compensation
        for 160
    improvements 146
    Landlord and Tenant
        (Amendment) Act,
        1980 141, 146–7, 160
    new tenancy, right to a 146–7, 153
    residential equity 146
    Residential Tenancies Act,
        2004 82
    security of tenure 73

maintenance see repair and
    maintenance
management companies 60,
    67–8, 251
management costs 227
maps 50
market conditions 10, 12, 235,
    241
marriage, termination on 135
mediation 10, 92–9
merger 133, 135, 197–8
mesne rates 124
monthly tenancies 15, 16, 122
mortgages in possession and
    VAT 272
multi-lets 117, 225, 230, 251
multiple occupants 79, 81–2,
    88
Murphy Report 102

negligence, damages for 250
new tenancy, right to a see also
    renewal, right of
    break in user 145
    business equity 144–58
    caretaker's agreements 43–4,
        145
    commercial leases 17, 144–58
    conditions 150, 156
    contracting out 43–4, 150–4
    damages 156
    defaults or acts by tenants 154
    disturbance, compensation
        for 156, 160
    duration of tenancies 148–9
    foreign businesses,
        encouragement of 145,
        141
    forms 151–4, 156, 166–7
    freehold, right to buy out 180
    good estate management,
        definition of 154
    improvements equity 147, 154
    integrated area plans,
        termination where building
        is in area with 156
    intention 156
    interpretation 143–4
    investment properties,
        problems with
        management of 149
    Landlord and Tenant
        (Amendment) Act, 1980
        18, 141, 144–58, 166–7
    Landlord and Tenant Law
        Reform Bill 2011 (draft)
        10, 12, 149
    Law Reform Commission 149
    licences 145, 150
    long possession equity 146–7,
        153

notice of acceptance of new
    tenancy, form for 167
notice of intention to claim
    relief, service of 156–8
occupation 143–6
office, use as an 150–1
overholdings 157
periodic tenancies 16
planning permission 155
procedure 156–8
punitive damages 156
remain in occupation,
    crystallisation of right
    to 157
rent 10, 149, 157
rent reviews 149
renunciation 150–4
Residential Tenancies Act, 2004
    17, 145–58
restrictions on right 10, 150–6
service 156–7
short-term renewals 145
State, restrictions on application
    to 154
sub-tenants 144
temporary break in
    occupation 145
tenements 17 144–58
terms and conditions 147–50,
    156–7
writing 10, 151, 156
nominees, leases granted to 184
non-payment of rent see arrears
    and non-payment of rent
notice see notice of termination;
    notice to quit; notices
notice of termination see also
    notice to quit
anti-social behaviour 86
bare licences 20
break clauses 136
contents of notice 84–5
definition 4
forms and precedents 165
Landlord and Tenant Act,
    1980 119, 165
Landlord and Tenant Law
    Reform Bill 2011
    (draft) 119
notice of intention to claim
    relief 119, 138
Part 4 tenancies 62–3, 81–2
Residential Tenancies Act, 2004
    84–5, 88
Residential Tenancies Board
    (RTB) 82, 84, 87–8, 92–3,
    103
service 138
sub-tenancies 84, 87
time limits 88, 119
validity 84, 92–3

notice to quit 119–26
  agents 120
  agricultural property 120–1
  arrears 120
  children reaching majority,
    repudiation by 120
  commercial tenancies 118–19
  companies, service on 120
  conduct, waiver by 124
  contents 120–1
  description of premises 121
  dispensing with
    requirement 120
  ejectment 120, 138
  ejectment civil bill for
    overholding 138
  events, termination on
    happening of stated 120
  forfeiture 119, 128
  form 120–1, 124–6
  freehold, right to buy 119–20
  gale days 121–2, 124–6
  house, definition of 121
  illegality 120
  intention 121
  Landlord and Tenant
    (Amendment) Act,
    1980 119
  length of notice 15, 121–2
  mesne rates 124
  method of service 122–3
  monthly tenancies 122
  notice period 121–2
  overholding 119, 138
  periodic tenancies 15, 119
  persons who may be
    served 12203
  quarterly tenancies 122
  reasonable notice 122
  refusal to quit 130
  rent 124, 127–8
  Residential Tenancies Act, 2004
    118–21
  sample notices 124–6
  service 120, 122–3
  surrender, service of notice
    of 119
  term of years of year certain,
    leases for 120
  urban lands, minimum notice
    for 121
  urgent situations 118–19
  waiver 124
  weekly tenancies 122
  where notice not required 120
  year to year, tenancies from 122
notices *see also* **notice of
    termination; notice to
    quit**
  arbitration 219–20

discontinuance 192, 207
forfeiture 116, 120, 128–9
freehold, buying 190–3, 194,
    199, 204–6, 208–9, 215,
    219–20
improvements 3, 108, 158–9, 168
information, requiring 177–8,
    190–1, 205–6
intention to claim relief 119,
    138, 156–8, 164–5, 176
long possession equity leases 82
new tenancy, acceptance of
    a 167
notice periods 57–8, 78–9,
    83–90, 97
prohibition notices 108
rent 102, 178, 208
rent review 237
Residential Tenancies Act, 2004
    57–8, 65, 83–90
section 14 notices 116, 128–9
service 58, 65, 83, 87–8, 192,
    199, 204, 237
Tenancy Tribunal 97
nuisance or annoyance 247 *see
    also* **anti-social behaviour**

occupation
  business equity 143–6
  conacre 38
  continuous occupation 81–2
  freehold, right to buy out 180
  multiple occupants 79, 81–2, 88
  new tenancy, right to 143–6
  own or families' occupation,
    landlord requires
    accommodation for own 76
  paramount occupation 38
  peaceful and exclusive
    occupation 66, 107
  permissive occupants 25, 133
  remain in occupation,
    crystallisation of right
    to 157
  tenements 143
offences
  deposits 101, 103
  Determination Orders 98–9
  false or misleading information,
    offence of providing 100
  fines 70, 98–9
  imprisonment 70, 98–9, 108
  registration 100–1
  rent books 108
  repairs 108
  Residential Tenancies Act, 2004
    70, 88
  Residential Tenancies Board
    (RTB) 98–101
  service 65, 88

**Office of Public Works in
    Ireland (OPW)** 188
office, use as an 150–1
old premises, repair of 113–14
online applications 97
**option, termination on
    exercise of** 136
oral agreements 7, 12, 105–6
overholding
  civil bills 138
  controlled dwellings 275–6
  definition 4
  ejectment civil bills on title 138
  freehold, right to buy out 186
  mesne rates 124
  new tenancy, right to a 157
  notice to quit 119, 138
  periodic tenancies 15
  Residential Tenancies Board
    (RTB), dispute resolution
    by 93
  termination 119, 125, 138
overriding obligations 11–12,
    49, 111
**own or families' occupation,
    landlord requires
    accommodation for
    own** 76

painting of premises 115
Pale of Dublin 5
parcels 4, 49–50
parliamentary franchise 37
parol evidence 4, 8
Part 4 tenancies
  continuous occupation 81–2
  definition 63–4
  further tenancies 80–1
  interpretation 63–4
  multiple occupants 81–2
  notice of termination 63, 75–80
  notice period 75, 85–6
  notice to quit 119
  Residential Tenancies Acts 61–4,
    75–83, 85–6
  security of tenure 62, 73
  service of notice 75
  termination 75–80, 85–6, 93
  terms 80
particulars, registration of 66,
    99–101
**peaceful and exclusive
    occupation** 66, 67
periodic tenancies 8, 15–16, 63
permissive occupants 25, 133
personal representatives 93,
    124, 210
plain language 11
planning permission 51, 52,
    155, 158, 162, 246

plant and machinery 227, 230
plate glass, insurance of 248
policy advice 101–2
possession, agreements to
    enter into 8
power of sale 41–2
PRTB *see* Residential Tenancies
    Board (RTB)
precedents *see* forms and
    precedents
predecessors in title, definition
    of 4, 143
pre-contract enquiries 48, 260,
    App 8, App 10
pre-emption, right of 241
premiums 4, 53–4, 264, 267, 270
Private Residential Tenancies
    Board (PRTB) *see* dispute
    resolution by Residential
    Tenancies Board (RTB);
    Residential Tenancies
    Board (RTB)
privity 57, 251
profits à prendre 38–9, 130
prohibition notices 108
promissory estoppel 22
Property Registration
    Authority Ireland
    (PRAI) 11, 199, 223–4
Property Services Regulatory
    Authority (PSRA) 251–2
proprietary estoppel 22
proprietary leases 179
public authorities 64, 67, 143,
    154, 188
public hearings 95
public liability cover 249
punitive damages 156
purchase price 10, 191, 195,
    199–202, 210

quarterly tenancies 122
quiet enjoyment/possession 4, 49
quit, notice to *see* notice to quit

rack rent 4, 137
rates 1, 50, 55–6, 189, 244
rebuilding, reinstatement and
    renewal 114, 135, 182–3,
    248–9
receivers 14, 272
recitals, definition of 4
reddendum 4, 50, 235, 237
redress scheme, introduction
    of 11, 119
re-entry 116, 119, 127–32
references 244–6
refurbishment and
    redevelopment 73, 76,
    259, 263, 265, 267

refuse receptacles, provision
    of 101
registration
    commercial leases 251–2
    compulsory registration 55
    deeds, registration of 6
    electronic conveyancing 10–11
    enforcement 102
    fees 100
    forms and precedents 100, 102
    freehold, right to buy out 195–8
    good practice guidelines 102–3
    Land Registry 11, 193, 195–8,
    202, 210
    landlord's obligations 66
    numbers 100
    offences 100–1
    online registration 100
    particulars 66, 99–101
    procedure 100
    Property Registration Authority 11
    Residential Tenancies Board
    (RTB) 10, 91–3, 99–101
    Registration of Deeds Act
    (Ireland), 1707 6
    Registration of Deeds and Title
    Act, 2006 10–11
    Registrar of Titles 187, 190,
    194–7, 199
    Registry of Deeds 11, 135, 179,
    197, 199, 210
    residence, right of 41–2
    Residential Tenancies Act,
    2004 10, 91–2
    rules 135
    stamp duty 53
    surrender 135
    Tenancy Management System,
    online registration
    under 100
    unregistered land 55
    VAT 266
reinstatement 114, 135, 182–3,
    248–9
relationships involving
    land other than
    tenancies 36–44
removal expenses for
    disturbance,
    compensation for 9
renewal *see also* new tenancy,
    right to a
    commercial leases 232
    development, possession
    required for 9
    Landlord and Tenant Act, 1931
    9, 15
    Landlord and Tenant
    (Amendment) Act, 1980
    140–1

Landlord and Tenant Law
    Reform Bill 2011 (draft) 12
    licences 20, 22
    periodic tenancies 15
    reinstatement, rebuilding and
    renewal 114, 135, 182–3,
    248–9
    right of renewal 9, 15, 140–1
rent *see also* arrears and non-
    payment of rent; ground
    rents; rent review clauses
    in commercial leases
    acceptance of rent 124, 226
    affordability 276
    alienation 241–2
    apportionment 183, 192–3,
    208–9
    books 106–7, 108
    calculation, statements on 67
    change of user 249
    controlled dwellings 273–7
    Deasy's Act 6, 50, 70–1
    demands for rent 124, 127
    enforcement 50
    forfeiture 127–8, 132, 137
    freehold, right to buy out 183–
    6, 188–9, 200–2, 205–6,
    208–9
    gale days 3, 121–2, 124–6, 137
    gross rent 149
    Housing (Private Rented
    Dwellings) Act, 1982 273–7
    improvements 157
    increases 94, 108, 158, 199,
    201, 237, 246
    Index 102
    information, notice
    requiring 178, 205–6
    instalments 137
    Landlord and Tenant
    (Amendment) Act, 1980
    178
    licences 19
    market rent, definition of 71
    new lease under 1980 Act,
    applications for 10, 149,
    156
    notice to quit 124, 128–9
    particulars, registration
    of 99–101
    predictability 103
    previous tenants, access to
    details paid by 103
    rack rent 4, 137
    reddendum 50
    rent-free periods 264
    Rent Pressure Zones 103
    Rent Restrictions Acts 273
    rent to buy schemes 271
    Rent Tribunal, role of 273–7

rent (*cont.*)
  repairs 106–8, 110, 117
  Residential Tenancies Acts 67,
      70–2, 103
  Residential Tenancies Board
      (RTB) 72–3, 91, 94–5
  reversionary leases 188–9
  service charges 57, 227, 230
  set-off 110, 117
  temporary convenience
      dwellings 107
  tenant's obligations 68
  termination 137–8
  VAT 264, 271
rent review clauses
  alienation 241–2
  arbitrators, costs of 237
  assignment 237, 246
  basis for review 237, 238–40
  commercial leases 136, 225,
      234–40
  downwards rent reviews 236
  economic conditions 241
  experts, costs of 237
  forms App 4
  freehold, right to buy out 189,
      203
  frequency 71–2
  goodwill 238
  guarantees 235–6
  improvements 92–3, 238
  independent review, provision
      for 236–7
  interpretation 237
  Law Reform Commission 235
  Law Society 235, 237
  market rent 236, 237
  new tenancy, right to a 150
  particulars, registration
      of 99–101
  parts of clause 238–40
  precedent 238–40
  recording revised rent 240
  reddendum 235
  Residential Tenancies Act, 2004
      71–2
  Residential Tenancies Board
      (RTB) 99, 103
  sample clause 235, 238–40
  service of notices 236
  stamp duty 240
  standard forms 235, 238–40
  terms and conditions 235, 238–40
  time is not of the essence 236
  upwards only 72, 235–6, 237
repairs 104–17
  advising clients 250–1
  age of building 114, 135
  better state of repair, putting
      in 251

character of building 135
collateral warranties 251
commercial leases 112, 117,
    225, 232, 250–1
Commission on the Private
    Rented Residential
    Sector 108
common law 104–6, 110–11
costs and expenses,
    reimbursement of 111
covenants 104–6, 109–10, 111–16
damages 109, 116, 117
Deasy's Act, 1860 104, 109, 117
deductions from rent 110, 117
deterioration, tenant's obligation
    not to cause 108
draft leases 112
duration of tenancies 104
enforcement 108
exterior 104, 112, 225, 251
fair wear and tear 115
fire or other accidents, surrender
    following 117
forfeiture 116, 117
freehold, right to buy out 185,
    189
FRI leases 225–6, 250–1
*Groome v Fodhla Printing
    Co* 112–13
Housing (Miscellaneous
    Provisions) Act, 1992 104,
    106–8
Housing (Rent Book) Regulations,
    1993 104, 106–7
Housing (Standards for Rented
    Houses) Regulations,
    2008 107–8
improvements 108, 114
indemnities for structural
    defects 251
inherent defects 114
injunctions 117
inspection 108, 111
insurance 251
interior 104, 112, 225, 250–1
interpretation of
    covenants 112–16
keep in repair 112–15
kind of tenant 114
Landlord and Tenant
    (Amendment) Act, 1980
    109–10
Landlord and Tenant Law
    Reform Bill 2011
    (draft) 105, 111
landlords
  notification 111
  obligations 66, 67, 104–5,
      108, 110, 116–17, 225
  remedies 116–17

latent and inherent defects 251
Law Reform Commission 111
licences 24
local authorities 108
locality 114
management companies 251
mandatory injunctions 117
notification of landlord 111
offences 108
old premises 113–14
oral tenancies 105–6
overriding obligations 111
painting of premises 115
privity 251
prohibition notices 108
proper state of repair 57
put in repair 114–16
rebuilding, renewal and
    improvements,
    distinguished from 114,
    135
re-entry 116
refurbishment and
    redevelopment 74, 76, 259,
    263, 265, 267
reimbursement of costs and
    expenses 111
re-letting, prevention of 108
remedies 116–17
rent
  books 106–7, 108
  deduction of costs, from 111
  increases 108
  set-off, against 117
rent review 225–6
replacement 114
repudiatory breach 117
residence, right of 41–2
residential covenants 111–12
residential leases 57–8
Residential Tenancies Act,
    2004 104–5, 108, 111–12,
    116
Residential Tenancies Board
    (RTB) 108
retaliatory action 108
sample covenants 111–16
sanitary facilities 107–8, 115
schedule of conditions 251
security of tenure 108
service charges 225, 226–7, 251
set-off 110, 117
shopping centres 251
specific performance 117
standards 107–8
statistics 108
statutory bodies 111
statutory framework 104–11
structure 104, 108, 115, 225,
    251

substantial repair 108
surrender under Deasy's Act, 1860 117
surveys 251
tenants
  obligations 68, 104–6, 108, 111–16
  remedies 117
tenements 109–10
termination 117
terms and conditions 150, 251
Whelan v Madigan 115–16
wilful waste, definition of 110
written agreements 105–6
research 91, 92, 101–2
residence, rights of 41–2
residential tenancies *see also* **Residential Tenancies Board (RTB); Residential Tenancies Act, 2004**
agreements 57–8
covenants to repair 111–12
drafting leases 57–8
Dublin Solicitors' Bar Association's draft agreement 58
freehold, right to buy out 179–83, 190, 193, 198, 200–1
instruction sheets 57
insurance 57
private residential tenancies register 100–1, 103
repairs 57, 111–12
residential equity 146
service charges 57
termination 79–80, 118–19
waste charges 57
Residential Tenancies Acts 2004 to 2016 10–11, 59–90
alienation 162
anti-social behaviour 58, 68, 85–6, 93
application of Act 59–60
approved housing bodies (AHBs) 61–2
arrears 70–1, 93
commencement 59
Commission on the Private Rented Residential Sector 10
contracting out 65, 82, 85
controlled dwellings 275–7
damages 82
danger of serious injury or death 86
definition of lease 64–5
definitions 62–5
dispute resolution 10, 58, 70–1, 88
disturbance, compensation for 160

duration of lease 59, 60, 73–4
dwelling, definition of 63
effluxion of time, termination by 132–3
exclusions 60, 73
fixed term tenancies 79–80
forfeiture 126
grievance procedure 82
hardship 82–3
housing co-operatives 61
improvements, compensation or 162
interpretation 59, 62–5, 83–4
Landlord and Tenant (Amendment) Act, 1980 140–1
landlords
  definition, of 64–5
  obligations 65–8, 82, 85
  termination, by 75–8, 84–5
long possession equity leases 82
management companies, referrals by 68
miscellaneous matters 88
multiple occupants 81–2, 88
new tenancy, right to a 17, 145–58
non-private dwellings 63
notice of termination 83–7, 88
notice periods 57–8, 83–90
notice to quit 118–21
offences 70, 88
Part 4 tenancies 61–4, 75–80
Residential Tenancies Act 2016 59, 67, 71, 77–8, 103
Residential Tenancies (Amendment) Act 2015 59–64, 68, 86
  commencement 61
  notice periods 86
Residential Tenancies Board (RTB) 10, 57–8, 60, 70–1, 78–9, 84, 88, 91–101
procedural requirements 83–7
prohibitions 88
redress 70–1
refuse receptacles, provision of 101
registration 10, 91–2
rent and rent reviews 67, 70–2, 103
repairs 104–5, 108, 111–12, 116
residential tenancy agreements 58
restrictive of user, covenants which are 162
security of tenure 10, 63, 74, 80
service of notices 58, 65, 83, 88
statutory obligations of tenants 57–8

sub-tenancies 74, 84, 87
tenancy, definition of 63
Tenancy Tribunal 10, 100
tenants
  definition, of 64–5
  obligations 65–6, 68–70, 83, 86
  termination, by 78–9, 86
termination 10, 57–8, 75–80, 83–90, 119–20
third parties, hardship to 82–3
transitional dwellings 62
Residential Tenancies (Amendment) Act, 2009 92
Residential Tenancies (Amendment) Bill, 2012 57–8
Residential Tenancies (Amendment) Act, 2015 96, 98, 103
Residential Tenancies Board (RTB) 91–103 *see also* **dispute resolution by Residential Tenancies Board (RTB)**
committees, establishment of 92
compensation 70–1
composition 91
costs and expenses 70, 92–3, 98, 100, 113, 114
Director 91
establishment 10, 91
false or misleading information, offence of providing 100
forms 99–101, App 1, App 2
functions 91–9
gender balance 91
guidelines for good practice, publication and development of 102–3
Housing (Private Rented Dwellings) At, 1982 274
information, collection and provision of 91–3, 95–6, 97–102
landlord's obligation 67
notice of termination 82, 84, 87–8, 92–3, 103
number of members 92
offences 98–9, 100–1
online registration 100
particulars, registration of 99–101
policy advice 102–3
private residential tenancies register 99–101, 102–3
procedure for registration 100
registration 91–2, 99–103, 108, App 1, App 2

INDEX

Residential Tenancies Board (RTB) (*cont.*)
registration numbers 100
re-naming 10, 62–3, 91, 103
rent levels, information on 92
rent review 99, 103
Rent Tribunal, transfer of functions of 273–4
repairs 108
research 91, 92, 101–2
Residential Tenancies Act, 2004 10, 57, 60, 70–1, 83, 84, 88, 91–2, 99–101
Revenue Commissioners, disclosure to 101
security of tenure 99, 103
standards 102
statistics 99
sub-tenancies 87, 93
Tenancy Management System, online registration under 99
termination 99, 100, 102–3
time limits 88
website 101
restrictive of user, covenants which are 162
Revenue Commissioners 101, 253
reverse premiums, definition of 4
reversionary interests 4, 15, 19–20, 185, 187, 188–9, 202, 246, 267
rights of way 196

sanitary facilities 107–8, 112, 116, 175
sanitary improvement certificates 175
searches 14, 52
secondment, employees on 36
security of tenure
20 years continuous occupation 73
alienation 274
assignment 240
fixed term tenancies 74, 79–80
improvements 73
long possession equity 73
opt outs 74
Part 4 tenancies 62, 74
particulars, registration of 99
premature termination, right of 73–4
repairs 108
Residential Tenancies Act, 2004 10, 63, 74, 80
Residential Tenancies Board (RTB) 99, 103

statutory rights 17
sub-tenancies 74, 240
temporary convenience lettings 17
termination 74, 79–80
seizure of land 14
servants/employees 30, 36
service
alive, where tenant is 122
burden of proof 65
companies 120, 123
costs 123
death of tenant 123
extension of time 157
family homes 123
limited liability companies 123
methods 121–2
new tenancy, right to a 156–9
notices 25, 58, 65, 75, 83–8, 122–3, 138, 192, 199, 204
notice of termination 75, 138
offences 65, 88
personal representatives 124
personal service 122
persons who may be served 122–3
post, by 122, 124
quit, notice to 120, 122–3
rent review 236
Residential Tenancies Act, 2004 58, 65, 83, 88
sub-tenancies 87
termination, notices of 75, 138
third parties, on 123
time limits 65, 157
time of the essence 236
who may serve 120
service charges
advance, quarterly payments in 227–8
amount, determination of 227–8
apportionment 227, 228, 233–4, 244
assignment 244
audits 228
balancing charge 228
certification 227–8, 244
components 275
conventional services 229
costs and expenses 227–33
covenants 229–30
discontinuance of services 227
dispute, potential areas of 230–3
fixed amount 233
fixed percentage 233
floor area, calculation by 233–4
FRI leases 225–6
future redevelopment costs 2
improvements 230

insurance 248
Law Society and RICS, notes on service charges by App 3
legal fees, recovery of 230
management costs 227
mopping up clauses 229
multi-let buildings 230
overpayments 227–8
rateable valuation 233
rent 57, 227, 230
repairs 225, 232, 251
reserve funds 230–1
residential leases 57
services to be included 228–30
setting up costs 230
shopping centres 234
sinking fund 230
staff costs 230
statutory requirements, compliance with 227
structure of building 229
underpayments 228
weighted floor area, calculation by 233
weighting 233
set-off 110, 117
shams 17–18, 22–4
sheriffs
Ordinary Sheriff 14
Revenue Sheriff 14
seizure 14
shops and shopping centres
anchor tenants 225, 234, 246
change of user 246–8
commercial leases 225–7, 231, 233
concessions 24, 29–35
covenants 162, 226, 233
drafting leases 50–1
franchises 40
licences 24, 26, 29–35
rent review 203
repairs 251
service charges 234
short-term and temporary lettings
commercial premises 17–18
duration 17–18
FRI leases 225–6
new tenancy, right to a 145
rent books 107
security of tenure 18
shams 17–18
temporary convenience lettings 17–18, 107, 145, 225–6, 274–5
tenement, definition of 17
VAT 287–8
side letters 225
signatures 9, 88, 101, 248

sinking funds 231
Sixth VAT Directive 253
small tenant farmers, economic
    and social conditions
    of 6
social and economic
    conditions 10, 12, 235,
    240
sources of law 12
specific performance 9, 56
spouses and civil partners 79,
    274, 277
staff costs 230
stamp duty
    certificates 53–5
    charities 54
    compulsory registration 55
    deeds 53–4
    eStamping 53–4
    Finance Act 2012, changes made
        by 53
    late stamping, penalties for 55
    premiums 53–4
    registration 53
    rent review clauses 240
standard forms 8, 225, 235,
    238–40 see also forms and
    precedents
standards
    Dublin Solicitors Bar Association
        Agreement 102
    Housing (Standards for Rented
        Houses) Regulations
        2017 107–8
    landlord's obligations 66, 68
    repair 107–8
    Residential Tenancies Board
        (RTB) 102
    sanitary facilities 107
state and state authorities 143,
    154, 188
Statute of Frauds (Ireland),
    1695 6, 8
statutory relief under
    Landlord and Tenant
    (Amendment) Act, 1980
    140–72
statutory tenancies 17
structure 104, 107–8, 115, 225,
    229, 251
students 102
subrogation and insurance 248,
    250
substratum 49–50
sub-tenancies 4, 245–6
    assignment 78, 80, 245–6
    commercial leases 245–6
    consent 69, 240–1, 245
    covenants and conditions 241–2,
        245

current tenant's position 245
definition of a tenancy 63
dispute resolution 87
draft leases 245
forfeiture 131, 132
freehold, right to buy out 185–
    8, 203
ground rents 179
head landlord's position 245
head tenancies, termination
    of 87
improvements, compensation
    for 157
new tenancy, right to a 144
notice of termination 87–8
partial sub-letting 245–6
proposed sub-tenant's
    position 245
purpose of restrictions 241–2
re-entry 131
references 245
rent, apportionment of 245
rent review clauses 246
Residential Tenancies Act,
    2004 74, 84, 87–8
Residential Tenancies Board
    (RTB) 87, 93
restrictions 241–2
security of tenure 74, 240
termination 78–9, 80, 87
time limits 88
withholding consent
    unreasonably 241
succession to tenancies 79,
    274–7
sufferance, tenancies at 15,
    16–17, 133
surrender
    assignment 134–5
    damages 134–5
    Deasy's Act 105, 117, 134–5
    deeds or notes in writing,
        by 134–5
    keys, handing over 135
    Landlord and Tenant Law
        Reform Bill (draft) 119
    merger 135
    notice to quit 121
    operation of law, by 135
    physical surrender 135
    registration 135
    Registry of Deeds 135
    repairs 117
surveys 232, 251

tax see also stamp duty; VAT
    collection 14
    supply incentives 10
    payment, of 68
telephone mediation 96

temporary lettings see short-
    term and temporary
    lettings
tenancy/lease, definition of 3,
    7, 12, 16, 17, 63–4, 181, 275
Tenancy Management System,
    online registration
    under 100
Tenancy Tribunal 10, 92–3, 95,
    100
tenant, definition of 143
tenants for life 41–2
tenant's obligations
    access for works, allowing 69
    anti-social behaviour 70
    assignment without consent 69
    charges or taxes, payment of 68
    deterioration, not to cause 69,
        108
    disbursements, landlord's
        entitlement to 70
    dwelling, use only as a 69
    identity of persons resident,
        notification of 69
    improvements without
        consent 69
    insurance, invalidating 69
    rent 68
    repairs 69, 104–6, 108, 111–16
    Residential Tenancies Act, 2004
        57–8, 65–6, 68–70, 83, 85–6
    statutory obligations, not to
        cause landlords to be in
        breach of 68
    sub-tenancies without
        consent 70
    termination by tenants 78–9, 86
    wear and tear 69
tenements
    alienation 161
    assignment 143
    business equity 144
    car parking 142
    companies 143
    controlled dwellings 275
    definition 5, 17, 141–3, 275
    filling stations 142
    improvements 157
    Landlord and Tenant
        (Amendment) Act,
        1980 141–4
    Landlord and Tenant Law
        Reform Bill 2011 (draft)
        142
    main purpose/user 141–2
    new tenancy, right to a 17,
        144–58
    occupation 143
    predecessors in title, definition
        of 143

tenements (*cont.*)
repairs 109–10
restrictive of user, covenants
which are 162
subsidiary and ancillary test 275
tenant, definition of 143
terms and conditions 141
term certain tenancies 14–15,
74, 79–80, 120
termination 119–39 *see also*
notice of termination;
notice to quit
6th months, within the first 79
actual termination 78, 157
age, condition and character of
building, termination due
to 135
arrears 78, 86, 102, 120, 132,
134–5, 137–8
assignment with consent 78, 80
break clauses 20, 136, 225, 241
collusion 88
commercial tenancies 119–20,
136
compensation 135
compulsory acquisition of
dangerous and derelict
sites 136
costs and expenses 123, 130–2,
138
court orders 135
dangerous premises 136
Deasy's Act, 1860 138
death of tenants 79, 132, 135
decrees or warrants for
possession 134–5
deemed termination 78, 116,
118–19
demands for possession 133–4
derelict sites 136
disclaimers 136
effluxion of time 119, 132–3,
138
ejectment for non-payment of
rent 137–8
event, occurrence of a
stated 135
eviction 11, 119, 2
execution of judgments or
decrees for possession 120,
134
fixed term tenancies 79–80
forfeiture 118–19
forms 102
grievance procedure 82
head tenancies 87
improvements 157
integrated area plans,
termination where building
is in area with 135, 156

interest, licence coupled with
an 20
Landlord and Tenant Law
Reform Bill 2011 (draft)
12, 119
legal proceedings 136–8
licences 20
liquidator's disclaimer 136
list of ways to terminate 118
marriage 135
merger 133, 135
options, exercise of 136
overholding 119, 125, 138
own or families' occupation,
landlord requires
accommodation for own 76
Part 4 tenancies 75–80
particulars, registration of 100
periodic tenancies 15–16
practical steps, summary of 139
premature termination 73–4
prohibitions 88
refurbish or renovate, landlord's
intention to 74, 76
rent 137–8
repairs 117
Residential Tenancies Act, 2004
10, 57–8, 75–80, 83–90,
118, 132
Residential Tenancies Board
(RTB) 93–100, 102–3
security of tenure 73–4, 79–80
sub-tenancies 78, 80, 87
succession to tenancy 78
suitable, accommodation no
longer 75–6
tenants, termination by 78–9,
86
terms and conditions 125–6
third parties, hardship to 82–3
urban renewal 136
voluntary renunciation
option 150, 153
warrants for possession 134, 138
website 101
terms and conditions *see also*
covenants
assignment 244–6
breach 49, 126
contracting out 10, 44, 150–4
covenants 48–9
damages 117
date of commencement of
terms 49
Deasy's Act 7
essential contents 8, 49–50
essential conditions 181–3
forfeiture 126, 137–8
freehold, right to buy out 181–6,
188–9, 190, 194, 198, 200–1

habendum 3, 50
initialling terms 8
instructions, taking 1, 49, 57–8
licences 21, 26, 31
new tenancy, right to a 147–50,
156
parcels 49–50
parol evidence 8
Part 4 tenancies 80
planning permission 155
reddendum 4, 50, 235, 237
rent review 235, 238–40
repairs 150, 251
sub-tenancies 244
standard forms 8, 225, 235,
238–40
tenements 141
termination 125–6
urban areas 156
writing 10, 151, 156
third parties 12, 20, 82–3, 93, 123
time limits
disturbance, compensation
for 160
extension of limits 73, 94, 138,
157, 164
improvements, compensation
for 158
notice of termination 119
Residential Tenancies Board
(RTB), dispute resolution
by 94, 95
service 65
time of the essence 236
tithes to Church of Ireland 6
title
certificates 218
drafting leases 52
ejectment civil bills on title 129,
137, 138
estoppel 17
evidence 57
predecessors in title, definition
of 4, 43
transfer of businesses 271
transitional dwellings 62
transparency 251–2
trespass 16, 19, 20, 124
trusts 42

under-tenancies *see*
sub-tenancies
undue influence 25
unregistered land 3, 55, 135,
193, 197
urban renewal 136
urban tenants 179–80
urgent situations 118–19
use, change of 52, 162, 244,
246–8

use of force 129–30
utilities 5

vacant leases 183, 187
VAT 253–72
  4A authorisation 259
  accounting 255–6, 259, 262, 266, 270
  adjustments 262–8, 266, 272
  assignment 245, 258, 259, 264–7, 269–70, 289–90
  Capital Goods Records 272
  Capital Goods Scheme 260–70, 272
  capital value 259
  cash receipt basis 256
  category 2 leases 260–5
  category 3 leases 265–7
  category 4 leases 267–9
  completion of residential tenancies, Revenue Concession on 272
  deductions 253, 257, 261–3, 265, 268, 272
  drafting leases 52
  Economic Value Test 259
  enquiries App 8
  entry, powers of 258
  European Union 253
  exclusive possession 258
  exemptions 254, 257, 259–64, 266–72
  fixed term tenancies 258
  freehold equivalents 260
  groups 269
  imports 254
  inspection powers 258
  input credit 257
  input VAT 253, 257, 265–6, 269, 272
  invoices 256
  legacy leases 260, 265–7, 269
  lettings 258–72
  liquidators, lettings by 272
  mixed use 262
  mortgages in possession, lettings by 272
  new leases 260–4
  operation of VAT regime 253–4
  opt to tax 260–9, 272
  output VAT 253, 257
  passport 263
  place of supply 255
  Practice Note Revised VAT Special Condition 3 and Pre-Contract VAT Enquiries App 7

  pre-contract enquiries 52, 260, App 8, App 10
  Pre-Contract Enquiries (Law Society) (2011) 260, App 8, App 10
  premiums 264, 267, 269
  property intervals 262–8
  rates 255, 259, 260, 264, 266
  receivers, lettings by 272
  records 258
  refurbishment/ redevelopment 259, 263, 265, 267
  registration for VAT 266
  related or connected parties 260, 268
  rent-free periods 267
  rent to buy schemes 271
  resales 253
  returns 253, 257
  Revenue Commissioners 253, 267–8
  reverse charge VAT 254
  reversionary interests 267
  self-supply 255
  short-term lettings 267–8
  Sixth VAT Directive 253
  Special Condition 3 (August 2011) (Law Society) App 7, App 8
  supply of goods and services 254–5, 261
  surrender 259, 265–7, 289–90
  taxable goods and services 254
  tenant's obligations 248
  tenant's VAT status 263–4
  transfer of businesses 271
  transitional measures 260–70
  Value Added Tax Consolidation Act 2010 253–72
  waiver of exemption 259, 260, 267–9
  what is subject to VAT 254–5
  works by tenants 264–5, 267, 269
  zero-rating 255
vesting
  arbitration 194–5, 196–7, 212–13
  certificates 194–8, 199, 202–3, 209, 211–13, 216–17
  consent 194, 211
  forms and precedents 194–8, 209, 211, 216–17
  freehold, right to buy out 193–7, 199, 202–3
vexatious or frivolous applications 95

voluntary renunciation option 150, 153

waiver
  definition 5
  notice to quit 124
  VAT exemptions 259, 260, 267–9
warrants for possession 134, 137
waste 57, 110
water 50, 57, 106, 112, 115,249
way, rights of 196
wayleaves, definition of 5
wear and tear 40, 69, 106, 108, 115
websites 53, 68, 84, 93, 95, 100, 101, 260
weekly tenancies 15, 16, 122
will, tenancies at 16
wills 41, 45
works *see also* **improvements; rebuilding, reinstatement and renewal; repairs**
  access, allowing 69
  fitting out 22, 40, 51, 56, 145, 228
  tenants, by 264–5, 267, 269
  undertakings 173
  VAT 264–5, 267, 269
writing or memorandum in writing
  correspondence 8
  Deasy's Act 7–8, 12, 14–15
  exceptions 12
  essential terms, examples of 8
  fee farm grants 14–15
  instructions, taking 45
  Land and Conveyancing Law Reform Act, 2009 7–8
  Landlord and Tenant Law Reform Bill (draft) 12, 14–15
  leases for lives renewable forever 14–15
  new tenancy, right to a 10, 151, 156
  periodic tenancies 9, 15
  possession, agreements to enter into 9
  repairs 105–6
  Statute of Frauds (Ireland), 1695 8

yearly tenancies 15, 122, 186–7, 200–2